Exam 70-622: *Supporting and Troubleshooting Applications on a Windows Vista® Client for Enterprise Support Technicians*

Objective	Chapter	Lesson
Deploying Windows Vista		
Analyze the business environment and select an appropriate deployment method.	2	3
Prepare a system for clean installation or upgrade.	1	1, 2, 3
Deploy Windows Vista from a custom image.	2	1, 2
Perform post-installation tasks.	3	1, 2
Troubleshoot deployment issues.	3	1, 2
Managing Windows Vista Security		
Configure and troubleshoot security for Windows Internet Explorer 7+.	5	1
Troubleshoot security configuration issues.	4, 6	Chapter 4, Lesson 3 Chapter 6, Lesson 2
Troubleshoot Windows Firewall issues.	10	1
Troubleshoot Windows Defender issues.	5	3
Apply security patches and updates.	5	2, 3
Configure and troubleshoot access to resources.	7	2, 3
Troubleshoot authentication issues.	7	1
Configure and troubleshoot User Account Control.	8	1, 2, 3
Managing and Maintaining Systems That Run Windows Vista		
Troubleshoot policy settings.	4	1, 2
Configure and manage the Task Scheduler.	6	3
Configure and troubleshoot Event Forwarding.	6	1
Apply and troubleshoot updates.	5	2
Troubleshoot performance and reliability issues.	6	2
Configuring and Troubleshooting Networking		
Configure and troubleshoot network protocols.	9	1, 2
Configure and troubleshoot network services at the client level.	9	1, 2
Configure and troubleshoot remote access.	12	1
Troubleshoot connectivity issues.	9	2
Configure and troubleshoot wireless networking.	11	1, 2
Configure network security.	10, 12	Chapter 10, Lesson 2 Chapter 12, Lessons 1, 2
Troubleshoot access to network resources.	9	2
Supporting and Maintaining Desktop Applications		
Support deployed applications	5	4
Troubleshoot software restrictions	4	3
Maintain desktop applications	5	4

Note: Exam objectives are subject to change at any time without prior notice and at Microsoft's sole discretion. Please visit the Microsoft Learning Certification Web site (*www.microsoft.com/learning/mcp/*) for the most current listing of exam objectives.

Microsoft®

MCITP Self-Paced Training Kit (Exam 70-622): Supporting and Troubleshooting Applications on a Windows Vista® Client for Enterprise Support Technicians

Tony Northrup and J.C. Mackin

PUBLISHED BY
Microsoft Press
A Division of Microsoft Corporation
One Microsoft Way
Redmond, Washington 98052-6399

Library of Congress Control Number: 2007931440

Printed and bound in the United States of America.

1 2 3 4 5 6 7 8 9   QWT   2 1 0 9 8 7

Distributed in Canada by H.B. Fenn and Company Ltd.

A CIP catalogue record for this book is available from the British Library.

Microsoft Press books are available through booksellers and distributors worldwide. For further information about international editions, contact your local Microsoft Corporation office or contact Microsoft Press International directly at fax (425) 936-7329. Visit our Web site at www.microsoft.com/mspress. Send comments to tkinput@microsoft.com.

Acquisitions Editor: Ken Jones
Developmental Editor: Jenny Moss Benson
Project Editor: Laura Sackerman
Editorial Production Services: nSight, Inc.

Body Part No. X13-92828

To Pancho Puce—never stop seeking perfection.

—Tony Northrup

Thanks to friends and family for all your support throughout this process.

—J.C. Mackin

About the Authors

Tony Northrup

Tony Northrup, MVP, MCSE, MCTS, and CISSP, is a Microsoft Windows consultant and author living in the Boston, Massachusetts, area. Tony started programming before Windows 1.0 was released but has focused on Windows administration and development for the last 15 years. He has written more than a dozen books covering Windows networking, security, and development. Among other titles, Tony is coauthor of the *Windows Server 2003 Resource Kit* and the *Windows Vista Resource Kit*.

When he's not consulting or writing, Tony enjoys remote-controlled flight, golf, and photography. Tony lives with his wife, Erica, his cat, Sam, and his dog, Sandi. You can learn more about Tony by visiting his technical blog at *http://www.vistaclues.com* or his personal website at *http://www.northrup.org*.

J.C. Mackin

J.C. Mackin, MCSE, MCDST, MCT, MSITP, is a writer, editor, consultant, and trainer who has been working with Microsoft networks since 1997. Books he has previously authored or coauthored include *MCSA/MCSE Self-Paced Training Kit (Exam 70-291): Implementing, Managing, and Maintaining a Microsoft® Windows Server™ 2003 Network Infrastructure* and *MCITP Self-Paced Training Kit (Exam 70-443): Designing a Database Server Infrastructure Using Microsoft SQL Server 2005*. When not working with computers, J.C. can be found with a panoramic camera photographing medieval villages in Italy or France. He holds a master's degree in telecommunications and network management.

Contents at a Glance

Table of Contents

What do you think of this book? We want to hear from you!

Microsoft is interested in hearing your feedback so we can continually improve our books and learning resources for you. To participate in a brief online survey, please visit:

www.microsoft.com/learning/booksurvey/

What do you think of this book? We want to hear from you!

Microsoft is interested in hearing your feedback so we can continually improve our books and learning resources for you. To participate in a brief online survey, please visit:

www.microsoft.com/learning/booksurvey/

Acknowledgments

This book was put together by a team of respected professionals, and we, the authors, would like to thank them each for the great job they did. At Microsoft, Ken Jones worked out our contracts, and Jenny Moss Benson and Laura Sackerman were our developmental editors. Carol Whitney at nSight was the project manager, coordinating the many other people who worked on the book. Among those, Kerin Foley and Joe Gustaitis were our copyeditors, who are responsible for making sure the book is readable and consistent, and Lindsey Valich and Paul Connelly provided additional proofreading.

Orin Thomas, Rozanne Murphy Whalen, and Bob Dean provided a technical review to help make the book as accurate as possible. Angela Montoya was our graphic artist, processing screenshots and converting our rough diagrams into the polished art you'll see throughout the book. Terrie Cundiff was our desktop publisher, largely responsible for creating a great presentation in the printed book. Jack Lewis created the index that you'll find at the back of the book.

Many other people helped with this book, even though they weren't formally part of the team. Tony Northrup would like to thank his friends, especially Tara Banks, Kristin Cavour, Chris and Diane Geggis, Bob Hogan, Bob Dean, and Samuel Jackson, for helping him enjoy his time away from the keyboard. The whole team at nSight deserves a second round of thanks for helping Tony finish off more than a couple bottles of wine (and pitchers of margaritas). Enjoy Costa Rica, Cindy! Tony would also like to thank his wife, Erica, for being so patient during many long days of writing, as well as Erica's family—Mike, Michelle, Sandi, and Raymond Edson. Finally, a special thanks to Jenny Lozier, her mother, and Mr. T, who must read this at a local retail outlet.

It makes a huge difference when you consider the people you work with to be friends. Having a great team not only improves the quality of the book, it makes it a more enjoyable experience. Writing this book was my most enjoyable project yet, and I hope I get the chance to work with everyone in the future.

Introduction

This training kit is designed for information technology (IT) support personnel who support Windows Vista at the Tier 1 or Tier 2 level in a wide range of environments and who plan to take the Microsoft Certified IT Professional (MCITP) exam 70-622. We assume that before you begin using this kit you have a solid foundation-level understanding of Microsoft Windows client operating systems and common Internet technologies.

By using this training kit, you will learn how to do the following:

- Create and deploy Windows Vista images
- Migrate users to Windows Vista computers
- Configure and manage Windows Vista security
- Perform routine maintenance of Windows Vista computers
- Configure and troubleshoot Windows Vista networking
- Implement and troubleshoot shared desktop technologies
- Implement and manage client software

Lab Setup Instructions

The exercises in this training kit require four computers or virtual machines:

- One Windows Server 2003 computer
- One Windows Vista (Enterprise, Business, or Ultimate) computer
- One Windows XP Professional computer (optional but strongly recommended)
- One computer with no software yet installed

All four computers must be physically connected to the same network. We recommend that you use an isolated network that is not part of your production network to do the practice exercises in this book. To minimize the time and expense of configuring physical computers, we recommend that you use virtual machines for all four computers. To run computers as virtual machines within Windows, you can use Virtual PC 2007, Virtual Server 2005 R2, or third-party virtual machine software. To download Virtual PC 2007, visit *http://www.microsoft.com /windows/downloads/virtualpc/default.mspx*. To download an evaluation of Virtual Server 2005 R2, visit *http://www.microsoft.com/technet/virtualserver/evaluation/default.mspx*.

Preparing the Windows Server 2003 Computer

Perform the following steps to prepare the Windows Server 2003 computer for the exercises in this training kit.

Check OS Version Requirements

In System Control Panel, verify that the operating system version is Windows Server 2003 Service Pack 1 or later. Download and install the latest service pack, if necessary.

Install the Windows Automated Installation Kit (WAIK)

1. Download the Windows Automated Installation Kit (WAIK) from *http://www.microsoft.com /downloads/details.aspx?familyid=C7D4BC6D-15F3-4284-9123-679830D629F2*. Note that the file to be downloaded is an IMG DVD image file. Use this IMG file to burn a DVD by using DVD burning software, mount the image as a DVD drive in Virtual PC, open the file using SlySloft Virtual CloneDrive, or open the file by using another third-party tool.

2. When you place the WAIK DVD in the DVD drive or mount the WAIK IMG file, the Welcome To Windows Automated Installation Kit window automatically appears. In this window, use the .NET Framework Setup and MSXML 6.0 Setup links to install these components, if necessary. (If either of these components is already installed on the local machine, you will not be given an Install option.)

3. Use the Windows AIK Setup link to install the WAIK.

Name the Computer

In the System Control Panel, specify the computer name as **dcsrv1**.

Configure TCP/IP Properties

In the Internet Protocol (TCP/IP) properties of the Local Area Connection, select the Use The Following IP Address option. Then, manually configure the computer with an IP address, such as 192.168.10.1. Finally, beneath the Use The Following DNS Server Addresses option, type this same chosen address as the preferred Domain Name System (DNS) server.

Add Server Roles

Click the Manage Your Server option on the Start menu. Then, in the Manage Your Server window, click the Add Or Remove A Role option to add the following roles one at a time. (For each role, enter any information provided below. Otherwise, leave all default options.)

- File Server
- Domain Controller (Active Directory directory service)
  - Full DNS Name for New Domain: **nwtraders.msft**.
  - Note that the DNS registration diagnostics are expected to fail. On the DNS Registration Diagnostics page of the Active Directory Installation Wizard, leave the default option to Install And Configure The DNS Server On This Computer.

- DHCP Server
    - ❑ Scope Name: Nwtraders.
    - ❑ IP Address Range: Choose a start IP address, an end IP address, and a subnet mask that are compatible with the IP address of your server and the network space of your organization. For example, if you have specified an address of 192.168.10.1 for the local server, you can specify the DHCP scope start IP address as 192.168.10.2, the end IP address as 192.168.10.254, and the subnet mask as 255.255.255.0.
    - ❑ Domain Name and DNS Servers: Specify the parent domain as **nwtraders.msft**. Type **dcsrv1** in the Server Name text box, click Resolve, and then click Add to add the IP address of the local server.

Authorize the DHCP Server

1. From the Start menu, point to Administrative Tools, and then click DHCP.
2. In the DHCP console tree, right-click the *dcsrv1.nwtraders.msft* node, and then click Authorize from the shortcut menu.

If your network has another DHCP server, you will need to disable it for your practice computers to be correctly configured. For this reason, it is extremely important that the computers you use are connected to an isolated network.

Create Personal User Accounts

1. In the Active Directory Users And Computers administrative tool, expand the *nwtraders.msft* node in the console tree.
2. Right-click the Users folder, point to New on the shortcut menu, and then click User.
3. In the New Object – User dialog box, enter the name and user logon name of an account that you will use as a *domain administrator* account throughout the exercises of this training kit. Click Next.
4. Enter a password of your choice, click Next, and then click Finish.
5. In the Active Directory Users And Computers console, locate the new account you have just created in the details pane. Right-click the account, and then click Add To A Group from the shortcut menu.
6. In the Select Group dialog box, type **Domain Admins**, and then press Enter. In the Active Directory message box, click OK.
7. Create a second domain account using the method just described, but do NOT add this account to any group other than the default Domain Users. Use this second account whenever the exercises in this training kit require you to log on to the domain as a standard user, not as a domain administrator.

Preparing the Windows Vista Computer

Perform the following steps to prepare your Windows Vista computer for the exercises in this training kit.

Check OS Version Requirements

In System Control Panel (found in the System And Maintenance category), verify that the operating system version is Windows Vista Enterprise, Business, or Ultimate. If necessary, choose the option to upgrade to one of these versions.

Name the Computer

In the System Control Panel, specify the computer name as **vista1**.

Configure Networking

- Enable File Sharing.

  In Control Panel, click Set Up File Sharing. In Network And Sharing Center, verify that the network is configured as a Private network and that File Sharing is enabled.
- Verify that the computer is set to obtain an address automatically.

  In Network And Sharing Center, click Manage Network Connections. In Network Connections, open the properties of the Local Area Connection. Verify that the Internet Protocol Version 4 (TCP/IPv4) properties specify the options to obtain an IP address *and* DNS server address automatically.

Preparing the Windows XP Professional Computer

Perform the following steps to prepare your Windows XP Professional computer for the exercises in this training kit.

Check OS Version Requirements

In System Control Panel (found in the Performance And Maintenance category), verify that the operating system version is Windows XP Professional Service Pack 2 or later. If necessary, upgrade the operating system or install the latest service pack.

Name the Computer

In the System Control Panel, specify the computer name as **Xpclient**.

Verify IP Address Settings

In the Network Connection Control Panel (found in the Network And Internet Connections category), open the properties of the Local Area Connection. Verify that the Internet Protocol (TCP/IP) properties specify the options to obtain an IP address *and* DNS server address automatically.

Using the CD

The companion CD included with this training kit contains the following:

- **Practice tests**   You can reinforce your understanding of how to configure Windows Vista by using electronic practice tests that you customize to meet your needs from the pool of Lesson Review questions in this book. Or you can practice for the 70-622 certification exam by using tests created from a pool of 300 realistic exam questions, which give you many practice exams to ensure that you are prepared.
- **An eBook**   An electronic version (eBook) of this book is included for when you do not want to carry the printed book with you. The eBook is in Portable Document Format (PDF), and you can view it by using Adobe Acrobat or Adobe Reader.
- **Microsoft webcasts**   Several Microsoft webcasts that contain information related to chapters within this book are included. Additional webcasts can be found at *www.microsoft.com/webcasts*.
- **Practice files**   Several lessons have accompanying files that you use when performing the practice exercises.
- **Software**   Software used when performing some of the practice exercises is included so that you don't need to download it.

How to Install the Practice Tests

To install the practice test software from the companion CD to your hard disk, do the following:

1. Insert the companion CD into your CD drive and accept the license agreement. A CD menu appears.

    NOTE If the CD menu does not appear

    If the CD menu or the license agreement does not appear, AutoRun might be disabled on your computer. Refer to the Readme.txt file on the CD-ROM for alternate installation instructions.

2. Click Practice Tests and follow the instructions on the screen.

How to Use the Practice Tests

To start the practice test software, follow these steps:

Click Start/All Programs/Microsoft Press Training Kit Exam Prep. A window appears that shows all the Microsoft Press training kit exam prep suites installed on your computer.

Double-click the lesson review or practice test you want to use.

NOTE Lesson reviews versus practice tests

Select the (70-622) Configuring Windows Vista Client *lesson review* to use the questions from the "Lesson Review" sections of this book. Select the (70-622) Configuring Windows Vista Client *practice test* to use a pool of 300 questions similar to those that appear on the 70-622 certification exam.

Lesson Review Options

When you start a lesson review, the Custom Mode dialog box appears so that you can configure your test. You can click OK to accept the defaults, or you can customize the number of questions you want, how the practice test software works, which exam objectives you want the questions to relate to, and whether you want your lesson review to be timed. If you are retaking a test, you can select whether you want to see all the questions again or only the questions you missed or did not answer.

After you click OK, your lesson review starts.

- To take the test, answer the questions and use the Next, Previous, and Go To buttons to move from question to question.
- After you answer an individual question, if you want to see which answers are correct—along with an explanation of each correct answer—click Explanation.
- If you prefer to wait until the end of the test to see how you did, answer all the questions, and then click Score Test. You will see a summary of the exam objectives you chose and the percentage of questions you got right overall and per objective. You can print a copy of your test, review your answers, or retake the test.

Practice Test Options

When you start a practice test, you choose whether to take the test in Certification Mode, Study Mode, or Custom Mode:

- **Certification Mode** Closely resembles the experience of taking a certification exam. The test has a set number of questions. It is timed, and you cannot pause and restart the timer.

- **Study Mode**   Creates an untimed test in which you can review the correct answers and the explanations after you answer each question.
- **Custom Mode**   Gives you full control over the test options so that you can customize them as you like.

In all modes the user interface when you are taking the test is basically the same but with different options enabled or disabled depending on the mode. The main options are discussed in the previous section, "Lesson Review Options."

When you review your answer to an individual practice test question, a "References" section is provided that lists where in the training kit you can find the information that relates to that question and provides links to other sources of information. After you click Test Results to score your entire practice test, you can click the Learning Plan tab to see a list of references for every objective.

How to Uninstall the Practice Tests

To uninstall the practice test software for a training kit, use the Add Or Remove Programs option (Windows XP) or the Program And Features option (Windows Vista) in Windows Control Panel.

Microsoft Certified Professional Program

The Microsoft certifications provide the best method to prove your command of current Microsoft products and technologies. The exams and corresponding certifications are developed to validate your mastery of critical competencies as you design and develop, or implement and support, solutions with Microsoft products and technologies. Computer professionals who become Microsoft-certified are recognized as experts and are sought after industrywide. Certification brings a variety of benefits to the individual and to employers and organizations.

MORE INFO   **All the Microsoft certifications**

For a full list of Microsoft certifications, go to *www.microsoft.com/learning/mcp/default.asp*.

Technical Support

Every effort has been made to ensure the accuracy of this book and the contents of the companion CD. If you have comments, questions, or ideas regarding this book or the companion CD, please send them to Microsoft Press by using either of the following methods:

E-mail: tkinput@microsoft.com

Postal Mail:

Microsoft Press
Attn: MCITP Self-Paced Training Kit (Exam 70-622): Supporting and Troubleshooting Applications on a Windows Vista Client for Enterprise Support Technicians, *Editor*
One Microsoft Way
Redmond, WA 98052–6399

For additional support information regarding this book and the CD-ROM (including answers to commonly asked questions about installation and use), visit the Microsoft Press Technical Support website at *www.microsoft.com/learning/support/books/*. To connect directly to the Microsoft Knowledge Base and enter a query, visit *http://support.microsoft.com/search/*. For support information regarding Microsoft software, connect to *http://support.microsoft.com.*

Chapter 1
Preparing for Windows Vista Deployment

Software deployment refers to the process of making software available for use—typically on many computers in the workplace. Operating system deployment certainly includes installation but is not limited to it. Deploying Windows Vista also refers to preparing the user's desktop environment so that the necessary configurations are set, so that the user's applications function properly, and so that the user's data is readily available.

In a business environment, deploying Windows Vista successfully across many desktop computers requires significant preparation. This preparation includes developing an understanding of the entire deployment process, ensuring that your target computers meet the hardware requirements of Windows Vista, planning for application compatibility, and taking preliminary steps to preserve data throughout the deployment process.

The topic of Windows Vista deployment is one of the main content areas on the 70-622 exam, and the first three chapters in this training kit are dedicated to this topic. After covering preinstallation tasks in Chapter 1, we'll move on to the actual deployment process in Chapter 2, "Deploying Windows Vista," and the postinstallation tasks in Chapter 3, "Troubleshooting Deployment Issues."

Exam objectives in this chapter:
- Prepare a system for clean installation or upgrade.

Lessons in this chapter:

Before You Begin

To complete the lessons in this chapter, you must have

- A Windows Vista Enterprise, Business, or Ultimate computer named Vista1.
- A Windows XP Professional computer named Xpclient.

Real World

JC Mackin

Before upgrading users' computers to a new operating system, I typically spend some time with them locating their essential files so that I can back up these files before the upgrade. However, users do occasionally forget about important files stored in well-hidden locations, especially when they are used to accessing this data automatically through an application. So, to keep users happy after the upgrade, ideally, you should ensure that they have a way of accessing *everything* on their old systems. You can certainly achieve this if you just back up their entire system in advance of the upgrade, and sometimes that is indeed the best solution. But what I prefer to do when I can is to back up only their user state and then replace the system's hard disk, moving the old one to an external enclosure that can be accessed directly if necessary.

Now, however, there's an even cooler way to let users have access to their old data. Microsoft's ImageX utility (introduced in Chapter 2, "Deploying Windows Vista") allows you to capture an image of the user's old system and then deploy that image anywhere—even inside a virtual machine. Users can then run the virtual machine in Virtual PC when they need to access something that wasn't backed up or even when—why not?—they're just feeling a little nostalgic for their old desktop.

Lesson 1: Overview of the Windows Deployment Process

To begin to deploy Windows Vista in your organization, you should preview the various phases of deployment and consider how these phases might be performed in light of your particular needs. Gaining an overview in this way is critical to managing the deployment process when it is later performed.

After this lesson, you will be able to:
- Describe the three phases of the deployment life cycle.
- Describe deployment challenges that require planning and preparation.

Estimated lesson time: 10 minutes

Overview of the Deployment Life Cycle

The deployment life cycle provides a model of the tasks needed to deploy an operating system successfully. You can view the desktop deployment life cycle, shown in Figure 1-1, as consisting of three phases: Plan, Build, and Deploy. Understanding these phases is essential to successfully managing and implementing the deployment process.

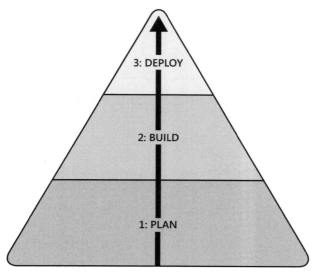

Figure 1-1 The deployment life cycle

- **Plan** During the Plan phase, organizations first assess their needs and then devise a specific deployment strategy that best meets those needs. For example, during this phase the deployment team should perform *hardware* assessment (to determine which computers are capable of being upgraded to Windows Vista) and *software* assessment (to determine which applications need to be upgraded for the newer operating system). The deployment team during this phase also determines the tools required to assist in the Build and Deploy phases of the project. These tools might include technologies used to deploy client images as well as those used to back up and restore user data.

As a result of the planning phase, a written document should be produced that outlines the deployment process details, such as a schedule for the deployment, an assessment of the current network configuration, where to store data during data migration, a pilot plan, and a rollout plan.

■ **Build**   The Build phase is the set-up phase in which the tools and technologies chosen for deployment are put into place, tested, and streamlined. This stage includes performing the actual hardware upgrades needed to support Windows Vista, developing the automated deployment solution, and developing and testing the disk images to be deployed.

■ **Deploy**   The Deploy phase is the period during which the team implements the deployment solution and ensures that this solution is stable and usable. This phase also includes procedures such as migrating user data that accompany the installation of the operating system on each user machine.

Quick Check
■ Which kinds of assessments are performed during the Plan phase?
Quick Check Answer
■ Hardware assessment and software assessment

Planning for Deployment Challenges

In most business environments, deploying a new operating system on business client desktops is not a simple task. Many interdependent requirements complicate the rollout procedure. In particular, it is essential to plan for the following challenges as you begin to prepare for deployment:

■ **Hardware upgrades**   Windows Vista has more advanced hardware requirements than do earlier versions of Windows. Before you can deploy Windows Vista in your organization, you need to investigate which client computers already meet these hardware requirements, which client computers should be upgraded to meet the requirements, and which computers need to be replaced altogether.

To begin, you need to plan and perform this investigation itself in a coordinated manner. Then, after you have completed the study, you will need to acquire budgetary approval for your hardware upgrade recommendations and create a plan to implement the hardware upgrades.

- **Application compatibility** As you prepare for Windows Vista deployment, you will need a plan to investigate and eliminate application compatibility problems in the new operating system.

  Each release of Windows includes new features and capabilities that affect how applications run. Although most programs written for earlier versions of Windows also work in Windows Vista, some older programs might run poorly or not at all. In cases where applications are critical to the business, you must perform testing in advance and take steps to ensure that they are functional after the rollout of the new operating system.

- **Migrating the user-state configuration** To adequately prepare for Windows Vista deployment, you must create a plan to preserve as much of each user's state as possible. Beyond simply aiming to back up the user's e-mail and other work-related data, you should devise a strategy that also preserves installed applications, application settings, printers, favorites, shortcuts, and any other features that the user has come to expect in his or her environment. Not doing so results in increased costs stemming from, among other factors, a loss of productivity and an increased strain on technical help resources.

- **Acquiring expertise and technical resources** Migrating many desktops to a new operating system requires significant resources in terms of infrastructure, expertise, people, and tools. These resources are often not easy to acquire and can delay the rollout procedure. If your organization does not already have the resources necessary to perform the migration, you must outline steps to obtain them as part of your deployment plan.

- **Minimizing cost** Your deployment plan should strive to minimize the cost of deployment. In general, cost increases with complexity, and complexity results when desktops are not standardized—when desktops of many types must be migrated. In addition, migration can significantly disrupt the work environment and increase costs by resulting in lost productivity. Other factors that contribute to the cost of deployment include the level of automation built into the deployment and the amount of resources that must be purchased in order to perform the deployment. Your deployment plan should thus propose a method that balances these various factors as a means to reduce overall costs.

Lesson Summary

- It is helpful to view the Windows Vista deployment process as consisting of three basic phases: Plan, Build, and Deploy.
- The Plan phase includes performing hardware assessment and application compatibility testing. It also includes creating a document that outlines the deployment strategy.
- The Build phase includes performing any necessary hardware upgrades, putting into place the technologies to be used during deployment, and testing the deployment processes.
- The Deploy phase includes the processes of installing the new operating systems on user desktops and migrating user data from old systems to new systems.

■   It is important to prepare for the many challenges that stand in the way of a successful deployment of Windows Vista. These challenges include acquiring the resources necessary to deploy the new operating system while at once minimizing the costs of the deployment.

Lesson Review

You can use the following questions to test your knowledge of the information in Lesson 1, "Overview of the Windows Deployment Process." The questions are also available on the companion CD if you prefer to review them in electronic form.

NOTE   Answers

Answers to these questions and explanations of why each answer choice is right or wrong are located in the "Answers" section at the end of the book.

---

1. Your deployment plan calls for the migration of 50 Windows XP computers to Windows Vista as soon as possible. The users who run these computers depend on Microsoft Office 2007 to perform their jobs. Which of the following steps should be taken first to ensure the success of the project?

   A.   Application compatibility testing

   B.   User interviews

   C.   User data migration

   D.   Hardware assessment

2. Which of the following user state elements is least essential to migrate during a typical deployment?

   A.   Desktop settings

   B.   Documents

   C.   Application settings

   D.   E-mail messages

Lesson 2: Verifying Windows Vista Hardware Requirements

Before you deploy Windows Vista in your organization, you will have to determine which computers already meet the hardware requirements of the new operating system and which ones do not. Fortunately, new tools are available that simplify this task.

After this lesson, you will be able to:

- Describe the difference between Windows Vista Capable and Windows Vista Premium Ready computers.
- Use the Windows Vista Upgrade Advisor (WVUA) to verify the readiness of an individual computer to run Windows Vista.
- Describe the function of the Windows Vista Hardware Assessment (WVHA) tool and how it differs from that of the WVUA.

Estimated lesson time: 20 minutes

Understanding Windows Vista Performance Levels

Assessing a network for the hardware readiness of Windows Vista is complicated by the fact that two sets of hardware specifications are defined for the operating system. Each set of specifications represents a different standard of performance.

If a PC meets the first, more basic set of hardware requirements, the computer is considered Windows Vista Capable, a designation whose program logo is shown in Figure 1-2. (This logo typically appears only on Windows XP computers purchased before the release of Windows Vista.) If a computer meets the more advanced set of requirements, the PC is considered Windows Vista Premium Ready. The Windows Vista Premium Ready logo, which also appears only on Windows XP computers purchased before the release of Windows Vista, is shown in Figure 1-3.

Figure 1-2   The Windows Vista Capable logo

Figure 1-3   The Windows Vista Premium Ready logo

Note that these designations are not mutually exclusive: A Windows Vista Premium Ready computer is also considered Windows Vista Capable.

Computers purchased after the release of Windows Vista can display their Windows Vista performance level with a different set of logos. The Windows Vista Basic logo, shown in Figure 1-4, is comparable to the Windows Vista Capable standard of performance. The standard Windows Vista logo, in turn, is comparable to that of Windows Vista Premium Ready. The Windows Vista logo is shown in Figure 1-5.

Figure 1-4   The Windows Vista Basic logo

Figure 1-5   The Windows Vista logo

In this text, we will refer to the two Windows Vista performance levels as Windows Vista Capable and Windows Vista Premium Ready.

Windows Vista Capable Requirements

A Windows Vista Capable computer is a computer that meets the minimum physical requirements necessary to run Windows Vista. A computer is considered Windows Vista Capable when it meets or exceeds the following specifications:

- 800 MHz 32-bit (x86) or 64-bit (x64) processor
- 512 MB system memory
- SVGA (800x600) video resolution
- DirectX 9-capable graphics processor
- Internal or external CD-ROM drive
- 20 GB hard disk drive, of which 15 GB must be free

Windows Vista Premium Ready Requirements

A Windows Vista Premium Ready computer runs at a higher level of performance than a Windows Vista Capable computer does and is also able to deliver the Windows Aero user experience.

Windows Aero is an optional user interface feature of Windows Vista that provides faster graphical rendering and an enhanced visual style. Aero is marked by a set of graphical user interface features such as menu bar translucency and screen thumbnails for Taskbar tiles.

Of more importance to the deployment team, however, is that Windows Vista Premium Ready computers leverage the graphics card to render graphics within the operating system. The result of this feature is that a good portion of the processing workload for Windows Vista Premium Ready computers is offloaded from the CPU to the graphics card. This process improves system performance by freeing up the CPU to perform more calculations.

A Windows Vista Premium Ready PC is one that meets or exceeds the following hardware requirements:

- 1 GHz 32-bit (x86) or 64-bit (x64) processor
- 1 GB of system memory
- Support for DirectX 9 graphics with a Windows Driver Display Model (WDDM) driver, adequate graphics memory (see note below), Pixel Shader 2.0, and 32 bits per pixel
- 40 GB of hard disk drive capacity with 15 GB of free space
- DVD-ROM Drive
- Audio output capability
- Internet access capability

NOTE **What is adequate graphics memory?**

Adequate graphics memory is defined as:

- 64 MB of graphics memory to support a single monitor at 1,310,720 or less.
- 128 MB of graphics memory to support a single monitor at resolutions of 2,304,000 pixels or less.
- 256 MB of graphics memory to support a single monitor at resolutions higher than 2,304,000 pixels.

■ Graphics memory bandwidth, as assessed by a tool such as the Windows Vista Upgrade Advisor, of at least 1,600 MB per second.

Beyond these specifications, certain optional Windows Vista features require additional hardware. For example, BitLocker Drive Encryption requires a Trusted Platform Module (TPM) 1.2 chip or a universal serial bus (USB) 2.0 flash drive. Tablet PC features require a computer that meets the Tablet PC specification (including an electromagnetic digitizer pen).

Choosing Performance Levels for Deployment

When performing a hardware assessment of your network and determining the readiness of client computers for Windows Vista, your deployment team will need to decide which computers should be upgraded to meet the standards of the Windows Vista Premium Ready program and which computers need only to meet the standards of the Windows Vista Capable program.

In general, users who work primarily with text, e-mail, and Office applications in their jobs will be perfectly capable of performing these job functions with a Windows Vista Capable computer. Because of the processing efficiency associated with Windows Vista Premium Ready computers, however, users such as graphics designers, whose jobs require greater processing power, should have their computers upgraded to meet the more stringent hardware requirements of the Windows Vista Premium Ready program.

Quick Check

1. How much RAM is required for a Windows Vista Capable computer?
2. How much RAM is required for a Windows Vista Premium Ready computer?

Quick Check Answers

1. 512 MB
2. 1 GB

Verifying Computer Hardware Requirements

In only some cases is it actually necessary to know the complete list of hardware requirements for Windows Vista. If, for example, you are building a new computer by assembling parts, or if you want to order a preassembled computer with upgraded components, you might need to ensure that the new computer is Windows Vista Capable or Windows Vista Premium Ready. Knowing the hardware requirements as you create or order the computer can be the best way to achieve this.

In many circumstances, however, knowing the specific requirements of each performance level is unnecessary. For example, if you are purchasing a standard preassembled computer, the computer's specifications typically designate the computer with either the Windows Vista Basic or the standard Windows Vista logo. In addition, if you want to check the status of a computer you already have, you can use software such as the WVUA or the WVHA tool to verify the performance level of the machine.

Verifying Requirements on an Individual Computer

If you need to determine whether a single Windows XP computer is Windows Vista Capable or Windows Vista Premium Ready, you can use the Windows Vista Upgrade Advisor (WVUA). When you run WVUA on a computer, it generates a detailed report that provides information and guidance about upgrading to Windows Vista. This information includes which steps must be taken, if any, to make the computer Windows Vista Capable or Premium Ready.

WVUA is a free tool that you can download from the Microsoft website and that is simple enough for end users to use. Although the complete report generated by WVUA is somewhat detailed, this report can be saved and e-mailed to an administrator for review.

Figure 1-6 shows a sample output screen from WVUA.

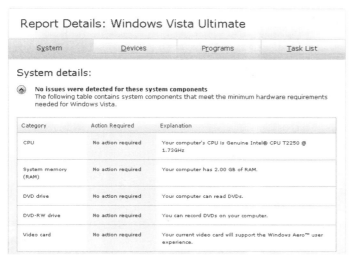

Figure 1-6   The Windows Vista Upgrade Advisor

A limitation of WVUA is that it runs separately on each computer and therefore does not scale well to mass deployments. For example, if your network includes 200 computers that you plan to upgrade to Windows Vista, it is not efficient to install and run WVUA on all 200 computers and then aggregate the results. In addition, WVUA requires physical access to each machine, which is not always feasible. Finally, a major limitation of WVUA is that it runs only on the 32-bit version of Windows XP and on Windows Vista. In other words, it does not run on Windows 95, Windows 98, Windows Me, Windows 2000, or the 64-bit version of Windows XP.

MORE INFO   Where do you get WVUA?

WVUA is included on the companion CD in the Software\WVUA folder.

You can also download WVUA from the Microsoft Download Center. To locate the WVUA download page, go to *http://download.microsoft.com* and search for "Windows Vista Upgrade Advisor."

Verifying Requirements on a Network

Windows Vista Hardware Assessment (WVHA) is a centrally managed tool that allows an administrator to determine whether other computers on the network are Windows Vista Capable or Premium Ready.

WVHA runs as a wizard-based tool. When running the WVHA Wizard, you specify domain administrator credentials for the domain or domains in which the computers are found or specify a local administrator account to be used by each local computer. WVHA then scans the network and stores information about the computers it finds in a SQL database. Upon doing this, WVHA assesses the hardware readiness of each computer for Windows Vista.

MORE INFO   Where do you get WVHA?

WVHA is included on the companion CD in the Software\WVHA folder.

You can also download WVHA from the Microsoft Download Center. To locate the WVHA download page, go to *http://download.microsoft.com* and search for "Windows Vista Hardware Assessment."

A page of the WVHA Wizard is shown in Figure 1-7.

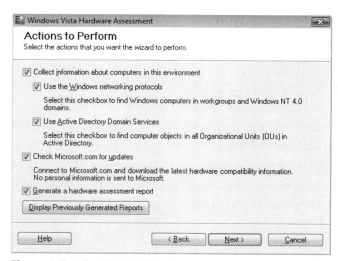

Figure 1-7   The WVHA Wizard

All of the results of the WVHA assessment are stored in a SQL database and are used to generate the following two documents:

■ **Excel Workbook**   This workbook contains spreadsheets providing the detailed results of the inventory and assessment.

■ **Readiness Report**   This report summarizes the results of the inventory and assessment. This report includes information about how many computers are ready for Windows Vista and, for computers that do not meet minimum requirements for Windows Vista, what hardware upgrades can be installed to make them ready.

Exam Tip   Although you don't need to know how to use the WVHA for the 70-622 exam, you do need to know what it is and what it is used for.

Practice: Assessing Windows Vista Hardware Readiness

In these practices, you will use the WVUA to verify the performance level of your computer. You should perform this practice on a Windows XP Professional computer (named Xpclient) if you have one available. If you don't have a Windows XP computer available, you can still run the tool on Windows Vista to see how it works.

▶ **Practice 1: Running the Windows Vista Upgrade Advisor**

In this practice, you will install and run the WVUA.

1. Install the WVUA.

MORE INFO   **Where do you get WVUA?**

WVUA is included on the companion CD in the Software\WVUA folder.

You can also download WVUA from the Microsoft Download Center. To locate the WVUA download page, go to *http://download.microsoft.com* and search for "Windows Vista Upgrade Advisor."

---

2. After installation is complete, launch the WVUA from the Start menu.
3. In the Windows Vista Upgrade Advisor window that appears, click the Start Scan button.
4. Wait for the scan to complete. This process can take up to five minutes.
5. When the scan completes, click the See Details button.
6. Spend a few minutes browsing the screens associated with each Windows Vista edition.
7. Click the link for Windows Vista Business, and then click the See Details button beneath System Requirements.
8. Answer the following question: Is any hardware upgrade required for your system to run Windows Vista?

9. Click Programs, and then answer the following question: Are there any installed applications with compatibility issues for Windows Vista?

10. Click the Save Report button. Note the default name and location assigned to the file, and then click Save.

11. Open the report file in Windows and review its contents.

12. Close the report file, and then close the Window Vista Upgrade Advisor.

Lesson Summary

- Microsoft defines two sets of hardware specifications for Windows Vista: Windows Vista Capable and Windows Vista Premium Ready. A Windows Vista Capable computer is one that is able to run Windows Vista at (at least) a basic level of performance. A Windows Vista Premium Ready computer is powerful enough to handle graphics efficiently and run the Windows Aero user experience.

- You can use the Windows Vista Upgrade Advisor (WVUA) on a single computer to determine its readiness to run Windows Vista.

- You can use Windows Vista Hardware Assessment (WVHA) to analyze all the computers in your network and determine their readiness to run Windows Vista.

Lesson Review

You can use the following questions to test your knowledge of the information in Lesson 2, "Verifying Windows Vista Hardware Requirements." The questions are also available on the companion CD if you prefer to review them in electronic form.

NOTE Answers

Answers to these questions and explanations of why each answer choice is right or wrong are located in the "Answers" section at the end of the book.

1. A user needs to upgrade her system to Windows Vista, and you want to verify that the computer meets the minimum hardware requirements. What is the best method to achieve this?

    A. Use the Application Compatibility Toolkit (ACT) 5.0.

    B. Use the Windows Vista Upgrade Advisor (WVUA).

    C. Use the Windows Vista Hardware Assessment (WVHA).

    D. Use the System Information tool to compare the local system hardware components to the requirements of Windows Vista that are published on the Microsoft website.

2. You need to create a report describing the readiness of all 50 computers in the Finance department to upgrade to Windows Vista. What is the most efficient way to achieve this?

    A. Create a script that queries the computers for system information and then compiles that information into a single document.

    B. Run the Windows Vista Upgrade Advisor (WVUA) on the Finance department computers and print the results.

    C. Use Windows Vista Hardware Assessment (WVHA) to generate an Excel Workbook and a Readiness Report that provide details about the hardware readiness of the computers for Windows Vista.

    D. User State Migration Tool (USMT) 3.0.

Lesson 3: Migrating Applications and Data

Before moving users to Windows Vista, you need to take steps to ensure that their essential applications will continue to function under the new operating system and also that the users' essential data and configuration settings will be preserved. Tools such as the Application Compatibility Toolkit (ACT), Windows Easy Transfer, and the User State Migration Tool (USMT) 3.0 will help you perform these tasks.

After this lesson, you will be able to:
- Describe the function of the Application Compatibility Toolkit 5.0.
- Describe the difference between a wipe-and-load migration and a side-by-side migration.
- Migrate user state data from one computer to another by using Windows Easy Transfer.
- Back up and restore user state data by using the User State Migration Tool.

Estimated lesson time: 30 minutes

Migrating Applications to Windows Vista

As part of the process of moving users to a new operating system, you should create and prioritize a list of their currently installed client applications that you need to migrate. You must then test each application that you decide to migrate to Windows Vista to ensure compatibility with the new operating system.

In Windows Vista, most of the new features that affect application compatibility are related to security improvements such as file and registry virtualization. If you don't plan to fix or work around these compatibility issues, users in the organization might be prevented from performing their roles, and core business functions might be impeded.

File and Registry Virtualization

Prior to Windows Vista, many applications—even those run by standard users—were run with administrator privileges. These elevated privileges were necessary because many applications write to system files and registry keys during the installation and running of the program. Often, in fact, if applications in Windows XP were configured to run with standard user privileges, they would fail to run properly because of insufficient access rights.

Running programs with administrator privileges nonetheless introduced a persistent and serious security hole in Windows installations. Malware such as worms and viruses could leverage the privileges of such a program to damage the system or install other undesirable features.

To fix this problem, Windows Vista introduced a background feature called file and registry virtualization. In Windows Vista, all applications by default run with standard user privileges. When a program attempts to write to a privileged area of the registry, the operation is redirected to a safe location reserved for each user. For example, registry operations to the global store (HKEY_LOCAL_MACHINE\Software) are redirected to a per-user location within the user's profile known as the virtual store (HKEY_USERS\<User SID>_Classes\VirtualStore\Machine\Software).

In addition to this security improvement, other Windows Vista features that might affect application compatibility include:

- Concerns with 64-bit versions of Windows Vista.
  - ❑ 16-bit applications and 32-bit drivers are not supported on 64-bit versions of Windows Vista.
  - ❑ Automatic registry and system file redirection is not supported in the 64-bit environment. These changes require that 64-bit applications must adhere to a stronger set of Windows Vista application standards.
- Applications that check operating system version.

Applications may check for a specific version of operating system, such as Microsoft Windows 98 Second Edition, Windows 2000, or Windows XP. Although the application might run correctly on Windows Vista, logic in the application might prevent the application from installing if a specific operating system version is not discovered.

Using the Microsoft Application Compatibility Toolkit 5.0

The Application Compatibility Toolkit (ACT) 5.0 is a set of tools that collects information about the applications installed on your network. After compiling a list of these installed applications, the ACT helps you understand application compatibility challenges by identifying which of these applications are compatible with Windows Vista and which require further testing.

When preparing for deployment-related application compatibility challenges, you can also use the ACT to achieve the following:

- Analyze your network's portfolio of applications, websites, and computers.
- Evaluate operating system deployments, the impact of operating system updates, and your compatibility with specific websites.
- Centrally manage compatibility evaluators and configuration settings.
- Prioritize application compatibility efforts with filtered reporting.
- Deploy automated mitigations to known compatibility issues.

MORE INFO   Where do you get ACT 5.0?

ACT 5.0 is included on the companion CD in the Software\ACT folder.

You can also download ACT from the Microsoft Download Center. To locate the ACT download page, go to *http://download.microsoft.com* and search for "Application Compatibility Toolkit." If you want to learn more about how to use the ACT, you can perform the ACT virtual lab in the "Suggested Practices" section at the end of this chapter.

Exam Tip   Although you don't need to know how to use the ACT for the 70-622 exam, you do need to know what it is and what it is used for.

Migrating Data to Windows Vista

Besides planning for the migration of applications, you also need to plan for the migration of data before you deploy Windows Vista. Typically, data that is migrated is first backed up from the source systems and then restored to the target systems during the deployment process. In general, the data that needs to be backed up includes user data, operating system data, and application data.

Choosing What to Back Up

When planning for your migration, you should identify the file types, files, folders, and settings that you want to migrate.

First, determine the standard file locations on each computer, such as My Documents, C:\Data, and company-specified locations, such as \EngineeringDrafts. Next, you should determine the nonstandard locations. For nonstandard locations, consider the following:

- **File types** Consider which file types need to be included and excluded from the migration. You can create this list based on common applications used in your organization. For example, Microsoft Word primarily uses .doc (and under Word 2007, the .docx) file name extension. However, it also uses other file types, such as templates (.dot files), less frequently.
- **Excluded locations** Consider the locations on the computer that should be excluded from the migration (for example, %windir% and Program Files).
- **New locations** Decide where files should be migrated to on the destination computer (for example, My Documents, a designated folder, or the original location).

After you catalog the files and folders that you want to back up, you should identify which system settings you want to migrate. These system settings might include desktop appearance and wallpaper, key repeat rates, Web browser home page, and e-mail account settings.

To help you decide which settings to migrate, you should consider what you might have learned from any previous migrations you have performed in the same environment and also the results of any surveys or tests that you have conducted. You should also consider the number of help desk calls related to operating system settings that you have had in the past and are able to handle in the future.

In general, you will want to migrate the settings that users need to perform in their jobs, the settings that make the work environment comfortable, and the settings that will reduce help desk calls after the migration. Do not underestimate the importance of migrating user preferences because users can spend a significant amount of time restoring items such as wallpaper, screen savers, and other customizable user-interface features. Most users do not remember how to reapply these settings, and though these items are not critical to migration success, migrating them increases user productivity and the overall satisfaction with the migration process.

Determining Where to Store Data

After you have compiled a list of the files and settings that will be transferred from the users' machines, you'll need to determine where this data will be stored during the migration process. The most suitable choice depends on whether you are performing a wipe-and-load migration or a side-by-side migration on the computers in question.

Wipe-and-Load Migration

In this type of migration, an individual computer is *upgraded* to Windows Vista. For such a scenario, the administrator typically migrates the user state from a source computer to an intermediate store. After installing the operating system, the administrator then migrates the user state back to the same source computer. Figure 1-8 depicts a wipe-and-load migration.

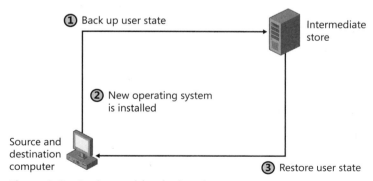

Figure 1-8 A wipe-and-load migration

NOTE   Complete PC backup

You should back up the entire contents of a computer before performing a wipe-and-load migration.

If you are performing a wipe-and-load migration, storing data on a locally attached drive is normally the best option in terms of performance. In this method you can store the data either on a separate partition on an internal hard disk or on a removable device such as a USB drive. However, if no local drive is available with sufficient space, you can choose to store the data on a network share instead.

NOTE   Storing user data on the OS partition

Believe it or not, the new Windows imaging (WIM) technology allows you—theoretically, at least—to store all the migration data on the very same drive as the one on which you will be installing Windows Vista. Because WIM file imaging is nondestructive, deploying a WIM file image on a drive will erase an existing file or folder only if the drive already contains a file or folder with the same name. However, this strategy makes little sense when you consider that, typically, when you choose to deploy a Windows Vista image, you will want to format the target drive beforehand. Formatting the drive, of course, will delete the migration data stored on the drive along with the rest of drive's contents.

Exam Tip   In some rare cases you might need to configure computers to dual-boot in Windows Vista and another operating system such as Windows XP. In this case, install each operating system on its own partition. If users will be accessing and working with the same data from both operating systems, you should keep that data separate from both operating systems on a third, separate partition.

Side-by-Side Migration

In this type of migration a user's computer is *replaced* with a more powerful model on which Windows Vista is installed. To begin this migration process, the administrator typically migrates the user state from the source computer to an intermediate store. After installing the operating system on the destination computer, the administrator then migrates the user state from the intermediate store to the destination computer. Figure 1-9 shows a side-by-side migration.

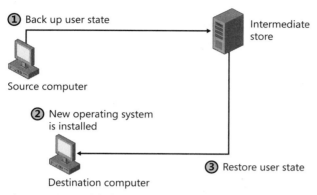

Figure 1-9   A side-by-side migration

If you are performing a side-by-side migration, storing the backed-up user data on a network share is typically the simplest and most manageable option. If storing on a network share is not feasible, you can choose instead to back up the user state data to a removable USB drive or other device that you can then physically transport to the new computer.

NOTE   Side-by-side with Windows Easy Transfer

When using Windows Easy Transfer to perform a side-by-side migration of computer settings, backing up to an intermediate store is not the best option. You can achieve much higher performance by establishing a direct connection between the computers with a Windows Easy Transfer cable (described in the next section).

After you decide where to back up the data, you next need to determine *how* to back up the data. The two most common tools for backing up user data during migration are Windows Easy Transfer and the USMT.

Migrating User Data with Windows Easy Transfer

Windows Easy Transfer is a tool whose purpose is to simplify the process of migrating a small number of users to Windows Vista in a secure fashion. Similar to the File and Settings Transfer Wizard in Windows XP, Windows Easy Transfer allows you to transfer data and settings from a Windows 2000 or Windows XP computer to a Windows Vista computer by any of the following means:

- **Windows Easy Transfer Cable**   A Windows Easy Transfer Cable is a special USB 2.0 cable designed to be used with the Windows Easy Transfer utility. This cable, which you can purchase online or at an electronics store, allows you to connect two computers from USB port to USB port. This data migration method works with Microsoft Windows 2000 (files only), Windows XP, and Windows Vista.

NOTE   **USB cables and Windows Easy Transfer**

You can't use an ordinary USB cable to transfer data between computers by using Windows Easy Transfer.

The advantage of this method is that it offers the best performance of any data migration method. A disadvantage is that it requires the computers to be located close enough to each other to be joined by a cable.

A Windows Easy Transfer cable is shown in Figure 1-10.

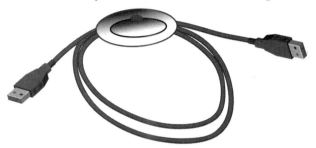

Figure 1-10   A Windows Easy Transfer cable

- **Local area network**   You can use Windows Easy Transfer to back up user state data to a network share, and then restore them to the target computer.
- **CD**   If the source computer is running Windows XP and has an attached CD recordable drive, you can use Windows Easy Transfer to back up user state data to a disc. Windows 2000 does not support CD burning.

NOTE   **DVD burning and Windows Easy Transfer**

Although this function is not related to Windows Vista deployment, you can use Windows Easy Transfer to transfer data from one Windows Vista computer to another. In this case you can burn the data to a CD *or* DVD at the source Windows Vista computer. DVD burning is not supported in Windows XP or Windows 2000.

- **Removable storage**   Windows Easy Transfer allows you to back data up to a locally attached USB drive or other drive. You can then physically transport the drive to the destination computer and restore the data from this drive.

What Can You Back Up with Windows Easy Transfer?

If you are migrating a user from a Windows XP computer, you can use Windows Easy Transfer to transfer the user's files and folders, user accounts and settings, e-mail contacts and messages, e-mail settings, program settings, Internet settings and favorites, music, pictures, and videos. Note that if you want to transfer program settings to Windows Vista, you must first install that program on the target Windows Vista-based computer before you run Windows Easy Transfer.

From Windows 2000 you can use Windows Easy Transfer only to transfer files to Windows Vista. You cannot transfer any settings.

NOTE   **Which service packs do I need?**

On the source computer, Windows Easy Transfer runs on Windows 2000 Service Pack 4 or later and Windows XP Service Pack 2 or later.

Using Windows Easy Transfer

Windows Easy Transfer is a wizard-based tool that provides its own instructions for use. However, it is useful to have an overview of the general process of transferring data by using this utility. This general process includes the following steps:

1. Running the tool on the destination (Windows Vista) computer by clicking Start, All Programs, Accessories, System Tools, and then Windows Easy Transfer

2. Using the wizard to help you transfer the Windows Easy Transfer program files to the source (Windows XP or Windows 2000) computer

3. Running MigWiz.exe (the Windows Easy Transfer executable) on the source computer

4. Transferring the files and settings from the source computer to the destination computer

The first page of the Windows Easy Transfer Wizard is shown in Figure 1-11.

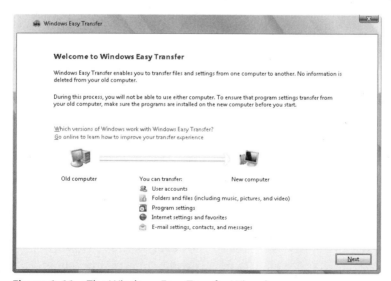

Figure 1-11   The Windows Easy Transfer Wizard

Migrating User Data with the User State Migration Tool 3.0

You can use the User State Migration Tool (USMT) 3.0 to migrate user accounts during large deployments of Windows Vista. USMT captures user accounts, including each user's settings and files, and then migrates these accounts to a new Windows installation. USMT is intended for administrators who are performing automated deployments. If you are migrating the user states of only a few computers, you can use Windows Easy Transfer instead.

Overview of USMT 3.0

USMT essentially refers to two command-line utilities (Scanstate and Loadstate), a set of customizable Extensible Markup Language (XML) files (MigApp.xml, MigSys.xml, and MigUser.xml), and various internal files. To migrate user state data by using USMT, first run Scanstate on the source computer to copy the data to an intermediate store. Then run Loadstate on the destination computer to copy the same data from the intermediate store.

By modifying the XML files, you can maintain a high degree of control over the migration process. For instance, you can specify what to copy and what not to copy, arbitrate conflicts between the source computer and destination computer, modify where the data is migrated to on the destination computer, emulate missing settings, and remove settings from the destination computer.

MORE INFO   **Where do you get USMT 3.0.1**

USMT 3.0.1 is included on the companion CD in the Software\USMT folder.

You can also download USMT 3.0.1 from the Microsoft Download Center. To locate the USMT 3.0.1 download page, go to *http://download.microsoft.com* and search for "USMT."

Exam Tip   Remember that you need to run Scanstate and Loadstate with administrative credentials. To achieve this in Windows Vista, remember first to open your command prompt by right-clicking Command Prompt in the Start menu and then clicking Run As Administrator.

The following section provides two examples of how USMT is used.

USMT Example #1: Migrating All Users and User Settings

To migrate all users and settings from one computer to another, perform the following steps:

1. Log on to the source computer as an administrator and type the following at a command prompt:

   ```
   scanstate \\fileserver\migration\mystore /i:miguser.xml /i:migapp.xml /o
   ```

   In this command, user and application settings are copied to the network location \\fileserver\migration\mystore. The switch /i is used to specify each .xml file that contains rules defining what to migrate. The first .xml file specified, Miguser.xml, is used to migrate user folders, files, and file types to computers running both Windows XP and Windows Vista. The second .xml file specified, Migapp.xml, is used to migrate application settings to computers running both Windows XP and Windows Vista. Finally, the switch /o overwrites any existing data in the store.

2. Log on to the destination computer as an administrator.

If you are migrating domain accounts, type the following at a command prompt:

```
loadstate \\fileserver\migration\mystore /i:miguser.xml /i:migapp.xml
```

If you are migrating local accounts along with domain accounts, type the following:

```
loadstate \\fileserver\migration\mystore /i:miguser.xml /i:migapp.xml /lac /lae
```

In these commands, user and application settings are copied from the network location \\fileserver\migration\mystore. In the latter command, the /lac switch specifies that if a user account is a local (nondomain) account and does *not* exist on the destination computer, USMT will create the account on the destination computer in a disabled state. To enable the account, you must also specify the /lae switch. If /lac is not specified, any local user accounts (that do not already exist on the destination computer) will not be migrated.

USMT Example #2: Migrating Two Domain Accounts (User1 and User2)

To migrate two domain accounts from one computer to another, perform the following steps:

1. Log on to the source computer as administrator and type the following at a command prompt:

```
scanstate \\fileserver\migration\mystore /ue:*\* /ui:domain1\user1 /ui:domain2\user2 /
i:miguser.xml
```

In this command, two domain users are copied to the network location \\fileserver\migration\mystore. The switch /ue is used to exclude certain users from being migrated, and since the argument "**" that follows signifies "all users in all domains," the command is actually specifying that *no* users should be migrated—*except* those included with the /ui (user include) switch.

2. Log on to the destination computer as an administrator and type the following at a command prompt:

```
loadstate \\fileserver\migration\mystore /i:miguser.xml /i:migapp.xml
```

In this command, two domain users and their settings are copied from the network location \\fileserver\migration\mystore.

Exam Tip   For the 70-622 exam, you should be able to understand all of the syntax in the previous Scanstate and Loadstate examples. In addition, you need to understand the following common switches:

❑ **/v**   Allows you to specify the level of verbosity (from 0 to 15) in the output of the Scanstate log.

❑ **/c**   Allows Scanstate to continue even if there are nonfatal errors.

❑ **/p**   Does not collect the user state but generates a space estimate file called Usmt-size.txt. To use this option, you must also specify the /nocompress switch.

❑ **/all**   Migrates all of the users on a computer.

Quick Check

■ In what way is USMT better than Windows Easy Transfer for migrating many users in a large-scale environment?

Quick Check Answer

■ USMT is far more customizable and gives you far greater control over the migration process than does Windows Easy Transfer.

Practice: Transferring Users by Using USMT 3.0.1

In these practices, you will use USMT 3.0.1 to move a user from a source Windows XP computer (Xpclient) to a target Windows Vista computer (Vista1). If you don't have a Windows XP computer, you can substitute another Windows Vista computer as the source computer.

▶ **Practice 1: Backing Up User Data with Scanstate**

In this practice, you will use the Scanstate utility to copy user data to a network share.

1. On Vista1, enable File Sharing in the Network And Sharing Center.

2. Using the ping command, ensure that Vista1 and Xpclient can communicate with each other.

3. Install USMT 3.0.1 on both XPClient and Vista1. Be sure to choose the version that corresponds to the appropriate operating system and architecture: x64 or x86.

MORE INFO   Where do you get USMT 3.0.1

USMT 3.0.1 is included on the companion CD in the Software\USMT folder.

You can also download USMT 3.0 from the Microsoft Download Center. To locate the USMT 3.0.1 download page, go to *http://download.microsoft.com* and search for "USMT."

---

4. Log on to Xpclient as an administrator. Create a local account named TestUser on the computer by using the User Accounts program in Control Panel.

5. Log on to Xpclient as TestUser. Modify the desktop background and save a new text file named Test in the My Documents folder.

6. On Xpclient, log back on with your administrator account.

7. On the root of the C drive, create a folder named USMTdata.

8. Open a command prompt.

9. At the command prompt, use the Cd command to navigate to the USMT program directory. For example, if you have installed USMT 3.0.1, type **cd "C:\Program Files \USMT301"**. (You can use the dir command to search the Program Files directory and determine the specific name of your USMT program directory.)

10. At a command prompt, type the following:

```
scanstate C:\USMTdata /i:miguser.xml /i:migapp.xml /c
```

▶ **Practice 2: Restoring User Data with Loadstate**

In this practice, you will transfer the newly created user account to Vista1.

1. Log on to Vista1 with an administrator account.

2. Copy the USMTdata folder from Xpclient to the root of the C drive on Vista1. You can perform this step any way you choose. For example, you can transport the folder by using a USB drive or by sharing the folder and copying its contents to the new location over the network.

3. On Vista1, open a command prompt by running it as Administrator. To do this, click the Start button, click All Programs, click Accessories, right-click Command Prompt, and then, from the shortcut menu, click Run As Administrator.

4. At the command prompt, use the Cd command to navigate to the USMT program directory. For example, if you have installed USMT 3.0.1, type **cd "C:\Program Files \USMT301"**. (You can use the dir command to search the Program Files directory and determine the specific name of your USMT directory.)

5. At the command prompt, type the following:

```
loadstate C:\USMTdata /i:miguser.xml /i:migapp.xml /c /lac /lae
```

6. Restart Vista1 and log on to the computer as TestUser. Have all the desktop settings been preserved? Can you find the Test document that you created?

7. Log off Vista1.

Lesson Summary

- If you are upgrading computers to Windows Vista in a business environment, you need to test currently installed applications to ensure their compatibility with the new operating system. The Application Compatibility Toolkit 5.0 can help you do this.

- A wipe-and-load migration involves changing an operating system without changing a computer. A side-by-side migration involves changing both the operating system and the computer.

- When you migrate users to Windows Vista, you need to preserve their data and settings from the old operating system. To achieve this, you can back up their user state data from the old system to an intermediate store. Then, on the new Windows Vista system, you need to restore that user state data from the intermediate store.

■ Windows Easy Transfer is a tool built into Windows Vista that simplifies the process of migrating the data of a few users to Windows Vista.

■ USMT 3.0 is a tool that includes two command-line utilities (Scanstate and Loadstate), a set of customizable XML files (MigApp.xml, MigSys.xml, and MigUser.xml), and various internal files. Because of its power and customizability, you can use USMT to back up and restore the data of many users during a migration to Windows Vista.

Lesson Review

You can use the following questions to test your knowledge of the information in Lesson 3, "Migrating Applications and Data." The questions are also available on the companion CD if you prefer to review them in electronic form.

NOTE   Answers

Answers to these questions and explanations of why each answer choice is right or wrong are located in the "Answers" section at the end of the book.

---

1. Your deployment team wants to evaluate the current software environment of your organization's network in order to determine which applications will and will not run on Windows Vista. Which of the following tools best allows you to achieve this?

   A. User State Migration Tool (USMT) 3.0

   B. Application Compatibility Toolkit (ACT) 5.0

   C. Windows Easy Transfer

   D. Windows Vista Hardware Assessment (WVHA)

2. You are migrating a single user to a new Windows Vista computer. Which tool should you use to migrate the user's data from her old computer to the new computer?

   A. Windows Easy Transfer

   B. User State Migration Tool (USMT) 3.0

   C. Complete PC Backup

   D. Windows Vista Upgrade Advisor (WVUA)

3. You want to use Loadstate to migrate user data from an intermediate store to a new Windows Vista computer. Which switch should you specify to ensure that Loadstate continues to migrate the data even if nonfatal errors occur during the migration process?

   A. /v

   B. /all

   C. /q

   D. /c

Chapter Review

To further practice and reinforce the skills you learned in this chapter, you can

- Review the chapter summary.
- Review the list of key terms introduced in this chapter.
- Complete the case scenario. This scenario sets up a real-world situation involving the topics of this chapter and asks you to create solutions.
- Complete the suggested practices.
- Take a practice test.

Chapter Summary

- In a business environment, it's especially important to prepare for the challenges that precede operating system deployment. These challenges include hardware assessment, application compatibility testing, and user state data migration.
- To determine whether a single Windows XP computer can be upgraded to Windows Vista, you can use the Windows Vista Upgrade Advisor. To analyze all the computers in your network and determine their readiness to run Windows Vista, you can use the Windows Vista Hardware Assessment (WVHA) tool.
- If you are upgrading computers to Windows Vista in a business environment, you need to test currently installed applications to ensure their compatibility with the new operating system. The Application Compatibility Toolkit 5.0 can assist you in this process.
- Windows Easy Transfer is a tool built into Windows Vista that simplifies the process of migrating the data of a few users to Windows Vista.
- USMT 3.0 is a tool that includes two command-line utilities (Scanstate and Loadstate), a set of customizable XML files (MigApp.xml, MigSys.xml, and MigUser.xml), and various internal files. Because of its power and customizability, you can use USMT to back up and restore the data of many users during a migration to Windows Vista.

Key Terms

Do you know what these key terms mean? You can check your answers by looking up the terms in the glossary at the end of the book.

- Windows Aero
- Windows Driver Display Model (WDDM)

Case Scenarios

In the following case scenario you will apply what you've learned in this chapter. You can find answers to these questions in the "Answers" section at the end of this book.

Case Scenario 1: Performing Upgrades

You are a computer support specialist in a medium-sized business. Your boss has asked you to begin upgrading company computers from Windows XP to Windows Vista. He wants you to begin by upgrading the computers that require no additional hardware purchases.

1. You begin by investigating the computers in the Customer Service department because the users in this department do not require high processing power. You already know that of the seven computers in the Customer Service department, four have 256 MB of RAM, two have 512 MB of RAM, and one has 1024 MB of RAM. On how many computers in the Customer Service department should you run the WVUA to determine hardware readiness for Windows Vista?

2. A few months later, your boss asks you to migrate 10 laptop users to new models running Windows Vista. He wants you to perform these migrations as quickly as possible. Which tool or set of tools should you use to achieve this?

Case Scenario 2: Migrating Data

You are a desktop support technician in a large company with 500 employees. You are working with a deployment team to begin Windows Vista rollout. Currently, you and your team are choosing details about the project.

1. Some computers that will be upgraded to Windows Vista have two internal hard disks. All have CD burners, and all have access to plentiful network storage. You want to standardize the data migration process as much as possible. To which location should you plan to back up user state data during the migration process?

2. Assume that your team will be performing a wipe-and-load migration on the computers that will be upgraded to Windows Vista. Which tool should you use to transfer user data during the migration process?

3. Which tool should you use to transfer user data for side-by-side migrations?

Suggested Practices

To help you successfully master the exam objectives presented in this chapter, complete the following tasks.

Perform a Migration

- **Practice 1: Upgrade a System**   On a Windows XP computer, use USMT 3.0 to back up user data to an intermediate store. Format the hard disk drive on the Windows XP computer, and then install Windows Vista from the product CD. Use USMT 3.0 to restore the user data to the Windows Vista computer.

- **Practice 2: Use the Windows Easy Transfer Cable**   Purchase a Windows Easy Transfer cable. Use the cable to connect two computers. Then, use Windows Easy Transfer to transfer user data from one computer to another.

Assess Network Hardware Readiness

- **Practice 1: Analyze Your Network's Readiness for Windows Vista**   Install the WVHA tool on a network computer. Use the tool to scan your network and analyze its computers' readiness for Windows Vista.

Watch a Webcast

- **Practice 1: Learn About Real Windows Vista Deployments**   Watch the webcast, "TechNet Webcast: How Microsoft IT Deployed Windows Vista (Level 300)" by Chad Lewis, available on the companion CD in the Webcasts folder.

Perform a Virtual Lab

- **Practice 1: Learn more about using the Application Compatibility Toolkit**   Go to *http:// msevents.microsoft.com* and search for "Event ID# 1032330298". Register and perform the virtual lab named "Windows Vista: Application Compatibility Toolkit 5.0 Virtual Lab."

- **Practice 2: Migrate Data from Windows XP to Windows Vista in a Virtual Environment**   Go to *http://msevents.microsoft.com* and search for "Event ID# 1032305599". Register and perform the virtual lab named "Migrating User State from Windows XP to Windows Vista Virtual Lab."

Take a Practice Test

The practice tests on this book's companion CD offer many options. For example, you can test yourself on just one exam objective, or you can test yourself on all the 70-622 certification exam content. You can set up the test so that it closely simulates the experience of taking a certification exam, or you can set it up in study mode so that you can look at the correct answers and explanations after you answer each question.

MORE INFO   Practice tests

For details about all the practice test options available, see the "How to Use the Practice Tests" section in this book's Introduction.

Chapter 2
Deploying Windows Vista

After you have performed the necessary preparations and backed up user data, you are ready to perform the actual Windows Vista deployment. In the past, large-scale Windows deployments were often performed by means of Remote Installation Services (RIS) or third-party imaging technologies. However, with Windows Vista, Microsoft has introduced a new process of installing and deploying Windows in a corporate environment. This change is reflected in a new suite of technologies (such as WIM files) and tools (such as ImageX) that support Windows Vista installation.

This chapter introduces you to many of these deployment procedures and tools that are new to Windows Vista. Armed with this knowledge, you can choose the deployment method that best suits the needs of your organization.

Exam objectives in this chapter:
- Analyze the business environment and select an appropriate deployment method.
- Deploy Windows Vista from a custom image.

Lessons in this chapter:

Before You Begin

To complete the lessons in this chapter, you must have completed the lab setup instructions provided in the book's Introduction. In particular, you need:

- A Windows Server 2003 domain controller named dcsrv1.nwtraders.msft on which you have installed the Windows Automated Installation Kit (WAIK). (You can download the WAIK from *http://download.microsoft.com*. Specific directions for downloading and installing the WAIK can be found in the introduction to this book.)
- A Windows Vista Business, Enterprise, or Ultimate computer named Vista1.
- A second computer named Vista2 on which no software or operating system is installed.

Real World

JC Mackin

The introduction of the new WIM imaging technology native to Windows is a huge development. Yes, of course it's nice that Windows now has its own built-in imaging and that you no longer have to buy third-party software when you want to image a computer. But that's not what's so great about it. To me, the best thing about WIM file imaging is that, unlike most imaging formats, it's almost completely hardware-independent. I can't tell you how many times the images I've made from third-party tools have become out-dated only because of a hardware change or a computer upgrade. Not only will the WIM file images I'm making with ImageX have a longer shelf life, but they're also usable right now on many more computers than my old images ever were. Beyond this, many tasks that were difficult to perform before are now suddenly made easy. Move a user to a new computer? No problem. Move your system to a partition with more space? Piece of cake. Edit an image offline? Go ahead.

And because this book is about Windows Vista, there's one other thing that you might not realize about WIM file imaging: with some limitations, you can actually use ImageX to make WIM files of your Windows XP computers as well. So by all means, break out of the book you're holding and start experimenting with these new technologies and tools—regardless of whether you have Windows Vista or XP computers to work with. Independent of any exams you might be preparing for, WIM files are going to be around for a long time, and you're going to need to develop some familiarity with them. In this particular case, I'm betting, you'll actually have some fun doing so.

Lesson 1: Understanding Windows Vista Deployment

Windows Vista introduces a significant change to the line of Windows operating systems in that it is deployed *only* by means of disk imaging technology. To support this new image-based deployment, Windows now includes a native Windows Imaging (WIM) format and many new associated tools.

Windows Vista is delivered on the product media in this new WIM format. You can install this Windows Vista image by using the Setup program on the Windows product DVD or, by using new tools, create customized images for automated deployment.

After this lesson, you will be able to:
- Understand the features and advantages of WIM file images.
- Understand the function of Windows Vista deployment tools such as Windows PE, ImageX, Windows System Image Manager (SIM), and Sysprep.

Estimated lesson time: 30 minutes

Introduction to WIM Files

At the center of the Windows deployment processes is the WIM file. A WIM file is technically not an image but a file containing one or more disk images in the WIM format. These images are file-based, which means that they are composed of collections of volume files and are not merely "sector-based" snapshots of disk data, as is common with many other disk imaging applications. The main advantage of file-based images over sector-based images is that you can modify them before, during, and after deployment.

Besides storing file data, WIM files include XML-based metadata describing the files and directories that make up each image. This metadata includes access control lists (ACLs), short/long file names, attributes, and other information used to restore an imaged volume.

Figure 2-1 shows the metadata associated with a specific WIM file.

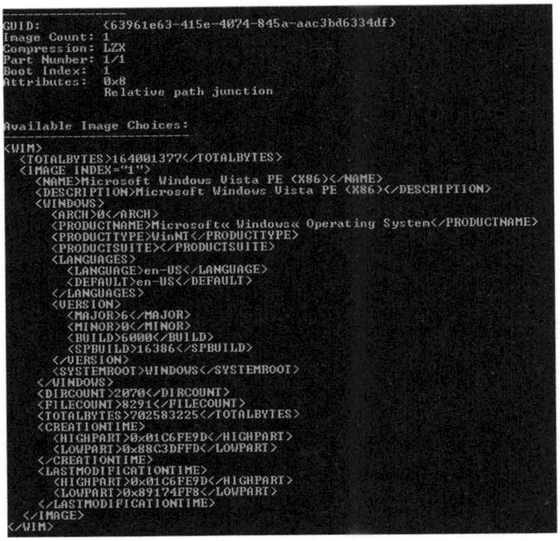

Figure 2-1   Viewing WIM file information

NOTE   Install.wim

The original image of Windows Vista stored on the Windows Vista DVD is contained in the file *install.wim*.

WIM files offer a number of additional Windows deployment advantages, including the following:

- Because the WIM image format is hardware-agnostic, you need only one image to support many hardware configurations or hardware abstraction layers (HALs). (Separate images, however, are needed for x86 and 64-bit operating systems.)
- WIM files allow images to be customized by scripts or automated by answer files upon installation.
- The WIM image format allows you to modify the contents of an image offline. You can add or delete certain operating system components, updates, and drivers without creating a new image.
- WIM files need to keep only one copy of disk files common to all the images stored in the file. This feature dramatically reduces the amount of storage space required to accommodate multiple images.

- You can start a computer from a disk image contained in a WIM file by marking an image as bootable.

- The WIM image format allows for nondestructive deployment. This means that you can leave data on the volume to which you apply the image because the application of the image does not erase the disk's existing contents.

- A WIM file image uses only as much space as the files that comprise it. Therefore, you can use WIM files to capture data on a volume with empty space and then migrate the data to a smaller volume.

- A WIM file can span multiple CDs or DVDs.

- WIM files support two types of compression—Xpress (fast) and LZX (high)—in addition to no compression (fastest).

WIM Files and Modularization

Windows Vista has been written to increase its modularity over previous versions of Windows. Because of this modularity, you can effectively add, remove, or swap many operating system components within any WIM file image. For example, unlike with previous versions of Windows, you don't need to obtain a language-specific version of Windows Vista if you want to view the interface in a language besides English. With Windows Vista, the interface language is simply a modular component that can be added or removed from any WIM file image.

Windows Vista Deployment Tools

The following section describes some of the main tools used to help deploy Windows Vista in the enterprise.

Windows Preinstallation Environment (Windows PE) 2.0

Windows PE 2.0, also known as WinPE, is a bootable and lightweight version of Windows that you can use to start a computer from a removable medium such as a CD or from a network source. Although the main purpose of Windows PE is to provide an environment from which to capture or apply a Windows image, you can also use it to troubleshoot or recover an installed operating system. In general, you can think of Windows PE as a replacement for bootable MS-DOS disks, but, unlike the 16-bit MS-DOS that requires its own set of drivers, the 32-bit Windows PE operating system leverages the drivers used in Windows Vista.

Windows PE can run many familiar (mostly command-line) programs and even communicate over IP networks. If you boot a computer from a typical Windows PE disk, a command prompt will appear from which you can run built-in tools and other programs you have made available.

NOTE   A lightweight Windows

Although installations of Windows PE vary in size, a typical installation requires about 100 MB of space in RAM. Because of its size, Windows PE cannot be run from a floppy disk.

NOTE   Windows Vista Setup and Windows PE

Windows PE provides the basis for all Windows Vista installations. Whenever you boot from the Windows Vista DVD and run the Setup program, Windows PE is actually running in the background.

Although Windows PE *starts* from the CD drive, Windows PE 2.0 does not actually *run* from the CD drive when it is fully booted. Windows PE 2.0 instead creates a RAM disk (a portion of RAM used as a drive), loads the operating system into that drive, and then runs from that RAM disk. This RAM disk is assigned the drive letter X.

NOTE   Replacing the CD in Windows PE

Because Windows PE loads into and runs from a RAM disk, you can remove the Windows PE CD and insert a second CD to access additional required drivers or software.

The X:\Windows\System32 folder contains many programs and utilities that you can execute in Windows PE. Although most of these tools are also used in the full version of Windows Vista, some tools—such as drvload, wdscapture, and wpeutil—are specific to Windows PE.

- **Drvload**   Adds out-of-box drivers to a booted Windows PE image
- **Wdscapture**   Allows you to capture an image and upload it into Windows Deployment Services (WDS)
- **Wpeutil**   Enables you to perform many functions, such as shut down or reboot Windows PE, enable or disable the firewall, configure language settings, and initialize a network

Besides these tools built into Windows PE, you can install additional Windows PE tools through the WAIK. These tools include the following:

- **Oscdimg**   Creates an ISO image of Windows PE
- **PEimg**   Used to view and modify the contents of a Windows PE image
- **BCDEdit**   Modifies the Boot Configuration Data (BCD) store, which controls the operating system loading preferences in multiboot systems

---

Exam Tip   Along with the other tools and technologies mentioned in this chapter, be sure to know these last six command-line tools for the exam.

> ## Quick Check
> 1. True or False? A single WIM file image can support only one type of HAL.
> 2. What advantage does Windows PE have over MS-DOS disks?
>
> ## Quick Check Answers
> 1. False. A single WIM file image can support different HALs; however, a single WIM file image can support only a 32-bit or a 64-bit CPU architecture, not both.
> 2. Windows PE can run off of a CD-ROM and leverages the drivers used for Windows Vista.

ImageX

ImageX is a command-line tool that you can use to capture, modify, and apply WIM images for deployment.

The main function of ImageX is to let you capture a volume to a WIM file image and to apply a WIM file image to a volume. For example, to capture an image, you can boot into Windows PE and use the command **imagex /capture C:** *wimfilename*.**wim** "*Image_Name*". To apply an image to a volume, use **imagex /apply** *wimfilename*.**wim 1**. (In this case, the value 1 indicates the index number of the image within the file wimfilename.wim.)

Another important feature of ImageX is that it lets you mount a WIM file image in the Windows file system so that you can modify the contents of that image. For example, you can mount an operating system image to add device drivers and then unmount it so that it is once again ready to be applied to a volume.

Windows System Image Manager (Windows SIM)

Windows System Image Manager (SIM) is the tool used to create unattended Windows Setup answer files. In Windows Vista answer files are XML-based documents used during Windows Setup to supply information needed by the Windows installation. For example, you can use Windows SIM to create an answer file that partitions and formats a disk before installing Windows or that changes the default setting for the Internet Explorer home page. By modifying settings in the answer file, you can also use Windows SIM to install third-party applications, device drivers, language packs, and other updates.

NOTE   **Windows XP Setup Manager**

As a means to create answer files for unattended installations, Windows SIM replaces the Setup Manager tool used with previous versions of Windows.

Window SIM uses catalog (.clg) files along with Windows images (WIM files) to display the available components and packages that can be added to an unattended answer file. Catalog files and WIM files contain configurable settings that you can modify once the component or package is added to an answer file.

IMPORTANT   Catalog (.clg) files

You need to re-create the catalog file associated with a Windows image whenever you update a WIM file image.

Figure 2-2 shows the Windows SIM tool.

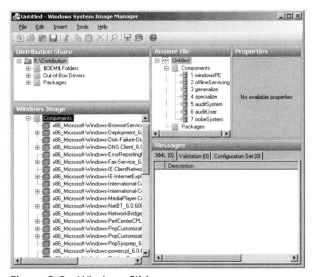

Figure 2-2   Windows SIM

NOTE   Windows Automated Installation Kit (WAIK)

Windows PE, ImageX, and Windows SIM are all made available through the Windows Automated Installation Kit (WAIK). You can download the WAIK through the Deployment Workbench tool or by searching for "WAIK" at *http://download.microsoft.com*.

User State Migration Tool (USMT) 3.0

You can use the User State Migration Tool (USMT) 3.0 (introduced in Chapter 1, "Preparing for Windows Deployment") to migrate user files and settings during large deployments of Windows XP and Windows Vista. USMT captures desktop settings, application settings, user accounts, and users' files, and then migrates these elements to a new Windows installation.

Application Compatibility Toolkit (ACT) 5.0

The Application Compatibility Toolkit (ACT) 5.0 (introduced in Chapter 1, "Preparing for Windows Deployment") is a set of tools that helps you resolve application compatibility issues related to deploying Windows Vista and Windows Updates. One of the functions of the ACT is to analyze the network for installed applications and identify which of these applications are compatible with Windows Vista.

Sysprep

The Sysprep tool generalizes a specific computer's installation so that it can be used on many other computers. Sysprep achieves this generalization by removing only those settings of the installation that would not be shared by other computers—settings such as the computer name, its domain membership, the time zone, the product key, the security identifier (SID), and various other user and machine settings. When you run Sysprep on an installation of Windows, a Sysprep image is generated, and the installation is said to be *Sysprepped*.

After you run Sysprep, the computer shuts down. The Sysprepped installation then resides on the hard disk, ready to be captured by ImageX into a WIM file and deployed to other computers.

Of course, the settings that are removed by Sysprep need to be replaced on each computer that uses the Sysprepped image. Some of these settings (such as the computer SID) are automatically regenerated when the installation boots for the first time after Sysprep has run. Other settings might be provided by an answer file you configure in advance and supply when the Sysprepped image first boots. All remaining settings needed by the system are provided by the user in Windows Welcome, an interactive wizard that appears during the first boot after Sysprep is run.

Business Desktop Deployment (BDD) 2007

Business Desktop Deployment (BDD) 2007 is a collection of tools and documentation used to support the automated deployment of Windows Vista and Microsoft Office in a corporate environment. The main tool of BDD 2007 is the Deployment Workbench (also known as the BDD Workbench), shown in Figure 2-3. The Deployment Workbench includes its own set of tools and documentation, along with pointers to other information and required tools online.

Using the tools available in and through the Deployment Workbench, BDD 2007 provides guidance to deploy Windows Vista in environments both with and without Systems Management Server (SMS). Complete automation is possible only with SMS, so these two deployment scenarios are known as Zero Touch Installation (ZTI) and Lite Touch Installation (LTI), respectively.

BDD includes pointers to download the USMT, ACT 5.0, and the WAIK.

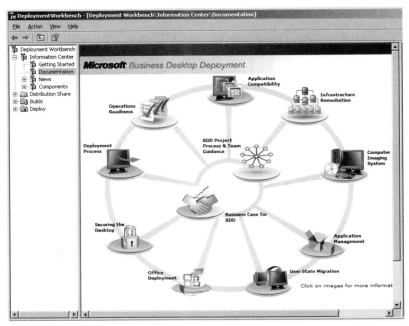

Figure 2-3   The Deployment Workbench

Windows Deployment Services (Windows DS or WDS)

Windows Deployment Services is a set of components that enables administrators to deploy WIM files over the network without having to be physically present at each computer. (An end user is normally present at the destination computer, but this end user does not require any technical expertise.)

NOTE   **WDS and RIS**

Windows Deployment Services is the updated and redesigned version of Remote Installation Services (RIS). To install WDS on a Windows Server 2003 computer, first install RIS. Then you can upgrade RIS by using a tool provided in the WAIK.

When WDS is configured, a client can boot without an operating system, search for and locate a WDS server on the network, and load a WIM file image from the WDS server.

Lesson Summary

- Windows Vista is installed only by means of new Windows images stored in WIM files. WIM files include one or more *file-based* images, which, unlike sector-based images, represent collections of files on a given volume.
- Windows PE is a bootable 32-bit environment that can run off of a CD-ROM and that replaces MS-DOS disks.
- ImageX is a new command-line tool used to capture and apply Windows images.
- Windows SIM is a new tool used to simplify the creation of answer files used with Windows Vista Setup.
- Pre-existing tools that have been upgraded for use with Windows Vista include Sysprep, the User State Migration Tool (USMT), and Windows Deployment Services (an update of RIS).

Lesson Review

You can use the following questions to test your knowledge of the information in Lesson 1, "Understanding Windows Vista Deployment." The questions are also available on the companion CD if you prefer to review them in electronic form.

NOTE Answers

Answers to these questions and explanations of why each answer choice is right or wrong are located in the "Answers" section at the end of the book.

---

1. Which of the following tools is necessary to perform an unattended installation of Windows Vista on multiple machines?
   A. The Windows Vista product DVD
   B. Windows SIM
   C. Sysprep
   D. Windows Deployment Services
2. You are dual-booting a machine between Windows Vista and Windows XP. Which tool should you use to change the default operating system from Windows XP to Windows Vista?
   A. BCDEdit
   B. Boot.ini
   C. PEimg
   D. Diskpart

Lesson 2: Using Windows Vista Deployment Tools

This lesson provides step-by-step instructions to use the Windows Vista deployment tools Windows PE, Sysprep, and ImageX. You can use these tools, which are heavily tested on the 70-622 exam, to prepare, capture, edit, and apply computer images for deployment.

In the lesson scenario, three computers are used. The first, called the *technician computer* (DCSRV1), has the Windows Automated Installation Kit (WAIK) installed. The second computer, called the *master computer* (Vista1), has Windows Vista installed and a fully configured master installation whose image we intend to capture for deployment. A third computer, called the *target computer* (Vista2), meets the hardware requirements for Windows Vista but does not have any operating system installed.

After this lesson, you will be able to:
- Create a Windows PE CD.
- Use Sysprep to prepare an installation to be imaged.
- Use ImageX to capture and apply a Windows image.

Estimated lesson time: 45 minutes

Creating Windows PE Media

To prepare to capture a WIM file image, you first need to create or obtain a Windows PE CD. You perform this procedure on the *technician computer* (on which you have installed the WAIK).

IMPORTANT   Remember to install the WAIK

Before you can perform the procedures in this lesson, you need to have installed the WAIK on a computer that we will call the *technician computer* in this chapter. In general, you can install the WAIK on any Windows XP, Windows Server 2003, or Windows Vista computer. To ensure compatibility with the hardware requirements and exercises for this training kit, however, you can use DCSRV1 as the technician computer.

You can download the WAIK at *http://download.microsoft.com*. See the introduction in this training kit for more information about how to download and install the WAIK.

You can find the resources you need to create a Windows PE CD in the PETools folder installed by the WAIK. This folder, in turn, is located in the Program Files\Windows AIK\Tools folder, as shown in Figure 2-4.

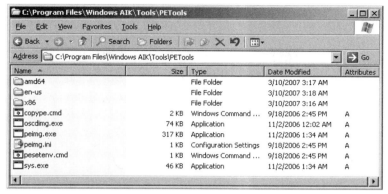

Figure 2-4   Windows PE tools

The Windows PE tools are command-line utilities, so to use them you will need to open a command prompt and navigate to the Program Files\Windows AIK\Tools\PETools directory. (Alternatively, you can simply open the Windows PE Tools Command Prompt that is available on the Start menu.)

1.   To begin the process, first use the script named Copype.cmd to install the Windows PE files into a new directory of your choice. When you run the Copype.cmd script, you need to include an argument of x86, amd64, or ia64 to specify the CPU architecture of the computer on which the Windows PE CD will be used.

     For example, to install the Windows PE files in a new C:\WinPE_x86 in preparation for an x86 CPU, type the following:

```
Copype.cmd
x86 C:\WinPE_x86
```

     After you run this command, the new WinPE_x86 directory will contain, among other files and folders, a directory named ISO. This ISO directory is important because it contains the eventual contents of the WinPE CD.

2.   For this reason, the next step in creating a Windows PE CD is to copy Imagex.exe (and any other tools you need on the eventual CD) to this ISO folder in the new directory. You can find three versions of the Imagex.exe tool, one for each of the supported CPU architectures (amd64, ia64, or x86). Each version is located in the Program Files\Windows AIK\Tools\ folder and in the subfolder named for the associated architecture (amd64, ia64, or x86). After you find the version of ImageX that corresponds to the CPU architecture of the master computer, copy the tool to the root of the ISO directory, to a new subfolder such as Tools, or to another location of your choice.

     For example, if you want Imagex.exe to appear in the root of the Windows PE CD, run the following command:

```
Copy "C:\Program files\Windows AIK\Tools\x86\imagex.exe" C:\WinPE_x86\ISO\
```

3. For ImageX, you should then create the Wimscript.ini configuration file in Notepad and place this file in the same directory (in our example, the root of the ISO folder) as Imagex.exe. The Wimscript.ini file includes two sections, the [ExclusionList] section and the [CompressionExclusionList] section.

   The [ExclusionList] section specifies which files should not be captured when you are performing a capture by using the ImageX tool. A typical exclusion list might resemble the following:

   ```
   [ExclusionList]
   ntfs.log
   hiberfil.sys
   pagefile.sys
   "System Volume Information"
   RECYCLER
   Windows\CSC
   ```

   The [CompressExclusionList] section of Wimscript.ini specifies which files or file types should not be compressed when you are compressing an image by using the ImageX tool. A typical compress exclusion list might look like the following:

   ```
   [CompressionExclusionList]
   *.mp3
   *.zip
   *.cab
   \WINDOWS\inf\*.pnf
   ```

4. After you have created the Wimscript.ini file, you are ready to make an .iso file of the ISO directory by using the Oscdimg command-line tool, which is available in the Program Files\Windows AIK\Tools\PETools\ directory. To make the Windows PE CD bootable, use the –b switch to specify the location of the boot sector file, etfsboot.com. Etfsboot.com is found in the root of the directory (such as WinPE_x86) created by the Copype.cmd script.

   For example, to create a bootable image file named winpe_x86.iso out of the contents of the C:\WinPE_x86\ISO folder (and to place this new .iso file in the C:\WinPE_x86 folder), navigate a command prompt to the PETools directory, and then type the following:

   ```
   Oscdimg -n –bc:\WinPE_x86\etfsboot.com c:\WinPE_x86\ISO c:\WinPE_x86\WinPE_x86.iso
   ```

   NOTE Oscdimg switches

   The –n switch in Oscdimg enables long file names in the .iso file. Note also that there is no space after the –b switch.

5. After you have created the .iso file, you can burn this file to a CD by using your favorite CD-burning software.

Quick Check

1. What is the name of the text file used to define file exclusions for ImageX?
2. What is the name of the script used to create a directory named ISO?
3. What is the Oscdimg utility used for?

Quick Check Answers

1. Wimscript.ini.
2. Copype.cmd.
3. Oscdimg turns a folder into an ISO file.

Exam Tip   For the 70-622 exam, you need to understand every step in the process of making a WinPE CD. You need to understand the role of the WAIK, of Copype.cmd, of Wimscript.ini, and of Oscdimg.

Capturing a WIM File Image

To capture a master image for deployment, you first need to prepare and generalize the master installation by running the Sysprep utility. Then you can start the master computer in WinPE and perform the capture by using ImageX.

Using Sysprep to Prepare a Master Installation

After you have created your master installation, you need to run the Sysprep utility with the Generalize option to remove information (such as event logs and unique SIDs) that is used only by the master computer. This process will leave the installation in a state suitable for capturing with ImageX and deploying to other computers.

You can find Sysprep.exe in Windows Vista in the Windows\System32\Sysprep folder. You can run the tool graphically or from the command line. To choose the Generalize option from the user interface, select the Generalize check box, as shown in Figure 2-5. To select the Generalize option from the command line, use the /generalize switch.

You will usually also want to select the Out-of-Box Experience (OOBE) option because this selection brings up Windows Welcome on first boot after Sysprep is run. Windows Welcome enables users to customize the computer by creating a new administrator account, naming the computer, selecting a time zone, and performing other tasks. To select the OOBE option from the user interface, select that option from the System Cleanup Action drop-down list box, as shown in Figure 2-5.

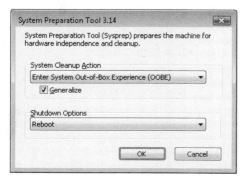

Figure 2-5   Preparing an image in Sysprep

To execute in the command line the same options chosen in Figure 2-5, type the following at a command prompt:

```
C:\Windows\System32\Sysprep\Sysprep.exe /oobe /generalize
```

NOTE   Sysprep Audit Mode

The alternative to selecting the OOBE option is to select the Audit Mode option. When the system enters audit mode after running Sysprep, Windows Welcome does not run. Instead, audit mode settings are read in a Windows Vista answer file, settings that allow administrators to add system-specific drivers and run programs from a local or network source. Then the system allows you to log on with the built-in Administrator account. Once logged on as Administrator, you can use audit mode to verify that a computer is fully functional before the computer is delivered to the end user. Then, after the computer's functionality has been verified, you can finally prepare the computer for the customer by running Sysprep with the /oobe switch. Note also that you need to understand the function of the Audit Mode option for the 70-622 exam.

NOTE   Resetting Windows activation

When you install Windows with a single-license product key, you have 30 days during which you must activate that installation of Windows. If you do not activate Windows within the 30-day period, Windows prevents users from logging on to the computer until Windows is activated.

The Sysprep /generalize command resets the activation clock to 0 and allows a fresh 30 days before activation is required—but only the first three times the command is run. After the third time you run the Sysprep /generalize command on any particular installation, the clock can no longer be reset.

Starting the Master Computer in Windows PE

To boot the master computer in Windows PE, configure the boot order in the basic input/output system (BIOS) so that the computer starts from the CD/DVD-ROM drive. Then simply place the Windows PE disk in the CD drive and boot the computer.

When Windows PE starts, you are given a command prompt, as shown in Figure 2-6.

Figure 2-6   Command prompt in Windows PE

Using ImageX to Capture a Master Installation

1. After you have booted in Windows PE, navigate by means of the command prompt to the directory on the Windows PE CD in which you have stored the Imagex.exe utility.

   For example, if your Windows PE CD is assigned the drive letter D and you have stored Imagex.exe in the root of the CD, type the following:

   ```
   cd d:
   ```

2. To capture a volume on a local hard disk to a WIM file with ImageX, use the /capture switch, point to the source volume to be captured, and specify the name and destination of the new WIM file (followed by a description in quotation marks if desired). In most cases you will also want to use the /compress switch to compress the volume. (Use "/compress fast" for faster compression.) Finally, you can use the /verify switch to check for errors and file duplication.

   For example, to capture with fast compression the C:\ volume to a file named MyNewImage.wim and then to store this WIM file on the same volume, you can type the following:

   ```
   imagex /compress fast /capture C: C:\MyNewImage.wim "my Vista Install" /verify
   ```

3. The new WIM file can then be copied to a network source for future deployment. For example, to map a network drive Z to a network share named \\ServerName\WIMfiles and then to copy the newly created WIM file to that drive, type the following commands (providing appropriate credentials when prompted):

```
Net use Z: \\ServerName\WIMfiles
Copy C:\MyNewImage.wim Z:
```

Exam Tip   You need to understand this procedure well for the 70-622 exam.

IMPORTANT   **Capturing multiple images**

WIM files can store more than one image. However, you use the Imagex /capture command only for the first volume captured to a WIM file. After that, you can capture additional volumes into the WIM file by means of the Imagex /append command.

Viewing WIM File Metadata

You can use ImageX to read the XML metadata associated with a WIM file. This metadata will tell you, among other things, how many images the WIM file contains, the description given to each image, and the index number associated with each image. For example, to view the metadata associated with the file C:\Images\MyNewImage.wim, type the following:

```
Imagex /info c:\Images\MyNewImage.wim
```

NOTE   **ImageX in Windows**

Although ImageX is used typically in Windows PE to capture a Windows Vista installation to a WIM file, you can use ImageX in Windows Vista to perform other functions (such as managing WIM files).

Viewing and Editing a WIM File Image Offline

You can use ImageX to mount a WIM file image in the Windows Vista file system for viewing and editing. To do so, first create a folder into which you will mount the WIM file image. Then use ImageX with the /mountrw switch, specifying the source WIM file, the index number of the desired image within the file, and the destination folder into which the image will be mounted.

For example, to mount the first image (index = 1) of the file C:\Images\MyNewImage.wim in the folder C:\mounted_images, type the following:

```
imagex /mountrw C:\Images\MyNewImage.wim 1 C:\mounted_images
```

After you mount an image, you can add and remove files to it by using Windows Explorer.

Note also that a mounted image is considered *offline* and thus cannot be applied until it is unmounted. To unmount an image, use ImageX with the /unmount switch and specify the folder used for mounting. (ImageX knows which WIM file is already mounted in the file system, so you don't need to specify the WIM file itself.) To save any changes you have made to the image during editing, you must use the /commit switch. Otherwise, any changes you have made will be discarded.

For example, to unmount the WIM file image mounted in C:\mounted_images and save any changes made offline, type the following:

```
imagex /unmount /commit c:\mounted_images
```

Deploying a WIM File Image

To deploy a WIM file image from a network share to a target computer, first boot the target computer by using the Windows PE CD. Then use the Diskpart utility to prepare the local hard disk. Finally, connect to the WIM file from across the network and apply the image by using ImageX.

Using Diskpart to Prepare a Disk for Image Deployment

In most cases you are going to deploy a new installation of Windows Vista onto a blank disk. Before you apply a WIM file image to a disk, you need to create a primary partition on that disk, set that partition as active, and then format the partition. You can perform all these steps in Windows PE by using the Diskpart command-line utility, available by default in the X:\Windows\System32 folder.

Exam Tip   You need to understand the function of Diskpart for the 70-622 exam.

For example, the following set of Diskpart commands selects the first hard disk (disk 0) in the computer, removes (cleans) all existing partition information from the disk, creates a new primary partition of 12,000 MB, sets this (first) partition as active, and then formats the new partition as an NTFS partition.

```
X:\windows\system32>
X:\windows\system32>diskpart
DISKPART>select disk 0
DISKPART>clean
DISKPART>create partition primary size=12000
DISKPART>select partition 1
DISKPART>active
DISKPART>format
DISKPART>exit
X:\windows\system32>
```

IMPORTANT Setting the active partition

Don't forget to set the partition as active. If you do not set the partition as active, you will not be able to boot the machine into any operating system you deploy on that partition.

NOTE Automated alternative to Diskpart

If you are installing Windows Vista from the product DVD, you can also prepare a disk by means of an answer file that is automatically processed before Setup runs.

Applying a WIM File Image

To connect to a WIM file on a network share from the target computer, first map a network drive to that share. Then you can either apply the selected image directly from the network drive, or you can copy the WIM file to the hard disk drive on the target computer and apply the desired image from the local source.

NOTE Nondestructive imaging

Because WIM file images are file-based and not sector-based, they do not overwrite existing data. As a result, if a WIM file image is stored in a particular C drive, you can apply that image to the very same C drive. To achieve this, of course, you need to make sure that enough free space exists on the C drive to accommodate both the WIM file and the applied image.

---

1. Use the Net Use command to map a network drive to the share on which the WIM file is stored. For example, the following commands map the drive letter Z to a network share named WIMfiles (found on a server named ServerName) and then copy the file MyNewImage.wim from drive Z to the local C drive:

    ```
    Net use Z: \\ServerName\WIMfiles
    Copy Z:\MyNewImage.wim C:
    ```

2. After this point you are ready to apply the image to the target computer by using ImageX. The following command applies the first image (index = 1) found in the file C:\MyNewImage.wim to the empty space in the rest of the C drive:

    ```
    Imagex.exe /apply C:\MyNewImage.wim 1 c:
    ```

    The image is now deployed, and you can boot the target computer into Windows Vista.

ImageX Switches

ImageX includes many command options that are useful for managing images. Because ImageX is a new and important tool, you could be tested on any of these options on the 70-622 exam. However, pay special attention to /append, /apply, /capture, /commit, /compress, /mountrw, and /unmount.

Table 2-1 presents an overview of the full range of these ImageX command switches.

Table 2-1   ImageX Command-Line Options

Switch	Description
/append	Appends a volume image into an existing WIM file
/apply	Applies a volume image to the specified drive
/capture	Captures a volume image into a new WIM file
/commit	Commits the changes made to a mounted WIM
/compress	Sets compression type to none, fast, or maximum
/config	Uses the specified file to set advanced options
/delete	Deletes an image from a WIM file with multiple images
/dir	Displays a list of files and folders within a volume image
/export	Transfers an image from one WIM file to another WIM file
/info	Returns the store's XML descriptions for the specified WIM
/ref	Sets WIM references for an apply operation
/scroll	Scrolls output for redirection
/split	Splits an existing WIM file into multiple read-only WIM parts
/verify	Verifies duplicate and extracted files
/mount	Mounts an image, with read-only access, to the specified directory
/mountrw	Mounts an image, with read-write access, to the specified directory
/unmount	Unmounts the image mounted to the specified directory
/?	Returns valid command-line parameters for ImageX

Practice: Capturing and Deploying a WIM File Image

In these practice exercises, you will use Windows PE, Sysprep, and ImageX to capture a Windows Vista installation and deploy it to another computer.

▶ **Practice 1: Creating a Windows PE CD**

In this practice, you will create a WinPE CD that you will later use to image the Vista1 computer.

1. On DCSRV1, open the Windows PE Tools Command Prompt by clicking Start, pointing to All Programs, pointing to Windows AIK, and then clicking Windows PE Tools Command Prompt.

2. In the Windows PE Tools Command Prompt, type the line below that corresponds to the CPU architecture of your Vista1 computer:

    ```
    Copype.cmd x86 C:\WinPE_x86
    Copype.cmd amd64 C:\WinPE_amd64
    Copype.cmd ia64 C:\WinPE_ia64
    ```

3. In the Windows PE Tools Command Prompt, type the line below that corresponds to the CPU architecture of your Vista1 computer:

    ```
    Copy "C:\Program files\Windows AIK\Tools\x86\imagex.exe" C:\WinPE_x86\ISO
    Copy "C:\Program files\Windows AIK\Tools\amd64\imagex.exe" C:\WinPE_amd64\ISO
    Copy "C:\Program files\Windows AIK\Tools\ia64\imagex.exe" C:\WinPE_ia64\ISO
    ```

4. In Notepad, create an empty file named Wimscript.ini and save it to the new WinPE_x86\ISO, WinPE_amd64\ISO, or WinPEia64\ISO folder, as appropriate.

5. Enter the following text into Wimscript.ini, and then save the file again:

    ```
    [ExclusionList]
    ntfs.log
    hiberfil.sys
    pagefile.sys
    "System Volume Information"
    RECYCLER
    Windows\CSC

    [CompressionExclusionList]
    *.mp3
    *.zip
    *.cab
    \WINDOWS\inf\*.pnf
    ```

6. In the Windows PE Tools Command Prompt, type the line below that corresponds to the CPU architecture of your Vista1 computer:

    ```
    Oscdimg -n -bc:\WinPE_x86\etfsboot.com c:\WinPE_x86\ISO
    c:\WinPE_x86\WinPE_x86.iso

    Oscdimg -n -bc:\WinPE_amd64\etfsboot.com c:\WinPE_x86\ISO
    c:\WinPE_amd64\WinPE_amd64.iso
    ```

```
Oscdimg -n -bc:\WinPE_ia64\etfsboot.com c:\WinPE_ia64\ISO
c:\WinPE_x86\WinPE_ia64.iso
```

7. Using software of your choice, burn the new .iso file to a CD (or mount the .iso in a virtual CD drive).

▶ **Practice 2: Generalizing a Windows Vista Installation with Sysprep**

In this practice, you will use Sysprep to generalize the installation of Windows Vista on the Vista1 computer.

1. Log on to Vista1 as an administrator and open a command prompt.

2. At the command prompt, type the following (if necessary, change the drive letter to correspond to the system root on your machine):

   cd c:\windows\system32\sysprep

3. At the command prompt, type the following:

   sysprep /generalize /oobe

   Sysprep runs, and the machine shuts down.

▶ **Practice 3: Capturing a WIM File Image**

In this practice, you will boot Vista1 in Windows PE and capture an image of the C drive to a network share.

1. On DCSRV1, create a folder in the root of the C drive called Images. Share the folder with the same share name. Assign Everyone the Full Control permission to the share. (Leave the default security settings on the Security tab.)

2. Insert your Windows PE CD into the CD-ROM drive of the Vista1 computer, power up the computer, and then boot the computer from the CD by hitting any key when prompted.

   The computer boots into the Windows PE operating system. When Windows PE finishes booting, a command prompt appears.

3. At the command prompt, type the following:

   net use z: \\dcsrv1.nwtraders.msft\images

4. When prompted, provide a set of administrator credentials for the NWTRADERS domain.

5. After the command completes successfully, navigate the command prompt to the root of the CD drive.

6. At the command prompt, type the following:

   imagex /compress fast /capture c: z:\MyImage.wim "Master Image" /verify

7. After the capture completes, type the following:

   wpeutil shutdown

   This is the command to shut down the local computer in Windows PE.

▶ **Practice 4: Applying a Capture**

In this practice, you will boot Vista2 into Windows PE and then apply the image captured in the previous practice.

1. Using the Windows PE CD, boot Vista2 into Windows PE.

2. After Windows PE boots, type the following:

    ```
    Diskpart
    ```

    This opens a Diskpart command prompt.

3. At the Diskpart command prompt, type the following sequence of commands, one at a time. Be sure to press the Enter key after typing each command.

    ```
    select disk 0
    clean
    create partition primary size=12000
    select partition 1
    active
    format
    exit
    ```

4. At the command prompt, type the following:

    ```
    net use z: \\dcsrv1.nwtraders.msft\images
    ```

5. When prompted, provide a set of administrator credentials for the NWTRADERS domain.

6. After the command completes successfully, navigate the command prompt to the root of the CD drive.

7. At the command prompt, type the following:

    ```
    Imagex /apply Z:\MyImage.wim 1 c:
    ```

8. After the command completes successfully, type the following:

    ```
    wpeutil reboot
    ```

    This is the command in Windows PE to reboot the local machine.

9. Verify that Vista2 boots successfully into Windows Welcome. Complete the Windows Welcome screens as desired, but be sure to name the computer Vista2.

10. Log on to Vista2 with the user account of your choice.

Lesson Summary

- To capture a master image for Windows deployment, first generalize the master installation by running the Sysprep utility. Then, start the master computer in Windows PE and perform the capture by using ImageX.

- To deploy a WIM file image to a target computer, first boot the target computer by using the Windows PE CD. Then use the Diskpart utility to prepare the local hard disk. Finally, connect to the WIM file and apply the image by using ImageX.

- You can use ImageX to mount a WIM file image in the Windows Vista file system for viewing and editing.

Lesson Review

You can use the following questions to test your knowledge of the information in Lesson 2, "Using Windows Vista Deployment Tools." The questions are also available on the companion CD if you prefer to review them in electronic form.

NOTE Answers

Answers to these questions and explanations of why each answer choice is right or wrong are located in the "Answers" section at the end of the book.

---

1. Which of the following tools do you need to burn an ISO file of a Windows PE CD?

    A. Sysprep

    B. Copype.cmd

    C. PEimg

    D. Oscdimg

2. Which of the following commands would you use to load a WIM file into the Windows file system for editing?

    A. imagex /mountrw

    B. imagex /mount

    C. imagex /export

    D. imagex /capture

Lesson 3: Designing a Network Environment

You can deploy Windows Vista through the product media, through network share distribution, through Windows Deployment Services, or through Systems Management Server (SMS). Each of these deployment methods is suitable for different network environments.

After this lesson, you will be able to:

■ Understand the various deployment methods for Windows Vista, the advantages and disadvantages of each, and the environments in which each is most suitable.

Estimated lesson time: 20 minutes

Windows Vista Deployment Methods

The Windows Vista operating system is typically deployed in one of four ways: by means of the product DVD, by means of a WIM file stored on a network share, by means of Windows Deployment Services, or by means of SMS 2003. Each of these four respective methods offers an increasing level of automation, but each method also requires an increasing amount of resources, expertise, and preparation. Deciding which method to use depends on the resources you have available, the size of your organization, and the number of deployments you need to make.

Booting from a DVD

The simplest method to deploy Windows Vista onto new hardware without requiring end-user interaction is to start the computer from the Windows Vista product DVD and supply an answer file named Autounattend.xml. In this case the answer file must be located at the root of an accessible universal serial bus (USB) Flash Device (UFD) drive or floppy disk.

Exam Tip   In order to perform an unattended installation from the Windows Vista product DVD, place an answer file named Autounattend.xml on a *USB drive* and boot the computer.

This deployment method is most suitable when no high-bandwidth connection to the destination computer is available (as might be the case with a branch office), when you are deploying Windows Vista onto a small number of computers, and when no IT personnel are available at the site of the target computer. Compared to other automated forms of deployment, this deployment method also requires the least amount of technical preparation, resources, and expertise at both source and destination sites.

However, deploying Windows Vista by means of the product DVD does have significant limitations. First, it requires more participation on the part of nontechnical end users than is ideal for operating system installations. If the target computer does not have a floppy disk drive or if you have distributed the Autounattend.xml through a network connection, the user's participation is significant; the user must place the answer file at the root of a UFD or floppy disk and boot the computer with that disk and the product DVD loaded. A second limitation of the media distribution method is that it does not allow for any additional drivers or updates (configuration sets) to be installed as part of Setup without significant technical expertise at the site of the end user. Finally, one last limitation of this deployment method is that physical media need to be distributed to every target computer, and installation can occur simultaneously only on as many computers as product DVDs you have available.

NOTE   Modifying install.wim

On the product DVD the file install.wim contains the default image of Windows Vista. For your own deployment needs, you can replace the default install.wim (and associated catalog files) with your own version and use this new version to create a custom Windows Vista Setup DVD.

Network Share Distribution

You can deploy Windows Vista to computers from a network share in one of two ways: by using the Setup program or by applying a WIM file image.

In the first method the contents of the Windows Vista product media are stored on the network share. You can then either keep the default version of install.wim or replace it (and associated catalog files) with an image of your own custom-configured master installation. Setup is then launched from the command prompt in Windows PE on the local machine. To specify an answer file, use the /unattend switch.

For example, if you have mapped a drive Y to the network share containing the installation files and saved an answer file named deploy_unattend.xml in the same share, you could boot the local computer by means of Windows PE and type the following:

```
Y:\setup.exe /unattend:deploy_unattend.xml
```

The second way to deploy Windows Vista by means of a network share is to store on that share the captured WIM file image of a Sysprepped master installation. In this case, you can even keep an answer file inside the installation in the following location: %WINDIR%\panther\unattend. (The name of the answer file must be Unattend.xml or Autounattend.xml.)

Then, on the target computer, you can apply the Windows image by means of Windows PE and ImageX. For example, if you have mapped a drive Y to the network share containing the WIM file images, you would boot the local computer by means of Windows PE and type the following:

```
Imagex /apply Y:\myimage.wim 1 c:
```

Deploying Windows Vista through a network share is a suitable solution when sufficient bandwidth exists to copy large (2 GB or more) files across the network, when you need to deploy more than a very few computers, and when the network environment does not include Active Directory directory service or SMS.

The main disadvantage of this method is that it is not completely automated. Instead, it requires someone at the site of the target computer with the technical expertise to boot into Windows PE and run appropriate commands at the command prompt. Unlike WDS, this solution does not automatically find the source files on the network and provide a menu of operating systems to download. Unlike SMS, this solution does not allow an administrator to deploy operating systems automatically to remote locations.

Besides this lack of automation, a second disadvantage of network share deployment is that it is not a managed solution. There is no central tool from which to manage and modify the Windows images stored at the network source. As a result, network share deployments are typically scalable only to network sizes of fewer than 50 computers.

Windows Deployment Services (WDS)

Unlike the network share deployment scenario, WDS allows an end user without any technical expertise to boot a computer with no operating system and simply select, from a menu, a Windows image to load. The target computer is able to find the WDS server and download this operating system menu from it by means of the Pre-boot eXecution Environment (PXE) boot process. PXE is a technology that leverages DHCP to locate a server during a computer's boot phase.

IMPORTANT   PXE-boot computers

For a WDS client computer to find a WDS server, the client computer needs to have a PXE-boot compatible network card.

WDS is a far more scalable and manageable solution than simply storing WIM files on a network. However, WDS does have the following fairly extensive infrastructure requirements:

- **Active Directory**   A Windows Deployment Services server must be either a member of an Active Directory domain or a domain controller for an Active Directory domain. The Active Directory domain and forest versions are irrelevant; all domain and forest configurations support Windows Deployment Services.
- **Dynamic Host Configuration Protocol (DHCP)**   You must have a working DHCP server with an active scope on the network because Windows Deployment Services uses PXE, which in turn, uses DHCP. The DHCP server does not have to be on the Windows Deployment Services server.

- **Domain Name System (DNS)**   A working DNS server on the network is required to run Windows Deployment Services. The DNS server does not have to be running on the Windows Deployment Services server.
- **Windows Server 2003 SP1 with WDS installed**   For Windows Server 2003, WDS is an update of RIS. RIS does not have to be configured, but it must be installed on the Windows Server 2003 computer for the WDS update to run. In addition, the WDS server requires an NTFS partition for the image store. This image store must be separate from the operating system files.
- **A high-speed, persistent connection between the WDS servers and the target computers**   Such a connection is necessary because of the size of the images being distributed to the target computers (500 MB–4 GB). In addition, these servers should be on adjacent subnets to the target computers to ensure high-speed connectivity.

Aside from the extensive infrastructure requirements of WDS, another limitation of this deployment solution is that it requires end-user participation. The administrator cannot simply choose to push an operating system to any desktop in the organization.

As a result of these limitations, WDS does not scale well to the largest corporate networks with multiple Active Directory domains, IP subnets, or physical sites.

Quick Check
- What are the server and infrastructure requirements for WDS?

Quick Check Answer
- Windows Server 2003 SP1 with WDS installed, Active Directory, DNS, DHCP, and a persistent high-speed connection

---

Systems Management Server (SMS)

When used in conjunction with the other deployment methods, SMS allows you to create a fully managed deployment solution for large organizations. Unlike other deployment options, SMS allows for a completely unattended operating system deployment and installation to remote computers.

SMS assists with the many tasks that are involved when you apply automated procedures to multiple servers and client computers, tasks such as:

- Selecting computers that have the hardware necessary for a given operating system and that you are ready to support.
- Distributing the operating system source files to all sites, including remote sites and sites without technical support staff.

- Monitoring the distribution to all sites.
- Providing the appropriate user rights for the upgrade.
- Automatically initiating the installation of software packages, with the possibility of having users control the timing.
- Resolving problems related to the distributions or installations.
- Reporting on the rate and success of deployment.
- Verifying that all computers in your organization have received the standardized operating system configuration.

Deploying Windows Vista with SMS requires that you have a high-speed, persistent connection between the servers and target computers used in the deployment process. Such a connection is necessary because of the size of the images SMS distributes to the target computers (500 MB–4 GB).

In addition, you will also need the following software:

- *SMS 2003 with SP2*. SMS 2003 with SP2 is required on all SMS site servers within the infrastructure before beginning deployment.
- *SMS 2003 Operating System Deployment (OSD) Feature Pack*. The SMS 2003 OSD Feature Pack is an add-on to SMS 2003 that provides the ability to capture, distribute, and install images to target computers and servers. The SMS 2003 OSD Feature Pack is required on one or more site servers within the organization (recommended) or on a target computer running the SMS 2003 Administrator Console.

Among the disadvantages of SMS is, first, that, unlike the other deployment methods mentioned, it is a separate product requiring a purchase beyond that of Windows Vista and Windows Server 2003. In addition, installing and configuring an SMS infrastructure requires significant technical expertise. A third disadvantage of SMS is that, unlike WDS, you can't use it to deploy an operating system onto a blank computer. The target computer requires SMS Advanced Client. (Because of this latter limitation, in fact, SMS is typically used in conjunction with WDS and not as a replacement for it.)

Lesson Summary

- There are several ways to deploy Windows Vista in corporate networks. Each method is suitable for different network environments.
- Distributing the Windows Vista product DVD with an answer file requires the least amount of preparation, technical expertise, and network resources. However, it is also the least scalable solution.
- Deploying Windows Vista through a network share requires less administrative overhead than some other solutions, but it is not fully automated and it is not manageable for large networks.

- Through WDS, you can pull a new operating system from the network onto an empty computer. This solution is suitable for medium-to-large networks, but it does not allow images to be pushed onto remote computers. In addition, WDS has strict infrastructure requirements, the most important of which are Active Directory and DHCP.

- SMS assists with deployment in large organizations. Among its many benefits is that it allows you to push operating system source files to remote locations without technical support staff. Disadvantages of SMS are that it is not a technology built into Windows, it does not allow deployment onto empty computers, and it requires significant technical expertise and preparation.

Lesson Review

You can use the following questions to test your knowledge of the information in Lesson 3, "Designing a Network Environment." The questions are also available on the companion CD if you prefer to review them in electronic form.

NOTE   Answers

Answers to these questions and explanations of why each answer choice is right or wrong are located in the "Answers" section at the end of the book.

---

1. You want to perform an unattended installation of Windows Vista by using the product DVD. Where should you keep the answer file, and what should you name it?

    A. Keep the file on a UFD and name the file Autounattend.xml.

    B. Keep the file on a floppy disk and name the file Autounattend.txt.

    C. Keep the file on the hard disk and name the file Autounattend.xml.

    D. Keep the file in the CD drive and name the file Autounattend.txt.

2. If the contents of the Windows Vista DVD have been copied to a share named \\server1\VSetup and an answer file named Unattend.xml is stored in the same directory, which commands should you type to initiate Setup from that network share?

    A. `net use z: \\server1\Vsetup`
       `Z:\setup.exe /unattended:Unattend.xml`

    B. `net use z: \\server1\Vsetup`
       `Imagex /unattend:Unattend.xml /apply z:\install.wim 1 c:`

    C. `net use z: \\server1\Vsetup`
       `Imagex /unattended:Unattend.xml /apply z:\install.wim 1 c:`

    D. `net use z: \\server1\Vsetup`
       `Z:\setup.exe /unattend:Unattend.xml`

Chapter Review

To further practice and reinforce the skills you learned in this chapter, you can

■ Review the chapter summary.

■ Review the list of key terms introduced in this chapter.

■ Complete the case scenarios. These scenarios set up real-world situations involving the topics of this chapter and ask you to create solutions.

■ Complete the suggested practices.

■ Take a practice test.

Chapter Summary

■ Windows Vista is installed by means of Windows images stored in WIM files.

■ Windows PE is a new bootable 32-bit environment that can run off of a CD-ROM and that replaces MS-DOS disks.

■ ImageX is a new command-line tool used to capture and apply Windows images. You can use ImageX to mount a WIM file image in the Windows Vista file system for viewing and editing.

■ To capture a master image for Windows deployment, first generalize the master installation by running the Sysprep utility. Then, start the master computer in Windows PE and perform the capture by using ImageX.

■ Windows Vista can be deployed through the product DVD, a network share, WDS, or SMS. Each of these deployment options is suitable in different network environments.

Key Terms

Do you know what these key terms mean? You can check your answers by looking up the terms in the glossary at the end of the book.

■ Catalog (.clg) file

■ ImageX

■ Sysprep

■ Windows Deployment Services (WDS)

■ Windows Imaging (.wim) file

■ Windows PE

■ Windows SIM

Case Scenarios

In the following case scenarios, you will apply what you've learned in this chapter. You can find answers to these questions in the "Answers" section at the end of this book.

Case Scenario 1: Choosing a Deployment Technology

Northwest Traders is a retail company that specializes in furniture imports from around the world. The company employs a total of 500 workers in its two branches in Seattle and Portland. Recently, the IT department has been asked to deploy Windows Vista onto all client computers in both branches.

The Northwest Traders network includes two Active Directory domains, sea.nwtraders.com and port.nwtraders.com, for each branch office.

1. Which technology would allow Northwest Traders to maintain a single centralized deployment infrastructure? Assume that a high-speed connection exists between the two sites.
2. The Seattle branch wants to maintain its own deployment infrastructure, but it doesn't want to make any additional software investment. It also wants to automate the deployment process as much as possible. Which deployment technology would you recommend?

Case Scenario 2: Preparing a Master Image

You are a desktop support technician for Contoso, Inc., a medium-sized advertising firm with 100 employees. You want to prepare a standard WIM file image to deploy Windows Vista to client computers from the network share. You have already performed testing with Windows Vista to ensure that it is compatible with the current client hardware and software, but the new operating system is no longer installed on any computer in the company.

1. If you have not yet taken any steps to prepare the image, what should you do first?
2. What is the last step you should perform before you image the master computer?
3. Which utility and switch should you use to image the master computer?

Suggested Practices

To help you successfully master the exam objectives presented in this chapter, complete the following tasks.

Work with WIM Files

■ **Practice 1: Capture a WIM File Image**   Use the ImageX utility to capture a WIM file image of the computer you use most often. It's simplest to choose a computer that uses only one partition, but you can also just image the system drive if you use more than one partition. Use high compression to store the image on a DVD or a network drive.

■ **Practice 2: Edit a WIM File Image**   Mount the new WIM file image in the file system. Add a new folder of data to the image.

■ **Practice 3: Deploy a WIM File**   Using the ImageX utility, deploy the image to another computer or virtual machine. Verify that the new folder of data is available.

Perform a Virtual Lab

■ **Practice 1: Learn to Create and Engineer Windows Images**   Go to *http://msevents .microsoft.com* and search for Event ID# 1032305600. Register and perform the virtual lab named "Windows Vista Image Engineering Virtual Lab."

■ **Practice 2: Learn to Use ImageX to Manage Windows Images**   Go to *http://msevents .microsoft.com* and search for Event ID# 1032305601. Register and perform the virtual lab named "Using ImageX to Manage Windows Image Files Virtual Lab."

■ **Practice 3: Learn to Customize Windows PE**   Go to *http://msevents.microsoft.com* and search for Event ID# 1032305602. Register and perform the virtual lab named "Customizing Windows Preinstallation Environment Virtual Lab."

■ **Practice 4: Learn How to Service a Windows Image Offline**   Go to *http://msevents .microsoft.com* and search for Event ID# 1032329676. Register and perform the virtual lab named "Windows Vista: Offline Servicing of Windows Images Using ImageX and PkgMgr Virtual Lab."

Watch a Webcast

For this task, watch the following webcasts, available in the Webcasts folder on the companion CD:

■ **Practice 1: Learn About Windows Vista Deployment**   Watch "TechNet Webcast: Windows Vista Deployment Overview (Level 2000)," by Chris Henley.

■ **Practice 2: Learn About Windows Vista Deployment Tools**   Watch "TechNet Webcast: Windows Vista Deployment Tools and Technologies (Level 2000)," by John Baker.

- **Practice 3: Learn About Windows PE**   Watch "TechNet Webcast: Windows Preinstallation Environment 2.0 for Windows Vista Deployment (Level 2000)," by Andy Zeigler.
- **Practice 4: Learn About Creating WIM File Images**   Watch "TechNet Webcast: Building a Windows Vista Image for Your Corporate Deployment (Level 2000)," by Glenn Fincher.
- **Practice 5: Learn More About Creating WIM File Images**   Watch "TechNet Webcast: Imaging Windows Vista (Level 2000)," by Chris Henley.

Take a Practice Test

The practice tests on this book's companion CD offer many options. For example, you can test yourself on just one exam objective, or you can test yourself on all the 70-622 certification exam content. You can set up the test so that it closely simulates the experience of taking a certification exam, or you can set it up in study mode so that you can look at the correct answers and explanations after you answer each question.

MORE INFO   Practice tests

For details about all the practice test options available, see the "How to Use the Practice Tests" section in this book's Introduction.

Chapter 3

Troubleshooting Deployment Issues

After you have deployed Windows Vista, the process of troubleshooting the deployment begins. Two of the most common areas in which problems appear after Windows Vista deployment are roaming user profiles and application compatibility. This chapter introduces you to methods you can use to resolve post-deployment problems in these two areas.

Exam objectives in this chapter:
- Perform post-installation tasks.
- Troubleshoot deployment issues.

Lessons in this chapter:

Before You Begin

To complete the lessons in this chapter, you must have

- A Microsoft Windows Server 2003 domain controller named dcsrv1.nwtraders.msft.
- Two Windows Vista Enterprise, Business, or Ultimate client computers named Vista1 and Vista2.
- A Windows XP Professional computer named Xpclient.

Lesson 1: Resolving User Profile Compatibility Issues

User profiles in Windows Vista by default are not compatible with user profiles in previous versions of Windows. Consequently, if you have configured roaming user profiles for your Windows domain, you will typically need to resolve user profile issues after you deploy Windows Vista. To allow roaming users to access their data in a consistent way across Windows versions, you should use a feature called Folder Redirection. Aside from promoting user profile compatibility between Windows versions, Folder Redirection provides a number of additional benefits, such as faster logon times, real-time data synchronization, and policy automation.

> **After this lesson, you will be able to:**
> - Understand the advantages and disadvantages of using roaming user profiles in Windows Vista.
> - Use Folder Redirection to resolve problems with user profiles in Windows Vista.
>
> **Estimated lesson time: 40 minutes**

Understanding User Profiles in Windows Vista

In general terms, a user profile simply refers to the collection of data that makes up a user's individual environment—data including a user's individual files, application settings, and desktop configuration. More specifically, a user profile refers to the contents of the personal folder, automatically created by Windows, that bears the name of an individual user. By default, this personal folder is created in the C:\Users folder when a user logs on to a Windows Vista computer for the first time. It contains subfolders such as Documents, Desktop, and Downloads, as well as a personal data file named Ntuser.dat. For example, by default, a user named SheilaB will store the data that makes up her personal environment in a folder named C:\Users\SheilaB.

The contents of the user profile folder are shown in Figure 3-1.

Figure 3-1   The user profile namespace

Although each user profile is stored in C:\Users by default, this default location is often not suitable for corporate environments, especially when users tend to switch computers. Ideally, users' documents and settings should follow them from computer to computer and not be restricted to a single computer or be dispersed among several computers. To allow documents and settings to roam with users in an organization in this way, network administrators have traditionally configured roaming user profiles in a domain environment. To configure domain user accounts with roaming user profiles, you simply need to modify the properties of those accounts so that the profiles are stored on a central network share instead of on the local machine. When you do this, the same personal folder containing a user's documents and settings is downloaded from the network share to the local computer when the user logs on, regardless of which domain computer the user logs on to. All changes made to the user profile are then copied back to the central network share when the user logs off.

Understanding User Profile Changes in Windows Vista

If you have used earlier versions of Windows, one of the differences you might have noticed about Windows Vista is that the default location of the user profile folders has moved. In Windows 2000, Windows XP, and Windows Server 2003, user profiles are stored by default in the C:\Documents and Settings folder, not in C:\Users as they are in Windows Vista. In addition, the contents of each user profile have been modified. For example, what was called My Documents in earlier versions of Windows is now simply called Documents, and several new subfolders, such as Downloads, Contacts, and Links, exist only in the Windows Vista user profiles.

Table 3-1 summarizes the many differences between Windows Vista and Windows XP user profiles. (Note that the folders mentioned in Table 3-1 are hidden by default.)

Table 3-1   Windows Vista Profile Changes

Windows Vista User Profile Folder Location (below \Users*username*\...)	Windows XP User Profile Folder Location (below Documents and Settings*username*\...)
...\AppData\Roaming	...\Application Data
N/A	...\Local Settings
...\AppData\Local	...\Local Settings\Application Data
...\AppData\Local\Microsoft\Windows\History	...\Local Settings\History
...\AppData\Local\Temp	...\Local Settings\Temp
...\AppData\Local\Microsoft\Windows\Temporary Internet Files	...\Local Settings\Temporary Internet Files
...\AppData\Roaming\Microsoft \Windows\Cookies	...\Cookies
...\AppData\Roaming\Microsoft\Windows\Network Shortcuts	...\Nethood
...\AppData\Roaming\Microsoft\Windows\Printer Shortcuts	...\PrintHood
...\AppData\Roaming\Microsoft\Windows\Recent	...\Recent
...\AppData\Roaming\Microsoft\Windows\Send To	...\SendTo
...\AppData\Roaming\Microsoft\Windows\Start Menu	...\Start Menu
...\AppData\Roaming\Microsoft\Windows\Templates	...\Templates
...\Contacts	Not applicable
...\Desktop	...\Desktop
...\Documents	...\My Documents
...\Downloads	Not applicable
...\Favorites	...\Favorites

Table 3-1   Windows Vista Profile Changes

Windows Vista User Profile Folder Location (below \Users*username*\...)	Windows XP User Profile Folder Location (below Documents and Settings*username*\...)
...\Music	...\My Music
...\Videos	...\My Videos
...\Pictures	...\My Pictures
...\Searches	Not applicable
...\Links	Not applicable
...\Saved Games	Not applicable

NOTE   The Public profile

The Public profile in Windows Vista is essentially a renamed version of the All Users profile in previous versions of Windows. The Public profile provides a way to add user data to all user profiles without editing each user profile individually. Adding a shortcut to the desktop of the Public profile, for example, would result in every user receiving the shortcut on their desktop when they log on.

Windows Vista and Windows XP Roaming Profiles

The fact that user profiles have changed so significantly is a very important consideration for Windows Vista deployment because Windows Vista and earlier versions of Windows *cannot share profiles for roaming users*. Whenever a user for whom you have configured a roaming user profile logs on to a Windows Vista computer, a second user profile folder named *username*.V2 is created on the central network share for use with just Windows Vista.

For instance, before Windows Vista deployment, if user MarkB is configured with a roaming user profile, he is able to log on to any Windows 2000, Windows XP, or Windows Server 2003 computer in his workplace and see—among other things—the same desktop and the same My Documents folder. On a central network share, all of MarkB's documents and settings are stored in a profile named MarkB. However, after you deploy Windows Vista in the organization, MarkB logs on to a Windows Vista computer but does not see any part of his familiar environment by default: his desktop has changed, and none of his documents can be found. On the central network share, a new folder named MarkB.V2 now appears alongside the MarkB folder. Any changes that MarkB makes to his new Windows Vista environment follow him to other Windows Vista computers, but these documents and settings are kept separate from those available to him in previous versions of Windows.

The side-by-side roaming user profile folders for Windows Vista and Windows XP are shown in Figure 3-2.

Figure 3-2   Roaming user profile for Windows XP and Windows Vista

Other Limitations of Roaming User Profiles   Besides the lack of default compatibility between Windows Vista roaming user profiles and those used in earlier versions of Windows, there are other important limitations related to traditional roaming user profiles in all versions of Windows:

- **Slow logon and logoff**   As a user configured with a roaming user profile logs on to a domain, all of the data stored in the user profile on the network share is copied to the local computer. This process can result in a slow logon, especially when the size of the user profile grows beyond 20 MB. When a user logs off the system, the same profile must be copied back to the network share; this process results in a slow logoff.

- **Lack of real-time data synchronization**   With roaming user profiles, changes a user makes to his or her documents and settings are copied back to the central network share only when the user logs off. This lack of real-time data synchronization can complicate matters for users who frequently switch systems while performing their jobs.

- **Network problems can disperse profile data**   If a user configured with a roaming user profile experiences network problems during logon, a new profile can automatically be created for that user on the local system. Any work saved during this logon session becomes unavailable to the user during future sessions if he or she is once again able to connect to the network share.

- **Lack of roaming user profile automation**   Although you can configure roaming user profiles on many existing accounts simultaneously, there is no method built into Windows that allows you to configure newly created users with a roaming user profile by default. This lack of automation results in increased administrative overhead and in increased opportunity for misconfiguration.

To address the limitations of roaming user profiles, you can use a feature called Folder Redirection—either in place of roaming user profiles or in addition to them.

Understanding Windows Vista Folder Redirection

Folder Redirection allows you to change the target location of user profile folders in a way that is transparent to the user. For example, if an administrator has redirected your C:\Users\Documents folder to a central network share, you will still see the Documents folder in the same location on your local computer. Whenever you open the Documents folder, however, the window reveals contents stored at the redirected location on the central network share.

You can configure and enforce Folder Redirection for domain users through Group Policy. The folders that you can redirect through Group Policy are shown in Figure 3-3.

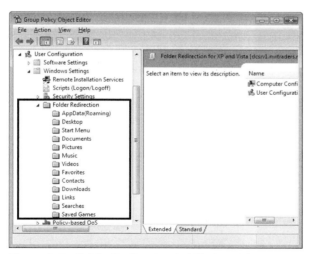

Figure 3-3   Folder Redirection in Windows Vista

When configured, Folder Redirection offers a number of important advantages over traditional roaming user profiles:

■ **Compatibility between Windows Vista and earlier versions of Windows** In Windows Vista, you can configure Folder Redirection in such a way that most of the important elements of a user profile are accessible across all recent Windows versions. For example, you can configure your Application Data, Desktop, Start Menu, and Documents/ My Documents folders to be redirected to a specific set of folders on a network server regardless of whether you log on to a Windows 2000, XP, or Vista computer. Folder Redirection is therefore an essential method of providing data consistency for users who roam among Windows Vista computers and Windows 2000, XP, or Server 2003 computers.

Exam Tip For the 70-622 exam, you need to know that Folder Redirection allows you to provide consistency between Windows Vista and Windows XP roaming user profiles.

■ **Faster logons** When you redirect folders such as the Documents folder, the redirected data is essentially separated from the user profile. This redirected data is never downloaded to the local computer at logon, even when you also configure roaming user profiles. Instead, the data is accessed only as needed—much as it would be accessed through a desktop shortcut to a network share. The desktop shortcut is part of the user profile, but the data behind the shortcut is not.

The same factor that allows for faster logons also allows for equally fast logoffs.

■ **Real-time data synchronization** By default, configuring Folder Redirection enables a feature called Offline Files. Offline Files allows a copy of the files contained in redirected folders to be stored locally, and when changes are made to the local copies, the changes are then automatically synchronized with the original source files. When you turn off Offline Files, the user connecting to the redirected data connects directly to the original source files and any edits the user makes to this data are made to the source data. In both configurations, Folder Redirection, when properly configured, allows users to witness any data changes they make to redirected data instantly on other computers they simultaneously log on to. Unlike with roaming user profiles, the changes made by users are not copied back to the source only when the user logs off.

■ **Network problems do not disperse data** If network problems prevent a user from connecting to a redirected folder, the user can access the local copies of the data made available from Offline Files. This data is then automatically synchronized when network connectivity is reestablished. If you turn off the Offline Files feature or if the data has never been synchronized, the user simply receives an error message and fails to connect to the source data. In either case, a faulty network connection does not lead to data being dispersed among separate user profiles for the redirected folders in question.

■ **Folder Redirection can be automated through Group Policy**   By configuring Folder Redirection in a domain environment through Group Policy, you can ensure that the feature will apply both to the current users and to the new users who fall under the scope of the policy.

Quick Check

1. Why does implementing Folder Redirection speed the logon times of users for whom roaming user profiles have been configured?
2. True or False? Folder Redirection can be used with or without roaming user profiles.

Quick Check Answers

1. Folder Redirection separates data from the roaming user profile so that less data needs to be downloaded to the local desktop.
2. True.

Real World

JC Mackin

I am often asked why organizations should use roaming user profiles at all if Folder Redirection can provide more reliable access to the same data. Well, in Windows XP and Windows 2000, the limitations of Folder Redirection were pretty substantial. Folder Redirection, in fact, could only be used to redirect four specific folders in the user profile. So I used to recommend that, if organizations wanted user profile data to roam with users, the organizations should implement roaming user profiles *in addition to* Folder Redirection.

However, with Windows Vista, Folder Redirection can now be used to redirect *all* folders in the user profile. So the question needs to be raised again—in a Windows Vista network do you still need to use roaming user profiles with Folder Redirection, or can you finally use Folder Redirection *in place of* roaming user profiles?

The answer isn't clear-cut because Folder Redirection, despite its many newfound virtues in Windows Vista, still does not redirect the personal data file Ntuser.dat, located in the root of the user profile folder. This file represents all the registry settings for a user, settings loaded into HKEY_CURRENT_USER when the user logs on. What kinds of settings are kept in Ntuser.dat? All the user-specific *settings* (as opposed to data files) in an interface: Desktop background settings, Control Panel settings, sound/audio settings, environmental variables, program preferences, and printer settings. (Note, however, that with Windows Vista, you can also now deploy printers to users through Group Policy.) The question of whether you want to use roaming user profiles in your organization, then, ultimately depends on how much you need users to preserve these settings as the users roam from computer to computer.

If I were going to make a general recommendation for your network, I would suggest using Group Policy to redirect all user profile folders to a central network share but also preserving any roaming user profiles you have already implemented (provided they . aren't causing too much of a technical headache). If, however, you have only Windows Vista clients and have never configured roaming user profiles, then I would recommend implementing only Folder Redirection and not roaming user profiles. If the need later arises for roaming user profiles, your users will let you know, and you can always implement the feature then.

Configuring Folder Redirection

Windows Vista includes a new Folder Redirection node for the Group Policy Management Console (GPMC) that allows you to configure Folder Redirection for clients running Windows Vista, Windows XP, and Windows 2000. You can choose the following settings for each folder listed in the Folder Redirection node:

- **Not Configured**   The Not Configured Folder Redirection setting is available to all folders listed in the snap-in. When you select this setting, you are returning the Folder Redirection policy for the named folder to its default state. Folders previously redirected with the policy will stay redirected. User folders on clients without any previous knowledge of the folder redirection policy will remain local, unless acted on by another policy.
- **Basic Redirection**   The Basic Redirection setting allows you to redirect the selected folder to the same share for all users.

■ **Advanced Redirection**   You use advanced redirection when you want to redirect the selected folder to different locations for different security groups. For example, you would use advanced folder redirection when you want to redirect folders belonging to the Accounting group to the Finance server and folders belonging to the Sales group to the Marketing server.

Figure 3-4 shows an example of a folder configured with advanced redirection. Note that the %username% environmental variable is used to provide a unique path based on each user's name.

Figure 3-4   Advanced folder redirection

Using the Follow The Documents Folder Setting

The Music, Pictures, and Videos folders support another Folder Redirection setting called Follow The Documents Folder. The Follow The Documents Folder setting redirects the Music, Pictures, and Videos folders as subfolders of the Documents folder. This folder redirection will make the selected folder inherit folder redirection options from the Documents folder and disable the folder redirection options for the selected folder.

The Follow The Documents Folder setting is shown in Figure 3-5.

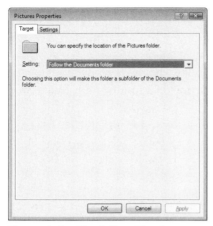

Figure 3-5   The Follow The Documents Folder setting

Configuring a Target Folder Location

If you have not opted to configure a folder to follow the Documents folder, you will need to configure the folder with a target location. Windows Vista provides four options when selecting a target folder location:

- **Create A Folder For Each User Under The Redirection Path**   This option will redirect the selected folder to the location you specify in the Root Path text box. Also, this option will add a folder named after the user logon name. For example, if you redirect the Documents folder to the root path of \\server\share, Folder Redirection will create the Documents folder under the path \\server\share\username.

- **Redirect To The Following Location**   This option redirects the named folder to the exact path listed in the root path. This has the capacity to redirect multiple users using the same share path for the redirected folder. For example, you could use this option so that multiple users have the same Desktop or Start Menu.

- **Redirect To The Local User Profile Location**   This option redirects the named folder to the local user profile. The local user profile for Windows Vista is Users\Username. The local user profile for Windows XP and Windows 2000 is Documents and Settings\username.

- **Redirect To The User's Home Directory**   This option, available only for the Documents folder, redirects the Documents folder to the home folder path configured in the properties of the user object. (A home folder is the default location some programs use to save files.)

These four target location settings are shown in Figure 3-6.

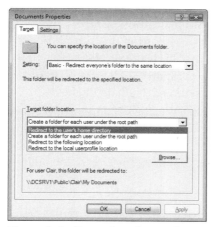

Figure 3-6   Target location settings

Configuring the Folder Redirection Settings Tab Options

The Folder Redirection Settings tab options, shown for the Documents folder in Figure 3-7, include both redirection settings and policy removal settings.

Figure 3-7   Folder Redirection Settings tab options

The following redirection settings are available on the Settings tab for folders you choose to redirect:

- **Grant The User Exclusive Rights To *\<Folder\>***   This option controls the NTFS permissions of the newly created *%username%* folder, allowing the user and Local System to have Full Control of the newly created folder. This is the default behavior.
- **Move The Contents Of *\<Folder\>* To The New Location**   Will move all the user data in the named folder to the redirected folder. This setting defaults to Enabled.
- **Also Apply Redirection Policy To Windows 2000, Windows 2000 Server, Windows XP, And Windows Server 2003 Operating Systems**   Directs the Folder Redirection management tool to write the redirection policy in a format recognized by the previous operating systems listed. When this setting is cleared, the tool writes the redirection policy in a format exclusive to Windows Vista.

Exam Tip   Although you might be tested on any of the Folder Redirection configuration settings, pay special attention to this last setting for the 70-622 exam.

The Settings tab also allows you to configure policy removal settings. These settings allow you to choose the behavior that occurs for redirected folders and their contents after a folder redirection policy no longer applies to a given user. A Folder Redirection policy might stop applying to a user, for example, when an administrator unlinks or deletes the policy or when the user joins a security group for which the policy is blocked.

The following policy removal settings are available:

- **Leave Folder In New Location When Policy Is Removed**   When you enable this option, the data a user has stored in the redirected location stays in that location once the policy no longer applies to that user.
- **Redirect The Folder Back To The Local User Profile Location When Policy Is Removed**   When you enable this option, the data a user has stored in the redirected location will be copied to the local user profile once the policy no longer applies to the user.

Exam Tip   Be sure to understand policy removal settings for the 70-622 exam.

Practice: Configuring Roaming User Profiles and Folder Redirection

In these practices, you will first join all three client computers (Vista1, Vista2, and Xpclient) to the domain. You will then create a new domain user account and configure a roaming user profile for that new user. Next, you will test the roaming user profile on the domain member computers Vista1, Vista2, and Xpclient. Finally, you will configure Folder Redirection and observe the difference in behavior between Folder Redirection and traditional roaming user profiles.

IMPORTANT This practice assumes that you have configured a DHCP server on DCSRV1 in the manner described in this book's Introduction and that you have configured all three clients to obtain an IP address automatically. If you have not configured a DHCP server, each client must specify DCSRV1 as its preferred DNS server.

▶ **Practice 1: Joining the Client Computers to the Domain**

In this practice, you will add the Vista1, Vista2, and Xpclient client computers to the NWTRADERS.MSFT domain.

1. Log on to Vista1 with an administrator account.
2. From the Start menu, right-click Computer, and then select Properties.
3. In the System window that appears, in the Computer Name, Domain, And Workgroup Settings area, click Change Settings.
4. If a User Account Control window appears, click Continue to grant the system the permission to perform this action.
5. In the Computer Name tab of the System Properties dialog box, click Change.
6. In the Computer Name/Domain Changes dialog box, select the Domain option button.
7. In the accompanying Domain text box, type **nwtraders.msft**, and then click OK.
8. In the Windows Security dialog box, enter the credentials of a domain administrator account, and then click OK.
9. Click OK (or Close, as appropriate) to close all open dialog boxes, and then choose the option to restart the computer now.
10. Log on to Vista2 with an administrator account, and then perform steps 2 through 9 to join Vista2 to the NWTRADERS domain.
11. Log on to Xpclient with an administrator account.
12. Right-click My Computer, and then select Properties.
13. In the System Properties dialog box, click the Computer Name tab.
14. In the Computer Name tab, click Change.
15. In the Computer Name Changes dialog box, select the Domain option button.
16. In the accompanying Domain text box, type **nwtraders.msft**, and then click OK.
17. In the new Computer Name Changes dialog box that appears, enter the credentials of a domain administrator account, and then click OK.
18. Click OK to close all open dialog boxes, and then choose the option to restart the computer now.

▶ **Practice 2: Creating a Roaming User Profile**

In this practice, you will first create a share named Profiles on DCSRV1. Then you will create a new domain user named RoamingUser in the NWTRADERS domain and configure the user with a roaming user profile.

1. Log on to DCSRV1 as an administrator.
2. On the C drive of DCSRV1, create a new folder named Profiles.
3. Open the Properties dialog box of the Profiles folder.
4. In the Sharing tab, select Share This Folder. Then configure permissions so that Everyone is assigned Full Control.
5. In the Security tab, use the Add button to add Authenticated Users to the Group Or User Names list. Then, assign the Full Control permission to the Authenticated Users group.
6. Click OK to close the Profiles Properties dialog box.
7. Open Active Directory Users And Computers.
8. In the console tree, right-click the Users container, point to New, and then click User.
9. In the New Object – User dialog box, type the following information:
   a. First Name: **Roaming**
   b. Last Name: **User**
   c. User Logon Name: **Roaminguser**
10. Click Next.
11. In the New Object – User dialog box, enter a password in the Password and Confirm Password text boxes.
12. Clear the User Must Change Password At Next Logon check box.
13. In the New Object – User dialog box, click Next, and then click Finish.
14. In the details pane of Active Directory Users And Computers, locate the new Roaming User domain user account you have just created and open its Properties dialog box.
15. In the Roaming User Properties dialog box, click the Profile tab.
16. In the Profile Path text box, type the following:
    \\dcsrv1\profiles\%username%
17. In the Roaming User Properties dialog box, click OK.

▶ **Practice 3: Testing the Roaming User Profile on Windows Vista Computers**

In this practice, you will log on to the NWTRADERS domain from a computer running Windows Vista. You'll then make a change to your desktop, log off, and observe the results when you log on to another domain member computer running Windows Vista. Finally, you will log on to a Windows XP computer and observe any changes.

1. Log on to the NWTRADERS domain from Vista1 with the Roaminguser user account.
2. Create a text file on the desktop named Test1, and then log off Vista1.

3. Log on to the NWTRADERS domain from Vista2 with the Roaminguser user account.
4. Verify that the file named Test1 appears on Roaminguser's desktop on Vista2.
5. Answer the following question: Did the file move from one computer to another?

   Answer: No, it is stored centrally on the server.
6. Log off Vista2.
7. Log on to DCSRV1 with an administrator account.
8. Navigate to the C drive, and open the Profiles folder.
9. Answer the following question: What is the name of the folder in which Roaminguser's data is being stored?

   Answer: Roaminguser.V2
10. Log on to the NWTRADERS domain from Xpclient with the Roaminguser user account.
11. Answer the following question: Why doesn't the Test1 file appear on the desktop on Xpclient?

    Answer: Because roaming user profiles are not compatible between Windows XP and Windows Vista
12. Log off Xpclient.
13. Return to DCSRV1 and navigate once more to C:\Profiles.
14. Answer the following question: Which new folder has appeared in Profiles since you logged on to the domain from the Windows XP computer?

    Answer: A folder named Roaminguser
15. Answer the following question: For which operating systems will this second folder hold roaming user profile data?

    Answer: For Windows 2000, Windows XP, and Windows Server 2003 computers

▶ **Practice 4: Configuring Folder Redirection for use with Windows XP and Windows Vista**

In this practice, you will create a Group Policy object (GPO) that redirects common folders to a central location.

1. Log on to the NWTRADERS domain from Vista1 with a domain administrator account.
2. Open the Start menu.
3. In the Start Search box, type **gpmc.msc**, and press Enter.
4. In the User Account Control message prompt, click Continue to grant the system the permission to perform this action.

   The Group Policy Management Console (GPMC) opens.
5. In the console tree, expand the Domains container.
6. Below the Domains folder, right-click the Nwtraders.msft domain, and then click Create A GPO In This Domain, And Link It Here.

7. In the New GPO window, type **Folder Redirection for XP and Vista**, and then click OK.

8. In the details pane of the GPMC, right-click the new GPO you have just created, and then click Edit.

   The Group Policy Object Editor opens.

9. In the console tree, below User Configuration, expand the Windows Settings container, and then expand the Folder Redirection container.

10. Take a minute to browse the various folders beneath the Folder Redirection container. These are the folders that you can redirect to any available location, such as a central server.

11. Open the Properties of the AppData(Roaming) folder.

12. In the Target tab, select the setting of Basic – Redirect Everyone's Folder To The Same Location.

13. In the Root Path text box, type **\\dcsrv1\profiles**.

14. In the Settings tab, select the check box next to Also Apply Redirection Policy To Windows 2000, Windows 2000 Server, Windows XP, And Windows Server 2003 Operating Systems.

15. This option makes the folder redirection compatible between Windows Vista and other operating systems.

16. Click OK.

17. If a Warning box appears, read the Warning, and then click Yes.

18. Perform steps 12 through 17 for the Desktop, Start Menu, and Documents folders.

19. Log off Vista1.

▶ **Practice 5: Testing Folder Redirection**

In this practice, you will log on to both Xpclient and Vista1 from a domain user account. You will then make changes to the user environment and observe the effects.

1. Log on to NWTRADERS from Xpclient as Roaminguser.

2. Create a text file on the desktop named Test2.

3. Log on to NWTRADERS from Vista1 as Roaminguser.

4. If you do not see the Test2 text file on the desktop, log off, and then log back on again.

5. When the Test2 file appears on the desktop on Vista1, create a new text file on the Vista1 desktop named Test3.

6. Switch to Xpclient.

   You should see Test3 on the desktop of Xpclient.

7. On Vista1, open the Documents folder, and then create a new text file named Test4 in that folder.

8. Switch to Xpclient, and then answer the following question: Where does Test4 appear on Xpclient?

    Answer: In the My Documents folder

9. Answer the following question: Files on the desktop and in the Documents/My Documents folder now have a modified icon. What does the new icon mean?

    Answer: The icon means that the Offline Files feature of Windows is allowing the operating system to use a local copy of the files. The original versions of these files are stored centrally on the server, and they are synchronized with the local copies.

10. Log off all machines.

Lesson Summary

- By default, roaming user profiles in Windows Vista are not compatible with those used in previous versions of Windows.

- By implementing the Folder Redirection feature through Group Policy, you can negate most incompatibilities between the roaming user profiles used in Windows Vista and those used in previous Windows versions.

- Folder Redirection also offers a number of additional advantages, such as improving logon times for roaming users, offering instantly synchronized data among multiple desktops, and allowing for automation through Group Policy.

- Folder Redirection can be used in place of roaming user profiles or in addition to them. When Folder Redirection is configured in place of roaming user profiles, the user settings stored in the file Ntuser.dat do not roam from desktop to desktop.

Lesson Review

You can use the following questions to test your knowledge of the information in Lesson 1, "Resolving User Profile Compatibility Issues." The questions are also available on the companion CD if you prefer to review them in electronic form.

NOTE Answers

Answers to these questions and explanations of why each answer choice is right or wrong are located in the "Answers" section at the end of the book.

---

1. You want to configure Folder Redirection for both Windows XP and Windows Vista clients on your network. How can you best achieve this?

    A. In Group Policy, configure separate Folder Redirection policies for the Windows XP clients and the Windows Vista clients.

    B. In Group Policy, configure a single Folder Redirection policy from a Windows Vista computer and choose the option to apply the redirection policy to Windows 2000, Windows XP, and Windows Server 2003 operating systems.

    C. In Group Policy, configure a single Folder Redirection policy from a Windows XP computer and choose the option to apply the redirection policy to Windows 2000, Windows XP, and Windows Server 2003 operating systems.

    D. In Group Policy, configure a single Folder Redirection policy from a Windows Server 2003 computer and choose the option to apply the redirection policy to Windows 2000, Windows XP, and Windows Server 2003 operating systems.

2. You are going to be removing a Folder Redirection policy. How can you ensure that users will be able to access the data now stored in redirected folders after the policy is removed?

    A. Before removing the Folder Redirection policy, select the option to redirect the folder back to the local user profile location after the policy is removed.

    B. After removing the Folder Redirection policy, select the option to redirect the folder back to the local user profile location after the policy is removed.

    C. Before removing the Folder Redirection policy, select the option to leave the folder in the new location when the policy is removed.

    D. After removing the Folder Redirection policy, select the option to leave the folder in the new location when the policy is removed.

3. You want to configure Folder Redirection so that users have access to the same data regardless of which desktop computer they log on to. Which of the following cannot be configured to roam with users by means of Folder Redirection alone? (Choose all that apply.)

    A. The Documents folder

    B. Files stored on the user's desktop

    C. Desktop background settings

    D. Files stored in personal folders created in the root of the C drive

Lesson 2: **Configuring Application Compatibility Settings**

Although your organization should perform extensive testing of critical applications in Windows Vista before deployment, some aspects of application compatibility tuning are performed after deployment. For example, if you find that a program runs more stably in Windows Vista only when configured to run in Windows XP compatibility mode, you can make this adjustment after Windows Vista is deployed. In addition, Group Policy settings that control how application compatibility problems are diagnosed become available only after Windows Vista is deployed.

After this lesson, you will be able to:

- Understand the features of Windows Vista that are most likely to cause application compatibility problems.
- Adjust the compatibility settings of a given program by using the Program Compatibility Wizard or the program's Compatibility tab.
- Configure Group Policy settings that affect how program compatibility issues are diagnosed in Windows Vista.

Estimated lesson time: 30 minutes

Understanding Application Compatibility

Each release of Windows includes new features and capabilities that affect how applications run. Before making adjustments to improve application compatibility, you should try to gain some understanding of the particular features in Windows Vista that are most likely to cause application compatibility problems. These particular features can generally be classified as security enhancements and operating system changes.

Security Enhancements Affecting Application Compatibility

Of the new security features in Windows Vista, the following are most likely to lead to compatibility problems with third-party applications:

- **User Account Control**   User Account Control (UAC) separates standard user privileges from administrator privileges in a way that helps reduce the effect of malware, unauthorized software installation, and unapproved system changes. If you are logged on as an administrator, UAC by default prompts you to confirm any task you want to perform that requires administrator privileges. If you are logged on as a standard user and attempt to perform a task that requires administrator privileges, UAC gives you an opportunity to enter administrator credentials instead of denying you the right to perform the task outright.

  UAC can introduce problems in applications that are not compliant with this technology enhancement. For this reason, it is important to test applications with UAC enabled before you deploy them.

- **File and Registry Virtualization (Windows Resource Protection)**   This new feature in Windows Vista receives any application requests to write to protected system files or registry locations and redirects these requests to safe and temporary locations. Although most applications can handle this redirection without any problem, some applications require full access to the protected areas and cannot handle the redirection process.

  File and registry virtualization is covered in more detail in Lesson 3, "Migrating Applications and Data," of Chapter 1, "Preparing for Windows Deployment."

- **Protected Mode**   Protected Mode is a feature of Internet Explorer 7 that protects computers from malware by restricting the browser's access within the registry and file system. Although Protected Mode helps maintain the integrity of client computers, it can affect the proper operation of older Internet and intranet applications.

Operating System Enhancement Affecting Application Compatibility

Of the many operating system changes introduced by Windows Vista, the following features are most likely to lead to application compatibility difficulties:

- **New system application programming interfaces (APIs)**   APIs expose layers of the Windows Vista operating system differently than they did in previous versions of Windows. Antivirus and firewall software are examples of applications that rely on these new APIs to monitor and protect Windows Vista.

  Applications that relied on outdated APIs will need to be upgraded or replaced for Windows Vista.

- **Windows Vista 64-bit**   Neither 16-bit applications nor 32-bit drivers are supported in the Windows Vista 64-bit environment. The automatic registry and system file redirection that allows some older applications to function in the 32-bit version of Windows Vista are not available for the 64-bit environment. For these reasons, new 64-bit applications must comply fully with Windows Vista application standards.
- **Operating system version**   Many older applications check for a specific version of Windows and stop responding when they fail to find this specific version. Features built into Windows Vista, such as the Program Compatibility Assistant (discussed in the next section), can usually resolve this type of issue automatically.

Using Windows Vista Built-in Compatibility Tools

Although you should perform extensive application compatibility testing before you deploy Windows Vista, compatibility problems might unexpectedly appear or persist after deployment. To help you improve the compatibility of older programs after deployment, Windows Vista provides three tools: the Program Compatibility Assistant, the Program Compatibility Wizard, and the Compatibility tab in a program's Properties dialog box.

- **Program Compatibility Assistant (PCA)**   The PCA is a tool that automatically appears when Windows Vista detects known compatibility issues in older programs. When it does appear, the PCA can offer to fix the problem the next time you run the program. For example, the PCA can resolve conflicts with UAC, or it can run the program in a mode that simulates earlier versions of Windows. If you agree to the changes PCA proposes, these changes are then performed automatically. Alternatively, if the compatibility issue detected is serious, the PCA can warn you or block the program from running.

  When the PCA recognizes a problem but cannot offer a fix, it gives you an option to check online for possible solutions, as shown in Figure 3-8.

Figure 3-8   The Program Compatibility Assistant

■ **Program Compatibility Wizard (PCW)**   The PCW is a Control Panel program you can use to configure the compatibility settings for an older program if you notice that the program is not running smoothly. For example, you can configure the program to run in a simulated environment of a previous version of Windows, to run with specific display settings, or to run with Administrator privileges.

To launch the wizard, in Control Panel, first click Programs, and then, in the Programs And Features category, click Use An Older Program With This Version Of Windows.

A page of the PCW is shown in Figure 3-9.

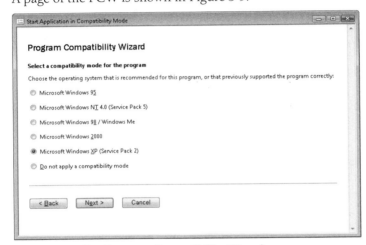

Figure 3-9   The Program Compatibility Wizard

___

CAUTION   Warning

Do not use the PCW on older antivirus programs, disk utilities, or other system programs because it might cause data loss or create a security risk.

___

■ **Compatibility tab**   As an alternative to running the PCW, you can simply configure compatibility settings in the Compatibility tab within the Properties sheet of any given program. The options provided on this tab are the same as those you can configure through the PCW.

The Compatibility tab is shown in Figure 3-10.

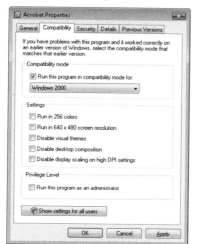

Figure 3-10 Compatibility properties

If changing the settings in the Compatibility tab does not fix the problem, go to the program manufacturer's website to see if there is an update for the program.

Alternate Hosting for Application Compatibility

In some cases your organization will need to support an application for which you cannot immediately resolve compatibility issues with Windows Vista. For example, if you are running a 64-bit version of Windows Vista, you will not be able to run 16-bit applications by merely adjusting the compatibility settings of the program. Until a newer, more compatible version of the application appears (or until your organization finds an alternate application), you must find a temporary fix for the application compatibility problem.

The most common temporary fix for unresolved application compatibility problems is simply to run the application within the old operating system in a virtual machine or on a remote server that can be accessed through Remote Desktop.

- **Virtual PC 2007** You can use Virtual PC to run applications on Windows Vista that function properly only with older versions of Windows. For example, if your organization needs to support a 16-bit application within a 64-bit version of Windows Vista, you can use Virtual PC 2007 to run the program within a virtual machine running a previous version of Windows. Although virtual machine software such as Virtual PC is required to run 16-bit applications in 64-bit versions of Windows Vista, the use of Virtual PC need not be reserved only for this purpose. Virtual PC also lets users keep a previous version of Windows until upgraded versions of older applications are developed. Whenever you need to support an older application that does not run smoothly in Windows Vista and that cannot be upgraded, you should consider running the application inside a virtual machine.

■ **Terminal Services for hosting applications** Hosting older applications on Terminal Services lets you deliver Windows-based applications, or the Windows desktop itself, to virtually any computer device on your network. Windows Vista clients can connect to these application-hosting environments through Remote Desktop.

■ **Virtual Server for hosting applications** With Virtual Server you can host legacy applications and allow remote connectivity from end users who need access to those applications. Virtual Server 2005 allows you to run any major x86 operating systems as a guest on a Windows Server 2003 machine. Windows Vista clients can then connect over the network to applications hosted on these operating systems.

Configuring Application Compatibility Diagnostics through Group Policy

After you deploy Windows Vista, many new Group Policy settings become available, including a set of policy options related to application compatibility diagnostics. To browse these new settings, open the GPMC on a Windows Vista computer joined to an Active Directory directory service domain. In a GPO, browse to Computer Configuration, Administrative Templates, System, Troubleshooting And Diagnostics, and Application Compatibility Diagnostics.

The Application Compatibility Diagnostics policy settings are shown in Figure 3-11.

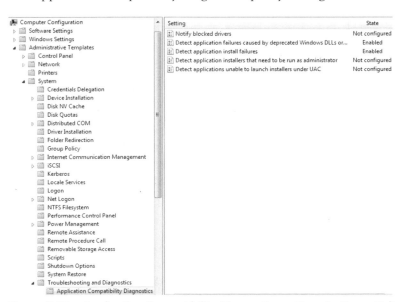

Figure 3-11 Application Compatibility Diagnostics settings in Group Policy

The Application Compatibility Diagnostics folder includes the following five policies:

- **Notify Blocked Drivers**   This policy setting determines whether the PCA will notify the user if drivers are blocked because of compatibility issues. If you enable this policy setting, the PCA will notify the user of blocked driver issues and give the user an option to check the Microsoft website for solutions. (This behavior is also the default behavior in Windows Vista.) If you disable this policy setting, the PCA will not notify the user of blocked driver issues. Note that if this policy setting is configured as disabled, the user will not be presented with solutions to blocked drivers.

- **Detect Application Failures Caused By Deprecated Windows DLLs Or COM Objects**   This policy setting determines whether the PCA will notify the user when a DLL load or COM object creation failure is detected in an application. If you enable this policy setting, the PCA detects programs trying to load legacy Microsoft Windows DLLs or creating legacy COM objects that are removed in this version of Windows. (This behavior is also the default behavior in Windows Vista.) When this failure is detected, after the program is terminated PCA notifies the user about this problem and provides an option to check the Microsoft website for solutions. If you disable this policy setting, the PCA does not detect programs trying to load legacy Windows DLLs or creating legacy COM objects.

- **Detect Application Install Failures**   This policy setting configures the PCA to notify the user when an application installation has failed. If you enable this policy setting, the PCA detects application installation failures and gives the user an option to restart the installer in Microsoft Windows XP compatibility mode. (This behavior is also the default behavior in Windows Vista.) If you disable this policy setting, the PCA will not detect program installation failures.

- **Detect Application Installers That Need To Be Run As Administrator**   This policy setting determines whether the PCA will notify the user when application installations have failed because they need to be run as administrator. If you enable this policy setting, the PCA will detect such installation failures and provide the user with an option to restart the installer programs as administrator. (This behavior is also the default behavior in Windows Vista.) If you disable this policy setting, the PCA will not notify users when installer program failures have occurred for this reason.

- **Detect Applications Unable To Launch Installers Under UAC**   This policy setting configures the PCA to notify the user when UAC is preventing an application from launching an installer (typically an updater program). If you enable this policy setting, the PCA detects programs that fail to launch installers and grants administrator privileges that allow this task to be performed the next time the program is run. (This behavior is also the default behavior in Windows Vista.) If you disable this policy setting, the PCA will not detect applications that fail to launch installers run under UAC.

Exam Tip   You need to understand these application compatibility diagnostics Group Policy settings for the 70-622 exam.

Exam Tip   Although unrelated to the topic of application compatibility, new Group Policy settings in Windows Vista also allow you to configure *device installation restrictions*. These policies, which you can configure post-deployment, let you control the types of devices that a user can install on a local system—and optionally let system administrators override these defined restrictions. You can browse Device Installation Restriction policy settings in a GPO by navigating to Computer Configuration, Administrative Templates, System, Device Installation, Device Installation Restrictions.

For the 70-622 exam, you need to know what Device Installation Restrictions policies do and where you find them.

Quick Check

1. True or False? Group Policy settings in Windows Vista allow you to configure the compatibility settings of a given program.
2. True or False? The only ways to run a 16-bit application on a 64-bit version of Windows is through either a virtual machine or a Terminal Services connection to another computer.

Quick Check Answers

1. False. Group Policy settings in Windows Vista allow you to configure only how the user is notified about application compatibility problems.
2. True.

Practice: Configuring Application Compatibility Diagnostics

In this practice, you will configure application compatibility settings in Group Policy.

▶ **Practice 1: Creating a Policy for Application Compatibility Settings**

In this practice, you will create a new GPO named Application Compatibility Diagnostics Policy. In the GPO you will enable two settings that enable particular behaviors in the PCA.

1. Start DCSRV1 and Vista1.

    Vista1 should already be joined to the domain NWTRADERS.

2. Log on to NWTRADERS from Vista1 as an administrator.

3. In the Start Search box of the Start menu, type **gpmc.msc**, and then press Enter.
   The Group Policy Management Console (GPMC) opens.

4. In the GPMC console tree, expand Forest: nwtraders.msft and then Domains.

5. Beneath the Domains container, right-click the Nwtraders.msft icon, and then click the option to Create A GPO In This Domain And Link It Here.
   The New GPO dialog box opens.

6. In the New GPO dialog box, type **Application Compatibility Diagnostics Policy**, and then click OK.

7. In the details pane of the GPMC, ensure that the Linked Group Policy Objects tab is selected. Then, in the list of GPOs, right-click Application Compatibility Diagnostics Policy, and then click Edit.
   A Group Policy Object Editor window opens.

8. In the console tree of the Group Policy Object Editor, navigate to Computer Configuration, Administrative Templates, System, Troubleshooting And Diagnostics, and then Application Compatibility Diagnostics.

9. In the details pane of the Group Policy Object Editor, double-click the policy named Detect Application Failures Caused By Deprecated DLLs Or COM Objects.
   The associated policy properties dialog box opens.

10. In the Setting tab of the policy properties dialog box, select Enabled.

11. In the Scenario Execution Level drop-down list box, ensure that Detection, Troubleshooting And Resolution is selected.

12. In the policy properties dialog box, click the Explain tab.

13. Take a few moments to read the explanation of the policy, and then click OK.
    The policy should now appear as Enabled.

14. In the details pane of the Group Policy Object Editor, double-click the policy named Detect Application Install Failures.

15. In the Settings tab of the policy properties dialog box, select Enabled.

16. Click the Explain tab.

17. Take a few moments to read the explanation of the policy, and then click OK.
    The policy should now appear as Enabled.

18. Close all open windows.

19. Shut down Vista1, and then shut down DCSRV1.

Lesson Summary

- Each release of Windows introduces new features that affect the compatibility of programs written for earlier operating systems. With Windows Vista, the features most likely to affect application compatibility include User Account Control (UAC), file and registry virtualization, and new system APIs.

- The Program Compatibility Assistant (PCA) is a tool that automatically appears when Windows Vista detects known compatibility issues in older programs. When it does appear, the PCA can offer to fix the problem the next time you run the program.

- The Program Compatibility Wizard (PCW) is a Control Panel program you can use to configure the compatibility settings for an older program. You can configure these same compatibility settings in the Compatibility tab of the program.

- If you need to support an application that is not compatible with Windows Vista, you can run the program in a compatible operating system within a virtual machine. Alternatively, you can use a Terminal Services connection to a computer running the application and a compatible operating system.

- Windows Vista introduces new Group Policy settings that allow you to determine how the PCA will diagnose and troubleshoot application compatibility problems.

Lesson Review

You can use the following questions to test your knowledge of the information in Lesson 2, "Configuring Application Compatibility Settings." The questions are also available on the companion CD if you prefer to review them in electronic form.

NOTE Answers

Answers to these questions and explanations of why each answer choice is right or wrong are located in the "Answers" section at the end of the book.

---

1. After upgrading the client computers in your organization from Windows XP to Windows Vista, you discover that a certain application installs without error but no longer runs properly in the new operating system. How can you ensure that users will receive any possible notifications telling them why the application has failed?

    A. In Group Policy, enable the Detect Application Failures Caused By Deprecated Windows DLLs Or COM Objects policy.

    B. In Group Policy, enable the Notify Blocked Drivers policy.

    C. In Group Policy, enable the Detect Application Install Failures policy.

    D. In Group Policy, enable the Detect Application Installers That Need To Be Run As Administrator policy.

2. Which of the following applications is least likely to run on the 32-bit version of Windows Vista without a software update?

   A. A 16-bit application written for Windows 2000

   B. A 32-bit application written for Windows XP that requires administrative privileges to run properly

   C. An application written for Windows 2000 that writes to a protected area of the registry

   D. An application written for Windows XP that writes to protected system files

Chapter Review

To further practice and reinforce the skills you learned in this chapter, you can

- Review the chapter summary.
- Review the list of key terms introduced in this chapter.
- Complete the case scenarios. These scenarios set up real-world situations involving the topics of this chapter and ask you to create solutions.
- Complete the suggested practices.
- Take a practice test.

Chapter Summary

- Roaming user profiles in Windows Vista are not compatible with those used in previous versions of Windows.
- By configuring Folder Redirection in Group Policy, you can allow users in an Active Directory domain to have access to the same personal data as they roam from desktops in Windows Vista to desktops in Windows 2000, Windows XP, and Windows Server 2003.
- The Program Compatibility Assistant (PCA) is a tool that automatically appears when Windows Vista detects known compatibility issues in older programs. When it does appear, the PCA can offer to fix the problem the next time you run the program.
- The Program Compatibility Wizard (PCW) is a Control Panel program you can use to configure the compatibility settings for an older program. You can configure these same compatibility settings on the Compatibility tab of the program.
- Windows Vista introduces new Group Policy settings that allow you to determine how the PCA will diagnose and troubleshoot application compatibility problems.

Key Terms

Do you know what these key terms mean? You can check your answers by looking up the terms in the glossary at the end of the book.

- Ntuser.dat
- roaming user profile
- User Account Control (UAC)
- user profile

Case Scenarios

In the following case scenarios, you will apply what you've learned in this chapter. You can find answers to these questions in the "Answers" section at the end of this book.

Case Scenario 1: Supporting Roaming Users in Windows Vista

You are a desktop support technician in a large company. The company has just deployed Windows Vista on client computers in the Sales department. Roaming user profiles have been implemented for the Sales department team members for several years, and all user profiles are stored on the network share \\server3\profiles. More than other users, the Sales department team members tend to log on to computers outside of their department, including computers running Windows XP.

1. Sales team members store all of their documents in the My Documents folder, but after Windows Vista is deployed, none of the users' familiar documents are available. How can you allow Sales team members access to their old data?

2. A Sales user whose user name is SallyB is logged on to a Windows XP computer. She tells you that she wants to browse her Windows Vista profile folders to locate a recently saved file. Where should you direct her to look? (Assume that Folder Redirection has not yet been configured.)

Case Scenario 2: Configuring Application Compatibility Settings

You are a computer support specialist in a business with 100 employees. You have just finished deploying Windows Vista to all client desktops and are currently fielding issues related to application compatibility.

1. A certain application used infrequently by the Advertising department was written for Windows XP. The application runs without problems on Windows Server 2003 but does not run at all in the Windows Vista environment. Assuming that no updates for the application are yet available, what is the first temporary remedy that you should investigate?

2. Users report that sometimes applications fail to install but that they receive no notification about the failure. What can you do to ensure that users receive notification when applications fail to install?

Suggested Practices

To help you successfully master the exam objectives presented in this chapter, complete the following tasks.

Configure Folder Redirection

■ **Practice: Compare Logon Times for Roaming User Profiles With and Without Folder Redirection** Configure a roaming user profile without Folder Redirection. Be sure to store the user profile on a network share. Add at least 20 MB of data to the Documents folder, and then calculate the time required to log on and log off the computer. Next, configure Folder Redirection to redirect the Documents folder to the network share. Calculate the time saved when logging on and logging off.

Perform a Virtual Lab

■ **Practice: Learn about Application Compatibility in Windows Vista** Go to *http://msevents .microsoft.com* and search for Event ID# 1032316592. Register and perform the virtual lab named "Windows Vista Readiness – Application Compatibility (TechNet) Virtual Lab."

Watch a Webcast

■ **Practice: Watch a Webcast About Application Compatibility in Windows Vista** Watch the Webcast "TechNet Webcast: Application Compatibility Considerations with Windows Vista (Level 200)," by Bryan Von Axelson, available on the companion CD in the Webcasts folder.

Take a Practice Test

The practice tests on this book's companion CD offer many options. For example, you can test yourself on just one exam objective, or you can test yourself on all the 70-622 certification exam content. You can set up the test so that it closely simulates the experience of taking a certification exam, or you can set it up in study mode so that you can look at the correct answers and explanations after you answer each question.

MORE INFO   **Practice tests**

For details about all the practice test options available, see the "How to Use the Practice Tests" section in this book's Introduction.

Chapter 4

Troubleshooting Group Policy Settings

Microsoft Windows uses Group Policy settings to make it easier to manage multiple computers. However, Group Policy settings in enterprise environments can be very complicated, with multiple layers of Group Policy objects (GPOs) affecting any given user or computer. Additionally, Group Policy becomes even more complicated with Windows Vista, because you can now use multiple local GPOs, even if you do not have an Active Directory directory service domain.

This chapter provides an overview of Group Policy, a description of how Windows Vista handles Group Policy processing differently from earlier versions of Windows, an overview of new and improved Group Policy settings, and guidance for isolating and troubleshooting Group Policy problems.

Exam objectives in this chapter:
- Troubleshoot policy settings.
- Troubleshoot security configuration issues.

Lessons in this chapter:

Before You Begin

To complete the lessons in this chapter, you should be familiar with managing Windows client computers in an Active Directory domain environment and be comfortable with the following tasks:

- Configuring Windows Server 2003 domain controllers.
- Adding Windows Vista computers to an Active Directory domain.
- Using the Group Policy Object Editor.
- Using the Event Viewer.
- Viewing and editing Extensible Markup Language (XML) files.
- Running commands at a command prompt.

Lesson 1: Group Policy Overview

One of Microsoft's goals for Windows Vista was to make almost every aspect of the operating system's behavior configurable using Group Policy settings. As a result, Windows Vista includes dozens of new Group Policy settings. Some aspects of Group Policy behavior have changed, too. For example, you can now configure multiple local GPOs, which simplifies managing computers in workgroup environments.

This lesson provides an overview of Group Policy objects (GPOs), Multiple Local Group Policy objects (MLGPOs), and administrative templates. Lesson 2, "Windows Vista Group Policy Settings," provides an overview of new Group Policy settings included with Windows Vista.

After this lesson, you will be able to:
- Describe Group Policy and determine when you might be able to use Group Policy to manage computers more efficiently.
- List operating systems that can be managed by Group Policy and describe how their behavior differs.
- Describe how domain administrators use Group Policy to manage users and client computers in a hierarchy.
- Describe how MLGPOs function in Windows Vista, list the different types of MLGPOs, and configure MLGPOs using the Group Policy Object Editor.
- Create and migrate administrative templates to the new format supported by Windows Vista.

Estimated lesson time: 30 minutes

What Is Group Policy?

Group Policy is a mechanism for consistently configuring thousands of different aspects of Windows operating systems. Home users, or business users with a small number of computers, can easily manage their computers' configurations using tools such as the Control Panel. However, organizations with dozens of computers or more, require a more efficient and reliable way to consistently configure computers.

To use Group Policy, administrators create GPOs and link them to containers such as an organizational unit (OU) within an Active Directory domain. A single GPO can contain one or more Group Policy settings, and those settings are automatically applied to users or computers in the containers that the GPO is linked to.

For example, a single GPO might contain definitions for the following Group Policy settings. Administrators could then configure these settings to be applied to all users in the domain, all users in the Marketing department, or a single user.

- Maximum password age: 30 days
- Minimum password length: 0 characters
- Account lockout threshold: five invalid logon attempts
- Turn on menu bar by default: Enabled

Any settings not defined in a GPO remain at their defaults.

Some of the settings you can define using Group Policy include the following:

- **Registry settings**   Any registry value can be defined by using existing or custom administrative templates, as described later in this lesson.
- **Security settings**   Group Policy settings provide control over all major security settings.
- **Windows Update settings**   You can configure Windows Update intervals or configure computers to use an internal Windows Server Update Services (WSUS) update distribution server.
- **Software restrictions**   Use software restrictions to control which program can run on your computers.
- **Software distribution**   You can distribute Windows Installer files, such as those included with almost all programs, to install new software on computers in your organization.
- **Computer and user scripts**   When Group Policy settings don't provide sufficient control, you can use Group Policy to launch custom scripts on computers.
- **Folder redirection**   Redirect important folders, such as the Users folder or just the Documents folder, to a server on your network. This can provide centralized management over user files.
- **Internet Explorer settings**   Configure browser settings to meet your organization's needs.

Group Policy settings are arranged hierarchically within a GPO. For example, Figure 4-1 shows the Group Policy Object Editor being used to configure the User Rights Assignment policies in the Local Computer Policy. The Group Policy Object Editor is the primary tool for editing GPOs, and the Local Computer Policy is the GPO that is automatically applied to all computers.

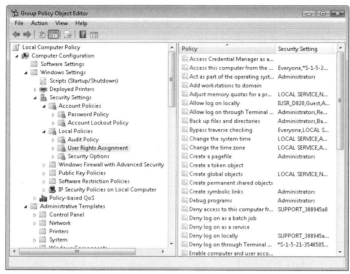

Figure 4-1   Group Policy settings are arranged in a hierarchy to make them easier to manage

Which Computers Can Use Group Policy?

Most recent business-oriented Windows operating systems support Group Policy, including:

- Windows 2000 Professional.
- Windows 2000 Server.
- Windows XP Professional.
- Windows Server 2003.
- Windows Server 2008.
- Windows Vista Business.
- Windows Vista Enterprise.
- Windows Vista Ultimate.

Consumer Windows operating systems, such as Windows XP Home and Windows Vista Home Basic and Home Premium, do not support Group Policy, nor do they support joining Active Directory domains.

How Are Group Policy Objects Applied in Domain Environments?

Although you can manage computers by editing local GPOs, you can also use Active Directory Group Policy to apply a single GPO to all computers, all users, or groups of computers and users. Figure 4-2 shows the Group Policy Management Console, a tool for managing GPOs in a domain environment. This example shows the fictional hq.contoso.com domain, which contains the standard Default Domain Policy that applies to all computers in a domain, and multiple custom OUs, to which you can link GPOs.

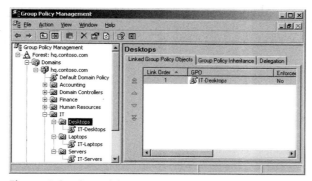

Figure 4-2   Organizing GPOs into a hierarchy in Active Directory domains

In Figure 4-2 you can see that the example hq.contoso.com domain has custom OUs named Accounting, Finance, Human Resources, and IT, as well as the standard Domain Controllers OU. The IT OU contains the Desktops, Laptops, and Servers OUs. Each of these OUs has its own GPO. If the IT department assigned a desktop computer to one of their users, that user would place the computer object in the hq.contoso.com\IT\Desktops OU. This would cause Group Policy to apply the following GPOs to the computer, in this order:

- Local GPO
- Default Domain Policy
- IT (if a GPO exists at this level)
- IT-Desktops

Settings in lower-level GPOs override settings in higher GPOs. Settings in domain GPOs always override local GPOs. Therefore, if passwords should expire in 40 days for most computers in your organization, you should enable that setting in the Default Domain Policy. If users in your IT departments should have their passwords expire in 30 days instead, you could define that setting in the IT Group Policy setting. Settings within the IT-Desktops, IT-Laptops, and IT-Servers GPOs should only be defined when different settings are required for different operating systems.

This hierarchy provides a great deal of flexibility when configuring computers in large organizations. Unfortunately, it can also complicate troubleshooting. For example, if a restrictive security setting is causing an application to fail, how can you determine which of the GPOs contains the setting? Fortunately, Windows Vista provides tools to quickly isolate such problems. Lesson 3, "Troubleshooting Group Policy Settings," covers this type of troubleshooting in more detail.

Multiple Local Group Policy Objects

Earlier versions of Windows supported applying multiple GPOs in Active Directory domains; however, computers that were not a member of a domain could have only a single local GPO. This local GPO applied to users, guests, and even administrators—making it difficult to restrict user settings while still allowing administrators to manage the computer.

Windows Vista adds the capability to apply multiple local GPOs (MLGPOs) to local users, which can make it much easier to manage computers that are not members of a domain but that are shared between multiple users. MLGPO is ideal for environments such as public Internet kiosks and shared library computers because you can apply a restrictive local GPO to public users while granting administrators higher privileges.

Types of MLGPOs

Windows Vista supports the following levels of local GPOs, from most general to most specific:

- **Local Computer Policy**   Exactly like the local GPO in earlier versions of Windows, settings in this GPO apply to the computer and all users on the computer. This is the only local GPO with Computer Configuration settings; the other GPOs have only User Configuration settings.
- **Administrators and Non-Administrators Local Group Policy**   Two separate GPOs, the Administrators local GPO applies to members of the Administrators local group, while the Non-Administrators local GPO applies to all other users. This makes it convenient to configure restrictive settings for standard users of a computer without affecting administrators.
- **User-specific Group Policy**   GPOs that apply to individual user accounts. You can create one for each user, but you cannot create local GPOs that apply to user groups other than Administrators and Non-Administrators.

As with domain GPOs, Windows Vista applies the most specific setting if MLGPOs have different values for the same setting. For example, if the Local Computer Policy GPO, the Non-Administrators local GPO, and the user-specific local GPO all define different values for the same setting, the user-specific GPO takes effect.

Exam Tip

Remember GPO priorities for the exam. From highest priority to lowest priority: OU-specific GPOs, the default domain GPO, site GPOs, the user-specific local GPO, the local Administrators or Non-Administrators GPO, and finally, the Local Computer Policy GPO.

Avoid using local GPOs in domain environments. It's much easier to manage and troubleshoot domain GPOs, especially as the number of computers in your domain grows. Use local GPOs only for computers that cannot join a domain but still require customized security settings.

How to Manage Multiple Local Group Policy Objects

To create and manage MLGPOs, follow these steps:

1. Click Start, type **mmc.exe**, and then press Enter.
2. In the Console1 window, click File, and then click Add/Remove Snap-in.
3. In the Add Or Remove Snap-ins dialog box, in the Available snap-ins list, click Group Policy Object Editor, and then click Add.
4. In the Select Group Policy Object dialog box, click Browse.
5. The Browse For A Group Policy Object dialog box appears. By default, the This Computer option is selected if your computer is a member of a workgroup, which refers to the local GPO. To select a different local GPO, click the Users tab, as shown in Figure 4-3. Then click Administrators, Non-Administrators, or the user you want to create the GPO for. Click OK.

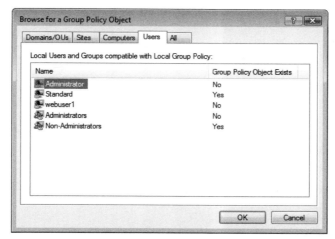

Figure 4-3   Using the Users tab in the Browse For A Group Policy Object dialog box to select local GPOs

6. Click Finish.
7. In the Add Or Remove Snap-ins dialog box, repeat steps 4–7 to add other GPOs to the same console. Then click OK.

To simplify managing local GPOs in the future, save your console for later use.

Understanding Administrative Templates

Microsoft provides thousands of standard Group Policy settings. However, administrators often need to create custom Group Policy settings that define registry entries for custom applications or Windows features that do not already have Group Policy settings.

Windows XP and earlier versions of Windows supported extending Group Policy by using administrative templates implemented by using .adm files. These administrative template files appear under the Administrative Templates node in the Group Policy Object Editor. Microsoft provided many standard administrative template files, and administrators could create their own administrative templates.

Administrative templates on Windows XP have several weaknesses:

- The .adm files use a proprietary file format that required using custom tools to create.
- Administrative templates support only one language per .adm file, which caused problems when an organization had administrators from different regions.
- Every time an administrator created a new GPO, all .adm template files were copied from the Windows XP workstation (they are stored in the %windir%\inf\ folder) to the Group Policy Template store within the domain. Then the template files were replicated between domain controllers. These template files could become quite large and cause problems replicating to domain controllers on slow links.

The following sections describe how Windows Vista improves on these weaknesses.

NOTE   The Group Policy Management Console

The Group Policy Management Console (GPMC) is now included with Windows Vista.

Administrative Template File Formats

Windows Vista implements administrative templates using .admx files, which are based on the open-standards XML file format. Windows Vista stores .admx files at %windir%\Policy-Definitions. For example, the following is an excerpt from the ControlPanelDisplay.admx file:

```
<?xml version="1.0" encoding="utf-8"?>
<!--  (c) 2006 Microsoft Corporation  -->
<policyDefinitions xmlns:xsd="http://www.w3.org/2001/XMLSchema"
xmlns:xsi="http://www.w3.org/2001/XMLSchema-instance" revision="1.0" schemaVersion="1.0"
xmlns="http://schemas.microsoft.com/GroupPolicy/2006/07/PolicyDefinitions">
  <policyNamespaces>
   <target prefix="controlpaneldisplay" namespace="Microsoft.Policies.ControlPanelDisplay" />
   <using prefix="windows" namespace="Microsoft.Policies.Windows" />
  </policyNamespaces>
  <resources minRequiredRevision="1.0" />
  <categories>
    <category name="Display" displayName="$(string.Display)">
      <parentCategory ref="windows:ControlPanel" />
    </category>
    <category name="Themes" displayName="$(string.Themes)">
      <parentCategory ref="Display" />
    </category>
  </categories>
```

```
    <policies>
       <policy name="CPL_Display_Disable" class="User"
displayName="$(string.CPL_Display_Disable)" explainText="$(string.NoDispCpl_Help)"
key="Software\Microsoft\Windows\CurrentVersion\Policies\System"
valueName="NoDispCPL">
          <parentCategory ref="Display" />
          <supportedOn ref="windows:SUPPORTED_Win2k" />
       </policy>
    </policies>
</policyDefinitions>
```

Notice that descriptions are defined using variables. For example:

```
    <policy name="Themes_Disable_Color_Select" class="User"
displayName="$(string.Themes_Disable_Color_Select)"
explainText="$(string.Themes_Disable_Color_Select_Help)"
key="Software\Microsoft\Windows\CurrentVersion\Policies\System"
valueName="NoColorChoice">
```

In this case, $(string.Themes_Disable_Color_Select) is a placeholder that refers to the Themes_Disable_Color_Select description contained in an administrative template language file (.adml). These files are stored in a region-specific subfolder of %windir%\PolicyDefinitions. For example, the English-language .adml files are stored at C:\Windows\PolicyDefinitions\en-US\ by default. Microsoft provides .adml files for all languages supported by Windows. If you create custom .admx files, you can also create custom .adml files to provide descriptions in every language used in your organization.

NOTE   When to use .adml files

All the standard administrative templates included with Windows Vista include separate .adml files. However, if you create custom .admx files, you don't need to use a .adml file if you need to support only a single language. Instead of using variables to define descriptions, just place the description in the .admx file itself.

In the previous example showing the Themes_Disable_Color_Select policy, the *$(string .Themes_Disable_Color_Select)* reference referred to the following in the C:\Windows\Policy-Definitions\en-US\ControlPanelDisplay.adml file:

```
<string id="Themes_Disable_Color_Select">Prohibit Theme color selection</string>
```

Exam Tip

For the exam, remember that only Windows Vista computers can open .admx files. Windows XP and earlier versions of Windows use .adm files. So, if you create custom Group Policy settings using .admx files, you will be able to edit them only from a Windows Vista computer.

How to Create a Central Store for Administrative Template Files

Unlike .adm files, .admx files are not stored in individual GPOs. In Active Directory environments you can create a central store location of .admx files that is accessible to anyone with permission to create or edit GPOs. Group Policy tools will continue to recognize custom .adm files associated with existing GPOs but will ignore any .adm file that has been superseded by .admx files: System.adm, Inetres.adm, Conf.adm, Wmplayer.adm, and Wuau.adm.

NOTE **Administrative templates and replication**

Storing administrative templates in GPOs caused problems with replication between domain controllers (especially across low-bandwidth links) because the storage was very inefficient. Storing administrative templates in a central location still requires replication, but it is much more efficient. To take advantage of the central store, all administrators need to be using Windows Vista because earlier versions of Windows can't read the .admx files.

Group Policy Object Editor automatically reads and displays Administrative Template policy settings based on .admx files that are stored either locally or in the optional .admx central store. Group Policy Object Editor will automatically display Administrative Template policy settings defined in custom .adm files stored in the GPO. You can still add or remove custom .adm files to a GPO with the Add/Remove Template menu option.

To create a central store, create the following folders on the domain controller currently acting in the PDC Emulator flexible single master operations (FSMO) role:

- **%SystemRoot%\sysvol\domain\policies\PolicyDefinitions**   You will use this folder to store the .admx language-neutral (.admx) files.
- **One or more %SystemRoot%\sysvol\domain\policies\PolicyDefinitions*MUI_culture* folders**   You will use these subfolders to store the .adml language-specific (.adml) files, mirroring the structure used on local computers.

MORE INFO **ISO language identifiers**

For a list of International Organization for Standardization (ISO) language identifiers that you should use to name the language-specific *MUI_culture* folders, visit *http://msdn2.microsoft.com /en-us/library/ms693062*.

After you create the central store and copy your administrative templates to it, the File Replication Service (FRS) automatically replicates the templates to all domain controllers. If the same administrative template exists in both the local folder and the central store, Windows Vista uses the template file from the central store.

How to Migrate Administrative Templates

If you created custom .adm files for earlier versions of Windows, you can use those same .adm files by using the Group Policy Object Editor in Windows Vista. However, if you modified one of the standard .adm files included with Windows XP, Windows Vista will ignore it. This happens because all .adm files included with Windows XP are built into Windows Vista.

NOTE   Using the Group Policy Object Editor with earlier versions of Windows

If you run the Group Policy Object Editor on Windows Server 2003, Windows XP, or Windows 2000, it will not correctly display new Windows Vista Administrative Template policy settings that might be enabled or disabled within a GPO. Instead, the registry values associated with these policy settings will be displayed under "Extra Registry Settings" in the Group Policy Object Editor.

When you run the Group Policy Object Editor from Windows Vista, .adm files appear under the Classic Administrative Templates node. Although you do not have to migrate these to .admx files, you might find it easier to manage Group Policy settings if you convert all templates to the .admx format. Microsoft provides a free tool called ADMX Migrator, shown in Figure 4-4, which was developed by FullArmor. ADMX Migrator is available at *http://www.microsoft.com/downloads/details.aspx?FamilyId=0F1EEC3D-10C4-4B5F-9625-97C2F731090C* on the Microsoft Download Center and can be installed on Windows Vista, Windows Server 2003 with Service Pack 1 or later, and Windows XP with Service Pack 2 or later (if MMC 3.0 and the .NET Framework 2.0 are installed) .

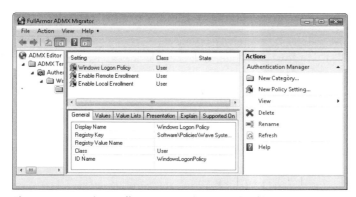

Figure 4-4   Using FullArmor to migrate .adm files to .admx files

Practice: Working with Local GPOs

In this practice, you will first enable Group Policy debugging logs to set up a practice in Lesson 3, "Troubleshooting Restrictive Security Settings." Then you will use MLGPOs to apply settings to a computer.

▶ **Practice 1: Enable Group Policy Debugging Logs**

In this practice, you enable Group Policy Object Editor debugging logs. This topic isn't covered until Lesson 3, "Troubleshooting Restrictive Security Settings," but enabling the debugging logs now will give you some information to analyze when you reach that lesson.

1. Log on to the Windows Vista computer.

2. Click Start and type **regedit**. Right-click Regedit on the Start menu, and then click Run As Administrator. Alternatively, you can type **regedit**, and then press Ctrl+Shift+Enter, which is a keyboard shortcut for launching a program with administrative credentials. Respond to the UAC prompt that appears.

3. Registry Editor opens. Browse to the HKLM\Software\Microsoft\Windows NT\Current-Version\Winlogon\ key.

4. Click the Edit menu, click New, and then click DWORD (32-bit) Value. Name the value GPEditDebugLevel. Then double-click the new value and set it to 10002 hex.

▶ **Practice 2: Applying Multiple Local Group Policy Objects**

In this practice, you configure MLGPOs and experiment with their behavior to determine the relative priority of each.

1. Log on to your computer as an administrator and create an account named Standard that is a member of the Users group.

   Create an MMC console with the Local Group Policy object, the Non-Administrators Group Policy object, and the Standard user Group Policy object by following these steps:

   a. Click Start, type **mmc.exe**, and then press Enter. Respond to the UAC prompt that appears.

   b. In the Console1 window, click File, and then click Add/Remove Snap-in.

   c. In the Add Or Remove Snap-ins dialog box, in the Available Snap-ins list, click Group Policy Object Editor, and then click Add.

   d. In the Select Group Policy Object dialog box, click Finish. This adds the Local Computer Policy object to the MMC console.

   e. In the Add Or Remove Snap-ins dialog box, with Group Policy Object Editor still selected, click Add again. Then click Browse.

   f. The Browse For A Group Policy Object dialog box appears. Click the Users tab. Then click Non-Administrators and click OK.

   g. Click Finish.

   h. In the Add Or Remove Snap-ins dialog box, click Add again. Then click Browse.

   i. The Browse For A Group Policy Object dialog box appears. Click the Users tab. Click Standard, and then click OK.

   j. Click Finish.

k. The Add Or Remove Snap-ins dialog box now shows three Local Group Policy objects. Click OK to create the MMC console.

Save the console to your desktop by clicking the File menu and clicking Save. In the Save As dialog box, change the filename to **Local Group Policy Objects** and click Save.

2. Expand the Local Computer Policy object. Then expand User Configuration, Administrative Templates, Desktop, and select the Desktop node. In the right pane, double-click Desktop Wallpaper.

3. In the Desktop Wallpaper Properties dialog box, select Enabled. In the Wallpaper Name box, type **%windir%\web\wallpaper\img4.jpg** (a black-and-white photo). Click the Wallpaper Style list, and then click Stretch. Click OK.

4. In the Local Group Policy Objects console, select the Local Computer\Non-Administrators Policy\User Configuration\Administrative Templates\Desktop\Desktop node. Then enable the Desktop Wallpaper setting. For the Wallpaper Name, type **%windir% \web\wallpaper\img26.jpg** (a picture showing colored circles). Set the Wallpaper Style list to Stretch. Click OK.

5. In the Local Group Policy Objects console, select the Local Computer\Standard Policy \User vb Configuration\Administrative Templates\Desktop\Desktop node. Then, enable the Desktop Wallpaper setting. For the Wallpaper Name, type **%windir%\web \wallpaper\img10.jpg** (a photo of a flower). Set the Wallpaper Style list to Stretch. Click OK.

6. Now that you have configured three wallpapers for each of the policies, log off the computer and log back on as the Standard user. Hold down the Windows key and press D to display the desktop.

Although there are three settings, each with a different wallpaper, the desktop displays an orange flower because that is what you selected in the user Group Policy object. When multiple policies have the same setting defined, Windows Vista always uses the setting from the most specific Group Policy object.

Lesson Summary

- Group Policy is a technology used to simplify managing multiple computers, whether they are part of an Active Directory domain or a workgroup.

- Windows 2000, Windows XP, Windows Server 2003, and Windows Vista computers can be managed by using Group Policy (with the exception of home versions of these operating systems).

- In Active Directory environments, GPOs are applied hierarchically to enable administrators to meet the specific needs of different groups within the organization.

- Windows Vista supports MLGPOs to provide flexible configuration for computers that are not members of a domain.

- Windows Vista supports an improved version of administrative templates, which are used to provide custom Group Policy settings. In Windows Vista, administrative templates use two files: the .admx file (which defines the registry settings and values that each Group Policy setting relates to) and the .adml file (which contains language-specific descriptions).

Lesson Review

You can use the following questions to test your knowledge of the information in Lesson 1, "Group Policy Overview." The questions are also available on the companion CD if you prefer to review them in electronic form.

NOTE   Answers

Answers to these questions and explanations of why each answer choice is right or wrong are located in the "Answers" section at the end of the book.

---

1. The user Marsha is a member of the Users group. Which of the following Group Policy objects (GPOs) would apply to Marsha? (Choose all that apply.)

    A. Local Computer GPO

    B. Administrators GPO

    C. Non-Administrators GPO

    D. Marsha user GPO

2. The user Sam is a member of the Administrators group. Several Local GPOs contain definitions for the same setting. Which GPO takes precedence?

    A. Local Computer GPO

    B. Administrators GPO

    C. Non-Administrators GPO

    D. Sam user GPO

3. You are the administrator for a small business network. You wanted to improve the security of the Windows Vista client computers, so you configured several of the Local GPOs on each computer for more restrictive settings. Later, your manager allocated the budget for you to purchase a domain controller. You added the computers to the Windows Server 2003 Active Directory domain and configured the Default Domain GPO, as well as a separate Domain GPO that applies to all mobile computers in your organization (named Mobile Computers). Some of the settings in your Domain GPOs conflict with settings in your Local GPOs. When there is a conflict for a user setting on a mobile computer, which of these GPOs will take effect?

    A. Default Domain Policy

    B. Mobile Computer Domain GPO

    C. Local Computer GPO

    D. Non-Administrators Local GPO

4. You are troubleshooting a problem with the Computer Configuration\Windows Settings\Security Settings\Local Policies\Audit Policies\Audit System Events setting. It is supposed to be enabled, but it is disabled on one of your computers. Which of these GPOs might be causing the problem? (Choose all that apply.)

    A. The user Local GPO

    B. The Local Computer GPO

    C. The Non-Administrators Local GPO

    D. The Default Domain GPO

Lesson 2: Windows Vista Group Policy Settings

One of Microsoft's goals for Windows Vista was to make almost every aspect of the operating system centrally manageable and configurable. As part of that goal, Microsoft added about 700 new Group Policy settings to the approximately 1800 settings that previously existed.

You don't need to memorize all 700 new settings, but you should be familiar with the types of settings that might affect the Windows Vista computers you manage. Group Policy settings that are covered on the exam are covered in more detail in the lessons that cover those specific topics.

After this lesson, you will be able to:

■ Describe the types of new Group Policy settings supported by Windows Vista.

■ Describe differences in how Windows Vista processes Group Policy and how you can configure Group Policy processing.

Estimated lesson time: 20 minutes

New Windows Vista Group Policy Settings

Windows Vista includes about 700 new Group Policy settings. The sections that follow describe the most important new categories and settings, divided into security, management, and desktop topics. You should spend several hours browsing these categories and experimenting with different settings in a lab environment.

MORE INFO   Complete list of Group Policy settings

For a complete list of all Group Policy settings in Windows Vista, see the Group Policy Settings Reference spreadsheet available from the Microsoft Download Center at *http://www.microsoft.com /downloads/details.aspx?FamilyID=41dc179b-3328-4350-ade1-c0d9289f09ef*.

Security Settings

Table 4-1 shows Group Policy categories related to security that have been extended in Windows Vista. In the following table, "CC" means Computer Configuration, "UC" means User Configuration, and "CC and UC" means the setting is available in both locations.

Table 4-1   New and Improved Group Policy Categories

Category	Location	Description
Attachment Manager	UC\Administrative Templates \Windows Components \Attachment Manager	Configures how e-mail clients handle risky attachments

Table 4-1   **New and Improved Group Policy Categories**

Category	Location	Description
BitLocker Drive Encryption	CC\Administrative Templates \Windows Components \BitLocker Drive Encryption	Configures BitLocker Drive Encryption
Device Installation	CC\Administrative Templates \System\Device Installation	Controls which devices (based on device class or device ID) can be installed
Network Sharing	UC\Administrative Templates \Windows Components \Network Sharing	Prevents users from sharing from within their profile paths
Removable Storage	CC and UC\Software\Policies \Microsoft\Windows \RemovableStorageDevices	Controls whether users can read or write removable storage devices, such as universal serial bus (USB) hard disks or flash drives
User Account Protection	CC\Windows Settings\Security Settings\Local Policies\Security Options	Configures User Account Control (UAC) behavior, which prompts users when programs require elevated privileges
Windows Defender	CC\Administrative Templates \Windows Components \Windows Defender	Configures Windows Defender, the antimalware component of Windows Vista
Windows Firewall with Advance Security	CC\Windows Settings\Security Settings\Windows Firewall with Advance Security	Configures Windows Firewall and Internet Protocol Security (IPSec) settings for filtering, authenticating, and encrypting network traffic
Windows Logon Options	CC and UC\Administrative Templates\Windows Components\Windows Logon Options	Displays message when logging on with cached credentials and configures behavior when logon hours expire

As shown in Figure 4-5, Windows Vista includes a new tool for configuring Windows Firewall and IPSec settings. Settings defined in this tool apply only to Windows Vista computers; Windows XP and earlier versions of Windows will not be affected. For more information, see Chapter 10, "Configuring and Troubleshooting Network Protocol Security."

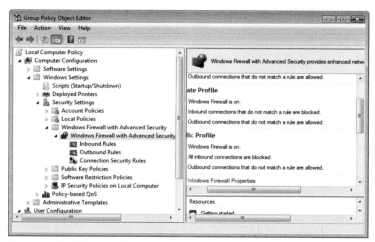

Figure 4-5 Using a single interface in the Group Policy Object Editor to configure both firewall and IPSec settings

The most useful Windows Vista–only security settings include:

- **CC\Administrative Templates\Windows Components\Credential User Interface\Require trusted path for credential elevation**   Enabling this setting causes Windows Vista to use the Secure Desktop when prompting users for administrative credentials using UAC. This helps to prevent Trojan horses or other malicious software from tricking the user into entering credentials. However, the Secure Desktop freezes and darkens the screen, which can be annoying for some users. The Secure Desktop should never cause application problems.

- **CC\Administrative Templates\System\Driver Installation\Allow non-administrators to install drivers for these device setup classes**   By default, any user can install devices that have drivers already staged in the Driver Store. However, only administrators can install drivers for other devices. If a user needs to install a device without providing administrative credentials, enable this setting and specify the device classes, such as printers or mice that mobile users often need.

MORE INFO   Device setup classes and globally unique identifiers

For a list of device setup classes and the globally unique identifiers (GUIDs) used to identify them in Group Policy settings, see "System-Supplied Device Setup Classes" in the Windows Driver Kit (WDK) at *http://msdn2.microsoft.com/en-US/library/ms791134.aspx*. For more information about drivers, see Chapter 3, "Deploying Windows Vista."

- **UC\Administrative Templates\System\Driver Installation\Code signing for device drivers**   Signed drivers have been tested by Microsoft, which helps to ensure that they are stable and secure. IT departments can also sign drivers that have been internally tested. Some organizations require that all drivers be signed before staging the driver to the Driver Store. If you are experiencing a problem installing a driver, this setting might be the cause of the problem. For more information about drivers, see Chapter 3, "Deploying Windows Vista."

Management Settings

Table 4-2 shows the new and improved Group Policy categories relating to managing Windows Vista clients. In this table, "CC" represents the Computer Configuration node, and "UC" represents the User Configuration node.

Table 4-2   New and Improved Group Policy Categories

Category	Location	Description
Disk Diagnostic	CC\Administrative Templates \System\Troubleshooting and Diagnostics\Disk Diagnostic	Configures how Windows Vista communicates to the user when disk problems occur.
Disk NV Cache	CC\Administrative Templates \System\Disk NV Cache	Configures the behavior of hybrid hard disks, which are a new type of storage that provides disk caching using flash memory.
Event Log Service	CC\Administrative Templates \Windows Components\Event Log Service	Configures the path, size, and behavior for built-in event logs.
Online Assistance	CC and UC\Administrative Templates\Online Assistance	Configures whether users can access active or untrusted help content.
Remote Assistance	CC\Administrative Templates \System\Remote Assistance	Configures Remote Assistance.
Search	CC\Administrative Templates \Windows Components\Search	Prevents which files are indexed by Search.
Terminal Services	CC and UC\Administrative Templates\Windows Components\Terminal Services	Configures the Remote Desktop client.
Troubleshooting and Diagnostics	CC\Administrative Templates \System\Troubleshooting and Diagnostics	Configures built-in diagnostics (which are enabled by default).
Windows Customer Experience Improvement Program	CC\Administrative Templates \Windows Components \Windows Customer Experience Improvement Program	Configures Customer Experience Improvement Program behavior.

Table 4-2   New and Improved Group Policy Categories

Category	Location	Description
Windows Error Reporting	CC and UC\Administrative Templates\Windows Components\Windows Error Reporting	Enables you to redirect Windows Error Reporting to an internal server.
Windows Update	CC\Administrative Templates \Windows Components \Windows Update	Among other settings for earlier versions of Windows, you can configure Windows Update Power Management to automatically wake the system to install scheduled updates or install Recommended Updates as well as Critical Updates.

The default values for these settings provide the best client manageability for most environments. However, you should make note of the following setting:

■ **CC\Administrative Templates\Windows Components\Windows Customer Experience Improvement Program\Allow Corporate redirection of Customer Experience Improvement uploads**   Some types of errors can generate Customer Experience Improvement reports, which are by default sent to Microsoft and used to identify the most serious bugs. If your organization uses a Microsoft Operations Manager (MOM) server, you can direct those reports to your internal server instead, which might be useful for internal troubleshooting. Use this setting to specify your MOM server.

Desktop Settings

Table 4-3 shows the new and improved Group Policy categories relating to managing Windows Vista clients. In this table, "CC" represents the Computer Configuration node, and "UC" represents the User Configuration node.

Table 4-3   New and Improved Group Policy Categories

Deployed Printers	CC and UC\Windows Settings \Deployed Printers	Configures network printer connections
Desktop	UC\Administrative Templates \Desktop	Configures desktop wallpaper
Desktop Windows Manager	UC\Administrative Templates \Windows Components\Desktop Windows Manager	Allows you to block desktop composition, Flip3D invocation, and window animations
Folder Redirection	UC and CC\Administrative Templates \System\Folder Redirection	Enables localization of redirected subfolders of Start menu and Documents

Table 4-3   New and Improved Group Policy Categories

Internet Explorer	CC and UC\Administrative Templates\Windows Components\Internet Explorer	Configures the Web browser built into Windows
Logon	CC\Administrative Templates\System\Logon	Configures the default domain, removes entry point for Fast User Switching, and turns off startup sound (among other settings available for earlier versions of Windows)
Offline Files	CC\Windows Settings\Network\Offline Files	Configures slow-link mode and disk space used for offline files (among other settings for earlier versions of Windows)
Performance Control Panel	CC and UC\Administrative Templates\System\Performance Control Panel	Disables access to the Performance Control Panel page
Power Management	CC\Administrative Templates\System\Power Management	Configures power management and other mobile settings
Programs	UC\Administrative Templates\Control Panel\Programs	Hides different aspects of the Programs Control Panel page
Regional and Language Options	CC and UC\Administrative Templates\Control Panel\Regional and Language Options	Restricts access to Regional and Language Options
Start Menu and Taskbar	UC\Administrative Templates\Start Menu and Taskbar	Locks down behavior of Start menu and taskbar
User Profiles	CC and UC\Administrative Templates\System\User Profiles	Configures behavior of roaming and locally cached profiles
Windows Explorer	UC\Administrative Templates\Windows Components\Windows Explorer	Configures behavior of Windows Explorer windows, such as Computer, Documents, and Pictures

Some of the most useful Windows Vista–only desktop settings include:

■ **CC or UC\Administrative Templates\Windows Components\Application Compatibility\Turn Off Program Compatibility Assistant**   The Program Compatibility Assistant (PCA) monitors applications for known compatibility problems. If the PCA detects a problem, it prompts the user with suggestions for recommended solutions. The PCA is a useful tool, especially for home and small business users. In enterprise environments where all applications are tested before deployment, it should be removed to prevent unnecessarily alarming the user. For more information about application compatibility, refer to Chapter 3, "Deploying Windows Vista."

- **CC or UC\Administrative Templates\Windows Components\AutoPlay Policies\Default behavior for AutoRun**   In previous versions of Windows, AutoPlay read the Autorun.inf file on any removable media that was connected to the computer and ran the referenced application. This is risky behavior, though, because a user who was tricked into connecting a USB flash drive, portable audio player, or other device that acted as removable storage might unknowingly run malicious software, such as a virus or Trojan horse. Instead of automatically running software, Windows Vista prompts the user to browse the files on the disk or to perform the AutoRun action. If this causes a problem for users, you can revert to the Windows XP behavior by enabling this setting and setting it to Automatically Execute AutoRun commands.

How to Configure Group Policy Processing

Windows XP clients processed Group Policy settings only during startup (for computer settings), logon (for user settings), and on a scheduled interval of every 90 minutes plus a random offset of up to 30 minutes. Windows Vista also processes Group Policy settings at these times. In addition, Windows Vista processes Group Policy when a computer returns from Sleep, when a mobile computer docks with a docking station, when a virtual private network (VPN) connection is established, and when a Windows Vista computer exits network quarantine.

You can use the following Group Policy settings to control Group Policy processing. Settings related to Group Policy processing are located in Computer Configuration\Administrative Templates\System\Group Policy. Those policies that are new in Windows Vista are:

- **Turn Off Local Group Policy Objects Processing**   Enable this policy setting to prevent Windows Vista from processing Local GPOs.
- **Startup Policy Processing Wait Time**   Enable this policy setting to configure how long Group Policy waits for network availability notifications during startup policy processing. The default wait time for Windows Vista computers is 30 seconds.
- **Wired Policy Processing**   Enables you to configure aspects of processing that apply when using a wired network connection, such as Fast Ethernet. Typically, these do not need to be modified because wired networks provide enough bandwidth that processing Group Policy should not have an undesirable effect. The similar Wireless Policy Processing setting, which is supported for Windows 2000 and later operating systems, is more useful because wireless networks tend to be bandwidth-limited.

Windows Vista continues to support other policies in the same location, which provide control over software installation, background refreshing, slow link detection, and many other aspects of Group Policy processing.

Practice: Using Domain GPOs

In this practice, you will configure and apply GPOs in an Active Directory domain environment.

▶ **Practice 1: Configuring Group Policy Settings in a Domain Environment**

In this practice, you configure Domain Group Policy settings and then experiment with them to determine their relative priority. To complete this practice, you must have completed Practice 1 of Lesson 1, "Group Policy Overview."

1. Configure a Windows Server 2003 computer as an Active Directory domain controller for the domain nwtraders.msft. Then, within the domain, use the Active Directory Users And Computers console to create an IT OU. Within the IT OU, create three OUs named Desktops, Laptops, and Servers. Your domain should now resemble that shown in Figure 4-6.

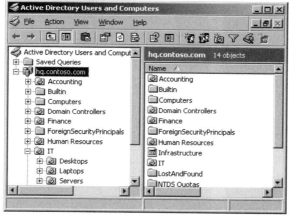

Figure 4-6   The only OUs required in the sample domain—the IT OU and the OUs it contains

2. Create a domain user named Standard and add that user to the Domain Users group. Assign a password to the user.

3. Join the computer you used in Practice 1 to a Windows Server 2003 Active Directory domain. The domain should be for testing only because you will be modifying important Group Policy settings.

4. Log on to the Windows Vista client computer using an account that is a member of the Domain Admins group. Click Start, type **gpmc.msc**, and then press Enter to open the Group Policy Management Console. Respond to the UAC prompt that appears.

5. Under the nwtraders.msft domain, right-click Default Domain Policy, and then click Edit.

6. The Group Policy Object Editor opens to display the Default Domain Policy, which affects all users and computers in the domain. Expand User Configuration, Administrative Templates, Desktop, and select the Desktop node. In the right pane, double-click Desktop Wallpaper. In the Desktop Wallpaper Properties dialog box, select Enabled. In

the Wallpaper Name box, type **%windir%\web\wallpaper\img15.jpg** (a picture of a fish). Click the Wallpaper Style list, and then click Stretch. Click OK.

7. Expand Computer Configuration, Administrative Templates, and Windows Components. Then select Windows Sidebar. In the right pane, double-click Turn Off Windows Sidebar. Enable the policy, and then click OK.

8. Close the Group Policy Object Editor.

9. In the Group Policy Management Console, right-click the IT\Laptops OU, and then click Create A GPO In This Domain, And Link It Here. Name the GPO IT-Laptops, and then click OK.

10. Right-click the new GPO, and then click Edit.

11. The Group Policy Object Editor opens to display the IT-Laptops policy, which affects only users and computers in the IT\Laptops OU. Expand User Configuration, Administrative Templates, Desktop, and select the Desktop node. In the right pane, double-click Desktop Wallpaper. In the Desktop Wallpaper Properties dialog box, select Enabled. In the Wallpaper Name box, type **%windir%\web\wallpaper\img13.jpg** (a picture of a bridge). Click the Wallpaper Style list, and then click Stretch. Click OK.

12. Expand Computer Configuration, Administrative Templates, and Windows Components. Select Windows Sidebar. In the right pane, double-click Turn Off Windows Sidebar. Disable the policy, and then click OK.

13. Under Computer Configuration, enable the Administrative Templates\Windows Components\Credential User Interface\Require Trusted Path For Credential Entry Policy.

▶ **Practice 2: Applying Group Policy Settings in a Domain Environment**

In this practice, you apply Group Policy settings to a client computer and analyze the behavior of multiple GPOs. To complete this practice, you must have already completed Practice 1.

1. On the Windows Vista client computer, open a command prompt. Run the command Gpupdate to immediately refresh Group Policy from your domain controller. This would happen automatically if you chose to wait long enough.

2. Log off the computer, and then log on again as the Standard domain user.

3. Note that the desktop background is a picture of a fish. This fish picture was applied to the Default Domain Policy, and it overrides all local policies. Although it was overridden in the IT-Laptops policy, the Standard domain user you logged on to the computer with is not part of the IT OU. Also note that the Sidebar is disabled because of the setting made to the Default Domain Policy.

4. From the domain controller, move the Windows Vista client computer account from the Computers node in Active Directory Users And Computers to the IT\Laptops OU. Click Yes when prompted.

5. From the Windows Vista client computer, open a command prompt and run **gpupdate /force**. Then log off and log back on for the changes to take effect (even though you refreshed Group Policy, settings such as enabling the Windows Sidebar can take effect only when the user logs on).

6. Note that the Windows Sidebar appears because the computer is now a member of the IT\Laptops OU. The desktop background did not change, however, because the user is not a member of the IT\OU.

Lesson Summary

■ Windows Vista supports over 700 new Group Policy settings, giving you better control over client security, manageability, and the user's desktop environment.

■ Windows Vista computers now process Group Policy settings during any power state change, when users connect to a VPN, when a computer is released from quarantine, and when a mobile computer is docked.

Lesson Review

You can use the following questions to test your knowledge of the information in Lesson 2, "Windows Vista Group Policy Settings." The questions are also available on the companion CD if you prefer to review them in electronic form.

NOTE Answers

Answers to these questions and explanations of why each answer choice is right or wrong are located in the "Answers" section at the end of the book.

1. In which of the following circumstances does Windows Vista process Group Policy? (Choose all that apply.)
    A. When a user logs on
    B. When a user connects using a virtual private network (VPN)
    C. When Group Policy is updated at a domain controller
    D. When a computer resumes from Sleep

2. Which of the following are new Group Policy capabilities in Windows Vista? (Choose all that apply.)
    A. Allow users to install specific classes of devices
    B. Block users from offering Remote Assistance
    C. Run specific programs when the user logs on
    D. Require the Secure Desktop when elevating privileges

3. Which of the Group Policy settings might you need to adjust from its default setting to provide compatibility with earlier versions of Windows?

   A. Computer Configuration\Administrative Templates\Windows Components \Credential User Interface\Require trusted path for credential elevation

   B. Computer or User Configuration\Administrative Templates\Windows Components \AutoPlay Policies\Default behavior for AutoRun

   C. Computer Configuration\Administrative Templates\Windows Components \Windows Customer Experience Improvement Program\Allow Corporate redirection of Customer Experience Improvement uploads

   D. Computer or User Configuration\Administrative Templates\Windows Components \Application Compatibility\Turn Off Program Compatibility Assistant

Lesson 3: Troubleshooting Group Policy Settings

Windows Vista computers will occasionally have problems processing Group Policy. This is especially true for mobile computers, which might be connected intermittently by VPNs, wireless networks, or dial-up connections.

Fortunately, Windows Vista provides several tools to help you identify the source of Group Policy problems. By default, Windows Vista records very detailed information in the event logs. Additionally, you can enable debugging logs if you have problems running the Group Policy Object Editor. If you see unexpected settings on a computer, the Resultant Set Of Policy, GPResult, and Security Configuration And Analysis tools can help you pinpoint the source of the setting.

This lesson describes the tools for troubleshooting Group Policy, as well as techniques for solving problems related to Group Policy–enforced software restrictions.

After this lesson, you will be able to:
- Manually refresh Group Policy settings.
- Use the Resultant Set Of Policy tool to determine the GPOs that define security settings applied to a computer.
- Describe the purpose of security templates and view the settings contained within a security template.
- Use the Security Configuration And Analysis tool to determine effective settings that do not match those contained within a security template.
- Use the GPResult tool at a command line to identify the GPOs that impact a computer.
- Examine Group Policy logs to isolate problems.
- Troubleshoot software restriction policies that prevent legitimate programs from running.
- Troubleshoot problems using logon scripts in Windows Vista.

Estimated lesson time: 45 minutes

How to Manually Refresh Group Policy

If you notice that Group Policy settings haven't been applied to a computer, your first step should be to refresh Group Policy. You can do this from a command line by running the GpUpdate command, as the following example shows:

```
GpUpdate Updating Policy...
User Policy update has completed successfully.
Computer Policy update has completed successfully.
```

Calling GpUpdate without any parameters refreshes policy and reapplies only changed settings. To force all settings to be overwritten, call **GpUpdate /Force**. Using the /force parameter often resolves problems related to Group Policy not taking effect.

If you know that a Group Policy setting requires the computer to restart (such as a software installation), you can refresh policy and restart the computer with a single command by calling **GpUpdate /Boot**. Modifying the following settings requires Windows Vista to be restarted:

- Turn off Tablet PC touch input
- Turn off Windows Defender
- Turn off legacy remote shutdown interface

The following Group Policy settings are applied only after the user logs off and logs back on (this needs to be done manually; you cannot do it automatically with GpUpdate):

- Do not allow window animations
- Do not allow desktop composition
- Do not allow Flip3D invocation
- Specify a default color
- Do not allow color changes
- Verbose vs. normal status messages
- Set action to take when logon hours expire
- Report when logon server was not available during user logon
- Custom user interface

How to Use the Resultant Set of Policy Tool

In organizations with complex Active Directory domains, it's common to find unexpected settings on a client computer. Most likely, the setting was defined by one of many domain GPOs. With Windows Vista, it might also be defined by different local GPOs. Before you can fix the problem, you need to identify the GPO that is the source of the setting.

You can use the Resultant Set Of Policy (RSoP) snap-in to identify the source of a Group Policy setting when more than one GPO affects a computer. If a policy setting is not what you expected, RSoP identifies the Group Policy object responsible for defining the policy.

To run RSoP, follow these steps:

1. Click Start and type **mmc**. Provide administrative credentials. You can run the RSoP with standard user privileges by running Rsop.msc directly, but you will be able to inspect only the User Configuration settings.

2. A blank MMC console appears. Click the File menu, and then click Add/Remove Snap-In.

3. In the Add Or Remove Snap-Ins dialog box, double-click Resultant Set Of Policy. Click OK.

4. Right-click Resultant Set Of Policy and click Generate RSoP Data.

5. The Resultant Set Of Policy Wizard appears. Click Next.

6. On the Mode Selection page, select Logging Mode, and then click Next.

Exam Tip

Use Planning Mode to anticipate the effect of Group Policy changes before you put them in place. Logging mode is more useful for troubleshooting, which is the focus of this exam objective.

---

7. To analyze the local computer, select This Computer. Otherwise, select Another Computer and specify the remote computer to analyze. Click Next.

8. To analyze the current user, select Current User. Otherwise, select Select A Specific User, and specify the user to analyze. Click Next.

9. On the Summary Of Selections page, click Next, and then click Finish.

You can view these same settings by simply running Rsop.msc with administrative privileges, but adding the RSoP snap-in to a blank MMC console is the only way to use the wizard to configure the snap-in.

With the RSoP snap-in open, you can browse settings on the current computer and determine their exact source. If a setting is not listed, it's because the setting isn't defined by any GPO. Figure 4-7 shows a setting that is defined by the Local Group Policy. As you can see, the user interface closely resembles the Group Policy Object Editor, which makes it very intuitive.

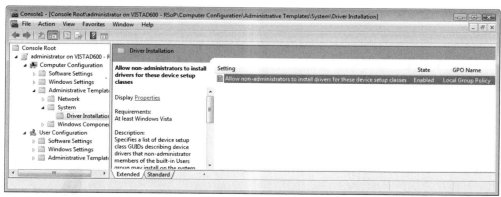

Figure 4-7 Resultant Set Of Policy identifies the source of any Group Policy setting

Note that many security settings are defined under both Computer Configuration and User Configuration. Be sure to check both sets of settings to identify the source of your problem.

What Are Security Templates?

Security templates are files that represent important aspects of a computer's security configuration. Although administrators can apply security templates directly to a computer without using Group Policy, Group Policy provides an extremely flexible and robust distribution mechanism for security templates. Using security templates and GPOs together, administrators can create complex security configurations and mix and match those configurations for each of the various roles computers serve in their organizations. When deployed across a network, security templates allow you to implement consistent, scalable, and reproducible security settings throughout your organization.

Security templates can be used only to configure a small subset of overall Group Policy settings. Specifically, security templates represent those settings contained in Computer Configuration\Windows Settings\Security Settings. Therefore, you cannot rely entirely on security templates to manage the configuration of computers in your organization.

Unlike earlier versions of Windows, Windows Vista does not provide standard security templates. However, you can make your own security templates or use the security templates included with the Windows Vista Security Guide. To download the Windows Vista Security Guide, visit *http://www.microsoft.com/downloads/details.aspx?FamilyId=A3D1BBED-7F35-4E72 -BFB5-B84A526C1565b.*

The Windows Vista Security Guide includes the following templates (each has an .inf extension):

- **Vista Default Security**   A security template that you can use to restore default security settings or compare your current settings to the default.
- **VSG EC Desktop, VSG EC Laptop, and VSG EC Domain**   Templates that the Windows Vista Security Guide team recommends for use in enterprise environments. EC stands for Enterprise Configuration.
- **VSG SSLF Desktop, VSG SSLF Laptop, and VSG SSLF Domain**   Templates that the Windows Vista Security Guide team recommends for organizations that are willing to sacrifice some functionality for improved security. SSLF stands for Specialized Security Limited Functionality.

After you install the Windows Vista Security Guide, the security templates will be located within your user account's Documents\Windows Vista Security Guide\GPOAccelerator Tool\Security Templates\ folder. Follow these steps to open the security templates in the Security Templates snap-in:

1.   Click Start and type **mmc**.

2. A blank MMC console appears. Click the File menu, and then click Add/Remove Snap-In.

3. In the Add Or Remove Snap-Ins dialog box, double-click Security Templates. Click OK.

4. Right-click Security Templates, and then click New Template Search Path.

5. In the Browse For Folder dialog box, expand your user folder, Documents, Windows Vista Security Guide, GPOAccelerator Tool, and then select Security Templates. Click OK.

6. Click the new folder in the Security Templates snap-in.

    Now you can browse or modify the security settings in each of the templates. For best results, copy standard templates before modifying them by right-clicking the template and then clicking Save As.

How to Use the Security Configuration And Analysis Tool

The Security Configuration And Analysis snap-in gives you an immediate, detailed list of security settings on a computer that do not meet your security requirements. Security template settings are presented alongside current system settings, and icons or remarks are used to highlight any areas where the current settings do not match the proposed level of security. Security Configuration And Analysis uses a database to perform analysis and configuration functions. Using a database gives you the ability to compare the current security settings against custom databases that are created by importing one or more security templates.

To analyze a computer's security settings by comparing them to a security template, complete the following steps:

1. Create a new Microsoft Management Console (MMC) console and add the Security Configuration And Analysis snap-in.

2. Right-click Security Configuration And Analysis, and then click Open Database.

3. In the Open Database dialog box, type a name for the new database, and then click Open.

4. In the Import Template dialog box, select a security template to import. Click Open.

5. If you want to import more than one security template, right-click Security Configuration And Analysis, and then click Import Template. Select the template to import, and then click Open. Repeat this process for each security template you want to import.

6. Right-click Security Configuration And Analysis, and then click Analyze Computer Now.

7. In the Perform Analysis dialog box, click OK.

After the analysis is complete, examine the results by expanding the nodes contained within the Security Configuration And Analysis node. As shown in Figure 4-8, the Database Setting column shows what's recommended in the template, and the Computer Setting column shows your setting.

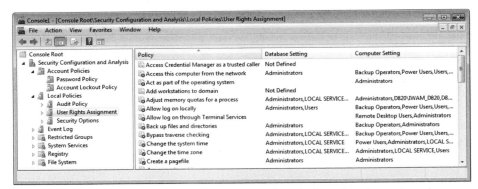

Figure 4-8   Using the Security Configuration And Analysis tool to determine where computer settings differ from settings in a security template

You can also use the Security Configuration And Analysis tool to apply security settings, although it is generally more effective to apply security settings by using GPOs. To apply settings from one or more security templates to a computer, follow these steps:

1.   Create a new MMC console and add the Security Configuration And Analysis snap-in.

2.   Right-click Security Configuration And Analysis, and then click Open Database.

3.   In the Open Database dialog box, type a name for the new database, and then click Open.

4.   In the Import Template dialog box, select a security template to import. Click Open.

5.   If you want to import more than one security template, right-click Security Configuration And Analysis, and then click Import Template. Select the template to import, and then click Open. Repeat this process for each security template you want to import.

6.   Right-click Security Configuration And Analysis, and then click Configure Computer Now.

7.   In the Configure System dialog box, click OK.

The Configuring Computer Security window appears while the security template is being applied. The security settings take effect immediately.

NOTE   Importing and exporting security templates

To import a security template into a GPO, right-click Computer Configuration\Windows Settings\Security Settings, and then click Import Policy. Click Export Policy to create a security template based on the security settings in a GPO.

How to Use the GPResult Tool

GPResult is a command-line tool that displays detailed information about user and computer policies. Although many administrators prefer graphical tools, GPResult is the best way to quickly determine what Group Policy objects were applied, in which order they were applied, and what security group memberships might have influenced which Group Policy objects the computer or user has permissions to access. Unlike other tools, GPResult displays policies that were filtered and shows why they were filtered. This is a common cause of problems relating to GPOs not being applied.

The following is an excerpt from a sample output from the GPResult tool:

```
RSOP data for HQ\Standard on VISTA : Logging Mode
----------------------------------------------------
OS Configuration:              Member Workstation
OS Version:                    6.0.6000
Site Name:                     N/A
Roaming Profile:               N/A
Local Profile:                 C:\Users\standard.HQ
Connected over a slow link?:   No
COMPUTER SETTINGS
------------------
    CN=VISTALAPTOP,OU=Laptops,OU=IT,DC=hq,DC=contoso,DC=com
    Last time Group Policy was applied: 1/9/2007 at 7:32:12 PM
    Group Policy was applied from:      2003-ad.hq.contoso.com
    Group Policy slow link threshold:   500 kbps
    Domain Name:                        HQ
    Domain Type:                        Windows 2000

    Applied Group Policy Objects
    -----------------------------
        IT-Laptops
        Default Domain Policy
        Local Group Policy

    The computer is a part of the following security groups
    --------------------------------------------------------
        BUILTIN\Administrators
        Everyone
        BUILTIN\Users
        NT AUTHORITY\NETWORK
        NT AUTHORITY\Authenticated Users
        This Organization
        VISTALAPTOP$
        Domain Computers
        System Mandatory LevelUSER SETTINGS
--------------
    CN=Standard Standard,CN=Users,DC=hq,DC=contoso,DC=com
    Last time Group Policy was applied: 1/9/2007 at 5:56:37 PM
    Group Policy was applied from:      2003-ad.hq.contoso.com
    Group Policy slow link threshold:   500 kbps
```

```
Domain Name:                            HQ
Domain Type:                            Windows 2000

Applied Group Policy Objects
----------------------------
    Default Domain Policy
    Local Group Policy\Non-Administrators
    Local Group Policy

The user is a part of the following security groups
---------------------------------------------------
    Domain Users
    Everyone
    BUILTIN\Users
    NT AUTHORITY\INTERACTIVE
    NT AUTHORITY\Authenticated Users
    This Organization
    LOCAL
    Medium Mandatory Level
```

When run with the /Z parameter, GPResult provides additional information about the computer, including:

- The resultant set of policies for both the user and the computer.
- Administrative templates.
- User security privileges.

The /Z parameter for GPResult creates so much output that much of it would scroll off before you could read it. Therefore, it is more effective to redirect the output to a text file. To view the full output of GPResult in Notepad, execute the following commands at a command prompt:

```
Gpresult /Z > Gpresult.txt
Notepad Gpresult.txt
```

You can run GPResult from a standard command prompt without administrative privileges. However, it will output only the user configuration. To view the computer configuration, you must open the command prompt with administrative privileges on the local computer.

Examining Group Policy Logs

Administrators need to be able to study how specific computers process Group Policy to identify the cause of any problems. To give administrators the information they need, Windows Vista records Group Policy data in several places:

- **System Event Log** Windows Vista records basic Group Policy processing information in the System Event Log. This information includes when the computer processed Group Policy, whether there were any changes, and whether processing was successful.

- **Applications And Service Logs\Microsoft\Windows\Group Policy\Operational Event Log**
  Windows Vista stores advanced Group Policy processing information in this event log.
  This information includes when Group Policy started and stopped processing and the
  details of any errors that occurred.
- **Group Policy Debugging Logs**   These logs are disabled by default, but they can be
  enabled to cause Windows Vista to record detailed information about using the Group
  Policy Object Editor, such as which domain controllers are contacted and which admin-
  istrative templates are loaded.

The sections that follow describe these logs and how to use them in more detail.

How to Use Event Viewer to Examine Group Policy Logs

Windows Vista records important aspects of Group Policy processing in the System Event Log
and the Applications And Service Logs\Microsoft\Windows\Group Policy\Operational
Event Log. As with earlier versions of Windows, the System Event Log records basic Group
Policy information, including the following events:

- **Event ID 1500**   "The Group Policy settings for the computer were processed successfully.
  There were no changes detected since the last successful processing of Group Policy."
- **Event ID 1501**   "The Group Policy settings for the user were processed successfully.
  There were no changes detected since the last successful processing of Group Policy."
- **Event ID 1502**   "The Group Policy settings for the computer were processed success-
  fully. New settings from 3 Group Policy objects were detected and applied."
- **Event ID 1503**   "The Group Policy settings for the user were processed successfully. New
  settings from 4 Group Policy objects were detected and applied."
- **Event ID 1129**   "The processing of Group Policy failed because of lack of network connectivity to a domain controller. This may be a transient condition..."
- **Event ID 1053**   "The processing of Group Policy failed. Windows could not resolve the
  user name. This could be caused by one or more of the following..."
- **Event ID 1055**   "The processing of Group Policy failed. Windows could not resolve the
  computer name. This could be caused by one or more of the following..."

The Group Policy Operational Event Log (located in the Event Viewer at Applications And Service Logs\Microsoft\Windows\Group Policy\Operational) replaces the Userenv.log file that
Windows XP used to record Group Policy processing information. In the Group Policy Operational Event Log, you can identify types of events by using the Event ID. All events in the
Group Policy Event Log will fall into one of the following ranges:

- **4000–4299**   Events that indicate Group Policy processing is beginning. For example,
  Event ID 4000 might have a description of "Starting computer boot policy processing for
  DOMAIN\computer," while Event ID 4001 might have a description of "Starting user

logon policy processing for computer\user." The specific Event ID indicates the type of Group Policy being processed and how the processing was initiated:

- ❏ 4000: Computer startup
- ❏ 4001: User logon
- ❏ 4002: Computer network change
- ❏ 4003: User network change
- ❏ 4004: Computer manual refresh
- ❏ 4005: User manual refresh
- ❏ 4006: Computer periodic refresh
- ❏ 4007: User periodic refresh

- **8000–8299**   Events that indicate that Group Policy processing has completed successfully. These events will always have an Event ID 4000 higher than the corresponding scenario start event. For example, Event ID 8000 might have a description of "Completed computer boot policy processing for DOMAIN\computer," while Event ID 8001 might have a description of "Completed user logon policy processing for computer\user." Notice that in the previous example Event ID 4000 corresponds to this example Event ID 8000, while Event ID 4001 corresponded to Event ID 8001. You can use this correlation to quickly determine the outcome of a specific processing session.

- **5000–5299**   Events that indicate Group Policy processing has completed successfully. These events will always have an Event ID 1000 higher than the corresponding scenario start event.

- **6000–6299**   Events that indicate a warning during Group Policy processing. These events will always have an Event ID 2000 higher than the corresponding scenario start event.

- **7000–7299**   Events that indicate Group Policy processing has completed with an error. These events will always have an Event ID 3000 higher than the corresponding scenario start event. For example, Event ID 7000 might have a description of "Computer boot policy processing failed for DOMAIN\computer in 121 seconds" and relate directly to the policy that started with Event ID 4000.

- **5300–5999**   Informational Group Policy events. For example:
  - ❏ Event ID 5315: How long it will be until the computer next processes Group Policy
  - ❏ Event ID 5326: How long it took to find a domain controller
  - ❏ Event ID 5327: The estimated bandwidth of a network connection

- **6300–6999**   Warning events. These Event IDs correlate to the informational Group Policy events in the 5300-5999 range, plus 1000. For example, Event ID 6326 indicates a warning while finding a domain controller.

- **7300–7999**   Error events. These Event IDs correlate to the informational Group Policy events in the 5300-5999 range, plus 2000. For example, Event ID 7326 indicates an error while finding a domain controller.

For each of these Events, Event Viewer provides two views: General and Details. When viewing an event, click the Details tab to view more detailed information, including the exact processing time, the domain controller being accessed, and the total number of Group Policy objects. As shown in Figure 4-9, the Details tab provides both a Friendly view and an XML view. The Friendly view is almost always more useful.

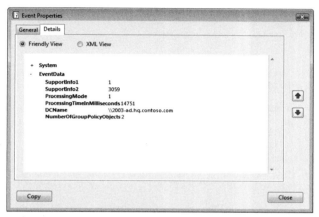

Figure 4-9   The Friendly view of the Details tab

For detailed information, read "Troubleshooting Group Policy Using Event Logs" at *http:// technet2.microsoft.com/WindowsVista/en/library/7e940882-33b7-43db-b097-f3752c84f67 f1033.mspx.*

How to Use the GPLogView Tool

If you would rather use a text file to analyze Group Policy events from the System and Group Policy event logs, you can use the GPLogView tool. GPLogView is not included with Windows Vista, but you can download it from *http://www.microsoft.com/downloads/details.aspx?FamilyId =BCFB1955-CA1D-4F00-9CFF-6F541BAD4563.*

The command-line options for this tool are:

- **-o** *output_file_name*   Output file name required for text, XML, or Hypertext Markup Language (HTML); not valid if -m is specified.
- **-n**   Do not output the activity id.
- **-p**   Display the process id and thread id associated with each event.
- **-a** *activity_id_guid*   Shows only events matching the given activity id.
- **-m**   Displays Group Policy events in real time. This mode is useful for monitoring Group Policy activity when attempting to re-create a problem.
- **-x**   Outputs the event in XML. The only options that can be combined with -x are -m and -a (but not both together).

- **-h**   Outputs the events in HTML format. The -m or -x options are not allowed, and -a and -n are allowed but not both together. You must specify -o option to name the output file.
- **-q** *Query_file_name*   Uses the query specified by query file.
- **-l** *Publisher_name*   If -q is specified, the publisher name must be specified.

After installation, GPLogView is located in the C:\Program Files\GroupPolicy LogView\ folder. To dump events to a text file, run the following command:

```
C:\Program Files\GroupPolicy Logview>gplogview -o gpevents.txt
Processing events...
Processed 10245 records.
```

This produces a large text file, which will resemble this shortened example:

```
2006-11-29 14:25:59.790 The Group Policy Client service is currently configured as a shared
service.
2006-11-29 14:25:59.790 Initializing and reading current service configuration for the Group
Policy Client service.
2006-11-29 14:25:59.790 Initializing service instance state to detect previous instances of
the service.
2006-11-29 14:25:59.790 A previous instance of the Group Policy Client Service has been
detected.
```

To create the file using XML (which would be useful if you planned to parse it with a script) along with an .xsl stylesheet, run the following command:

```
Gplogview -o gpevents.xml -x
```

To create the file using HTML (which would be useful for browsing the file manually, as shown in Figure 4-10), run the following command:

```
Gplogview -o gpevents.htm -h
```

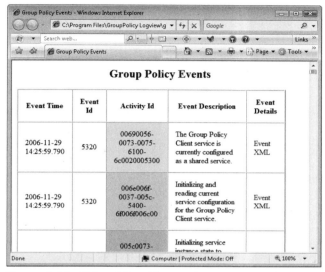

Figure 4-10   Using GPLogView to dump Group Policy events to an HTML file

How to View Group Policy Editor Debugging Logs

The logging in Event Viewer is sufficient for troubleshooting most Group Policy problems, and it is enabled by default. However, if you need more detailed information to troubleshoot a problem using the Group Policy Object Editor (such as loading custom administrative templates), you can enable debug logging by creating the following REG_DWORD registry value and setting it to 0x10002 (65538):

HKLM\Software\Microsoft\Windows NT\CurrentVersion\Winlogon\GPEditDebugLevel

After adding this value, Windows Vista creates a GpEdit.log file in the %windir%\debug\usermode\ folder the next time you edit Group Policy settings.

The GpEdit.log file includes very detailed information about the inner workings of the Group Policy Object Editor. For example, the following excerpt shows that the Group Policy Object Editor successfully loaded the ActiveXInstallService .admx and .adml files:

```
GPEDIT(b04.aac) 14:36:32:979 PDX parser: Parsing file
'C:\Windows\PolicyDefinitions\ActiveXInstallService.admx'.
GPEDIT(b04.aac) 14:36:32:983 PDX parser: Obtained appropriate PDX resource
file 'C:\Windows\PolicyDefinitions\en-US\ActiveXInstallService.adml' for
language 'en-US'.
GPEDIT(b04.aac) 14:36:32:983 PDX parser: Parsing resource file
'C:\Windows\PolicyDefinitions\en-US\ActiveXInstallService.adml'.
GPEDIT(b04.aac) 14:36:32:984 PDX parser: Parsing resource file
completed successfully.
GPEDIT(b04.aac) 14:36:32:984 PDX parser: Successfully parsed file.
```

The following excerpt shows that the computer running the Group Policy Object Editor did not have any Windows XP .adm files in the standard locations:

```
GPEDIT(b04.aac) 14:36:34:038 CParseManager::BuildFileList: No '**.adm'
files found in 'C:\Windows\inf'.
GPEDIT(b04.aac) 14:36:34:039 CParseManager::BuildFileList: Path not found,
 'C:\Windows\System32\GroupPolicy\Adm'.
```

The following excerpt shows that the Group Policy Object Editor skipped several .adm files stored on the domain controller because they are built into Windows Vista:

```
GPEDIT(e10.8a8) 15:06:24:753 File excluded from parsing:
'\\hq.contoso.com\sysvol\hq.contoso.com\Policies
\{31B2F340-016D-11D2-945F-00C04FB984F9}\Adm\conf.adm'.
GPEDIT(e10.8a8) 15:06:24:753 File excluded from parsing:
 '\\hq.contoso.com\sysvol\hq.contoso.com\Policies
\{31B2F340-016D-11D2-945F-00C04FB984F9}\Adm\inetres.adm'.
GPEDIT(e10.8a8) 15:06:24:753 File excluded from parsing:
 '\\hq.contoso.com\sysvol\hq.contoso.com\Policies
\{31B2F340-016D-11D2-945F-00C04FB984F9}\Adm\system.adm'.
GPEDIT(e10.8a8) 15:06:24:753 File excluded from parsing:
'\\hq.contoso.com\sysvol\hq.contoso.com\Policies
\{31B2F340-016D-11D2-945F-00C04FB984F9}\Adm\wmplayer.adm'.
GPEDIT(e10.8a8) 15:06:24:753 File excluded from parsing:
'\\hq.contoso.com\sysvol\hq.contoso.com\Policies
\{31B2F340-016D-11D2-945F-00C04FB984F9}\Adm\wuau.adm'.
```

The following excerpt shows exactly which GPO and domain controller were being accessed:

```
GPEDIT(ff0.a38) 16:05:02:080 CGroupPolicyObject::OpenDSGPO: GPO Path:
 LDAP://2003-ad.hq.contoso.com/cn={31B2F340-016D-11D2-945F-
00C04FB984F9},cn=policies,cn=system,DC=hq,DC=contoso,DC=com
GPEDIT(ff0.a38) 16:05:02:080 CGroupPolicyObject::OpenDSGPO: Flags:  1
GPEDIT(ff0.a38) 16:05:02:080 CGroupPolicyObject::OpenDSGPO:
Using server 2003-ad.hq.contoso.com
```

The GPEdit.log file can grow very large. Therefore, you should leave debugging enabled only when you are troubleshooting problems using the Group Policy Object Editor. To disable debugging, delete the HKLM\Software\Microsoft\Windows NT\CurrentVersion\Winlogon \GPEditDebugLevel registry value.

Group Policy Troubleshooting Checklist

If you find a user or computer with an unexpected Group Policy setting, use the following checklist to identify the source:

- Verify that GPOs that should be applied are not being blocked.
- Verify that no overriding policy that is set at a higher level of Active Directory has been set to No Override. If Block and No Override are both used, No Override takes precedence. Active Directory administrators use these settings to block default GPO hierarchy priorities.

- Verify that the user or computer is not a member of any security group for which the Apply Group Policy permission is set to Deny.
- Verify that the user or computer is a member of at least one security group for which the Apply Group Policy permission is set to Allow.
- Verify that the user or computer is a member of at least one security group for which the Read permission is set to Allow.

Troubleshooting Software Restriction Policies

Software restriction policies are a feature in Windows XP and later versions of Windows that can regulate which software users can run on a computer. Organizations use software restriction policies to protect users from running malicious software; by limiting users only to trusted software, the organization greatly reduces security risks. Additionally, they relieve the user of the burden of deciding which software is safe to run.

However, software restriction policies can inadvertently block a legitimate application. If this happens, you'll see the dialog box shown in Figure 4-11. If you attempt to run a blocked program from a command prompt, you'll see the message, "The system cannot execute the specified program."

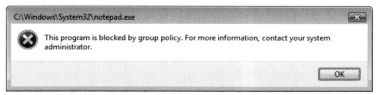

Figure 4-11 An indication that a software restriction policy has blocked your application

How Domain Administrators Use Software Restriction Policies

With software restriction policies, administrators can protect Windows computers from untrusted software by specifying the software permitted to run. Depending on the configuration, administrators can block specific applications, or they can choose to block all unapproved applications. If administrators choose to block all unapproved applications, they must then create exceptions to this default security level by creating software restriction policy rules for specific software.

Software restriction policies can be defined using domain or local GPOs and for either computers or individual users. Software restriction policies provide a number of ways to identify software (such as hashes, certificates, paths, and Internet zones), and they provide a policy-based infrastructure to enforce decisions about whether the identified software can run. With software restriction policies, when users run software programs, they must adhere to the guidelines that administrators set up.

With software restriction policies, domain administrators can control the ability of software to run on users' computers. For example, if domain administrators are concerned about users receiving viruses through e-mail, they can apply a policy setting that does not allow certain file types to run in the e-mail attachment folder. Domain administrators can even restrict policies based on users, allowing only certain users on a computer to run an application.

Because of the flexibility provided by software restrictions, it can be difficult to identify the cause when an application doesn't run.

MORE INFO   Software restriction policies

The 70-622 exam and this book are focused on troubleshooting software restriction policies. For information about designing and creating software restriction policies, read "Windows Vista: Using Software Restriction Policies to Protect Against Unauthorized Software" at *http://technet.microsoft .com/en-us/windowsvista/aa940985.aspx*.

New Features of Software Restriction Policies in Windows Vista

Windows Vista includes several improvements to software restriction policies, including:

- **An additional default security level, Basic User**   As shown in Figure 4-12, administrators can now use software restriction policies to cause programs to run with Basic User privileges only. In the Group Policy setting, the term "Basic User" refers to "Standard User" privileges in Windows Vista. In other words, when this security level is applied to an application, the user will not be able to elevate privileges using the UAC prompt. This allows the application to run but helps reduce the risk that the application will be used to modify important computer settings. You cannot select the Basic User security level for certificate rules.

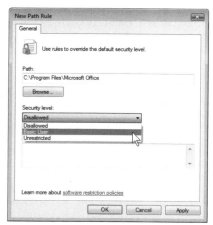

Figure 4-12   The Basic User security level

- **Support for SHA256 hash rules**   When you create a hash rule using a Windows Vista computer, it generates two hashes: either MD5 or SHA-1 (used by earlier versions of Windows) and SHA-256 (used by Windows Vista computers). SHA-256 is simply a more secure hashing algorithm.

- **Certificate rules can be enabled using the Enforcement Properties dialog box**   Certificate rules enable administrators to configure software restriction policies by comparing the certificates used to create digital signatures on a program file to a list of approved certificates. This can be a slow process, however. In Windows Vista you can enable certificate rules using the Enforcement Properties dialog box, as shown in Figure 4-13, which you access by double-clicking Computer Configuration\Windows Settings\Security Settings\Software Restrictions\Enforcement.

Figure 4-13   The Enforcement Properties dialog box

Otherwise, software restriction policies function similar to the way they did for Windows XP and Windows Server 2003.

How to Configure Software Restriction Policies

To configure software restriction policies, open a GPO in the Group Policy Object Editor and select the Computer Configuration\Windows Settings\Security Settings\Software Restriction Policies node. If the node contains no objects, software restriction policies have not been defined within that GPO. Thus, they are not the cause of any problems you might be experiencing. To create a software restriction policy, right-click Software Restriction Policies, and then click New Software Restriction Policies.

You can view the default software restriction policy security level by selecting the Computer Configuration\Windows Settings\Security Settings\Software Restrictions\Security Levels node. In the right pane you will see three security levels listed: Disallowed, Basic User (new in Windows Vista), and Unrestricted. The default level defines how Windows Vista responds to any software that doesn't have an exception created for it. The current default level is signified using a small check mark on the icon. If it hasn't been changed, Unrestricted will be selected, which allows any software to run.

How to Troubleshoot Software Restriction Policies Using the Event Log

You can quickly identify the software restriction policy blocking a program from running by examining the Application Event Log. Within the Application Event Log, find Event ID 866, as demonstrated in Figure 4-14. This event lists the GUID (a 32-byte hexadecimal value) of the policy that blocked the program.

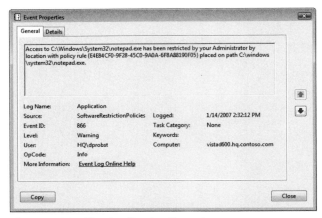

Figure 4-14   The Application Event Log

After finding the GUID of the software restriction policy that blocked your program, use the GPResult command-line tool to identify the GPO containing the rule. To identify the rule, follow these steps:

1. Open a command prompt with administrative privileges.

2. Run the following command:

```
Gpresult /Z > gpresult.txt
```

3. Open the Gpresult.txt file in Notepad by running the following command at the command prompt:

```
Notepad gpresult.txt
```

4. In Notepad, search for the first four digits of the GUID you identified. Notepad jumps to the GUID, which resembles the following:

```
GPO: Default Domain Policy
KeyName:
Software\Policies\Microsoft\Windows\Safer\CodeIdentifiers\0\Paths\{e4e84cf0-9f28-45c0-
9a0a-6f8a88190f05}\Description
```

```
Value:      0, 0
State:      Enabled
```

5.   Identify the GPO name, which is listed just above the KeyName. In this example, the software restriction policy causing the problem is defined in the Default Domain Policy.

After you have determined the GPO name, you should analyze the GPO to identify the specific policy affecting your computer, as described in the next section.

How to Manually Troubleshoot Software Restriction Policies

To determine the source of a software restriction policy problem, first use the RSoP tool to query the problem computer's current configuration. Then determine whether the default level might be causing your problem based on the default level:

- **Unrestricted**   If you are experiencing a problem running software and the default level is Unrestricted, it means that an exception has been created to block your application from running. Continue troubleshooting by examining the Software Restriction Policies\Additional Rules node.

- **Basic User**   Allows programs to run as a standard user, without administrative privileges. If your application normally requires administrative privileges, or it initiates a UAC prompt when you run it, the Basic User default level will cause it to fail. To allow the application to run, create a rule for the program and configure the security level as Unrestricted.

- **Disallowed**   Prevents all programs from running unless an exception has been created for the program under the Additional Rules node. If the default level is Disallowed, check the Software Restriction Policies\Enforcement policy. If All Software Files is selected instead of All Software Files Except Libraries, it will be very difficult to run any software. Selecting All Software Files in the Enforcement Policies dialog box requires administrators to specify every dynamic-link library (DLL) a program might use—a very difficult task.

After determining the default level, check the Software Restriction Policies\Additional Rules node. By default, this node within Computer Configuration includes two rules that allow Windows components and programs installed by administrators to run. Removing either of these two rules could cause serious problems if the default level is set to Disallowed or Basic User:

- **%HKEY_LOCAL_MACHINE\SOFTWARE\Microsoft\Windows NT\CurrentVersion \SystemRoot%**   Refers to the C:\Windows\ folder

- **%HKEY_LOCAL_MACHINE\SOFTWARE\Microsoft\Windows\CurrentVersion\ProgramFilesDir%** Refers to the C:\Program Files\ folder

If either of these rules have been removed and the default level is set to Disallowed or Basic User, that could be the source of your problems (they don't exist by default under User Configuration, however). Any rules other than those two have been manually added by an administrator.

Inspect each software restriction rule for one that might match the software you are attempting to run. Pay particular attention to wildcard characters in path rules, in which a question mark (?) or asterisk (*) replace parts of the path. If used incorrectly, a wildcard character can unintentionally block a great deal of programs.

Often, multiple rules might match a specific program. Some of those rules might block the program, while others allow the program. When multiple path rules match, the most specific match takes precedence over the most general match. For example, given the following list of rules that match the C:\Windows\System32\Notepad.exe file, the last rule would take precedence:

- *.exe
- C:\Windows\System32*.exe
- C:\Windows\System32\Notepad.exe

Given that example, if the first rule blocked all .exe files, and the last rule specifically allowed Notepad.exe, Notepad.exe will be allowed to run.

When multiple types of rules match a single program, they are evaluated in this order:

- Default rule
- Internet zone rule
- Path rule
- Hash rule
- Certificate rule

In other words, a hash rule always overrides the default rule, and a certificate rule always overrides a matching hash rule.

After making changes to a software restriction policy, restart the computer to make the change take effect.

How to Enable Advanced Logging of Software Restriction Policies

The Application Event Log shows only programs that are blocked. If you want to view both programs that are blocked and programs that are allowed, enable advanced logging.

To enable advanced logging of software restriction policies, add a String registry value to the following location and set the value to the log file path: HKLM\SOFTWARE\Policies \Microsoft\Windows\Safer\CodeIdentifiers.

After adding the registry value, Windows Vista immediately begins logging (you do not have to log off or reboot). The log file shows every program that the user runs that is evaluated by software restriction policies. For example, consider the following log file:

```
cmd.exe (PID = 3128) identified C:\Windows\system32\notepad.exe as
Disallowed using path rule, Guid = {e4e84cf0-9f28-45c0-9a0a-6f8a88190f05}
cmd.exe (PID = 3128) identified C:\Windows\system32\calc.exe as
```

```
Unrestricted using path rule, Guid = {191cd7fa-f240-4a17-8986-94d480a6c8ca}
cmd.exe (PID = 3128) identified C:\Windows\system32\whoami.exe as
Unrestricted using path rule, Guid = {191cd7fa-f240-4a17-8986-94d480a6c8ca}
```

In this example three programs were run from the command prompt (Cmd.exe). A software restriction policy blocked Notepad.exe, as shown in the first log file line. The second and third log file lines show that Calc.exe and Whoami.exe were allowed. You can use the GUID to quickly identify the responsible GPO by using GPResult, as described in the previous section.

Real World

Tony Northrup

Once, a Domain Admin at my company created a software restriction policy for the lab domain that blocked just about everything, including administrative tools used to manage Group Policy. If you get stuck like this, start Safe Mode, and then log on as a member of the local Administrators group. Windows Vista ignores software restrictions for local administrators in Safe Mode.

Troubleshooting Logon Scripts

If you use Group Policy settings to configure logon scripts, they might behave differently under Windows Vista than they did in previous versions of Windows. In Windows Vista, UAC can cause problems with logon scripts because Windows Vista might start running the logon script before logon has completed.

To work around this problem, Microsoft provides the launchapp.wsf script. The launchapp.wsf runs instead of your normal logon script, and it schedules the normal logon script as a scheduled task that begins after the user logs on. The launchapp.wsf script is available in Appendix A of "Deploying Group Policy Using Windows Vista" at *http://technet2.microsoft .com/WindowsVista/en/library/5ae8da2a-878e-48db-a3c1-4be6ac7cf7631033.mspx*. That paper also provides instructions for configuring the script.

Practice: Troubleshooting Group Policy Settings

In this practice, you will use the tools built into Windows Vista to determine the source of Group Policy settings.

▶ **Practice 1: Determine the Source of a Configuration Setting**

In this practice, you must determine the Group Policy object that defines the user's background. To complete this practice, you must have completed all earlier practices in this chapter.

1. Log on to the Windows Vista computer using the Standard domain user account.

2. Click Start and type **rsop.msc**. Right-click Rsop, and then click Run As Administrator.

3. Because you added the computer to the IT\Laptops OU in the previous lesson and that OU has a GPO linked to it that requires the Secure Desktop, a User Account Control dialog box appears informing you that you have to type your credentials on the authentic Windows logon screen. Click I Want To Complete This Action.

4. Press Ctrl+Alt+Del to open the Secure Desktop. Then provide administrative credentials to your domain.

5. The Resultant Set Of Policy console appears. Browse to User Configuration\Administrative Templates\Desktop\Desktop. In the right pane, notice that the Desktop Wallpaper setting is enabled and the GPO Name is Default Domain Policy. This identifies the source of the desktop background.

6. In the right pane, double-click the Desktop Wallpaper policy. Then click the Precedence tab. Notice that two GPOs are listed. The Default Domain Policy that you edited in Lesson 2, "Windows Vista Group Policy Settings," is listed at the top because it has the highest priority. The Local Group Policy that you edited in Lesson 1, "Group Policy Overview," is second because local policies always have a lower priority than domain policies. Click OK.

7. Browse to Computer Configuration\Administrative Templates\Windows Components \Windows Sidebar. Notice that the Turn Off Windows Sidebar setting is defined by the IT-Laptops OU. Double-click this setting, and then click the Precedence tab. Notice that it is enabled by the Default Domain Policy but disabled by the higher-priority IT-Laptops GPO.

▶ **Practice 2: Examine the Group Policy Logs**

In this practice, you must examine the Group Policy log files.

1. Log on to the Windows Vista computer using the Standard domain user account.

2. Click Start, and then click Computer. Browse to the C:\Windows\Debug\UserMode folder. Double-click the GPEdit file to open it in Notepad.

3. Browse the debug log. Notice that it does not contain data relating to Group Policy being refreshed. Instead, it contains details about loading .admx and .adml files, as well as other tasks related to using the Group Policy Object Editor.

▶ **Practice 3: Examine Security Settings**

In this practice, you will analyze a computer's security settings by using the Security Configuration And Analysis snap-in.

1. Log on to a Windows Vista computer that is a member of a domain.

2. Download and install the Windows Vista Security Guide from *http://www.microsoft.com /downloads/details.aspx?FamilyID=a3d1bbed-7f35-4e72-bfb5-b84a526c1565&DisplayLang=en.*

3. Create a new MMC console with administrative privileges and add the Security Configuration And Analysis snap-in.

4. Right-click Security Configuration And Analysis, and then click Open Database.

5. In the Open Database dialog box, type **newdb**, and then click Open.

6. In the Import Template dialog box, select Documents\Windows Vista Security Guide \GPOAccelerator Tool\Security Templates\VSG SSLF Domain. If you launched the MMC console with a different user account, this folder will be located under the C:\Users\<*username*>\ folder of the account you used to install the Windows Vista Security Guide. Click Open.

7. Right-click Security Configuration And Analysis, and then click Analyze Computer Now.

8. In the Perform Analysis dialog box, click OK.

9. Expand Security Configuration And Analysis, and then expand Account Policies.

10. Select Password Policy.

11. Notice the policies listed in the right pane. The policies that do not meet or exceed the settings specified in the VSG SSLF Domain.inf security template are marked with a red X, as shown in Figure 4-15.

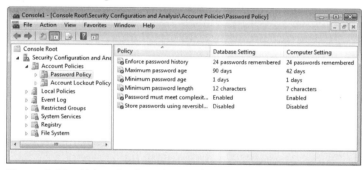

Figure 4-15   Using the Security Configuration And Analysis tool to identify deficient settings

Lesson Summary

- Use the GPUpdate command-line tool to refresh Group Policy. Some settings cannot take effect until after the user logs off and logs back on, while other settings require the computer to be restarted.

- You can use the Resultant Set Of Policy tool to determine which GPO takes effect for any given setting on a computer.

- Security Templates are files that store a limited set of security configuration settings.

- You can use the Security Configuration And Analysis tool to compare a computer's current configuration to a security template.

- Use the GPResult tool to determine GPOs that are applied and filtered.

- Windows Vista adds a significant amount of information to different Group Policy logs. You can use this information to troubleshoot problems applying GPOs. Additionally, you can enable debug logging for the Group Policy Object Editor if you have problems using that tool.

- Administrators use software restriction policies to control which software users can run. This can cause problems with legitimate software, however. Fortunately, you can use Event Viewer to isolate the GPO that is the source of a software restriction policy, enabling domain administrators to correct the policy or add an exception for the required program.

- For many years domain administrators have used Group Policy logon scripts to perform configuration that wasn't possible using other Group Policy settings. Due to authentication changes in Windows Vista, Group Policy logon scripts might not run correctly. To fix these problems, use the launchapp.wsf script, available for download from Microsoft.com.

Lesson Review

You can use the following questions to test your knowledge of the information in Lesson 3, "Troubleshooting Restrictive Security Settings." The questions are also available on the companion CD if you prefer to review them in electronic form.

NOTE   Answers

Answers to these questions and explanations of why each answer choice is right or wrong are located in the "Answers" section at the end of the book.

---

1. You see the following event information in the Group Policy\Operational node of Event Viewer:

   ```
   Source: Group Policy
   Event ID: 4006
   Level: Information
   Description: Starting periodic processing for computer WORKGROUP\CONTOSO1. Activity id:
   {ED6EA197-60E6-45AD-9651-B9BE916D055E}
   ```

   Which Event IDs might indicate the resolution of that processing? (Choose all that apply.)
   - A. 8006
   - B. 4006
   - C. 6006
   - D. 4007

2. Basic User is a valid security level for which of the following software restriction types? (Choose all that apply.)

    A. Certificate

    B. Hash

    C. Path

    D. Network Zone

3. You need to validate that a computer's security settings match those provided by a standard security template. Domain administrators provide you with your organization's security template. Which of the following settings might be defined within the security template?

    A. Software restriction policies

    B. Specifying which users can change the time zone on the computer

    C. Logon scripts

    D. Internet Explorer settings

4. A user is complaining that an important application cannot run. The user is receiving the error message, "This program is blocked by group policy. For more information, contact your system administrator." Which tools can you use to determine the Group Policy object (GPO)? (Choose all that apply.)

    A. Security Templates

    B. Event Viewer

    C. Security Configuration And Analysis

    D. GPResult

Chapter Review

To further practice and reinforce the skills you learned in this chapter, you can

- Review the chapter summary.
- Review the list of key terms introduced in this chapter.
- Complete the case scenarios. These scenarios set up real-world situations involving the topics of this chapter and ask you to create a solution.
- Complete the suggested practices.
- Take a practice test.

Chapter Summary

- To operate efficiently, IT departments must configure computers securely and consistently. This would be impossible if administrators had to manually configure hundreds or thousands of client computers. To enable large organizations to manage computers, Windows supports Group Policy. Group Policy can be applied locally (using different levels in Windows Vista) or, for better efficiency, within an Active Directory domain. Although Windows Vista supports thousands of standard Group Policy settings, administrators can create custom administrative templates to deploy custom settings.

- Windows Vista includes hundreds of new settings to enable administrators to configure almost any aspect of the operating system. In particular, these settings are useful for configuring security, manageability, and the behavior of the user's desktop environment. Windows Vista also includes improvements that will help mobile computers stay up-to-date with Group Policy settings in domain environments. Specifically, Windows Vista applies updated Group Policy settings during power state changes, when connecting to an internal network remotely, when docking and undocking, and when exiting network quarantine.

- Sometimes mistakes in configuring or applying Group Policy settings appear as problems on client computers. Fortunately, Windows Vista includes many tools for identifying the source of the problem. Once you've identified the source of the problem, you can pass it up to domain administrators who will make the necessary changes. The most important troubleshooting tool is Event Viewer, which contains detailed information about Group Policy processing and rules that are applied (including software restriction rules that prevent programs from running). Additionally, you can use the graphical Resultant Set Of Policy tool or the command-line GPResult tool to determine which GPOs apply which settings to a computer. Finally, for determining how a computer's configuration differs from a security template, you can use the Security Configuration And Analysis tool.

Key Terms

Do you know what these key terms mean? You can check your answers by looking up the terms in the glossary at the end of the book.

- administrative template
- Group Policy
- Group Policy object (GPO)
- Multiple Local Group Policy objects (MLGPOs)
- security template

Case Scenarios

In the following case scenarios, you will apply what you've learned about how to configure and troubleshoot Group Policy settings. You can find answers to these questions in the "Answers" section at the end of this book.

Case Scenario 1: Configuring a Windows Vista Computer for a Kiosk

You are a systems administrator for Southridge Video, a video rental chain. Recently, management decided to offer at every outlet computer kiosks that customers could use to search the *http://www.southridgevideo.com* public website to determine whether videos are currently available.

You set up a series of meetings to determine the requirements for the kiosks.

Interviews

Following is a list of company personnel interviewed and their statements:

- **Ezio Alboni, IT Manager** "This is an awful idea... let's put public computers in every store so hackers can use them to crack into our internal network. Worse yet, maybe they'll figure out how to surf to some inappropriate website. Well, we don't have a choice in the matter, so just try to figure something out where you can really lock the computer down. Do everything you can to keep people from using them to get into our internal network."

- **Lori Penor, Chief Security Officer** "Look, you're not going to be able to put together an unhackable computer. All I ask is that you limit your risk as much as possible. Plan on someone eventually getting elevated privileges and make your design decisions to minimize the risk of them getting something valuable when they do. Also keep in mind that the attackers will have physical access to the computers, so they might perform physical attacks like adding a keyboard logging device or booting into some cracking tools from a flash drive or CD."

Questions

Answer the following questions for your manager:

1. Which operating system will you use?
2. How will you configure the computer—using the Control Panel, Local Group Policy, or Domain Group Policy?
3. How can you reduce the risk of an attacker booting into another operating system using removable storage?

Case Scenario 2: Troubleshooting Group Policy Objects

You are a desktop support technician working for Fabrikam, Inc. Recently, Active Directory administrators made some organizational changes. Specifically, they created a new OU for a group of temporary employees who will be performing data entry for several weeks. The OU contains the user accounts for the temporary employees and provides software restrictions that prevent the users from running anything except several work-related programs.

Carol Philips is the manager of the temporary employees. Today you answered a support call from Carol. Apparently, she can't open her favorite instant messaging application.

You tell her you need 20 minutes to investigate the problem. During that time, you call a couple of your coworkers.

Interviews

Following is a list of company personnel interviewed and their statements:

- **Simon Rapier, Active Directory domain administrator** "The other day they had me create the Temps OU, and then I created a dozen user accounts and put them in that OU. After the desktop deployment guys set the computers up, I moved the computer accounts into that OU, too. I see there's a GPO linked to that OU, but Arlene set that up."
- **Arlene Huff, Client Security Manager** "Yes, I set up the GPO for the Temps OU. The manager of that group, Carol Philips, gave me a list of programs that the temporary staff should be able to run. I blocked all programs by default and created rules for each of the approved programs using the hashes of the executables. I configured the software restrictions within the User Configuration node."

Questions

Answer the following questions for your manager:

1. What tools would you use to determine which GPO was causing the software restriction?
2. Can you create a local GPO to override the domain GPO software restrictions?
3. If you had to guess, what do you think is causing the problem? Why?

Suggested Practices

To successfully master the objectives covered by this chapter, complete the following tasks:

Troubleshoot Policy Settings

For this task, you should complete at least Practices 1, 2, 3, and 4. If you want a better understanding of how administrative templates can be deployed in multilingual organizations, complete Practice 5 as well.

- **Practice 1** Complete two virtual labs: "Windows Vista: Managing Windows Longhorn Server and Windows Vista using Group Policy Virtual Lab" at *http://msevents.microsoft.com/CUI/WebCastEventDetails.aspx?EventID=1032329674* and "Exploring New Group Policy Settings in Vista Virtual Lab" at *http://msevents.microsoft.com/CUI/WebCastEventDetails.aspx?EventID=1032305609*.
- **Practice 2** If you work in an Active Directory domain environment, run the Resultant Set of Policy tool. Determine how many GPOs impact your computer and user account. What does this tell you about your organization's Active Directory design?
- **Practice 3** Run both the GPResult and Resultant Set of Policy tool as standard users, without elevating privileges using UAC. How does the output differ from when you have administrative privileges?
- **Practice 4** Examine the standard .admx and .adml files included with Windows Vista.
- **Practice 5** If you have access to a computer in an Active Directory environment, analyze the event logs to determine whether any problems have ever occurred applying Group Policy. What was the source of those problems? What are the event IDs that indicated the problem occurred?
- **Practice 6** Create a custom .admx file with two .adml files for different languages. Configure a Windows Vista client computer in the second language and notice that it automatically displays the preferred language.

Troubleshoot Security Configuration Issues

For this task, you should complete all three practices to gain experience troubleshooting security configuration problems.

- **Practice 1** Using the default security templates provided with the Windows Vista Security guide, determine which security settings on your current computer have been modified from the default.
- **Practice 2** Examine the System, Security, and Application event logs on your computer for any events that might indicate problems caused by restrictive security settings. Determine the source of these problems. If you can't find any relevant events, examine a Windows Vista client computer that has been in use for several months.

■ **Practice 3** Imagine that your organization has standardized desktop client configuration based on the Enterprise Configuration (EC) security templates included with the Windows Vista Security Guide. Then, audit the settings on your computer to determine which settings do not meet your organization's requirements.

Take a Practice Test

The practice tests on this book's companion CD offer many options. For example, you can test yourself on just the content covered in this chapter, or you can test yourself on all the 70-622 certification exam content. You can set up the test so that it closely simulates the experience of taking a certification exam, or you can set it up in study mode so that you can look at the correct answers and explanations after you answer each question.

MORE INFO Practice tests

For details about all the practice test options available, see "How to Use the Practice Tests" in this book's Introduction.

Chapter 5

Protecting Internet Explorer and Other Applications

In recent years more and more security compromises are initiated when users visit a website. For example, websites might trick the user into providing confidential information, or they might exploit a vulnerability in the browser to run code without the user's explicit permission. In Windows Vista, Microsoft Internet Explorer 7.0 includes several features to reduce this risk.

Although Windows Vista is designed to minimize security risks out of the box, attackers are constantly developing new security vulnerabilities. To adapt to changing security risks, you must deploy updates to your client computers. Additionally, Windows Defender (a tool that helps give users control over the software installed on their computers) requires Windows Vista to regularly install updated definitions.

This chapter describes how to manage Internet Explorer, how to best deploy updates to Windows Vista client computers, and how to troubleshoot problems with Windows Defender.

Exam objectives in this chapter:
- Configure and troubleshoot security for Windows Internet Explorer 7+.
- Troubleshoot Windows Defender issues.
- Apply security patches and updates.
- Apply and troubleshoot updates.
- Support deployed applications.
- Maintain desktop applications.

Lessons in this chapter:

Before You Begin

To complete the lessons in this chapter, you should be familiar with Windows Vista and be comfortable with the following tasks:

■ Installing Windows Vista and joining a domain

■ Configuring Group Policy settings

■ Performing basic configuration tasks of Microsoft Windows Server 2003 domain controllers

To complete the practice exercises in this chapter, you should have

■ A lab environment with one Windows Server 2003 domain controller, one Windows Vista client computer that is a member of that domain, and, optionally, a second Windows Vista client computer that is not a member of a domain.

Lesson 1: Configuring and Troubleshooting Internet Explorer Security

Internet Explorer is one of the most important components of the Windows Vista operating system because it provides access to Web applications on both the public Internet and on internal intranets. However, because it might be used to access untrusted websites, security is a serious concern. In the past, attackers have used websites to trick users into disclosing private information, to gain elevated privileges on client computers, and to distribute malware.

How Internet Explorer Works in 64-bit Versions of Windows Vista

Because it provides a wider data bus, allowing many times greater scalability, 64-bit computing is the future. Right now, however, most users run 32-bit versions of Windows.

Unfortunately, although 64-bit versions of Windows are fundamentally superior, in the real world they do have some compatibility problems. In particular, 64-bit versions of Internet Explorer can't use 32-bit components (such as ActiveX controls, which might provide critical functionality for many websites). Although 64-bit components are becoming more common, some critical components still aren't available for 64-bit.

For that reason, the 32-bit version of Internet Explorer is the default even in 64-bit versions of Windows. If a user instead chooses to use the 64-bit version of Internet Explorer (there's also a shortcut for it on the Start menu), test any problematic webpages in the 32-bit version of Internet Explorer before doing any troubleshooting.

MORE INFO   Deploying Internet Explorer

To deploy preconfigured versions of Internet Explorer, you can use the Internet Explorer Administration Kit. For more information, visit *http://technet.microsoft.com/en-us/ie/bb219556.aspx*.

After this lesson, you will be able to:
- Configure add-ons in Internet Explorer (including ActiveX controls) and troubleshoot problems related to add-ons.
- Describe and configure Protected Mode.
- Resolve problems related to Secure Sockets Layer (SSL) certificates.

Estimated lesson time: 40 minutes

Internet Explorer Add-Ons

Add-ons extend Internet Explorer capabilities to enable websites to provide much richer, more interactive content. For example, the following are commonly used add-ons:

- **Shockwave Flash** An add-on that enables complex animations, games, and other interactive capabilities
- **Windows Media Player** An add-on that enables webpages to integrate audio and video
- **Microsoft Virtual Server VMRC Control** An add-on that enables users to remotely control a remote virtual machine from within Internet Explorer

The sections that follow describe how to configure add-ons and troubleshoot problems related to add-ons.

How to Enable and Disable Add-Ons

After starting Internet Explorer, you can disable or delete add-ons by following these steps:

1. Click the Tools button on the toolbar, click Manage Add-Ons, and then click Enable Or Disable Add-Ons.

2. The Manage Add-Ons dialog box appears, as shown in Figure 5-1.

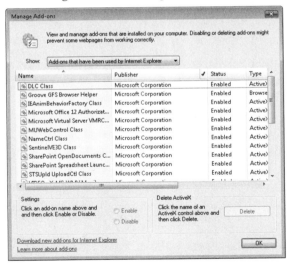

Figure 5-1   The Manage Add-Ons dialog box

3. In the Manage Add-Ons dialog box, select an add-on, and then select Disable to prevent the add-on from automatically loading. If the add-on is an ActiveX control, you can click Delete to permanently remove it.

   If an add-on is causing serious enough problems that you can't start Internet Explorer, you can disable the add-on without opening Internet Explorer by following these steps:

4. Click Start, and then click Control Panel.
5. Click the Network And Internet link.
6. Under Internet Options, click the Manage Browser Add-Ons link.
7. The Internet Properties dialog box appears.
8. Click the Manage Add-Ons button.
9. At the Manage Add-Ons dialog box, select an add-on. Then, select Disable and click OK to prevent the add-on from automatically loading.

How to Start Internet Explorer Without Add-Ons

A buggy or malicious add-on can cause problems with starting Internet Explorer. To work around this problem and launch Internet Explorer without add-ons, follow these steps:

1. Click Start. Then, click All Programs, Accessories, and System Tools.
2. Click Internet Explorer (No Add-Ons).

    Internet Explorer starts with all add-ons disabled. If a webpage opens a new window when you click on a link, that new window will also have add-ons disabled. Add-ons will automatically be enabled the next time you start Internet Explorer using the standard shortcut.

Alternatively, you can manually launch Internet Explorer using the −extoff parameter by clicking Start, typing **iexplore −extoff**, and pressing Enter.

You cannot manage add-ons when you start Internet Explorer in No Add-Ons mode. If you need to disable an add-on without opening Internet Explorer, follow the steps to use Control Panel, as described in the previous section.

How to Configure Add-Ons in Active Directory Domain Environments

As with earlier versions of Internet Explorer, you can use the Group Policy settings in User Configuration\Administrative Templates\Windows Components\Internet Explorer\Security Features\Add-on Management to enable or disable specific add-ons throughout your organization. Typically, you need to use two settings in this group to block all unapproved add-ons in your organization:

- **Add-On List** Enable this setting, and then specify the approved add-ons in your organization. To specify an add-on, provide the class identifier (CLSID) for the add-on you need to add as the Value Name in the Add-On List. The CLSID should be in brackets, such as "{BDB57FF2-79B9-4205-9447-F5FE85F37312}." You can find the CLSID for an add-on by reading the <object> tag from the Hypertext Markup Language (HTML) of a webpage that references the add-on. To specify that the add-on should be denied, specify a Value of 0. To allow an add-on, specify a Value of 1. To both allow an add-on and permit users to manage the add-on, specify a Value of 2.

- ■ **Deny All Add-Ons Unless Specifically Allowed In The Add-On List**   After specifying the add-ons you want to allow in the Add-On List setting, enable this policy to automatically block all other add-ons. You can use the combination of these two settings to block all unapproved add-ons.

Two other Group Policy settings related to add-on management are located within both User Configuration and Computer Configuration at Administrative Templates\Windows Components\Internet Explorer. The settings that relate to managing add-ons are:

- ■ **Turn Off Crash Detection**   By default, Internet Explorer will detect an add-on that crashes and disable it the next time you start Internet Explorer. If you have a problematic add-on that is required for a critical Web application, you can enable this policy to ensure that even a failing add-on continues to run.
- ■ **Do Not Allow Users To Enable Or Disable Add-Ons**   By default, users can open the Manage Add-Ons dialog box and enable or disable add-ons. If you enable this policy, they won't be able to configure add-ons.

How to Configure ActiveX Add-Ons

ActiveX is a technology that enables powerful applications with rich user interfaces to run within a Web browser. For that reason, many organizations have developed ActiveX components as part of a Web application. For the same reason, many attackers have created ActiveX components to abuse the platform's capabilities. Some examples of ActiveX controls include:

- ■ A component that enables you to manage virtual computers from a Microsoft Virtual Server webpage.
- ■ A Microsoft Update component that scans your computer for missing updates.
- ■ Shockwave Flash, which many websites use to publish complex animations and games.

Earlier versions of Internet Explorer installed ActiveX controls without prompting the users. This provided an excellent experience for websites that used ActiveX controls because the user was able to enjoy the control's features without manually choosing to install it. However, malware developers soon abused this capability by creating malicious ActiveX controls that installed software on the user's computer or changed other settings, such as the user's home page.

To enable you to use critical ActiveX controls while blocking potentially dangerous ActiveX controls, Microsoft built strong ActiveX management capabilities into Internet Explorer. The sections that follow describe how to configure ActiveX on a single computer and within an enterprise.

How to Configure ActiveX Opt-in   In Internet Explorer 7, ActiveX controls are not installed by default. Instead, when users visit a webpage that includes an ActiveX control, they will see an information bar that informs them that an ActiveX control is required. Users will then have to click the information bar and click Install ActiveX Control. If the users do nothing, Internet Explorer does not install the ActiveX control. Figure 5-2 shows the Genuine Microsoft Software webpage, which requires users to install an ActiveX control before their copy of Windows can be validated as genuine.

Figure 5-2   The Genuine Microsoft Software page

After the user clicks Install ActiveX Control, the user needs to respond to a User Account Control (UAC) prompt for administrative credentials. Then the user receives a second security warning from Internet Explorer, as shown in Figure 5-3. If the user confirms this security warning, Internet Explorer installs and runs the ActiveX control.

Figure 5-3   A second security warning

ActiveX Opt-in is enabled by default for the Internet and Restricted Sites zones but disabled by default for the Local Intranet and Trusted Sites zones. Therefore, any websites on your local intranet should be able to install ActiveX controls without prompting the user. To change the setting default for a zone, follow these steps:

1. Open Internet Explorer. Click the Tools button on the toolbar, and then click Internet Options.

2. In the Internet Options dialog box, click the Security tab. Select the zone you want to edit, and then click the Custom Level button.

3. Scroll down in the Settings list. Under ActiveX Controls And Plug-Ins, change the setting for the first option, which is Allow Previously Unused ActiveX Controls To Run Without Prompt. If this is disabled, ActiveX Opt-in is enabled.

Exam Tip

The name "ActiveX Opt-in" can be confusing. Enabling ActiveX Opt-in causes Internet Explorer to *not* install ActiveX controls by default, instead requiring the user to explicitly choose to configure the add-on.

---

4. Click OK twice.

ActiveX Opt-in applies to most ActiveX controls. However, it does not apply for ActiveX controls on the preapproved list. The preapproved list is maintained in the registry at HKEY_LOCAL_MACHINE\SOFTWARE\Microsoft\Windows\CurrentVersion\Ext\Pre-Approved. Within this key there are several subkeys, each with a Class ID (CLSID) of a pre-approved ActiveX control. You can identify an ActiveX control's CLSID by viewing the source of a webpage and searching for the <object> tag. For best results, try searching the source of a webpage for the phrase "<object."

How to Configure ActiveX on a Single Computer   The previous section described how to configure ActiveX Opt-in on a single computer. In addition to that setting, you can configure several other per-zone settings related to ActiveX from the Security Settings dialog box:

- **Automatic Prompting For ActiveX Controls**   This setting is disabled by default for all zones. If you choose to enable this setting, it bypasses the information bar and instead actively prompts the user to install the ActiveX control.

- **Download Signed ActiveX Controls**   The developer can sign ActiveX controls. Typically, signed ActiveX controls are more trustworthy than unsigned controls, but you shouldn't trust all signed ActiveX controls. By default, this setting is set to prompt the user. You can reduce the number of prompts the user receives by changing this to Enable.

- **Download Unsigned ActiveX Controls**   By default, unsigned ActiveX controls are disabled. If you must distribute an unsigned ActiveX control, add the site that requires the control to your Trusted Sites list and change this setting for the Trusted Sites zone to Prompt.

- **Initialize And Script ActiveX Controls Not Marked As Safe For Scripting**   This setting is disabled by default for all zones. You should enable it only if you experience a problem with a specific ActiveX control, and the developer informs you that this setting is required. In that case you should add the site to the Trusted Sites list and enable this control only for that zone.

- **Run ActiveX Controls And Plug-Ins** This setting controls whether ActiveX controls will run, regardless of how other settings are defined. In other words, if this setting is disabled, users will not be able to run ActiveX controls, even using ActiveX Opt-in. This setting is enabled for all zones except for the Restricted Sites zone.

- **Script ActiveX Controls Marked Safe For Scripting** Some ActiveX controls are marked safe for scripting by the developer. This setting is enabled for all zones except for the Restricted Sites zone. Typically, you should leave this at the default setting. Because the developer chooses whether the control is marked safe for scripting, this marking does not indicate that the ActiveX control is more trustworthy than any other control.

How to Manage ActiveX Add-Ons on a Single Computer To configure ActiveX on a single computer, follow these steps:

1. Open Internet Explorer.
2. Click the Tools button on the toolbar, click Manage Add-Ons, and then click Enable Or Disable Add-Ons.

   The Manage Add-Ons dialog box appears.
3. Click the Show list, and then click Downloaded ActiveX Controls.
4. Select the ActiveX control you want to manage. Then select:
   - ❑ Disable to disable the ActiveX control.
   - ❑ Delete to remove the ActiveX control.
5. Click OK.

How to Configure ActiveX Installer Service Some critical Web applications might require ActiveX controls to run. This can be a challenge if your users lack administrative credentials because UAC requires administrative credentials to install ActiveX controls (although any user can access an ActiveX control after it is installed).

Fortunately, you can use the ActiveX Installer Service to enable standard users to install specific ActiveX controls. The ActiveX Installer Service is a Windows component but is not installed by default. To enable the ActiveX Installer Service on a computer, follow these steps:

1. Click Start, and then click Control Panel.
2. Click the Programs link.
3. Click the Turn Windows Features On Or Off link and reply to the UAC prompt that appears.
4. In the Windows Features dialog box, select the ActiveX Installer Service check box. Click OK.
5. Restart the computer if prompted.
6. Use the Services console (Services.msc) to start the ActiveX Installer (AxInstSV) service and configure it to start automatically. It is set to start manually by default.

After enabling the ActiveX Installer Service on a computer, configure the list of sites approved to install ActiveX controls by following these steps:

1. Open the Group Policy Object (GPO) in the Group Policy Object Editor.

2. Browse to Computer Configuration\Administrative Templates\Windows Components \ActiveX Installer Service.

3. Double-click the Approved Installation Sites For ActiveX Controls setting. Enable it.

4. Click the Show button to specify host Uniform Resource Locators (URLs) that are allowed to distribute ActiveX controls. In the Show Contents dialog box, click Add and configure the host URLs:

   ❏ Configure each item name as the hostname of the website from which clients will download the updated ActiveX controls, such as *http://activex.microsoft.com*.

   ❏ Configure each value name using four numbers separated by commas (such as "2,1,0,0"). These values are described later in this section.

5. Click OK to save the setting for the new policy.

When you configure the list of approved installation sites for ActiveX Controls, you configure a name and value pair for each site. The name will always be the URL of the site hosting the ActiveX control, such as *http://activex.microsoft.com*. The value consists of four numbers:

■ **Trusted ActiveX Controls**   Define the first number as 0 to block trusted ActiveX controls from being installed, as 1 to prompt the user to install trusted ActiveX controls, or as 2 to automatically install ActiveX controls without prompting the user.

■ **Signed ActiveX Controls**   Define the second number as 0 to block signed ActiveX controls from being installed, as 1 to prompt the user to install signed ActiveX controls, or as 2 to automatically install signed ActiveX controls without prompting the user.

■ **Unsigned ActiveX Controls**   Define the third number as 0 to block unsigned ActiveX controls from being installed or define this number as 1 to prompt the user to install unsigned ActiveX controls. You cannot configure unsigned ActiveX controls to be automatically installed.

■ **Server Certificate Policy**   Set this value to zero to cause the ActiveX Installer Service to abort installation if there are any certificate errors. Alternatively, you can set it to 256 to ignore an unknown CA, 512 to ignore invalid certificate usage, 4096 to ignore an unknown common name in the certificate, or 8192 to ignore an expired certificate. Add these numbers together to ignore multiple types of certificate errors.

For example, the numbers 2,1,0,0 would cause the ActiveX Installer Service to silently install trusted ActiveX controls, prompt the user for signed controls, never install unsigned controls, and abort installation if any Hypertext Transfer Protocol Secure (HTTPS) certificate error occurs.

When a user attempts to install an ActiveX control that has not been approved, the ActiveX Installer Service creates an event in the Application Log with an Event ID of 4097 and a source of AxInstallService. To be automatically notified when users need ActiveX controls that haven't been approved, configure a trigger for these events. For more information, read Chapter 6, "Monitoring Client Computers."

Protected Mode

Before Windows Vista, many computers were compromised when websites containing malicious code succeeded in abusing the Web browsers of visitors to run code on the client computer. Because any new process spawned by an existing process inherits the privileges of the parent process and the Web browser ran with the user's full privileges, maliciously spawned processes received the same privilege as the user. With the user's elevated privileges, the malicious process could install software and transfer confidential documents.

In Windows Vista, Internet Explorer hopes to reduce this type of risk using a feature called Protected Mode. With Protected Mode, Internet Explorer 7 runs with very limited privileges on the local computer—even fewer privileges than those that the standard user has in Windows Vista. Therefore, even if malicious code on a website were to successfully abuse Internet Explorer to spawn a process, that malicious process would have privileges only to access the Temporary Internet Files folder and a few other locations—it would not be able to install software, reconfigure the computer, or read the user's documents.

For example, most users log on to Windows XP computers with administrative privileges. If a website exploits a vulnerability in Windows Vista that hasn't been fixed with an update and successfully launches a process to install spyware, the spyware installation process would have full administrator privileges to the local computer. On a Windows Vista computer the spyware install process would have minimal privileges—even less than those of a standard user—regardless of whether the user was logged on as an administrator.

Protected Mode is a form of defense-in-depth. Protected Mode is a factor only if malicious code successfully compromises the Web browser and runs. In these cases, Protected Mode limits the damage the process can do without the user's permission. Protected Mode is not available when Internet Explorer 7 is installed on Windows XP because it requires several security features unique to Windows Vista.

The sections that follow provide more information about Protected Mode.

How Protected Mode Works

One of the Windows Vista features that enables Protected Mode is Mandatory Integrity Control (MIC). MIC labels processes, folders, files, and registry keys using one of four integrity access levels (ILs), as shown in Table 5-1. Internet Explorer runs with a low IL, which means it can access only other low IL resources without the user's permission.

Table 5-1   Mandatory Integrity Control Levels

IL	System Privileges
System	System. Processes have unlimited access to the computer.
High	Administrative. Processes can install files to the Program Files folder and write to sensitive registry areas like HKEY_LOCAL_MACHINE.
Medium	User. Processes can create and modify files in the user's Documents folder and write to user-specific areas of the registry, such as HKEY_CURRENT_USER. Most files and folders on a computer have a medium integrity level because any object without a mandatory label has an implied default integrity level of Medium.
Low	Untrusted. Processes can only write to low integrity locations, such as the Temporary Internet Files\Low folder or the HKEY_CURRENT_USER\Software\LowRegistry key.

Low IL resources that Internet Explorer in Protected Mode can access include:

- The History folder.
- The Cookies folder.
- The Favorites folder.
- The %userprofile%\AppData\Local\Microsoft\Windows\Temporary Internet Files\Low \ folder.
- The Windows temporary files folders.
- The HKEY_CURRENT_USER\Software\Microsoft\Internet Explorer\LowRegistry key.

Using a feature called User Interface Privilege Isolation (UIPI), low IL also prevents Internet Explorer (or a malicious process launched by Internet Explorer) from sending window messages to other applications. This reduces the risk of shatter attacks, in which a process attempts to elevate privileges by directly attacking another process with higher privileges.

Unfortunately, it's not only malicious software that needs to elevate privileges. Often, legitimate websites and user tasks require more privileges than Protected Mode provides by default. Some user tasks, such as viewing the source code of a page, also require elevated privileges. In these circumstances, Internet Explorer prompts the user to grant additional privileges. Figure 5-4 shows the dialog box that appears if the user clicks the View menu and then clicks Source; Internet Explorer needs permission because it has to launch Notepad, an external application, to show the source code. Low IL processes cannot launch external applications.

Figure 5-4   Internet Explorer prompts the user before granting elevated privileges

The warning dialog box shown in Figure 5-4 shows a yellow banner, indicating that the privileges requested require a medium IL (standard user privileges). A red banner can also appear, indicating that the privileges require a high IL (administrative privileges). Protected Mode protects Internet Explorer extensions, too, limiting the damage that could be done if an extension is malicious or contains a security vulnerability.

How the Protected Mode Compatibility Layer Works

To minimize both the number of privilege elevation requests and the number of compatibility problems, Protected Mode provides a compatibility layer. The compatibility layer redirects requests for protected resources to safer locations. For example, any requests for the My Documents folder (known as the Documents folder in Windows Vista) are automatically redirected to \%userprofile%\AppData\Local\Microsoft\Windows\Temporary Internet Files\Virtualized. The first time an add-on attempts to write to a protected object, the compatibility layer copies the object to a safe location and accesses the copy. All future requests for the same protected file will access the copy.

The compatibility layer applies only to Internet Explorer add-ons written for earlier versions of Windows because anything written for Windows Vista would natively access files in the preferred locations.

How to Enable Compatibility Logging

Some Web applications and Internet Explorer add-ons developed for earlier versions of Internet Explorer will have compatibility problems when you run them with Internet Explorer 7 and Windows Vista. One way to identify the exact compatibility problem is to enable compatibility logging using Group Policy. To enable compatibility logging on your local computer, follow these steps:

1. Click Start, type **gpedit.msc**, and then press Enter. Provide administrative credentials when prompted.

2. In the Group Policy Object Editor, browse to User Configuration\Administrative Templates\Windows Components\Internet Explorer\. If you need to enable compatibility logging for all users on the computer, browse to Computer Configuration\Administrative Templates\Windows Components\Internet Explorer\.

3. Double-click the Turn On Compatibility Logging setting. Select Enabled, and then click OK.

4. Restart Internet Explorer if it is currently open.

With compatibility logging enabled, you should reproduce the problem you are experiencing. You can then view events in the Event Viewer snap-in under Applications And Service Logs\Internet Explorer. Some events, such as Event ID 1037, will not have a description unless you also install the Application Compatibility Toolkit.

MORE INFO   Compatibility logging

For more information about compatibility logging, read "Finding Security Compatibility Issues in Internet Explorer 7" at *http://msdn.microsoft.com/library/en-us/IETechCol/cols/dnexpie /ie7_compat_log.asp*.

How to Disable Protected Mode

If you are concerned that Internet Explorer Protected Mode is causing problems with a Web application, you can temporarily disable it to test the application. Protected Mode is enabled on a zone-by-zone basis and is disabled by default for trusted sites.

To disable Protected Mode, follow these steps:

1. Open Internet Explorer.

2. Click the Tools button on the toolbar, and then click Internet Options.

3. Click the Security tab.

4. Select the zone for which you want to disable Protected Mode. Then, clear the Enable Protected Mode check box.

5. Click OK.

If the application works when Protected Mode is disabled, the problem is probably related to Protected Mode. In that case, you should reenable Protected Mode and work with the application developer to solve the problems in the Web application. Alternatively, you could add the site to the Trusted Sites zone, thus permanently disabling Protected Mode for that site.

How to Troubleshoot Certificate Problems

Certificates are used for several security-related tasks in Internet Explorer:

- **Encrypting traffic**   The most common use for certificates in Internet Explorer. Many websites, especially e-commerce websites that accept credit card numbers, have a Secure Sockets Layer (SSL) certificate installed. This SSL certificate enables HTTPS communications, which behave similar to HTTP, but with encryption and authentication. With standard, unencrypted HTTP, if an attacker has access to the network, the attacker can read all data transferred to and from the server. With encrypted HTTPS, an attacker can capture the traffic, but it will be encrypted and cannot be decrypted without the server's private certificate.

- **Authenticating the server**   SSL certificates authenticate the server by allowing the client to verify that the certificate was issued by a trusted certification authority (CA) and that the name in the certificate matches the hostname used to access the site. This helps to prevent man-in-the-middle attacks, whereby an attacker tricks a client computer into visiting a malicious server that impersonates the legitimate server. Websites on the public Internet typically have SSL certificates issued by a third-party CA that is trusted by default in Internet Explorer. Intranet websites can use certificates issued by an internal CA as long as client computers are configured to trust the internal CA.

- **Authenticating the client**   Intranet websites can issue certificates to clients on their network and use the client certificates to authenticate internal websites. When using Active Directory Group Policy, it is very easy to distribute client certificates throughout your enterprise.

If Internet Explorer detects a problem with a certificate, it displays the message, "There is a problem with this website's security certificate," as shown in Figure 5-5.

Figure 5-5   How Internet Explorer detects mismatched SSL certificates

The following list describes common problems that can occur when using certificates in Internet Explorer and how to troubleshoot them:

- **The security certificate presented by this website was issued for a different website's address**   In this case, there are several possible causes:
    - ❏ The hostname you are using to access the website is not the website's primary address. For example, you might be attempting to access the website by IP address. Alternatively, you might be accessing an alternative hostname, such as "constoso.com" instead of "www.contoso.com."
    - ❏ The server is impersonating a server with a different hostname. For example, an attacker might have set up a website to impersonate www.fabrikam.com. However, the attacker is using a different SSL certificate on the website. Earlier versions of Internet Explorer show a less intimidating error message, so many users might have bypassed the error and continued to the malicious site.
    - ❏ The server administrator made a mistake. For example, the administrator might have mistyped the server's hostname when requesting the certificate, or the administrator might have installed the wrong certificate on the server.
- **The certificate has expired**   Certificates have a limited lifespan—usually one to five years. If the certificate has expired, the server administrator should request an updated certificate and apply it to the server.
- **Internet Explorer is not configured to trust the certificate authority**   Anyone, including attackers, can create their own CA and issue certificates. Therefore, Internet Explorer does not trust all CAs by default. Instead, Internet Explorer trusts only a handful of public CAs. If the certificate was issued by an untrusted CA and the website is on the public Internet, the server administrator should acquire a certificate from a trusted CA. If the website is on your intranet, a client administrator should configure Internet Explorer to trust the issuing CA. In Active Directory directory service domains, member computers automatically trust enterprise CAs. For more information, complete the practices at the end of this lesson.

Practice: Troubleshoot Certificate Problems

In this practice, you first configure the ActiveX Installer Service to trust ActiveX controls from MSN. Then, you will practice troubleshooting certificate-related problems by generating an untrusted certificate, viewing how Internet Explorer responds to that certificate, and then configuring Internet Explorer to trust the certificate.

▶ **Practice 1: Automate the Installation of an ActiveX Control**

In this practice, you configure the ActiveX Installer Service to automatically install an ActiveX control used by MSN.com.

1. Log on as a standard user and open Internet Explorer. Visit *http://music.msn.com/client/install.aspx*. Click Install.

2. Click the Information Bar, and then click Install ActiveX Control. The UAC prompt appears, indicating that a standard user would be unable to install the add-on. Click Cancel.

3. Follow these steps to install the ActiveX Installer Service:

   a. Click Start, and then click Control Panel.

   b. Click the Programs link.

   c. Click the Turn Windows Features On Or Off link and reply to the UAC prompt that appears.

   d. In the Windows Features dialog box, select ActiveX Installer Service check box. Click OK.

   e. If prompted, do not restart the computer.

4. Follow these steps to configure Microsoft.com as a trusted installer:

   a. Use administrative privileges to open the local GPO in the Group Policy Object Editor.

   b. Browse to Computer Configuration\Administrative Templates\Windows Components\ActiveX Installer Service.

   c. Double-click the Approved Installation Sites For ActiveX Controls setting. Select Enable.

   d. Click the Show button.

   e. Click Add. Specify a value name of **http://entimg.msn.com/** and a value of **2,2,1,0**.

   NOTE Source URL and CLSID of an ActiveX control

   You can determine the source URL and CLSID of the ActiveX control by viewing the source of the webpage that installs the ActiveX control. Then, within the source, search for the phrase "<object".

   ---

   f. Click OK three times to save the setting for the new policy.

5. Restart your computer to complete the installation of the ActiveX Installer Service and to apply the updated Group Policy settings.

6. Log back on as a standard user. Open Internet Explorer and visit *http://music.msn.com /client/install.aspx* again. Click Install. Then, click the Information Bar, and click Install ActiveX Control. Notice that this time, although Internet Explorer prompts you to confirm the installation, no UAC prompt appears. After the ActiveX control is installed, click the information bar again to activate the control.

7. In Internet Explorer, click the Tools button on the toolbar, click Manage Add-Ons, and then click Enable Or Disable Add-Ons.

8. In the Manage Add-Ons dialog box, click the Show list, and then click Downloaded ActiveX Controls. Notice that the newly installed ActiveX control appears on the list.

▶ **Practice 2: Simulate an Invalid Certificate**

In this practice, you open a webpage using a hostname other than the common name specified in the SSL certificate and view how Internet Explorer handles it.

1. Open Internet Explorer. In the Address bar, type **https://www.microsoft.com**. Press Enter.

    When prompted to display nonsecure items, click No.

2. Internet Explorer opens the *www.microsoft.com* home page using encrypted HTTPS. Note the gold lock in the Address bar, as shown in Figure 5-6.

Figure 5-6 The gold lock in the address bar, which signifies that communications with the site are encrypted and the certificate is valid

3. Click the gold lock in the address bar to display the website identification. Notice that the identification page displays "www.microsoft.com," which exactly matches the hostname you typed in the address bar.

4. In the Address bar, type **https://microsoft.com**. Notice that this time the hostname does not begin with "www." Press Enter.

    Internet Explorer displays the There Is A Problem With This Website's Security Certificate webpage. This happens because the hostname in the certificate, www.microsoft.com, does not exactly match the hostname you typed in the address bar, microsoft.com. Users would see this same error message if they attempted to visit a site that was impersonating another site.

▶ **Practice 3: Issue an Untrusted Certificate**

In this practice, you must issue an internal certificate to a Web server and determine how Windows Vista handles it both as a member of the domain and from outside the domain.

1. Connect to a Windows Server 2003 Active Directory domain controller in a test environment and log on as an administrator.

2. Certificate Services requires Internet Information Services (IIS). Therefore, you need to install the Application Server role if it is not already installed. Click Start, click Administrative Tools, and then click Manage Your Server. If the Application Server role is already installed, skip to step Otherwise, click Add Or Remove A Role to start the Configure Your Server Wizard.

3. On the Preliminary Steps page, click Next.

4. On the Server Role page, select Application Server (IIS, ASP.NET), and then click Next. Follow the prompts that appear to install IIS with ASP.NET enabled. Finally, click Finish.

5. After you have installed IIS, click Start, click Control Panel, and then click Add Or Remove Programs. Click Add/Remove Windows Components.

6. If the Certificate Services check box is already selected, skip to step Otherwise, select the Certificate Services check box, click Yes to close the Microsoft Certificate Services message box, and then click Next.

7. On the CA Type page, leave Enterprise Root CA selected, and then click Next.

8. On the CA Identifying Information page, type the hostname for your CA (such as DCSRV1.nwtraders.msft), and then click Next to accept the default settings. If prompted to stop IIS, click Yes.

9. On the Certificate Database Settings page, click Next. Respond to any prompts that appear to complete the installation of Certificate Services. Finally, click Finish.

10. Click Start, click All Programs, click Administrative Tools, and then click IIS Manager.

11. In the IIS Manager, expand your computer and expand Web Sites. Then, right-click Default Web Site and click Properties.

12. In the Default Web Site Properties dialog box, click the Directory Security tab. Then, click the Server Certificate button.

13. The Web Server Certificate Wizard appears. On the Welcome To The Web Server Certificate Wizard page, click Next.

14. On the Server Certificate page, select Create A New Certificate, and then click Next.

15. On the Delayed Or Immediate Request page, select Send The Request Immediately To An Online Certification Authority. Then, click Next.

16. On the Name And Security Settings page, accept the default settings by clicking Next.

17. On the Organization Information page, type **Northwind Traders** in the Organization box and type **IT** in the Organizational Unit box. Then, click Next.

18. On the Your Site's Common Name page, note that the default setting matches the site's computer name. This setting is extremely important because it must exactly match the name that users type to access your website. Computer names work well on intranet sites, but for public Internet sites the common name should resemble "www.nwtraders.com." Click Next to accept the default setting because this site will be accessed like an intranet site.

19. On the Geographical Information page, enter your geographic information. Then, click Next.

20. On the SSL Port page, accept the default standard setting of 44. Then, click Next.

21. On the Choose A Certification Authority page, verify that the CA listed matches the domain controller. Click Next.

22. On the Certificate Request Submission page, click Next.

23. On the Completing The Web Server Certificate Wizard page, click Finish.

24. In the Default Web Site Properties dialog box, click OK.

25. Now you have configured your domain controller as a Web server with an SSL certificate. On your Windows Vista client computer, open Internet Explorer. In the address bar, enter https://*common_name*, where *common_name* is the name you entered in step 19 (such as https://dcsrv1). Press Enter.

    Internet Explorer opens the page. Notice that the gold lock icon appears in the address bar, signifying that the SSL certificate is valid.

26. On a second Windows Vista computer that is not a member of your domain, open Internet Explorer. Alternatively, if you do not have a second computer, you can temporarily remove your Windows Vista computer from the domain. In Internet Explorer, enter https://*common_name* and press Enter.

    Internet Explorer displays a warning message indicating that the certificate was not issued by a trusted certificate authority, as shown in Figure 5-7.

Figure 5-7   The warning message given by Internet Explorer if it doesn't trust the certificate authority

Now, continue working with Practice 4 to resolve this problem.

▶ **Practice 4: Trust a Certificate Authority**

In this practice, you must export your CA's root certificate and trust that certificate on your nondomain Windows Vista computer so that you can open the SSL-encrypted website without a warning. To complete this practice, you must have completed Practice 2.

1. On your domain controller, in the Certification Authority console, right-click your server, and then click Properties.
2. Click the General tab. Click Certificate #0, and then click the View Certificate button.
3. In the Certificate dialog box, click the Details tab. Then, click Copy To File.
4. The Certificate Export Wizard appears. Click Next.
5. On the Export File Format page, accept the default export format, and then click Next.
6. On the File To Export tab, type **C:\root.cer**, and then click Next.
7. Click Finish. Then, click OK twice.
8. On your Windows Vista client computer that is not a member of your test domain, open Internet Explorer. In Internet Explorer, click the Tools button on the toolbar, and then click Internet Options.

9. In the Internet Options dialog box, click the Content tab, and then click Certificates.

10. In the Certificates dialog box, click the Trusted Root Certification Authorities tab. Then, click the Import button.

11. The Certificate Import Wizard appears. On the Welcome To The Certificate Import Wizard page, click Next.

12. On the File To Import page, click the Browse button. In the Open dialog box, type ***server_name*\c$\root.cer**. Then, click Open. Click Next.

13. On the Certificate Store page, notice that the Certificate Import Wizard will import the certificate into the Trusted Root Certification Authorities store by default. This is the correct place. Click Next.

14. On the Completing The Certificate Import Wizard page, click Finish.

15. A Security Warning dialog box appears. Click Yes to install the certificate. Then, click OK.

16. Click Close, and then click OK.

17. In Internet Explorer, enter https://*common_name*, and press Enter.

    Internet Explorer opens the page. Notice that the gold lock icon appears in the address bar, signifying that the SSL certificate is valid. Because this computer is not a member of the Active Directory domain, you had to manually trust the root certificate. Then, all certificates issued by that CA will be trusted. If the computer had been a member of the Active Directory domain, Group Policy would have caused the computer to automatically trust the enterprise CA.

Lesson Summary

■ Web application developers often use Internet Explorer add-ons to extend the Web browser's capabilities. However, some add-ons can cause reliability problems, and others might compromise your organization's security. Fortunately, Internet Explorer provides tools to disable add-ons and delete ActiveX controls. If an add-on is preventing Internet Explorer from starting, you can start Internet Explorer with all add-ons disabled.

■ Protected Mode is one of Internet Explorer 7.0's most significant security improvements, and it's available only when using Windows Vista. By default, Protected Mode causes Internet Explorer to run with low privileges, which prevents Internet Explorer (or any process launched by Internet Explorer) from accessing most resources on the computer. The user must confirm permissions if Internet Explorer or an add-on require elevated privileges.

■ Many websites use certificates to authenticate the Web server and to provide encrypted communications. Certificates are extremely important for websites that provide access to confidential information or that collect private information from users (such as credit card numbers). The most common certificate problem is a nonmatching server hostname, which can typically be resolved by providing the hostname listed in the certificate. For servers on your intranet, users might experience certificate problems if the computer hasn't been correctly configured to trust the CA.

Lesson Review

You can use the following questions to test your knowledge of the information in Lesson 1, "Configuring and Troubleshooting Internet Explorer Security." The questions are also available on the companion CD if you prefer to review them in electronic form.

NOTE Answers

Answers to these questions and explanations of why each answer choice is right or wrong are located in the "Answers" section at the end of the book.

---

1. A user is attempting to visit one of the many internal websites run by your IT department. The user's shortcut is set up to use SSL by default. Today, when the user attempted to open the page, Internet Explorer showed the user the following message:

   There is a problem with this website's security certificate.
   The security certificate presented by this website was issued
   for a different website's address.

   Which of the following might cause this message? (Choose all that apply.)
   A. The certificate is expired.
   B. An attacker is redirecting traffic to a malicious Web server.
   C. Internet Explorer no longer trusts the CA that issued the certificate.
   D. The website certificate was issued for a different hostname than that stored in the user's shortcut.

2. Which of the following would Internet Explorer block by default (until confirmed by a user)? (Choose all that apply.)
   A. Animated GIFs
   B. Background music in a webpage
   C. Video embedded in a webpage
   D. Viewing the source code of a webpage

3. Which of the following types of requests would the Internet Explorer compatibility layer redirect to a virtualized location?

    A. Storing a cookie

    B. Storing a file in the Documents folder

    C. Prompting the user to choose a file to upload to a website

    D. Storing a file in the Temporary Internet Files folder

4. You receive a support call from a user attempting to access an internal webpage. The user recently upgraded to Windows Vista; previously, the user had been using Windows XP and Internet Explorer 6.0. The webpage contains an ActiveX control, but it isn't appearing on the webpage for the user. Which of the following are valid ways for the user to resolve the problem? (Choose two. Each correct answer is a complete solution.)

    A. Right-click the page, and then click Run ActiveX Control.

    B. Click the Information Bar, and then click Run ActiveX Control.

    C. Add the site to the Trusted Sites list.

    D. Clear the Enable Protected Mode check box in the Internet Security dialog box.

Lesson 2: Updating Software

Because security threats are constantly evolving, Microsoft must regularly release updates to Windows Vista. Deploying and managing these updates are some of the most important security tasks an IT department can perform. To simplify this task, Windows Vista includes several improved update capabilities compared to Windows XP:

- Windows Update is a stand-alone tool instead of a webpage.
- Windows Update will immediately connect to an update server the first time Windows Vista connects to a network.
- Windows Update automatically installs drivers for devices that are using generic drivers or that do not have any driver installed.
- Administrators can configure Windows Update to automatically install recommended updates as well as critical updates.
- Now non-administrators can approve update installations without providing administrative credentials.
- Windows Update can wake a computer from sleep to install updates, so users no longer need to leave their computers running to enable updates to be installed overnight.

This lesson describes the different techniques for deploying updates to Windows Vista computers and explains how to install and manage updates and how to troubleshoot update problems.

After this lesson, you will be able to:
- Choose a deployment technique for distributing updates within your organization.
- Install updates automatically, manually, and to new computers.
- Troubleshoot problems installing updates.
- Uninstall updates.

Estimated lesson time: 30 minutes

Methods for Deploying Updates

Microsoft provides several techniques for applying updates:

- **Directly from Microsoft**   For home users and small businesses, Windows Vista is configured to automatically retrieve updates directly from Microsoft. This method is suitable only for smaller networks with fewer than 50 computers.

- **Windows Server Update Services (WSUS)**   WSUS enables administrators to approve updates before distributing them to computers on an intranet. Optionally, updates can be stored and retrieved from a central location on the local network, reducing Internet usage when downloading updates. This approach requires at least one infrastructure server.
- **Microsoft Systems Management Server (SMS)**   The preferred method for distributing software and updates in large, enterprise networks, SMS provides highly customizable, centralized control over update deployment, with the ability to audit and inventory client systems. SMS typically requires several infrastructure services.

The sections that follow describe each of these deployment methods in more detail.

Windows Update Client

Whether you download updates from Microsoft or use WSUS, the Windows Update client is responsible for downloading and installing updates on Windows Vista computers. The Windows Update client replaces the Automatic Updates client available in earlier versions of Windows. Both Windows Update in Windows Vista and Automatic Updates in previous versions of Windows operate the same way: they download and install updates from Microsoft or an internal WSUS server. Both clients install updates at a scheduled time and automatically restart the computer if necessary. If the computer is turned off at that time, the updates can be installed as soon as the computer is turned on. Alternatively, Windows Update can wake a computer from sleep and install the updates at the specified time if the computer hardware supports it.

The Windows Update client provides for a great deal of control over its behavior. You can configure individual computers by using the Control Panel\Security\Windows Update\Change Settings page, as described in "How to Configure Windows Update Using Graphical Tools" later in this section. Networks that use Active Directory can specify the configuration of each Windows Update client by using Group Policy, as described in "How to Configure Windows Update Using Group Policy Settings."

After the Windows Update client downloads updates, the client checks the digital signature and the Secure Hash Algorithm (SHA1) hash on the updates to verify that they have not been modified.

Windows Server Update Services

Windows Server Update Services (WSUS) is a version of the Microsoft Update service that you can host on your private network. WSUS connects to the Windows Update site, downloads information about available updates, and adds them to a list of updates that require administrative approval.

After an administrator approves and prioritizes these updates, WSUS automatically makes them available to any computer running Windows Update (or the Automatic Updates client on earlier versions of Windows). Windows Update (when properly configured) then checks the WSUS server and automatically downloads and installs updates as configured by the administrators. As shown in Figure 5-8, you can distribute WSUS across multiple servers and locations to scale to enterprise needs. WSUS meets the needs of medium-sized organizations and many enterprises.

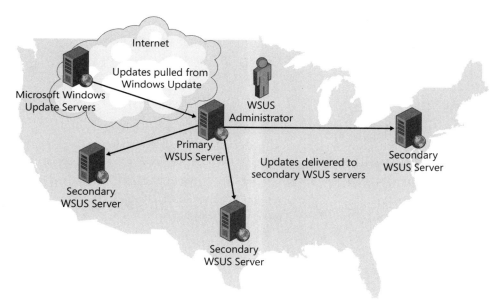

Figure 5-8 WSUS can scale to support thousands of computers

You must install WSUS on at least one infrastructure server, and you manage it by using a Web browser. To deploy updates to Windows Vista computers, you must have WSUS Service Pack 1 or later installed on your server.

MORE INFO   Windows Server Update Services (WSUS)

For more information about update management with WSUS and to download WSUS, visit *http://www.microsoft.com/wsus/*.

Systems Management Server

Microsoft Systems Management Server (SMS) 2003 is a tool for efficiently managing, distributing, and inventorying software in enterprise environments. Although WSUS is sufficient to meet the needs of medium-sized organizations, SMS can supplement WSUS in enterprise organizations that manage hundreds or thousands of computers.

MORE INFO   Systems Management Server (SMS)

For more information about SMS, visit the SMS website at *http://www.microsoft.com/smserver*.

MORE INFO   Using SMS for update management

For information about using SMS for update management, refer to the article "Patch Management Using Systems Management Server 2003" at *http://www.microsoft.com/technet/itsolutions/cits/mo /swdist/pmsms/2003/pmsms031.mspx*.

How to Install Updates

Ideally, you would install all current updates immediately when you deploy new computers. After deployment, you can manually install updates, but you'll be much more efficient if you choose an automatic deployment technique. For situations that require complete control over update installation but still must be automated, you can script update installations.

How to Apply Updates to New Computers

When you deploy new computers, you should deploy them with as many recent updates as possible. Even though Windows Vista immediately checks for updates the first time it starts (rather than waiting for the scheduled automatic update time), this provides improved security for the computer the first time it starts, rather than waiting for it to retrieve updates after startup.

You can use the following techniques, in order of most secure to least secure, to apply updates to new computers:

- **Integrate updates into Windows Vista setup files**   If you use an automatic deployment technology such as the Microsoft Solution Accelerator for Business Desktop Deployment 2007 (BDD), you can ensure that updates are present during setup by installing Windows Vista and all updates on a lab computer and then using Windows PE and the XImage tool to create an operating system image (a .wim file) that you can deploy to new computers.

MORE INFO   Solution Accelerator for Business Desktop Deployment 2007 (BDD)

For more information about BDD, visit *http://www.microsoft.com/technet/desktopdeployment /bdd/2007/*.

- **Install updates automatically during setup** Using scripting, you can install updates automatically during setup. Ideally, you would distribute the update files with your Windows Vista installation media or on the distribution server. You can use BDD to configure updates for installation during setup, or you can manually configure updates using one of the following techniques:

  ❑ Use the Windows System Image Manager to add a RunSynchronous command to an Unattend.xml answer file in your Windows Vista image. RunSynchronous commands are available in the Microsoft-Windows-Setup and the Microsoft-Windows-Deployment components.

  ❑ Edit the %windir%\Setup\Scripts\SetupComplete.cmd file in your Windows Vista image. Windows Vista runs any commands in this file after Windows Setup completes. Commands in the SetupComplete.cmd file are executed with local system privilege. You cannot reboot the system and resume running SetupComplete.cmd; therefore, you must install all updates in a single pass.

- **Manually install updates using removable media** One of the best ways to minimize the risk of a new computer being attacked before it installs updates is to deploy computers while disconnected from the network, using removable media. If you choose this approach, you should also use removable media to install updates before connecting the computer to the public Internet.

- **Use WSUS to apply updates to new computers** After Windows Vista starts the first time, it immediately attempts to download updates (rather than waiting for the scheduled Windows Update time). Therefore, even with the default settings, the time new computers spend without updates is minimized. To further minimize this, ask your WSUS administrators to configure the most critical updates with a deadline. The deadline forces new computers downloading the updates to install the critical updates and then immediately restart to apply them.

How to Manually Apply Updates

In previous versions of Windows, you could apply updates by visiting the *http://windowsupdate .com* website. In Windows Vista, you must follow these steps:

1. Click Start, click All Programs, and then click Windows Update.
2. The Windows Update window appears. Click the Check For Updates link.
3. If any updates are available, click Install Updates, as shown in Figure 5-9. To install optional updates, click View Available Updates.

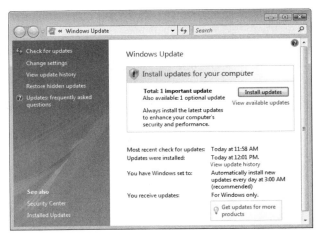

Figure 5-9   Using the Windows Update tool to check for updates

NOTE   If an update is not listed

If an update does not appear on the list, it might have been hidden. To fix this, click the Restore Hidden Updates link in the Windows Update window.

4. Windows Updates downloads and installs the available updates.
5. If required, restart the computer by clicking Restart Now.

    If you choose not to immediately restart the computer, Windows Update will regularly prompt the user to restart, as shown in Figure 5-10. The user can postpone the update prompt for up to four hours. Administrative credentials are not required to install updates.

Figure 5-10   The reminder from Windows Update that updates are waiting for the computer to be restarted

How to Automatically Apply Updates

You can configure automatic updates by using either graphical, interactive tools or by using Group Policy. The sections that follow describe each of these techniques.

How to Configure Windows Update Using Graphical Tools   During an interactive setup, Windows Vista prompts users to choose update settings. Setup recommends enabling automatic updates. To manually configure automatic updates on a computer, follow these steps (which require administrative privileges):

1. Click Start, and then click Control Panel.
2. Click the Security link.
3. Under Windows Update, click the Turn Automatic Updating On Or Off link.
4. Adjust the settings, including whether updates are installed automatically and the time they are installed, and then click OK.

How to Configure Windows Update Using Group Policy Settings   You can configure Windows Update client settings using local or domain Group Policy settings. This is useful for the following tasks:

- Configuring computers to use a local WSUS server
- Configuring automatic installation of updates at a specific time of day
- Configuring how often to check for updates
- Configuring update notifications, including whether non-administrators receive update notifications
- Configure client computers as part of a WSUS target group, which you can use to deploy different updates to different groups of computers

Windows Update settings are located at Computer Configuration\Administrative Templates \Windows Components\Windows Update. The Windows Update Group Policy settings are:

- **Configure Automatic Updates**   Specifies whether client computers will receive security updates and other important downloads through the Windows Update service. You also use this setting to configure whether the updates are installed automatically and what time of day the installation occurs.
- **Specify Intranet Microsoft Update Service Location**   Specifies the location of your WSUS server.
- **Automatic Updates Detection Frequency**   Specifies how frequently the Windows Update client checks for new updates. By default, this is a random time between 17 and 22 hours.
- **Allow Non-Administrators To Receive Update Notifications**   Determines whether all users or only administrators will receive update notifications. Non-administrators can install updates using the Windows Update client.

- **Allow Automatic Updates Immediate Installation**   Specifies whether Windows Update will immediately install updates that don't require the computer to be restarted.

- **Turn On Recommended Updates Via Automatic Updates**   Determines whether client computers install both critical and recommended updates, which might include updated drivers.

- **No Auto-Restart For Scheduled Automatic Updates**   Specifies that to complete a scheduled installation, Windows Update will wait for the computer to be restarted by any user who is logged on instead of causing the computer to restart automatically.

- **Re-Prompt For Restart With Scheduled Installations**   Specifies how often the Windows Update client prompts the user to restart. Depending on other configuration settings, users might have the option of delaying a scheduled restart. However, the Windows Update client will automatically remind them to restart based on the frequency configured in this setting.

- **Delay Restart For Scheduled Installations**   Specifies how long the Windows Update client waits before automatically restarting.

- **Reschedule Automatic Updates Scheduled Installations**   Specifies the amount of time for Windows Update to wait, following system startup, before continuing with a scheduled installation that was missed previously. If you don't specify this amount of time, a missed scheduled installation will occur one minute after the computer is next started.

- **Enable Client-Side Targeting**   Specifies which group the computer is a member of. This option is useful only if you are using WUS; you cannot use this option with SUS.

- **Enabling Windows Update Power Management To Automatically Wake Up The System To Install Scheduled Updates**   If people in your organization tend to shut down their computers when they leave the office, enable this setting to configure computers with supported hardware to automatically start up and install an update at the scheduled time. Computers will not wake up unless there is an update to be installed. If the computer is on battery power, the computer will automatically return to Sleep after two minutes.

Additionally, the following two settings are available at the same location under User Configuration (which you can use to specify per-user settings) in addition to Computer Configuration:

- **Do Not Display 'Install Updates And Shut Down' Option In Shut Down Windows Dialog Box**   Specifies whether Windows XP with Service Pack 2 or later shows the Install Updates And Shut Down option.

- **Do Not Adjust Default Option To 'Install Updates And Shut Down' In Shut Down Windows Dialog Box**   Specifies whether Windows XP with Service Pack 2 or later automatically changes the default shutdown option to Install Updates And Shut Down when Windows Update is waiting to install an update.

Finally, the last user setting is available only at User Configuration\Administrative Templates\Windows Components\Windows Update:

- **Remove Access To Use All Windows Update Features**   When enabled, prevents user from accessing the Windows Update interface.

How to Script Updates

Windows Vista opens MSU files with the Windows Update Standalone Installer (Wusa.exe). To install an update from a script, run the script with administrative privileges, call Wusa and provide the path to the MSU file. For example, you can install an update named Windows6.0-KB929761-x86.msu in the current directory by running the following command:

```
wusa Windows6.0-KB929761-x86.msu
```

Additionally, Wusa supports the following standard command-line options:

- **/?, /h, or /help**   Displays the command-line options.
- **/quiet**   Quiet mode. This is the same as unattended mode, but no status or error messages are displayed. Use quiet mode when installing an update as part of a script.
- **/norestart**   Does not restart when installation has completed. Use this parameter when installing multiple updates simultaneously. All but the last update installed should have the /norestart parameter.

Scripting is not usually the best way to install updates on an ongoing basis. Instead, you should use Windows Update, WSUS, or SMS. However, you might create a script to install updates on new computers or to install updates on computers that cannot participate in your standard update distribution method.

How to Troubleshoot Problems Installing Updates

Occasionally, you might experience a problem installing an update. Fortunately, Windows Vista provides detailed information about update installations. The sections that follow describe how to troubleshoot problems with Windows Update and Restart Manager.

How to Troubleshoot Windows Update

Occasionally, you might discover a client that isn't automatically installing updates correctly. You can identify missing updates using an automated tool such as the Microsoft Baseline Security Analyzer (MBSA).

MORE INFO   Microsoft Baseline Security Analyzer (MBSA)

For more information about MBSA and to download the free tool, visit *http://www.microsoft.com/ mbsa/*.

Alternatively, you can manually identify problems installing updates by viewing the update history. To view the update history, follow these steps:

1. Click Start, click All Programs, and then click Windows Update.
2. The Windows Update window appears. Click the View Update History link.
3. The View Update History window appears, as shown in Figure 5-11. To view the details of an update, double-click it.

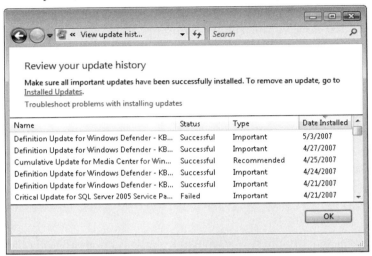

Figure 5-11   Reviewing an update history with the Windows Update tool

To identify the source of the problem causing an update to fail, follow these steps:

1. Examine the %windir%\WindowsUpdate.log file to verify that the client is contacting the correct update server and to identify any error messages. For detailed information about how to read the WindowsUpdate.log file, refer to Microsoft Knowledge Base article 902093 at *http://support.microsoft.com/kb/902093/*.

2. If your organization uses WSUS, verify that the client can connect to the WSUS server by opening a Web browser and visiting http://<*WSUSServerName*>/iuident.cab. If you are prompted to download the file, this means that the client can reach the WSUS server, and it is not a connectivity issue. Otherwise, you could have a name resolution or connectivity issue, or WSUS is not configured correctly.

MORE INFO   **Troubleshooting WSUS**

For more information about troubleshooting WSUS, visit *http://technet2.microsoft.com /WindowsServer/en/library/b23562a8-1a97-45c0-833e-084cd463d0371033.mspx?mfr*.

---

3. If you use Group Policy to configure the Windows Update client, use the Resultant Set of Policy (RSOP) tool (Rsop.msc) to verify the configuration. Within RSOP, browse to the Computer Configuration\Administrative Templates\Windows Compo-

nents\Windows Update node and verify the configuration settings. Figure 5-12 shows the RSOP snap-in.

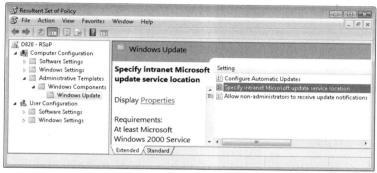

Figure 5-12   The RSOP snap-in

If you have identified a problem and made a configuration change that you hope will resolve it, restart the Windows Update service on the client computer to make the change take effect and begin another update cycle. You can do this using the Services console or by running the following two commands:

```
net stop wuauserv
net start wuauserv
```

Within 6 to 10 minutes, Windows Update will attempt to contact your update server.

How to Troubleshoot Restart Manager

Windows Vista includes Windows Installer 4.0, a new version of the application installation infrastructure that is not available for earlier versions of Windows. One of the most significant improvements in Windows Installer 4.0 is Restart Manager. Installation routines can communicate with Restart Manager to indicate which files need to be updated. Restart Manager then coordinates updating the files while minimizing the impact on the user.

The need to update a file that is already in use is one of the most common reasons a user is required to restart a computer. Restart Manager strives to reduce this requirement by closing and restarting programs and services that have files in use. Although some installations will always require the computer to be restarted (especially if they need to upgrade system files that are in use), Restart Manager should minimize this requirement. In Windows Vista all installers must take advantage of the Restart Manager for the program to receive Certified for Windows Vista status.

To diagnose a problem with Restart Manager, open Event Viewer and view the following event logs:

■ Windows Logs\Application

■   Applications and Services Logs\Microsoft\Windows\RestartManager\Operational

Search for Warning or Error events with a source of RestartManager. The following is an example of a Warning event with Event ID 10010:

```
Application 'C:\Program Files\Microsoft Office\OFFICE11\OUTLOOK.EXE'
(pid 5592) cannot be restarted - Application SID does not match
Conductor SID.
```

You can also view general Windows Update events in the Application log. Search for events with a source of MsiInstaller.

How to Remove Updates

Occasionally, an update might cause compatibility problems. If you experience problems with an application or Windows feature after installing updates and one of the updates was directly related to the problem you are experiencing, you can uninstall the update to determine whether it is related to the problem.

How to Manually Remove an Update

To remove an update, follow these steps:

1. Use Windows Update to view the update history, as described in "How to Troubleshoot Windows Update" earlier in this chapter. View the details of each update to identify the update that might be causing a problem. Make note of the Knowledge Base (KB) number for the update.

2. Click Start, and then click Control Panel.

3. Under Programs, click the Uninstall A Program link.

4. Under Tasks (in the upper-left corner of the window), click the View Installed Updates link.

5. Select the update you want to remove by using the KB number you noted in step 1. Then, click Uninstall, as shown in Figure 5-13.

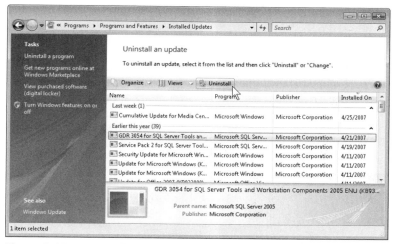

Figure 5-13   Uninstalling an update to determine whether it is the source of a problem

6. Follow the prompts that appear and restart the computer if required.

If removing the update does not resolve the problem, you should reapply the update. If removing the update does solve the problem, contact the application developer (in the case of a program incompatibility) or your Microsoft support representative to inform them of the incompatibility. The update probably fixes a different problem, and therefore you should make every effort to fix the compatibility problem and install the update.

How to Remove an Update using WSUS

If you use Windows Software Update Services (WSUS) to distribute updates internally, you might be able to remove the update from the WSUS server to prevent it from being distributed. Many updates do not support being removed. To remove an update for a group of computers or all computers with WUSA, follow these steps:

1. View the WSUS Updates page.
2. Select the update, and then click Change Approval under Update Tasks.
3. Click the Approval list, and then click Remove (if available).
4. Click OK.

How to Recover a Computer that Won't Start

If an update prevents Windows Vista from starting correctly, you can use the Startup Repair tool to quickly restore the computer. To run Startup Repair, follow these steps:

1. Insert the Windows Vista DVD in your computer.

2. Restart your computer. When prompted to boot from the DVD, press any key. If you are not prompted to boot from the DVD, you might have to configure your computer's startup sequence.

   Windows Vista Setup loads.

3. When prompted, select your regional preferences and keyboard layout, and then click Next.

4. Click Repair Your Computer.

   System Recovery scans your hard disks for Windows Vista installations.

5. If the standard Windows Vista drivers do not detect a hard disk because the disk requires drivers that were not included with Windows Vista, click the Load Drivers button to load the drivers, and then select an operating system to repair. Click Next.

6. If Windows failed to start during its last attempt, Windows Vista launches the Startup Repair tool automatically. Otherwise, the Choose A Recovery Tool page appears. Click Startup Repair, and then follow the prompts that appear.

7. After the Startup Repair tool completes its diagnosis and repair, click Click Here For Diagnostic And Repair Details. At the bottom of the report, Startup Repair lists a root cause, if found, and any steps taken to repair the problem.

If Startup Repair does not repair the problem, repeat steps 1–5. Then, in the System Recovery Options dialog box, click System Restore and follow the prompts that appear. Windows Vista automatically creates a System Restore point before any update is installed, so restoring a System Restore point effectively uninstalls any updates.

Practice: Distribute Updates

In this lab, you configure a Windows Vista client to download updates from a WSUS server.

▶ **Practice 1: Distribute Updates with Windows Server Update Services**

In this practice, you install WSUS on a server, approve updates, and then configure a Windows Vista client to retrieve updates from that server.

1. Log on to a Windows Server 2003 computer as an administrator. If necessary, add the Application Server role (a requirement of WSUS).

2. Visit *http://www.microsoft.com/wsus/* to download and install the latest version of WSUS on your Windows Server 2003 computer.

3. Configure WSUS to install updates only after you approve them. Then, open the WSUS management webpage and approve several recent updates that need to be installed on your Windows Vista computer.

4. Log on to your Windows Vista computer. If you have installed any of the updates you approved within WSUS, uninstall them now using the Control Panel.

5. Click Start, type **Mmc**, and then press Enter.

6. An empty MMC console opens.

7. Click File, and then click Add/Remove Snap-In. From the Available Snap-Ins list, select Group Policy Object Editor. Click Add.

8. On the Welcome To The Group Policy Wizard page, click Browse. Select the Default Domain Policy, and then click OK. Click Finish.

9. In the Add Or Remove Snap-In dialog box, click OK.

10. In the Group Policy Object Editor snap-in, browse to Computer Configuration\Administrative Templates\Windows Components\Windows Update. Specify the policy settings shown in Table 5-2.

Table 5-2   Sample Policy Settings

Policy	Setting
Specify Intranet Microsoft Update Service Location	Enabled. Also, specify your WSUS server name in the Set The Intranet Update Service For Detecting Updates box.
Configure Automatic Updates	Enabled. Also, set Configure Automatic Updating to 4.
Enable Recommended Updates Via Automatic Updates	Enabled.
Enabling Windows Update Power Management To Automatically Wake Up The System To Install Scheduled Updates	Enabled.

11. Click start, type **gpupdate /force**, and press Enter. This retrieves the latest Group Policy settings from the domain controller.

12. Wait a few minutes for Windows Vista to display a notification bubble informing the user of the presence of updates. Allow them to be automatically installed and the computer to restart.

Lesson Summary

■ Microsoft provides three techniques for distributing updates: the Windows Update client (built into Windows Vista), Windows Server Update Services (a free tool that can be installed on a Windows Server 2003 computer), and Systems Management Tool (an enterprise software distribution tool). These tools are designed for small, medium, and large organizations, respectively.

■ You can install updates interactively using the Windows Update tool. This would be very time-consuming, however. Instead, you should configure Windows Update either using graphical tools or by using Group Policy settings. If you need to install updates immediately (for example, as soon as a user logs on), you can create scripts that install updates.

- If you have a problem installing an update, you can diagnose the problem by viewing the Windows Update history, by analyzing the %windir%\WindowsUpdate.log file, or by examining WSUS logs. You can often resolve simple problems by restarting the Windows Update service.

- If you discover a compatibility problem after deploying an update, you can manually remove it or use WSUS to uninstall it.

Lesson Review

You can use the following questions to test your knowledge of the information in Lesson 2, "Updating Software." The questions are also available on the companion CD if you prefer to review them in electronic form.

NOTE Answers

Answers to these questions and explanations of why each answer choice is right or wrong are located in the "Answers" section at the end of the book.

---

1. Which of the following would you recommend for distributing updates to a small business with five Windows Vista client computers?
    A. Instructing employees to manually launch Windows Update when they experience problems
    B. Configuring Windows Update on each computer to download updates directly from Microsoft
    C. Installing WSUS and configuring Windows Update to download updates from the WSUS server
    D. Deploying updates using SMS and WSUS

2. You are working for a medium-sized organization that manages about 100 client computers. The IT department insists on testing all updates before they are applied to computers. Which of the following would you recommend for distributing updates within this organization?
    A. Instructing employees to manually launch Windows Update when they experience problems
    B. Configuring Windows Update on each computer to download updates directly from Microsoft
    C. Installing WSUS and configuring Windows Update to download updates from the WSUS server
    D. Deploying updates using SMS and WSUS

3. You are creating a batch file that installs updates when a Windows Vista computer starts for the first time. How should you do this?

   A. Call Update.exe and provide the path to the update file.

   B. Call Msiexec.exe and provide the path to the update file.

   C. Run the executable file included with the update.

   D. Call Wusa.exe and provide the path to the update file.

Lesson 3: Troubleshooting Windows Defender

Windows Defender, which is also available as a free download for Windows XP, is a tool that informs users about changes programs make to their computers and gives users greater control over which programs are installed. One of Windows Defender's goals is to reduce the impact of spyware and potentially unwanted programs.

However, as with many features that improve security, Windows Defender can cause compatibility problems. This lesson describes how to diagnose and resolve problems using Windows Defender.

After this lesson, you will be able to:
- Troubleshoot problems downloading Windows Defender definitions.
- Identify changes that Windows Defender has blocked.
- Avoid Windows Defender alerts for necessary programs.

Estimated lesson time: 15 minutes

How to Troubleshoot Problems Downloading Definitions

If Windows Defender cannot download updates, the most likely cause is that a firewall is blocking access to Windows Update. Often, network administrators block Windows Update because the organization uses WSUS to approve updates, and client computers should never retrieve updates directly from Microsoft.

To identify the source of the problem, first examine the System event log for information about updates. To view the System event log, follow these steps:

1. Click Start. Right-click Computer, and then click Manage. Provide administrative credentials at the UAC prompt.
2. Under System Tools, expand Event Viewer, Windows Logs, and then select System.

Within the System event log, view events with a source of "Windows Defender." The following shows an event with an Event ID of 2000, in which Windows Defender successfully installed a definition update:

```
Windows Defender signature version has been updated.
    Current Signature Version: 1.15.2224.9
    Previous Signature Version: 1.15.2220.1
    Update Source: User
    Signature Type: AntiSpyware
    Update Type: Delta
    User: NT AUTHORITY\SYSTEM
    Current Engine Version: 1.1.2101.0
    Previous Engine Version: 1.1.2101.0
```

Windows Defender uses Event ID 2002 to log updates to the Windows Defender engine itself.

Next, examine the %windir%\WindowsUpdate.log file for error messages, and then search related Microsoft Knowledge Base articles for more information about errors in the Windows-Update.log file. This log file will typically have thousands of entries, but you can quickly find the Windows Defender–related entries by searching for the phrase "Windows Defender." The following example shows a successful Windows Defender definition update (with some fields omitted for simplicity):

```
DnldMgr      **************
DnldMgr      ** START **  DnldMgr: Downloading updates [CallerId = AutomaticUpdates]
DnldMgr      *********
DnldMgr       * Call ID = {DA5A072F-A9F9-43B4-B67B-5435D3301B01}
DnldMgr       * Priority = 2, Interactive = 0, Owner is system = 1,
 Explicit proxy = 0, Proxy session id = -1, ServiceId =
{7971F918-A847-4430-9279-4A52D1EFE18D}
DnldMgr       * Updates to download = 1
Agent         *  Title = Definition Update 1.14.1921.2 for Windows Defender (KB915597)
Agent         *  UpdateId = {EAF6F766-3E8B-4F45-B50F-9F30EF004044}.100
Agent         *     Bundles 1 updates:
Agent         *        {B47FBF08-503F-428C-96BB-11509FBDF3A5}.100
DtaStor      Update service properties: service registered with AU is
 {7971F918-A847-4430-9279-4A52D1EFE18D}
DnldMgr      ***********  DnldMgr: New download job [UpdateId =
{B47FBF08-503F-428C-96BB-11509FBDF3A5}.100]  ***********
DnldMgr       * BITS job initialized, JobId = {99086C54-EAD1-4093-A226-92F021003FCF}
DnldMgr       * Downloading from http://au.download.windowsupdate.com/msdownload/update
/v3-19990518/cabpool/mpas-fe_7e35a762b4eb36bdef0bcfddafbafc1dc750dd54.exe
 to C:\Windows\SoftwareDistribution\Download
\714d679af4e2c432e404256a7e7e0782
\7e35a762b4eb36bdef0bcfddafbafc1dc750dd54 (full file).
Agent        *********
Agent        ** END **  Agent: Downloading updates [CallerId = AutomaticUpdates]
Agent        **************
Report       REPORT EVENT: {712F6CF3-4DAC-4DBD-AA73-7AB74B5DC419}
2006-11-29 16:17:13:272-0500     1     147     101
{00000000-0000-0000-0000-000000000000}     0     0
AutomaticUpdates     Success     Software Synchronization
Windows Update Client successfully detected 2 updates.
```

As you can see from this log file excerpt, the Windows Defender update agent logs the exact source and destination location. If you experience a problem downloading definitions, you can attempt to download the specified update file (*http://au.download.windowsupdate.com/msdownload/update/v3-19990518/cabpool/mpas-fe_7e35a762b4eb36bdef0bcfddafbafc1dc750dd54.exe* in the sample log file) directly from the computer by using Internet Explorer. If you can't download the file in Internet Explorer, the Windows Defender update agent also won't be able to download the file.

If you can't manually reach the file by using Internet Explorer, verify the following:

- You can use a Web browser to reach the public Internet.

- If your computer is a member of a domain, it has the latest version of the domain Group Policy settings. You can refresh these settings by running **gpupdate /force** with administrative privileges. These settings might configure the Windows Update client to retrieve updates from a WSUS server instead of downloading them directly from Microsoft.

- Any firewalls allow HTTP requests to the windowsupdate.com domain and subdomains (that is, download.windowsupdate.com).

- Internet Explorer is not configured to block requests to the windowsupdate.com domain. To verify that the problem is not related to the Internet Explorer configuration, add http://*.windowsupdate.com/ to the computer's Trusted Sites list.

How to Identify Changes Blocked by Windows Defender

Windows Defender adds events to the System event log when it detects changes that require the user's confirmation. Within the System event log, view events with a source of "Windows Defender." The following shows an event with an Event ID of 3004, in which Windows Defender blocked the installation of a program that registered an icon in the system tray:

```
Windows Defender Real-Time Protection agent has detected changes.
Microsoft recommends you analyze the software that made these changes
for potential risks. You can use information about how these programs
 operate to choose whether to allow them to run or remove them from
your computer.  Allow changes only if you trust the program or the
software publisher. Windows Defender can't undo changes that you allow.
 For more information please see the following:
Not Applicable
     Scan ID: {14DC2DCC-A5C9-47CF-90EC-0B01BF0C7B58}
     User: computer\user
     Name: Unknown
     ID:
     Severity ID:
     Category ID:
     Path Found: regkey:HKLM\Software\Microsoft\Windows\CurrentVersion\Run
\\SigmatelSysTrayApp;runkey:HKLM\Software\Microsoft\Windows
\CurrentVersion\Run\\SigmatelSysTrayApp;file:C:\Windows\sttray.exe
     Alert Type: Unclassified software
     Detection Type:
```

Shortly thereafter, the System event log might show an event with an Event ID of 3005, which will show how the user chose to handle the change. The following example event demonstrates that the user approved the previous change, as evidenced by the Ignore action:

```
Windows Defender Real-Time Protection agent has taken action to protect
 this machine from spyware or other potentially unwanted software.
 For more information please see the following:
Not Applicable
```

```
Scan ID: {14DC2DCC-A5C9-47CF-90EC-0B01BF0C7B58}
User: computer\user
Name: Unknown
ID:
Severity ID:
Category ID:
Alert Type: Unclassified software
Action: Ignore
```

You can use the Scan ID to match related Windows Defender events.

How to Work Around False Alarms

It is possible for Windows Defender to warn users about a file that you consider to be trustworthy. You can selectively avoid these warnings by trusting specific files and folders or by disabling different types of real-time protection. Making these changes always requires administrator privileges.

The sections that follow describe different techniques for avoiding these false alarms. Whenever possible, ignore specific files and folders that cause problems in your organization. Only disable real-time protection or heuristics if the Windows Defender warnings are extremely problematic and frequent.

NOTE Tracking Windows Defender changes

Malware might attempt to change the Windows Defender configuration to avoid detection. So that you can track all Windows Defender configuration changes, it adds events with a source of "Windows Defender" and an Event ID of 5007 to the System event log.

How to Ignore Specific Files and Folders

To configure Windows Defender to ignore specific files or folders, follow these steps:

1. Start Windows Defender. Then, click Tools on the toolbar.
2. Click the Options link.
3. Scroll down to the Advanced Options section.
4. Under Do Not Scan These Files Or Locations, click the Add button. In the Browse For Files Or Folders dialog box, select the file or folder you want Windows Defender to ignore. Click OK.

NOTE Where to find Document folders

The Browse For Files Or Folders dialog box doesn't show users' Documents folders. However, you can find these under C:\Users by default.

---

5.   Click Save.

Windows Vista will not scan the specified files or folders.

How to Ignore Specific Types of Real-Time Protection

Windows Defender monitors many aspects of the operating system. You can disable any of these aspects if they prove problematic in your organization because of a large number of false alarms.

1.   Start Windows Defender. Then, click Tools on the toolbar.
2.   Click the Options link.
3.   Scroll down to the Real-Time Protection Options section. Clear the check boxes for the specific types of protection you want to disable:

❑   **Auto Start**   Monitors changes to the list of programs that start automatically when Windows starts or when a user logs on. This is one of the most important configuration settings to monitor; if unwanted software adds itself to the Auto Start list, it will continue to run after restarting the computer.

❑   **System Configuration (Settings)**   Monitors changes to the system configuration. This is important to leave enabled because many types of unwanted software attempt to change aspects of the computer's configuration.

❑   **Internet Explorer Add-Ons**   Monitors changes to Internet Explorer add-ons. Typically, you should leave this enabled even if you have a custom add-on that you need installed. If this is disabled, unwanted software might be able to install add-ons, which can change how webpages appear.

❑   **Internet Explorer Configurations (Settings)**   Monitors changes to Internet Explorer configuration. This is very important, because changes to the Web browser configuration could disable important security settings, exposing weaknesses that other unwanted software might abuse.

❑   **Internet Explorer Downloads**   Monitors files that users download with Internet Explorer. Many unwanted software installations are initiated when a user intentionally downloads a program because the program contains unwanted, bundled software. Disabling this type of real-time protection increases the likelihood of users accidentally installing unwanted software. You should clear this setting only if you have tightly configured Internet Explorer to prevent users from downloading unwanted software.

❑   **Services And Drivers**   Monitors additions and changes to services and drivers. Services and drivers can start automatically and run with system-level privileges, so it is important to keep this real-time protection enabled.

❑   **Application Execution**   Monitors when unknown applications run.

- ❑ **Application Registration**   Monitors when an application installs itself.
- ❑ **Windows Add-Ons**   Monitors new components that register themselves as add-ons.
- ❑ **Software That Has Not Yet Been Classified For Risks**   Monitors software that does not yet have a Windows Defender definition. This capability allows Windows Defender to detect potentially unwanted software that Microsoft has not analyzed.
- ❑ **Changes Made To Your Computer By Software That Is Permitted To Run**   This is the only form of real-time protection that is disabled by default. You can enable this for additional security; however, users can find it annoying.

4. Click Save.

Windows Vista will not perform the types of scans for which you cleared the associated check boxes. If you must disable some form of real-time protection to troubleshoot an issue, disable one form of real-time protection at a time and test the problem to verify that it is fixed. Avoid disabling real-time protection unnecessarily to reduce security risks.

How to Ignore False Alarms for Unknown Software

Windows Vista can use heuristics to alert users to unknown software running. Unknown software includes any program that Microsoft has not yet analyzed and provided a definition for. If you determine that Windows Defender frequently alerts users to problems detected using heuristics, you can disable this feature by clearing the Use Heuristics To Detect Potentially Harmful Or Unwanted Behavior By Software That Hasn't Been Analyzed For Risks check box on the Windows Defender Options page.

Practice: Distribute Updates and Analyze Windows Defender Problems

In this practice, you configure a Windows Vista client to download updates from a WSUS server. Then you simulate the installation of an application by monitoring changes to a file that Windows Defender protects.

▶ **Practice 1: Analyze Windows Defender Changes**

In this practice, you perform a change that Windows Defender will detect as potentially unwanted. Then you examine the System event log to identify how Windows Defender records the attempted change.

1. Log on to your Windows Vista test computer.
2. Click Start. Type **notepad %windir%\system32\drivers\etc\hosts**. Press Ctrl+Shift+Enter to run Notepad with administrative privileges. Respond to the UAC prompt.

    Notepad opens your Hosts file, which is one of the files Windows Defender monitors.

3. At the top of the file, type **# Testing Windows Defender**. Save the file and close Notepad.

4. Click Start, right-click Computer, and then click Manage. Respond to the UAC prompt. Windows Vista opens Computer Management.

5. Expand Event Viewer, Windows Logs, and then select System.

6. Identify the Windows Defender event that describes the change you made to the Hosts file.

In production environments you can use this technique to identify important or dangerous change attempts that Windows Defender might have blocked.

Lesson Summary

- To troubleshoot problems downloading updated Windows Defender definitions, view the System event log. For more detailed information, analyze the %windir%\Windows-update.log file.

- To identify changes that Windows Defender has blocked, search the System event log for events with a source of "Windows Defender."

- You should test programs before deploying them to Windows Vista clients to verify that they work properly with Windows Defender. If Windows Defender does block legitimate changes made by one of your programs, you can configure Windows Defender to ignore the change to prevent problems when you deploy the program.

Lesson Review

You can use the following questions to test your knowledge of the information in Lesson 3, "Troubleshooting Windows Defender." The questions are also available on the companion CD if you prefer to review them in electronic form.

NOTE Answers

Answers to these questions and explanations of why each answer choice is right or wrong are located in the "Answers" section at the end of the book.

1. A user complains that an application installed incorrectly. How can you determine whether Windows Defender blocked any aspect of the application installation? (Choose two. Each correct answer is a complete solution.)

   A. Examine the System event log.

   B. Examine the Application event log.

   C. Examine the Security event log.

   D. View the Windows Defender History.

2. Where would you look to identify whether Windows Defender was experiencing problems downloading updated definitions from Microsoft?

   A. The System event log

   B. The Application event log

   C. The Security event log

   D. The Windows Defender History

3. Which of the following types of changes might Windows Defender alert the user to? (Choose all that apply.)

   A. A new service being installed

   B. A program that automatically starts

   C. A Microsoft Word document that contains a macro

   D. An Internet Explorer Add-on being installed

Lesson 4: Supporting Applications

Windows Vista alone isn't enough for most users—they need applications as well. Although every application has unique support requirements, all applications have some things in common. This lesson describes the most common way to deploy, install, and uninstall applications and explains how to configure multiple monitors to give users more desktop space and how to configure the Windows Sidebar.

> **After this lesson, you will be able to:**
> - Deploy and install applications.
> - Configure and maintain applications.
> - Run the Microsoft Support Diagnostic Tool.
>
> **Estimated lesson time: 15 minutes**

Deploying Applications

Before users can run most applications, they must be installed. To simplify installation, Windows Vista (as well as earlier versions of Windows) includes Windows Installer. Windows Installer allows you to install programs manually, from a script, or using Group Policy software distribution. The sections that follow provide an overview of Windows Installer and instructions for installing Windows Installer packages.

Windows Installer

Windows Installer is a Windows component that makes it easy to install, update, and uninstall programs. Windows Installer relies on a special file format with an .MSI file extension that contains all the files and settings required to install an application. Almost all applications developed in recent years include an .MSI file to allow the application to be deployed with Windows Installer.

If an application provides a Windows Installer package, you can deploy it in several ways:

- Manually, using a wizard interface. You can start the manual setup simply by double-clicking the .MSI file from the computer you want to install the program on. This technique resembles running the Setup.exe file included with most software installer's programs.
- Automatically, from a script using the MsiExec.exe tool. All Windows Installer packages can be automatically installed without prompting the user.
- Using Group Policy Software Distribution. Group Policy only supports distributing .MSI files, so many organizations often repackage an application in an .MSI file if it does not already include one.

MORE INFO   Repackaging programs

For more information about repackaging programs, refer to the Microsoft Solution Accelerator for Business Desktop Deployment 2007 at *http://www.microsoft.com/technet/desktopdeployment/bdd/2007/*.

- Using Microsoft Systems Management Server (SMS).

MORE INFO   SMS

For more information about SMS, visit *http://www.microsoft.com/sms*.

Using the MsiExec.exe Tool

You can use MsiExec.exe to install Windows Installer packages automatically. For example, to install a Windows Installer package named Update.MSI without prompting the user, you would run the following command:

```
Msiexec /package Update.msi /quiet
```

Similarly, to uninstall the same file, you would run the following command:

```
Msiexec /uninstall Update.msi /quiet
```

MsiExec.exe also supports the following useful parameters:

- **/norestart**   Prevents Windows from restarting, even if the application requires it. Use this parameter when you will be installing several programs in sequence and you don't want Windows to restart until after all programs have been installed.
- **/promptrestart**   Prompts the user to restart the computer only if a restart is necessary.
- **/forcerestart**   Always restarts the computer after installation, even if it is not required. You might use this if you previously used /norestart to install another program.

If you experience a problem during an automatic installation with the /quiet parameter, MsiExec does not inform the user of the problem; it just fails quietly. By default, MsiExec adds events to the Application event log with a source of MsiInstaller after any successful installation or unsuccessful installation attempt. For example, event ID 11925 indicates that an installation failed because the package requires administrative privileges to install, and the user lacked those privileges, and it would include a description resembling the following:

```
Product: Microsoft Baseline Security Analyzer 2.1 -- Error 1925.
You do not have sufficient privileges to complete this installation
for all users of the machine.  Log on as administrator and then
retry this installation.
```

Similarly, Event ID 11730 indicates that an uninstallation failed because the user lacked sufficient privileges, and it includes a description resembling the following:

```
Product: Microsoft Baseline Security Analyzer 2.1 -- Error 1730.
You must be an Administrator to remove this application. To remove
this application, you can log on as an Administrator, or contact your technical support group
for assistance.
```

A successful installation generates a message with Event ID 11707, with a description resembling the following:

```
Product: Microsoft Baseline Security Analyzer 2.1 -
Installation completed successfully.
```

The Application event log provides most of the troubleshooting information you will need. However, you can use the */l <log_file_name>* parameter with MsiExec to create a detailed text log file, as the following example demonstrates. Typically, this information contains the same information as the events in the Application event log.

```
Msiexec /uninstall Update.msi /quiet /l install_log.txt
```

For complete usage information, click Start, type **Msiexec**, and then press Enter.

Using Group Policy Software Distribution

In Active Directory environments, you can use Group Policy Software Distribution to deploy Windows Installer packages to member computers. To deploy a package using Group Policy, follow these steps:

1. Open the Group Policy Object Editor for the Group Policy Object you want to use to distribute the software.
2. Expand either Computer Configuration or User Configuration, and then select Software Settings.
3. Right-click Software Installation, click New, and then click Package.
4. In the Open dialog box, type the UNC path to the .MSI package you want to deploy, and then click Open. It's important that you specify the location with a UNC path (such as *server**share**package.msi*) that all clients can also use to access the .MSI file.
5. In the Deploy Software dialog box, select one of the following options:
   - ❑ **Published**   Make the application available to users from the Control Panel. Publishing is an option only when deploying the package using the User Configuration node of the Group Policy object.
   - ❑ **Assigned**   Automatically install the application with the default settings the next time Group Policy is applied. If you added the package under Computer Configuration, it will be installed regardless of which user logs on. If you install the package under User Configuration, it will be installed only when that user logs on.

❑ **Advanced** Configure additional options by immediately viewing the package properties. You can also configure settings by viewing the package properties later.

6. Click OK.

7. In the left pane of the Group Policy Object Editor, click Software Installation. You will see your Windows Installer package in the right pane.

To edit the settings of a package after adding it to Group Policy, click the Software Installation node in the Group Policy Object Editor. In the right pane, right-click the package, and then click Properties.

One of the most useful settings is found on the Deployment tab; by selecting the Uninstall This Application When It Falls Out Of The Scope Of Management check box, you configure Group Policy to automatically remove the program if the Group Policy object no longer applies to a user or computer. For example, you could use this to automatically uninstall accounting software if a member of the Accounting organizational unit (OU) moved to the Human Resources OU.

Configuring Applications and the Desktop Environment

Some applications and environments require special configuration, such as changing environment variables. Another common configuration request is using multiple monitors, enabling users to maximize two or more windows on different displays. Additionally, Windows Vista includes a new application platform called Windows Sidebar that you need to know how to disable or configure. The sections that follow describe each of these features.

Configuring Environment Variables

Environment variables are settings that are universal to Windows or to a user that applications reference to identify the location of system files, user documents, temporary files, and many other settings. Typically, you should leave environment variables at their default settings to provide the greatest application compatibility because some applications simply assume that the user has environment variables set to the default values.

You can view environment variables from a command prompt by running the Set command, as the following example shows:

```
C:\>Set
ALLUSERSPROFILE=C:\ProgramData
APPDATA=C:\Users\user1\AppData\Roaming
CommonProgramFiles=C:\Program Files\Common Files
COMPUTERNAME=D820
ComSpec=C:\Windows\system32\cmd.exe
HOMEDRIVE=C:
HOMEPATH=\Users\user1
LOCALAPPDATA=C:\Users\user1\AppData\Local
LOGONSERVER=\\D820
```

```
NUMBER_OF_PROCESSORS=2
Path=C:\Windows\system32;C:\Windows;C:\Program Files\Microsoft SQL Server\90\DTS\Binn\;
ProgramData=C:\ProgramData
ProgramFiles=C:\Program Files
PUBLIC=C:\Users\Public
SystemDrive=C:
SystemRoot=C:\Windows
TEMP=C:\Users\user1\AppData\Local\Temp
TMP=C:\Users\user1\AppData\Local\Temp
USERDOMAIN=D820
USERNAME=user1
USERPROFILE=C:\Users\user1
windir=C:\Windows
```

You can also use the Set command to change environment variables. For example, to change the temporary folder to C:\Temp for the current user, you could run the following command:

```
set TEMP=C:\temp
```

You can also change environment variables using the System Properties dialog box by following these steps:

1. Click Start, right-click Computer, and then click Properties.
2. Click the Advanced System Settings link, and then respond to the UAC prompt that appears.
3. Click the Advanced tab, and then click the Environment Variables button.
4. The Environment Variables dialog box appears, as shown in Figure 5-14.

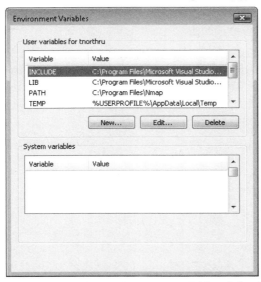

Figure 5-14   The Environment Variables dialog box

5. Select the environment variable you want to change, and then click Edit.

6. Type the new value, and then click OK.

7. Click OK again to close the Environment Variables dialog box, and then click OK again to close the System Properties dialog box.

You can reference environment variables in scripts by surrounding the environment variable name with percent symbols. For example, running the following command at a command prompt would display the name of the current domain:

```
echo %userdomain%
```

Configuring Multiple Monitors

One of the best ways to increase the usefulness of Windows is to double the desktop space by adding a second monitor. If you do add a second monitor, you have two options for configuring it:

- **Mirrored** The same desktop shows on both monitors. This is primarily useful for putting on a presentation when a mobile computer is connected to a projector. By mirroring both screens, the presenter can face the audience and look at the built-in display while being assured that the display on the projector matches exactly. To configure an extended desktop, open the Display Properties dialog box, select the new monitor, and then clear the Extend The Desktop Onto This Monitor check box.

- **Extended desktop** Windows Vista extends the desktop across two monitors, allowing the user to move windows between the displays. For example, a user could keep e-mail open on one screen and Microsoft Word on another, or a developer could keep his or her development open on one screen and reference files on the other. To configure an extended desktop, open the Display Properties dialog box, select the new monitor, and then select the Extend The Desktop Onto This Monitor check box. Then, click the monitor that you want to have the taskbar and Start menu and select the This Is My Main Monitor check box.

To open the Display Properties dialog box, follow these steps:

1. Click Start, and then click Control Panel.

2. Under Appearance And Personalization, click the Adjust Screen Resolution link.

3. Make your configuration changes, and then click OK.

Configuring Windows Sidebar

Windows Sidebar provides a platform for Windows Sidebar Gadgets, as shown in Figure 5-15. Gadgets are visually small applications that reside on the Sidebar or that you can remove to float on the desktop. Windows Vista includes several gadgets, and you can download others from *http://gallery.live.com/results.aspx?l=1*.

Figure 5-15   Windows Sidebar Gadgets

You can control the Sidebar by using Group Policy. Sidebar Group Policy settings are located in both Computer Configuration and User Configuration at Administrative Templates\Windows Components\Windows Sidebar. You can configure the following settings:

- **Override The More Gadgets Link**   By right-clicking the Sidebar, clicking Add Gadgets, and then clicking Get More Gadgets Online, users visit a Microsoft site where they can download new gadgets. Enable this setting to provide your own link for more gadgets (for example, to allow users to download gadgets from an intranet website).
- **Turn Off Windows Sidebar**   Enable this setting to prevent Windows Sidebar from running.
- **Disable Unpacking And Installation Of Gadgets That Are Not Digitally Signed**   Enable this setting to prevent Windows Sidebar from running gadgets that are not digitally signed. If you leave this setting at the default (disabled), Sidebar will warn users that a gadget is not digitally signed but still allow it to be installed.
- **Turn Off User Installed Windows Sidebar Gadgets**   Enable this setting to prevent users from installing their own gadgets.

The Microsoft Support Diagnostic Tool

The Microsoft Support Diagnostic Tool (MSDT) is a Windows Vista feature that Microsoft Support might instruct you to use to gather information about a problem. This can speed the troubleshooting process by decreasing the amount of information users must convey using the phone or e-mail. The tool collects some information by prompting the user and also gathers other information automatically based on computer settings and recorded events. Microsoft Support will provide a pass key and incident number for the user to enter into the tool to allow the tool to retrieve problem-specific configuration settings.

If configured by Microsoft Support, MSDT will download and run other diagnostic tools. After gathering the required information, MSDT can send the information to Microsoft across the Internet. If the computer with the problem isn't connected to the Internet, you can save the data to removable storage, such as a universal serial bus (USB) flash drive, and then send the data to Microsoft using a different computer.

You need to start MSDT only when instructed by Microsoft Support. In that case, they will direct you to the MSDT webpage, which will allow you to launch the tool. You must have administrative privileges to launch MSDT (you will receive a User Account Control prompt). To manually run MSDT, follow these steps:

1. Click Start, type **MSDT**, and then press Enter.
2. Respond to the UAC prompt that appears.
   MSDT appears.
3. On the Which Computer Has A Problem page, click This Computer or A Different Computer.
4. On the Type Your Pass Key page, type the pass key provided by Microsoft support.
   MSDT will connect to Microsoft to retrieve problem-specific information and diagnostic tools.
5. Follow the prompts that appear (the specific steps will vary depending on the nature of the problem).

Practice: Automating Software Installations

In this practice, you automate a software installation using a batch file, which you might do in a production environment to automatically install a program using a logon script.

▶ **Practice 1: Automatically Installing a Windows Installer Package**

In this practice, you use MsiExec to automatically install and then uninstall a Windows Installer package using a script.

1. Visit *http://www.microsoft.com/mbsa/* and download the latest version of the Microsoft Baseline Security Advisor (MBSA) from Microsoft. Save it to your Windows Vista computer without running it. Make note of the name and the path of the .MSI file.
2. Open Notepad and create a new batch file named InstallApp.bat. Save the file in your Documents folder.
3. Use Notepad to add the following line to your batch file and save the file:
   msiexec /package <*path*>\<*filename*>.msi /passive

   For example, if you saved the MBSA .MSI file as mbsasetup-en.msi in the root of your C drive, you would add the following line to your batch file:
   ```
   msiexec /package C:\mbsasetup-en.msi /passive
   ```

4. Now, double-click the InstallApp.bat file from Explorer. Wait a few moments while Windows Installer begins to install MBSA. Respond to the UAC prompt that appears. Because you used the /passive parameter, Windows Installer will display a progress bar and a UAC prompt, but it will not prompt you for any configuration information. Instead, Windows Installer will use the default settings.

5. After several minutes, verify that MBSA is installed correctly by clicking Start, All Programs, and then clicking Microsoft Baseline Security Advisor to launch the tool. Close the tool after you verify that it runs correctly.

6. Use Notepad to add the replace the current command in your batch file with the following command:

   msiexec /uninstall *<path>**<filename>*.msi /quiet

7. Now, right-click the InstallApp.bat file in Explorer, and then click Run As Administrator. Respond to the UAC prompt that appears. Because you are using /quiet this time, Windows Installer cannot provide a UAC prompt to gain administrative credentials, and you must run it with sufficient privileges.

   The batch file starts Windows Installer, which uninstalls MBSA without prompting you.

8. Wait several minutes, and then verify that MBSA was uninstalled correctly by looking for the shortcut on the Start menu.

Lesson Summary

- Windows Installer simplifies the installation and management of Windows applications. Applications are distributed in Windows Installer packages, which are files that use an .MSI file extension. Although you can install a Windows Installer package by simply double-clicking it, you can also automate the installation using the MsiExec command-line tool or by using Group Policy software distribution.

- Windows Vista stores some computer-wide and user-wide settings in environment variables. For example, applications can determine the current temporary directory by accessing the %TEMP% environment variable. You can change environment variables using the Set command-line utility or using the System Properties dialog box. If you need to configure a user for multiple monitors side-by-side, view the Desktop Properties dialog box, select the new monitor, and then select the Extend The Desktop Onto This Monitor check box. If a user wants to mirror the display on a projector, clear that check box.

- If you need to escalate a problem to Microsoft Support, they might request that you run the Microsoft Support Diagnostic Tool. Although the specific steps are problem-specific, you can start the tool by clicking Start, typing **MSDT**, and then pressing Enter.

Lesson Review

You can use the following questions to test your knowledge of the information in Lesson 4, "Supporting Applications." The questions are also available on the companion CD if you prefer to review them in electronic form.

NOTE Answers

Answers to these questions and explanations of why each answer choice is right or wrong are located in the "Answers" section at the end of the book.

---

1. You are a desktop support engineer. You need to distribute a Windows Installer package to the mobile computer user's OU in your Active Directory domain. To prevent the large download from occurring when users are connected to the internal network using a low-bandwidth connection, you want users to manually initiate the installation. Which of the following software distribution options should you choose?

   A. Published under Computer Configuration

   B. Published under User Configuration

   C. Assigned under Computer Configuration

   D. Assigned under User Configuration

2. You are a Windows Vista systems administrator. You need to create a logon script that installs a Windows Installer package without prompting the user. Which of the following tools would you use to install the package?

   A. FC

   B. RACAgent

   C. WUAgent

   D. MSIExec

3. Your chief security officer has decided that users should not be able to run any Windows Sidebar Gadgets. Which is the most effective way to implement this?

   A. In the Default Domain Group Policy Object, disable the Turn Off User Installed Windows Sidebar Gadgets policy.

   B. In the Default Domain Group Policy Object, enable the Turn Off User Installed Windows Sidebar Gadgets policy.

   C. In the Default Domain Group Policy Object, enable the Turn Off Windows Sidebar policy.

   D. Use a software restriction to block all *.gadget programs.

Chapter Review

To further practice and reinforce the skills you learned in this chapter, you can

- Review the chapter summary.
- Review the list of key terms introduced in this chapter.
- Complete the case scenarios. These scenarios set up real-world situations involving the topics of this chapter and ask you to create a solution.
- Complete the suggested practices.
- Take a practice test.

Chapter Summary

- Internet Explorer is one of the most important tools in Windows Vista because it provides users access to Web applications and the Internet. Therefore, it's vital that you know how to configure Internet Explorer and troubleshoot common problems. Historically, many users have experienced problems with add-ons, which extend Internet Explorer's capabilities but also have the potential to behave unreliably or maliciously. Fortunately, Internet Explorer gives administrators complete control over which add-ons can be installed, as well as the capability to quickly start Internet Explorer without any add-ons. To reduce security risks when using Internet Explorer, Protected Mode runs Internet Explorer with minimal privileges. If a webpage, Internet Explorer, an add-on, or any process launched from within Internet Explorer requires elevated privileges, the elevation must be approved before Internet Explorer can take action. To provide privacy and authentication, many websites use SSL certificates. Therefore, it's vital that you understand the causes of common certificate problems and how to fix these problems.

- Over time, computers can become less secure because attackers might discover new vulnerabilities. To maintain the security of your computers, you must regularly install updates. Microsoft provides several techniques for distributing updates throughout an organization. You should be familiar with these techniques, as well as the tools for troubleshooting problems deploying updates.

- To reduce the risk of potentially unwanted software, Windows Defender prompts users when some types of software attempt to make changes. Users can then choose to allow or block a change. To avoid compatibility problems, you should test applications with Windows Defender enabled and configure Windows Defender to ignore changes made by the applications your users require.

- Windows Installer makes it much simpler to install programs on Windows Vista. Most programs include a Windows Installer package in an .MSI file. With this .MSI file, you can manually install it just like a standard Setup.exe file, you can distribute it using Group Policy software distribution, or you can install it using the MsiExec.exe command-line tool. Applications use environment variables to determine computer settings such as the user's home directory, the location of system files, and where temporary files should be stored.

Key Terms

Do you know what these key terms mean? You can check your answers by looking up the terms in the glossary at the end of the book.

- ActiveX
- Mandatory Integrity Control (MIC)
- Protected Mode
- Protected Mode Compatibility Layer
- Restart Manager
- Windows Defender
- Windows Server Update Services (WSUS)

Case Scenarios

In the following case scenarios, you will apply what you've learned about how to manage Internet Explorer and Windows Update. You can find answers to these questions in the "Answers" section at the end of this book.

Case Scenario 1: Unwanted Internet Explorer Add-On

You are a systems administrator for Humongous Insurance. Recently, one of your brokers called the support desk because he was experiencing odd problems when using Internet Explorer. Specifically, his home page had changed, and the pop-up blocker no longer seemed to be working.

Your manager is concerned that this will be more than an isolated incident and asks you to interview key people and then come to his office to make recommendations about how to deal with this type of problem in the future.

Interviews

Following is a list of company personnel interviewed and their statements:

- **David Barber, Broker**   "I had installed an add-on because it said it would make browsing the Web faster. I didn't notice any improvement. After that, though, my Internet Explorer home page changed, and I began to get a lot of advertisements popping up on my screen."

- **Julian Price, Internet Development Project Manager**   "We recently converted all of our internal software to the ASP.NET Web application platform. To do some of the more complicated stuff, we install custom client-side add-ons in Internet Explorer. So, whatever you do, don't block all add-ons. We use add-ons internally, and we update them regularly, so we really need users to be able to install the add-ons automatically."

Questions

Answer the following questions for your manager:

1. If this comes up again, what's the best way to remove the unwanted add-on?
2. Are there any features enabled by default in Windows Vista that protect users from unwanted add-ons? What are they?
3. What's the best way to prevent unwanted add-ons in the future?

Case Scenario 2: Distribute Updates

You are a systems administrator working at the administrative offices of Fourth Coffee, a small shop with three Windows XP computers, three Windows Vista computers, and a Windows Server 2003 domain controller. Recently, an update caused a compatibility problem with Fourth Coffee's internal accounting program. Currently, all computers are configured to download updates from Microsoft and automatically install them overnight.

Your manager has asked you to find a way to test updates before they're deployed to the computers in your organization.

Questions

Answer the following questions for your manager:

1. How can you test updates before they're deployed?
2. Would your recommended deployment technology require any infrastructure?
3. Will your recommended deployment technology work with both the Windows XP and Windows Vista computers?
4. How can you configure the client computers to use your new deployment technology?

Suggested Practices

To successfully master the objectives covered by this chapter, complete the following tasks.

Configuring and Troubleshooting Internet Explorer

For this task, you should complete at least Practices 1 through 3. If you want in-depth knowledge of how Internet Explorer handles both legitimate and malicious changes, complete Practice 4 as well.

- **Practice 1: Manage Add-ons**   On your day-to-day computer, open Internet Explorer and view the Manage Add-Ons dialog box. Examine the different add-ons that are already installed.

- **Practice 2: Browsing Without Add-ons**   Launch Internet Explorer with add-ons disabled. Browse to your favorite websites and notice any differences caused by the missing add-ons.

- **Practice 3: Applications that Internet Explorer Has Virtualized**   On your day-to-day computer, use Explorer to browse \%userprofile%\AppData\Local\Microsoft\Windows\Temporary Internet Files\Virtualized\ and its subfolders. Make note of the applications that the Internet Explorer compatibility layer has virtualized and the types of files that were virtualized.

- **Practice 4: Browsing Dangerous Websites**   Perform a fresh installation of Windows Vista. Browse to your favorite websites and notice how the Information Bar, Protected Mode, and UAC work together to protect the user from potentially unwanted add-ons. Next, use Internet Explorer to browse to potentially dangerous websites that might try to install malicious software and view how Internet Explorer responds (hint: search for combinations of words such as "crack," "hack," "warez," and "serials").

Updating Software

For this task, you should complete all three practices to gain experience analyzing update installations.

- **Practice 1: Remove an Update**   Uninstall a recent update, and then reinstall it.
- **Practice 2: View the System Event Log**   Examine the System event log and identify any updates that have been recently installed.
- **Practice 3: Examine the WindowsUpdate.log File**   Examine the %windir%\WindowsUpdate.log file and identify any updates that have been recently installed.

Troubleshoot Windows Defender issues

For this task, you should complete all three practices to gain experience with Windows Defender.

- **Practice 1** On a test computer with Windows Defender enabled, download and install a program that includes potentially unwanted software. For example, you might install a peer-to-peer file sharing application. Monitor Windows Defender notifications. Choose to reject any changes made by the potentially unwanted software.

- **Practice 2** Using the same potentially unwanted software, configure Windows Defender to ignore the software so that it installs correctly without alerting the user.

- **Practice 3** Examine the Windows Defender history and the System event log to analyze changes monitored by Windows Defender during the software installation.

Take a Practice Test

The practice tests on this book's companion CD offer many options. For example, you can test yourself on just the content covered in this chapter, or you can test yourself on all the 70-622 certification exam content. You can set up the test so that it closely simulates the experience of taking a certification exam, or you can set it up in study mode so that you can look at the correct answers and explanations after you answer each question.

MORE INFO   Practice tests

For details about all the practice test options available, see "How to Use the Practice Tests" in this book's Introduction.

Chapter 6
Monitoring Client Computers

Windows Vista should be the most reliable version of Windows ever. However, computers are never perfect—the combination of complex hardware, widely varying accessories, and custom applications inevitably leads to problems. Because you can't create a completely problem-free IT environment, you must plan to quickly identify and resolve problems when they do occur. Windows Vista includes several features that enable administrators to monitor and respond to problems.

First, Windows Vista can forward events between computers, enabling you to collect on your workstation significant events from across your network. Additionally, you can monitor minute details of computers in real time using Performance Monitor. With Reliability Monitor, you can view a computer's history of changes and problems, which will often identify the source of a problem when the user can't list possible causes. If Reliability Monitor doesn't point to a cause, you can use data collector sets to gather configuration data and performance information about a computer for later analysis. Finally, for reoccurring problems, you can use Task Scheduler to automatically respond to events or proactively run tools that help to prevent problems.

Exam objectives in this chapter:
- Configure and troubleshoot Event Forwarding.
- Troubleshoot performance and reliability issues.
- Configure and manage the Task Scheduler.

Lessons in this chapter:

Before You Begin

To complete the lessons in this chapter, you should be familiar with Windows Vista and be comfortable with the following tasks:

- Installing Windows Vista and joining a domain
- Configuring Group Policy settings
- Performing basic configuration tasks of Windows Server 2003 domain controllers

To complete Practice 1 in Lesson 1, you'll need:

- Two Windows Vista Enterprise, Business, or Ultimate client computers named Vista1 and Vista2.

Lesson 1: Monitoring Events in an Enterprise

In Windows both the operating system and applications add events to event logs. Most of these events are informational (such as an event indicating that the computer is starting up) and can be safely ignored. However, very important events are often buried within thousands of insignificant events. These important events might indicate an impending hard disk failure, a security compromise, or a user who cannot access critical network resources.

Every Windows computer has a local event log. Because enterprises often have thousands of computers, each with its own local event log, monitoring significant events was very difficult with earlier versions of Windows. Event forwarding in Windows Vista makes it much easier for enterprises to manage local event logs. With event forwarding, you can configure Windows Vista computers to forward important events to a central location. You can then more easily monitor and respond to these centralized events.

This lesson describes how to configure and manage event forwarding.

After this lesson, you will be able to:
- Describe how Windows Vista improves event logging.
- Describe how event forwarding works.
- Configure event forwarding in Active Directory directory service environments.
- Configure event forwarding in workgroup environments.
- Troubleshoot event forwarding.

Estimated lesson time: 30 minutes

Event Logging Improvements in Windows Vista

As part of Microsoft's efforts to make Windows Vista more manageable in enterprise environments, Windows Vista includes several important improvements to event logging:

- **Overview And Summary pane**   Event Viewer now provides a summary of all logs, as shown in Figure 6-1.

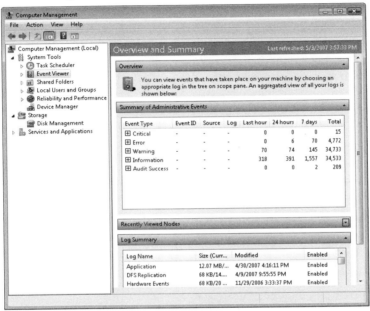

Figure 6-1   The Overview And Summary pane, which is new to Event Viewer in Windows Vista

- **More granular log files**   Besides the traditional System, Security, and Application logs, Windows Vista includes dozens of new component-specific event logs. Some examples of these new logs are: Backup, Diagnostics-Networking, Group Policy, OfflineFiles, RemoteAssistance, and WindowsUpdateClient.

- **Event forwarding**   If a new event matches criteria you specify, Windows Vista can forward it to a remote computer.

- **Event triggers**   If a new event matches criteria you specify, Windows Vista can respond to the event by sending an e-mail or running a program. This enables you to automatically respond to events. For example, you might create a script that runs Disk Cleanup if an event indicating low disk space appears.

- **Event filtering**   You can create custom filters in Event Viewer that show only the events you are most interested in. You can filter events by severity, source, Event ID, and several other criteria.

- **Custom views** You can create custom log files by specifying filtering criteria that matches events you are most interested in.
- **Trace and debug logs** In addition to the standard logs, Windows Vista includes trace and debug logs that are disabled and hidden by default. If you enable and show these logs, you can view detailed information that can be useful to developers when trouble-shooting complex problems.

How Event Forwarding Works

Event forwarding uses Hypertext Transfer Protocol (HTTP) or Hypertext Transfer Protocol Secure (HTTPS) (the same protocol used to browse websites) to send events from a client computer (the computer that is configured to forward events) to a server (the computer that is configured to collect events). Even though HTTP is normally unencrypted, event forwarding sends communications encrypted with the Microsoft Negotiate security support provider (SSP) in workgroup environments or the Microsoft Kerberos SSP in domain environments. HTTPS uses a Secure Sockets Layer (SSL) certificate (which you will need to generate) to provide an additional layer of encryption. This additional layer of encryption is unnecessary in most environments.

MORE INFO SSP providers

For more information about SSP providers, read *http://msdn2.microsoft.com/en-us/library /aa380502.aspx*.

Exam Tip For the exam, the most important thing to remember is that event forwarding uses encryption even if you choose the HTTP protocol. That's counter-intuitive because when you use HTTP to browse the Web, it's always unencrypted.

How to Configure Event Forwarding in Active Directory Domains

To forward events, you must configure both the forwarding and collecting computers. The forwarding computer is the computer that generates the events, and the collecting computer is the management workstation that administrators will use to monitor events. The configuration you create for forwarding and collecting events is called an event subscription.

Event forwarding is not enabled by default on Windows Vista. Before you can use event forwarding, both the forwarding and collecting computer must have two services running:

- Windows Remote Management
- Windows Event Collector

Additionally, the forwarding computer must have a Windows Firewall exception for the HTTP protocol. Depending on the event delivery optimization technique you choose, you might also have to configure a Windows Firewall exception for the collecting computer. Fortunately, Windows Vista provides tools that automate the configuration of forwarding and collecting computers.

The sections that follow describe step-by-step how to configure computers for event forwarding.

How to Configure the Forwarding Computer

To configure a Windows Vista computer to forward events, follow these steps on the forwarding computer:

1. Open an elevated command prompt by clicking Start, typing **cmd**, and pressing Ctrl+Shift+Enter. Respond to the User Account Control (UAC) prompt that appears.

2. At the command prompt, run the following command to configure the Windows Remote Management service:

   ```
   C:\>winrm quickconfig
   WinRM is not set up to allow remote access to this machine for management.
   The following changes must be made:

   Set the WinRM service type to delayed auto start.
   Start the WinRM service.
   Create a WinRM listener on HTTP://* to accept WS-Man requests to any IP on this
   machine.
   Enable the WinRM firewall exception.

   Make these changes [y/n]?
   ```

3. Type **Y**, and then press Enter.

   WinRm (the Windows Remote Management command-line tool) configures the computer to accept WS-Management requests from other computers. This involves making the following changes:

   ❑ Sets the Windows Remote Management (WS-Management) service to Automatic (Delayed Start) and starts the service.

   ❑ Configures a Windows Remote Management HTTP listener.

   ❑ Creates a Windows Firewall exception to allow incoming connections to the Windows Remote Management service using HTTP on Transmission Control Protocol (TCP) port 80. This exception applies only to the Domain and Private profiles; traffic will still be blocked while the computer is connected to Public networks.

Next, you must add the computer account of the collector computer to the local Administrators group on each of the forwarding computers by following these steps on the forwarding computer:

1. Click Start, right-click Computer, and then click Manage. Respond to the UAC prompt that appears.

2. Under System Tools, expand Local Users And Groups. Then, select Groups. Double-click Event Log Readers.

3. In the Event Log Readers Properties dialog box, click Add.

4. In the Select Users, Computers, Or Groups dialog box, click the Object Types button. By default, it searches only Users and Groups. However, we need to add the collecting computer account. Select the Computers check box and clear the Groups and Users check boxes. Click OK.

5. In the Select Users, Computers, Or Groups dialog box, type the name of the collecting computer. Then, click OK.

6. Click OK again to close the Event Log Readers Properties dialog box.

Alternatively, you could perform this step from an elevated command prompt or a batch file by running the following command:

```
Net localgroup "Event Log Readers" <computer_name>$@<domain_name> /add
```

For example, to add the computer VISTA1 in the nwtraders.msft domain, you would run the following command:

```
Net localgroup "Event Log Readers" vista1$@nwtraders.msft /add
The command completed successfully.
```

How to Configure the Collecting Computer

To configure a Windows Vista computer to collect events, follow these steps:

1. Open an elevated command prompt by clicking Start, typing **cmd**, and pressing Ctrl+Shift+Enter. Respond to the UAC prompt that appears.

2. At the command prompt, run the following command to configure the Windows Event Collector service:

```
wecutil qc
```

Windows Server 2008 will include the ability to collect forwarded events also. However, versions of Windows released prior to Windows Vista do not support acting as a collecting computer or as a forwarding computer.

How to Create an Event Subscription

Subscriptions, as shown in Figure 6-2, are configured on a collecting computer and retrieve events from forwarding computers.

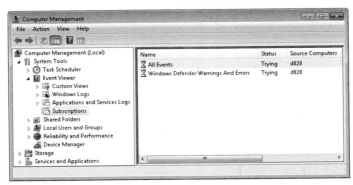

Figure 6-2   Subscriptions forward events to a management computer

To create a subscription on a collecting computer, follow these steps:

1. In Event Viewer, right-click Subscriptions, and then click Create Subscription.

2. In the Event Viewer dialog box, click Yes to configure the Windows Event Collector service, as shown in Figure 6-3 (if prompted).

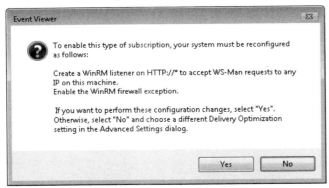

Figure 6-3   Pushing events from the forwarding computer to the collecting computer

•   The Subscription Properties dialog box appears.

3. In the Subscription Name box, type a name for the subscription. Optionally, type a description.

4. Optionally, click the Destination Log list and select the log in which you want to store the forwarded events.

5. Click the Add button. In the Select Computer dialog box, type the name of the computer that will be forwarding events. Then, click OK.

6. In the Subscription Properties dialog box, click the forwarding computer in the Source Computers list. Then, click Test. Click OK when Event Viewer verifies connectivity.

NOTE **"Error: Source status unavailable" message**

The Subscription Properties dialog box will always show the message "Error: Source status unavailable" until you have saved the subscription.

---

7. Click the Select Events button and create the query filter. Click OK.
8. Click the Advanced button to open the Advanced Subscription Settings dialog box. You can configure three types of subscriptions:
   - ❑ **Normal**   This option ensures reliable delivery of events and does not attempt to conserve bandwidth. It is the appropriate choice unless you need tighter control over bandwidth usage or need forwarded events delivered as quickly as possible. It uses pull delivery mode (where the collecting computer contacts the forwarding computer) and downloads five events at a time unless 15 minutes pass, in which case it downloads any events that are available.
   - ❑ **Minimize Bandwidth**   This option reduces the network bandwidth consumed by event delivery and is a good choice if you are using event forwarding across a wide area network or on a large number of computers on a local area network. It uses push delivery mode (where the forwarding computer contacts the collecting computer) to forward events every six hours.
   - ❑ **Minimize Latency**   This option ensures that events are delivered with minimal delay. It is an appropriate choice if you are collecting alerts or critical events. It uses push delivery mode and sets a batch timeout of 30 seconds.

   Additionally, you can use this dialog box to configure the user account the subscription uses. Whether you use the default Machine Account setting or you specify a user, you will need to ensure that the account is a member of the forwarding computer's Event Log Readers group.
9. Click OK.
10. In the Subscription Properties dialog box, click OK.

By default, normal event subscriptions check for new events every 15 minutes. You can decrease this interval to reduce the delay in retrieving events. However, there is no graphical interface for configuring the delay; you must use the command-line Wecutil tool that you initially used to configure the collecting computer.

To adjust the event subscription delay, first create your subscription using Event Viewer. Then, run the following two commands at an elevated command prompt:

```
wecutil ss <subscription_name> /cm:custom
wecutil ss <subscription_name> /hi:<milliseconds_delay>
```

For example, if you created a subscription named "Critical Events" and you wanted the delay to be one minute, you would run the following commands:

```
wecutil ss "Critical Events" /cm:custom
wecutil ss "Critical Events" /hi:6000
```

Now, if you open the Subscription Properties dialog box and click the Advanced button, the Advanced Subscription Settings dialog box will show the Event Delivery Optimization setting as Custom, as shown in Figure 6-4. This option button is not selectable using the graphical interface.

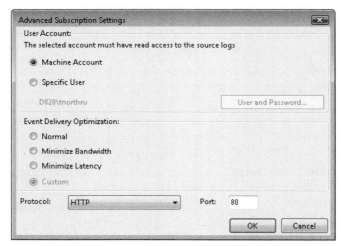

Figure 6-4 Custom Event Delivery Optimization Wecutil after configuration

If you need to check the interval, run the following command:

```
wecutil gs <subscription_name>
```

For example, to verify that the interval for the "Critical Events" subscription is one minute, you would run the following command and look for the HeartbeatInterval value:

```
wecutil gs "Critical Events"
```

The Minimize Bandwidth and Minimize Latency options both batch a default number of items at a time. You can determine the value of this default by typing the following command at a command prompt:

```
winrm get winrm/config
```

How to Configure Event Forwarding to use HTTPS

To configure event forwarding to use the encrypted HTTPS protocol, you must perform the following additional tasks on the forwarding computer in addition to those described in the section entitled "How to Configure the Forwarding Computer" earlier in this chapter:

- Configure the computer with a computer certificate. You can do this automatically in Active Directory environments by using an enterprise CA.
- Create a Windows Firewall exception for TCP port 443.
- Run the following command at an elevated command prompt:

```
winrm quickconfig -transport:https
```

On the collecting computer, you must modify the subscription properties to use HTTPS rather than HTTP. Additionally, the collecting computer must trust the certification authority (CA) that issued the computer certificate—this will happen automatically if the certificate was issued by an enterprise CA and both the forwarding computer and the collecting computer are part of the same Active Directory domain.

For detailed instructions, see Practice 4 in this lesson. If you have configured Minimize Bandwidth or Minimize Latency Event Delivery Optimization for the subscription, you must also configure a computer certificate and an HTTPS Windows Firewall exception on the collecting computer.

Real World

Tony Northrup

Windows Vista stores a great deal of very useful information in the event log, but there's even more useless information in there. For event forwarding, you should focus only on those events that you can proactively respond to.

To identify those useful events that you might want to forward, examine the event log each time a user calls with a problem. Was there an event that appeared either shortly before or after the problem occurred? If so, and if the event only appears during problem scenarios, you should configure that event for forwarding.

How to Configure Event Forwarding in Workgroup Environments

Typically, event forwarding is required only in large environments that use Active Directory domains. However, you can also configure event forwarding in workgroup environments. The process is very similar to that used in Active Directory environments, with the following exceptions:

- You must add a Windows Firewall exception for Remote Event Log Management on each forwarding computer.

- You must add an account with administrator privileges to the Event Log Readers local group on each forwarding computer. You must specify this account in the Configure Advanced Subscription Settings dialog box when creating a subscription on the collector computer.

- On each collecting computer, run the following command to allow the forwarding computers to use NTLM authentication:

  ```
  winrm set winrm/config/client @{TrustedHosts="<forwarding_computers>"}
  ```

  Provide a comma-separated list of forwarding computers for the *<forwarding computers>* value in the previous example. Alternatively, you can provide a wildcard, such as msft*.

Exam Tip

For the exam, remember that you must configure the TrustedHosts parameter on the collecting computer, not the forwarding computer. This is counter-intuitive and might be hard to remember.

How to Troubleshoot Event Forwarding

If event forwarding doesn't seem to function properly, follow these steps to troubleshoot the problem:

1. Verify that you have waited long enough for the event to be forwarded. Forwarding events using the Normal setting can take up to 15 minutes. The delay might be longer if either the forwarding or the collecting computer has recently restarted because the Windows Remote Management service is set to start automatically, but with a delay so that it doesn't impact startup performance. The 15 minute counter doesn't start until after the Windows Remote Management service has started.

2. Check the Applications And Services Logs\Microsoft\Windows\Eventlog-ForwardPlugin \Operational event log and verify that the subscription was created successfully. Event ID 100 indicates a new subscription, while Event ID 103 indicates a subscription has been unsubscribed.

3. Verify that the subscription is Active. On the collecting computer, browse to Event Viewer\Subscriptions. The subscription status should be Active. If it is not, double-click it and examine the status in the Subscription Properties dialog box to determine the source of the problem.

4. Verify that the forwarding computer has the Windows Remote Management listener properly configured. From an elevated command prompt, run the following command:

   ```
   Winrm enumerate winrm/config/Listener
   ```

If the Windows Remote Management listener isn't configured, there will be no output. If the Windows Remote Management listener is properly configured for HTTP, the output will resemble the following:

```
Listener
    Address = *
    Transport = HTTP
    Port = 80
    Hostname
    Enabled = true
    URLPrefix = wsman
    CertificateThumbprint
    ListeningOn = 127.0.0.1, 192.168.1.214, ::1, fe80::100:7f:ffe%9,
fe80::5efe:192.168.1.214%10
```

If the Windows Remote Management listener is properly configured for HTTPS, the output will resemble the following (note that the host name must match the name the event collector uses to identify the computer):

```
Listener
    Address = *
    Transport = HTTPS
    Port = 443
    Hostname = vista1.nwtraders.msft
    Enabled = true
    URLPrefix = wsman
    CertificateThumbprint = 52 31 db a8 45 50 1f 29 d9 3e 16 f0 da 82 ae 94 18 8f 61 5e
    ListeningOn = 127.0.0.1, 192.168.1.214, ::1, fe80::100:7f:ffe%9,
fe80::5efe:192.168.1.214%10
```

5. Verify that the collecting computer can connect to Windows Remote Management on the forwarding computer. From an elevated command prompt on the collecting computer, run the following command:

    Winrm id –remote:*<computer_name>*.*<domain_name>*

    For example, if the forwarding computer is named vista1.nwtraders.msft, you would run the following command:

    ```
    Winrm id –remote:vista.nwtraders.msft
    IdentifyResponse
        ProtocolVersion = http://schemas.dmtf.org/wbem/wsman/1/wsman.xsd
        ProductVender = Microsoft Corporation
        ProductVersion = OS: 6.0.6000 SP: 0.0 Stack: 1.0
    ```

    If you receive the message "WS-Management could not connect to the specified destination," verify that the Windows Remote Management service is started on the forwarding computer and that no firewall is blocking connections between the two computers.

6. Verify that the user account you configured the subscription to use has privileges on the forwarding computer. If necessary, enable failure security auditing on the remote computer, wait for events to be forwarded, and then examine the Security event log for logon failures. Additionally, you can temporarily configure the subscription to use a Domain

Admin account—if the subscription works with the Domain Admin account, the source of your problem is definitely related to authentication. Troubleshoot the authentication problem and reconfigure the subscription to use the original user account.

7. If the subscription is configured to use Machine Account authentication, verify that the collecting computer's account is a member of the forwarding computer's Event Log Readers local group. If the subscription is configured to use a different user account, that account must be in the forwarding computer's Event Log Readers local group.

8. Verify that the following services are started on the forwarding computer:
    - ❑ Windows Remote Management (WS-Management)
    - ❑ Windows Event Collector

9. Verify that the Windows Event Collector service is started on the collecting computer.

10. Verify Windows Firewall settings on the forwarding computer: ·
    - ❑ Verify that the Windows Remote Management (HTTP-In) firewall exception is enabled.
    - ❑ If you are using HTTPS instead of HTTP, verify that you have created and enabled a custom firewall exception for TCP port 443.
    - ❑ Verify that the forwarding computer and the collecting computer are both connected to Private or Domain networks, rather than to Public networks. To verify the network profile, click Start, right-click Network, and then click Properties. In the Network And Sharing Center, the profile type will appear after the network name. If it shows Public Network, click the Customize button and change the profile type to Private.

11. In addition to the forwarding computer, verify that the Windows Remote Management (HTTP-In) firewall exception is enabled on the collecting computer.

12. Verify that a network firewall is not blocking traffic by testing connectivity:
    - ❑ Because the forwarding computer must have HTTP and possibly HTTPS available, you can attempt to connect to it from the collecting computer by using Microsoft Internet Explorer—simply type **http://computername** (or **HTTPS (Hypertext Transfer Protocol Secure)://computername** if you are using HTTPS) in the Address bar. If the firewall on the forwarding computer is correctly configured, you will receive an HTTP 404 error, and Internet Explorer will display the message "The webpage cannot be found." If Internet Explorer displays the message "Internet Explorer cannot display the webpage," the firewall exception on the forwarding computer has not been enabled.

13. Verify that the event query is valid by following these steps:
    a. View the subscription properties and click the Select Events button.
    b. Select the XML tab, select the contents of the query, and press Ctrl+C to copy it to the Clipboard.

   c. Open a second instance of Event Viewer. Right-click Event Viewer, and then click Connect To Another Computer. Select the forwarding computer, and then click OK.

   d. Right-click Custom Views, and then click Create Custom View.

   e. In the Create Custom View dialog box, select the XML tab. Select the Edit Query Manually check box, and click Yes when prompted.

   f. Click the query box and press Ctrl+V to paste the query. Then, click OK.

   g. The new custom view appears and shows the matching events. If any events have appeared since you created the event forwarder, they should have been forwarded. If there are no new events, the problem is your forwarding criteria. Try creating a custom view that matches the events you want to forward and then importing that into a new subscription.

Practice: Forward Events Between Computers

In this practice, you configure event forwarding between two computers using the default settings. Then you update the configuration to use HTTPS instead of HTTP.

▶ **Practice 1: Configuring a Computer to Collect Events**

In this practice, you configure a computer to collect events.

1. Log on to the Windows Vista computer that you want to use to collect events using a domain account with administrative privileges.

2. Open an elevated command prompt by clicking Start, typing **cmd**, and pressing Ctrl+Shift+Enter. Respond to the UAC prompt that appears.

3. At the command prompt, run the following command to configure the Windows Event Collector service:

wecutil qc

4. When prompted to change the service startup mode to Delay-Start, type **Y** and press Enter.

▶ **Practice 2: Configuring a Computer to Forward Events**

In this practice, you configure a Windows Vista computer to forward events to the collecting computer. To complete this practice, you must have completed Practice 1.

1. Log on to the Windows Vista computer that you want to use to forward events using a domain account with administrative privileges.

2. Open an elevated command prompt by clicking Start, typing **cmd**, and pressing Ctrl+Shift+Enter. Respond to the UAC prompt that appears.

3. At the command prompt, run the following command to configure the Windows Remote Management service:

winrm quickconfig

4. When prompted to change the service startup mode, create the WinRM listener, enable the firewall exception, type **Y**, and press Enter.

5. Verify that you have updated the Windows Firewall configuration by following these steps:

   a. Click Start, and then click Control Panel.

   b. Click the Security link.

   c. Click the Windows Firewall link.

   d. Click the Change Settings link.

   e. Select the Exceptions tab. In the Program Or Port list, verify that the Windows Remote Management check box is selected.

   f. Click OK.

6. Verify that the Windows Remote Management service is configured to automatically start by following these steps:

   a. Click Start, type **services.msc**, and press Enter. Respond to the UAC prompt that appears.

   b. In the Services console, select the Windows Remote Management (WS-Management) service. Verify that it is started and that the Startup Type is set to Automatic (Delayed Start).

7. Now, you need to grant the collecting computer permission to read this computer's event log. If you skipped this step, you would need to configure the subscription to use an administrative user account. To grant access to the collecting computer account, follow these steps:

   a. Click Start, right-click Computer, and then click Manage. Respond to the UAC prompt that appears.

   b. Under System Tools, expand Local Users And Groups. Then, select Groups. Double-click Event Log Readers.

   c. In the Event Log Readers Properties dialog box, click Add.

   d. In the Select Users, Computers, Or Groups dialog box, click the Object Types button. By default, it searches only Users and Groups. However, we need to add the collecting computer account. Select the Computers check box and clear the Groups and Users check boxes. Click OK.

   e. In the Select Users, Computers, Or Groups dialog box, type the name of the collecting computer. Then, click OK.

   f. Click OK again to close the Event Log Readers Properties dialog box.

▶ **Practice 3: Configuring an Event Subscription**

In this practice, you create an event subscription to gather events from the forwarding computer. To complete this practice, you must have completed Practices 1 and 2.

1. Log on to the Windows Vista computer that you want to use to collect events using a domain account with administrative privileges.

2. Click Start, right-click Computer, and then click Manage. Respond to the UAC prompt that appears.

3. In the Computer Management console, expand System Tools, expand Event Viewer, right-click Subscriptions, and then click Create Subscription.

4. In the Event Viewer dialog box, click Yes to configure the Windows Event Collector service (if prompted).

   The Subscription Properties dialog box appears.

5. In the Subscription Name box, type **Windows Defender Warnings And Errors**.

6. Click the Add button. In the Select Computer dialog box, type the name of the computer that will be forwarding events. Then, click OK.

7. In the Subscription Properties dialog box, click the forwarding computer in the Source Computers list. Then, click Test. Click OK when Event Viewer verifies connectivity.

8. Click the Select Events button. In the Query Filter dialog box, select the Error, Critical, and Warning check boxes. Click By Source. Then, click the Event Sources list and select Windows Defender (as shown in Figure 6-5). Click OK.

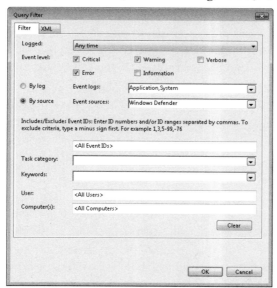

Figure 6-5 Configuring the Query Filter to forward important Windows Defender events

9. Click the Advanced button to open the Advanced Subscription Settings dialog box. Note that it is configured to use the Machine Account by default. This will work because we have added this computer's domain account to the forwarding computer's Event Log

Readers local group. Also note that the subscription is configured by default to use Normal Event Delivery Optimization using the HTTP protocol. Click OK.

10. In the Subscription Properties dialog box, click OK.

    Next, generate a Windows Defender event on the forwarding computer by following these steps:

11. Log on to the forwarding computer.

12. Click Start and type **notepad %windir%\system32\drivers\etc\hosts**. Press Ctrl+Shift+Enter to open Notepad with administrative privileges. Respond to the UAC prompt that appears.

13. In Notepad, type a space anywhere in the file to cause the Hosts file to be updated. Then, save the file by clicking File, and then clicking Save.

14. While still using the forwarding computer, open Event Viewer and check the System log. You should see a *Warning* event with a source of Windows Defender.

15. Using the collecting computer, select the Forwarded Events event log. If you don't immediately see the Windows Defender event, wait a few minutes—it might take up to 15 minutes for the event to appear.

▶ **Practice 4: Configuring a Computer to Forward Events by Using HTTPS**

In this practice, you configure a collecting computer to use HTTPS and then troubleshoot the connectivity problem. Then, you assign a computer certificate to the forwarding computer, enable a Windows Firewall exception for HTTPS, and configure the Windows Remote Management service to use HTTPS. To complete this practice, you must have completed Practices 1 through 3.

1. On the collecting computer, select the *Subscriptions* node in Event Viewer.

2. Double-click your Windows Defender Warnings And Errors subscription. Click the Advanced button in the Subscription Properties dialog box.

3. In the Advanced Subscription Settings dialog box, click the Protocol list and select HTTPS. Notice that the Port number automatically changes from 80 to 443. Click OK twice.

4. With the *Subscriptions* node in Event Viewer selected, notice that the Status of the Windows Defender Warnings And Errors subscription is Trying rather than Active. Trying indicates that Event Viewer cannot connect to the forwarding computer. Double-click the subscription and notice the status, which should resemble the following:

```
[VISTA1.nwtraders.msft] - Trying - Last retry time: 2/14/2007 10:07:36 AM. Code
(0x80338012): WS-Management could not connect to the specified destination:
(VISTA1.nwtraders.msft:443). Next retry time: 2/14/2007 10:12:36 AM.
```

This error indicates that the forwarding computer either isn't connected to the network or isn't accepting HTTPS connections.

5. To resolve this problem, you need to configure the forwarding computer to accept HTTPS connections. This requires the forwarding computer to have a computer certificate. Install a computer certificate by following these steps:

   a. Install Certificate Services on your domain controller. For detailed instructions, refer to Practice 3 of Lesson 1, "Configuring and Troubleshooting Internet Explorer Security" in Chapter 5, "Protecting Internet Explorer and Other Applications." If Certificate Services was not previously installed, restart both the forwarding computer and the collecting computer so they trust the new CA.

   b. On the Windows Vista forwarding computer, log on using a domain account. Click Start, type **mmc**, and then press Enter.

      A blank MMC console appears.

   c. Click the File menu, and then click Add/Remove Snap-In.

   d. In the Add Or Remove Snap-Ins dialog box, click Certificates, and then click Add.

      In the Certificates Snap-In Wizard, click Computer Account, and then click Next. Then, click Local Computer and click Finish.

   e. Click OK to close the Add Or Remove Snap-Ins dialog box.

   f. Expand Certificates (Local Computer), and then expand Personal. Right-click Certificates, click All Tasks, and then click Request New Certificate.

   g. On the Before You Begin page of the Certificate Enrollment Wizard, click Next.

   h. On the Request Certificates page, select Computer, and then click Enroll.

   i. On the Certificate Installation Results page, click Finish.

      Your computer now has a computer certificate and is ready to enable HTTPS.

6. After you configure the SSL certificate, HTTPS can accept incoming connections. However, Windows Firewall is still configured to block incoming HTTPS connections by default. Follow these steps to allow incoming HTTPS connections:

   a. On the forwarding computer, click Start, type **firewall**, and then click Windows Firewall With Advanced Security. Respond to the UAC prompt that appears.

   b. In the Windows Firewall With Advanced Security console, select Inbound Rules.

   c. In the Actions pane, click the New Rule link.

      The New Inbound Rule Wizard appears.

   d. On the Rule Type page, select Port. Then, click Next.

   e. On the Protocols And Ports page, verify that TCP is selected. In the Specific Local Ports text box, type **443** (the port HTTPS uses by default). Then, click Next.

   f. On the Action page, verify that Allow The Connection is selected. Then, click Next.

   g. On the Profile page, clear the Public check box. You typically need to use event forwarding only when connected to a Domain or Private network, and allowing incoming connections on the Public network increases security risks. Click Next.

    h. On the Name page, type **Windows Remote Management (HTTPS-In)**. The exact name doesn't matter, but this name matches the format of the default Windows Remote Management (HTTP-In) rule. Then, click Finish.

    i. Because you no longer need them, disable the two Windows Remote Management (HTTP-In) exceptions. You will need to reenable these if you plan to use HTTP instead of HTTPS in the future.

7. On the forwarding computer, run the following command at an elevated command prompt:

winrm quickconfig –transport:https

8. When prompted, type **y**, and then press Enter.

9. Switch to the collecting computer. Double-click the Windows Defender Warnings And Errors subscription to open it.

10. In the Subscription Properties dialog box, click Retry to test the connection using HTTPS.

This time, the collecting computer should be able to connect to the forwarding computer. The status changes to Active.

Lesson Summary

- Windows Vista improves event logging by providing an overview and summary page, numerous and granular log files, event forwarding, event triggers, event filtering, custom views, and trace and debug logs.

- Event forwarding uses HTTP by default, allowing it to easily pass through most firewalls. You can also configure event forwarding to use HTTPS. However, communications are encrypted with standard HTTP.

- To configure event forwarding in a domain, run the "winrm quickconfig" command at the forwarding computer and run the "wecutil qc" command on the collecting computer. Then, add the collecting computer's account to the forwarding computer's Event Log Readers group.

- To configure event forwarding in a workgroup, follow the same steps you would in a domain. Additionally, you will need to add a Windows Firewall exception for the Remote Event Log Management service on each forwarding computer, add a user account with administrator privileges to the forwarding computer's Event Log Readers group, and run the "winrm set" command to configure the collecting computer to trust the forwarding computers.

- To troubleshoot event forwarding, verify that you have waited long enough, verify that subscriptions are active, check the Windows Remote Management configuration on both the forwarding and collecting computers, and verify that the user account you specified for the subscription is a member of the forwarding computer's Event Log Readers group.

Lesson Review

You can use the following questions to test your knowledge of the information in Lesson 1, "Monitoring Events in an Enterprise." The questions are also available on the companion CD if you prefer to review them in electronic form.

NOTE   Answers

Answers to these questions and explanations of why each answer choice is right or wrong are located in the "Answers" section at the end of the book.

1. When starting with the default configuration of a computer, which of the following steps are required to enable event forwarding? (Choose all that apply.)

    A. Start the Windows Rights Management service on the forwarding computer.

    B. Start the Windows Rights Management service on the collecting computer.

    C. Configure Internet Information Services on the forwarding computer.

    D. Enable a Windows Firewall exception on the forwarding computer.

    E. Nothing is required; event forwarding is enabled by default.

2. Which tool would you use to configure a subscription to use a 10-minute interval?

    A. Event Viewer

    B. Winrm

    C. Wecutil

    D. Wevutil

3. What is the standard interval for a subscription with a bandwidth optimization setting of Minimize Latency?

    A. 30 seconds

    B. 15 minutes

    C. 30 minutes

    D. 6 hours

4. Which of the following tasks do you need to perform in an Active Directory domain environment to enable a computer to collect events from another computer?

    A. Run the following command on the collecting computer:

        ```
        winrm set winrm/config/client @{TrustedHosts="<forwarding_computers>"}
        ```

    B. Run the following command on the forwarding computer:

        ```
        winrm set winrm/config/client @{TrustedHosts="<collecting_computers>"}
        ```

    C. Add the forwarding computer's machine account to the Event Log Readers local group.

    D. Add the collecting computer's machine account to the Event Log Readers local group.

Lesson 2: Troubleshooting Performance, Reliability, and Security Problems

When users experience problems, you need to know how to quickly identify the source of the problems. Fortunately, in Windows Vista you no longer need to dig through Event Viewer for clues. In addition to Performance Monitor, Windows Vista includes data collector sets, reports, and the Reliability Monitor. Each of these tools enables you to quickly evaluate a computer's configuration, existing problems, and changes that might have caused those problems.

After this lesson, you will be able to:

- Use Performance Monitor to examine real-time statistics and compare logged data to a performance baseline.
- Use data collector sets to generate reports that provide detailed information about a computer's configuration and the problems it's experiencing.
- Use Reliability Monitor to determine when a computer began having problems and what changes might have contributed to those problems.

Estimated lesson time: 45 minutes

Performance Monitor

Like earlier versions of Windows, the Performance Monitor snap-in graphically displays real-time data, as shown in Figure 6-6.

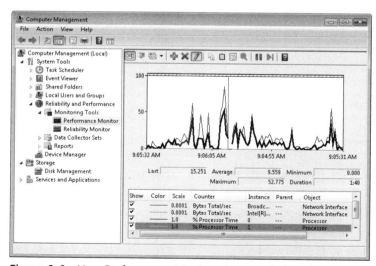

Figure 6-6   How Performance Monitor shows real-time data

The sections that follow describe how to monitor real-time data, how to configure the Performance Monitor chart, and how to compare multiple graphs.

How to Monitor Real-Time Performance Data

To open Performance Monitor, follow these steps:

1. Click Start, right-click Computer, and then click Manage.
2. Expand System Tools, expand Reliability And Performance, and then expand Monitoring Tools. Select Performance Monitor.
3. Add counters to the real-time graph by clicking the green plus button on the toolbar. You can also display data from other computers on the network.

Each line on the graph appears in a different color. To make it easier to view a specific graph, select a counter and press Ctrl+H. The selected counter appears bold and in black on the graph.

Performance Monitor automatically assigns line colors and styles to the counters you select. To manually configure line colors and styles, follow these steps:

1. Click the Action menu, and then click Properties.
   The Performance Monitor Properties dialog box appears.
2. Click the Data tab.
3. In the Counters list, select the counter you want to configure. Then, adjust the Color, Width, and Style.
4. To increase the height of the graph for a counter, click the Scale list and click a higher number. To decrease the height of a graph, click the Scale list and click a lower number.
5. You can also adjust the scale for all counters by clicking the Graph tab and changing the Maximum and Minimum values in the Vertical Scale group.
6. Click OK.

If you keep multiple Performance Monitor windows open simultaneously, you can make it easier to quickly distinguish between the windows by changing the background color on the chart using the Appearance tab in the Performance Monitor Properties dialog box.

How to Control How Much Data Appears in the Graph

By default, Performance Monitor updates the graphs once per second and displays 100 seconds of data. To display data over a longer period of time, you can increase the sampling interval or increase the amount of data displayed on the graph at once. To adjust these settings, follow these steps in Performance Monitor:

1. Click the Action menu, and then click Properties.
   The Performance Monitor Properties dialog box appears.

2. In the General tab, in the Graph Elements group, adjust the Sample Every box to change how frequently the graph updates. Use a longer interval (such as five seconds) to show a smoother, less jagged graph that is updated less frequently. If you are connecting to a computer across a network, longer intervals reduce bandwidth usage.

3. Adjust the Duration box to change how much data is displayed in the graph before Performance Monitor begins overwriting the graph on the left portion of the chart. To display one full hour of data in the graph, set the duration to 3,600. To display one full day of data in the graph, set the duration to 86,400. If you increase the Duration box, you should also increase the Sample Every box.

4. Click OK.

By default, Performance Monitor begins overwriting graphed data on the left portion of the chart after the specified duration has been reached. When graphing data over a long period of time, it's typically easier to see the chart scroll from right to left, similar to the way Task Manager shows data. To configure the Performance Monitor graph to scroll data, follow these steps:

1. Click the Action menu, and then click Properties.

   The Performance Monitor Properties dialog box appears.

2. Click the Graph tab. In the Scroll Style group, select Scroll.

3. Click OK.

Although the line chart shows the most information, you can select from the following chart types by clicking the Change Graph Type button on the toolbar or by pressing Ctrl+G:

- **Line**   The default setting, this shows values over time as lines on the chart.
- **Histogram bar**   This shows a bar graph with the most recent values for each counter displayed. If you have a large number of values and you're primarily interested in the current value (rather than the value of each counter over time), this will be earlier to read than the line chart.
- **Report**   This text report lists each current value.
- **Area**   Shows a line chart with the area under each line filled in using a solid color. This chart type is available only when viewing logged data.
- **Stacked Area**   Similar to the area chart, the stacked chart adds values on top of each other, rather than overlapping them.

How to Compare Multiple Graphs

By running Performance Monitor with the /sys parameter, you can visually compare two Performance Monitor logs (for example, to compare performance logs taken before and after making changes). To overlay two Performance Monitor windows, follow these steps:

1. Click Start, type **perfmon /sys**, and then press Enter. Respond to the UAC prompt that appears. Configure the Performance Monitor window to display the data you want to compare.

NOTE   Compare menu

Notice that Performance Monitor includes the Compare menu. This appears only if you run it with the /sys parameter.

---

2. Click Start, type **perfmon /sys**, and then press Enter. Respond to the UAC prompt that appears to open the second Performance Monitor window. Configure the new Performance Monitor window to display the second set of data you want to compare.

3. In either Performance Monitor window, click the Compare menu, click Set Transparency, and then click 70% Transparency.

4. Using the transparent Performance Monitor window, click the Compare menu, and then click Snap To Compare.

Performance Monitor displays the two windows on top of each other. Because the top window is partially transparent, you can see the underlying window to compare the data. If you click the window, you will always access the top window. However, you can select either window by clicking the taskbar button. You are free to move either window as well, and you can return to the Compare menu to realign them later.

Data Collector Sets and Reports

Previous versions of Windows enabled you to log performance counter data and view it later. Windows Vista greatly expands this capability. Now you can create a data collector set to log the following types of information:

- Performance counters and alerts (just like in previous versions of Windows)
- Event trace data showing detailed debugging information
- Registry settings showing system and application configuration

After running a data collector set, you can view the performance counters in Performance Monitor, and you can view a summary of the other collected information in a report. The sections that follow describe how to create data collector sets and how to use reports.

Built-in Data Collector Sets

Windows Vista includes several built-in data collector sets located at Reliability And Performance\Data Collector Sets\System:

- **System Performance**   Logs processor, disk, memory, and network performance counters and kernel tracing. Use this data collector set when troubleshooting a slow computer or intermittent performance problems.

- **System Diagnostics**   Logs all the information included in the System Performance data collector set, plus detailed system information. Use this data collector set when troubleshooting reliability problems such as problematic hardware, driver failures, or Stop errors (also known as blue screens). As shown in Figure 6-7, the report generated by the data collector set provides a summary of error conditions on the system without requiring you to manually browse Event Viewer and Device Manager.

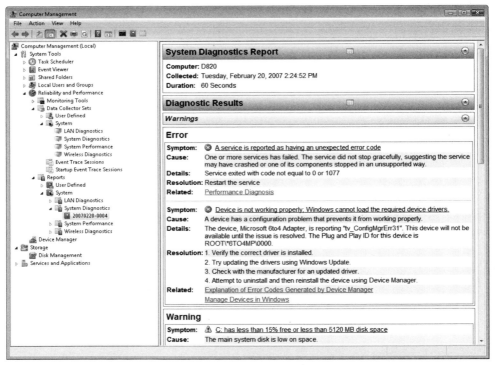

Figure 6-7 The System Diagnostics Report

- **LAN Diagnostics**   Logs network performance counters, network configuration data, and important diagnostics tracing. Use this data collector set when troubleshooting complex network problems, such as network time-outs, poor network performance, or virtual private network (VPN) connectivity problems.

- **Wireless Diagnostics**   Logs the same information as the LAN Diagnostics data collector set, plus information relevant to troubleshooting wireless network connections. Use this data collector set only when troubleshooting network problems that occur when connected to a wireless network.

To use a data collector set, right-click it, and then click Start. The System Performance and System Diagnostics data collector sets stop automatically after a minute, while the LAN Diagnostics and Wireless Diagnostics data collector sets can run indefinitely. If you are troubleshooting a network problem, you should attempt to reproduce the problem after starting the data collector set. To manually stop a data collector set, right-click it, and then click Stop.

After running a data collector set, you can view a summary of the data gathered in the *Reliability And Performance\Reports* node. To view the most recent report for a data collector set, right-click the data collector set, and then click Latest Report. Reports are automatically named using the format *yyyymmdd-####*.

To minimize the performance impact of data logging, log the least amount of information required. For example, you should use System Performance instead of System Diagnostics whenever possible because System Performance includes fewer counters.

When a problem is difficult to reproduce and is not performance related, you should err on the side of logging too much data to minimize the chance that you will miss important information.

How to Create a Data Collector Set by Using a Standard Template

You can save performance data to a log and then view and analyze the data in Performance Monitor at any time. It's important to create a baseline by logging performance data before making changes that you think might have a performance impact. After making the changes, you can compare new performance data to the original performance data to determine whether your changes were beneficial.

To save performance data, follow these steps:

1. Under Reliability And Performance, expand Data Collector Sets.
2. Right-click User Defined, click New, and then click Data Collector Set.
   The Create New Data Collector Set Wizard appears.
3. On the How Would You Like To Create This New Data Collector Set page, type a name for the set. Make sure Create From A Template is selected. Then, click Next.

4. On the Which Template Would You Like To Use page, choose from one of the three standard templates (or Browse to select a custom template), and click Next:

    ❑ **Basic**   Logs all Processor performance counters, stores a copy of the HKLM\Software\Microsoft\Windows NT\CurrentVersion registry key, and performs a Windows Kernel Trace.

    ❑ **System Diagnostics**   Logs 13 useful performance counters (including processor, disk, memory, and network counters), stores a copy of dozens of important configuration settings, and performs a Windows Kernel Trace. By default, System Diagnostics logs data for one minute, giving you a snapshot of the computer's status.

    ❑ **System Performance**   Logs 14 useful performance counters (including the same counters logged by the System Diagnostics template) and performs a Windows Kernel Trace. System Performance logs data for one minute.

5. On the Where Would You Like The Data To Be Saved page, click Next to accept the default location for the data (%systemdrive%\perflogs\test).

6. On the Create The Data Collector Set page, leave Run As set to <Default> to run it using the current user's credentials, or click the Change button to specify other administrative credentials. Select one of three options before clicking the Finish button:

    ❑ **Open Properties For This Data Collector Set**   Immediately customize the Data Collector Set.

    ❑ **Start This Data Collector Set Now**   Immediately begin logging data without customizing the Data Collector Set.

    ❑ **Save And Close**   Close the Data Collector Set without starting it. You can edit the properties and start it at any time after saving it.

Custom data collector sets are always available under the *User Defined* node within Data Collector Sets.

How to Create a Custom Data Collector Set

After creating a new data collector set, you can modify it to log additional data sources by right-clicking the data collector set, clicking New, and then clicking Data Collector to open the Create New Data Collector Wizard. On the What Type Of Data Collector Would You Like To Create page, type a name for the data collector, select the type, and then click Next.

You can choose from the following types of data collectors (each of which provides different options in the Create New Data Collector Wizard):

- **Performance Counter Data Collector** Logs data for any performance counter available when using the Performance Monitor console. You can add as many counters as you like to a data collector. You can assign a sample interval (15 seconds, by default) to the data collector.

- **Event Trace Data Collector** Stores events from an event trace provider that match a particular filter. Windows Vista provides dozens of event trace providers that are capable of logging even the most minute aspects of the computer's behavior. For best results, simply add all event trace providers that might relate to the problem you are troubleshooting. If the data collector logs a large amount of unnecessary data, you can use the provider properties to filter which trace events are stored.

- **Configuration Data Collector** Stores a copy of specific registry keys, management paths, files, or the system state. If you are troubleshooting application problems or if you need to be aware of application settings, add the registry keys using a configuration data collector. To add a management path, file, or system state, create the data collector without specifying a registry key using the wizard. Then, view the new data collector properties, and select the Management Paths, File Capture, or State Capture tab.

- **Performance Counter Alert** Generates an alert when a performance counter is above or below a specified threshold.

You can add as many data collectors to a data collector set as required.

How to Save Performance Data

After creating a data collector set, you can gather the data specified in the Data Collector Set by right-clicking it and clicking Start. Depending on the settings configured in the Stop Condition tab of the data collector set's properties dialog box, the logging might stop after a set amount of time or it might continue indefinitely. If it does not stop automatically, you can manually stop it by right-clicking it and clicking Stop.

How to View Saved Performance Data in a Report

After using a data collector set to gather information and then stopping the data collector set, you can view the gathered information. To view a summary of the data saved using a data collector set, right-click the data collector set, and then click Latest Report. As shown in Figure 6-8, the console expands the *Reports* node and selects the report generated when the data collector set ran. You can expand each section to find more detailed information.

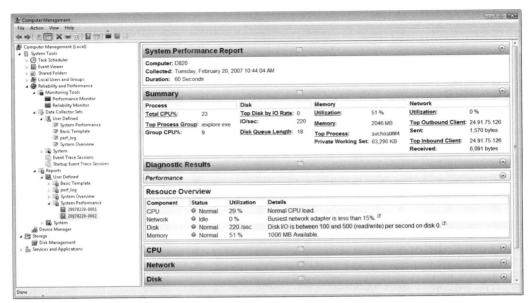

Figure 6-8   How reports summarize information gathered by a data collector set

If the data collector set included performance counters, you can also view them using the Performance Monitor snap-in by following these steps:

1. Under Reliability And Performance, expand Monitoring Tools, and then select Performance Monitor.

2. Click the Action menu, and then click Properties. In the Performance Monitor Properties dialog box, click the Source tab. You can also click the View Log Data button on the toolbar or press Ctrl+L.

3. Under Data Source, select Log Files. Then, click Add. By default, Windows Vista stores data collector set data in the C:\Perflogs\ folder. Browse to select the data collector set data (the folder corresponds to the report name), and then click Open.

4. Optionally, click the Time Range button and narrow the range of data you want to analyze.

5. Click OK.

6. Performance Monitor shows the logged data instead of real-time data. To narrow the time range shown, click and drag your cursor over the graph to select a time range. Then, right-click the graph and click Zoom To, as shown in Figure 6-9.

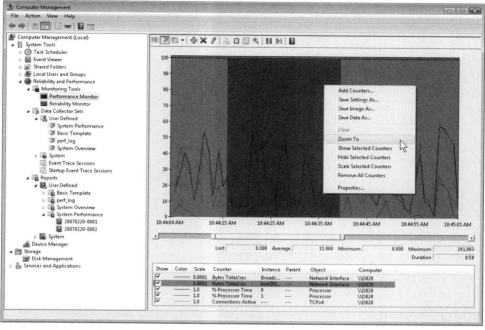

Figure 6-9 Using the Zoom To feature to analyze a narrow time span

7. The horizontal bar beneath the graph illustrates the currently selected time range. Drag the left and right sides of the bar to expand the selected time range. Then, right-click the graph and click Zoom To again to change the selection.

Reliability Monitor

One of the biggest challenges of troubleshooting problems on user computers is identifying recent changes that might be the cause of the problems. Although it's commonplace to ask users what they have recently changed, many users might not remember or even be aware of important changes. Event Viewer will reveal many of these changes, but it could take hours of digging to identify significant events.

Windows Vista includes the Reliability Monitor to enable support personnel to quickly identify important changes and failures. Figure 6-10 shows the Reliability Monitor for a computer that is used to test application and hardware compatibility with Windows Vista and thus has a large number of failures. The chart at the top of the page shows a number from 1 (representing the least stable computer) to 10 (representing an extremely stable computer).

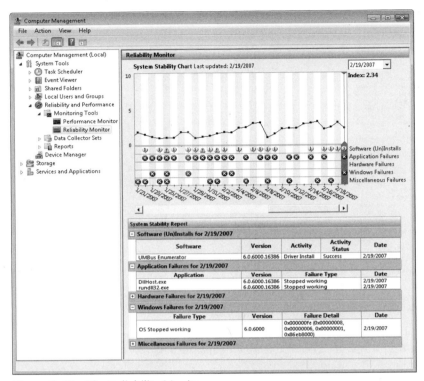

Figure 6-10   The Reliability Monitor

To open Reliability Monitor, follow these steps:

1. Click Start, right-click Computer, and then click Manage. Respond to the UAC prompt that appears.

2. In the Computer Management console, expand System Tools, Reliability And Performance, Monitoring Tools, and then select Reliability Monitor.

NOTE   Opening the Reliability And Performance console

You can also open the Reliability And Performance console from the Administrative Tools folder on your Start menu. To open it directly, click Start, type a few letters of the tool name (such as **Reli**), and press Enter when it appears at the top of the Start menu.

The chart at the top of Reliability Monitor shows one data point for each day. The rows below the chart show icons for successful and unsuccessful software installations, application failures, hardware failures, Windows failures, and other miscellaneous failures. Click a day to view the day's details in the System Stability Report below the chart.

You can analyze the System Stability Chart to determine approximately when stability problems began—the point will be indicated by a decreasing stability index. Starting at the first day on which the stability began decreasing, examine software installs and uninstalls for each previous day. Consider uninstalling any new applications or updates that might be causing the problems. Additionally, you can check Event Viewer for other configuration changes that might have been made around the time the problems began to occur.

The Reliability Monitor displays data gathered by the Reliability Analysis Component (RAC), which is implemented using RACAgent.exe. RACAgent.exe runs once an hour using a hidden scheduled task. To view the scheduled task, open Task Scheduler, click the View menu, and then select Show Hidden Tasks. Then, browse to Task Scheduler Library\Microsoft\Windows\RAC.

Practice: Collect and Analyze Performance Data

In this practice, you collect performance data using a data collector set and then analyze it by using a report and Performance Monitor.

▶ **Practice 1: Perform System Diagnostics**

In this practice, you collect performance data by using a built-in data collector set.

1. Click Start, right-click Computer, and then click Manage. Respond to the UAC prompt that appears.

2. In the Computer Management console, expand System Tools, Reliability And Performance, Data Collector Sets, and then System.

3. Right-click System Diagnostics, and then click Start. Notice that a green arrow appears on the System Diagnostics icon.

4. While the System Diagnostics data collector set is running, click System Diagnostics. Browse through the various data collectors. In particular, view the properties of the following data collectors:

   ❑ Performance Counter

   ❑ NT Kernel

   ❑ Operating System

   ❑ UAC Settings

   ❑ Windows Update Settings

5. The green arrow will disappear from the System Diagnostics icon after the data collector set has finished running in one minute. Now, right-click System Diagnostics, and click Latest Report.

6. Examine the Diagnostic Results section and investigate any error or warning conditions. Then, investigate each of the other sections of the report to identify the following pieces of information:

   ❑ Processor utilization

- ❑ The number of processors and whether the processors are hyper-threaded or not
- ❑ Memory utilization
- ❑ Total physical memory
- ❑ Whether the operating system architecture is 32-bit or 64-bit
- ❑ The name of the workgroup or domain the computer is a member of
- ❑ The name of the antispyware, antivirus, and firewall software installed, if any
- ❑ Whether UAC is enabled
- ❑ Whether the Computer Browser, Server, Workstation, and Windows Update services are running
- ❑ Which service is using the most processor time
- ❑ Whether IRQ 3 is in use
- ❑ The Windows Experience Index rating for the processor, memory, and hard disk
- ❑ Basic input/output system (BIOS) type and version
- ❑ The Internet Protocol (IP) address that is sending the most bytes to the local computer
- ❑ The number of IPv4 and IPv6 connections
- ❑ The file causing the most disk input/output (I/O)
- ❑ The application with the largest working set

▶ **Practice 2: Create a Performance Graph**

In this practice, you use Performance Monitor to graphically analyze data gathered in Practice 1.

1. In the Computer Management console, select the System Tools\Reliability And Performance\Monitoring Tools\Performance Monitor node.

2. Click the View Log Data button on the toolbar to open the Performance Monitor Properties dialog box to the Source tab.

3. Select Log Files. Then, click Add. Select the C:\Perflogs\System\Diagnostics*yyyym-mdd-####*\Performance Counter.blg file to open the performance counter log created when you ran the System Diagnostics data collector set. Click Open.

4. Click OK to return to Performance Monitor.

   Now you are viewing the logged performance data. However, because you have not added any counters to the chart, nothing is visible.

5. Click the Add button on the toolbar. Add the following counters to the chart, and then click OK:
   - ❑ IPv4\Datagrams/sec
   - ❑ IPv6\Datagrams/sec
   - ❑ Memory\% Committed Bytes In Use
   - ❑ PhysicalDisk\Disk Bytes/sec

> ❑ Processor\% Processor Time
> ❑ System\Processes

6. Press Ctrl+H to highlight the selected counter. Browse through the available counters and examine their performance during the one-minute log period.

7. Drag your mouse horizontally across the middle of the chart to select about 30 seconds of the chart. Then, right-click the chart and click Zoom To. Notice that the chart displays a smaller period of time.

8. Use the slider below the chart to select the entire chart time period. Then, right-click the chart and click Zoom To.

Lesson Summary

- You can use Performance Monitor to analyze system statistics in real time, or you can use it to analyze data logged using a data collector set.

- Data collector sets and reports gather performance and configuration data about a computer and enable you to easily analyze that information using reports or Performance Monitor.

- Reliability Monitor tracks a computer's stability over time, displays a summary of that stability, and displays factors that might contribute to stability problems, such as newly installed programs.

Lesson Review

You can use the following questions to test your knowledge of the information in Lesson 2, "Troubleshooting Performance, Reliability, and Security Problems." The questions are also available on the companion CD if you prefer to review them in electronic form.

NOTE Answers

Answers to these questions and explanations of why each answer choice is right or wrong are located in the "Answers" section at the end of the book.

---

1. How can you overlay two Performance Monitor windows?

   A. Open Performance Monitor from within the Computer Management console.

   B. Run Perfmon /sys.

   C. Open the Reliability And Performance Monitor from Administrative Tools. Then, click the control box in the upper-left corner and select Compare.

   D. Open an elevated command prompt, and run Perfmon /compare.

2. Which of the following built-in data collector sets could you use to monitor processor utilization? (Choose all that apply.)

    A. LAN Diagnostics

    B. System Diagnostics

    C. System Performance

    D. Wireless Diagnostics

3. Which of the following built-in data collector sets could you use to generate a report that detailed malfunctioning hardware devices?

    A. LAN Diagnostics

    B. System Diagnostics

    C. System Performance

    D. Wireless Diagnostics

Lesson 3: Using Task Scheduler

In Windows Vista, Task Scheduler is useful for much more than running a program or script at a specific time of day. Task Scheduler now has the ability to respond to a variety of different triggers, including the operating system starting or stopping or specific events appearing in an event log. Besides simply running programs, Task Scheduler can now display a message to the user or send an e-mail. Additionally, the tool is more reliable, scalable, and secure than it was in earlier versions of Windows.

After this lesson, you will be able to:
- Describe how Task Scheduler has improved in Windows Vista.
- Use Task Scheduler to create a new task.
- Use the SchTasks.exe command-line tool to create a new task.
- Manage existing tasks with Task Scheduler.
- Troubleshoot problems with scheduled tasks.

Estimated lesson time: 20 minutes

Task Scheduler Improvements in Windows Vista

The most important improvements in the Windows Vista version of Task Scheduler are:

- **User interface**   As shown in Figure 6-11, the new Task Scheduler includes a completely new interface. Task Scheduler now organizes tasks based on technology and provides a summary of previously run tasks and active tasks.

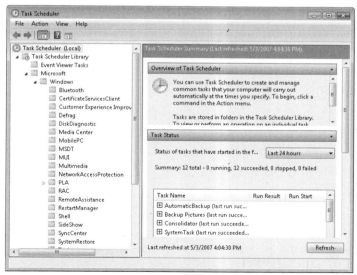

Figure 6-11   The new interface in Task Scheduler in Windows Vista

- **Triggers**   In Windows Vista, Task Scheduler provides more flexible scheduling options, including the ability to run a series of tasks one after another as a chain. You can schedule tasks to run when the computer shuts down or starts up. Failed tasks can be automatically retried. You can also run a task when an event that matches specific criteria is added to the event log.
- **Actions**   Besides simply running programs, scheduled tasks can display a message to the user or send an e-mail.
- **Security**   Task Scheduler now stores passwords using the Windows Vista Credentials Manager, helping to protect the credentials you configure to run tasks.
- **Manageability**   In Windows Vista, you can configure tasks to send an e-mail if the task fails. Additionally, Task Scheduler provides a detailed history of scheduled tasks.

Task Scheduler still provides backward compatibility for tasks created in Windows XP and tasks created using the At command-line tool.

How to Create Tasks with the Task Scheduler Tool

To create a scheduled task, follow these steps:

1. Launch Task Scheduler by clicking Start, All Programs, Accessories, System Tools, and then Task Scheduler. Respond to the UAC prompt that appears.
2. Task Scheduler appears.
3. In the console tree, select and then right-click Task Scheduler. Click Create Task.
4. In the General tab of the Create Task dialog box, as shown in Figure 6-12, type a name for the task. You can configure the following security settings from this tab:

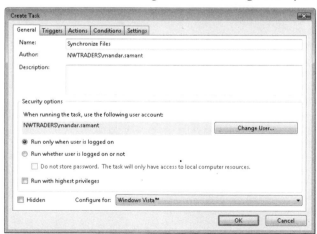

Figure 6-12   Using the General tab to configure security settings for a task

❑ By default, the task will run using the current user account with least privileges. To change the user, click the Change User Or Group button. To configure the task to run with elevated privileges (as if you had responded to a UAC prompt), select the Run With Highest Privileges check box.

❑ By default, new tasks run only when the user is logged on—this enables the task to interact with the user if necessary. If the task can run without user interaction, select Run Whether User Is Logged On Or Not. This prevents tasks from displaying any user interface, which is useful if you are scheduling a script to run and you don't want the user to see the command prompt.

❑ If you select the Do Not Store Password check box, Task Scheduler will not store the credentials supplied on the local computer but will discard them after properly authenticating the user. When required to run the task, the Task Scheduler service will use the Service-for-User (S4U) extensions to the Kerberos authentication protocol to retrieve the user's token. Selecting the Do Not Store Password check box prevents the scheduled task from accessing network resources or encrypted files. Selecting the Do Not Store Password check box also requires that the user have the Log On As A Batch Job user right.

❑ If you want the task to not be visible by default in Task Scheduler, select the Hidden check box.

5. In the Triggers tab of the Create Task dialog box, click the New button to configure at least one trigger. If you don't configure a trigger, the task will never run (but you could launch it manually). You can configure the following security settings from the New Trigger dialog box, as shown in Figure 6-13:

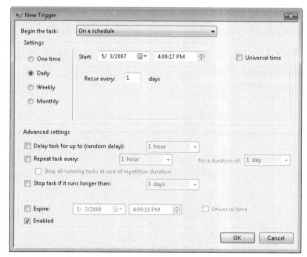

Figure 6-13 The New Trigger dialog box

❑ If you click the Begin The Task list and select On A Schedule, you can configure the task to run on a regular basis, such as daily or weekly. To avoid running the same task on multiple computers at exactly the same moment (which would be useful if the task accesses a network resource that might become overloaded), select the Delay Task For Up To check box.

❑ To configure tasks to run based on user actions, from the Begin The Task list select At Log On, At Startup, On Workstation Lock, or On Workstation Unlock. To avoid slowing down the computer during the user's task, select the Delay Task For check box.

❑ To configure a task to run when the computer is not in use, click the Begin The Task list and select On Idle. This is useful for tasks that might make the computer less responsive when a user is actively using it.

❑ To configure a task to run when a user connects or disconnects from a remote session, select On Connection To User Session or On Disconnect From User Session.

❑ To run a task when an event appears, select On An Event from the Begin The Task list. Then, select Basic if your event criteria requires only matching a specific event log, event source, or event ID. If you require more complex matching criteria, select Custom, and then click the New Event Filter button.

❑ To configure a task to run when a task is created or edited, select At Task Creation/Modification from the Begin The Task list. This is primarily useful for auditing scheduled tasks or automating the management of Task Scheduler.

6. In the Actions tab of the Create Task dialog box, click the New button to configure at least one action. If you don't configure an action, nothing will happen when the event is triggered. You can configure the following security settings from the New Action dialog box, as shown in Figure 6-14:

Figure 6-14 Security settings in the New Action dialog box

❑ If you select Start A Program from the Action list, you can run an application or script. Simply click the Browse button and select the program that you want to run.

❑ If you select Send An E-mail from the Action list, you can have the task send an e-mail when it is triggered. You will need to configure the From, To, Subject, and Text boxes, as well as the address of the mail server. To include a log file as part of the e-mail, click the Browse button and select the file.

❑ If you select Display A Message from the Action list, type a Title and Message. Task Scheduler displays the message to the user when the task is triggered.

7. In the Conditions tab of the Create Task dialog box, as shown in Figure 6-15, you can specify criteria that must be met in addition to any triggers you have configured. This enables you to configure the task to run only if the computer is idle for a specific amount of time and to configure the task to stop if the user returns to the computer, run only if the mobile computer is plugged in, or run only if a specific network connection is available.

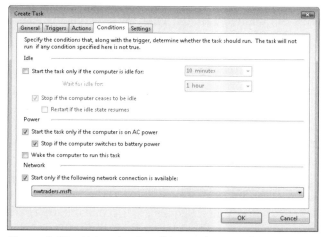

Figure 6-15   Using the Conditions tab to configure conditions to further refine the circumstances that trigger a task

8. In the Settings tab of the Create Task dialog box, as shown in Figure 6-16, you can configure the following:

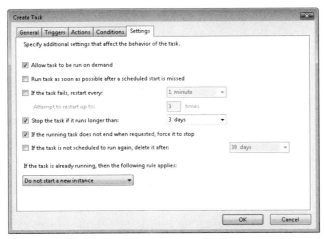

Figure 6-16   Using the Settings tab to configure tasks to automatically restart

- ❑ Whether users can manually launch a task by selecting the Allow Task To Be Run On Demand check box.
- ❑ The task to run as soon as possible after a scheduled start is missed (for example, if the computer is shut down) by selecting the Run Task As Soon As Possible After A Scheduled Start Is Missed.
- ❑ The task to automatically restart if it fails by selecting the If The Task Fails, Restart Every check box and selecting an interval. This is useful if the task relies on an external resource that might not always be available, such as a network connection or an external hard disk.
- ❑ Task Manager to stop the task if it runs longer than a specified amount of time by selecting the Stop The Task If It Runs Longer Than check box and the If The Running Task Does Not End When Requested, Force It To Stop check box.
- ❑ Task Manager to delete automatically by selecting the If The Task Is Not Scheduled To Run Again, Delete It After check box.
- ❑ Whether multiple instances of the task can run by selecting a nondefault setting from the If The Task Is Already Running list.

9. Click OK to create your new task.

How to Create Tasks with the SchTasks.exe Command-Line Tool

Although the Scheduled Tasks console is by far the simplest way to schedule tasks, if you need to schedule tasks (or perform other task management activities) from a command-line or from a script, you can use the SchTasks.exe command-line tool.

SchTasks.exe supports the following parameters:

- **/Create**   Create a new task.
- **/Delete**   Delete an existing task.
- **/Query**   View tasks.
- **/Change**   Modify an existing task.
- **/Run**   Launch an existing scheduled task.
- **/End**   Stop a currently running task.

For detailed information about any of these tasks, run the command at a command prompt with the /? parameter. For example, to view detailed information about creating a new task, you would run the following command:

```
SchTasks.exe /Create /?
```

To create a new task named "Launch Notepad" that runs hourly (starting now) with the current user's credentials, you could use the following command:

```
SchTasks.exe /create /sc hourly /tn "Launch Notepad" /tr Notepad.exe
SUCCESS: The scheduled task "Launch Notepad" has successfully been created.
```

To delete the same task, you would run the following command:

```
C:\Windows\system32>schtasks /delete /tn "Launch Notepad"
WARNING: Are you sure you want to remove the task "Launch Notepad" (Y/N)? y SUCCESS: The
scheduled task "Launch Notepad" was successfully deleted.
```

How to Manage Existing Tasks

Managing tasks with the Task Scheduler tool uses the same user interface for creating tasks. Within Task Scheduler, custom tasks are located in the *Task Scheduler\Task Scheduler Library* node.

Additionally, Microsoft includes dozens of default scheduled tasks located under Task Scheduler\Task Scheduler Library\Microsoft. You can modify some aspects of these tasks if you need to change their scheduled time or other settings affecting their performance. Some of the scheduled tasks you might want to modify include the following:

- **Task Scheduler Library\Microsoft\Windows\Defrag\ScheduledDefrag**   Automatically defragments your hard disk at 1 A.M. every Wednesday or the next time the computer is plugged in and idle. This task automatically stops if the computer ceases to be idle.
- **Task Scheduler Library\Microsoft\Windows\Shell\CrawlStartPages**   When your computer is idle and plugged in, this task indexes files on your computer for fast searching.
- **Task Scheduler Library\Microsoft\Windows\SystemRestore\SR**   Creates a system restore point every day at midnight and at system startup.

■ **Task Scheduler Library\Microsoft\Windows\WindowsBackup\AutomaticBackup**   This task is created when a user schedules an automatic backup. You can update this task's configuration using the Backup Status And Configuration tool.

Some tasks are hidden by default. To view these tasks, click the View menu in Task Scheduler, and then select Show Hidden Tasks.

NOTE   Group Policy settings

You cannot use the Group Policy settings located under both Computer Configuration and User Configuration at Administrative Templates\Windows Components\Task Scheduler to configure Windows Vista. These settings apply only to earlier versions of Windows.

How to Troubleshoot Problems Running Tasks

You can quickly view the last result of a scheduled task by selecting Task Scheduler Library in the Task Scheduler Tool. The Last Run Time and the Last Run Result columns reveal when the task was last started and whether the task completed successfully. Note that some tasks misreport the status when they complete; for example, the AutomaticBackup scheduled task always appears to have run successfully even if it was unable to perform a backup (you should use the Backup Status And Configuration tool to accurately view whether backups ran).

To view detailed information about a task, double-click the task, and then click the History tab. As shown in Figure 6-17, the History tab displays the results of every scheduled task. Each entry corresponds to an event in the TaskScheduler\Operational event log for that specific scheduled task.

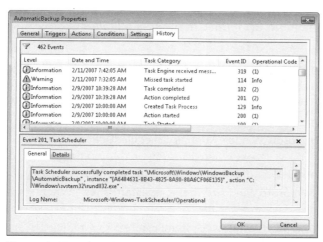

Figure 6-17   The History tab, which reveals whether the task ran successfully in the past

To view a detailed history of all the actions Task Scheduler has taken, view the Applications And Services Logs\Microsoft\Windows\TaskScheduler\Operational log file in Event Viewer. In particular, the following event IDs are useful:

- **100 – Task Started and 200 – Action Started**   Appear when a scheduled task starts.
- **102 – Task Completed and 201 – Action Completed**   Appear when a scheduled task is completed.
- **114 – Missed Task Started**   Appears when a scheduled task was unable to run (perhaps because the computer was shut down or on battery power) but is being restarted.
- **322 – Launch Request Ignored, Instance Already Running**   Appears when a previously run task hasn't finished and the task is configured to not run multiple instances simultaneously.
- **326 – Launch Condition Not Met, Computer On Batteries**   The scheduled task was configured to run only when the user was logged on. If this is a default scheduled task, it will automatically run later.
- **332 – Launch Condition Not Met, User Not Logged-On**   The scheduled task was configured to run only when the user was logged on. If this is a default scheduled task, it will automatically run later.
- **101 – Task Start Failed, 103 – Action Start Failed, 103 – Task Failed To Start, and 203 – Action Failed To Start**   Appear when Scheduled Tasks cannot start a task.
- **126– Task Restarted On Failure**   Appears after a task fails and it has been configured to automatically restart.

A typical event log includes a large number of warning and error events. Most of these can be safely disregarded because they are probably caused by default scheduled tasks that are configured to automatically restart later.

Practice: Create and Manage a Scheduled Task

In this practice, you create a scheduled task that launches Notepad on a regular basis. Then, you update the scheduled task to launch when an event occurs. Next, you analyze the history and System event log for events added by Scheduled Task. Finally, you remove the scheduled task.

▶ **Practice 1: Create a Scheduled Task**

In this practice, you create a scheduled task that opens Notepad every five minutes.

1. Launch Task Scheduler by clicking Start, All Programs, Accessories, System Tools, and then Task Scheduler. Respond to the UAC prompt that appears.
2. In the console tree, select and then right-click Task Scheduler. Click Create Task.
3. In the General tab of the Create Task dialog box, type **Launch Notepad** in the Name box.

4. Click the Triggers tab, and then click the New button. Under Settings, click Daily. Under Advanced Settings, select the Repeat Task Every check box, and set the delay to 5 Minutes. Click OK to close the New Trigger dialog box.

5. In the Create Task dialog box, click the Actions tab, and then click the New button.

6. In the New Action dialog box, click the Browse button and select %windir%\notepad.exe. Click OK.

7. In the Conditions tab of the Create Task dialog box, clear the Start The Task Only If The Computer Is On AC Power check box. Changing this setting will allow the task to run even if you're using a mobile computer that's not plugged in.

8. Click OK to finish creating the task.

9. In Task Scheduler, select Task Scheduler Library. In the middle pane, notice that your new task is listed. (If you do not see your new task, right-click Task Scheduler Library, and then click Refresh to update the task listing.) Make note of the Next Run Time—this is the next time the task will automatically run.

10. Right-click your task, and then click Run. Notice that Notepad immediately appears.

11. In Task Scheduler, in the Actions pane, click Refresh. Notice that the Last Run Time has been updated. The Next Run Time doesn't change; this is always based on the last scheduled running.

12. Wait until the Next Run Time and close Notepad when it appears.

▶ **Practice 2: Configure an Event as a Trigger**

In this practice, you examine the task history and event viewer to analyze whether the task was successfully launched. To complete this practice, you must have completed Practice 1.

1. In Task Scheduler, double-click your scheduled task.

2. Click the Triggers tab. Then, click New.

3. In the New Trigger dialog box, click the Begin The Task list, and then click On An Event.

4. Click the Log list, and then click System. Next, click the Source list, and then click Windows Defender. Click OK to create the new trigger.

    This new trigger will cause the scheduled task to run each time a new Windows Defender event is added.

5. Double-click the Daily trigger. Then, in the Edit Trigger dialog box, clear the Repeat Task Every check box to prevent the task from opening Notepad every five minutes. Click OK.

    Note that you can have multiple triggers enabled simultaneously.

6. Click OK.

7. Now, generate a Windows Defender event. Click Start and type **notepad %windir%\system32\drivers\etc\hosts**. Press Ctrl+Shift+Enter to open Notepad with administrative privileges. Respond to the UAC prompt that appears. In Notepad, type a space

anywhere in the file to cause the Hosts file to be updated. Then, save the file by clicking File, and then clicking Save.

A second instance of Notepad opens immediately because Windows Defender generated an event.

8. Close both Notepad windows.

▶ **Practice 3: Analyze a Scheduled Task**

In this practice, you examine the task history and event viewer to analyze whether the task was successfully launched. To complete this practice, you must have completed Practice

1. In Task Scheduler, double-click the task to open the task properties. In the General tab, click Run Whether User Is Logged On Or Not. Then, click OK. Type your username and password when prompted.

2. Right-click your task, and then click Run. Notice that Notepad does not appear.

3. Press Ctrl+Alt+Del, and then click Start Task Manager. Click the Processes tab. Then, click the Show Processes From All Users button and respond to the UAC prompt that appears. Now that Task Manager is showing processes for all users, click the Image Name column to sort by process name and find Notepad.exe to verify that Task Scheduler launched it correctly. If this were a script, the scheduled task would end after it completed. However, because it is a windowed application and is waiting on a user response, it will continue to run indefinitely.

4. In Task Manager, right-click the Notepad.exe process, and then click End Process.

5. Click your scheduled task. Then, in the lower-middle pane, click the History tab. Browse the events. Notice that multiple events are created each time a task is started.

6. Click Start, right-click Computer, and then click Manage. Respond to the UAC prompt that appears.

7. In the Computer Management console, expand System Tools, Event Viewer, Applications And Services Logs, Microsoft, Windows, and TaskScheduler, and then click Operational. Notice that the events shown here correspond directly to the events shown in the Task Scheduler history but that events for other tasks are also shown.

▶ **Practice 4: Disable and Delete a Scheduled Task**

In this practice, you disable and then delete your scheduled task.

1. In Task Scheduler, right-click your scheduled task, and then click Disable. With this setting the task will not be run if any of the trigger conditions are matched. However, users could still manually launch the task.

2. Right-click the scheduled task and click Delete. This permanently removes the task.

Lesson Summary

- Task Scheduler in Windows Vista includes an improved user interface, new triggers (such as starting a task when a specific event appears), new actions (such as sending an e-mail), better security, and improved manageability.

- To create a task, launch Task Scheduler, click Create Task, and then provide the details for the task.

- To create a task with the SchTasks.exe command-line tool, run it at a command prompt with elevated privileges and use the /Create parameter.

- To manage existing tasks, use the Task Scheduler console or the SchTasks.exe command-line tool.

- If you experience a problem running a scheduled task, you can isolate the cause of the problem by viewing the task history and the event log.

Lesson Review

You can use the following questions to test your knowledge of the information in Lesson 3, "Using Task Scheduler." The questions are also available on the companion CD if you prefer to review them in electronic form.

NOTE Answers

Answers to these questions and explanations of why each answer choice is right or wrong are located in the "Answers" section at the end of the book.

1. Which of the following are valid ways to start a scheduled task? (Choose all that apply.)
   A. Daily at a specific time
   B. When the user launches e-mail
   C. When the screen saver starts
   D. When the computer has been idle for 10 minutes

2. You need to create a scheduled task from a command file (also known as a batch file). Which of the following tools should you use?
   A. Task Scheduler
   B. At.exe
   C. SchTasks.exe
   D. TaskMgr.exe

3. Which of the following actions can you take from a scheduled task? (Choose all that apply.)

   A. Start a program.

   B. Restart the computer.

   C. Send an e-mail.

   D. Display a message to the user.

Chapter Review

To further practice and reinforce the skills you learned in this chapter, you can perform the following tasks:

- Review the chapter summary.
- Review the list of key terms introduced in this chapter.
- Complete the case scenarios. These scenarios set up real-world situations involving the topics of this chapter and ask you to create a solution.
- Complete the suggested practices.
- Take a practice test.

Chapter Summary

- The Windows Vista event log contains a great deal of valuable information, including events that describe problems that have already occurred or might occur soon. By monitoring these events using event forwarding, you can respond to problems more quickly or prevent them from becoming critical.
- Data collector sets are a new feature in Windows Vista that you can use to quickly capture a snapshot of a computer's status. This can be extremely useful when you are troubleshooting problems that can't be isolated based on the event log. Another new feature is the Reliability Monitor, which graphically charts a computer's stability over time. Using the Reliability Monitor, you can determine when problems began to arise on a computer and what changes might have contributed to those problems.
- Like earlier versions of Windows, you can use Task Scheduler to run programs at a specific time of day. With Windows Vista, you can also launch Task Scheduler when the computer starts, shuts down, or when a specific event occurs. Besides running programs, tasks can display messages to users or send an e-mail. To manage tasks from the command line, use the SchTasks.exe tool.

Key Terms

Do you know what these key terms mean? You can check your answers by looking up the terms in the glossary at the end of the book.

- event forwarding
- pull delivery mode
- push delivery mode

Case Scenarios

In the following case scenarios, you will apply what you've learned about how to monitor and troubleshoot Windows Vista computers. You can find answers to these questions in the "Answers" section at the end of this book.

Case Scenario 1: Monitoring Kiosk Computers

You are a systems administrator at the Baldwin Museum of Science. In addition to managing computers used by internal staff, you manage several Windows Vista computers that are configured as kiosks in the museum's front lobby. Visitors to the museum can use these computers to browse a limited number of websites with science-related content. Desktop security restrictions limit the applications users can run and the websites they can visit.

The museum attracts a large audience of intelligent, computer-savvy visitors. Unfortunately, some of them have taken it as a challenge to break into the kiosk computers. For example, you recently happened upon an attacker using an internal wireless connection to attack a kiosk computer across the network. You noticed the attack because you happened to discover an event in the event log, as shown in Figure 6-18.

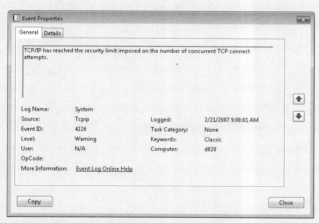

Figure 6-18   An event indicating an active attack in your organization

Questions

Answer the following questions for your manager:

1. You manage several kiosk computers. How can you easily monitor all of their event logs for this particular event?
2. Which bandwidth optimization technique should you use for event forwarding?

3. If this event appears, you need to know about it immediately. How can you be actively notified of an attack?

Case Scenario 2: Troubleshooting Client Computer Problems

You are a desktop support technician working at Woodgrove Bank. Several times a day you get support calls from users who are experiencing problems on their computers. Because the users' skills are focused on banking, they typically know very little about managing computers.

Unfortunately, the users' lack of computer experience makes troubleshooting more difficult. Users often cannot describe the exact problem they are having. Additionally, they are typically unable to correlate the installation of a new program or a new piece of hardware with the appearance of recurring problems.

Interviews

Following is a list of company personnel interviewed and their statements:

- **Stuart Railson, Desktop Support Technician**   "These users are so hard to help. This guy complained that his computer was crashing every day, and he has this attitude like it's my fault. So I look into it, and I discover that he took it upon himself to upgrade one of his drivers—and of course that driver is causing the blue screens. It sure was a pain to find the exact source of the problem, though, because this user had made a bunch of changes to his computer. Digging through that event log is tough."

- **Angela Barbariol, IT Manager**   "As you know, all of our client computers are running Windows 2000 Professional or Windows XP Professional. They're working well, and I'm hesitant to upgrade unless there is a significant benefit. For example, if you can demonstrate that you'd be able to more rapidly solve user problems, I'd seriously consider upgrading."

Questions

Answer the following questions for your manager:

1. Could Windows Vista help you identify changes users had made that might contribute to a problem? If so, what feature would do that?

2. Does Windows Vista have a way to take a snapshot of the system configuration so that you can quickly analyze it and identify any potential problems, such as driver failures? How do you use that feature? Can we extend it to capture the configuration of our internal applications?

Suggested Practices

To successfully master the objectives covered in this chapter, complete the following tasks.

Configure and Troubleshoot Event Forwarding

For this task, you should complete at least Practices 1 and 2. If you want a better understanding of how to configure event forwarding in an enterprise, complete Practice 3 as well. Completing these configuration tasks will also help you with your troubleshooting skills because problems are bound to arise when configuring nondefault event forwarding.

- **Practice 1: Forward Events in a Workgroup**   Configure a workgroup computer to forward events to another workgroup computer.
- **Practice 2: Forward Events Using Different Optimization Techniques**   Configure a forwarding computer to send events to a collecting computer using each of the three standard bandwidth optimization techniques. Then, customize the event forwarding configuration by reducing the time required to forward events by half.
- **Practice 3: Configure Event Forwarding by Using Group Policy**   Use Group Policy to configure multiple client computers to forward events to a collecting computer. For the greatest scalability, use logon scripts to configure the forwarding computers—it would be too time-consuming to manually configure forwarding computers in an enterprise.

Troubleshoot Performance and Reliability Issues

For this objective, you should complete all three practices to gain experience troubleshooting performance and reliability issues.

- **Practice 1: Run Standard Data Collector Sets**   Run each standard data collector set on several production computers. Analyze the report generated by each.
- **Practice 2: Run Reliability Monitor**   Run Reliability Monitor on several production computers. How stable are the computers? Can you identify the cause of any stability problems?
- **Practice 3: Create a Custom Data Collector Set**   Using several applications that your organization uses internally, create a data collector set that gathers each of the application's configuration settings.

Configure and Manage the Task Scheduler

For this objective, you should complete all three practices.

- **Practice 1: Create a Scheduled Task to Send an E-mail**   Create scheduled tasks that send you an e-mail each time the computer starts or shuts down.

- **Practice 2: Examine Default Scheduled Tasks**   Examine the default scheduled tasks, including the hidden scheduled tasks. For each task, think about why Microsoft chose to configure the triggers and conditions the way they did.
- **Practice 3: Examine the Task Scheduler History**   On a production computer, examine the Task Scheduler history to identify tasks that failed. Determine whether each failure is acceptable because it will run again later or whether the failure requires an administrator to resolve the problem.

Take a Practice Test

The practice tests on this book's companion CD offer many options. For example, you can test yourself on just the content covered in this chapter, or you can test yourself on all the 70-622 certification exam content. You can set up the test so that it closely simulates the experience of taking a certification exam, or you can set it up in study mode so that you can look at the correct answers and explanations after you answer each question.

MORE INFO   **Practice tests**

For details about all the practice test options available, see "How to Use the Practice Tests" in this book's Introduction.

Chapter 7

Authenticating, Authorizing, and Auditing Access to Resources

You can use access control, also known as authorization, to control which users can access a file, registry key, printer, or other object. Before authorization can be effective, the operating system must validate a user's identity using a process known as authentication. Although authentication and authorization work together to provide data security, they can also cause problems by blocking access to authorized users.

This chapter describes how to configure authentication and authorization and how to troubleshoot related security problems.

Exam objectives in this chapter:
- Troubleshoot authentication issues.
- Configure and troubleshoot access to resources.

Lessons in this chapter:

Before You Begin

To complete the lessons in this chapter, you should be familiar with Windows Vista and be comfortable with the following tasks:

- Installing Windows Vista and joining a domain
- Configuring Group Policy settings
- Performing basic configuration tasks of Microsoft Windows Server 2003 domain controllers

To complete all the practices in this chapter, you should have two networked Windows Vista computers.

Lesson 1: Authenticating Users

Before a user can log on to a Windows Vista computer, connect to a shared folder, or browse a protected website, the resource must validate the user's identity using a process known as authentication. Windows Vista supports a variety of authentication techniques, including the traditional user name and password, smart cards, and third-party authentication components. Additionally, Windows Vista can authenticate users against the local user database or an Active Directory directory service domain.

This lesson provides a basic background in authentication technologies and then describes how to audit logons and troubleshoot authentication problems.

After this lesson, you will be able to:

- Describe authentication and list common authentication techniques.
- Describe how the Windows Vista logon architecture differs from earlier versions of Windows.
- Describe how Windows Vista provides an improved infrastructure for smart cards.
- Manually add user names and passwords to Credential Manager to enable automatic authentication to network resources.
- Troubleshoot authentication issues.

Estimated lesson time: 20 minutes

What Is Authentication?

Authentication is the process of identifying a user. In home environments authentication is often as simple as clicking a user name at the Windows Vista logon screen. However, in enterprise environments almost all authentication requests require users to provide both a user name (to identify themselves) and a password (to prove that they really are that person).

Windows Vista also supports authentication using a smart card. The smart card, which is about the size of a credit card, contains a chip that stores a certificate that uniquely identifies the user. As long as a user doesn't give the smart card to someone else, inserting the smart card into a computer sufficiently proves the user's identity. Typically, users also need to type a password or personal identification number (PIN) to prove that they aren't using someone else's smart card. When you combine two forms of authentication (such as both typing a password and providing a smart card), it's called multifactor authentication. Multifactor authentication is much more secure than single-factor authentication.

Biometrics is another popular form of authentication. Although a password proves your identity by testing "something you know" and a smart card tests "something you have," biometrics test "something you are" by examining a unique feature of your physiology. Today the most common biometric authentication mechanisms are fingerprint readers (now built into many mobile computers) and retinal scanners.

NOTE Biometrics

Biometrics are the most secure and reliable authentication method because you cannot lose or forget your authentication. However, it's also the least commonly used method. Reliable biometric readers are too expensive for many organizations, and some users dislike biometric readers because they feel the devices violate their privacy.

The New Windows Vista Logon Architecture

Logging on to Windows provides access to local resources (including Encrypting File System [EFS]-encrypted files) and, in Active Directory environments, protected network resources. Many organizations require more than a user name and password to authenticate users. For example, they might require multifactor authentication using both a password and biometric identification or a smart card.

In Windows XP and earlier versions of Windows, implementing custom authentication methods required developers to completely rewrite the Graphical Identification and Authentication (GINA) interface. Often, the effort required did not justify the benefits provided by strong authentication, and the project was abandoned. Additionally, Windows XP only supported a single GINA interface.

With Windows Vista developers can now provide custom authentication methods by creating a new credential provider. This requires significantly less development effort, meaning more organizations will offer custom authentication methods for Windows Vista.

NOTE Upgrading authentication from Windows XP

If you used custom authentication (such as a fingerprint scanner) with Windows XP, you will need updated software to work with Windows Vista. Because Windows Vista does not include the GINA interface, custom GINA interface implementations for Windows XP will not work. Windows Vista does include a smart card credential provider, so you might not need custom software to use smart cards.

The new architecture also enables credential providers to be integrated throughout the user experience. For example, the same code used to implement a fingerprint authentication scheme at the Windows logon screen can be used to prompt the user for a fingerprint when accessing a particular corporate resource. The same prompt also can be used by applications that use the new credential user interface application programming interface (API).

Additionally, the Windows logon user interface can use multiple credential providers simultaneously, providing greater flexibility for environments that might have different authentication requirements for different users. For example, you can have most users log on using a user name and password but require your IT department to use smart cards.

Smart Card Improvements

Both Windows 2000 and Windows XP support authentication by means of smart cards. However, previous versions of Windows required administrators to deploy and maintain additional components, such as cryptography modules and communications support for card readers, to support their smart card infrastructure. Smart card improvements in Windows Vista both simplify and improve smart card management.

To simplify development of smart card software tools (which is typically done by the smart card provider), a common cryptographic service provider (CSP) implements all the standard back-end cryptographic functions that hardware and software developers need. In addition, integrated third-party card modules make it easier to rapidly deploy a smart card solution and enable protected, predictable communications between the CSP and other components of the smart card infrastructure. Microsoft is also working with smart card providers to improve the technology by certifying smart card modules and making module updates available with Windows Update.

Additionally, smart card users will need to enter their PINs less frequently because of Kerberos improvements, and users will be able to reset their PINs without calling the support desk.

To assist users who access their smart cards infrequently, Windows Vista stores a copy of smart card certificates (just the public key—private keys are never copied from a smart card) within Credential Manager. This enables Credential Manager to notify the user that the certificates on the smart card are going to expire, allowing the user to renew the certificates prior to expiration. This will help prevent problems in which users who rarely need to use smart cards discover that they don't work when they do finally need them.

Real World: Smart Card Improvements

Tony Northrup

If you're wondering how all these smart card improvements in Windows Vista will help you, you're probably not alone. As an administrator, you still can't just buy a stack of smart cards and start using them. You'll need to work with a third-party smart card provider, just like you would for earlier versions of Windows. It's the developers at the third-party smart card provider that will really appreciate the improvements because it'll make their jobs easier and make their smart card software much more elegant.

Even though it's developers who benefit the most from these improvements, they're still important for you to understand.

How to Use Credential Manager

Credential Manager is a single-sign on feature, originally for Windows Server 2003 and Windows XP, that enables users to input user names and passwords for multiple network resources and applications. When different resources require authentication, Windows can then automatically provide the credentials without requiring the user to type them.

In Windows Vista, Credential Manager can roam stored user names and passwords between multiple Windows Vista computers in an Active Directory domain. Windows Vista stores credentials in the user's Active Directory user object. This enables users to store credentials once and use them from any logon session within the Active Directory domain. For example, if you connect to a password-protected web server and you select the Remember My Password check box, Microsoft Internet Explorer will be able to retrieve your saved password later, even if you log on to a different computer. Although earlier versions of Windows will not be able to access the stored credentials, it won't cause any problems if a user does log on to Windows XP.

Users can take advantage of Credential Manager without even being aware of it. For example, each time a user connects to a shared folder or printer and selects the Reconnect At Logon check box, Windows Vista automatically stores that user's credentials within Credential Manager. Similarly, if a user authenticates to a website that requires authentication and selects the Remember My Password check box in the Internet Explorer authentication dialog box, Internet Explorer stores the user name and password in Credential Manager.

MORE INFO   Credential roaming

For detailed information about credential roaming, read "Configuring and Troubleshooting Certificate Services Client-Credential Roaming" at *http://www.microsoft.com/technet/security/guidance/cryptographyetc/client-credential-roaming/implementation-differences.mspx*.

Windows Vista automatically adds credentials used to connect to shared folders to the Credential Manager. However, you might want to manually add a user name and password so that Windows Vista can automatically provide those credentials for a group of computers in a different domain. To manually add a user name and password to Credential Manager, follow these steps:

1. Click Start, and then click Control Panel.
2. Click the User Accounts link. Then, click the User Accounts link again.
3. In the left pane, click the Manage Your Network Passwords link.

   The Stored User Names And Passwords dialog box appears, as shown in Figure 7-1. You can also open this tool by running the case-sensitive command **rundll32.exe keymgr.dll,KRShowKeyMgr**.

Figure 7-1   Using Credential Manager to automatically authenticate to resources that require credentials other than those you use to log on

4.   Click Add.

The Stored Credential Properties dialog box appears.

5.   In the Log On To box, type the name used to identify the network resource. You can use an asterisk (*) as a wildcard. For example, to use the credential for all resources in the contoso.com domain, you could type *.contoso.com.

6.   In the User Name and Password boxes, type your user credentials.

7.   In the Credential Type group, select A Windows Logon Credential if you are connecting to a shared folder, printer, or other Windows network resource. If you are connecting to a website, select A Web Site Or Program Credential. Figure 7-2 demonstrates how to complete the Stored Credential Properties dialog box.

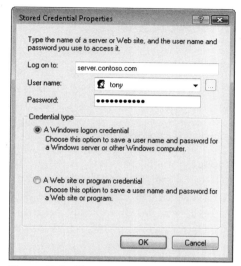

Figure 7-2   The Stored Credential Properties dialog box

NOTE **Websites that Credential Manager can automatically authenticate**

The only websites that Credential Manager can automatically authenticate to are those that use Hypertext Transfer Protocol (HTTP) authentication. When visiting the site, the web browser will open a dialog box to prompt for credentials. Credential Manager cannot remember your user name and password for websites that use an HTML form for authentication (such as those that have a special logon page), which is much more common. Credential Manager can also remember .NET Passport credentials.

---

   8. Click OK, and then click Close to save your changes.

You can also manually back up and restore credentials using the Stored User Names And Passwords dialog box.

How to Troubleshoot Authentication Issues

Sometimes users might experience problems authenticating to resources that are more complex than mistyping a password or leaving the Caps Lock key on. The sections that follow describe troubleshooting techniques that can help you better isolate authentication problems.

Real World: UAC Compatibility Problems

Tony Northrup

Users often confuse authentication and authorization issues. This isn't a surprise because both types of problems can show the exact same error message: Access Is Denied. Because User Account Control (UAC) limits the user's privileges and many applications were not designed to work with UAC, security errors are bound to be even more frequent in Windows Vista than they were in Windows XP.

Most UAC-related problems are authorization-related, not authentication-related. If the user doesn't receive a UAC prompt at all but still receives a security error, it's definitely an authorization problem. If the user receives a UAC prompt and the user's credentials are accepted (or if the user logs on as an administrator and only needs to click the Continue button), it's definitely an authorization problem. UAC problems will be authentication-related only if UAC prompts a user for credentials and rejects the user's password. For information about troubleshooting authorization problems, read Lesson 3, "Troubleshooting Authorization Problems and Auditing User Access."

How to Troubleshoot Authentication Problems

By default, Windows Vista does not add an event to the event log when a user provides incorrect credentials (such as when a user mistypes a password). Therefore, when troubleshooting authentication problems, your first step should be to enable auditing for logon events so that you can gather more information about the credentials the user provided and the resource being accessed.

Windows Vista (and earlier versions of Windows) provides two separate authentication auditing policies:

- **Audit Logon Events** Audits authentication attempts for local resources, such as a user logging on locally, elevating privileges using a UAC prompt, or connecting over the network (including connecting using Remote Desktop or connecting to a shared folder). All authentication attempts will be audited, regardless of whether the authentication attempt uses a domain account or a local user account.

■ **Audit Account Logon Events** Audits domain authentications. No matter which computer the user authenticates to, these events appear only on the domain controller that handled the authentication request. Typically, you do not need to enable auditing of account logon events when troubleshooting authentication issues on Windows Vista computers. However, success auditing of these events is enabled for domain controllers by default.

To log failed authentication attempts, you must enable auditing by following these steps:

1. Click Start, click All Programs, click Administrative Tools, and then click Local Security Policy. Respond to the UAC prompt that appears. If you are not automatically prompted with a UAC prompt, you will need to right-click the Local Security Policy icon, and then click Run As Administrator.
2. In the Local Security Policy console, expand Local Policies, and then select Audit Policy.
3. In the right pane, double-click Audit Logon Events.
4. In the Audit Logon Events Properties dialog box, select the Failure check box to add an event to the Security event log each time a user provides invalid credentials. If you also want to log successful authentication attempts (which will include authentication attempts from services and other nonuser entities), select the Success check box.
5. Click OK.
6. Restart your computer to apply the changes.

With auditing enabled, you can view audit events in Event Viewer by following these steps:

1. Click Start, right-click Computer, and then click Manage. Respond to the UAC prompt that appears.
2. Expand System Tools, Windows Logs, and then select Security.
   Event Viewer displays all security events. To view only successful logons, click the Filter Current Log link in the Actions pane, and show only Event ID 4624. To view only unsuccessful logon attempts, click the Filter Current Log link, and show only Event ID 4625.

Figure 7-3 shows an example of a logon audit failure that occurred when the user provided invalid credentials at a UAC prompt. Notice that the Caller Process Name (listed under Process Information) is Consent.exe, the UAC process.

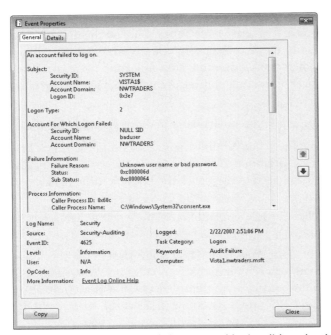

Figure 7-3   A logon audit failure caused by invalid credentials

Audits from failed authentication attempts from across the network resemble the following. In particular, the Account Name, Account Domain, Workstation Name, and Source Network Address are useful for identifying the origin computer.

```
An account failed to log on.

Subject:
    Security ID:        NULL SID
    Account Name:       -
    Account Domain:     -
    Logon ID:           0x0

Logon Type:             3

Account For Which Logon Failed:
    Security ID:        NULL SID
    Account Name:       baduser
    Account Domain:     NWTRADERS
Failure Information:
    Failure Reason:     Unknown user name or bad password.
    Status:             0xc000006d
    Sub Status:         0xc0000064

Process Information:
    Caller Process ID:  0x0
```

```
Caller Process Name:    -

Network Information:
   Workstation Name:
   CONTOSO-DC      Source Network Address: 192.168.1.212
   Source Port:            4953

Detailed Authentication Information:
   Logon Process:              NtLmSsp
   Authentication Package:     NTLM
   Transited Services:         -
   Package Name (NTLM only):   -
   Key Length:                 0
```

When you are authenticating to network resources, authentication failures are always logged on the server, not on the client. For example, if you attempt to connect to a shared folder and you mistype the password, the event won't appear in your local event log—it will appear in the event log of the computer sharing the folder.

NOTE Don't trust the reported computer name

The computer sending the authentication attempt communicates its own workstation name. Therefore, if the attack is malicious, the workstation name might be intentionally invalid. The IP address should always be correct, however.

How to Troubleshoot Network Authentication Issues

To improve network security, network administrators often require 802.1X authentication before allowing client computers to connect to either wireless or wired networks. 802.1X authentication works at the network infrastructure layer to provide full network access only to computers that are able to authenticate. For example, on most wireless networks client computers must be configured with a network security key or a certificate in order to connect to the wireless access point. On wired networks, network switches that support 802.1X allow a newly connected computer to access only a limited number of servers until the computer is authenticated.

Network authentication can be a problem if Group Policy settings are used to distribute the certificates required for network authentication because the client computer must first connect to the network to retrieve the certificate. To work around this requirement for 802.1X-protected wireless networks, connect client computers to a wired network long enough to update Group Policy settings.

If your organization requires authentication for wired networks (a less common requirement than requiring wireless authentication), work with the domain administrators to identify a procedure for temporarily connecting to the network when wired 802.1X authentication fails. This process might involve connecting the computer across a virtual private network (VPN), manually importing the client certificate on the client computer, or using a smart card to authenticate to the network.

How to Troubleshoot an Untrusted Certification Authority

Certificates, such as those issued by an enterprise certification authority (CA), are often used for authentication. Windows Vista can store certificates locally to authenticate a user or the computer itself, and users can carry certificates with them on smart cards. Typically, domain administrators should manage certificates, and settings should be propagated to client computers using Group Policy settings. However, if you receive an error informing you that the CA that issued a certificate is not trusted, you can view existing CAs and then import the CA's certificate to configure Windows Vista to trust any certificates issued by the CA.

To view trusted CAs, follow these steps:

1. Click Start, type **mmc**, and then press Enter to open a blank Microsoft Management Console. Respond to the UAC prompt if it appears.
2. Click File, and then click Add/Remove Snap-in.
3. Select Certificates and click Add.
4. If prompted, select My User Account, and then click Finish.
5. Click OK to close the Add Or Remove Snap-Ins dialog box.
6. Expand Certificates – Current User, expand Trusted Root Certification Authorities, and then select Certificates.

   The middle pane shows a list of trusted CAs. By default, this includes more than 10 default public CAs. Additionally, it should include any internal CAs used by your organization. If your organization has an enterprise CA and it does not appear on this list, contact the domain administrator for assistance because the CA trust should be configured by using Group Policy.

Alternatively, you can manually trust a CA by following these steps from within the Certificates snap-in:

1. Below Trusted Root Certification Authorities, right-click Certificates, click All Tasks, and then click Import.

   The Certificate Import Wizard appears.
2. On the Welcome To The Certificate Import Wizard page, click Next.
3. On the File To Import page, click Browse. Select your CA certificate (which can be provided by the CA administrator or exported from a computer that trusts the CA), and then click Next.
4. On the Certificate Store page, accept the default certificate store (Trusted Root Certification Authorities), and then click Next.

5. On the Completing The Certificate Import Wizard page, click Finish.

   If prompted with a security warning, click Yes.

6. Click OK to confirm that the import was successful.

   Now your user account will trust any certificates issued by the CA.

Practice: Save Credentials for Future Use

In this practice, you use Credential Manager to store credentials, enabling you to automatically authenticate to a remote computer.

▶ **Practice 1: Use Credential Manager**

In this practice, you use Credential Manager to save credentials for future use.

1. Log on to a Windows Vista computer. Create a new user account with the user name MyLocalUser and assign a password. This account will not exist on any network computers. Therefore, when connecting to remote computers, the user will always need to provide alternate credentials.

2. On a remote computer, create a shared folder. Make note of the server and share name.

3. Log on as MyLocalUser.

4. Click Start, and then click Computer. Then, click Map Network Drive.

5. In the Map Network Drive dialog box, type \\server\share to attempt to connect to the share you created in step 2. Click Finish.

6. When the Connect To Server dialog box appears, click Cancel twice.

   This dialog box appeared because your current account did not have privileges on the remote server, and you had not entered credentials in Credential Manager.

NOTE   Manually configure the credentials for this practice

For the purpose of this practice, you should manually configure the credentials using Credential Manager. However, a much easier way to accomplish the same thing is to complete the *User Name* and *Password* fields, and then select the Remember My Password check box. This causes Windows Explorer to automatically store the credentials.

---

7. Click Start, and then click Control Panel.

8. Click the User Accounts link. Then, click the User Accounts link again.

9. In the left pane, click the Manage Your Network Passwords link.

   The Stored User Names And Passwords dialog box appears.

10. Click Add.

    The Stored Credential Properties dialog box appears.

11. In the Log On To box, type the name of the server that you attempted to connect to in step 5.

12. In the User Name and Password boxes, type your administrative credentials to the remote server.

13. Click OK. Then, click Close.

14. Click Start, and then click Computer. Then, click Map Network Drive.

15. In the Map Network Drive dialog box, type *server**share* to attempt to connect to the same share you specified in step 5. Clear the Reconnect At Logon check box, and then click Finish.

    Windows Explorer automatically connects to the shared folder without prompting you for credentials. Instead of requiring you to type the user name and password, it retrieved them from Credential Manager.

Lesson Summary

- Authentication is the process of identifying a user and proving the user's identity.

- Windows Vista has a new logon architecture that replaces the Graphical Identification and Authentication (GINA) interface with one or more credential providers.

- Windows Vista provides an improved infrastructure for managing smart cards and for developing smart card software.

- Credential Manager stores user credentials to provide automatic authentication during future attempts to access a resource. You can manually add credentials using the Stored User Names And Passwords tool in Control Panel.

- When troubleshooting user authentication issues, you should enable failure logon auditing, reproduce the authentication problem, and then examine the Security event log for details of the authentication failure. When troubleshooting network authentication issues, verify that Group Policy settings have been updated and work with network administrators to resolve the problem. When troubleshooting a problem with an untrusted CA, import the CA's certificate into the list of trusted root CAs.

Lesson Review

You can use the following questions to test your knowledge of the information in Lesson 1, "Authenticating Users." The questions are also available on the companion CD if you prefer to review them in electronic form.

NOTE **Answers**

Answers to these questions and explanations of why each answer choice is right or wrong are located in the "Answers" section at the end of the book.

1. Which of the following might support automatic authentication using Credential Manager? (Choose all that apply.)

    A. Connecting to a shared folder

    B. Connecting to a shared printer

    C. Authenticating to a website that uses an HTML form

    D. Authenticating to a website that prompts for user credentials using a dialog box

2. Which of the following statements about smart card support in Windows Vista is true?

    A. Windows Vista supports smart card authentication components created for Windows XP.

    B. Windows Vista has smart card authentication built in.

    C. Smart cards store a user name and password.

    D. A user must be a member of the Domain Admins group to reset the personal identification number (PIN) on a smart card.

3. Which of the following types of auditing would you enable to track when a user mistypes his or her user name and password when logging on to a Windows Vista domain member computer using a local user account?

    A. Audit Logon Events, Success

    B. Audit Logon Events, Failure

    C. Audit Account Logon Events, Success

    D. Audit Account Logon Events, Failure

4. Which of the following events would be logged in the local event log if you enabled auditing for successful and failed logon attempts? (Choose all that apply.)

    A. Logging on locally to a Windows Vista computer

    B. Typing a user name and password at a remote website

    C. Connecting to a remote shared folder

    D. Elevating privileges at a User Account Control (UAC) prompt

Lesson 2: Using Encryption to Control Access to Data

If an attacker has physical access to data, that person can easily circumvent operating system security features such as NTFS file permissions. However, with encryption you can protect data even if it falls into the wrong hands.

Encryption makes data completely unreadable without a valid decryption key. With encryption, attackers need access to both the data and the decryption key before they can access your private files. Windows Vista provides two file encryption technologies: EFS (for encrypting individual files and folders) and BitLocker (for encrypting the entire system drive). In many environments you will need to use both together.

This lesson describes how to configure and troubleshoot EFS and BitLocker.

> **After this lesson, you will be able to:**
> - Configure EFS, grant multiple users access to EFS-encrypted files, and back up and recover EFS certificates.
> - Describe how BitLocker encryption differs from EFS, enable BitLocker, and recover data on a BitLocker-encrypted volume.
>
> **Estimated lesson time: 40 minutes**

Encrypting File System (EFS)

EFS is a file encryption technology (supported only on NTFS volumes) that protects files from offline attacks such as hard disk theft. Because EFS works at the file system level, EFS is entirely transparent to end users and applications. In fact, the encryption is apparent only when a user who doesn't have a decryption key attempts to access an encrypted file. In that case, the file is completely inaccessible.

EFS is designed to protect sensitive data on mobile or shared computers, which are more susceptible to attack by techniques that circumvent the restrictions of access control lists (ACLs) such as file permissions. An attacker can steal a computer, remove the hard disk drives, place the drives in another system, and gain access to the stored files (even if they're protected by file permissions). When the attacker does not have the decryption key, however, files encrypted by EFS appear as unintelligible characters.

In most ways, EFS in Windows Vista is exactly the same as it was in Windows XP. Windows Vista adds the ability to store both user and recovery keys on smart cards. As an administrator, you can even store domain recovery keys on a smart card, enabling you to quickly recover EFS-encrypted files from a user's computer.

NOTE Versions of Windows Vista that do not support EFS

Windows Vista Starter, Windows Vista Home Basic, and Windows Vista Home Premium do not support EFS.

How to Encrypt a Folder with EFS

With EFS, you can encrypt specific files and folders. To enable EFS for a folder, follow these steps:

1. Click Start, and then click Computer.

   A Windows Explorer window opens to the user's profile.

2. Right-click the folder you want to encrypt, and then click Properties. For example, if you want to encrypt the user's profile, expand C:\Users\, right-click the user's profile folder, and then click Properties.

3. In the General tab, click the Advanced button.

4. In the Advanced Attributes dialog box, select the Encrypt Contents To Secure Data check box.

5. Click OK twice.

6. In the Confirm Attribute Changes dialog box, accept the default setting to encrypt subfolders by clicking OK.

NOTE Recognizing EFS-encrypted files and folders in Windows Explorer

In Windows Explorer, EFS-encrypted files and folders are colored green. Other users can still browse EFS-encrypted folders, but they will not be able to access EFS-encrypted files.

During the encryption process you might receive errors that a file (such as NTUSER.dat, the user registry hive) is currently in use. Additionally, to prevent users from encrypting a file that might stop the computer from starting, you cannot encrypt any file that is marked with the *System* attribute. Encrypted files cannot be compressed with NTFS compression.

NOTE EFS-encrypted files cannot be indexed

EFS-encrypted files are not indexed and will not be returned with search results. You can enable indexing of some encrypted files by opening the Indexing Options tool in Control Panel, clicking Advanced, and then selecting the Index Encrypted Files check box. However, this still does not index EFS-encrypted files. Nothing allows you to index EFS-encrypted files because Search indexes files as the system rather than your user account and therefore can't decrypt your files.

How to Create and Back Up EFS Certificates

EFS uses certificates to encrypt and decrypt data. If you lose an EFS certificate, you will be unable to decrypt your files. Therefore, it is extremely important to back up EFS certificates.

The backup tools built into Windows automatically back up your certificates. Additionally, Windows Vista provides a wizard interface for manually creating and backing up EFS certificates. To use the interface, follow these steps:

1. Click Start, and then click Control Panel.
2. Click the User Accounts link. Then, click the User Accounts link again.
3. In the left pane, click the Manage Your File Encryption Certificates link. The Encrypting File System Wizard appears.
4. On the Manage Your File Encryption Certificates page, click Next.
5. On the Select Or Create A File Encryption Certificate page, as shown in Figure 7-4, select Use This Certificate if an EFS certificate already exists (Windows Vista automatically generates a certificate the first time a user encrypts a file) and you want to back it up. To select a different certificate than the default, click the Select Certificate button. If you want to manually generate a certificate, select Create A New Certificate.

Figure 7-4   Using the Encrypting File System Wizard to back up EFS certificates

6. If you are creating a new certificate, the Which Type Of Certificate Do You Want To Create page appears. If you want to use a smart card to store the certificate, insert your smart card and select A Self-Signed Certificate Stored On My Smart Card. If your domain has an enterprise CA available, select A Certificate Issued By My Domain's Certification

Authority. Otherwise, leave the default setting of A Self-Signed Certificate Stored On My Computer selected. Click Next.

7. On the Back Up The Certificate And Key page, click the Browse button to select an unencrypted folder to save the certificate. For best results, you should save it to removable media that will be stored securely. Then, complete the Password and Confirm Password boxes. Click Next.

8. If the Update Your Previously Encrypted Files page appears, it means some files were encrypted with a different key than you selected. To avoid problems decrypting files in the future, you should always update encrypted files. Select the All Logical Drives check box, and then click Next. The Encrypting File System Wizard updates the keys associated with all encrypted files. This might take a few minutes, or it might take several hours, depending on how many files need to be updated.

   The Encrypting File System Wizard backs up your key and saves it to the specified file. Keep this file safe.

9. On the last page, click Close.

To restore an EFS certificate, simply double-click the certificate. Then, follow the steps in the Certificate Import Wizard. For step-by-step instructions, read Practice 3 at the end of this lesson.

As an alternative to using Control Panel, you can back up EFS certificates in Windows Explorer by following these steps:

1. Open Windows Explorer and select a file that you have encrypted. You must select a file and not a folder.

2. Right-click the file, and then select Properties.

3. Click Advanced in the General tab.

4. Click Details in the Advanced Attributes dialog box to open the User Access dialog box.

5. Select your user name, and then click Back Up Keys to open the Certificate Export Wizard.

6. Click Next to select the file format to use.

7. Click Next and enter a password to protect the key. Repeat the entry, and then click Next.

8. Enter a path and file name to save the file to or browse for a path. Click Next.

9. Click Finish to export the certificate, and then click OK to confirm that it was saved successfully.

Anyone with access to an EFS certificate can decrypt that user's files. Therefore, it is extremely important to keep the backup secure.

How to Grant an Additional User Access to an EFS-Encrypted File

By default, only the user who encrypted a file is able to access it. However, Windows Vista (as well as Windows XP and Windows Server 2003, but not Windows 2000) allows you to grant more than one user access to an EFS-encrypted file. This is possible because EFS doesn't encrypt files using the user's personal EFS key; instead EFS encrypts files with a File Encryption Key (FEK), and then encrypts the FEK with the user's personal EFS key. Therefore, decryption requires two separate keys. However, the FEK key can be encrypted multiple times for different users and each user will be able to access his or her own encrypted copy of the FEK key to decrypt files.

To allow encrypted files to be shared between users on a computer, follow these steps:

1. In Windows Explorer, right-click the file, and then click Properties.
2. In the General tab, click the Advanced button.
3. In the Advanced Attributes dialog box, click the Details button.

   The User Access dialog box appears, showing the users who have access to the file and the users who can act as recovery agents.
4. Click the Add button.

   The Encrypting File System dialog box appears and displays a list of users who have logged on to the local computer and who have an EFS certificate. A domain administrator can generate EFS certificates, or Windows Vista will automatically generate one the first time a user encrypts a file.
5. To add a domain user who is not in the list but who has a valid encryption certificate, click the Find User button. If EFS informs you that no appropriate certificates correspond to the selected user, the user has not been granted an EFS certificate. The user can generate by encrypting a file, or a domain administrator can distribute an EFS certificate to the user.

NOTE   Manually importing a certificate

If a user has a certificate but you can't find it, you can manually import it. First, have the user export the certificate as described in the previous section. Then, import the certificate as described in the next section.

---

6. Select the user you want to add, and then click OK.
7. Repeat steps 3–5 to add more users. Then, click OK three times.

You cannot share encrypted folders with multiple users, only individual files. In fact, you cannot even share multiple encrypted files in a single action—you must share each individual file. However, you can use the Cipher.exe command-line tool to automate the process of sharing files.

Granting a user EFS access to a file does not override NTFS permissions. Therefore, if a user still lacks the file permissions to access a file, Windows Vista will still prevent that user from accessing a file.

Any users who have access to an EFS-encrypted file can, in turn, grant other users access to the file.

NOTE   EFS doesn't affect sharing across a network

EFS has no effect on sharing files and folders across a network. Therefore, you only need to follow these steps to share a folder with another local user on the same computer.

How to Import Personal Certificates

You can share encrypted files with other users if you have the certificate for the other user. To allow another user to use a file that you have encrypted, you need to import the user's certificate onto your computer and add the user's name to the list of users who are permitted access to the file, as described in the previous section.

To import a user certificate, follow these steps:

1. Click Start, type **mmc**, and then press Enter to open a blank Microsoft Management Console. Respond to the UAC prompt that appears.
2. Click File, and then click Add/Remove Snap-In.
3. Select Certificates and click Add. Select My User Account and click Finish. Click OK to close the Add Or Remove Snap-ins dialog box.
4. Select Certificates, and then expand Trusted People.
5. Under Trusted People, right-click Certificates. On the All Tasks menu, click Import to open the Certificate Import Wizard.
6. Click Next, and then browse to the location of the certificate you want to import.
7. Select the certificate, and then click Next.
8. Type the password for the certificate, and then click Next.
9. Click Next to place the certificate in the Trusted People store.
10. Click Finish to complete the import.
11. Click OK to acknowledge the successful import, and then exit the MMC.

Now you can grant that user access to EFS-encrypted files.

How to Recover to an EFS-Encrypted File Using a Data Recovery Agent

EFS grants data recovery agents (DRAs) permission to decrypt files so that an administrator can restore an encrypted file if the user loses his or her EFS key. By default, workgroup computers configure the local Administrator account as the DRA. In domain environments domain administrators will configure one or more user accounts as DRAs for the entire domain.

Because DRA certificates are not automatically copied when an administrator logs on to a computer, the process of copying the DRA certificate and recovering an EFS-encrypted file is somewhat lengthy (but straightforward). To recover an EFS-encrypted file, follow these steps:

1. First, you need to obtain a copy of the DRA certificate. By default, this is stored in the Administrator user account on the first domain controller in the domain. Using the DRA account, log on to the administrator account on the first domain controller in the domain.

2. Click Start, and then click Run. Type **mmc**, and then press Enter. Respond to the UAC prompt that appears.

3. Click File, and then click Add/Remove Snap-In.

4. Click Add.

    A list of all the registered snap-ins on the current computer appears.

5. Double-click the Certificates snap-in.

6. If the Certificates Snap-In Wizard appears, select My User Account, and then click Finish. Click OK.

    The MMC console now shows the Certificates snap-in.

7. Browse to Certificates – Current User\Personal\Certificates. In the details pane, right-click the domain DRA certificate, click All Tasks, and then click Export (as shown in Figure 7-5). By default, this is the Administrator certificate that is also signed by the Administrator, and it has the Intended Purpose shown as File Recovery.

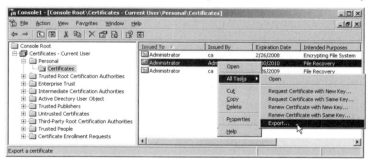

Figure 7-5   Recovering EFS-encrypted files

8. In the Certificate Export Wizard, click Next.

9. On the Export Private Key page, select Yes, Export The Private Key. Then, click Next.

10. On the Export File Format page, accept the default settings shown in Figure 7-6, and then click Next. For security reasons, you might want to select the Delete The Private Key If The Export Is Successful check box, and then store the private key on removable

media in a safe location. Then, use the removable media when you need to recover an EFS-encrypted file.

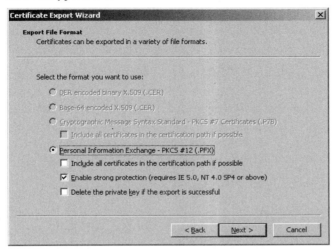

Figure 7-6   Using the default .PFX file format for the DRA recovery key

11.   On the Password page, type a recovery password twice. Click Next.

12.   On the File To Export page, type a file name to store the recovery password on removable media. Click Next.

13.   On the Completing The Certificate Export Wizard page, click Finish. Then, click OK.

Now you are ready to import the DRA key on the client computer that requires recovery. Log on to the client computer and follow these steps:

1.   Click Start, and then click Run. Type **mmc**, and then press Enter.

2.   Click File, and then click Add/Remove Snap-In. Respond to the UAC prompt that appears.

3.   Click Add.

   A list of all the registered snap-ins on the current computer appears.

4.   Double-click the Certificates snap-in.

5.   In the Certificates Snap-In Wizard, select My User Account, and then click Finish. Click OK.

   The MMC console now shows the Certificates snap-in.

6.   Right-click Certificates – Current User\Personal\Certificates, click All Tasks, and then click Import.

7.   In the Certificate Import Wizard, click Next.

8. On the File To Import page, click Browse. In the Open dialog box, click the file types list (above the Open button) and select Personal Information Exchange. Then, select the DRA key file and click Open. Click Next.

9. On the Password page, type the password you used to protect the DRA key. Click Next.

10. On the Certificate Store page, leave the default selection to store the certificate in the Personal store. Click Next.

11. Click Finish, and then click OK.

Now you can open or decrypt the files just as if you had been added as an authorized user. To decrypt the files, view the properties for the file or folder and clear the Encrypt Contents To Secure Data check box. After clicking OK twice, Windows Vista will use the DRA key to decrypt the files. Now that the files are unencrypted, the user who owns the files should immediately reencrypt them.

NOTE   Decrypting recovered files

If you use Windows Backup, files recovered from backup media will still be encrypted with EFS. Simply recover the files to a computer and have the DRA log on to that computer to decrypt them.

After recovering files, remove any copies of your DRA. Because the DRA can be used to decrypt any file in your domain, it's critical that you not leave a copy of it on a user's computer.

BitLocker

NTFS file permissions provide access control when the operating system is online. EFS supplements NTFS file permissions by using encryption to provide access control that is in effect even if an attacker bypasses the operating system (for example, by starting the computer from a bootable DVD). BitLocker Drive Encryption, like EFS, uses encryption. However, BitLocker has several key differences from EFS:

- BitLocker encrypts the entire system volume, including all user and system files. EFS cannot encrypt system files.

- BitLocker protects the computer at startup before the operating system starts. After the operating system starts, BitLocker is completely transparent.

- BitLocker provides computer-specific encryption, not user-specific encryption. Therefore, you still need to use EFS to protect private files from other valid users.

- BitLocker can protect the integrity of the operating system, helping to prevent rootkits and offline attacks that modify system files.

NOTE Editions of Windows Vista containing BitLocker

BitLocker is a feature of Windows Vista Enterprise and Windows Vista Ultimate. It is not supported on other editions of Windows Vista.

How to Configure BitLocker Partitions

BitLocker requires at least two NTFS volumes: a boot volume with at least 1.5 GB of free space and a system volume that can consume the rest of the space on the physical disk. The system volume is typically labeled the C drive, and the BitLocker Drive Preparation Tool automatically labels the boot volume S. If you do not configure these partitions prior to installing Windows Vista, you can use the BitLocker Drive Preparation Tool.

Exam Tip

BitLocker encrypts only the system volume. Therefore, if a computer has two hard disks and you need to encrypt data on any volume other than the system volume, you will need to use EFS.

The BitLocker Drive Preparation Tool is available only as a Windows Ultimate Extra. Therefore, you can't use it with a Windows Vista Enterprise computer. To install the BitLocker Drive Preparation Tool, follow these steps:

1. Click Start, click All Programs, and then click Windows Update.
2. Click Check For Updates.
3. Under There Are Windows Ultimate Extras Available For Download, click View Available Extras. If this link does not appear, the BitLocker Drive Preparation Tool might already be installed.
4. On the Choose The Updates You Want To Install page, under Windows Ultimate Extras, select the BitLocker And EFS Enhancements check box. Then, click Install. Respond to the UAC prompt that appears.

After installing the BitLocker Drive Preparation Tool, follow these steps to configure your computer's partitions for BitLocker:

1. Click Start, All Programs, Accessories, System Tools, and BitLocker, and then click BitLocker Drive Preparation Tool. Respond to the UAC prompt that appears.
2. Click I Accept.

   If you see the message shown in Figure 7-7, the BitLocker Drive Preparation Tool found a condition that prevents it from repartitioning your disk. Specifically, the BitLocker Drive Preparation Tool requires about 10 percent free disk space and needs to be able to create a new 1.5-GB partition from free, contiguous disk space. To solve the problem, first use the Disk Cleanup Wizard to clear up as much free space as possible. If you still receive the error, disable hibernation and remove all paging files from the system drive. Then, restart the computer and delete the C:\Pagefile.sys and C:\Hiberfil.sys files (the BitLocker Drive Preparation Tool cannot move these files in order to create the required contiguous free space). Then, attempt to run the BitLocker Drive Preparation Tool again. If you are successful, remember to reenable hibernation and reconfigure the page file.

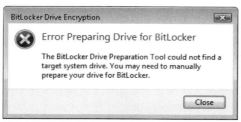

Figure 7-7   A generic error indicating insufficient disk space or immovable files

3. On the Preparing Drive For BitLocker page, click Continue.

    The BitLocker Drive Preparation Tool shrinks your C drive and then creates a new S partition, marks it active, and copies the necessary files to the new S partition.

4. Click Finish.

5. Click Restart Now to restart your computer.

Now the computer has a small boot partition—separate from the system partition—that meets the disk partitioning requirements for BitLocker.

How to Use BitLocker with TPM Hardware

If available, BitLocker seals the symmetric encryption key in a Trusted Platform Module (TPM) 1.2 chip (available in some newer computers). If the computer does not have a TPM chip, BitLocker stores the encryption key on a universal serial bus (USB) flash drive that must be provided every time the computer starts or resumes from hibernation.

Many TPM-equipped computers have the TPM chip disabled in the basic input/output system (BIOS). Before you can use it, you must enter the computer's BIOS settings and enable it. After you enable the TPM chip, BitLocker will perform the TPM initialization automatically. To allow you to manually initialize TPM chips and turn them on or off at the operating system level, Windows Vista includes the TPM Management snap-in, as shown in Figure 7-8. To use it, open a blank MMC console and add the snap-in.

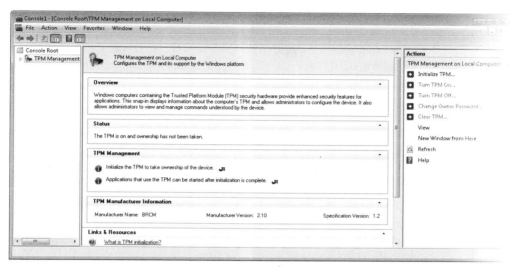

Figure 7-8   Using the TPM Management snap-in to manually initialize a TPM

NOTE   BitLocker initializes a TPM by itself

Because BitLocker handles the TPM initialization for you, the TPM Management snap-in is not dis-cussed further in this book.

BitLocker has two modes available on computers with TPM hardware:

- **TPM only**   This mode is transparent to the user, and the user logon experience is exactly the same as it was before BitLocker was enabled. During startup, BitLocker communi-cates with the TPM hardware to validate the integrity of the computer and operating sys-tem. However, if the TPM is missing or changed, if the hard disk is moved to a different computer, or if critical startup files have changed, BitLocker will enter recovery mode. In recovery mode, the user needs to enter a 40-digit recovery key or insert a USB flash drive with a recovery key stored on it to regain access to the data. TPM only mode provides protection from hard-disk theft with no user training necessary.

- **TPM with startup key**   In this mode, TPM performs the same integrity checks as TPM only mode but also requires the user to provide a startup key to log on to the computer. A startup key can either be physical (a USB flash drive with a machine-readable key writ-ten to it) or personal (a password set by the user). This provides protection from both hard-disk theft and stolen computers (assuming the computer was shut down or locked); however, it requires some effort from the user.

When TPM hardware is available, BitLocker validates the integrity of the computer and operating system by storing "measurements" of various parts of the computer and operating system in the TPM chip. In its default configuration, BitLocker instructs the TPM to measure the master boot record, the active boot partition, the boot sector, the Windows Boot Manager, and the BitLocker storage root key. Each time the computer is booted, the TPM computes the SHA-1 hash of the measured code and compares this to the hash stored in the TPM from the previous boot. If the hashes match, the boot process continues; if the hashes do not match, the boot process halts. At the conclusion of a successful boot process, the TPM releases the storage root key to BitLocker; BitLocker decrypts data as Windows reads it from the protected volume. Because no other operating system can do this (even an alternate instance of Windows Vista), the TPM never releases the key, and therefore, the volume remains a useless encrypted blob. Any attempts to modify the protected volume will render it unbootable.

How to Enable the Use of BitLocker on Computers Without TPM

If TPM hardware is not available, BitLocker can store decryption keys on a USB flash drive instead of using a built-in TPM module. Using BitLocker in this configuration can be risky, however, because if the user loses the USB flash drive, the encrypted volume will no longer be accessible, and the computer will not be able to start without the recovery key. Windows Vista does not make this option available by default.

To use BitLocker encryption on a computer without a compatible TPM, you will need to change a computer Group Policy setting by following these steps:

1. Open the Group Policy Object Editor by clicking Start, typing **gpedit.msc**, and pressing Enter. Respond to the UAC prompt that appears.
2. Navigate to Computer Configuration\Administrative Templates\Windows Components\BitLocker Drive Encryption.
3. Enable the Control Panel Setup: Enable Advanced Startup Options setting. Then, select the Allow BitLocker Without A Compatible TPM check box.

If you plan to deploy BitLocker in an enterprise using USB flash drives instead of TPM, you should deploy this setting with domain-based Group Policy settings.

How to Enable BitLocker Encryption

Individual users can enable BitLocker from Control Panel, but most enterprises should use Active Directory to manage keys.

MORE INFO Configuring Active Directory to back up BitLocker

For detailed instructions on how to configure Active Directory to back up BitLocker and TPM recovery information, read "Configuring Active Directory to Back up Windows BitLocker Drive Encryption and Trusted Platform Module Recovery Information" at *http://go.microsoft.com/fwlink/?LinkId=78953*.

To enable BitLocker from Control Panel, follow these steps:

1. Perform a full backup of the computer. Then, run a check of the integrity of the Bit-Locker partition using ChkDsk.

2. Open Control Panel. Click the Security link. Under BitLocker Drive Encryption, click the Protect Your Computer By Encrypting Data On Your Disk link. Respond to the UAC prompt that appears.

3. On the BitLocker Drive Encryption page, click Turn On BitLocker.

4. If available (the choice can be blocked by a Group Policy setting), in the Set BitLocker Startup Preferences dialog box, select your authentication choice. The choices will vary depending on whether the computer has a TPM chip built in. As shown in Figure 7-9, your choices are:

Figure 7-9 Startup options in BitLocker

- ❑ **Use BitLocker Without Additional Keys**   Uses the TPM to verify the integrity of the operating system at every startup. This option does not prompt the user during startup, providing completely transparent protection.

- ❑ **Require PIN At Every Startup**   Uses the TPM to verify the integrity of the operating system at startup and requires the user to type a PIN to verify the user's identity. This option provides additional protection but can inconvenience the user.

- ❑ **Require Startup USB Key At Every Startup**   Does not require TPM hardware. This option requires the user to insert a USB key containing the decryption key at startup. Alternatively, users can type a recovery key to gain access to the encrypted system partition.

5. If you chose to use a USB key, the Save Your Startup Key dialog box appears. Select the startup key, and then click Save.

6. On the Save The Recovery Password page, choose the destination (a USB drive, a local or remote folder, or a printer) to save your recovery password. The recovery password is a small text file containing brief instructions, a drive label and password ID, and the 48-digit recovery password. Save the password and the recovery key on separate devices and store them in different locations. Click Next.

7. On the Encrypt The Volume page, select the Run BitLocker System Check check box and click Continue if you are ready to begin encryption. Click Restart Now. Upon rebooting, BitLocker will ensure that the computer is fully compatible and ready to be encrypted.

8. BitLocker displays a special screen confirming that the key material was loaded. Now that this has been confirmed, BitLocker will begin encrypting the C drive after Windows Vista starts, and BitLocker will be enabled.

BitLocker encrypts the drive in the background so that you can continue using the computer.

How to Manage BitLocker Keys on a Local Computer

To manage keys on the local computer, follow these steps:

1. Open Control Panel and click the Security link. Under BitLocker Drive Encryption, click the Manage BitLocker Keys link. Respond to the UAC prompt that appears.

2. In the BitLocker Drive Encryption window, click Manage BitLocker Keys.

Using this tool, you can perform the following actions (which vary depending on the authentication type chosen):

- **Duplicate the Recovery Password**   Provides the following options:
  - ❑ Save The Password On A USB Drive
  - ❑ Save The Password In A Folder
  - ❑ Print The Password
- **Duplicate the Startup Key**   When you use a USB startup key for authentication, this allows you to create a second USB startup key with an identical key.
- **Reset the PIN**   When you use a PIN for authentication, this allows you to change the PIN.

To manage BitLocker from an elevated command prompt or from a remote computer, use the Manage-bde.wsf script (included with Windows Vista in the System32 folder). Use Cscript.exe to run Manage-bde.wsf, as the following example demonstrates.

```
C:\>cd \Windows\system32
C:\Windows\system32>cscript manage-bde.wsf -status
Microsoft (R) Windows Script Host Version 5.7
Copyright (C) Microsoft Corporation. All rights reserved.

Disk volumes that can be protected with
```

```
BitLocker Drive Encryption:
Volume C: []
[OS Volume]

    Size:                 698.64 GB
    Conversion Status:    Fully Decrypted
    Percentage Encrypted: 0%
    Encryption Method:    None
    Protection Status:    Protection Off
    Lock Status:          Unlocked
    Automatic Unlock:     Disabled
    Key Protectors:       None Found
```

For detailed information about how to use Manage-bde.wsf, run it with the -? parameter.

How to Recover Data Protected By BitLocker

When you use BitLocker, the system partition will be locked if the encryption key is not available, causing BitLocker to enter recovery mode. Likely causes of the encryption key not being available include:

- Modification of one of the boot files.
- BIOS is modified and the TPM disabled.
- TPM is cleared.
- An attempt is made to boot without the TPM, PIN, or USB key being available.
- The BitLocker-encrypted disk is moved to a new computer.

After the drive is locked, you can only boot to recovery mode, as shown in Figure 7-10. On most keyboards you can use the standard number keys from 0–9. However, on some non-English keyboards you need to use the function keys by pressing F1 for the digit 1, F2 for the digit 2, and so forth, with F10 being the digit 0.

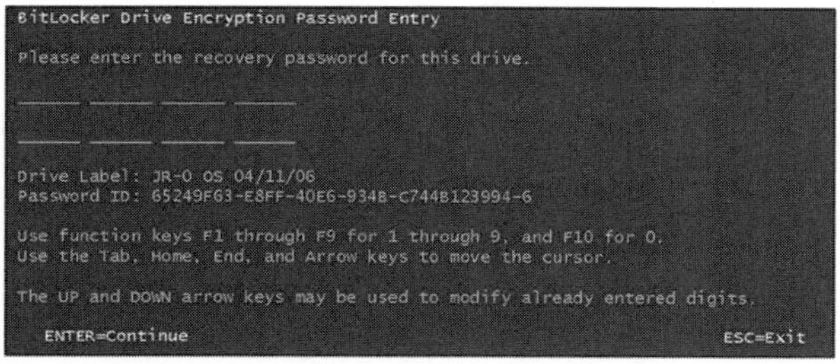

Figure 7-10   Gaining access to a BitLocker-encrypted drive by typing a 48-character recovery password

If you have the recovery key on a USB flash drive, you can insert the recovery key and press the Esc key to restart the computer. BitLocker reads the recovery key automatically during startup.

If you cancel out of recovery, the Windows Boot Manager will provide instructions for using Startup Repair to automatically fix a startup problem. Do not follow these instructions; Startup Repair cannot access the encrypted volume. Instead, restart the computer and enter the recovery key.

Additionally, you can use the BitLocker Repair Tool to help recover data from an encrypted volume. For more information, see *http://support.microsoft.com/kb/928201*.

NOTE   Backing up encrypted drives

It's especially important to regularly back up BitLocker-encrypted drives. Note, however, that your backups might not be encrypted by default. This applies to Complete PC Backups, as well. Although Complete PC Backups make a copy of your entire disk, BitLocker functions at a lower level than Complete PC. Therefore, when Complete PC reads the disk, it reads the BitLocker-decrypted version of the disk.

How to Disable or Remove BitLocker Drive Encryption

Because BitLocker intercepts the boot process and looks for changes to any of the early boot files, it can cause problems in the following nonattack scenarios:

- Upgrading or replacing the motherboard or TPM
- Installing a new operating system that changes the master boot record or the boot manager
- Moving a BitLocker-encrypted disk to another TPM-enabled computer
- Repartitioning the hard disk
- Updating the BIOS
- Third-party updates that occur outside the operating system (such as hardware firmware updates)

To avoid entering BitLocker recovery mode, you can temporarily disable BitLocker, which allows you to change the TPM and upgrade the operating system. When you reenable BitLocker, the same encryption keys will be used. You can also choose to decrypt the BitLocker-protected volume, which will completely remove BitLocker protection. You can reenable BitLocker only by repeating the process to create new keys and reencrypt the volume.

To temporarily disable BitLocker or permanently decrypt the BitLocker-protected volume, follow these steps:

1. Log on to the computer as Administrator.
2. From Control Panel, open BitLocker Drive Encryption.
3. Click Turn Off BitLocker for the volume that has BitLocker enabled.
4. Choose Disable BitLocker Drive Encryption to use a clear key (See Figure 7-11). To completely remove BitLocker, choose Decrypt The Volume.

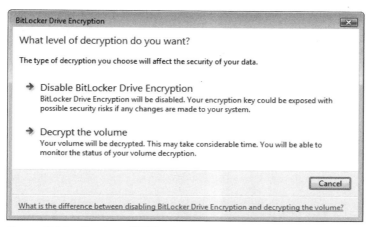

Figure 7-11 Turning off BitLocker

Troubleshooting BitLocker Problems

Several common BitLocker problems are actually "features." The problems occur because Bit-Locker is designed to provide protection from specific types of attacks. Often, these legitimate uses resemble attacks and cause BitLocker to refuse to allow the computer to start or the Bit-Locker encryption to prevent you from accessing files:

- **The operating system fails to start in a dual-boot configuration** You can dual-boot a computer after enabling BitLocker. However, the second operating system instance must be configured on a different partition. You cannot dual-boot to a second operating system installed on the same partition.

  ***NOTE* Dual-booting with BitLocker enabled**

  Many people use BitLocker purely to protect Windows Vista from Windows XP. If you dual-boot between Windows XP and Windows Vista, Windows XP will erase the Windows Vista restore points and shadow copies. However, if you enable BitLocker for the Windows Vista partition (even if you then disable the security features), Windows XP won't touch the Windows Vista partition.

- **The operating system fails to start if you move the hard disk to a different computer** Bit-Locker is designed to protect data from offline attacks, such as attacks that bypass operating system security by connecting the hard disk to a different computer. The new computer will be unable to decrypt the data (even if it has a TPM chip in it). Before moving a BitLocker-encrypted disk to a different computer, disable BitLocker. Reenable BitLocker after transferring the disk. Alternatively, you can use the recovery key to start Windows after moving the hard disk to the new computer.

■ **The data on the hard disk is unreadable using standard disk recovery tools**   For the same reasons stated in the previous bullet point, BitLocker files are unreadable using standard disk recovery tools. Someday recovery tools that support decrypting BitLocker files using a recovery key might be available. As of the time of this writing, your only opportunity for recovering BitLocker-encrypted files is to start Windows Vista using the BitLocker recovery key. For this reason it is very important to regularly back up BitLocker-encrypted volumes.

Practice: Encrypt and Recover Encrypted Data

In this practice, you simulate the recovery of a lost EFS encryption certificate.

Practice 1: Encrypt Data

In this practice, you encrypt a file. Windows Vista will automatically generate an EFS key if you don't already have one.

1. Log on to a Windows Vista computer as a standard user.
2. Create a file named Encrypted.txt in your Documents folder.
3. Right-click the Encrypted.txt file, and then click Properties.
4. In the General tab of the Properties dialog box, click the Advanced button.
5. Select the Encrypt Contents To Secure Data check box, and then click OK. Click OK again.
6. In the Encryption Warning dialog box, select Encrypt The File Only, and then click OK. Notice that Windows Explorer displays the Encrypted.txt file in green.
7. Double-click the Encrypted.txt file to open it in Notepad. Then, add the text "**This file is encrypted.**" Save the file and close Notepad.
8. Double-click the file to verify that you can open it, and then close Notepad again.

Now you have encrypted a file, and no user can access it without your EFS key.

Practice 2: Back Up an EFS Key

In Practice 1, you encrypted a file. In this practice, you will back up the EFS key that was automatically generated when you encrypted the file. Then, you will delete the original key and determine whether you can access the EFS-encrypted file. To complete this practice, you must have completed Practice 1.

1. Click Start, and then click Control Panel.
2. Click the User Accounts link. Click the User Accounts link again.
3. In the left pane, click the Manage Your File Encryption Certificates link. The Encrypting File System Wizard appears.

4.   On the Manage Your File Encryption Certificates page, click Next.

5.   On the Select Or Create A File Encryption Certificate page, leave the default certificate (your EFS certificate) selected, and then click Next.

6.   On the Back Up The Certificate And Key page, click the Browse button and select the Documents folder. For the filename, type **EFS-cert-backup.pfx**. Click Save. Then, type a complex password in the *Password* and *Confirm Password* fields. Click Next.

7.   If the Update Your Previously Encrypted Files page appears, leave all check boxes cleared, and then click Next.

8.   On the Encrypting File System page, click Close.

9.   In Windows Explorer, open your Documents folder and verify that the EFS certificate was correctly exported.

Now that you have backed up your EFS key, you can safely lose it. Simulate a corrupted or lost key by following these steps to delete it:

1.   Click Start, type **mmc**, and then press Enter to open a blank Microsoft Management Console.

2.   Click File, and then click Add/Remove Snap-in.

3.   Select Certificates and click Add. Click OK.

4.   Expand Certificates – Current User, expand Personal, and then select Certificates.

5.   In the middle pane, right-click your EFS certificate, and then click Delete.

6.   In the Certificates dialog box, click Yes to confirm that you want to delete the certificate.

7.   Log off the current desktop session, and then log back on. Windows Vista caches the user's EFS certificate. Thus, if you remained logged on, you would still be able to open your encrypted file.

8.   Open the Documents folder and double-click the Encrypted.txt file. Notepad should appear and display an Access Is Denied error message. This indicates that the file is encrypted, but you don't have a valid EFS certificate.

Practice 3: Recover Encrypted Data

In this practice, you recover a lost EFS key and use it to access encrypted data. To complete this practice, you must have completed Practices 1 and 2.

1.   In the Documents folder, double-click the EFS-cert-backup.pfx file that you created in Practice 2.

     The Certificate Import Wizard appears.

2.   On the Welcome To The Certificate Import Wizard page, click Next.

3.   On the File To Import page, click Next.

4. On the Password page, type the password you assigned to the certificate. Then, click Next.

5. On the Certificate Store page, click Next.

6. On the Completing The Certificate Import Wizard page, click Finish.

7. Click OK to confirm that the import was successful.

8. Open the Documents folder and double-click the Encrypted.txt file. Notepad should appear and display the contents of the file, indicating that you successfully recovered the EFS key and can now access encrypted files.

Lesson Summary

- Use EFS to encrypt individual files and folders. Because encrypted files will be unavailable if the user loses his or her EFS certificate, it's important to have a backup EFS certificate and a recovery key. In environments where multiple users log on to a single computer, you can grant multiple users access to EFS-encrypted files.

- Use BitLocker to encrypt the entire system volume. If available, BitLocker makes use of TPM hardware to seal the encryption key. BitLocker then works with the TPM hardware during computer startup to verify the integrity of the computer and operating system. If TPM hardware is available, you can optionally require the user to insert a USB flash drive with a special key or type a password to gain access to the BitLocker-encrypted volume. BitLocker is disabled by default on computers without TPM hardware, but you can enable BitLocker without TPM hardware by using Group Policy settings. If TPM hardware is not available, users are required to insert a USB flash drive or a recovery key to start Windows Vista.

Lesson Review

You can use the following questions to test your knowledge of the information in Lesson 2, "Using Encryption to Control Access to Data." The questions are also available on the companion CD if you prefer to review them in electronic form.

NOTE Answers

Answers to these questions and explanations of why each answer choice is right or wrong are located in the "Answers" section at the end of the book.

1. Which tool would you use to back up an Encrypting File System (EFS) certificate?
   A. BitLocker Drive Encryption
   B. Computer Management
   C. Certificates
   D. Services

2. In the Certificates console, which node would you access to back up the data recovery agent (DRA) certificate?
   A. *Certificates – Current User\Personal\Certificates*
   B. *Certificates – Current User\Active Directory User Object*
   C. *Certificates (Local Computer)\Personal\Certificates*
   D. *Certificates (Local Computer)\Active Directory User Object*

3. Which of the following partitions will the BitLocker Drive Preparation Tool create? (Choose all that apply)
   A. A 1.5-GB C:\ volume
   B. A C:\ volume that uses all available space
   C. A 1.5-GB S:\ volume
   D. A 2.1-GB S:\ volume

4. Using the default settings, which of the following BitLocker configurations is available? (Choose all that apply.)
   A. Use BitLocker with a Trusted Platform Module (TPM) but without additional keys.
   B. Use BitLocker with a Trusted Platform Module (TPM) and require a personal identification number (PIN) at every startup.
   C. Use BitLocker without a Trusted Platform Module (TPM) and require a personal identification number (PIN) at every startup.
   D. Use BitLocker without a Trusted Platform Module (TPM) and require a universal serial bus (USB) key at every startup.

Lesson 3: Troubleshooting Authorization Problems and Auditing User Access

With Windows Vista, more and more environments will grant users only standard user privileges. In other words, most people won't be logging on as local administrators any more. Applications created for Windows Vista should handle this perfectly because they will have been designed to run with limited privileges. However, many applications created before Windows Vista was released will have problems with insufficient privileges because they assume that the user will run the application as an administrator.

This lesson describes how to identify and resolve these privilege problems. It is not a full discussion of application compatibility concepts; instead, it focuses on using auditing to identify authorization problems.

After this lesson, you will be able to:
- Describe how Windows Vista provides more granular auditing.
- Troubleshoot problems related to permissions.

Estimated lesson time: 20 minutes

Windows Vista Auditing Enhancements

In Windows XP and earlier versions of Windows the only way to enable auditing was to use the Audit Policy section of the Group Policy settings, as described in Lesson 1, "Authenticating Users." That's an easy and efficient way to configure auditing, but it provides access only to the following types of auditing:

- Audit Account Logon Events
- Audit Account Management
- Audit Directory Service Access
- Audit Logon Events
- Audit Object Access
- Audit Policy Change
- Audit Privilege Use
- Audit Process Tracking
- Audit System Events

The drawback to these categories is that they are very broad. For example, the Audit Logon Events policy enables auditing for a wide range of events, including logons, logoffs, account lockouts, and Internet Protocol Security (IPSec). Therefore, enabling the Audit Logon Events policy causes Windows Vista to add a large number of events that might not relate to your troubleshooting.

Although Windows Vista supports the same broad auditing categories when configured with Group Policy settings, Windows Vista also provides the AuditPol.exe tool to enable auditing for very specific events. This reduces the number of irrelevant events, potentially reducing the "noise" generated by false-positive auditing events.

To view the new categories, run the following command from an administrative command prompt:

```
auditpol /get /category:*
System audit policy
Category/Subcategory                    Setting
System
  Security System Extension             No Auditing
  System Integrity                      Success and Failure
  IPsec Driver                          No Auditing
  Other System Events                   Success and Failure
  Security State Change                 Success
Logon/Logoff
  Logon                                 Success
  Logoff                                Success
  Account Lockout                       Success
  IPsec Main Mode                       No Auditing
  IPsec Quick Mode                      No Auditing
  IPsec Extended Mode                   No Auditing
  Special Logon                         Success
  Other Logon/Logoff Events             No Auditing
Object Access
  File System                           No Auditing
  Registry                              No Auditing
  Kernel Object                         No Auditing
  SAM                                   No Auditing
  Certification Services                No Auditing
  Application Generated                 No Auditing
  Handle Manipulation                   No Auditing
  File Share                            No Auditing
  Filtering Platform Packet Drop        No Auditing
  Filtering Platform Connection         No Auditing
  Other Object Access Events            No Auditing
Privilege Use
  Sensitive Privilege Use               No Auditing
  Non Sensitive Privilege Use           No Auditing
  Other Privilege Use Events            No Auditing
Detailed Tracking
  Process Termination                   No Auditing
  DPAPI Activity                        No Auditing
  RPC Events                            No Auditing
  Process Creation                      No Auditing
Policy Change
  Audit Policy Change                   Success
```

```
    Authentication Policy Change        Success
    Authorization Policy Change         No Auditing
    MPSSVC Rule-Level Policy Change     No Auditing
    Filtering Platform Policy Change    No Auditing
    Other Policy Change Events          No Auditing
Account Management
    User Account Management             Success
    Computer Account Management         No Auditing
    Security Group Management           Success
    Distribution Group Management       No Auditing
    Application Group Management        No Auditing
    Other Account Management Events     No Auditing
DS Access
    Directory Service Changes           No Auditing
    Directory Service Replication       No Auditing
    Detailed Directory Service Replication  No Auditing
    Directory Service Access            No Auditing
Account Logon
    Kerberos Ticket Events              No Auditing
    Other Account Logon Events          No Auditing
    Credential Validation               No Auditing
```

You can use the "Auditpol /set" command to enable granular auditing. For example, to add an event when a user attempts to log on but provides invalid credentials, run the following command:

```
auditpol /set /subcategory:"logon" /failure:enable
```

Similarly, to audit successful logoffs, run the following command:

```
auditpol /set /subcategory:"logoff" /success:enable
```

MORE INFO   Using Group Policy to configure auditing

For information about how to configure auditing in Active Directory environments using Group Policy settings, read Microsoft Knowledge Base article 921469, "How to use Group Policy to configure detailed security auditing settings for Windows Vista client computers in a Windows Server 2003 domain or in a Windows 2000 domain" at *http://support.microsoft.com/kb/921469*.

Troubleshooting Problems Related to Permissions

To troubleshoot problems accessing resources, follow these four high-level steps:

1. Enable failure object access auditing on the computer that contains the resource being accessed.

2. Enable failure auditing on the specific resource being accessed.

3. Test access to the resource and examine the Security event log to determine the resource being accessed and the type of access required. Modify permissions as necessary and repeat the test until the problem no longer occurs.

4. Disable failure object access auditing on the resource and the computer.

The sections that follow describe each of these four steps.

How to Isolate the Source of a Problem

Windows Vista provides several layers of permissions. For example, a file could be protected from local users by using both NTFS file permissions and EFS encryption. A shared folder could be protected by both NTFS file permissions and share permissions. Therefore, there might be multiple causes when troubleshooting an Access Denied error message. Additionally, the restrictive permissions might be in one or more places.

Unfortunately, users will receive the same error message regardless of the exact cause of the problem. Figure 7-12 shows the error message Windows Explorer displays when a user tries to create a file but lacks either NTFS or share permissions. If the user attempts to read or write a file within an application, that application will generate its own error.

Figure 7-12   Windows Explorer error messages do not indicate the source of a permissions problem

When troubleshooting an access denied problem with a local folder, follow these high-level steps:

1. Determine the effective NTFS permissions on the shared folder by following the steps in the section entitled "How to Determine Effective NTFS Permissions" later in this chapter. If these permissions do not allow you to perform the action you are attempting, then the NTFS permissions are too restrictive. Have the server administrator edit the folder properties (using the Security tab of the folder's properties dialog box) and grant the user account, or a group the user belongs to, at least Read NTFS permissions.

2. If problems persist after granting additional NTFS permissions, or if NTFS permissions seem sufficient, determine whether EFS is enabled for the file. If EFS is enabled, add the user attempting to access the file as an authorized user by following the steps in the section of this chapter entitled "How to Grant an Additional User Access to an EFS-encrypted File."

When troubleshooting an access denied problem with a shared folder, follow these high-level steps:

1. Verify that you can select the mapped drive in Windows Explorer. If you can select it and view the free space or any files in the folder, you have at least the Read share permission. If you cannot select the shared folder, you lack share permissions. Have the server administrator edit the shared folder properties (using the Sharing tab of the folder's properties dialog box) and grant the user account, or a group the user belongs to, at least the Read shared folder permissions.

2. Determine the effective NTFS permissions on the shared folder by following the steps in the next section, "How to Determine Effective NTFS Permissions." If these permissions do not allow you to perform the action you are attempting, the NTFS permissions are too restrictive. Have the server administrator edit the folder properties (using the Security tab of the folder's properties dialog box) and grant the user account, or a group the user belongs to, at least Read NTFS permissions.

3. If problems persist after granting additional NTFS permissions, grant additional permissions (such as the Change share permission) to the shared folder.

If you are reading or writing files using Windows Explorer, determining your required permissions is straightforward. Obviously, you need Read permission to open a file and Modify permission to edit a file. However, if you are experiencing an access denied message within an application, determining the required permissions can be much more complicated. As an administrator, you can't always determine exactly which files the application is accessing or whether the application needs to read or write the files. Some applications might request the ability to edit a file even though the application needs only to read the file, further complicating the troubleshooting process. To identify exactly what file permissions an application requires, follow the steps described in the section entitled "How to Use Auditing to Identify Permission Requirements" later in this chapter.

How to Determine Effective NTFS Permissions

Because of group memberships, permissions can be complicated to calculate. For example, if Mary is a member of both the Accounting group and the Managers group, she might have Read permission to a file through her membership in Accounting, Write permission to a file through her membership in the Managers group, and Full Control permission for her specific membership account. In this case the permissions would be cumulative, and Mary would have

Full Control effective permission. However, if any of those permissions were changed to No Access, that permission would override all other settings.

Although you can manually determine a user's effective permissions, it is quicker and more reliable to use Windows Vista. To determine the effective NTFS permissions on a file or folder (including files and folders located in a shared folder), follow these steps:

1. Open Windows Explorer. Then, right-click the file or folder, and then click Properties.
2. Click the Security tab.
3. Click Advanced.
4. Click the Effective Permissions tab.
5. Click Select. Type the name of the user or group that you want to test, and then click OK.

    Windows Vista displays the effective NTFS permissions. Selected check boxes indicate the user has that permission. Check boxes that are not selected indicate the user lacks that permission. Figure 7-13 shows that the user Yan Li has Read Only access to the C:\Users folder.

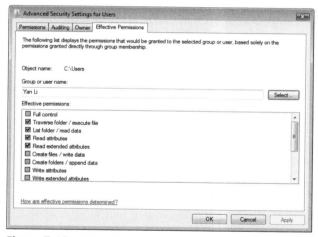

Figure 7-13 Using the Advanced Security Settings dialog box to determine effective NTFS permissions

How to Use Auditing to Identify Permission Requirements

If insufficient file or registry permissions are causing problems, you can use auditing to identify the exact resource Windows Vista is denying access to. The sections that follow describe how to enable failure object access auditing, how to enable auditing on folders and registry keys, and how to use Event Viewer to analyze the auditing events.

NOTE   Downloading Process Monitor

Process Monitor, a free download from Microsoft.com, is an extremely useful tool for determining which resources an application accesses. To download Process Monitor, visit *http://www.microsoft.com/technet/sysinternals/utilities/processmonitor.mspx*.

How to Enable Failure Object Access Auditing   By default, Windows Vista does not add an event to the event log when ACLs prevent a user from accessing a resource (such as a file or registry key that has been configured with overly restrictive permissions). To log failed attempts to access resources, you must enable auditing by following these steps on the computer that contains the resources (for example, to troubleshoot access to a shared folder, you would configure these settings on the file server and not on the client):

1. Click Start, click All Programs, click Administrative Tools, and then click Local Security Policy. Respond to the UAC prompt that appears. If you are not automatically prompted with a UAC prompt, you will need to right-click the Local Security Policy icon, and then click Run As Administrator.
2. In the Local Security Policy console, expand Local Policies, and then select Audit Policy.
3. In the right pane, double-click Audit Object Access.
4. In the Audit Object Access Properties dialog box, select the Failure check box, and then click OK.

NOTE   Using Audit Object Access policy

You should never enable Success auditing for the Audit Object Access policy—this can cause an extremely large number of events to occur. If you do enable Success auditing, enable it only for a very small number of objects, such as a single file that you need to monitor.

---

5. Restart your computer to apply the changes.

Alternatively, you could run the following command to enable just failure file auditing:

```
auditpol /set /subcategory:"file system" /failure:enable
```

Or use the following command to enable just failure registry auditing:

```
auditpol /set /subcategory:"registry" /failure:enable
```

How to Enable and Disable Failure Auditing on a Folder   To enable failure auditing for files, follow these steps:

1. Click Start, and then click Computer.
2. Right-click the file or folder you want to monitor, and then click Properties. If you're not sure which file can't be accessed, you can select the entire C drive (or any other drive). Enabling auditing for a large number of resources will affect performance, but because

you will leave it enabled only for the duration of this test, this will not be a significant problem.

3. In the Properties dialog box, click the Security tab. Then, click the Advanced button.

4. In the Advanced Security Settings dialog box, click the Auditing tab. Then, click the Continue button. Respond to the UAC prompt that appears.

5. Click the Add button.

6. In the Select User Or Group dialog box, type the name of the user whom you will use to test the resources access problem. Click OK.

7. In the Auditing Entry dialog box, select the Full Control/Failed check box, as shown in Figure 7-14. Then, click OK.

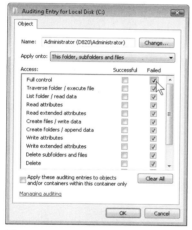

Figure 7-14   Enable failure auditing to identify overly restrictive permissions

8. Click OK again. If you are unable to apply updated auditing settings to any location, click Continue.

9. Click OK.

After performing your tests and analyzing the Security event log to identify resources that lack sufficient permissions, you should follow these steps to disable auditing:

1. In Windows Explorer, right-click the file or folder you are auditing, and then click Properties.

2. In the Properties dialog box, click the Security tab. Then, click the Advanced button.

3. In the Advanced Security Settings dialog box, click the Auditing tab. Then, click the Continue button. Respond to the UAC prompt that appears.

4. Select the auditing entry, and then click the Remove button.

5. Click OK. If you are unable to apply updated auditing settings to any location, click Continue.

6. Click OK twice more.

How to Enable and Disable Failure Auditing on the Registry   To enable failure auditing for a registry key, follow these steps:

1. Click Start and type **Regedit**. Right-click Regedit in the Start menu, and then click Run As Administrator. Respond to the UAC prompt that appears.
2. Right-click HKEY_CURRENT_USER, and then click Permissions.
3. In the Permissions dialog box, click the Advanced button.
4. In the Advanced Security Settings dialog box, click the Auditing tab. Then, click the Add button.
5. In the Select User Or Group dialog box, type the name of the user whom you will use to test the resource's access problem. Click OK.
6. In the Auditing Entry dialog box, select the Full Control/Failed check box. Click OK.
7. Click OK twice more.
8. Repeat steps 2–7 for the HKEY_LOCAL_MACHINE hive. You can audit any of the hives, but most of the important settings are located either in HKEY_CURRENT_USER or HKEY_LOCAL_MACHINE.

After performing your tests and analyzing the Security event log to identify resources that lack sufficient permissions, you should follow these steps to disable auditing:

1. Right-click the key you enabled auditing for, and then click Permissions.
2. In the Permissions dialog box, click the Advanced button.
3. In the Advanced Security Settings dialog box, click the Auditing tab.
4. Click the auditing entry, and then click Remove.
5. Click OK twice.

NOTE   Auditing printers and services

You cannot enable auditing on printers, services, or most other objects.

How to Examine Event Viewer to Isolate the Problem   With failure auditing enabled for object access, attempt to access the resource. Then, follow these steps to view the failure audit events in Event Viewer:

1. Click Start, right-click Computer, and then click Manage. Respond to the UAC prompt that appears.
2. Expand System Tools, Event Viewer, Windows Logs, and then select Security.
3. In the Actions pane, click the Filter Current Log link. In the Filter Current Log dialog box, click the Keywords list, and select the Audit Failure check box. Click OK.

    Event Viewer displays only the failure audits.

Audit Failure events list the object that the user attempted to access and the exact action that the user attempted to take. For example, the following event description (with Event ID 4656) shows that the user mandar.samant attempted to use Regedit.exe to add a subkey to HKEY_LOCAL_MACHINE\SOFTWARE\Policies:

```
A handle to an object was requested.

Subject:
    Security ID:            NWTRADERS\mandar.samant
    Account Name:           mandar.samant
    Account Domain:         NWTRADERS
    Logon ID:               0x2a7d2

Object:
    Object Server:          Security
    Object Type:            Key
    Object Name:            \REGISTRY\MACHINE\SOFTWARE\Policies
    Handle ID:              0x0

Process Information:
    Process ID:             0xc14
    Process Name:           C:\Windows\regedit.exe

Access Request Information:
    Transaction ID:         {00000000-0000-0000-0000-000000000000}
    Accesses:               Create sub-key

    Access Mask:                    0x4
    Privileges Used for Access Check: -
    Restricted SID Count:           0
```

Similarly, the following event description (with Event ID 4656) shows that the same user attempted to use the command prompt (Cmd.exe) to create a file at C:\attack-attempt.txt:

```
A handle to an object was requested.

Subject:
    Security ID:            NWTRADERS\mandar.samant
    Account Name:           mandar.samant
    Account Domain:         NWTRADERS
    Logon ID:               0x2a7d2

Object:
    Object Server:          Security
    Object Type:            File
    Object Name:            C:\attack-attempt.txt
    Handle ID:              0x0

Process Information:
    Process ID:             0xd7c
    Process Name:           C:\Windows\System32\cmd.exe
```

```
Access Request Information:
  Transaction ID:         {00000000-0000-0000-0000-000000000000}
  Accesses:               READ_CONTROL
              SYNCHRONIZE
              WriteData (or AddFile)
              AppendData (or AddSubdirectory or CreatePipeInstance)
              WriteEA
              ReadAttributes
              WriteAttributes

  Access Mask:                      0x120196
  Privileges Used for Access Check:  -
  Restricted SID Count:             0
```

After identifying the permissions required by the user, grant the user the minimum permission required to access the resource. Typically, the most efficient way to do this is to modify the object's permissions. For example, if an attempt to read a registry key was blocked, you should grant the user (or a group the user belongs to, if multiple users will need to access the same resource) Read access. Grant Write access only if the application requires it.

How to Disable Failure Auditing

You should never leave auditing enabled unnecessarily because it generates irrelevant security events and slows the computer's performance. After completing troubleshooting, disable failure auditing for any resources you earlier enabled, and then disable the Audit Object Access audit policy using the Local Security Policy console. Then, restart the computer to make the changes take effect.

If you enabled auditing with the AuditPol.exe command, simply rerun the same command but replace "enable" with "disable." To disable all types of failure auditing from the command prompt, run the following command:

```
auditpol /set /category:* /failure:disable
```

Practice: Identify File Permission Problems

In this practice, you use auditing to determine which files a program needs access to.

▶ **Practice 1: Enable Failure Object Access Auditing**

In this practice, you enable Audit Object Access for failure events only.

1. Log on to your Windows Vista test computer.
2. Click Start, click All Programs, click Administrative Tools, and then click Local Security Policy. Respond to the UAC prompt that appears. If you are not automatically prompted with a UAC prompt, you will need to right-click the Local Security Policy icon, and then click Run As Administrator.
3. In the Local Security Policy console, expand Local Policies, and then select Audit Policy.

4. In the right pane, double-click Audit Object Access.

5. In the Audit Object Access Properties dialog box, select the Failure check box, and then click OK.

6. Restart your computer to apply the changes.

▶ **Practice 2: Enable Failure Auditing for Files**

In this practice, you enable failure auditing on a portion of the file system. To complete this practice, you must have completed Practice 1.

1. Click Start, and then click Computer.

2. Right-click the C:\Program Files\ folder, and then click Properties.

3. In the Program Files Properties dialog box, click the Security tab. Then, click the Advanced button.

4. In the Advanced Security Settings dialog box, click the Auditing tab. Then, click the Continue button. Respond to the UAC prompt that appears.

5. Click the Add button.

6. In the Select User Or Group dialog box, type the name of the user whom you will use to test the resource's access problem. Click OK.

7. In the Auditing Entry dialog box, select the Full Control/Failed check box. Then, select the Apply These Auditing Entries To Objects And/Or Containers Within This Container Only check box. Click OK.

8. Click OK twice more.

▶ **Practice 3: Reproduce and Isolate the Problem**

In this practice, you run a provided batch file to simulate a program that requires additional privileges. Then, you examine the Security event log to determine what folders require additional access.

1. Log on to your Windows Vista test computer using a user account with standard user privileges (the account should not be a member of the Administrators group).

2. In the Chapter 07 folder, double-click the test-permissions.bat file. (All practice files can be installed from the Practice_Files folder on the CD accompanying this book.) A command window appears briefly. Running this batch file simulates running a program that requires access to a protected portion of the file system.

3. Click Start, right-click Computer, and then click Manage. Respond to the UAC prompt that appears.

4. Expand System Tools, Event Viewer, Windows Logs, and then select Security.

5. Browse the Security event log to identify the file system audit failure. View the Object section of the event description to identify the exact file that was being created. Then, examine the Access Request Information section of the event description to determine what action the program was trying to take.

Now you will modify file permissions to grant the user the access required to run the batch file.

6. Click Start, and then click Computer. Browse to the folder containing the file you identified in step 4. Right-click it, and then click Properties.

7. In the Properties dialog box, click the Security tab. Then, click Edit. Respond to the UAC prompt that appears.

8. Click the Add button. In the Select User Or Group dialog box, type the name of the user whom you will use to test the resources access problem. Click OK.

9. In the Permissions dialog box, with the newly added user selected, select the Allow/ Modify check box. Then, click OK twice to grant the user access to write to the folder.

10. From the CD accompanying this book, double-click the test-permissions.bat file to determine whether the test program can create the required files. Use Windows Explorer to verify that the C:\Program Files\Common Files\Services\Temp.tmp file was created successfully.

In this practice, you identified the exact file that a program needed to create to function properly and granted the user permissions required to run the program. In the real world you might need to grant access to several resources, requiring you to repeatedly grant permissions, retest the program, and then grant additional permissions.

▶ **Practice 4: Disable Auditing**

Now that you have used auditing to identify the file permissions required by a program, you should disable failure auditing.

1. In Windows Explorer, right-click the C:\Program Files folder, and then click Properties.

2. In the Properties dialog box, click the Security tab. Then, click the Advanced button.

3. In the Advanced Security Settings dialog box, click the Auditing tab. Then, click the Continue button. Respond to the UAC prompt that appears.

4. Select the auditing entry, and then click the Remove button.

5. Click OK. If you are unable to apply updated auditing settings to any location, click Continue.

6. Click OK twice more.

7. Click Start, type **local**, right-click the Local Security Policy icon, and then click Run As Administrator. Respond to the UAC prompt that appears.

8. In the Local Security Policy console, expand Local Policies, and then select Audit Policy.

9. In the right pane, double-click Audit Object Access.

10. In the Audit Object Access Properties dialog box, clear the Failure check box, and then click OK.

11. Restart your computer to apply the changes.

Lesson Summary

■ Windows Vista is compatible with Group Policy auditing settings used with earlier versions of Windows. Additionally, Windows Vista provides the AuditPol.exe command-line tool to specify more granular auditing subcategories.

■ To troubleshoot problems related to permissions, first verify the file and registry permissions that you know are required. If you don't know exactly which file and registry keys are required, enable failure object access auditing, enable failure auditing on all files or registry keys, and then re-create the problem. Then, examine the Security event log to determine which resources generated failure audit events. Adjust the permissions on those objects and rerun the test until the application works. Finally, disable auditing.

Lesson Review

You can use the following questions to test your knowledge of the information in Lesson 3, "Troubleshooting Authorization Problems and Auditing User Access." The questions are also available on the companion CD if you prefer to review them in electronic form.

NOTE   Answers

Answers to these questions and explanations of why each answer choice is right or wrong are located in the "Answers" section at the end of the book.

---

1. You need to determine which users are attempting to access a file. Which audit policy should you enable?

    A. Audit System Events

    B. Audit Privilege Use

    C. Audit Process Tracking

    D. Audit Object Access

2. Which tool would you use to configure auditing settings from the command line or from a script?

    A. SecPol.msc

    B. AuditPol.exe

    C. Mmc.exe

    D. ReLog.exe

3. You configure auditing for file accesses. Which of the following pieces of information about the file access are recorded in the event log? (Choose all that apply.)

    A. The time the user accessed the file

    B. The process that accessed the file

    C. The user name that accessed the file

    D. Whether the file access attempt was read-only or needed to update the file

Chapter Review

To further practice and reinforce the skills you learned in this chapter, you can

- Review the chapter summary.
- Review the list of key terms introduced in this chapter.
- Complete the case scenarios. These scenarios set up real-world situations involving the topics of this chapter and ask you to create a solution.
- Complete the suggested practices.
- Take a practice test.

Chapter Summary

- Authentication is the process of identifying a user and validating the user's identity. To troubleshoot authentication problems, enable failure auditing for Account Logon Events, and then examine the Security event log.
- Encryption provides data protection even if an attacker bypasses operating system security. Windows Vista includes two encryption technologies: EFS and BitLocker. EFS encrypts individual files and folders, while BitLocker encrypts the entire system volume.
- You can use auditing to troubleshoot authorization problems. First, enable failure object access auditing, enable failure auditing on all files or registry keys, and then re-create the problem. Then, examine the Security event log to determine which resources generated failure audit events. Adjust the permissions on those objects and rerun the test until the application works. Finally, disable auditing.

Key Terms

Do you know what these key terms mean? You can check your answers by looking up the terms in the glossary at the end of the book.

- BitLocker Drive Encryption
- cryptographic service provider (CSP)
- Encrypting File System (EFS)
- multifactor authentication
- rootkit
- single sign-on

Case Scenarios

In the following case scenarios, you will apply what you've learned about how to implement and apply security. You can find answers to these questions in the "Answers" section at the end of this book.

Case Scenario 1: Recommend Data Protection Technologies

You are a desktop support technician at Wingtip Toys. Recently, Adina Hagege, your organization's CEO, stopped you in the hallway to ask a couple of quick questions.

Questions

Answer the following questions for your CEO.

1.   "Can you give me a quick second opinion about something? I travel almost constantly, and I keep the company financials and all the plans for our new toys on my laptop. The IT department says they have file permissions set up so that only I can view these files. Is that good enough to protect me if someone steals my laptop?"

2.   "Is there some way I can protect my data even if my laptop is stolen? What are my options?"

3.   "Sometimes I share files with people across the network. Which of those technologies will allow me to share files this way?"

Case Scenario 2: Troubleshoot Permission Problems

You are a desktop support technician at Fourth Coffee. One of your finance users, Ken Malcolmson, calls to complain that a program he's trying to run doesn't work properly. Ken tells you about the problem:

"I downloaded this tool, ExcelAnalyzer.exe, to analyze one of my spreadsheets. It doesn't need to be installed or anything, I just run the executable file and then pick the spreadsheet that I need to analyze. It's giving me an Access Denied error, however, when I attempt to generate a report. What's wrong?"

You verify that Ken is logged on as a member of the standard Users group and is not an administrator. You test the ExcelAnalyzer.exe tool, and you don't receive a UAC prompt.

Questions

Answer the following questions about Ken's problem.

1.   Is this an authentication problem or an authorization problem?

2.   Why is UAC not prompting Ken to elevate privileges?

3.   How can you solve Ken's problem?

Suggested Practices

To successfully master the objectives covered in this chapter, complete the following tasks.

Troubleshoot Authentication Issues

For this task, you should complete both practices.

■ **Practice 1: Examining Real-World Authentication Problems**   Visit *http://windowshelp .microsoft.com/communities/newsgroups/en-us/* and browse the following two news-groups. In each, look for authentication problems. Read the posts to determine how administrators solved their problems:

  ❑ Windows Vista Administration, Accounts, And Passwords
  ❑ Windows Vista Security

■ **Practice 2: Examining Real-World Auditing Events**   On your production computer, enable success and failure auditing for the Audit Logon Events policy. Leave this enabled for several days, and then analyze the audit events in the Security event log to identify the types of events that are added during normal computer usage.

Configure and Troubleshoot Access to Resources

For this task, you should complete Practice 1. If you want a better understanding of BitLocker, complete Practices 2 and 3.

■ **Practice 1: Recovering an EFS-Encrypted File**   In a domain environment, use EFS to encrypt a file. Then, copy the domain DRA key to that computer and use a different account to recover the encrypted file.

■ **Practice 2: Bypassing Operating System Security with a Bootable CD**   Enable BitLocker Drive Encryption on a Windows Vista computer. Then, search the Internet for a free .ISO file for a bootable operating system and burn the .ISO file to a CD or DVD. Restart the computer from the bootable media and attempt to view files on the BitLocker-protected volume.

■ **Practice 3: Bypassing Operating System Security by Removing the Hard Disk**   Enable Bit-Locker Drive Encryption on a Windows Vista computer. Then, connect the hard disk to a different computer and attempt to load Windows. When prompted, provide the recovery key.

Take a Practice Test

The practice tests on this book's companion CD offer many options. For example, you can test yourself on just the content covered in this chapter, or you can test yourself on all the 70-622 certification exam content. You can set up the test so that it closely simulates the experience of taking a certification exam, or you can set it up in study mode so that you can look at the correct answers and explanations after you answer each question.

MORE INFO   **Practice tests**

For details about all the practice test options available, see "How to Use the Practice Tests" in this book's Introduction.

Chapter 8

Understanding and Configuring User Account Control

User Account Control (UAC) is one of the most noticeable new features that Windows Vista introduces to the Windows line of operating systems, and because it is new, it is heavily tested on the 70-622 exam. Fortunately, UAC is also easy to understand. Once you know how the feature works and the settings that control its behavior, you will have little difficulty handling UAC on the test or in the real world.

Exam objectives in this chapter:
- Configure and troubleshoot User Account Control.

Lessons in this chapter:

Before You Begin

To complete the lessons in this chapter, you must have

- A Windows Server 2003 domain controller named dcsrv1.nwtraders.msft.
- A Windows Vista Enterprise, Business, or Ultimate client computer named Vista1 that is a member of the Nwtraders.msft domain.

Real World

JC Mackin

Two questions. First, how many of you work for organizations in which all users are configured to be administrators of their own computers? Next, how many of you work for organizations in which computers often get infected by spyware, viruses, and other malware? I'm guessing that more of you who answered yes to the first question also answered yes to the second question. What's the connection between the two? Plain and simple: logging on as an administrator in Windows XP and Windows 2000 leaves you more vulnerable to damaging, network-based attacks. This problem has a name—the administrator problem—and it's been known for years.

Microsoft tried to address the problem in the past by encouraging users in Windows XP to log on without local administrative privileges and to use tools such as the Runas command whenever such privileges were needed. But this prescription turned out to be unfeasible for most users. To fix the administrator problem, what really needed to change was the underlying vulnerability that caused it, and this, in turn, required a drastic redesign of the way user accounts interacted with Windows.

The result of this redesign process is a Windows Vista feature called User Account Control (UAC), which is enabled by default. In UAC even administrators run without administrative privileges most of the time, and administrators must give consent before any administrative task is performed. Meanwhile, nonadministrators, now officially called standard users in Windows Vista, can perform any administrative task simply by entering administrative credentials when needed.

If these changes sound like a bit of a pain to get used to, well, that is precisely the idea: UAC is a *bit* of a pain designed to prevent the much larger pain of having your computer taken over by an Internet invader. Like a law requiring you to fasten your seat belt, UAC seems a little inconvenient and constraining at first, but in no time you'll get used to it and even grow to appreciate the feature for the improved security it brings.

Lesson 1: Understanding User Account Control

User Account Control is the Windows Vista feature that displays messages whenever you want to perform an administrative task. Understanding this feature in its entirety requires you to grasp new concepts such as elevation, Admin Approval Mode, access tokens, UAC prompts, UAC shields, and the Secure Desktop.

After this lesson, you will be able to:
- ■ Understand the purpose of User Account Control.
- ■ Understand the components of User Account Control.

Estimated lesson time: 30 minutes

What is User Account Control?

User Account Control (UAC) is a security feature designed to minimize the danger of running Windows Vista as an administrator and to maximize the convenience of running Windows Vista as a standard user. In previous versions of Windows, the risks of logging on as an administrator were significant, yet this practice was widespread. Meanwhile, running as a standard user was generally safe, but the inconveniences prevented many from doing so.

Running as Local Administrator in Windows XP

In previous versions of Windows, Trojan horses and other malware (malicious software) could leverage the credentials of a locally logged-on administrator to damage a system. For example, if you were logged on to Windows XP as an administrator and unknowingly downloaded a Trojan horse from a network source, this malware could use your administrative privileges to reformat your hard disk drive, delete all your files, or create a hidden administrator account on the local system.

The main reason that users in previous versions of Windows often ran as administrators despite these dangers is that many common tasks, such as installing an application or adding a printer, required (and still require today) a user to have administrative privileges on the local machine. In fact, some applications cannot even run properly unless the users have administrative privileges on the local machine. Because in previous versions of Windows there was no easy way to log on as a standard user and "elevate" to an administrator when necessary, organizations whose users occasionally needed administrative privileges simply tended to configure their users as administrators on their local machines.

NOTE   What is elevation?

In Windows Vista, the term "elevation" is used when a user adopts administrative privileges to perform a task.

NOTE   Local administrators

When we refer to administrators in this chapter, we are referring to members of the Administrators group on any Windows Vista computer. By default, the first account you create on a Windows Vista computer is a member of this Administrators group. In addition, within an Active Directory domain, domain administrators are also members of the Administrators group on each computer that is a member of the domain. Members of the Administrators group on each local machine are typically called local administrators. The local administrator account named Administrator is disabled by default in Windows Vista.

How UAC Fixes the Administrator Problem

UAC in Windows Vista minimizes the severity of the administrator problem in two ways. First, to inhibit malware from secretly leveraging a logged-on administrator's privileges, UAC by default enables Admin Approval Mode during administrator sessions. This mode requires administrators to approve all tasks (such as writing to a protected area of the registry) that require administrative privileges. (Because administrators running in Admin Approval Mode must approve all administrative tasks, they are also known as consent admins.) Second, to reduce the inconvenience of running as a standard user, UAC by default allows all standard users to perform administrative tasks as long as they can provide administrator credentials when prompted.

IMPORTANT   Running as a standard user is still safer

Though UAC certainly reduces the dangers of running as an administrator in Windows Vista, running as a standard user is still safer. Therefore, Microsoft recommends that even users requiring administrative privileges run as standard users whenever possible.

NOTE Power Users in Windows XP and Windows Vista

The Power Users group in Windows XP was designed to enable members of this group to perform system tasks, such as installing applications, without granting full administrator permissions. Power Users also had write access to areas of the file system and registry that normally only allow administrator access. Power Users enabled some level of application compatibility; unfortunately, this did not address the problem of some applications requiring unnecessary privileges and user rights. UAC does not make use of the Power Users group, and the permissions granted to the Power Users group on Windows XP have been removed from Windows Vista. Instead, UAC enables standard users to perform all common configuration tasks. The Power Users group, however, is still available for backward compatibility with other versions of Windows. To use the Power Users group on Windows Vista, you need to apply a new security template to change the default permissions on both system folders and the registry to grant Power Users group permissions equivalent to those in Windows XP.

Quick Check

1. Which kinds of accounts occasionally require elevation in Windows Vista, standard users, administrators, or both?
2. True or False? A consent admin is an administrator running in Admin Approval Mode.

Quick Check Answers

1. Both
2. True

Understanding the Differences Between Standard Users and Administrators in Windows Vista

The primary difference between a standard user and an administrator in Windows Vista is the level of access the user has over core, protected areas of the computer. For example, standard users by default cannot write to the system root (typically, the C:\Windows folder) or to most areas of the registry, but administrators can. In addition, administrators can change the system state, turn off the firewall, configure security policy, install a service or a driver that affects every user on the computer, and install software for the entire computer. Standard users can perform these particular tasks only if they are able to provide valid administrative credentials when prompted.

Table 8-1 details some of the tasks a standard user can perform and what tasks require elevation to an administrator account.

Table 8-1   Comparing Rights of Standard Users and Administrators

Standard Users	Administrators
Establish a local area network connection	Install and uninstall applications
Establish and configure a wireless connection	Install a driver for a device (for example, a digital camera driver)
Modify display settings	Install Windows updates
Users cannot defragment the hard disk drive, but a service does this on their behalf	Configure Parental Controls
Play CD/DVD media (configurable with Group Policy)	Install an ActiveX control
Burn CD/DVD media (configurable with Group Policy)	Open the Windows Firewall Control Panel
Change the desktop background for the current user	Change a user's account type
Open the Date and Time Control Panel and change the time zone	Modify UAC settings in the Security Policy Editor snap-in (secpol.msc)
Use Remote Desktop to connect to another computer	Configure Remote Desktop access
Change user's own account password	Add or remove a user account
Configure battery power options	Copy or move files into the Program Files or Windows directory
Configure Accessibility options	Schedule automated tasks
Restore user's backed-up files	Restore system backed-up files
Set-up computer synchronization with a mobile device (smart phone, laptop, or Personal Digital Assistant [PDA])	Configure Automatic Updates
Connect and configure a Bluetooth device	Browse to another user's directory

IMPORTANT   Local administrator accounts in Windows Vista

On new installations, by default, the first user account created is a consent admin—a local administrator account in Admin Approval Mode (UAC-enabled). All subsequent accounts are then created as standard users. The built-in Administrator account is disabled by default in Windows Vista. If Windows Vista determines during an upgrade from Windows XP that the built-in Administrator is the only active local administrator account, Windows Vista leaves the account enabled and places the account in Admin Approval Mode.

IMPORTANT   The Administrator account and Safe Mode

The built-in Administrator account, by default, cannot log on to the computer in Safe Mode. If the computer is not a member of a domain and the last local administrator account is inadvertently demoted, disabled, or deleted, Windows Vista automatically enables the built-in Administrator account in Safe Mode to allow for disaster recovery. If the computer is a member of a domain, Windows Vista does not automatically enable the built-in Administrator account in Safe Mode even after the last local administrator account is deleted. In this case, log on to the computer as a domain administrator in Safe Mode With Networking and create a new local administrator account for the machine.

Understanding the Windows Vista Logon

To best understand UAC, you need to understand the Windows Vista logon process. When a standard user logs on to a Windows Vista computer, the user is granted an access token. You can think of an access token as an entrance ticket that grants this user permission to roam freely in certain nonprotected areas of the operating system. However, when an administrator logs on to Windows Vista, the administrator is granted *two* access tokens: a standard user access token to access the nonprotected areas of the operating system and a full administrator access token to access the core areas.

Figure 8-1 illustrates how the logon process for an administrator differs from the logon process for a standard user.

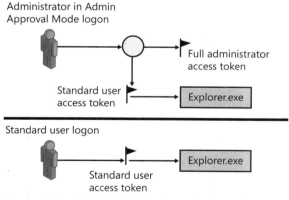

Figure 8-1   Administrator and standard user logons

Although administrators are granted two access tokens during Windows Vista logon, only the standard user access token is used to launch the desktop process, Explorer.exe. Explorer.exe, importantly, is also the parent process from which all other user-initiated processes inherit their access token. As a result, all applications launched by an administrator run as a standard user by default unless the administrator provides consent to approve an application's use of a full administrator access token.

Quick Check

1. Under what conditions is the built-in Administrator account enabled in Windows Vista after an upgrade from Windows XP?
2. True or False? In Windows XP, all applications launched by an administrator run with administrator privileges by default.
3. What kind of an access token is used when you perform a task requiring elevation?
4. What kind of access token is used when an administrator launches an application in Windows Vista?

Quick Check Answers

1. When no other administrator account exists on the local machine
2. True
3. A full administrator access token
4. A standard user access token

Understanding the UAC Elevation Prompts

With UAC enabled, Windows Vista prompts the user before launching a program or task that requires a full administrator access token. This prompt ensures that no malicious application can silently install.

The Consent Prompt

The consent prompt is presented when a user logged on as a consent admin attempts to perform a task that requires the user's administrative access token. Figure 8-2 shows the User Account Control consent prompt.

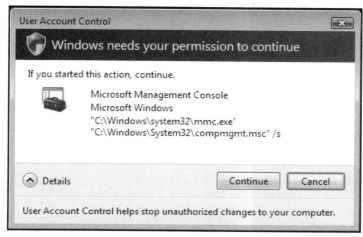

Figure 8-2   A UAC consent prompt

The Credential Prompt

The credential prompt is presented when a standard user attempts to perform a task that requires an administrative access token. Figure 8-3 shows the User Account Control consent prompt.

Figure 8-3   A UAC credential prompt

The UAC Multicolored Shield Icon

Some Windows Vista configuration elements, such as the Date And Time program in Control Panel, contain a mix of administrator and standard user operations. Standard users, for example, can view the clock and change the time zone, but a full administrator access token is required to change the local system time.

In such a case, a multicolored shield icon is displayed on the buttons that require elevation. Buttons on which there is no such shield signify functions that standard users can perform without administrative privileges.

Figure 8-4 displays the Date And Time tab of the Date And Time program in Control Panel. In the figure you can see that the *Change Date And Time* function requires elevation, but the *Change Time Zone* function does not.

Figure 8-4   The UAC shield icon

UAC Prompt Color Coding

UAC elevation prompts are color-coded as red, blue/green, gray, or yellow to identify the associated security risk. The following describes the meanings of each of these colors:

- **Blue/green**   The application requesting elevation is a Windows Vista administrative program such as a Control Panel program.
- **Gray**   The application is trusted by the local computer.

- **Red**   The application is from a blocked publisher or is blocked by Group Policy.
- **Yellow**   The application is unidentified. It is neither blocked nor trusted by the local computer.

Figure 8-5 shows an example of a yellow consent prompt.

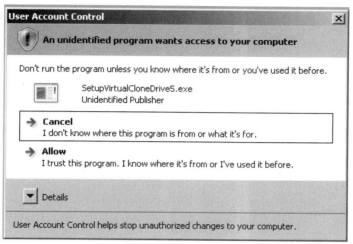

Figure 8-5   A UAC consent prompt for an unidentified application

UAC Prompts and the Secure Desktop

When a program requests elevation, the user's desktop by default is switched to a UAC feature called the Secure Desktop. The Secure Desktop dims all the elements of the user desktop except for the UAC prompt and disables all other user activity. Only when the user clicks Continue or Cancel does the desktop switch back to the user desktop.

The Secure Desktop is enabled by default in Windows Vista and can be configured locally with the Local Security Policy Editor snap-in (secpol.msc) or centrally with Group Policy. See Lesson 2, "Configuring User Account Control," for more information about configuring this option.

Quick Check

1. Which UAC prompt do standard users typically see?
2. Which UAC prompt do administrators typically see?
3. Which UAC prompt color signifies an elevation request by an application that is neither blocked nor trusted?

> **Quick Check Answers**
> 1. Credential prompt
> 2. Consent prompt
> 3. Yellow

Practice: Exploring UAC Features

In this practice, you will compare the UAC features that appear by default when you are logged on as an administrator to those that appear by default when you are logged on as a standard user.

▶ **Practice 1: Reviewing the Default UAC Features for Administrators**

In this practice, you will log on to Windows Vista as an administrator and review the default user interface features of UAC.

1. Log on to Vista1 as an administrator.
2. In Control Panel, click the Change Keyboards Or Other Input Methods link.
3. In the Regional And Language Options dialog box, click Change Keyboards.
4. In the Text Services And Input Language dialog box, click Add.
5. In the Add Input Languages dialog box, expand English (United States), and then select the United States-International keyboard check box.
6. Click OK to close all open dialog boxes.
7. Answer the following question: Does adding a keyboard require elevation in Windows Vista?

    Answer: No, because if elevation were required, you would have been prompted for elevation.
8. From the Start menu, right-click Computer, and then, from the shortcut menu, click Manage.
9. Answer the following questions:

    a. Does opening the Computer Management console require elevation?

    Answer: Yes, because you have been prompted for elevation.

    b. Which type of elevation prompt appears?

    Answer: A consent prompt

    c. Aside from the elevation prompt, which is the only feature in the desktop with which you are able to interact?

    Answer: The Language bar

      d. What is the name of the feature that blocks access to desktop elements whenever an elevation prompt is displayed?

          Answer: The Secure Desktop

      e. Why is the elevation prompt blue/green?

          Answer: The blue/green color signifies that the program requesting elevation is an element of Windows Vista, such as an administrative tool or a Control Panel program.

      f. How can you find out the location of the program requiring elevation?

          Answer: On the consent prompt, click the down arrow next to Details.

10. In the User Account Control message box (consent prompt), click Continue.

11. In the Computer Management console, browse to and expand the *Local Users And Groups* node.

12. Right-click the Users folder, and then click New User from the shortcut menu.

13. In the New User dialog box, enter a user name and password of your choice for the new user.

14. Clear the User Must Change Password At Next Logon check box, and then click Create.

15. Close the New User dialog box and verify that the new user you created is listed in the details pane.

16. Answer the following question: Why weren't you prompted for elevation when you created the new user?

    Answer: You were not prompted for elevation because Computer Management is already running with a full administrator access token.

17. Close Computer Management.

18. Open Control Panel. Click some links that have a shield next to them, and then click some links that do not have a shield next to them.

19. Answer the following question: What does the multicolored shield icon signify when you see it in the user interface?

    Answer: The multicolored shield signifies that clicking the associated tool or command requires elevation.

20. Log off Vista1.

▶ Practice 2: Reviewing the Default UAC Features for Standard Users

In this practice, you will log on to Windows Vista as a standard user and review the default user interface features of UAC.

1. Log on to Vista1 as a standard user. You can use the local user account you just created in the last practice. For example, if you just created an account named JuergenS, you can log on by specifying Vista1\JuergenS as the user name.

2. From the Start menu, right-click Computer, and then click Manage from the shortcut menu.

3. Answer the following question: What kind of elevation prompt appears?

   Answer: A credential prompt

4. In the User Account Control prompt, enter the credentials of an administrator account, and then click OK.

5. In Computer Management, create a new user account as described in the previous practice.

6. Answer the following question: If you have logged on as a standard user, why are you able to create a user account?

   Answer: You can perform administrative tasks such as creating user accounts in Computer Management because you are running Computer Management with administrator credentials.

7. Close Computer Management.

8. Open Control Panel.

9. Answer the following question: As a standard user, which type of prompt appears whenever you click a link next to a multicolored shield?

   Answer: A credential prompt

10. Close Control Panel.

11. From the Start menu, right-click an accessory such as Calculator or Command Prompt.

12. Answer the following question: As a standard user, which type of prompt appears whenever you choose to run a program as administrator?

    Answer: A credential prompt

13. Close all open windows and log off Vista1.

Lesson Summary

- In previous versions of Windows, staying logged on as an administrator increased the risk of a damaging attack by malware. This problem was known as the administrator problem.

- User Account Control (UAC) minimizes the severity of the administrator problem by warning administrators before changes are made to protected areas of the system. This particular aspect of UAC is known as Admin Approval Mode. UAC also allows standard users to perform administrative tasks if they can provide administrative credentials before doing so.

■ When UAC is enabled, both administrators and standard users rely on a standard user access token to perform nonadministrative tasks. When a task requires administrative privileges, administrators can "elevate" by providing consent to use a full administrator access token. Standard users can "elevate," too by providing administrative credentials.

■ The consent prompt is the elevation prompt that administrators see by default. The credential prompt is the elevation prompt that standard users see by default. These prompts are color-coded to identify the security risk of the elevation request. By default, in a feature known as the Secure Desktop, UAC freezes everything on the desktop except the elevation prompt.

■ In the Windows Vista user interface, a multicolored shield signifies a task that requires elevation.

Lesson Review

You can use the following questions to test your knowledge of the information in Lesson 1, "Understanding User Account Control." The questions are also available on the companion CD if you prefer to review them in electronic form.

NOTE   Answers

Answers to these questions and explanations of why each answer choice is right or wrong are located in the "Answers" section at the end of the book.

---

1. After you upgrade a computer to Windows Vista from Windows XP, you find that you can no longer log on with the built-in Administrator account. You verify that the profile for Administrator is still present on the Windows Vista computer. You want to use the built-in Administrator account in Windows Vista along with the user's profile inherited from Windows XP. What should you do?

    A. Enable the built-in Administrator account

    B. Log on to Windows Vista as Administrator in Safe Mode

    C. Migrate the files and settings to a standard user account

    D. Migrate the files and settings to an administrator account

2. A manager in your organization occasionally needs to perform tasks that require administrative privileges on his Windows Vista computer. Up to now he has been calling tech support every few days to have a desktop support technician perform such tasks for him. You want to allow the manager to perform these tasks on his own while minimizing security risks. What should you do? (Assume that User Account Control [UAC] is enabled.)

    A. Configure the manager's user account as an administrator account.

    B. Provide the manager with the user name and password of an administrator account with enough privileges to perform the needed tasks. Instruct him to log on with this account whenever he needs to perform administrative tasks.

    C. Provide the manager with the user name and password of an administrator account with enough privileges to perform the needed tasks. Instruct him to use this account from now on.

    D. Provide the manager with the user name and password of an administrator account with enough privileges to perform the needed tasks. Instruct the user to log on with his usual account and provide the credentials at a credential prompt when needed.

Lesson 2: Configuring User Account Control

In Windows Vista the out-of-box behavior for UAC results from the default settings defined in a computer's Local Security Policy. Although a domain administrator can configure these settings in Group Policy also, no UAC settings are defined by default at the Group Policy level.

As a desktop support specialist, you need to know how to configure UAC policy settings both for an individual computer and for groups of computers in a domain environment. Also important to know is that, because UAC is a new feature in Windows Vista, you will find many questions related to UAC policy settings on the 70-622 exam.

After this lesson, you will be able to:
- Enable and disable User Account Control in Control Panel.
- Configure User Account Control in Local Security Policy or a Group Policy object (GPO).
- Use the Run As Administrator option to open an administrator command prompt or run any program with administrative privileges.

Estimated lesson time: 30 minutes

Turning UAC On and Off in Control Panel

Although it is recommend that you leave UAC on, it is also important for you to know how to turn the feature on and off quickly. The standard way to turn UAC on and off is through Control Panel. In Control Panel, for domain-joined computers first click the User Accounts link, and then click the User Accounts link again. For computers not joined to a domain, click the User And Family Safety link, and then click the User Accounts link.

This step introduces the User Accounts page, as shown in Figure 8-6.

In the User Accounts window, click the Turn User Account Control On Or Off link. Doing so opens the Turn User Account Control On Or Off dialog box, as shown in Figure 8-7.

To turn UAC off, clear the Use User Account Control To Make Your Computer More Secure check box. You will need to restart your computer before the new setting will take effect.

Figure 8-6   Turning UAC on or off in Control Panel

Figure 8-7   Turning UAC on or off

When UAC is turned off, the Security Center displays a Windows Security Alert shield in the System Tray. You can then double-click the alert to turn UAC on in Security Center. To turn UAC on in Security Center, click the Turn On Now button in the User Account Control area, as shown in Figure 8-8.

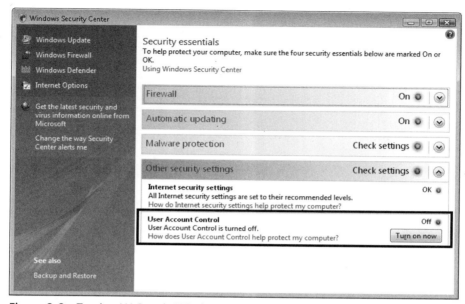

Figure 8-8   Turning UAC on in Windows Security Center

Locating UAC Policy Settings

UAC policy settings can be defined in an individual computer's Local Security Policy or in a GPO.

To locate UAC policy settings in Local Security Policy, first open the Local Security Policy console by typing **secpol.msc** at a command prompt, in Start Search, or in the Run box. (Alternatively, you can open Local Security Policy in Administrative Tools available in Control Panel classic view.) Then, in the Local Security Policy console, browse the console tree to Local Policies, and then to Security Options. To see the UAC policy settings, in the details pane, scroll to the bottom of the list of security options. These settings are shown in Figure 8-9.

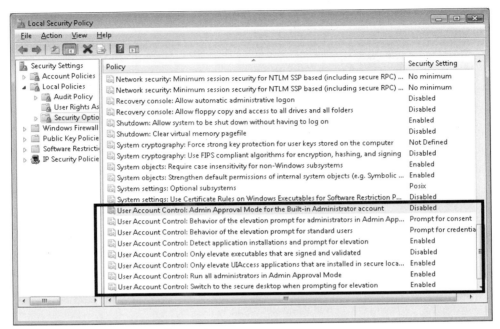

Figure 8-9 UAC security policy settings

To locate UAC policy settings in Group Policy, you can use the Group Policy Management Console (GPMC) on any domain member computer running Windows Vista. To open the GPMC, you can type **gpmc.msc** at a command prompt, in Start Search, or in the Run box. Then, in the GPMC console tree, right-click any GPO and select Edit from the shortcut menu. Next, in the Group Policy Object Editor window that appears, browse the console tree to Computer Configuration, Windows Settings, Security Settings, Local Security Policy, and then finally Security Options. In the details pane you will see the same UAC policy settings as those that appear in Figure 8-9.

Configuring UAC Policy Settings

In both Local Security Policy and GPOs, nine configurable policy settings are available for UAC. The following section describes each of these nine policies for UAC and the options available for each policy.

1. User Account Control: Admin Approval Mode For The Built-In Administrator Account This security setting, shown in Figure 8-10, determines the behavior of Admin Approval Mode for the built-in Administrator account.

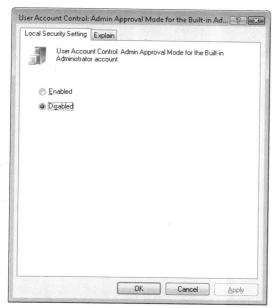

Figure 8-10   UAC security policy setting for the built-in Administrator account

The built-in Administrator account is distinctive in a number of ways. First, the account itself is disabled by default (unless no other administrator account exists). Second, you can configure its UAC settings separately from those of other administrators. Finally, it is the only account in Windows Vista for which the UAC feature is entirely disabled by default. This means that when the Administrator account is enabled, it runs as it did in Windows XP. For this reason and others, it is by far the least secure account in Windows Vista.

Two options are available for this policy setting:

❏   Enabled: The built-in Administrator will log on in Admin Approval Mode. By default, any operation that requires elevation of privilege will prompt the consent admin to choose either Permit or Deny.

❏   Disabled: The built-in Administrator will log on in Windows XP-compatible mode and run all applications by default with full administrative privilege.

By default, the policy setting is set to Disabled for new installations and for upgrades where the built-in Administrator is not the only local active administrator on the computer. However, the policy is set to Enabled for upgrades when Windows Vista determines that the built-in Administrator account is the only active local administrator on the computer. (If Windows Vista determines this, the built-in Administrator account is also kept enabled following the upgrade.)

2. User Account Control: Behavior Of The Elevation Prompt For Administrators In Admin
    Approval Mode

    This security policy setting, shown in Figure 8-11, determines the behavior of the eleva-
    tion prompt for administrators. It is, in other words, the setting that determines UAC
    behavior for all administrators except for the built-in Administrator account.

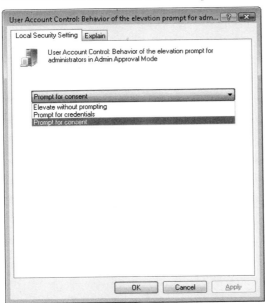

Figure 8-11   UAC security policy setting for administrators

The options available in this policy setting are:

- ❑ Prompt For Consent: An operation that requires elevation of privilege will prompt
  the consent admin to select either Permit or Deny. If the consent admin selects Permit, the operation will continue with the highest available privilege. This option
  allows users to enter their names and passwords to perform a privileged task.

- ❑ Prompt For Credentials: An operation that requires elevation of privilege will
  prompt the consent admin to enter a user name and password. If the user enters
  valid credentials, the operation will continue with the applicable privilege.

- ❑ Elevate Without Prompting: This option allows the consent admin to perform an
  operation that requires elevation without consent or credentials. Note: You should
  use this scenario only in the most constrained environments.

By default, this policy setting is set to Prompt For Consent.

Exam Tip Although you could be tested on any of the nine policy settings listed in this section, this last policy setting is one of the most heavily tested on the 70-622 exam.

---

3. User Account Control: Behavior Of The Elevation Prompt For Standard Users

This security setting, shown in Figure 8-12, determines the behavior of the elevation prompt for standard users. For most corporate users this is the setting that in fact determines the UAC experience.

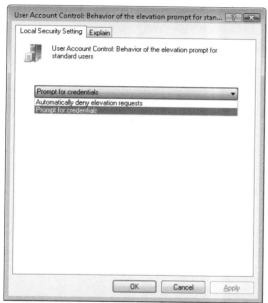

Figure 8-12 UAC security policy setting for standard users

The options available in this security policy setting are:

- ❏ Prompt For Credentials: An operation that requires elevation of privilege will prompt the user to enter an administrative user name and password. If the user enters valid credentials, the operation will continue with the applicable privilege.
- ❏ Automatically Deny Elevation Requests: This option results in an access denied error message being returned to the standard user when the user tries to perform an operation that requires elevation of privilege. Most enterprises running desktops as standard user will configure this policy to reduce help desk calls.

The default setting for this policy is Prompt For Credentials for Vista Home, Vista Business, and Vista Ultimate and Automatically Deny Elevation Requests for Vista Enterprise.

Exam Tip   Expect to see questions about this policy setting and its options for the 70-622 exam.

---

4. User Account Control: Detect Application Installations And Prompt For Elevation

    This security setting determines the behavior of application installation detection for the entire system.

    The options for this policy setting are:

    ❏ Enabled: Application installation packages that require an elevation of privilege to install are automatically detected and trigger an elevation prompt.

    ❏ Disabled: Application installation packages are not automatically detected.

    The default setting for this policy is Enabled for Windows Vista Home, Business, and Ultimate and Disabled for Windows Vista Enterprise.

NOTE   Managed software installation

This policy setting is intended to reduce unapproved application installations for organizations that do not manage software installation. Enterprises managing software installation through Group Policy or Systems Management Server (SMS) do not need this feature.

---

5. User Account Control: Only Elevate Executables That Are Signed And Validated

    This security setting will enforce digital certificate signature checks on any interactive application that requests elevation of privilege. Enterprise administrators can manage the list of allowed applications by controlling the certificates copied to the local computer's Trusted Publisher Store.

    The options for this policy setting are:

    ❏ Enabled: Requires the certificate of a given executable to be validated before the executable is permitted to run.

    ❏ Disabled: Does not enforce certificate chain validation before a given executable is permitted to run.

    By default, this policy setting is set to Disabled.

6. User Account Control: Only Elevate UIAccess Applications That Are Installed In Secure Locations

    This security setting will enforce the requirement that applications that request execution with a UIAccess integrity level (by means of a marking of UIAccess=true in their application manifests) must reside in a secure location on the file system. Secure locations are limited to the following directories:

    ❏ ...\Program Files\, including subdirectories

    ❏ ...\Windows\system32\

❑ For 64-bit versions of Windows Vista, the x86 program files folder (...\Program Files (x86)) including subdirectories for 64-bit versions of Windows

Windows already enforces a digital signature check on any interactive application that requests execution with UIAccess integrity level regardless of the state of this policy setting. This policy simply provides additional security by restricting the location of such applications.

The options for this policy setting are:

❑ Enabled: An application will launch with UIAccess integrity only if it resides in a secure location in the file system.

❑ Disabled: An application will launch with UIAccess integrity even if it does not reside in a secure location in the file system.

By default, this policy setting is set to Enabled.

7. User Account Control: Run All Administrators In Admin Approval Mode

This security setting, shown in Figure 8-13, determines the behavior of all UAC policies for the entire system. Although the policy name refers only to administrators, disabling this policy will also disable the credential prompts for standard users. In fact, UAC features in general depend on this policy being left in the Enabled state. When you disable UAC in Control Panel, this is the only policy setting whose status changes to Disabled.

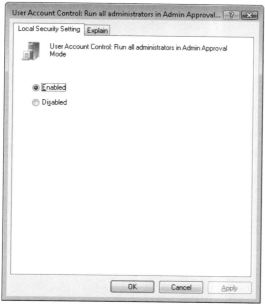

Figure 8-13   Security policy setting for enabling and disabling UAC

The options for this policy setting are:

❑ Enabled: Admin Approval Mode and all other UAC policies are dependent on this option being enabled. Changing this setting requires a system reboot.

❑ Disabled: Admin Approval Mode user type and all related UAC policies will be disabled. Note: The Security Center will notify you that the overall security of the operating system has been reduced.

By default, this policy setting is set to Enabled.

Exam Tip   This is an important policy setting. Be sure to understand it for the 70-622 exam.

---

8. User Account Control: Switch To The Secure Desktop When Prompting For Elevation

This security setting determines whether the elevation request will prompt on the interactive users desktop or the Secure Desktop.

The options for this policy setting are:

❑ Enabled: All elevation requests by default will enable the Secure Desktop.

❑ Disabled: Elevation requests will not enable the Secure Desktop. The interactive desktop is left active.

By default, this policy setting is set to Enabled.

9. User Account Control: Virtualize File And Registry Write Failures To Per-User Locations

This security setting enables the redirection of legacy application write failures to defined locations in both the registry and file system. This feature mitigates those applications that historically ran as administrator and wrote run-time application data back to either %ProgramFiles%, %Windir%; %Windir%\system32 or HKLM\Software\....

Virtualization facilitates the running of pre-Windows Vista (legacy) applications that historically failed to run with standard user privileges. An administrator running only Windows Vista-compliant applications might choose to disable this feature because it is unnecessary.

The options for this policy setting are:

❏ Enabled: Facilitates the run-time redirection of application write failures to defined user locations for both the file system and registry.

❏ Disabled: Applications that write data to protected locations will simply fail as they did in previous versions of Windows.

By default, this policy is set to Enabled.

Running a Command Prompt as Administrator

When administrators open a command prompt with UAC enabled, they are not prompted for elevation as with other administrative utilities. The reason that no elevation is required is that the command prompt by default runs in a standard user mode, even for administrators. If, after this command prompt opens, administrators then try to perform an administrative task by entering a command, they will be greeted by the message that "The requested operation requires elevation," as shown in Figure 8-14.

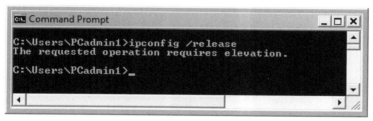

Figure 8-14   The command prompt by default runs without elevated privileges

If administrators want to perform an administrative task by means of the command prompt, they have to use the *Run As Administrator* option. To do so, right-click Command Prompt in the Start menu, and then select Run As Administrator from the shortcut menu, as shown in Figure 8-15.

The resulting command prompt that opens is distinguished as an administrator command prompt by its title bar title, "Administrator: Command Prompt," as shown in Figure 8-16.

Using such an administrator command prompt, an administrator can perform administrative tasks without needing to approve each task in a separate consent prompt.

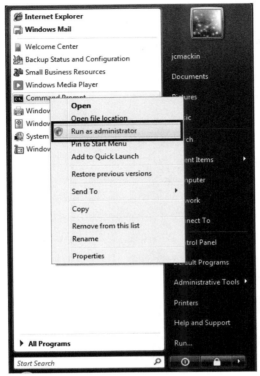

Figure 8-15   Running a command prompt as administrator

Figure 8-16   An administrator command prompt

Running Older Applications as Administrator

Some applications written for earlier versions of Windows require administrative privileges to function as expected. Because UAC prevents applications from running with administrative privileges by default, you might need to use the Run As Administrator option with some programs until a new version written for Windows Vista is released. In this case the procedure to run the program as administrator is exactly the same as running a command prompt as an administrator: simply right-click the program's icon, and then select Run As Administrator from the shortcut menu.

Alternatively, you can configure a program to always run with administrative privileges by selecting that option in the Compatibility tab of the program's properties dialog box.

NOTE Application Information service

Applications in Windows Vista that require use of the full administrator access token also require that the Application Information service be running. If this service is stopped, users might be unable to launch applications they require to perform desired tasks.

Quick Check
1. Which is the only policy setting whose status changes when you disable UAC in Control Panel?
2. True or False? A standard user cannot run a command prompt as an administrator.

Quick Check Answers
1. User Account Control: Run all administrators in Admin Approval Mode. (The status automatically changes to Disabled.)
2. False.

Practice: Configuring UAC Settings in Windows Vista

In this practice, you will disable UAC in Windows Vista, and then observe the effects. Finally, you will create a group policy that enables UAC at the domain level.

▶ **Practice 1: Disabling UAC**

In this practice, you will note the default security options for UAC in Local Security Policy, and then you will turn off UAC.

1. Log on to NWTRADERS from Vista1 as an administrator.
2. In the Start Search box, type **secpol.msc**, and then press Enter.
3. In the User Account Control prompt, click Continue.
4. In the Local Security Policy console, in the console tree, expand Local Policies, and then select Security Options.
5. Locate the nine User Account Control policy settings in the details pane. These settings should appear at the bottom of the list of security options.

6. Spend a few minutes reviewing these security options. Note which ones are enabled and which are disabled.

7. Answer the following question: Which is the only User Account Control security option that is disabled by default in Local Security Policy?

   Answer: The only UAC security setting disabled by default is named User Account Control: Only Elevate Executables That Are Signed And Validated.

8. Close the Local Security Policy console.

9. In Control Panel, click the User Accounts link, and then click the User Accounts link again.

10. In the Make Changes To Your Account window, click the Turn User Account Control On Or Off link.

11. In the User Account Control Prompt, click Continue.

12. In the Turn On User Account Control To Make Your Computer More Secure dialog box, clear the Use User Account Control To Help Protect Your Computer check box.

13. Click OK.

14. In the Microsoft Windows box, click Restart Now.

▶ **Practice 2: Exploring Windows Vista with UAC Disabled**

In this practice, you will log on to Windows Vista with UAC disabled and note the difference in behavior.

1. After the computer has finished rebooting from the previous practice, log back on to Vista1 as an administrator.

2. Open Control Panel.

3. In Control Panel, click some links next to which you see a multicolored shield.

4. Answer the following question: How has the behavior of Windows Vista changed for your administrator account now that you have turned off UAC?

   Answer: The consent prompt no longer appears when you attempt to perform a task that requires elevation.

5. Open the Local Security Policy console, and then browse the User Account Control security options.

6. Answer the following question: Which UAC security option or options have changed since you turned off User Account Control?

   Answer: The only option that has changed is User Account Control: Run All Administrators In Admin Approval Mode.

   The status is now set to Disabled.

7. Log off Vista1, and then log back on as any standard user. You can use the standard user account that you created in the practice in Lesson 1, "Understanding User Account Control," or you can use a domain user account such as NWTRADERS\SheilaE.

8. Open Control Panel.

9. In Control Panel, click the Security link.

10. Click the links next to which you see a multicolored shield and observe the effects.

11. Answer the following questions:

   a. Are standard users prompted for elevation when UAC is turned off?

      Answer: No

   b. Are you blocked from seeing administrative dialog boxes?

      Answer: No

   c. What is distinctive about these dialog boxes?

      Answer: All options are dimmed.

12. Close Control Panel.

13. From the Start menu, right-click Computer, and then click Manage.

14. Answer the following question: Are you allowed to open Computer Management as a standard user when you don't provide credentials for elevation?

      Answer: Yes

15. In Computer Management, expand the *Local Users And Groups* node, and then select the Users folder.

16. Right-click the Users folder, and then click New User.

17. Use the New User dialog box to fill in a user name and password for a new user.

18. Click Create.

19. Answer the following question: When UAC is turned off and you are logged on as a standard user, are you able to create a new user account?

      Answer: No

20. Log off Vista1.

▶ **Practice 3: Enabling UAC at the Domain Level**

In this practice, you will create a GPO that enables UAC on all computers in the domain.

1. Log on to the NWTRADERS domain from Vista1 with an administrator account.

2. Type the keystroke Windows button + R to open the Run box.

3. In the Run box, type **gpmc.msc**, and then click OK.

4. In the Group Policy Management console tree, right-click the nwtraders.msft domain, and then click Create A GPO In This Domain, And Link It Here from the shortcut menu.

5. In the New GPO dialog box, type **UAC Enabled**, and then click OK.

6. Click OK to dismiss the Group Policy Management Console message box.

7. In the console tree, right-click UAC Enabled, and then click Edit from the shortcut menu.

8. In the Group Policy Object Editor window, browse the console tree to Computer Configuration, Windows Settings, Security Settings, Local Policies, Security Options.

9. In the details pane, locate and double-click the security policy option named User Account Control: Run All Administrators In Admin Approval Mode.

10. In the dialog box that opens, select the Define This Policy check box, and then select Enabled.

11. Click OK.

12. Open a command prompt.

13. At the command prompt, type **gpupdate**.

14. After the group policy update has completed successfully, restart Vista1.

15. Log back on to NWTRADERS from Vista1 as an administrator.

16. Open the Local Security Policy console, and then browse the User Account Control security options. (Note that an elevation prompt appears when you attempt to open the Local Security Policy console. User Account Control has been turned back on.)

17. Locate and open the security policy named User Account Control: Run All Administrators In Admin Approval Mode.

18. Answer the following question: How has the setting changed since you created the UAC Enabled GPO?

    Answer: The setting is now set to Enabled, and you can no longer modify the setting because it is dimmed.

19. Log off Vista1.

Lesson Summary

■ You can turn UAC on and off in Control Panel.

■ UAC settings are controlled in Local Security Policy or a GPO.

■ You can modify nine UAC policy settings. These settings control, among other things, the nature of the elevation prompts for administrators and standard users.

■ To perform administrative tasks from a command prompt, you should open the command prompt with the Run As Administrator option.

■ You might need to use the Run As Administrator option to allow older applications to run properly in Windows Vista.

Lesson Review

You can use the following questions to test your knowledge of the information in Lesson 2, "Configuring User Account Control." The questions are also available on the companion CD if you prefer to review them in electronic form.

NOTE Answers

Answers to these questions and explanations of why each answer choice is right or wrong are located in the "Answers" section at the end of the book.

---

1. You are a desktop support technician for a company with 100 employees. The company network consists of a single Active Directory domain. All client computers in the company are running Windows Vista. Right now, all standard users are denied access to administrative tools. However, you want to give standard users the opportunity to enter administrative credentials at a prompt so that these users can occasionally perform administrative tasks. What should you do?

    A. In a domain-level Group Policy object (GPO), set the User Account Control: Behavior Of The Elevation Prompt For Administrators In Admin Approval Mode policy to Prompt For Credentials.

    B. In a domain-level GPO, set the User Account Control: Behavior Of The Elevation Prompt For Standard Users policy to Prompt For Credentials.

    C. In a domain-level GPO, set the User Account Control: Run All Administrators In Admin Approval Mode policy to Disabled.

    D. In a domain-level GPO, set the User Account Control: Behavior Of The Elevation Prompt For Standard Users policy to Automatically Deny Elevation Requests.

2. You do not want the administrators in your Active Directory domain to be prompted for consent every time they perform an administrative task. How can you achieve this?

    A. In a domain-level GPO, set the User Account Control: Behavior Of The Elevation Prompt For Administrators In Admin Approval Mode policy to Prompt For Consent.

    B. In a domain-level GPO, set the User Account Control: Behavior Of The Elevation Prompt For Administrators In Admin Approval Mode policy to Prompt For Credentials.

    C. In a domain-level GPO, set the User Account Control: Behavior Of The Elevation Prompt For Administrators In Admin Approval Mode policy to Elevate Without Prompting.

    D. In a domain-level GPO, set the User Account Control: Run All Administrators In Admin Approval Mode policy to Disabled.

3. You are a desktop support technician for a company whose network consists of a single Active Directory domain and 100 Windows Vista clients. Currently, neither standard users nor administrators are ever prompted when they attempt to access an administrative tool. You want to ensure that standard users are prompted for credentials and that administrators are prompted for consent whenever these users attempt to perform a task that requires administrative privileges. What should you do?

    A. In a domain-level GPO, set the User Account Control: Behavior Of The Elevation Prompt For Administrators In Admin Approval Mode policy to Prompt For Consent.

    B. In a domain-level GPO, set the User Account Control: Behavior Of The Elevation Prompt For Administrators In Admin Approval Mode policy to Prompt For Credentials.

    C. In a domain-level GPO, set the User Account Control: Behavior Of The Elevation Prompt For Standard Users policy to Prompt For Credentials.

    D. In a domain-level GPO, set the User Account Control: Run All Administrators In Admin Approval Mode policy to Enabled.

Chapter Review

To further practice and reinforce the skills you learned in this chapter, you can

- Review the chapter summary.
- Review the list of key terms introduced in this chapter.
- Complete the case scenarios. These scenarios set up real-world situations involving the topics of this chapter and ask you to create solutions.
- Complete the suggested practices.
- Take a practice test.

Chapter Summary

- The purpose of User Account Control is to prevent viruses, Trojan horses, and other malware from exploiting the privileges of a locally logged-on administrator.
- Both administrators and standard users normally run only with standard user privileges in Windows Vista. When a task requires administrative privileges, administrators can "elevate" by providing consent to perform that one specific task. Standard users can "elevate," too by providing administrative credentials.
- In the Windows Vista user interface, a multicolored shield signifies a task that requires elevation.
- You can turn UAC on and off in Control Panel.
- UAC can be configured in Local Security Policy or a Group Policy object (GPO). The configurable settings allow you to control, among other things, the nature of the elevation prompts for administrators and standard users.

Key Terms

Do you know what these key terms mean? You can check your answers by looking up the terms in the glossary at the end of the book.

- access token
- Admin Approval Mode
- consent admin
- consent prompt
- credential prompt
- elevation
- standard users

Case Scenarios

In the following case scenarios, you will apply what you've learned in this chapter. You can find answers to these questions in the "Answers" section at the end of this book.

Case Scenario 1: Configuring User Account Control

You are a desktop support technician for a large company whose network consists of a single Active Directory domain. You have recently deployed Windows Vista and have left UAC enabled.

1. You find that some users are disabling UAC on their machines. Which Group Policy setting should you use to enforce UAC on all user desktops?
2. You do not want standard users to be prompted to provide administrator credentials when they click an administrative tool. Which Group Policy setting should you use to prevent such a prompt from appearing?

Case Scenario 2: Troubleshooting User Account Control

You work as a desktop support technician. Your company has recently deployed Windows Vista, and you have been tasked with the responsibility of helping troubleshoot problems that arise as a result of UAC.

1. Another tech support specialist finds that he cannot release an IP address from a command prompt even when he is logged on as an administrator. What should you tell him to do?
2. A certain application written for Windows XP frequently generates elevation requests in Windows Vista. What can you do to allow the program to run without generating these elevation prompts?

Suggested Practices

To help you successfully master the exam objectives presented in this chapter, complete the following tasks.

Explore User Account Control Policy Settings

■ **Practice: Alter UAC Settings in Local Security Policy**   In Local Security Policy, experiment with different settings for the nine UAC policies available. For example, force the built-in Administrator account to run in Admin Approval Mode or allow administrators to elevate without prompting.

Perform a Virtual Lab

- **Practice: Learn About User Account Control in Windows Vista**   Go to *http://msevents*
  .microsoft.com and search for Event ID# 1032305607. Register and perform the virtual
  lab named "Exploring New User Account Control in Windows Vista Virtual Lab."

Watch a Webcast

- **Practice: Watch a Webcast About User Account Control**   Watch the webcast, "TechNet
  Webcast: User Account Control in Windows Vista (Level 200)," by Keith Combs, available on the companion CD in the Webcasts folder.

Take a Practice Test

The practice tests on this book's companion CD offer many options. For example, you can test
yourself on just one exam objective, or you can test yourself on all the 70-622 certification
exam content. You can set up the test so that it closely simulates the experience of taking a certification exam, or you can set it up in study mode so that you can look at the correct answers
and explanations after you answer each question.

MORE INFO   Practice tests

For details about all the practice test options available, see the "How to Use the Practice Tests" section in this book's Introduction.

Chapter 9

Configuring and Troubleshooting Client Connectivity

Because users depend on network resources in order to use critical applications such as e-mail, you must be able to quickly diagnose common network problems. Windows Vista can automatically diagnose many common problems and includes tools that you can use to manually test other conditions. This chapter will teach you how to configure network settings on Windows Vista computers and how to troubleshoot problems when they arise.

Exam objectives in this chapter:
- Configure and troubleshoot network protocols.
- Configure and troubleshoot network services at the client.
- Troubleshoot access to network resources.
- Troubleshoot connectivity issues.

Lessons in this chapter:

Before You Begin

To complete the lessons in this chapter, you should be familiar with Windows Vista and be comfortable with the following tasks:

- Installing Windows Vista
- Physically connecting a computer to a network

Lesson 1: Configuring Client Networking

In most environments, Windows Vista computers will automatically configure their network settings. You can literally connect a Windows Vista computer to almost any network using the default settings and get instant access to the local network and the Internet. Nonetheless, many large networks require customized settings. Therefore, it is important for you to understand how to manually configure Windows Vista networking.

After this lesson, you will be able to:
- List the important improvements to Windows Vista networking.
- Examine the current network configuration of a Windows Vista computer.
- Configure IP settings on a Windows Vista computer.
- Configure Network Discovery and Sharing.

Estimated lesson time: 25 minutes

Networking Changes in Windows Vista

Some of the most significant improvements in Windows Vista relate to networking. These improvements include:

- **Core improvements** Windows Vista offers improved network performance, especially across high-bandwidth, high-latency links such as wide area network (WAN) links or satellite connections. Essentially, Windows Vista is capable of more fully utilizing all available bandwidth than earlier versions of Microsoft Windows. Windows Vista also includes changes to the algorithms that work around network problems, increasing reliability.

- **IPv6** Windows Vista enables Internet Protocol version 6 (IPv6) by default. Several operating system components, such as Windows Meeting Space and other peer-to-peer components, use IPv6. As a result, as soon as you set up a Windows Vista computer on your network you'll see IPv6 traffic. You don't necessarily need to configure IPv6 on your network nor on the computers, however. You can configure it automatically using Dynamic Host Configuration Protocol version 6 (DHCPv6), but Windows Vista will automatically configure if you are not currently managing IPv6 on your network.

- **802.1X network authentication** Windows Vista supports 802.1X authentication for both wired and wireless networks. Clients can authenticate themselves using a user name and password or a certificate, which can be stored locally on the computer or on a smart card. Most wireless networks use 802.1X authentication, and some new wired network equipment also supports it.

- **Wireless networking**   Windows Vista includes several minor improvements to wireless networking. Additionally, the new user interface makes it easier for users to connect to wireless networks and manage their network connections.
- **SMB 2.0**   Server Message Block (SMB), also known as the Common Internet File System (CIFS), is the file-sharing protocol used by default on Windows-based computers. SMB 2.0 is more efficient and supports symbolic links. You can take advantage of SMB 2.0 only when communicating between Windows Vista or later operating systems.
- **Network And Sharing Center**   As shown in Figure 9-1, Windows Vista includes a new user interface for managing network connections by graphically showing you to which network you're connected and whether you can reach the Internet. To open Network And Sharing Center, click a network icon in the system tray, and then click the Network And Sharing Center link. Alternatively, you can click Start, right-click Network, and then click Properties.

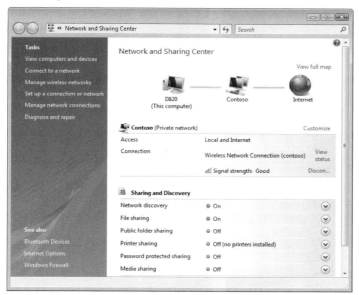

Figure 9-1   Network And Sharing Center

- **Network Map**   As shown in Figure 9-2, Network Map provides a diagram of the current network and the components Windows Vista is able to discover. You can access Network Map by clicking the View Full Map link in Network And Sharing Center. Although Network Map is disabled by default in domain environments, an administrator can use Group Policy settings to enable it.

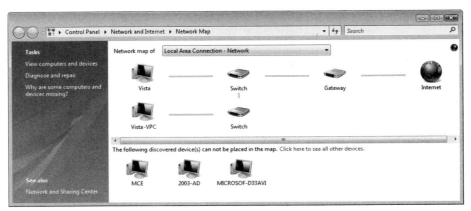

Figure 9-2   Network Map

■ **Network Explorer**   As shown in Figure 9-3, you can use Network Explorer to browse
your local network. It doesn't look much different than My Network Places in Windows
XP, but it uses Web Services Dynamic Discovery (WS-Discovery), Universal Plug and
Play (UPnP)/Simple Service Discovery Protocol (SSDP), and Link Layer Topology Discovery (LLTD) to find networked computers and devices (in addition to the NetBIOS
browsing used by earlier versions of Windows). This provides more reliable network
browsing than was available with earlier versions of Windows. To open Network
Explorer, click the Start button, and then click Network. Network Explorer is available
only if Network Discovery is enabled.

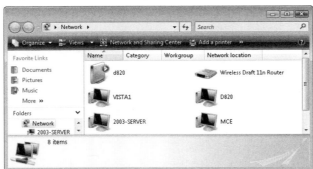

Figure 9-3   Network Explorer

■ **Networking icons**   Instead of one icon in the system tray for each network adapter,
Windows Vista shows a single icon that represents cumulative connectivity provided
by all network adapters. Figure 9-4 shows the four states of the network icon.

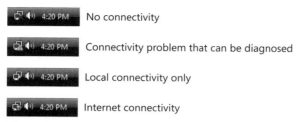

No connectivity

Connectivity problem that can be diagnosed

Local connectivity only

Internet connectivity

Figure 9-4   Windows Vista network icons show cumulative connectivity

- **Connect To A Network Wizard**   Users can connect to a wireless network, a virtual private network (VPN), or a dial-up connection by clicking Start, and then clicking Connect To. As shown in Figure 9-5, the wizard interface is extremely straightforward.

Figure 9-5   The Connect To A Network Wizard

- **Network Access Protection (NAP)**   To help protect internal networks from worms that infect mobile computers, NAP can check the health of a Windows Vista computer before allowing it unlimited access to the network. NAP requires Windows Server 2008 and will not be discussed in detail in this book.

- **Network location types**   In Windows Vista you can label networks as Public, Private, or Domain. All networks are Public by default. Administrators can manually upgrade a network from Public to Private, which would be useful to allow sharing across a home network. If the computer can connect to a domain controller, Windows Vista automatically changes the network type to Domain. By default, Windows Firewall blocks all incoming connections from Public networks. This enables you to configure firewall exceptions for private or domain networks while still protecting users who connect to unprotected wireless hotspots.

- **Policy-based quality of service (QoS)**   QoS enables Windows Vista to prioritize traffic in order to give real-time traffic, such as streaming audio, video, or Voice over IP (VoIP), priority over other types of traffic. Although earlier versions of Windows allowed individual applications to use QoS, Windows Vista gives systems administrators complete control over QoS without requiring applications to have built-in support.

■ **Windows Firewall and IPSec**   Windows Vista provides a single user interface for managing both Windows Firewall and Internet Protocol Security (IPSec). You can now manage both features using Group Policy settings or command-line scripting.

■ **Windows Connect Now**   Windows Connect Now, first included with Windows XP Service Pack 2, enables you to store wireless network settings on a USB flash drive (UFD) and configure a wireless client by connecting the UFD. Rather than leaving networks unprotected, you can use Windows Connect Now to quickly configure new computers or computers of guests with the security settings required to connect to your encrypted wireless network.

How to Identify the Current Network Configuration

You can view the current network configuration from the graphical user interface by following these steps:

1. Click Start, right-click Network, and then click Properties.

2. In Network And Sharing Center, click the View Status link next to the network adapter you want to examine.

3. In the Connection Status dialog box, click Details.

4. The Network Connection Details dialog box appears, as shown in Figure 9-6. This dialog box shows the current IP addresses, subnet mask, default gateway, Domain Name System (DNS) server, MAC address, and whether DHCP is enabled.

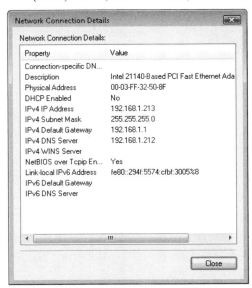

Figure 9-6   The Network Connection Details dialog box

5. Click Close twice to return to Network And Sharing Center.

The quickest way to identify the current network configuration is to open a command prompt and run the command **ipconfig /all**. The output will resemble the following:

```
Windows IP Configuration

   Host Name . . . . . . . . . . . . : Vista1
   Primary Dns Suffix  . . . . . . . : hq.contoso.com
   Node Type . . . . . . . . . . . . : Hybrid
   IP Routing Enabled. . . . . . . . : No
   WINS Proxy Enabled. . . . . . . . : No
   DNS Suffix Search List. . . . . . : hq.contoso.com
                                       contoso.com


Ethernet adapter Local Area Connection:

   Connection-specific DNS Suffix  . : contoso.com
   Description . . . . . . . . . . . : NVIDIA nForce Networking Controller
   Physical Address. . . . . . . . . : 00-13-D3-3B-50-8F
   DHCP Enabled. . . . . . . . . . . : Yes
   Autoconfiguration Enabled . . . . : Yes
   Link-local IPv6 Address . . . . . : fe80::a54b:d9d7:1a10:c1eb%10(Preferred)
   IPv4 Address. . . . . . . . . . . : 192.168.1.132(Preferred)
   Subnet Mask . . . . . . . . . . . : 255.255.255.0
   Lease Obtained. . . . . . . . . . : Wednesday, September 27, 2006 2:08:58 PM
   Lease Expires . . . . . . . . . . : Friday, September 29, 2006 2:08:56 PM
   Default Gateway . . . . . . . . . : 192.168.1.1
   DHCP Server . . . . . . . . . . . : 192.168.1.1
   DHCPv6 IAID . . . . . . . . . . . : 234886099
   DNS Servers . . . . . . . . . . . : 192.168.1.210
   NetBIOS over Tcpip. . . . . . . . : Enabled
```

Ipconfig /all provides all of the information provided in the Network Connection Details dialog box, plus information about the DHCP lease. The DHCP lease is the period of time the dynamically assigned IP address configuration is valid.

How to Configure IP Settings

Today, client computers are almost never configured manually. Instead, almost all networks rely on DHCP to automatically assign IP addresses to computers when they connect to a network. You can configure Windows Server computers as DHCP servers, and most routers have a DHCP server built in. Routers designed for home use always have DHCP enabled by default, enabling home users to connect computers to the network without manually configuring IP settings.

If you can't use DHCP, you can automate the manual configuration of IP settings by using the Netsh command-line tool in a script. The sections that follow describe how DHCP works and how to manually configure IP settings.

How DHCP Works

Windows Vista computers are configured to act as DHCP clients by default. Therefore, a newly installed Windows Vista computer can connect to the local network, obtain an IP address, and connect to network resources (including the Internet) without any network configuration. Figure 9-7 illustrates the process a client computer goes through to retrieve IP configuration settings from a DHCP server at startup.

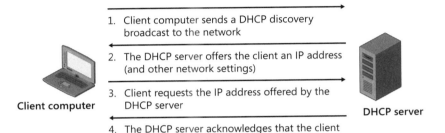

1. Client computer sends a DHCP discovery broadcast to the network
2. The DHCP server offers the client an IP address (and other network settings)
3. Client requests the IP address offered by the DHCP server
4. The DHCP server acknowledges that the client has a valid DHCP lease for the address

Client computer

DHCP server

Figure 9-7   How client computers typically retrieve IP configuration settings from a DHCP server

DHCP clients can't use the assigned IP address forever, however. DHCP servers specify a DHCP lease period. Windows Vista computers attempt to renew that lease when it is half-expired, which gives the DHCP server the opportunity to provide a different IP address if administrators have changed the network configuration. The process of renewing DHCP leases is completely transparent to the user and administrators.

DHCP is enabled by default. Therefore, to act as a DHCP client, all you need to do is turn on a Windows Vista computer and connect it to a network. If you have manually assigned an IP address, you can return a computer to the default setting of acting as a DHCP client by following these steps:

1. Click Start, right-click Network, and then click Properties.
2. In the left pane of Network And Sharing Center, click the Manage Network Connections link.
3. Right-click the network adapter you want to configure, and then click Properties. Respond to the User Account Control (UAC) prompt that appears.
4. Click Internet Protocol Version 4, and then click Properties.
5. The Internet Protocol Version 4 (TCP/IPv4) Properties dialog box appears.
6. In the General tab, select Obtain An IP Address Automatically. Then, select Obtain DNS Server Address Automatically.
7. Click OK, and then click Close.

How to Manually Configure IP Settings

Some environments do not provide a DHCP server, requiring you to manually configure IP address settings for every client computer. To manually configure IP address settings, follow these steps:

1. Click Start, right-click Network, and then click Properties.
2. In the left pane, click the Manage Network Connections link.
3. Right-click the network adapter you want to configure, and then click Properties. Respond to the UAC prompt that appears.

   The network connection properties dialog box appears. From this dialog box you can configure several network components. Typically, you will need to configure only IPv4 and IPv6.

   To configure IPv4 settings from the network connection name Properties dialog box, follow these steps:

   a. Click Internet Protocol Version 4, and then click Properties.
   b. In the Internet Protocol Version 4 Properties dialog box, select Use The Following IP Address.

4. Complete the *IP Address*, *Subnet Mask*, *Default Gateway*, and *DNS servers* fields with the values provided by your network administrator. These values are unique for every computer, but Figure 9-8 shows an example of a configuration. If you need to configure multiple IP addresses, gateways, more than two DNS servers, or Windows Internet Name Service (WINS) servers, click the Advanced button.

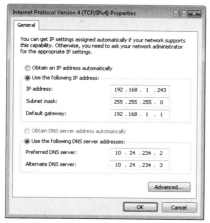

Figure 9-8 Manually configuring IPv4 address settings

5. Click OK.

To configure IPv6 settings from the network connection properties dialog box, follow these steps:

1. Click Internet Protocol Version 6, and then click Properties.

2. In the Internet Protocol Version 6 Properties dialog box, select Use The Following IPv6 Address.

3. Complete the *IPv6 Address*, *Subnet Prefix Length*, *Default Gateway*, and *DNS servers* fields with the values provided by your network administrator. These values are unique for every computer, but Figure 9-9 shows an example configuration. If you need to configure multiple IP addresses, gateways, or DNS servers, click the Advanced button.

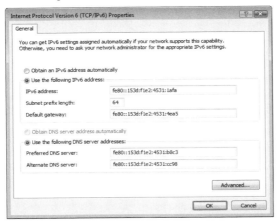

Figure 9-9   Manually configuring IPv6 address settings

NOTE   **IPv6 and WINS**

IPv6 never uses WINS servers.

---

4. Click OK.

Because of the time required to manually configure network settings, the high chance for human error, and the need to manually update settings every time network configurations change, you should use manually configured IP address settings only for servers or computers in test environments.

In some lab environments you might want to use scripts (also known as batch files or command files) to configure IP settings on Windows Vista computers. Windows Vista includes the Netsh command-line tool for this purpose. For more information about Netsh, run **Netsh /?** from a command prompt.

How to Configure Alternate IP Address Settings

Mobile computers often connect to different networks at different times. Because Windows Vista can define only one set of manual IP address settings, it would be very difficult to connect to multiple networks where different manually configured IP addresses are required. In fact, users would need to adjust settings manually each time they connected to a different network.

You can, however, use manual IP address settings for a single network (such as your company's internal network) and rely on DHCP to assign addresses for all other networks your mobile computer might connect to. When you configure an alternate configuration, Windows Vista always attempts to acquire an address using DHCP. If no DHCP server is available, Windows Vista assigns the manually configured alternate configuration.

To configure an alternate configuration, follow these steps:

1. Click Start, right-click Network, and then click Properties.
2. In the left pane, click the Manage Network Connections link.
3. Right-click the network adapter you want to configure, and then click Properties. Respond to the UAC prompt that appears.
4. Click Internet Protocol Version 4, and then click Properties.
5. The Internet Protocol Version 4 (TCP/IPv4) Properties dialog box appears.
6. In the General tab, select Obtain An IP Address Automatically if it is not already selected. If you have manually configured an IP address, make note of the settings.
7. Click the Alternate Configuration tab. By default, Automatic Private IP Address (APIPA) is selected. APIPA is described later in this section. To manually configure IP address settings that will be used when a DHCP server is unavailable, click User Configured, and then type the IP address settings provided by your network administrator.

APIPA Addressing

By default, if a Windows Vista computer is configured to use DHCP and a DHCP server is not available and you have not configured alternate IP address settings, Windows Vista assigns an Automatic Private IP Address (APIPA) address. APIPA addresses are always in the range 169.254.0.0 through 169.254.255.255. APIPA allows computers that don't have IP address settings to communicate across a local area network (LAN). However, APIPA is rarely used (intentionally) on production networks, and an APIPA address is typically considered a side effect of a connectivity problem. For more information about troubleshooting network configuration problems, see Lesson 2, "Troubleshooting Connectivity Problems."

Exam Tip
Memorize the APIPA address range!

How to Configure Sharing And Discovery

The Sharing And Discovery section of Network And Sharing Center provides easy access for enabling and disabling networking features. To open Network And Sharing Center, click Start, right-click Network, and then click Properties. You can use Network And Sharing Center to enable or disable the following settings:

- **Network Discovery**   Enables browsing of network resources and allows other computers on the network to discover your computer. Network Discovery is enabled by default on Private networks but disabled on Public networks (to reduce security risks) and on Domain networks (because browsing of network resources uses Active Directory directory service instead).

- **File Sharing**   Enables sharing of folders and printers across the network. File Sharing is disabled by default. Windows Vista automatically enables File Sharing the first time a user shares a folder on the network.

- **Public Folder Sharing**   The Public folder is traditionally used to share files with other users of the same computer. However, you can choose to turn on sharing so that people across the network can connect to the Public folder and either read or modify files. By default, this is disabled for all network types.

- **Printer Sharing**   Controls whether users on the network can connect to your printer. By default, this is disabled for all network types. Windows Vista automatically enables Printer Sharing the first time a user shares a printer on the network.

- **Password Protected Sharing**   Requires users to have a user account to connect to shared resources. By default, this is disabled for all network types.

- **Media Sharing**   Enables computers and network devices to access shared music, pictures, and videos on the computer. Typically, this is used by devices such as Xbox 360s, which home users can use to view media on televisions across the network. By default, this is disabled for all network types.

To enable or disable any feature from within Network And Sharing Center, expand it to display the full description (as shown in Figure 9-10), click the desired setting, and then click Apply. Any changes you make apply only to that specific type of network. For example, if you enable Printer Sharing while connected to a Domain network, Printer Sharing will be enabled only while you are connected to the domain. If you later connect to a Public or Private network, you will need to reenable Printer Sharing for that network type.

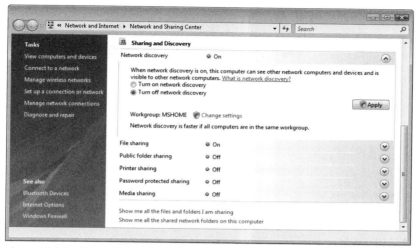

Figure 9-10 Using Network And Sharing Center to enable and disable network features

Practices: Examine and Modify Network Configuration

In this practice, you examine your current network settings, switch from automatic to manual IP addressing (or vice versa), and then revert to your original settings.

▶ **Practice 1: Examine Your Network Configuration**

In this practice, you examine your current computer's network configuration.

1. Click Start, right-click Network, and then click Properties.
    Network And Sharing Center appears.
2. Use Network And Sharing Center to answer the following questions:
    ❑ Are you connected to the Internet?
    ❑ Is your local network type Private, Public, or Domain?
    ❑ Are you connected to a wireless network? If so, what is the name and signal strength of the network?
    ❑ Is Network Discovery enabled?
    ❑ Is File Sharing enabled?
3. Click the View Status link next to your network adapter.
4. In the Local Area Connection Status dialog box, click the Details button.
5. Use the Network Connection Details dialog box to answer the following questions (make note of each setting for the next practice):
    ❑ Does the computer have an automatic or manual IP address configuration?
    ❑ What is the computer's current IP address?

❑ What is the IP address of the default gateway?

❑ What is the DNS server's IP address?

▶ **Practice 2: Configure Your Network Settings**

In this practice, you must switch from an automatic to a manual IP address configuration (or vice versa). To complete this practice, you must have completed Practice 1.

1. Click Start, click Network, and then click Properties.

2. Click the View Status link next to your network adapter.

3. Click the Properties button. Respond to the UAC prompt that appears.

4. Click Internet Protocol Version 4 (TCP/IPv4). Then, click Properties.

5. If Use The Following IP Address is selected, select Obtain an IP Address Automatically. Then, select Obtain DNS Server Address Automatically. Click OK. This configures the computer to use a DHCP server rather than a manual IP address configuration.

6. If Obtain An IP Address Automatically is selected, select Use The Following IP address. Then fill in all fields using the settings you identified in Practice 1. This configures the computer to use a manual IP address configuration with the same IP settings it had been manually configured to use.

7. Click Close twice to return to Network And Sharing Center.

8. Wait a few minutes for Network And Sharing Center to refresh its settings using the new network configuration. Then repeat steps 2–7 to return your computer to its original settings.

Lesson Summary

■ Windows Vista includes significant improvements to networking, including improved efficiency, simpler user interfaces, automatic diagnosis of network problems, and having IPv6 enabled by default.

■ To view the current network configuration, open Network And Sharing Center and click View Status. Alternatively, you can run the command **Ipconfig /all** from a command prompt.

■ Typically, you do not need to manually configure IP address settings because a DHCP server automatically provides them to your Windows Vista client computers. However, you can manually configure IP settings by viewing the network adapter properties, clicking Internet Protocol Version 4 or Internet Protocol Version 6, and then clicking Properties.

■ To configure Network Discovery, Sharing, and other networking features, use Network And Sharing Center to enable or disable them.

Lesson Review

You can use the following questions to test your knowledge of the information in Lesson 1, "Configuring Client Networking." The questions are also available on the companion CD if you prefer to review them in electronic form.

NOTE Answers

Answers to these questions and explanations of why each answer choice is right or wrong are located in the "Answers" section at the end of the book.

---

1. In the Network Connection Details dialog box, you see DHCP Enabled: Yes. What does this mean?
    A. The computer shares an IP address with other Windows Vista computers.
    B. An administrator manually configured the computer with an IP address.
    C. The computer generates a random IP address.
    D. The computer is configured to retrieve an IP address from a DHCP server.

2. Which of the following tools can you use to determine a computer's current IP address? (Choose all that apply.)
    A. Network And Sharing Center
    B. IPConfig
    C. Network Map
    D. Network Explorer

3. A user calls with a problem. When she clicks Start, and then clicks Network, nothing appears. What is the most likely cause of this problem?
    A. Her computer is configured to use DHCP.
    B. Her computer is configured to use a manually assigned IP address.
    C. Network Discovery is disabled.
    D. Network Mapping is disabled.

4. In which of the following network types is Network Discovery enabled by default?
    A. Public
    B. Private
    C. Domain
    D. Wireless

Lesson 2: Troubleshooting Network Problems

Although most client computers receive their network settings from a DHCP server completely automatically, networks are still very complex. If a network adapter, network cable, switch, router, Internet connection, or server fails, it will appear to a user that the user can't connect to a network. Often, this means that the user can't do his or her job, making it critical that you identify and solve the problem quickly.

This lesson describes how to identify the source of network problems and, when possible, resolve the problem.

After this lesson, you will be able to:

■ Use Windows Network Diagnostics to automatically troubleshoot common network problems.

■ Use Ping, PathPing, PortQry, and Nslookup to manually troubleshoot network problems.

■ Troubleshoot problems connecting to shared folders.

■ Troubleshoot an APIPA address.

■ Troubleshoot a name resolution problem.

■ Troubleshoot a network or application connectivity problem.

Estimated lesson time: 30 minutes

How to Use Windows Network Diagnostics

Windows Vista includes diagnostic tools that automate the process of testing for common network problems. Windows Vista can also automatically fix many network problems that are configuration-related or that simply require the network adapter to be reset.

There are several ways to launch Windows Network Diagnostics:

■ In the system tray, right-click the network icon and click Diagnose And Repair, as shown in Figure 9-11.

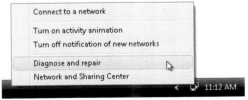

Figure 9-11   The Diagnose And Repair feature

- Open Network And Sharing Center. On the Network Map, click the link with an X over it (as shown in Figure 9-12).

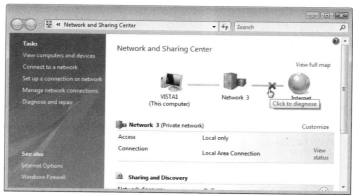

Figure 9-12   Clicking a broken link in Network And Sharing Center to diagnose a problem

- Open Network And Sharing Center. In the left pane, click the Diagnose And Repair link.
- Open Network And Sharing Center. Click the View Status link for the network adapter experiencing problems. Then, click Diagnose.
- Open Help And Support. Then, click Troubleshooting. Click the link under Networking that most closely describes the problem, and then select the Click To Open Network Diagnostics link.
- Open Internet Explorer when the Internet is unavailable. On the error page that appears, click Diagnose Connection Problems.
- Click Start, type **rundll32.exe ndfapi,NdfRunDllDiagnoseIncident** (a case-sensitive command), and then press Enter.

After Windows Network Diagnostics completes diagnostics, it displays a list of detected problems. For example, Figure 9-13 shows that the computer was connected to the network properly but that the DNS server was unavailable. An unavailable DNS server resembles a complete connectivity failure because no computers identified by a hostname will be available; however, solving the problem requires either configuring a different DNS server IP address or bringing the DNS server back online.

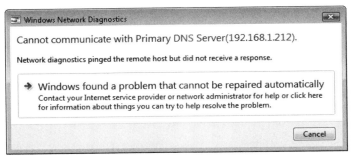

Figure 9-13   Using Windows Network Diagnostics to quickly identify problems that would be time-consuming for a person to isolate

Figure 9-14 shows a problem that Windows Network Diagnostics can solve: a disabled network adapter. In this scenario the user simply needs to click Enable The Network Adapter to solve the problem. Windows Network Diagnostics also provides the option of connecting to a different network to gain connectivity.

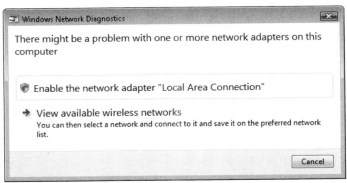

Figure 9-14   Windows Network Diagnostics can automatically solve some configuration problems

Network Troubleshooting Tools

If Windows Network Diagnostics does not isolate the source of the problem, Windows Vista provides many tools you can use to perform manual troubleshooting. The sections that follow describe the most important tools. Later, this chapter will describe how to use each tool to troubleshoot specific network problems.

Ping

Ping is the best-known network diagnostic tool. Unfortunately, as more and more computers and routers block Internet Control Message Protocol (ICMP; the network protocol Ping uses) requests, it has become less useful over time. Ping still works on most LANs, however.

To use Ping, open a command prompt and run the command "Ping hostname." For example:

```
C:\>ping www.contoso.com
Pinging contoso.com [207.46.197.32] with 32 bytes of data:

Reply from 207.46.197.32: bytes=32 time=95ms TTL=105
Reply from 207.46.197.32: bytes=32 time=210ms TTL=105
Reply from 207.46.197.32: bytes=32 time=234ms TTL=105
Reply from 207.46.197.32: bytes=32 time=258ms TTL=105

Ping statistics for 207.46.197.32:
    Packets: Sent = 4, Received = 4, Lost = 0 (0% loss),
Approximate round trip times in milli-seconds:
    Minimum = 95ms, Maximum = 258ms, Average = 199ms
```

Ping tells you several useful things. If you receive replies, you know that the network host is turned on and connected to the network. The time, measured in milliseconds (ms), indicates the round-trip latency between you and the remote host. If the latency is greater than a second, all network communications will probably seem very slow.

Many hosts do not respond to Ping requests even though they are online. For example, the Microsoft.com web servers drop ICMP requests even though they are online and will respond to web requests, as the following sample demonstrates:

```
C:\>ping www.microsoft.com
Pinging lb1.www.microsoft.com [10.46.20.60] with 32 bytes of data:

Request timed out.
Request timed out.
Request timed out.
Request timed out.

Ping statistics for 10.46.20.60:
    Packets: Sent = 4, Received = 0, Lost = 4 (100% loss),
```

PathPing

Although Ping uses ICMP to test connectivity to a specific host, PathPing uses ICMP to test connectivity to a remote host and all routers between you and the remote host. This can help you identify problems in the way your network is routing traffic, such as routing loops (where traffic crosses the same router more than once), a failed router (which might make it seem like the entire network has failed), or poor network performance. Figure 9-15 demonstrates how PathPing functions.

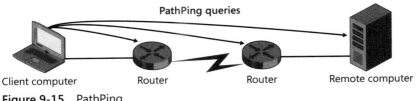

Figure 9-15 PathPing

NOTE PathPing vs. Tracert

Windows Vista still includes Tracert (pronounced "Trace Route"), but PathPing does everything Tracert does and is more powerful, so you should use PathPing instead.

Use PathPing in the exact same way as Ping. PathPing will attempt to list every router between you and the destination (just as Tracert would). Then, PathPing spends a few minutes calculating statistics for the entire route.

```
C:\>pathping www.contoso.com
Tracing route to contoso.com [10.46.196.103]
over a maximum of 30 hops:
  0  contoso-test [192.168.1.207]
  1  10.211.240.1
  2  10.128.191.245
  3  10.128.191.73
  4  10.125.39.213
  5  gbr1-p70.cb1ma.ip.contoso.com [10.123.40.98]
  6  tbr2-p013501.cb1ma.ip.contoso.com [10.122.11.201]
  7  tbr2-p012101.cgcil.ip.contoso.com [10.122.10.106]
  8  gbr4-p50.st6wa.ip.contoso.com [10.122.2.54]
  9  gar1-p370.stwwa.ip.contoso.com [10.123.203.177]
 10  10.127.70.6
 11  10.46.33.225
 12  10.46.36.210
 13  10.46.155.17
 14  10.46.129.51
 15  10.46.196.103

Computing statistics for 625 seconds...
              Source to Here   This Node/Link
Hop  RTT    Lost/Sent = Pct   Lost/Sent = Pct   Address
  0                                              contoso-test [192.168.1.207]
                                0/ 100 =  0%    |
  1   50ms     1/ 100 =  1%     1/ 100 =  1%    10.211.24.1
                                0/ 100 =  0%    |
  2   50ms     0/ 100 =  0%     0/ 100 =  0%    10.128.19.245
                                0/ 100 =  0%    |
  3   50ms     2/ 100 =  2%     2/ 100 =  2%    10.128.19.73
                                0/ 100 =  0%    |
  4   44ms     0/ 100 =  0%     0/ 100 =  0%    10.12.39.213
                                0/ 100 =  0%    |
```

```
 5    46ms      0/ 100 =   0%     0/ 100 =   0%  gbr1-p70.cb1ma.ip.contoso.com [10.12.40.98]
                                  0/ 100 =   0%   |
 6    40ms      2/ 100 =   2%     2/ 100 =   2%  tbr2-p013501.cb1ma.ip.contoso.com [10.12.11.201]
                                  0/ 100 =   0%   |
 7    62ms      1/ 100 =   1%     1/ 100 =   1%  tbr2-p012101.cgcil.ip.contoso.com [10.12.10.106]
                                  0/ 100 =   0%   |
 8   107ms      2/ 100 =   2%     2/ 100 =   2%  gbr4-p50.st6wa.ip.contoso.com [10.12.2.54]
                                  0/ 100 =   0%   |
 9   111ms      0/ 100 =   0%     0/ 100 =   0%  gar1-p370.stwwa.ip.contoso.com [10.12.203.177]
                                  0/ 100 =   0%   |
10   118ms      0/ 100 =   0%     0/ 100 =   0%  10.12.70.6
                                  0/ 100 =   0%   |
11   ---      100/ 100 =100%    100/ 100 =100%  10.46.33.225
                                  0/ 100 =   0%   |
12   ---      100/ 100 =100%    100/ 100 =100%  10.46.36.210
                                  0/ 100 =   0%   |
13   123ms      0/ 100 =   0%     0/ 100 =   0%  10.46.155.17
                                  0/ 100 =   0%   |
14   127ms      0/ 100 =   0%     0/ 100 =   0%  10.46.129.51
                                  1/ 100 =   1%   |
15   125ms      1/ 100 =   1%     0/ 100 =   0%  10.46.196.103

Trace complete.
```

NOTE Network lingo

The term "hop" is another name for a router or gateway.

If the statistics show a single router with an extremely high latency, that node might be causing network problems. Typically, a router with high latency will increase the latency for every router listed afterward. However, only the first router is experiencing the problem. If one router has high latency but the routers listed afterward have low latency, the latency probably isn't the sign of a problem. Routers handle ICMP requests at a lower priority than other traffic, so high latency shown by PathPing isn't always indicative of overall latency.

You can often determine from the name of the router whether it is on your internal network, the network of your Internet service provider (ISP), or elsewhere on the Internet. If it is on your internal network or your ISP's network, contact your network administrator for troubleshooting assistance. If it is somewhere else on the network, there is probably nothing you can do but wait for the administrators of the router to solve the problem.

To speed up the display of PathPing, use the −d command option to keep PathPing from attempting to resolve the name of each intermediate router address.

PortQry

Ping uses ICMP packets to test whether a remote computer is connected to the network. However, even if a computer responds to ICMP packets, it doesn't tell you whether the computer is running the network service that you need. For example, if you're having a problem downloading your e-mail, you really need to test whether the mail service itself is responding, not whether the mail server is responding to ICMP requests.

PortQry tests whether a specific network service is running on a server. To use PortQry, open a command prompt and run the following command:

```
portqry -n destination -e portnumber
```

For example, to test Hypertext Transfer Protocol (HTTP) connectivity to www.microsoft.com, type the following command at the command line:

```
portqry -n www.microsoft.com -e 80
```

This command produces output that is similar to the following example:

```
Querying target system called:
 www.microsoft.com
Attempting to resolve name to IP address...
Name resolved to 10.209.68.190
TCP port 80 (http service): LISTENING
```

Unfortunately, PortQry is not included with any version of Windows, including Windows Vista. Instead, you must download it from Microsoft.com at *http://www.microsoft.com/downloads/details.aspx?FamilyID=89811747-C74B-4638-A2D5-AC828BDC6983*. When deploying Windows Vista, consider adding PortQry to the %windir%\system32\ folder so that it is readily available for troubleshooting.

If you are using a computer that does not have PortQry installed, you can use Telnet to test a remote service. For more information, read "How to Troubleshoot Application Connectivity Problems" later in this lesson.

Nslookup

Use Nslookup to test whether your DNS server can properly resolve a hostname to an IP address. For example:

```
C:\>nslookup contoso.com
Server:  dns.fabrikam.com
Address:  192.168.1.1:53

Non-authoritative answer:
Name:    contoso.com
Addresses:  207.46.232.182, 207.46.197.32
```

In the previous example the client contacted the default DNS server (192.168.1.1) and successfully received a response indicating that contoso.com has two IP addresses: 207.46.232.182 and 207.46.197.32. This indicates that the DNS server is working correctly.

NOTE Round-robin DNS addressing

Some hostnames, including contoso.com and microsoft.com, resolve to multiple IP addresses. Your web browser is smart enough to connect to a different address if the first address isn't working properly, allowing multiple web servers with different IP addresses to respond to requests for the same hostname. This provides both scalability and redundancy.

The following response to the same query would indicate that the DNS server could not find an IP address for the contoso.com hostname:

```
*** dns.fabrikam.com can't find contoso.com: Non-existent domain
```

The following response indicates that no DNS server is responding:

```
Server:  dns.fabrikam.com
Address:  192.168.1.1:53

DNS request timed out.
    timeout was 2 seconds.
DNS request timed out.
    timeout was 2 seconds.
*** Request to dns.fabrikam.com timed-out
```

Use Nslookup any time you think a network problem might be caused by a failed DNS server or invalid name resolution.

How to Troubleshoot Problems Connecting to Shared Folders and Printers

If you're having a problem connecting to a shared folder or printer, first follow the troubleshooting steps outlined in Chapter 7, "Authenticating, Authorizing, and Auditing Access to Resources." Most often, these problems are related to insufficient privileges.

If you can't connect to the server at all, you might have a connectivity problem. For example, Windows Explorer displays the error message shown in Figure 9-16 if it cannot reach a server. Clicking the Diagnose button launches Windows Network Diagnostics, which is a good first step in troubleshooting.

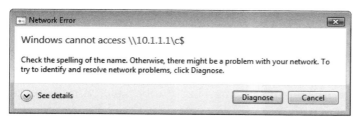

Figure 9-16   An error message indicating a network connectivity problem

Problems connecting to shared folders or printers are often caused by one of the following:

- Windows Firewall or another software firewall is blocking traffic at the client or server.
- A network firewall between the client and server is blocking traffic.
- Name-resolution problems prevent the client from obtaining the server's IP address.
- The server is offline.

First, start troubleshooting from the client computer. If the server is a Windows Vista computer and you have administrator access to it, you can also troubleshoot from the server. The sections that follow provide detailed troubleshooting steps from the client and server.

How to Troubleshoot File and Printer Sharing from the Client Computer

Follow these steps to troubleshoot problems connecting to shared files and printers:

1. If you can connect to the shared folder but receive an Access Is Denied message when attempting to open the folder, your user account has permission to access the share but lacks NTFS permissions for the folder. Contact the server administrator to grant the necessary NTFS file permissions. If the server is a Windows Vista computer, see "How to Troubleshoot File and Printer Sharing from the Server Computer" later in this lesson.

2. Verify that you can resolve the server's name correctly. At a command prompt, type **Ping** hostname. If Ping displays an IP address, as shown below, you can resolve the server's name correctly. It does not matter whether the server replies to the pings. If this step fails, it indicates a name-resolution problem. Contact your Active Directory or DNS administrator.

   ```
   ping server
   Pinging server [10.1.42.22] with 32 bytes of data:
   ```

   NOTE Nslookup vs. Ping

   You could use Nslookup to test name resolution instead of Ping. However, Ping is more useful in this case because it resolves names in exactly the same way that Windows Vista resolves the name when connecting to a shared folder. Although Nslookup only queries your DNS server, Ping checks the local Hosts file, queries the DNS server, queries a WINS server if one is available, and even resolves names of devices on the local network that aren't listed in DNS.

   ---

3. From a command prompt, run the command **net use \\server** to attempt to establish a connection to the server itself without connecting to the shared resource. If it succeeds, network connectivity is not a problem. However, your user account probably lacks privileges to connect to the shared resource. Have the server administrator grant your account the necessary share permissions. As described in Chapter 7, "Authenticating, Authorizing, and Auditing Access to Resources," share permissions are separate from NTFS file permissions.

4. Use Telnet or PortQry to test whether your computer can connect to TCP port 445 of the remote computer. If you cannot connect using TCP port 445, test TCP port 139. For instructions on how to test for connectivity using a specific port, see the section of this chapter entitled "How to Troubleshoot Application Connectivity Problems." If you cannot connect using either TCP port 139 or TCP port 445, verify that File And Printer Sharing is enabled on the server. Then, verify that the server has a firewall exception for TCP ports 139 and 445 or that an exception in Windows Firewall is enabled for File And Printer Sharing. For more information about configuring Windows Firewall, see Chapter 10, "Managing Network Security."

5. Attempt to connect to the server using an account with administrative credentials on the server. If you can connect with a different account, your normal account lacks sufficient privileges. Have the server administrator grant your account the necessary privileges.

If you are still unable to connect, continue troubleshooting from the server. If you do not have access to the server, contact the server administrator for assistance.

How to Troubleshoot File and Printer Sharing from the Server Computer

To troubleshoot file and printer sharing from a Windows Vista computer that is sharing the folder or printer, follow these steps:

NOTE Troubleshooting stand-alone computers

These steps assume that the computer is a member of an Active Directory domain. Troubleshooting steps for stand-alone computers differ.

---

1. Verify that the folder or printer is shared. Right-click the object, and then click Sharing. If it does not indicate that the object is already shared, share the object, and then attempt to connect from the client.

2. If you are sharing a folder and it is not already shared, right-click the folder and click Share. In the File Sharing Wizard, click Change Sharing Permissions. If the File Sharing Wizard does not appear, the Server service is not running. Continue with the next step. Otherwise, verify that the user account attempting to connect to the share appears on the list or that the user account is a member of a group that appears on the list. If the account is not on the list, add it to the list. Click Share, and then click Done.

3. Verify that the Server service is running. The Server service must be started and set to start automatically for file and printer sharing to work.

4. From Network And Sharing Center, verify that File Sharing or Printer Sharing (whichever is applicable) is turned on.

5. Verify that users have the necessary permission to access the resources. Right-click the object, and then click Properties. In the Properties dialog box, click the Security tab. Verify that the user account attempting to connect to the share appears on the list or that the user account is a member of a group that appears on the list. If the account is not on the list, add it to the list.

6. Check the Windows Firewall exceptions to verify that it is configured properly by following these steps:

    a. Click Start, and then click Control Panel.

    b. Click Security, and then click Windows Firewall.

    c. In the Windows Firewall dialog box, note the Network Location. Click Change Settings.

    d. In the Windows Firewall Settings dialog box, click the Exceptions tab. Verify that the File And Printer Sharing check box is selected.

    e. If the File And Printer Sharing exception is enabled, it applies only for the current network profile. For example, if Windows Firewall indicated that your Network Location was Domain Network, you might not have the File And Printer Sharing exception enabled when connected to Private or Public networks. Additionally, Windows Firewall will, by default, allow file and printer sharing traffic from the local network only when connected to a Private or Public network.

How to Troubleshoot an APIPA Address

If you discover that Windows Vista has assigned an APIPA address (any address in the range 169.254.0.0 through 169.254.255.255), you know that Windows Vista was unable to contact a DHCP server. This could be caused by several problems:

■ The DHCP server was temporarily unavailable.

■ The computer was not properly connected to the network.

■ The computer was not authorized to connect to the network.

As with most connectivity issues, you should use Windows Network Diagnostics as your first troubleshooting step. If that does not solve the problem, verify that the computer is connected to the local network and that the network hardware is functioning properly. Then, follow these steps to attempt to retrieve an IP address from a DHCP server:

1. Click Start. Type **cmd**, right-click Cmd in the Start menu, and then click Run As Administrator. Respond to the UAC prompt that appears. This opens an administrative command prompt, which is required to renew the IP address.

2. At the elevated command prompt, run the following two commands:

```
ipconfig /release
ipconfig /renew
```

These first command causes Windows Vista to drop the current IP configuration (if it has one), and the second command attempts to contact a DHCP server to retrieve a new configuration. If the network adapter still has an APIPA address after running these commands and you are connected to the network, the DHCP server is offline. Bring a DHCP server online, and then restart the computer. If the network does not use a DHCP server, configure a static or alternate IPv4 address provided by your network administrator.

Real World

Tony Northrup

If you can't get an address from the DHCP server but you do seem to be connected to the network, try manually configuring an IP address on the computer. First, log on to a computer that is working properly on the network and make note of its IP address, subnet mask, default gateway, and DNS server addresses. Then, change the last digit of the IP address and try to ping the new address. If you don't get a response (indicating that the IP address might not be currently in use), use the newly identified IP address and network settings to manually configure the IP address on the computer you're troubleshooting. If everything works properly with the new configuration, you know the problem is just the DHCP server and not the network infrastructure.

After using this technique to determine whether the DHCP server is the cause of the problem, you should immediately reconfigure the computer to act as a DHCP client. Even if you ping an IP address and it returns nothing, it might still be in use—not all computers respond to pings. Additionally, it's possible that a computer would later start up and use that IP address because manually assigning the IP address wouldn't register it as being in use with the DHCP server.

How to Troubleshoot Name Resolution Problems

Before two computers can communicate, the client must translate the server's hostname (such as www.contoso.com) to an IP address (such as 192.168.10.233 or the IPv6 address 2001:db8::1). This translation is called name resolution. Most of the time, a DNS server performs the name resolution and returns the IP address to the client computer.

As with most network problems, you should use Windows Network Diagnostics as your first troubleshooting step. If that does not solve the problem, verify that the computer is connected to the local network, and then follow these steps:

1. Verify that you can connect to other computers using IP addresses. If you cannot connect to servers by using their IP address, the source of your problems is network connectivity rather than name resolution. To test this, open a command prompt and run the command **ipconfig**. Make note of the default gateway. Then, attempt to ping the default gateway. For example, if the default gateway is 192.168.1.1, you could run the following command from a command prompt:

   ```
   ping 192.168.1.1
   ```

   If you receive replies, you are definitely connected to the network, and your problem is probably related to name resolution. If you don't receive a reply, you might not be connected to the network. Before troubleshooting the problem as a name resolution problem, verify that the computer is connected properly to the local network.

2. Open a command prompt and use Nslookup (a tool for testing name resolution) to look up the hostname you are attempting to contact, as the following example shows:

   ```
   nslookup www.microsoft.com
   ```

   Examine the output:

   ❏ If Nslookup resolves the name, name resolution isn't the problem. However, the server might be offline, a firewall might be blocking your traffic, the program you're using might be misconfigured, or the DNS server database is incorrect and returning an invalid IP address.

   ❏ If Nslookup displays only "DNS request timed out" (and doesn't later resolve the name), your DNS servers are not responding. First, run Nslookup again to make sure it's not an intermittent problem. Then, verify that your computer has the correct IP addresses listed for the DNS servers. If the DNS server IP addresses are correct, the DNS servers or the network they are connected to are offline.

   NOTE Finding the correct DNS server configuration

   If you're not sure what the DNS servers are supposed to be, check the configuration of a working computer on the same network.

   ❏ If Nslookup displays the message, "Default servers are not available," the computer does not have a DNS server configured. Update the client network configuration with DNS server IP addresses or configure the computer to acquire an address automatically, as described in "How DHCP Works" in Lesson 1, "Configuring Client Networking." DHCP will almost always assign DNS servers to clients.

Real World

Tony Northrup

Here's a tip to work around name resolution problems: if the DNS server isn't working correctly and you need to reach a particular server by name, you can add the name and IP address to the computer's Hosts text file. The Hosts file (it doesn't have a file extension) is located at %windir%\system32\drivers\etc\Hosts.

First, use the Nslookup command on a working computer to look up the server's IP address. Then, add it to the Hosts file.

To open the Hosts file, run Notepad by using administrative permissions. Then, open the Notepad %windir%\system32\drivers\etc\hosts file (it does not have a file extension). To add an entry to the Hosts file to enable name resolution without using DNS, add lines to the bottom of the Hosts file, as demonstrated here for IPv4 and IPv6 addresses:

```
192.168.1.10    www.contoso.com
2001:db8::1      mail.fabrikam.com
```

Save the hosts file, restart the web browser (if necessary), and Windows Vista will contact the IP address you specified instead of trying to query the DNS server. Don't forget to remove the line from the Hosts file when the DNS is working correctly—otherwise, the user won't be able to reach the server when its IP address changes.

How to Troubleshoot Connectivity Problems

Network connectivity problems prevent any application from accessing a network resource, while application connectivity problems prevent only specific applications from accessing resources. Most network connectivity problems result from one of the following issues:

- Failed network adapter
- Failed network hardware
- Failed network connection
- Faulty network cables
- Misconfigured network hardware
- Misconfigured network adapter

Application connectivity problems, however, tend to result from one of these issues (starting with the most likely):

- The remote service is not running. For example, if you're trying to remotely control a computer, Remote Desktop might not be enabled on the remote computer.

- The remote server has a firewall configured that is blocking that application's communications from the client computer.

- A firewall between the client and server computer is blocking that application's communications.

- Windows Firewall on the local computer might be configured to block the application's traffic.

- The remote service has been configured to use a nondefault port number. For example, web servers typically use TCP port 80, but some administrators might configure TCP port 81 or a different port.

The sections that follow describe how to troubleshoot network and application connectivity problems.

How to Troubleshoot Network Connectivity Problems

To identify the source of a connectivity problem, follow these steps and answer the questions until you are directed to a different section:

1. Open Network And Sharing Center by clicking Start, clicking Network, and then clicking Network And Sharing Center.

2. If a red X is displayed over a network link, click the link to start Windows Network Diagnostics and follow the prompts that appear. If the red X is between the network and the Internet, the problem is with the Internet connection and not the local computer. Contact the network administrator for assistance.

3. If no network adapters appear, either a network adapter isn't present, the hardware has failed, or the driver is not functioning. Restart the computer. If the network adapter is still not available, use Device Manager (drvmgmt.msc) to diagnose the problem. If possible, update the driver.

   ❑ Can other computers connect to the same network? If not, the problem is with the network and not the computer you're troubleshooting. Contact the network administrator for assistance.

   ❑ Can you connect to other network resources? For example, if you can browse the web but you can't connect to a shared folder, you are probably experiencing an application connectivity problem. For more information, read "How to Troubleshoot Application Connectivity Problems" later in this lesson.

4. Open a command prompt and run **Ipconfig /all**. Examine the output:

5. If the computer has an IP address in the range 169.254.0.0 through 169.254.255.255, the computer is configured to use DHCP addressing, but a DHCP server was not available. Follow the instructions in the section of this chapter entitled "How to Troubleshoot an APIPA Address."

6. If you have a valid IP address but do not have a default gateway or a DNS server, the problem is caused by an invalid IP configuration. If the computer has a DHCP-assigned IP address, run **ipconfig /release** and **ipconfig /renew** from an administrative command prompt. If the computer has a manually configured IP address, obtain the correct configuration from a network administrator.

7. If no network adapters are listed, the computer either lacks a network adapter or (more likely) does not have a valid driver installed. Use Device Manager to identify the network adapter, and then install an updated driver. If the hardware has failed, replace the network adapter (or add a new network adapter if the network adapter is built in).

8. If all network adapters show a Media State of Media Disconnected, the computer is not physically connected to a network. Connect the computer to a wired or wireless network. If you are connected to a wired network and you still see this error, disconnect and reconnect both ends of the network cable. If the problem continues, replace the network cable. Attempt to connect a different computer to the same network cable; if the new computer can connect successfully, the original computer has a failed network adapter. If neither computer can connect successfully, the problem is with the network wiring, the network switch, or the network hub. Replace the network hardware as necessary.

9. If all network adapters show DHCP Enabled: No in the display of the **ipconfig /all** command, the network adapter might be misconfigured. If DHCP is disabled, the computer has a static IPv4 address, which is an unusual configuration for client computers. Update the network adapter IPv4 configuration to Obtain An IP Address Automatically and Obtain DNS Server Address Automatically, as described in Lesson 1, "Configuring Client Networking." Then, configure the Alternate Configuration tab of the IP Properties dialog box with the current static IP configuration.

10. If you have a valid IP address and you can ping your default gateway, open a command prompt and run the command "Nslookup *servername*." If Nslookup cannot successfully resolve a valid name and does not display an answer similar to the following, you have a name-resolution problem. See "How to Troubleshoot Name Resolution Problems" in this lesson.

```
C:\>nslookup contoso.com
Non-authoritative answer:
Name:    contoso.com
Addresses:  10.46.232.182, 10.46.130.117
```

Those troubleshooting steps should allow you to identify the cause of most network problems.

How to Troubleshoot Application Connectivity Problems

If one application (or network protocol) works correctly but others don't, you are experiencing an application connectivity issue. To troubleshoot this type of problem, follow these steps:

1. First, make sure that you do not have a name-resolution problem by using Nslookup to query the server name you are trying to contact. If Nslookup cannot resolve the name, see "How to Troubleshoot Name Resolution Problems" in this lesson.

2. Often, a firewall might block your application's communications. Before you can test whether this is the case, you must identify the network protocol and port number used by the application. Table 9-1 lists port numbers for common applications. If you are not sure which port numbers your application uses, consult the application's manual or contact the technical support team.

Table 9-1   Default Port Assignments for Common Services and Tasks

Service Name or Task	UDP	TCP
Web servers, HTTP, and Internet Information Services (IIS)		80
Web servers that use Hypertext Transfer Protocol Secure (HTTPS)		443
File Transfer Protocol (FTP) servers		20, 21
DNS queries	53	53
DHCP client		67
File and printer sharing	137	139, 445
Internet Relay Chat (IRC)		6667
Incoming e-mail: Internet Mail Access Protocol (IMAP)		143
Incoming e-mail: IMAP (Secure Sockets Layer [SSL])		993
Incoming e-mail: Post Office Protocol 3 (POP3)		110
Incoming e-mail: POP3 (SSL)		995
Outgoing e-mail: Simple Mail Transfer Protocol (SMTP)		25
Connecting to an Active Directory domain controller	389, 53, 88	135, 389, 636, 3268, 3269, 53, 88, 445
Network Management: Simple Network Management Protocol (SNMP)	161, 162	
SQL Server		1433
Telnet		23
Terminal Server, Remote Desktop, and Remote Assistance		3389

3. After you identify the port numbers required by your application, test whether you can manually connect to that port on the server. If it is a TCP port, you can use either PortQry

or Telnet. To test a TCP port with Telnet (the only tool built into Windows Vista), run the following command:

```
Telnet hostname_or_address TCP_port
```

For example, to determine if you can connect to the web server at www.microsoft.com (which uses port 80), you would run the following command:

```
Telnet www.microsoft.com 80
```

If the command prompt clears or if you receive text from the remote service, you successfully established a connection, which means you do not have an application connectivity problem. Instead, you might have an authentication problem, or there might be a problem with the client or server software.

If Telnet displays "Could not open connection to the host," this verifies that you do indeed have an application connectivity issue. Either the server is offline or a misconfigured firewall is blocking the application's network traffic. Follow these steps to continue troubleshooting the problem:

1. Verify that the server is online by connecting to a different service running on the same server. For example, if you are attempting to connect to a web server and you know that the server has File Sharing enabled, attempt to connect to a shared folder. If you can connect to a different service, the problem is almost certainly a firewall configuration problem on the server. If you don't know of another service running on the server, contact the server administrator to verify that it's running.

2. Attempt to connect from different computers on the same and different subnets. If you can connect from a computer on the same subnet, the problem is caused by a firewall or application configuration problem on your computer—read Chapter 10, "Managing Network Security," and verify that a firewall exception is created either for your application or for the port numbers it uses. If you can connect from a client computer on a different subnet but not from the same subnet, a firewall on the network or on the server is probably filtering traffic from your client network. Contact a network administrator for assistance.

Practice: Troubleshoot Network Problems

In this practice, you troubleshoot two common network problems.

▶ **Practice 1: Solve a Simple Network Problem**

In this practice, you run a batch file to generate a networking problem, and then you troubleshoot it using Windows Network Diagnostics. This practice simulates a network problem on your computer. Before you run it, verify that you are connected to the network and can access network resources and be prepared to be disconnected from the network.

1. Browse to the Chapter 09 folder. (The practice files for this book can be installed from the Practice_Files folder on the companion CD.) Right-click the Lesson2-Practice1.bat file, and then click Run As Administrator. Respond to the UAC prompt that appears.

2. You can ignore the command window that appears; the batch file just simulates a networking failure. Now, you will troubleshoot the problem.

3. Open Internet Explorer and attempt to view a website. Notice that the Internet is not available.

4. Click Start, right-click Network, and then click Properties.

5. Network And Sharing Center appears and displays the Network Map.

6. Click the red X on the network map, which indicates that you are not connected to the LAN.

7. When Windows Network Diagnostics identifies the problem, click the solution to solve it. Respond to the UAC prompt that appears.

   Windows Network Diagnostics fixes the network problem.

▶ **Practice 2: Solve a More Complicated Network Problem**

In this practice, you must you run a batch file to generate a networking problem, and then you troubleshoot it using multiple tools. This practice simulates a network problem on your computer. Before you run it, verify that you are connected to the network and can access network resources, and be prepared to be disconnected from the network.

1. Browse to the Chapter 09 folder. (The practice files for this book can be installed from the Practice_Files folder on the companion CD.) Right-click the Lesson2-Practice2.bat file, and then click Run As Administrator. Respond to the UAC prompt that appears.

   You can ignore the command window that appears; the batch file just simulates a networking failure. Now, you will troubleshoot the problem.

2. Open Internet Explorer and attempt to view a website. Notice that the Internet is not available.

3. On the Internet Explorer error page that appears, click Diagnose Connection Problems. Windows Network Diagnostics attempts to identify the problem.

4. Make note of the problem that Windows Network Diagnostics displays. Then, click the suggested solution to attempt to solve it. Respond to the UAC prompt that appears.

   Windows Network Diagnostics attempts to resolve the problem by applying the potential solution you clicked.

5. Return to Internet Explorer and attempt to access the Internet again. Notice that the problem is still not resolved. Cancel Windows Network Diagnostics when it retests the network.

6. Open a command prompt by clicking Start, typing **Cmd**, and then pressing Enter.

7. Type **Ipconfig /all** and press Enter to view the current network configuration.

8. Attempt to ping the default gateway. The default gateway should respond, indicating that you are successfully connected to your LAN.

9. Run the command **Nslookup www.microsoft.com**. Notice that the DNS server does not respond, indicating one of several possible problems:

    ❑ The DNS server is offline.

    ❑ A network connecting your computer to the DNS server is offline.

    ❑ Your computer has the wrong DNS server address configured.

10. First, verify that the DNS server IP address is correct. You can find the correct DNS server address in the file %windir%\system32\previous_ip_configuration.txt. Double-click this file and make note of the correct DNS server address. Normally, you would get this from your network administrator, but the batch file you ran saved this copy of your previous network configuration automatically.

11. Because the DNS server IP address is different, you need to update it. Click Start, right-click Network, and then click Properties.

12. In Network And Sharing Center, besides your network adapter, click the View Status link.

13. Click the Properties button and respond to the UAC prompt that appears.

14. Click Internet Protocol Version 4 (TCP/IPv4), and then click Properties.

15. Configure the network settings to match those in the %windir%\system32\previous _ip_configuration.txt file. If you use DHCP, click Obtain DNS Server Address Automatically to return the interface to using the DNS server configuration provided by the DHCP server.

16. Click OK, and then click Close twice.

17. Return to Internet Explorer and verify that you can connect to the Internet.

Lesson Summary

- Windows Network Diagnostics can automatically identify many common network problems. Windows Network Diagnostics can be launched from many places, and it often prompts the user to run it when a network problem is detected.

- Use Ping to test connectivity to a remote host. PathPing functions similarly but also lists the routers between you and the remote host. Use PortQry or Telnet to determine whether a remote server is listening for connections on a specific port. Use Nslookup to troubleshoot DNS name resolution problems.

- You can troubleshoot problems connecting to shared folders from either the client or the server. Most often the problem is related to insufficient privileges. However, the server might be offline, Windows Firewall might be blocking the connection, or a network firewall might be filtering the network traffic.

- APIPA addresses are in the range 169.254.0.0 through 169.254.255.255. If a computer is assigned one of these addresses, it means that the computer is configured to receive a DHCP address, but a DHCP server was not available. You can resolve this problem by verifying that a DHCP server is online, and then refreshing the DHCP configuration by running **ipconfig /release** and then **ipconfig /renew**.

- Name resolution problems occur when both the client and server are online, but the client cannot determine the server's IP address. Typically, name resolution problems are caused by an incorrect DNS server configuration on the client, a DNS server that is offline, or a DNS server that has an incorrect IP address listed for the server.

- Connectivity problems can be caused by either the network or the application. Network connectivity problems prevent any traffic from being sent. Application connectivity problems block just the application's specific traffic. Typically, application connectivity problems occur because a Windows Firewall exception was not created on the server or a network firewall is blocking the application's communications.

Lesson Review

You can use the following questions to test your knowledge of the information in Lesson 2, "Troubleshooting Network Problems." The questions are also available on the companion CD if you prefer to review them in electronic form.

NOTE Answers

Answers to these questions and explanations of why each answer choice is right or wrong are located in the "Answers" section at the end of the book.

1. Microsoft Outlook gives you an error message when you attempt to download your mail. You verify that you can connect to other computers on the network. Which tools could you use to determine whether the mail server is responding to incoming e-mail requests? (Choose all that apply.)
   A. Ping
   B. Telnet
   C. PortQry
   D. PathPing

2. Which of the following IP addresses would indicate that a client computer could not retrieve an IP address from a DHCP server and did not have an alternate configuration?
   A. 10.24.68.20
   B. 127.0.0.1
   C. 192.168.22.93
   D. 169.254.43.98

3. Which tool would you use to determine whether a connectivity problem you are currently experiencing is related to name resolution?

   A. Nslookup

   B. Ipconfig

   C. Ping

   D. Netstat

Chapter Review

To further practice and reinforce the skills you learned in this chapter, you can

- Review the chapter summary.
- Review the list of key terms introduced in this chapter.
- Complete the case scenarios. These scenarios set up real-world situations involving the topics of this chapter and ask you to create a solution.
- Complete the suggested practices.
- Take a practice test.

Chapter Summary

- Most of the time, client computers receive an IP address from a DHCP server. If your network administrators inform you that you must use manual IP addressing, you can configure the IP address by viewing the network adapter's properties. For mobile computers, you can configure an alternate configuration so that the computer uses a manually assigned IP address only if a DHCP server is not available.
- Windows Vista includes Windows Network Diagnostics, a tool that can automatically diagnose common network problems. Windows Network Diagnostics should always be your first troubleshooting step. If that does not allow you to identify the problem, you can use Ping, PathPing, PortQry, and Nslookup to determine whether the problem is a network connectivity problem, an application connectivity problem, or a name resolution problem.

Key Terms

Do you know what these key terms mean? You can check your answers by looking up the terms in the glossary at the end of the book.

- Automatic Private IP Address (APIPA)
- latency
- Media Access Control (MAC) address
- name resolution

Case Scenarios

In the following case scenarios, you will apply what you've learned about how to configure network settings and troubleshoot network problems. You can find answers to these questions in the "Answers" section at the end of this book.

Case Scenario 1: Choosing a Network Configuration Method

You are a desktop support technician for Contoso Pharmaceuticals. Contoso is opening a new branch in Tulsa, Oklahoma, and is looking for your guidance about how to configure network settings on client computers.

Interviews

Following is a list of company personnel interviewed and their statements:

- **Elizabeth A. Andersen, Network Manager** "Right now, we're planning to allocate the 192.168.123.0 network for the Tulsa branch. As usual, I'll set up a router at 192.168.123.1 for the DSL connection. Eventually, we plan to add a second router to a satellite connection, and I'll want you to configure the client computers to use that as a backup. So, just be prepared to add a new router in the not-so-distant future."

- **Cristian Petculescu, IT Manager** "We're going to deploy a small Windows Server 2003 DNS server at the location. For best performance, you should configure that local DNS server as their primary server. You should configure our main DNS server as a secondary server, however."

Questions

Answer the following questions for your manager:

1. What configuration method should you use to configure the client network settings? Why?

2. Do the client computers need to be part of an Active Directory domain to support automatic IP addressing?

Case Scenario 2: Troubleshooting a Network Problem

You are a desktop support technician for Contoso Pharmaceuticals. Recently, you helped deploy 20 Windows Vista computers to a new location in Tulsa, Oklahoma. One of the users, Gordon L. Hee, calls you for help with a networking problem:

"My network is down."

Questions

Answer the following questions about the troubleshooting process:

1. What is the first step you should have Gordon take?

2. How can you determine whether the problem is with the local network or the WAN?

3. How can you determine whether Gordon's problem is a name resolution problem?

Suggested Practices

To successfully master the Configuring and Troubleshooting Networking exam objective, complete the following tasks.

Configure and Troubleshoot Network Protocols

For this task, you should complete all three practices.

- **Practice 1: Examine Real-World Networking Problems** Visit *http://windowshelp* *.microsoft.com/communities/newsgroups/en-us/* and browse the Windows Vista Network and Sharing newsgroup. Read the posts to determine how people solved their different network problems.

- **Practice 2: Examine Real-World Network Configurations** Separately, connect to your home and work networks. Examine the network configuration for each. Does it use DHCP or manual IP addressing? Do you have more than one DNS server available? What is the IP address of your default gateway?

- **Practice 3: Testing the Effectiveness of Ping** Try pinging your default gateway, DNS servers, computers on your local network, and web servers on the Internet. Which of those responds to ping requests and which ignore ping requests?

Configure and Troubleshoot Network Services at the Client

For this task, you should complete all four practices.

- **Practice 1: Using Nslookup** Use Nslookup to query several hostnames: www.microsoft.com, www.conotoso.com, and not-valid.contoso.com.

- **Practice 2: Using Ipconfig to Determine When the IP Address Was Assigned** Use Ipconfig to determine the IP address of your DHCP server and make note of how long ago you received your IP address. Ping the DHCP server.

- **Practice 3: Using Ipconfig To Receive a New IP Address** Use Ipconfig to view your current IP address. Then, use Ipconfig to release and renew your IP address. Did you get the same IP address or a different IP address?

- **Practice 4: Watch a Webcast on Network Diagnostics** Watch the "TechNet Webcast: Network Diagnostics in Windows Vista (Level 200)," by Kevin Remde at *http:// www.microsoft.com/cui/eventdetail.aspx?eventID=1032334112.*

Troubleshoot Access to Network Resources

For this task, you should complete both practices.

- **Practice 1: Sharing Folders on Public Networks**   While connected to a Private network, share a folder or printer, and then connect to it from a remote computer. Next, change the network type to Public. Can you still connect to the shared folder or printer?
- **Practice 2: Using Network Discovery**   Use Network Explorer to browse network resources with Network Discovery disabled. Then, enable it and immediately attempt to use Network Explorer. Wait 10 minutes and try Network Explorer again. Note that some devices might take a few minutes to appear.

Troubleshoot Connectivity Issues

For this task, you should complete the following practice.

- **Practice 1: Fix Network Problems**   Have a friend induce one of the following network problems. Then, use the tools built into Windows Vista to diagnose and repair the problem.
  - ❑ Computer is unplugged from the LAN.
  - ❑ Wireless network adapter is turned off (using the laptop's hardware switch).
  - ❑ Network adapter is disabled.
  - ❑ Router is disconnected from the Internet.
  - ❑ DNS server is unavailable or misconfigured.
  - ❑ Default gateway is offline.

Take a Practice Test

The practice tests on this book's companion CD offer many options. For example, you can test yourself on just the content covered in this chapter, or you can test yourself on all the 70-622 certification exam content. You can set up the test so that it closely simulates the experience of taking a certification exam, or you can set it up in study mode so that you can look at the correct answers and explanations after you answer each question.

MORE INFO   **Practice tests**

For details about all the practice test options available, see "How to Use the Practice Tests" in this book's Introduction.

Chapter 10
Managing Network Security

The topic of network security is enormous, but the amount you need to know about it for the 70-622 exam is limited. The 70-622 exam assumes you already understand the basics of configuring Windows Firewall in both Control Panel and the Windows Firewall With Advanced Security (WFAS) console. For this exam you just need to go a little deeper. Most significantly, you need to show that you understand how to configure Internet Protocol Security (IPSec) through both IPSec policies and Connection Security Rules (a new feature in Windows Vista). Beyond IPSec, you need to demonstrate that you can apply some of your Windows Firewall configuration skills to simple troubleshooting scenarios.

Exam objectives in this chapter:
- Configure network security.
- Troubleshoot Windows Firewall issues.

Lessons in this chapter:

Before You Begin

To complete the lessons in this chapter, you must have

- A Windows Server 2003 domain controller named dcsrv1.nwtraders.msft.
- Two Windows Vista Business, Enterprise, or Ultimate computers named Vista1 and Vista2. Both Vista1 and Vista2 are members of the Nwtraders.msft domain.
- A basic understanding of Windows networking and Group Policy.

Real World

JC Mackin

IPSec policies used to be the only way to secure data on the wire as it was sent among computers on a Windows network. You would think that a technology like that would be adopted universally, but it wasn't. IPSec policies, fairly or not, were perceived as being difficult to implement and manage. Despite the benefits of the feature, many businesses simply avoided using IPSec policies, even when their security needs seemed to call for it.

Now, in Windows Vista, Connection Security Rules help solve the "IPSec problem" by lowering the barrier to entry for IPSec. Connection Security Rules really do make IPSec easy and reliable, and I expect that in a few years many more businesses will use them to deploy IPSec on their networks. So, given this new and easy way to deploy IPSec, you can just forget about having to learn the old and troublesome IPSec policies, right? Wrong.

For all of their virtues, Connection Security Rules also have some significant limitations. Yes, they are very easy to configure. However, you can use Connection Security Rules only to secure *all* traffic to or from a specified source. You can't use them, as you can use IPSec policies, to secure just a certain type of traffic, such as e-mail, instant messaging, or Telnet. In addition, if you need clients only to respond to IPSec and not to request it—that kind of situation is still best handled by the default IPSec policy "Client (Respond Only)." Finally, it's essential to remember that Connection Security Rules by default don't encrypt anything. To configure them to encrypt data, you need to dig into the feature much more deeply, at which point the "ease of implementation" factor is greatly reduced. Because of the limitations of Connection Security Rules, IPSec policies are going to be around for years, so it's best that you learn to use them.

So, given that IPSec policies and Connection Security Rules will coexist as IPSec deployment methods, I have a word of practical advice concerning the two: whenever possible, avoid mixing IPSec policies and Connection Security Rules at a single physical site. Technically, they are indeed compatible with each other, but from an administrative and troubleshooting point of view, using both at the same time is something of a nightmare. I have the ripped-out tufts of hair to prove it.

Lesson 1: Securing Network Traffic

IP Security (IPSec) is a means to protect network data by ensuring its authenticity, its confidentiality, or both. In Windows Vista, you have a choice of implementing IPSec on your network either through IPSec policies or Connection Security Rules. For the 70-622 exam, you need to understand how to configure IPSec through both of these methods.

> **After this lesson, you will be able to:**
> - Deploy IPSec on a network through an IPSec policy.
> - Deploy IPSec on a network through Connection Security Rules.
>
> **Estimated lesson time: 60 minutes**

What is IPSec?

IPSec is essentially a way to provide security for data sent between two clients on an IP network. IPSec is not just a Windows feature; the Windows implementation of IPSec is based on standards developed by the Internet Engineering Task Force (IETF) IPSec working group. IPSec protects data between two IP addresses by providing the following services:

- Data Authentication
  - ❑ Data origin authentication. You can configure IPSec to ensure that each packet you receive from a trusted party originates in fact from that party and is not spoofed.
  - ❑ Data integrity. You can use IPSec to ensure that data is not altered in transit.
  - ❑ Anti-replay protection. You can configure IPSec to verify that each packet received is unique and not duplicated.
- Encryption
  - ❑ You can use IPSec to encrypt network data so that the data is unreadable if captured in transit.

In Windows Vista, IPSec is enforced either by *IPSec policies or Connection Security Rules.* IPSec policies by default attempt to negotiate both authentication and encryption services. Connection Security Rules by default attempt to negotiate only authentication services. However, you can configure IPSec policies and Connection Security Rules to provide a combination of these data protection services.

NOTE **IPSec beyond Windows**

Because it is an interoperable standard, IPSec can be implemented to secure communications between Windows and non-Windows computers.

IPSec Policies

IPSec policies define how a computer or group of computers handle secure communications. You can assign an IPSec policy either to an individual computer in Local Security Policy or to a group of computers in Group Policy. Although you may define many IPSec policies for use on a computer or network, only one policy is ever assigned to a computer at any given time.

Figure 10-1 shows a Group Policy object (GPO) in which an IPSec policy is assigned.

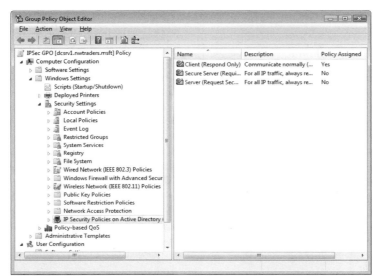

Figure 10-1   IPSec policies in a GPO

Every IPSec policy is comprised of one or more IPSec policy *rules* that determine when IP traffic should be protected. These rules in turn are comprised of IP *filters* and *filter actions*. Filters define a source or destination address, address range, computer name, TCP/UDP port, or server type (DNS, WINS, DHCP, default gateway). If traffic leaving or arriving at a computer on which a policy is assigned matches one of the assigned policy's IP filters, the corresponding filter action is applied. Possible filter actions are *block, permit,* or *negotiate security.* When matching a source or destination address, the most specific IPSec policy rule always takes precedence.

NOTE   How is security negotiated?

"Negotiate Security" is a general option for a filter action, but you can then specifically choose the way security is negotiated for that filter action. For example, should encryption or merely authentication (data integrity) be negotiated? What is the order of preference for encryption technologies or hashing algorithms? Is it okay to fall back to unsecured communications if no common protocol for security can be agreed upon? Because there are so many ways that you can choose to negoti-ate security for a filter action, it is possible to define many distinct rules for which the Negotiate Security option has been selected. Remember also that security can be successfully negotiated only when both ends of an IPSec connection can agree on the particular services and algorithms used to protect the data.

Figure 10-2 shows how IPSec policies are comprised of rules, filters, and filter actions.

IPSec Policy

	IP Filter Lists	Filter Actions
IPSec Policy Rule #1	Telnet Traffic from 192.168.3.32 POP3 Traffic from 192.168.3.200	Negotiate Security (Require Encryption)
IPSec Policy Rule #2	All Telnet Traffic All POP3 Traffic	Block
IPSec Policy Rule #3	All Traffic	Negotiate Security (Request Authentication)

Most Specific ↓ Least Specific

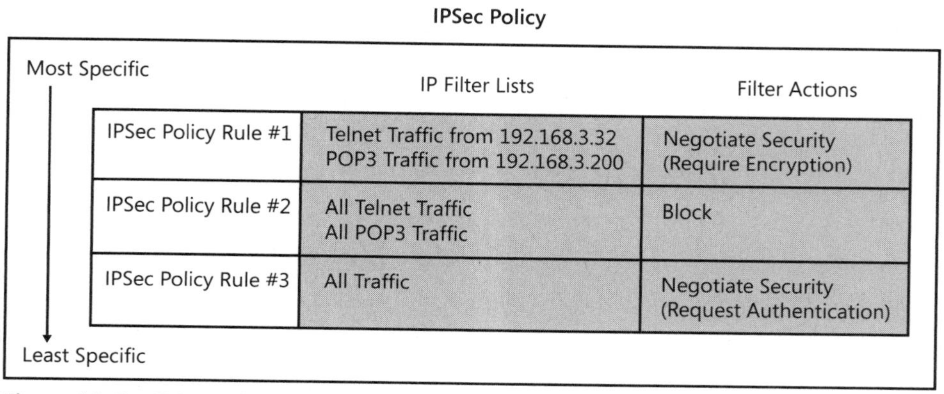

Figure 10-2   IPSec policies, rules, filters, and filter actions

IPSec Policy Example   If you want to require that the local computer send and accept POP3 (basic e-mail) traffic only to and from the address 192.168.10.5 and also that this POP3 traffic always be encrypted, you should write two rules in a single IPSec policy. The first rule should encrypt traffic sent over TCP port 110 (POP3's port) to and from the address 192.168.10.5, and the second rule should block *all* traffic sent over TCP port 110. This pair of rules produces the desired effect because when Windows evaluates an IPSec policy, the more specific rule takes precedence. If POP3 traffic is sent to or originates from 192.168.10.5, the communica-tion matches the first rule and is negotiated according to the first rule's filter action. If POP3 traffic is sent to or originates from any other IP address, the second, more general rule is trig-gered, and the communication will be blocked according to the second rule's filter action.

Figure 10-3 shows how these rules appear in such a policy.

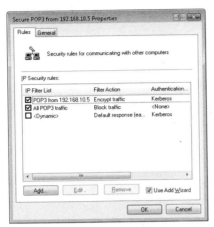

Figure 10-3   An example IPSec policy

NOTE   IP filter lists

In the example above only one IP filter is attached to each rule because only one destination (192.168.10.5) is specified. However, you can attach many IP filters to each rule—for example, to encrypt POP3 traffic from several specified servers. An IP filter list is the set of IP filters within an IPSec policy rule to which a filter action applies. Regardless of whether an IP filter list includes a single IP filter or many IP filters, you associate only a single filter action with an IP filter list and IPSec policy rule.

Quick Check

1.   Does every IPSec policy rule have an IP filter list?
2.   In terms of its function within an IPSec policy, what does a filter action do?

Quick Check Answers

1.   Yes, even if the list has only one IP filter.
2.   A filter action determines whether the traffic captured by an IP filter in a given policy rule is permitted, blocked, encrypted, or authenticated.

Connection Security Rules

You can also use Connection Security Rules to configure IPSec settings for specific connections between a local computer and other computers. Like IPSec policies, Connection Security Rules evaluate network traffic and then block, allow, or negotiate security for messages based on the criteria you establish. Unlike IPSec policies, however, Connection Security Rules do not include filters or filter actions. The features provided by filters and filter actions are built into each Connection Security Rule, but the filtering capabilities in Connection Security Rules are not as powerful as those of IPSec policies. Connection Security Rules do not apply to types of IP traffic, such as IP traffic that passes over port 23. Instead, they apply to all IP traffic originating from or destined for certain IP addresses, subnets, or servers on the network.

A Connection Security Rule first authenticates the computers defined in the rule before they begin communication and then secures the information sent between these two authenticated computers. If you have configured a Connection Security Rule that requires security for a given connection and the two computers in question cannot authenticate each other, the connection is blocked.

By default, Connection Security Rules provide only data authentication security (data origin authentication, data integrity, and anti-replay security). For this reason, Connection Security Rules are typically said only to authenticate connections. However, you can also configure data encryption for Connection Security Rules so that the connections in question are truly secured and not merely authenticated.

Figure 10-4 shows a Connection Security Rule that requires secure communications within a given domain.

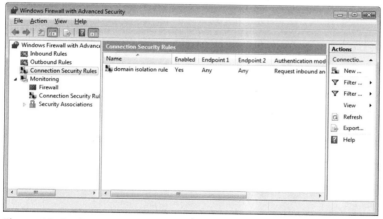

Figure 10-4   A Connection Security Rule

NOTE   Exporting Connection Security Rules

Connection Security Rules defined in the WFAS console apply only to the local Windows Vista computer. However, by using the *Export Policy* and *Import Policy* functions in the WFAS console, you can create one set of Connection Security Rules and export them to many computers in your organization.

Security Associations

After two computers negotiate an IPSec connection, whether through IPSec policies or Connection Security Rules, the data sent between those computers is secured in what is known a Security Association (SA). Security for an SA is provided by the two IPSec protocols—Authentication Header (AH) and Encapsulating Security Payload (ESP). These protocols provide data and identity protection for each IP packet in an SA. AH provides data origin authentication, data integrity, and anti-replay protection for the entire IP packet. ESP provides *data encryption,* data origin authentication, data integrity, and anti-replay protection for the ESP payload. To secure data within any SA, you can use either AH alone, ESP alone, or AH and ESP together.

How IPSec Connections Are Established

To establish SAs dynamically between IPSec peers, the Internet Key Exchange (IKE) protocol is used. IKE establishes a mutually agreeable policy that defines the SA, a policy that includes its security services, protection mechanisms, and cryptographic keys between communicating peers. In establishing the SA, IKE also provides the keying and negotiation for the IPSec security protocols AH and ESP.

To ensure successful and secure communication, IKE performs a two-phase negotiation operation, each with its own SAs. Phase 1 negotiation is known as *main mode* negotiation, and Phase 2 is known as *quick mode* negotiation. The IKE main mode SA protects the IKE negotiation itself. The SAs created during the second IKE negotiation phase are known as the quick mode SAs. The quick mode SAs protect application traffic.

We can summarize the steps for establishing an IPSec connection in the following way:

1. Set up a main mode SA.
2. Agree upon the terms of communication and encryption algorithm.
3. Create a quick mode SA.
4. Send data.

How to Configure an IPSec Policy

In Group Policy, three IPSec policies are predefined. You can thus configure an IPSec policy by assigning any one of these predefined policies described below.

- **Client (Respond Only)**   When you assign this policy to a computer through a GPO, that computer will never initiate a request to establish an IPSec communications channel with another computer. However, any computer to which you assign the Client policy will negotiate and establish IPSec communications when requested by another computer. You typically assign this policy to intranet computers that need to communicate with secured servers but that do not need to protect all traffic.

- **Server (Request Security)** You should assign this policy to computers for which encryption is preferred but not required. With this policy the computer accepts unsecured traffic but always attempts to secure additional communications by requesting security from the original sender. This policy allows the entire communication to be unsecured if the other computer is not IPSec-enabled. For example, communication to specific servers can be secure while allowing the server to communicate in an unsecured manner to accommodate a mixture of clients (some of which support IPSec and some of which do not).

- **Secure Server (Require Security)** You should assign this policy to intranet servers that require secure communications such as a server that transmits highly sensitive data.

To assign an IPSec policy within Local Security Policy or a GPO, right-click the policy, and then click Assign from the shortcut menu, as shown in Figure 10-5.

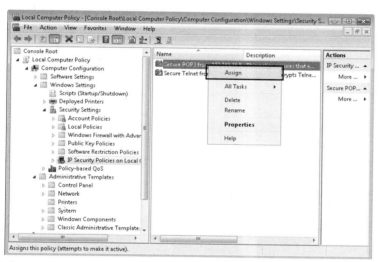

Figure 10-5 Assigning an IPSec policy in a GPO

You can assign only one IPSec policy to a computer at a time. If you assign a second IPSec policy to a computer, the first IPSec policy automatically becomes unassigned. If Group Policy assigns an IPSec policy to a computer, the computer ignores any IPSec policy assigned in Local Security Policy.

Creating a New IPSec Policy

To create a new custom IPSec policy, first open Local Security Policy or a GPO. In the console tree below Security Settings, right-click the IP *Security Policies* node, and then click Create IP Security Policy, as shown in Figure 10-6. (You can find Security Settings in a GPO beneath the Windows Settings folder.) This procedure launches the IP Security Policy Wizard.

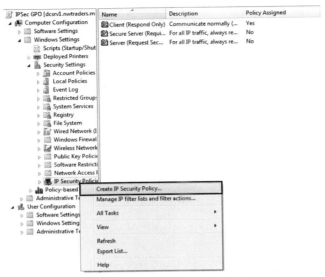

Figure 10-6   Creating a new IPSec policy in a GPO

The IP Security Policy Wizard simply gives you an opportunity to create an "empty" policy, to name that IPSec policy, and to enable the Default Response Rule. (The Default Response Rule is read only by previous versions of Windows and not by Windows Vista. For those operating systems, the rule provides a default action for an IPSec policy when no other IPSec policy filters apply.)

NOTE   Importing and exporting an IPSec policy

Why is the Default Response Rule included in the IP Security Policy Wizard if this rule does not even apply to Windows Vista? Policies can be exported. If you right-click the IPSec *Security Policies* node, you will see the option to import or export an IPSec policy. These options allow you to move IPSec policies from one computer to another or from a computer to a GPO (and vice versa). For this reason, you will see the option to enable the Default Response Rule even when, for example, you create a new IPSec policy in Local Security Policy on a Windows Vista machine. You could define such a policy on a Windows Vista machine and then export it to a Windows XP machine or to a GPO governing computers running previous versions of Windows.

After you have created the IPSec policy, you can configure the policy through its properties. Most important, you can add rules to the policy by clicking the Add button in the Rules tab in the Properties dialog box for the policy, as shown in Figure 10-7. This procedure launches the Create IP Security Rule Wizard.

Figure 10-7   Launching the Create IP Security Rule Wizard

Using the Create IP Security Rule Wizard

The bulk of IPSec policy configuration involves creating and configuring IPSec rules for that policy. To create and configure these rules, use the Create IP Security Rule Wizard.

The following section describes the five main pages of the Create IP Security Rule Wizard.

1. Tunnel Endpoint page

    Configure this page only when you want to use IPSec to create a "tunnel" or virtual private network (VPN) connection. (Configuring a tunnel is beyond the scope of the 70-622 exam and this training kit.)

2. Network Type page

    Use this page if you want to limit the rule to either the local area network or remote access connections.

3. IP Filter List page

    Use this page to specify the set of IP Filters you want to attach to the rule. In Group Policy, two IP filter lists are predefined for IPSec policy rules: All ICMP Traffic and All IP Traffic. To create a new IP filter list, click the Add button on the IP Filter List page, as shown in Figure 10-8. This procedure opens the IP Filter List dialog box.

NOTE   What is ICMP traffic?

ICMP (Internet Control Message Protocol) is a messaging feature of IP that allows Ping and Tracert to function. ICMP traffic typically refers to Ping and Tracert traffic.

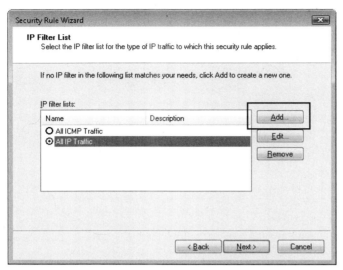

Figure 10-8   Creating a new IP filter list to attach to an IPSec policy rule

To create a new IP filter to add to the new IP filter list you are creating, click the Add button in the IP Filter List dialog box, as shown in Figure 10-9. This procedure, in turn, launches the IP Filter Wizard.

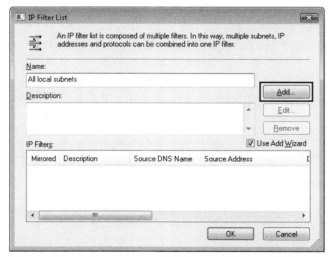

Figure 10-9   Creating a new IP filter to add to an IP filter list

Use the IP Filter Wizard to define IP traffic according to source and destination. You can specify a source and destination according to IP address, DNS name, server function (such as any DHCP server, DNS server, WINS server, or default gateway), and IP protocol type (including TCP/UDP port number).

You can also use the IP Filter Wizard to create a "mirrored" filter. A mirrored filter matches the source and destination with the exact opposite addresses, so that, for example, you can easily configure a filter that captures POP3 traffic sent to and from the local address. To configure your filter as a mirrored filter, leave the Mirrored check box selected on the first page of the IP Filter Wizard, as shown in Figure 10-10.

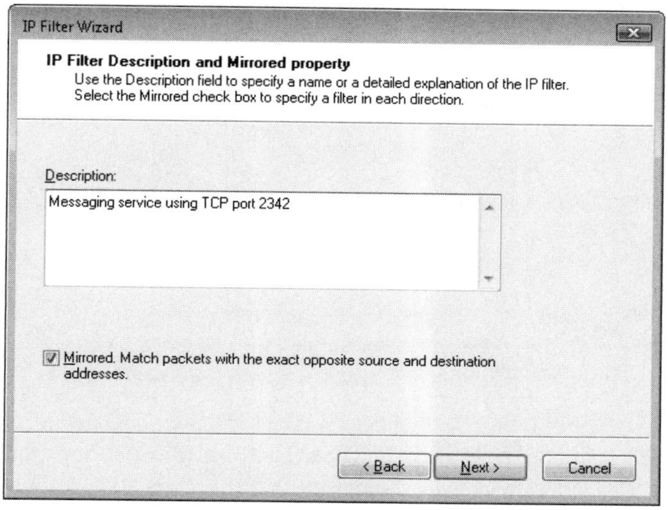

Figure 10-10   Creating a mirrored IP filter

Exam Tip   Most network applications depend on two-way communications and therefore require a mirrored filter for their traffic to be adequately secured. If you have configured a filter with the proper source and destination but your IPSec rule still isn't working as expected, the problem could be that you have not configured the filter as a mirrored filter.

4. Filter Action page

    After you have attached the desired IP filter list to the rule, you can specify a filter action for the rule in the Security Rule Wizard. In Group Policy the following three IP filters are predefined for IPSec policy rules:

    ❏ Permit – This filter action permits the IP packets to pass through unsecured.

    ❏ Request Security (Optional) – This filter action permits the IP packets to pass through unsecured but requests that clients negotiate security (preferably encryption).

    ❏ Require Security – This filter action triggers the local computer to request secure communications from the client source of the IP packets. If security methods (including encryption) cannot be established, the local computer will stop communicating with that client.

    To create a new filter action, click the Add button on the Filter Action page, as shown in Figure 10-11. This procedure launches the Filter Action Wizard.

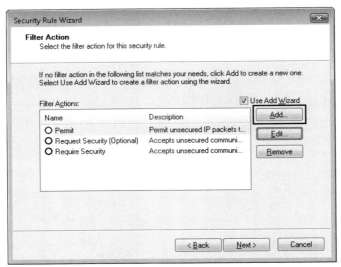

Figure 10-11   Creating a new filter action

5. Authentication Method page

Security can be negotiated only after the IPSec clients are authenticated. By default, IPSec rules rely on Active Directory directory service and the Kerberos protocol to authenticate clients. However, you can also specify a certificate infrastructure or a preshared key as a means to authenticate IPSec clients. To select the authentication method for IPSec, you can use the Authentication Method page of the Security Rule Wizard, as shown in Figure 10-12.

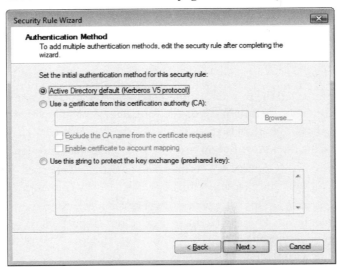

Figure 10-12   Specifying an authentication method for a new IPSec policy rule

Managing IP Filter Lists and Filter Actions

The IP filters, IP filter lists, and filter actions you create for an IPSec rule can be shared with other IPSec rules. You can also create and configure these features outside of the Security Rule Wizard. To do so, right-click the *IP Security Policies* node in Local Security Policy or a GPO, and then click Manage IP Filter Lists And Filter Actions, as shown in Figure 10-13.

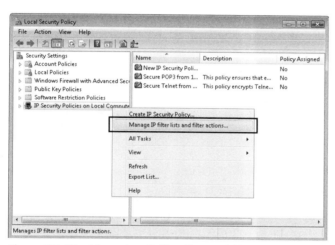

Figure 10-13   Managing IP filter lists and filter actions

Creating and Configuring a Connection Security Rule

To create a Connection Security Rule in the WFAS console tree, right-click the *Connection Security Rules* node, and then click New Rule from the shortcut menu. (Be sure to select the *Connection Security Rules* node directly beneath the root node in the console tree and not the *Connection Security Rules* node beneath the *Monitoring* node.)

This procedure, which launches the New Connection Security Rule Wizard, is shown in Figure 10-14.

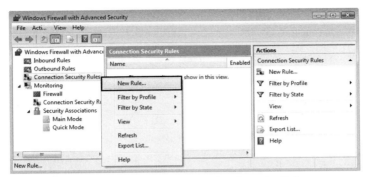

Figure 10-14   Creating a new Connection Security Rule

Using the New Connection Security Rule Wizard

The specific pages you see when you use the New Connection Security Rule Wizard depend on the type of rule you choose to create on the first page. The following section describes the six pages you would find when creating a custom rule.

■ **Rule Type page**   As shown in Figure 10-15, the Rule Type page allows you to create any of five rule types.

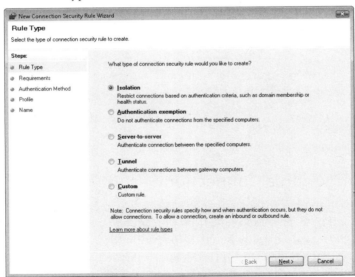

Figure 10-15   Choosing a Connection Security Rule type

These five rule types are described below:

❏ **Isolation rule**   This is a general rule used to authenticate all traffic for select network profiles (network location types). When the network type defined for the local computer in Network And Sharing Center corresponds to one of the profiles selected for the rule, the local computer attempts to negotiate security as defined in the rule. The three profiles defined are Domain, Private, and Public.

❏ **Authentication Exemption rule**   You can use this rule type to exempt specific computers or a group or range of IP addresses (computers) from being required to authenticate themselves, regardless of other Connection Security Rules. This rule type is commonly used to grant access to infrastructure computers that the local computer must communicate with before authentications can be performed. It is also used for other computers that cannot use the form of authentication you configured for this policy and profile.

To create an authentication exemption rule, you only need to specify the computers by name or IP address and then name the rule.

❏ **Server-To-Server rule**   This rule type allows you to authenticate the communications between IP addresses or sets of addresses, including specific computers and subnets.

❏ **Tunnel rule**   Use this rule type to secure communications between VPN endpoints.

❏ **Custom rule**   Use this rule type to create a rule that requires special settings or a combination of features from the various rule types.

■ **Endpoints page**   Use this page to specify the remote computers with which you want to negotiate an IPSec connection.

■ **Requirements page**   Use this page to specify whether authenticated communication should be required or merely requested with the endpoints specified. As an alternative, you can require authentication for inbound connections but only request them for outbound connections. Finally, on this page you can also configure an authentication exemption for the specified endpoints.

■ **Authentication Method page**   This page allows you to specify the method by which computer endpoints are authenticated. The first option is Default. When you choose this selection, the authentication method used by the connection is the one specified in the properties of the *Windows Firewall With Advanced Security* node in the root of the WFAS console. Other authentication options you can select include Kerberos (Active Directory) authentication for both computers and users, Kerberos authentication for computers only, a computer certificate from a certificate infrastructure, or the Advanced authentication option. The Advanced option allows you to configure an order of preference of authentication methods for both users and computers. It also allows you to configure these authentication methods as optional.

■ **Profile page**   The Profile page allows you to limit the local network location types to which the rule will apply. The profiles you can enable for the rule are Domain, Private, and Public.

■ **Name page**   The Name page allows you to name the new Connection Security Rule and (optionally) to provide a description.

Configuring IPSec Settings in the WFAS Console

Besides creating Connection Security Rules on your network, you also have to define the IPSec Settings in the Windows Firewall properties. To access these settings, first open the properties of the *Windows Firewall With Advanced Security* node in the root of the WFAS console tree, as shown in Figure 10-16. (The WFAS console itself is available in Administrative Tools.)

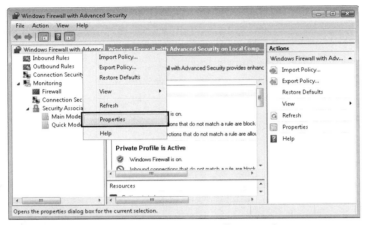

Figure 10-16   Opening Windows Firewall properties

Then, in the properties dialog box that opens, click the IPSec Settings tab, as shown in Figure 10-17.

Figure 10-17   Configuring IPSec settings

Through this tab you can configure two aspects of IPSec: IPSec defaults and ICMP exemptions.

■ **IPSec defaults**   Clicking the Customize button opens the Customize IPSec Settings dialog box, as shown in Figure 10-18. From this dialog box you can set new default parameters for key negotiation, for data protection, and for authentication method.

Figure 10-18   Setting IPSec defaults

For example, to configure data encryption for Connection Security Rules, first select Advanced in the Data Protection area, and then click Customize. This procedure opens the Customize Data Protection Settings dialog box, as shown in Figure 10-19. Next, in this dialog box, select the Require Encryption For All Connection Security Rules That Use These Settings check box, and then click OK.

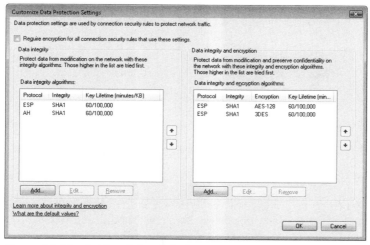

Figure 10-19   Setting IPSec defaults

- **ICMP exemptions**   Use this setting in the IPSec Settings tab to prevent ICMP (Ping and Tracert) messages from being authenticated or encrypted, or both. Keeping ICMP messages unprotected allows you to perform basic network troubleshooting when IPSec cannot be successfully negotiated.

Practice: Deploying IPSec Through IPSec Policies and Connection Security Rules

In the first stage of this practice, you will install Telnet services, and then configure an IPSec policy to encrypt Telnet traffic between Vista1 and Vista2. In the second stage you will create a Connection Security Rule that authenticates all network traffic between the same two computers.

▶ **Practice 1: Installing Telnet Services**

In this practice, you will install Telnet services on both Vista1 and Vista2.

1. Log on to NWTRADERS from Vista1 as an administrator.
2. Insert the Windows Vista Product DVD into the local hard disk drive.
3. In Control Panel, click Programs, and then, in Programs and Features, click Turn Windows Features On Or Off.
4. In the User Account Control (UAC) dialog box, click Continue.
   The Windows Features window opens.
5. After the list of features appears in the window, select both the Telnet Client and Telnet Server check boxes, and then click OK.
6. After the installation has completed, from Administrative Tools, open the Services console. In the UAC dialog box, click Continue.
7. In the Services console, locate, and then double-click Telnet to open its properties.
8. In the Telnet Properties dialog box, change the Startup Type to Automatic, and then click Apply.
9. In the Service Status area, click Start.
10. When the Service Status has changed to Started, click OK to close the Telnet Properties dialog box, and then close the Services console.
11. In Control Panel, click System And Maintenance, then click Administrative Tools, and then double-click Computer Management.
12. In the UAC dialog box, click Continue.
13. In the Computer Management console tree, expand Local Users And Groups, and then select the Groups folder.
14. In the details pane, double-click TelnetClients.
15. In the TelnetClients Properties dialog box, click the Add button.

16. In the Select Users, Computers, Or Groups dialog box, in the Enter The Object Names To Select text box, type **Domain Admins**, and then click OK.

17. In the TelnetClients Properties dialog box, click OK.

18. Log off Vista1.

19. Log on to NWTRADERS on Vista2, and then perform steps 2 through 18 on Vista2.

▶ **Practice 2: Creating an IPSec Policy**

In this practice, you will create a GPO and an IPSec policy that you will later configure to encrypt Telnet traffic in the Nwtraders.msft domain.

1. Log on to Nwtraders from Vista1 as a domain administrator.

2. From the Start menu, type **gpmc.msc** in Start Search, and then Enter.

3. In the UAC dialog box, click Continue.

4. In the Group Policy Management console tree, navigate to the Nwtraders.msft domain.

5. Right-click the *Nwtraders.msft* node and select Create A GPO In This Domain And Link It Here.

6. In the New GPO box, type **IPSec GPO**, and then click OK.

7. In the GPMC console, in the details pane, right-click the IPSec GPO, and then click Edit from the shortcut menu.

8. In the Group Policy Object Editor window, navigate to Computer Configuration, Windows Settings, Security Settings, and IP Security Policies On Active Directory.

9. Right-click the IP *Security Policies* node, and then click Create IP Security Policy on the shortcut menu.

    The IP Security Policy Wizard opens.

10. Click Next.

11. On the IP Security Policy Name page, type **Nwtraders IPSec Policy**.

12. In the *Description* field, type **This IPSec policy encrypts Telnet traffic**.

13. Click Next.

14. On the Requests For Secure Communications Page, read all of the text on the page, and then click Next.

15. Click Finish.

    The Nwtraders IPSec Policy Properties dialog box appears.

16. Leave all windows open and continue to Practice 3.

▶ **Practice 3: Creating an IPSec Policy Rule and Filter**

In this practice, you will configure the newly created Nwtraders IPSec Policy with rules that require high security for Telnet traffic. In the process you will run the Security Rule Wizard, the IP Filter Wizard, and the Filter Action Wizard.

1. While you are still logged on to Vista1, in the Nwtraders IPSec Policy dialog box, click Add.

   The Create IP Security Rule Wizard opens. (This wizard is also called the Security Rule Wizard.)

2. Read all of the text on the first page, and then click Next.

3. On the Tunnel Endpoint page, read all of the text on the page, and then click Next.

4. On the Network Type page, read all of the text on the page, and then click Next.

5. On the IP Filter List page, read all of the text on the page, and then click the Add button.

   The IP Filter List dialog box opens.

6. In the Name text box, type **Encrypt Telnet Filter List**, and then click Add.

   The IP Filter Wizard opens.

7. Click Next.

8. On the IP Filter Description And Mirrored Property page, read all of the text on the page, and then click Next.

9. On the IP Traffic Source page, leave the default selection of Any IP Address, and then click Next.

10. On the IP Traffic Destination page, leave the default of Any IP Address, and then click Next.

11. On the IP Protocol Type page, select TCP from the Select A Protocol Type drop-down list box, and then click Next.

    Telnet runs on TCP port 23, so you need to specify both TCP and the appropriate port.

12. On the IP Protocol Port page, select To This Port, and then type **23** in the accompanying text box. (Leave From Any Port selected.)

13. Click Next, and then click Finish to close the IP Filter Wizard.

14. In the IP Filter List dialog box, click OK.

    The IP Filter List page of the Security Rule Wizard reappears.

15. In the IP Filter Lists area, select the Encrypt Telnet Filter List option button, and then click Next.

16. On the Filter Action page, read all of the text on the page, and then click Add.

    The Filter Action Wizard opens. Leave this wizard open and continue to Practice 4.

▶ **Practice 4: Using the Filter Action Wizard**

In this practice, you use the Filter Action Wizard to configure a custom filter action to apply to Telnet traffic. Although the default filter actions available in Group Policy are usually adequate for creating IPSec rules, it is a good idea to configure higher security for Telnet. In addition, you need to be familiar with the IP Security Filter Action Wizard for the 70-622 exam.

1. On the Welcome To The IP Security Filter Action Wizard page, read all of the text on the page, and then click Next.

2. On the Filter Action Name page, in the Name text box, type **Require High Authentication and Encryption**.

3. In the *Description* field, type **Require AH authentication and 3DES encryption**.

4. Click Next.

5. On the Filter Action General Options page, ensure that Negotiate Security is selected, and then click Next.

6. On the Communication With Computers That Do Not Support IPSec page, ensure that Do Not Allow Unsecured Communication is selected, and then click Next.

7. On the IP Traffic Security page, select Custom and then Settings.

8. In the Custom Security Method Settings dialog box, select the Data And Address Integrity Without Encryption (AH) check box.

9. In the Session Key Settings area, select both Generate A New Key Every check boxes.

10. Ensure that the Data Integrity And Encryption (ESP) check box is selected, and then click OK. (Also note that 3DES is the selected encryption algorithm.)

11. On the IP Traffic Security page, click Next.

12. On the Completing The IP Security Filter Action Wizard page, click Finish.

13. On the Filter Action page of the Security Rule Wizard, in the list of Filter Actions, select Require High Authentication And Encryption, and then click Next.

14. On the Authentication Method page of the Security Rule Wizard, leave the default as Active Directory Default, and then click Next.

    The Completing The Security Rule Wizard page appears.

15. Click Finish.

16. In the Nwtraders IPSec Policy Properties dialog box, click OK.

17. In the Group Policy Object Editor, right-click the Nwtraders IPSec Policy, and then click Assign from the shortcut menu.

18. On Vista1 and Vista2, run the Gpupdate command at a command prompt.

▶ **Practice 5: Testing the New IPSec Policy**

In this practice, you will initiate a Telnet session from Vista1 to Vista2. You will then verify that data authentication and encryption are applied to the Telnet session.

1. On Vista1, open a command prompt.

2. At the command prompt, type **telnet vista2**.

3. A Telnet session to the Telnet server on Vista2 begins.

4. On Vista1, from the Start menu, point to Administrative Tools, and then click Windows Firewall With Advanced Security.

5. In the User Account Control prompt, click Continue.

6. In the WFAS console tree, navigate to Monitoring→Security Associations.

7. Beneath the *Security Associations* node, select the Main Mode folder and then the Quick Mode folder. You will see that an SA appears in the details pane when you select each folder. Spend a few moments browsing the information displayed about these SAs. If the quick mode SA disappears, enter a command such as **dir** at the Telnet prompt to reestablish it.

8. Answer the following question: How do you know that the quick mode SA is securing Telnet traffic in particular?

   Answer: Because the remote port is specified as port 23.

9. At the Telnet prompt, type **exit**.

   You now want to unlink the IPSec GPO so that it does not interfere with the next practice.

10. Open the Group Policy Management console. In the UAC dialog box, click Continue.

11. In the Group Policy Management console tree, browse to the Nwtraders.msft domain.

12. In the details pane, right-click the GPO named IPSec GPO, and then click Link Enabled.

13. In the Group Policy Management message box, click OK to change the Link Enabled status.

14. Verify that the Link Enabled Status of IPSec GPO is now set to No.

15. Close the Group Policy Management console.

16. At a command prompt on both Vista1 and Vista2, run the Gpupdate command.

▶ Practice 6: Implementing IPSec Through Connection Security Rules

In this practice, you will configure Connection Security Rules on both Vista1 and Vista2 so that all IP traffic between those clients is authenticated.

1. If you have not already done so, log on to Nwtraders from Vista1 as an administrator.

2. In the WFAS console tree, select the *Connection Security Rules* node that appears just below the parent node (not the one that appears below the *Monitoring* node).

3. Right-click the *Connection Security Rules* node, and then click New Rule from the shortcut menu.

   The New Connection Security Rule Wizard appears.

4. On the Rule Type page, read all of the text on the page, and then, leaving the default selection of Isolation, click Next.

5. On the Requirements page, read all of the text on the page, and then click Next.

6. On the Authentication Method page, leave the default selection, and then click Next.

7. On the Profile page, leave the default selections, and then click Next.

8. On the Name page, type **Request Data Authentication**, and then click Finish.

9. Perform steps 1 through 8 on Vista2.

10. In the WFAS console of Vista2, navigate to Monitoring➔Security Associations.

11. Beneath Security Associations, select the Main Mode and Quick Mode folders to ensure that no SAs have yet been established.

12. From the Start menu of Vista2, type **\\vista1** in Start Search, and then press Enter.
    A window appears that displays the network shares available on Vista1.

13. In the WFAS console, select the Main Mode folder and then the Quick Mode folder. You will now see that an SA appears in the details pane when each folder is selected. Spend a few moments browsing the information displayed about these SAs.

14. Answer the following question: Which SA reveals that no ESP confidentiality has been negotiated for the connection?
    Answer: The quick mode SA.

15. Answer the following question: Can you configure a Connection Security Rule that will encrypt only Telnet traffic?
    Answer: No. Connection Security Rules are not port-specific.
    You should now disable the rules you just created so that they do not interfere with any other practices in this book.

16. In the WFAS console of both Vista1 and Vista2, select the *Connection Security Rules* node directly beneath the parent node in the console tree. Then, in the details pane, right-click the Request Data Authentication rule and click Disable Rule from the shortcut menu.

17. Close all open windows.

Lesson Summary

- IPSec allows you to protect network traffic by providing data authentication or encryption, or both.

- In Windows Vista networks you can implement IPSec either through IPSec policies or through Connection Security Rules.

- As a means to deploy IPSec, IPSec policies are more powerful but also more difficult to configure than Connection Security Rules.

- IPSec policies, which are deployed through Local Computer Policy or a GPO, are made up of a set of IPSec rules. Each IPSec rule in turn is comprised of one IP filter list and one filter action. The filter list defines the type of traffic to which the filter action is applied. Filter actions are allow, block, and negotiate security (authenticate or encrypt, or both).

- Connection Security Rules protect all traffic between particular sources and destinations. By default, Connection Security Rules do not encrypt data but only ensure data integrity. You can create Connection Security Rules in the WFAS console.

Lesson Review

You can use the following questions to test your knowledge of the information in Lesson 1, "Securing Network Traffic." The questions are also available on the companion CD if you prefer to review them in electronic form.

NOTE Answers

Answers to these questions and explanations of why each answer choice is right or wrong are located in the "Answers" section at the end of the book.

1. You want to require encryption between your computer and a remote server named Srv3, whose address is 192.168.10.5. Both computers are in the Active Directory domain Nwtraders.com. You configure an IPSec policy and IP filter specifying your address as the source and the server's address as the destination. You create a filter action that requires encryption, and you specify Kerberos as the authentication method. However, after you apply the policy on both computers, you find that network traffic is being encrypted only from your computer to Srv3, not from Srv3 to your computer. What should you do?

    A. Configure the IP filter as a mirrored filter.

    B. Specify a computer certificate as the authentication method.

    C. Specify a preshared key as the authentication method.

    D. Change the filter action so that security is only required and not requested.

2. You want to ensure the integrity of all data reaching ClientA from other computers in the Nwtraders domain. However, you don't want to block traffic originating from sources outside the domain. What should you do?

    A. Configure a Connection Security Rule on ClientA that requires authentication for inbound and outbound connections. Configure Kerberos as the authentication method.

    B. Configure a Connection Security Rule on ClientA that requires authentication for inbound connections and requests authentication for outbound connections. Configure Kerberos as the authentication method.

    C. Configure a Connection Security Rule on ClientA that requests authentication for inbound and outbound connections. Configure a computer certificate as the authentication method.

    D. Configure a Connection Security Rule on ClientA that requests authentication for inbound and outbound connections. Configure Kerberos as the authentication method.

Lesson 2: Troubleshooting Windows Firewall

You can configure Windows Firewall by using a number of tools. By using Control Panel, you can create exceptions to allow specific types of traffic to pass through the firewall to the local computer. By using the WFAS console, you can create inbound and outbound rules to allow specific types of traffic to pass through the firewall either to or from the local computer. Combine these two tools with a third, Group Policy, and you have a quite a few configuration settings to review when troubleshooting Windows Firewall.

You need to master only a few Windows Firewall troubleshooting concepts for the test. These concepts are all related to the basic Windows Firewall configuration options available in Control Panel, the WFAS console, and Group Policy.

After this lesson, you will be able to:
- Perform basic troubleshooting of Windows Firewall by using Control Panel, the WFAS console, and Group Policy.

Estimated lesson time: 10 minutes

How Windows Firewall Works

By default, Windows Firewall blocks connections to the local computer originating from an external source. Exceptions (also known as allow rules) are then made to allow any desired incoming connections, such as traffic to local network shares or traffic for approved network applications.

After exceptions are defined, Windows Firewall inspects all incoming packets and compares them against this list of allowed traffic. If a packet matches an entry in the exception list, Windows Firewall passes the packet to the TCP/IP protocol for further processing. If the packet does not match an entry in the list, Windows Firewall discards the packet and, if logging is enabled, creates an entry in the Windows Firewall logging file.

The function of firewall exceptions is illustrated in Figure 10-20.

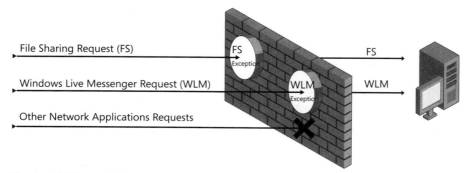

Figure 10-20   Windows Firewall blocks incoming traffic unless exceptions are made

Using Windows Firewall Troubleshooting Tools

You can troubleshoot firewall exceptions and other Windows Firewall features through three tools: the Windows Firewall Control Panel, Group Policy, and the WFAS console.

Troubleshooting Windows Firewall through Control Panel

As shown in Figure 10-21, you can perform the most common configuration and troubleshooting functions—turning the firewall on or off and configuring firewall exceptions—in Control Panel.

Figure 10-21   Basic Windows Firewall configuration in Control Panel

To configure an exception, click Allow A Program Through Windows Firewall. This opens the Windows Firewall Settings dialog box, as shown in Figure 10-22. In the Exceptions tab, simply select the program whose exception you want to configure. If the program is a custom application that is not already listed, you can add that program by clicking Add Program (if you have an instance of the program installed locally) or Add Port (if you know the TCP or UDP port used by the application).

To prevent any firewall exceptions from being configured at all, click the General tab, and then select the option to block all incoming connections.

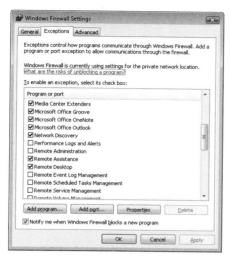

Figure 10-22   Adding exceptions to Windows Firewall

Exam Tip   Many of the questions about troubleshooting Windows Firewall you will see on the 70-622 exam are related to this concept of configuring firewall exceptions: if a network application is not functioning as expected, be sure to configure a firewall exception to allow the application to communicate with the local computer. If the application is listed in the Exceptions tab of the Windows Firewall Settings dialog box, simply select the application. If the application is not listed, either browse to the program locally or add the relevant port. Also remember that in the WFAS console, exceptions are known as allow rules.

Troubleshooting Windows Firewall with Group Policy

When you are troubleshooting Windows Firewall, be sure to review Group Policy and Local Computer Policy settings because these settings affect the Windows Firewall configuration.

Group Policy in particular provides a WFAS node beneath Computer ConfigurationWindows SettingsSecurity Settings, as shown in Figure 10-23.

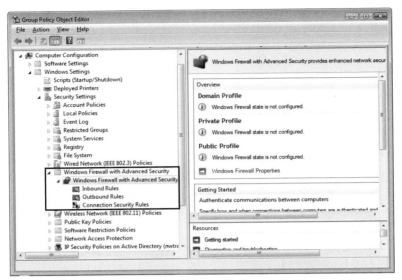

Figure 10-23 The WFAS node in Group Policy

The WFAS node in Group Policy allows you to configure WFAS settings for all computers at the site, domain, or organizational unit level. If you configure WFAS locally but do not observe the resulting behavior you expect, be sure to verify that no Group Policy settings configured in the WFAS node are conflicting with the local configuration.

Both Group Policy and Local Computer Policy also allow you to configure many Windows Firewall–related settings in Administrative Templates. To locate these settings in a local or Group Policy object, navigate to Computer ConfigurationAdministrative TemplatesNetworkNetwork ConnectionsWindows Firewall, as shown in Figure 10-24.

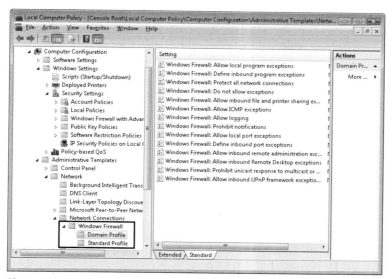

Figure 10-24   Windows Firewall configuration options in Administrative Templates

Through Administrative Templates you can configure the following Windows Firewall–related policy settings:

- **Windows Firewall: Allow Authenticated IPSec Bypass**   This policy setting allows the computers you specify to bypass the local Windows Firewall if they can authenticate by using IPSec. (Note that unlike the other settings mentioned in this list, this policy setting appears at the root of the Windows Firewall folder in Administrative Templates.)

- **Windows Firewall: Allow Local Program Exceptions**   This policy setting allows administrators to use the Windows Firewall Control Panel to define a local program exceptions list. The setting does not affect the WFAS console.

- **Windows Firewall: Define Inbound Program Exceptions**   This policy setting allows you to define firewall exceptions for a set list of programs.

- **Windows Firewall: Protect All Network Connections**   This setting allows you to force Windows Firewall into an "on" or "off" state.

- **Windows Firewall: Do Not Allow Exceptions**   If you enable this policy setting in the Windows Firewall component of Control Panel, the Don't Allow Exceptions check box is selected, and administrators cannot clear it.

- **Windows Firewall: Allow Inbound File And Printer Sharing Exception**   If you enable this policy setting, Windows Firewall opens these ports so that this computer can receive print jobs and requests for access to shared files.

- **Windows Firewall: Allow ICMP Exceptions**   This policy setting allows you to define the specific type of Internet Control Message Protocol (ICMP) message types that Windows Firewall allows.

- **Windows Firewall: Allow Logging**   This policy setting allows Windows Firewall to record information about the unsolicited incoming messages that it receives. If you enable this policy setting, Windows Firewall writes the information to a log file.

- **Windows Firewall: Prohibit Notifications**   This policy setting prevents Windows Firewall from displaying notifications to the user when a program requests that Windows Firewall add the program to the program exceptions list.

- **Windows Firewall: Allow Local Port Exceptions**   This policy setting allows administrators to use Control Panel to define a local port exceptions list. If you disable this policy setting, the Windows Firewall component in Control Panel does not allow administrators to define a local port exceptions list. However, local administrators will still be allowed to create firewall rules in the WFAS console.

- **Windows Firewall: Define Inbound Port Exceptions**   This policy setting allows you to define firewall exceptions for specific ports.

- **Windows Firewall: Allow Inbound Remote Administration Exception**   This policy setting allows remote administration of the local computer by using administrative tools such as the Microsoft Management Console (MMC) and Windows Management Instrumentation (WMI).

- **Windows Firewall: Allow Inbound Remote Desktop Exceptions**   This policy setting allows the local computer to receive inbound Remote Desktop requests (through TCP port 3389). If you disable this policy setting, Windows Firewall blocks this port, which prevents this computer from receiving Remote Desktop requests.

- **Windows Firewall: Prohibit Unicast Response To Multicast Or Broadcast Requests**   This policy setting prevents the local computer from receiving unicast responses to its outgoing multicast or broadcast messages. (This policy does not affect DHCP.)

- **Windows Firewall: Allow Inbound UPnP Framework Exceptions**   This policy setting allows the local computer to receive unsolicited inbound Plug and Play messages sent by network devices, such as routers with built-in firewalls.

Exam Tip   You could be tested on any of these policy settings mentioned above. Pay special attention to Allow ICMP Exceptions, Allow Logging, and Prohibit Notifications.

Troubleshooting Windows Firewall through the WFAS Console

The WFAS console is the main troubleshooting tool for Windows Firewall. You can use the WFAS console to perform advanced troubleshooting procedures such as determining the active firewall profile, reviewing local firewall properties, verifying inbound and outbound rules, and verifying Connection Security Rules.

Determining the Active Firewall Profile One of the first steps in troubleshooting Windows Firewall problems is to verify which firewall profile is active on the local computer.

Profiles allow you to apply different Windows Firewall settings and rules to different network locations. Using profiles, for example, Windows Firewall can automatically allow incoming traffic for a specific desktop management tool when the computer is on domain networks but block similar traffic when the computer is connected to public or private networks.

There are three network location types: domain, public, and private. A network is classified as the domain network location type if the computer is a member of a domain and uses that particular connection to authenticate to a domain controller. For all other connections, Windows Vista asks you to identify the network as either public or private. The public profile is intended for use when in public locations such as airports or coffee shops. For public networks, file sharing, network browsing, and network discovery are turned off. The private network location is intended for use when connected at a home or office and behind an edge device. Private networks allow network browsing, network discovery, and file sharing; for this reason they are less secure. To classify a network as a private network, the user must have administrator credentials to identify the network as private. Until you configure a network connection as private, the network is classified as public.

NOTE Changing the network location

To change the network location type of a network, open Network And Sharing Center and click Customize.

Exam Tip For the 70-622 exam, you need to know that the public profile (network location type) prevents network browsing, network discovery, and file sharing and that the private profile allows these same features.

Because firewall rules and properties (along with Local Computer Policy and Group Policy settings) are defined for specific firewall profiles, these settings produce the expected behavior only when the active profile of the local computer matches the profile for which the settings are defined. Although a computer may be connected to multiple network locations at the same time, only one profile can be active at a time. To view which profile is active, click the *Monitoring* node in the WFAS console. In the details pane one profile will be expanded and labeled active. You will find the active profile named directly above the text "Firewall State," as shown in Figure 10-25.

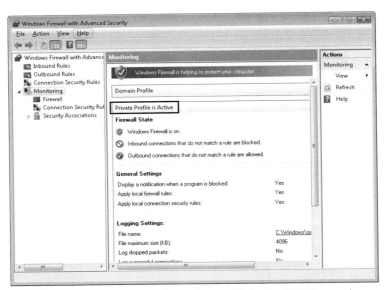

Figure 10-25   Determining the active profile in the WFAS console

Reviewing Firewall Properties   After you know the active profile on the local computer, you can verify the firewall properties for that profile. The settings configured in the properties of the *Windows Firewall With Advanced Security* node in the WFAS console affect the following behaviors for each profile:

- Whether incoming or outgoing connections as a whole are blocked.
- Whether a notification occurs when an incoming network program is blocked.
- Whether the local computer will allow unicast responses to any broadcast or multicast messages that it sends on the network.
- Whether logging is performed for dropped packets.

If you are troubleshooting any of these behaviors, be sure to review these settings.

Verifying Firewall Rules   If a network program cannot communicate with the local computer, verify that there is an active inbound allow rule for that program in the active profile. To verify that there is an active allow rule, in the WFAS console tree browse to Monitoring→Firewall. (Also be sure to verify that no active inbound block rules are affecting the program.) If you see no active allow rule for the program, go to the Inbound Rules node and create a new rule for that program.

Similarly, if the local computer cannot connect to a remote source, use the *Firewall* node to verify that no active outbound block rule affects the connection.

Finally, remember that you can configure rules in the WFAS console that allow a connection only if the connection is secured by IPSec. In such cases an inbound connection might be blocked not because of a Windows Firewall configuration error but because IPSec cannot authenticate the remote client.

Verifying Connection Security Rules   Connection Security Rules can block a program even if firewall rules allow it. For example, if a Connection Security Rule requires that all traffic be authenticated, traffic from a network source that cannot be authenticated will be dropped even if you have created an allow rule for the traffic in question.

For this reason you need to review Connection Security Rules when you are troubleshooting Windows Firewall. If you need to allow traffic from a remote source that cannot be authenticated, be sure to configure an exemption for that remote source. Alternatively, you can modify Connection Security Rules so that they only request but do not require authentication.

Quick Check

1. What is the main difference between firewall exceptions configured in Control Panel and firewall rules configured in the WFAS console?
2. Name three features disabled when the public profile is active.

Quick Check Answers

1. Exceptions define only inbound traffic that is allowed. Rules are much more flexible. They define either inbound or outbound traffic that is either allowed or denied. Firewall rules can also be configured to allow connections from authenticated, IPSec-aware clients.
2. Network discovery, network browsing, and file sharing.

Lesson Summary

- The tools used to troubleshoot Windows Firewall are the same as those used to configure it: Control Panel, the WFAS console, and Group Policy.

- Windows Firewall by default blocks incoming connections to the local computer. If a network program is unable to connect to local computer, you need to ensure that a firewall exception for that program has been created.

- You can use Group Policy to centrally enforce virtually any setting for Windows Firewall. When troubleshooting Windows Firewall, therefore, be sure to review the settings that are enforced by Group Policy.

- Many firewall settings are profile-specific. For this reason, when troubleshooting Windows Firewall, be sure to determine which profile is active.

- Use the WFAS console to perform advanced troubleshooting procedures such as determining the active firewall profile, reviewing local firewall properties, verifying inbound and outbound rules, and verifying Connection Security Rules.

Lesson Review

You can use the following questions to test your knowledge of the information in Lesson 2, "Troubleshooting Windows Firewall." The questions are also available on the companion CD if you prefer to review them in electronic form.

NOTE   Answers

Answers to these questions and explanations of why each answer choice is right or wrong are located in the "Answers" section at the end of the book.

---

1. You install a custom client network application on PC1, but you find that you are not able to receive messages from any other computers running the same application. Which of the following actions is most likely to fix the problem?

    A. Configure Group Policy to prevent unsigned drivers from being installed in the domain.

    B. Determine the port over which the application communicates and configure an exception for that port.

    C. In WFAS, create an inbound rule that allows secure connections to all computers in the local domain.

    D. In WFAS, create an outbound rule that allows connections to all computers in the local domain.

2. You work as a desktop support technician in a company whose network consists of a single Active Directory domain. You want to prevent messages from appearing on user desktops whenever Windows Firewall blocks an incoming program. What should you do?

    A. In Group Policy, configure the Windows Firewall: Do Not Allow Exceptions setting to Enabled.

    B. In Group Policy, configure the Windows Firewall: Do Not Allow Exceptions setting to Disabled.

    C. In Group Policy, configure the Windows Firewall: Prohibit Notifications setting to Enabled.

    D. In Group Policy, configure the Windows Firewall: Prohibit Notifications setting to Disabled.

Chapter Review

To further practice and reinforce the skills you learned in this chapter, you can

- Review the chapter summary.
- Review the list of key terms introduced in this chapter.
- Complete the case scenario. This scenario sets up a real-world situation involving the topics of this chapter and asks you to create solutions.
- Complete the suggested practices.
- Take a practice test.

Chapter Summary

- IPSec allows you to protect network traffic by providing data authentication or encryption, or both.
- In Windows Vista networks you can implement IPSec either through IPSec policies or through Connection Security Rules. As a means to deploy IPSec, IPSec policies are more powerful but are also more difficult to configure than Connection Security Rules.
- Windows Firewall by default blocks incoming connections to the local computer. If a desired network program is unable to connect to a local computer, you need to ensure that a firewall exception for that program has been created.
- You can use Group Policy to centrally enforce virtually any setting for Windows Firewall. When troubleshooting Windows Firewall, therefore, be sure to review the settings that are enforced by Group Policy.
- Use the WFAS console to perform advanced troubleshooting procedures such as determining the active firewall profile, reviewing local firewall properties, verifying inbound and outbound rules, and verifying Connection Security Rules.

Key Terms

Do you know what these key terms mean? You can check your answers by looking up the terms in the glossary at the end of the book.

- Firewall exception
- Internet Control Message Protocol (ICMP)
- Internet Protocol Security (IPSec)
- Kerberos

Case Scenario

In the following case scenario, you will apply what you've learned in this chapter. You can find answers to these questions in the "Answers" section at the end of this book.

Case Scenario: Troubleshooting Network Security

You are a desktop support technician for a company whose network consists of a single Active Directory domain, Fabrikam.com. Recently, network administrators have begun to implement tighter security rules on the network. These security changes include mandatory IPSec authentication on all finance servers and stricter Windows Firewall rules. You have been tasked with troubleshooting any new security problems uncovered by calls to the help desk.

1. A user calls in to complain that a certain network application is no longer able to communicate with other clients. What is the first step you should take to troubleshoot the problem?

2. A manager in the Marketing department needs to connect to a finance server but can't. Which default IPSec policy can you assign in Group Policy to allow users such as the marketing manager to communicate with servers that require security? You do not want the IPSec policy to affect communications with other computers and servers that do not require security.

3. A manager in the Research department wants to ensure that all connections to the server named Res1 are authenticted and protected. What step can you perform on Res1 to satisfy the manager's request?

Suggested Practices

To help you successfully master the exam objectives presented in this chapter, complete the following tasks.

Deploy IPSec

■ **Practice: Deploy IPSec in Different Ways**   In an Active Directory domain, configure and assign an IPSec policy that requires the securest methods of authentication and encryption. Make a note of any disruptions or difficulty in network communication. Then, unassign the IPSec policy and deploy a Connection Security Rule through Group Policy that also requires the securest methods of authentication and encryption. Again, make a note of any disruptions or difficulty in network communication.

Perform a Virtual Lab

■ **Practice: Learn about Managing Network Security in Windows Vista**   Go to *http://msev-ents.microsoft.com* and search for Event ID# 1032329277. Register and perform the virtual lab named "Managing Network Security Using Windows Firewall with Advanced Security Virtual Lab."

Watch a Webcast

■ **Practice: Watch a Webcast About Deploying IPSec**   Watch the webcast, "Deploying IPSec with Windows Vista," by John Baker, available on the companion CD in the Webcasts folder.

Take a Practice Test

The practice tests on this book's companion CD offer many options. For example, you can test yourself on just one exam objective, or you can test yourself on all the 70-622 certification exam content. You can set up the test so that it closely simulates the experience of taking a certification exam, or you can set it up in study mode so that you can look at the correct answers and explanations after you answer each question.

MORE INFO   Practice tests

For details about all the practice test options available, see the "How to Use the Practice Tests" section in this book's Introduction.

Chapter 11
Configuring and Troubleshooting Wireless Networking

Wireless networks are becoming increasingly common, and most mobile computers regularly connect to one or more wireless networks. Many traveling users connect to dozens of wireless networks—some at the office, some in their home, and some at public wireless hotspots in coffee shops or airports.

To ensure that users can stay connected while they are mobile, you must understand how to configure and troubleshoot wireless networks. This lesson teaches you how to connect to encrypted and unencrypted wireless networks and how to troubleshoot problems.

Exam objectives in this chapter:
- Configure and troubleshoot wireless networking.

Lessons in this chapter:

Before You Begin

To complete the lessons in this chapter, you should be familiar with Windows Vista and be comfortable with the following tasks:

- Installing Windows Vista
- Configuring a wireless access point
- Performing basic administration tasks on a Microsoft Windows Server 2003–based domain controller

To complete the practices in this chapter, you must have a wireless access point and a Windows Vista computer with a wireless network adapter.

To complete Practice 2 in Lesson 2, "Advanced Wireless Configuration and Troubleshooting," you must also have configured your Windows Server 2003 domain controller as an enterprise certification authority (CA). For detailed instructions, see Practice 3 of Lesson 1, "Configuring and Troubleshooting Internet Explorer Security," in Chapter 5, "Protecting Internet Explorer and Other Applications."

Lesson 1: Configuring Wireless Networking

One of the biggest improvements in Windows Vista is the simplified user interface for connecting to wireless networks. This lesson provides an overview of wireless networking and describes how to connect to most wireless networks with Windows Vista.

After this lesson, you will be able to:
- Describe wireless networking.
- List the improvements Windows Vista offers for wireless networking.
- Describe the different standards available to protect wireless networks.
- Connect to wireless networks.
- Modify the configuration of an existing wireless network.

Estimated lesson time: 20 minutes

Wireless Networking Overview

For most users, mobile computers are much more useful when they're connected to a network. Even if traveling users can only briefly connect to a network between flights, the network access gives them the opportunity to send and receive e-mail, check for important news, and synchronize files.

Although many airports and hotels offer wired network connections that mobile users can access, wired networks don't scale well because you need a separate network port for every user. Additionally, wired network ports are difficult to maintain in public places because the wires can be broken, or the ports can be physically jammed with something (it doesn't take long for someone to stick some gum into a network port).

Wireless networks, on the other hand, are much more efficient. A single wireless access point can service a radius of several hundred feet and potentially grant hundreds of individuals network access. The wireless access point can be physically secured in a closet, protecting it from damage. Additionally, users don't need to carry an Ethernet cable to connect to the network.

For these reasons, and the fact that services can charge money for access to wireless networks, public wireless networks have become very common (and now completely cover many metropolitan areas). Wireless networks have also become very popular in home environments, allowing users to instantly network an entire home without running Ethernet cable through their walls—a very expensive proposition. Additionally, wireless networks in the home allow users to use their mobile computers casually from their couch or backyard.

The primary benefit of wireless networks is that users don't need to physically connect a network cable. Unfortunately, this is also the primary drawback. Wireless networks are much more vulnerable to attacks than wired networks because attackers don't need physical access to the inside of a building to connect to a network. An attacker can connect to a wireless network from the parking lot, the street, or a nearby building. Fortunately, Windows Vista supports wireless network security technologies that provide protection that can meet most organizations' security requirements.

Wireless Networking Improvements

Windows Vista provides several wireless network improvements. The biggest change is that wireless auto configuration is now implemented in the WLAN AutoConfig service, which dynamically selects the wireless network that the computer connects to, based either on user preferences or on default settings. This includes automatically selecting and connecting to a more preferred wireless network when it becomes available.

Changes to the wireless networking behavior include:

- **Friendlier user interfaces**   It's now much easier for users to connect to and configure wireless networks.
- **Single sign-on**   Domain administrators can configure a Single Sign-on profile, allowing users to connect to a wireless network as part of the logon process. This enables users to connect to a wireless network and then to the domain in a single step, allowing Group Policy updates, execution of logon scripts, and wireless client domain joins.
- **WPA2 support**   Windows Vista supports WPA2, an update to the Wi-Fi Protected Access (WPA) wireless security standard (described in the next section). Windows XP requires an administrator to install updates before computers can connect to WPA2-protected networks.
- **Support for hidden wireless networks**   Some networks do not broadcast a service set identifier (SSID)—typically, administrators choose this configuration out of a mistaken understanding that it might be more secure. Earlier versions of Windows would always connect to preferred wireless networks that broadcast an SSID before connecting to preferred wireless networks that did not broadcast, even if the hidden network had a higher priority. Windows Vista connects to preferred wireless networks based on their priority, regardless of whether they broadcast an SSID.
- **Integration with Network Access Protection (NAP)**   WPA2-Enterprise, WPA-Enterprise, and dynamic Wired Equivalent Protection (WEP) connections that use 802.1X authentication can leverage NAP (a network security feature that requires Windows Server 2008) to prevent wireless clients that do not meet with health requirements, such as having critical security updates installed, from gaining unlimited access to a private network.

Additionally, troubleshooting wireless connection problems is now easier because wireless connections:

- Support the Network Diagnostics Framework, which attempts to diagnose and fix common problems.
- Record detailed information in the Event Log if a wireless connection attempt fails.
- Prompt the user to send diagnostic information to Microsoft for analysis and improvement.

Wireless Networking Security

Many wireless networks are unencrypted and unauthenticated—they completely lack any security features. Wired networks are typically unencrypted, too (at least at Layer 2), but it's not a significant problem because an attacker would need to physically connect an Ethernet cable to the network to gain access, and most organizations stop unauthorized people from walking into their buildings. With a wireless network, however, an attacker can physically connect to the network from the organization's lobby, parking lot, or even a nearby building.

To provide even a minimal level of protection, wireless networks need both authentication (to allow only authorized computers to connect) and encryption (to prevent attackers from viewing network traffic). All wireless security standards provide both authentication and encryption, but some are much more secure than others.

Windows Vista supports the following wireless security standards:

- **No security**   Many consumer wireless access points are configured with wireless networking enabled without security by default. As a result, unprotected wireless networks are common. Not requiring security makes it extremely convenient to connect to a network because the user does not need to provide a passphrase or key. However, the security risks are significant. Anyone within several hundred feet of the wireless access point can connect to it and possibly abuse it. Additionally, attackers can view any traffic sent to or from the wireless access point, including e-mails, instant messages, and any other unencrypted traffic.

Real World: Unprotected Wireless Networks

Tony Northrup

If someone commits a crime using the Internet, often the primary evidence law enforcement officials have regarding the perpetrator's identity is that person's IP address. Knowing the IP address, the law enforcement officials contact the Internet service provider (ISP) and issue a subpoena to force the ISP to reveal the subscriber who was assigned that IP address at the time of the crime.

Many would-be criminals are aware of this and avoid using a personal Internet connection to commit crimes. Often, they'll find an unprotected wireless network that offers Internet access, and they will abuse that connection. Then, law enforcement officials will trace the origin back to the owner of the wireless network rather than to the criminal. So by leaving a wireless network unprotected, you might be helping a criminal avoid the authorities.

- **Wired Equivalent Protection (WEP)** WEP, available using either 64-bit or 128-bit encryption, was the original wireless security standard. It's still commonly used because it's almost universally supported—almost every operating system, wireless access point, wireless bridge, or other wireless network device (such as printers and home media extenders) supports WEP. Although WEP offers better protection than using no wireless security, it is easily cracked by a knowledgeable attacker. 128-bit WEP offers significantly better protection than 64-bit WEP, but either can typically be cracked within just a few minutes. Regardless, using WEP is still safer than not using any wireless security because WEP will prevent casual users from abusing your network.

- **Wi-Fi Protected Access (WPA)** WPA is the successor to WEP, offering significantly better protection. WPA is not as universally supported as WEP, however, so if you have non-Windows wireless clients or wireless devices that do not support WEP, you might need to upgrade them to support WPA. Windows Vista supports both WPA-Personal and WPA-Enterprise:

  ❑ WPA-PSK (for preshared key), also known as WPA-Personal, is intended for home environments. WPA-PSK requires a user to enter an 8-character to 63-character passphrase into every wireless client. WPA converts the passphrase to a 256-bit key.

❑ WPA-EAP (Extensible Authentication Protocol), also known as WPA-Enterprise, relies on a back-end server running Remote Authentication Dial-In User Service (RADIUS) for authentication. The RADIUS server can then authenticate the user to the Active Directory directory service or by verifying a certificate. WPA-EAP enables very flexible authentication, and Windows Vista enables users to use a smart card to connect to a WPA-Enterprise–protected network.

■ **WPA2** WPA2 (also known as IEEE 802.11i) is an updated version of WPA, offering improved security and better protection from attacks. Like WPA, WPA2 is available as both WPA2-PSK and WPA2-EAP.

Windows Vista includes support for WEP, WPA, and WPA2 built-in. Windows XP can support both WPA and WPA2 by installing updates available from Microsoft.com. Recent versions of Linux and Mac OS are capable of supporting WEP, WPA, and WPA2.

Connecting to Wireless Networks

There are several ways to connect to wireless networks: manually, using Group Policy, and using scripts. The sections that follow describe each of these techniques.

Manually Connecting to a Wireless Network that is in Range

To connect to a wireless network that is currently in range, follow these steps:

1. Click Start, and then click Connect To.

   NOTE WLAN AutoConfig service must be started

   The WLAN AutoConfig service must be started for wireless networks to be available. This service by default is set to start automatically.

2. The Connect To A Network Wizard appears. Select the wireless network you want to connect to, and then click Connect.

   NOTE Appearance of networks that don't broadcast an SSID

   In Windows Vista, networks that are configured to not broadcast an SSID will appear as Unnamed Network, allowing you to connect to the network.

3. If the network does not broadcast an SSID, you will see the Type The Network Name (SSID) For The Network page. Type the network name, and then click Next.

4. If the network is not encrypted, click Connect Anyway.

5. If the network is encrypted, you will see the Type The Network Security Key Or Pass-phrase page. Type the security key. Alternatively, if you have saved network settings to a universal serial bus (USB) flash drive, you can connect it now. Click Connect.

6. Windows Vista will connect to the network, and then display the Successfully Connected To SSID page. Click Close.

Now you'll be able to use the wireless network. If you want to disconnect from the wireless network, you can follow these steps to connect to a different wireless network or simply click Start, and then Connect To, select your current wireless network connection, and then click Disconnect.

Manually Creating a New Wireless Network Profile

The easiest way to connect to a wireless network is to click Start, click Connect To, and follow the prompts that appear. However, that only works if the wireless network is currently in range and broadcasting an SSID. If you want to preconfigure a wireless network so that Windows Vista can automatically connect to it later when the network is in range, follow these steps:

1. Click Start, and then click Connect To.

   The Connect To A Network Wizard appears.

2. On the Disconnect Or Connect To Another Network page, near the bottom-right corner, click the Set Up A Connection Or Network link.

3. On the Choose A Connection Option page, click Manually Connect To A Wireless Network, as shown in Figure 11-1. Click Next.

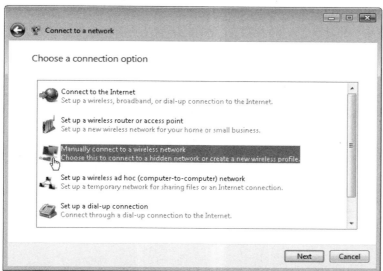

Figure 11-1 Manually connecting to a wireless network

4. On the Enter Information For The Wireless Network You Want To Add page, type the Network Name (which is the wireless network's SSID), choose the security settings, and choose whether to save the network connection. If the wireless network does not broadcast an SSID, select the Connect Even If The Network Is Not Broadcasting check box, as shown in Figure 11-2. Click Next.

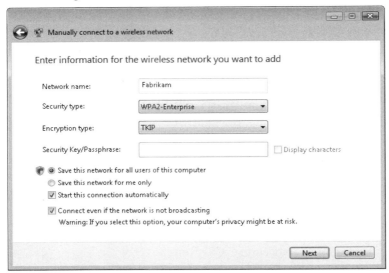

Figure 11-2   Preconfiguring a wireless network connection

5. If a User Account Control (UAC) prompt appears, respond to it.
6. Click Close.

As described in Lesson 1, "Configuring Wireless Networking," you can also preconfigure wireless networks using Group Policy settings or scripts.

Real World: Not Broadcasting an SSID

Tony Northrup

When wireless networks were new, some security experts told administrators that they should turn off SSID broadcasting to reduce security risks. It seemed like a good idea because if a wireless access point does not broadcast an SSID, client computers won't automatically detect it.

> The problem is, turning off SSID broadcasting makes it more difficult for legitimate users to connect to the wireless network. It doesn't make it any more difficult for an attacker, however. Although the ability to connect to wireless networks that don't broadcast an SSID is not built into the operating system, free tools are available on the Internet that immediately detect wireless networks that aren't broadcasting an SSID.

Connecting to Wireless Networks Using Group Policy Settings

Manually connecting to a wireless network works well when you're configuring a small number of computers. In Active Directory environments you should use Group Policy settings to configure client computers instead. For best results, you should have Windows Server 2003 with Service Pack 1 or later installed on your domain controllers because Microsoft extended support for wireless Group Policy settings when it released Service Pack 1.

Before you can configure wireless networks for Windows Vista client computers, you need to extend the Active Directory schema using the 802.11Schema.ldf file included on the companion CD. If you do not have access to the companion CD, you can copy the schema file from *http://www.microsoft.com/technet/network/wifi/vista_ad_ext.mspx*. To extend the schema, follow these steps:

1. Copy the 802.11Schema.ldf file to a folder on a domain controller.
2. Log on to the domain controller with Domain Admin privileges and open a command prompt.
3. Select the folder containing the 802.11Schema.ldf file and run the following command (where *Dist_Name_of_AD_Domain* is the distinguished name of the Active Directory domain, such as "DC=contoso,DC=com" for the contoso.com Active Directory domain):

   ```
   ldifde -i -v -k -f 802.11Schema.ldf -c DC=X "Dist_Name_of_AD_Domain"
   ```
4. Restart the domain controller.

After you have extended the schema, you can configure a wireless network policy from a Windows Vista client computer by following these steps:

1. Open the Active Directory Group Policy Object (GPO) in the Group Policy Object Editor.
2. Expand Computer Configuration, Windows Settings, Security Settings, and then click Wireless Network (IEEE 802.11) Policies.

3. Select and right-click Wireless Network (IEEE 802.11) Policies, and then click Create A New Windows Vista Policy.

4. The New Vista Wireless Network Policy Properties dialog box appears, as shown in Figure 11-3.

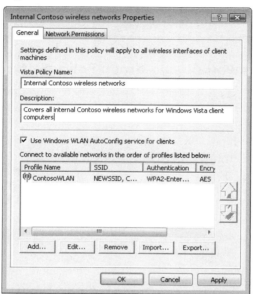

Figure 11-3   Using Group Policy settings to configure Windows Vista wireless network clients

5. To add an infrastructure network, click Add, and then click Infrastructure to open the Connection tab of the New Profile Properties dialog box. In the Network Names list, select NEWSSID (the default name), and then click Remove. Next, type a valid internal SSID in the Network Names box, and then click Add. Repeat this to configure multiple SSIDs for a single profile. If the network is hidden, select the Connect Even If The Network Is Not Broadcasting check box.

6. In the New Profile Properties dialog box, click the Security tab. Use this tab to configure the wireless network authentication and encryption settings. Click OK.

These settings will configure client computers to automatically connect to your internal wireless networks and to not connect to other wireless networks.

Connecting to Wireless Networks Using Scripts

You can also configure wireless settings using commands in the **netsh wlan** context of the Netsh command-line tool, which enables you to create scripts that connect to different wireless networks (whether encrypted or not). To list available wireless networks, run the following command:

```
Netsh wlan show networks
Interface Name : Wireless Network Connection
There are 2 networks currently visible

SSID 1 : Nwtraders1
    Network Type          : Infrastructure
    Authentication        : Open
    Encryption            : None

SSID 1 : Nwtraders2
    Network Type          : Infrastructure
    Authentication        : Open
    Encryption            : WEP
```

Before you can connect to a wireless network using Netsh, you must have a profile saved for that network. Profiles contain the SSID and security information required to connect to a network. If you have previously connected to a network, the computer will have a profile for that network saved. If a computer has never connected to a wireless network, you need to save a profile before you can use Netsh to connect to it. You can save a profile from one computer to an Extensible Markup Language (XML) file, and then distribute the XML file to other computers in your network. To save a profile, run the following command after manually connecting to a network:

```
Netsh wlan export profile name="SSID"
```

Before you can connect to a new wireless network, you can load a profile from a file. The following example demonstrates how to create a wireless profile (which is saved as an XML file) from a script or the command line:

```
Netsh wlan add profile filename="C:\profiles\nwtraders1.xml"
```

To quickly connect to a wireless network, use the **netsh wlan connect** command and specify a wireless profile name (which must be configured or added previously). The following examples demonstrate different but equivalent syntaxes for connecting to a wireless network with the Nwtraders1 SSIDs (service set identifiers):

```
Netsh wlan connect Nwtraders1
Netsh wlan connect Nwtraders1 interface="Wireless Network Connection"
```

Note that you need to specify the interface name only if you have multiple wireless network adapters, which is very rare. You can use the following command to disconnect from all wireless networks:

```
Netsh wlan disconnect
```

You can use scripts and profiles to simplify for your users the process of connecting to private wireless networks. Ideally, you should use scripts and profiles to save users from ever needing to type wireless security keys.

You can also use Netsh to allow or block access to wireless networks based on their SSIDs. For example, the following command allows access to a wireless network with the Nwtraders1 SSIDs (service set identifiers):

```
Netsh wlan add filter permission=allow ssid=Nwtraders1 networktype=infrastructure
```

Similarly, the following command blocks access to the Contoso wireless network:

```
Netsh wlan add filter permission=block ssid=Contoso networktype=adhoc
```

To block all ad hoc networks, use the Denyall permission, as the following example demonstrates:

```
Netsh wlan add filter permission=denyall networktype=adhoc
```

To prevent Windows Vista from automatically connecting to wireless networks, run the following command:

```
Netsh wlan set autoconfig enabled=no interface="Wireless Network Connection"
```

Netsh has many other commands for configuring wireless networking. For more information, run the following at a command prompt:

```
Netsh wlan help
```

Reconfiguring a Wireless Network

Earlier in this lesson you learned how to connect to and configure a new wireless network. After you first connect to the network, Windows Vista stores those settings for future connections. If the configuration of the wireless access point changes, you might not be able to connect to it in the future.

To change the configuration of a wireless network after the original configuration, follow these steps:

1. Click Start, right-click Network, and then click Properties.
2. In the left pane, click the Manage Wireless Networks link.
3. Right-click the network you want to reconfigure, and then click Properties.
   The Wireless Network Properties dialog box appears.
4. As shown in Figure 11-4, you can use the Connection tab to specify whether Windows Vista will automatically connect to the network when it is in range (assuming no other wireless connection already exists).

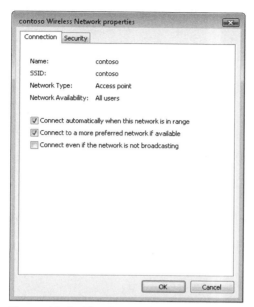

Figure 11-4   The Connection tab of the Wireless Network Properties dialog box

5. As shown in Figure 11-5, you can use the Security tab to specify the security and encryption types for this connection. Depending on the security type, Windows Vista will show other options in the dialog box.

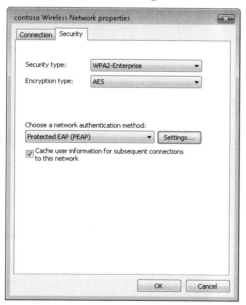

Figure 11-5   Using the Wireless Network Properties dialog box to change security settings

6. Click OK.

After reconfiguring the network connection, attempt to reconnect to the network to verify your settings.

Practice: Connect to Wireless Networks

In these practices, you connect to three types of wireless networks.

▶ **Practice 1: Configure an Unencrypted Wireless Access Point**

In this practice, you connect to an unencrypted wireless network. To complete this practice, you must have a wireless access point and a Windows Vista computer with a wireless network adapter.

1. Access your wireless access point's configuration page. Typically, you can manage wireless access points using a Web browser. Specify an SSID of "Contoso" with no network security.

2. On your Windows Vista computer, click Start, and then click Connect To.
    The Connect To A Network Wizard appears.

3. On the Disconnect Or Connect To Another Network page, select Contoso, and then click Connect.

4. On the Contoso Is An Unsecured Network page, click Connect Anyway.

5. On the Successfully Connected To Contoso page, click Close.

6. On the Select A Location For The Contoso Network, click Work, and then respond to the UAC prompt that appears. Notice that you need to provide administrative credentials if you select a Work or Home network type (which are both equivalent to Private network) but not if you select a Public network type.

7. On the Successfully Set Network Settings page, click Close.

Notice that it was very easy to connect to an unsecured wireless network; you required no knowledge of the wireless network at all. Windows Vista detected the network and allowed you to connect to it. Also notice that standard users without administrative credentials could configure the new network only as Public, meaning their computer would be more protected from threats that might exist on the network.

▶ **Practice 2: Configure a WEP-encrypted Wireless Access Point**

In this practice, you connect to a WEP-encrypted wireless network. To complete this practice, you must have a wireless access point and a Windows Vista computer with a wireless network adapter.

1. Access your wireless access point's configuration page. Typically, you can manage wireless access points using a Web browser. Specify an SSID of "Contoso2" with WEP or

WEP Open security. Provide a complex key if your wireless access point does not automatically generate one for you, and make note of that key.

2. On your Windows Vista computer, click Start, and then click Connect To.

    The Connect To A Network Wizard appears.

3. On the Disconnect Or Connect To Another Network page, notice that Contoso2 is shown as a secure network. Select Contoso2, and then click Connect.

4. On the Type The Network Security Key Or Passphrase For Contoso2 page, provide the same security key you provided at the wireless access point. Then, click Connect.

5. On the Successfully Connected To Contoso2 page, click Close.

6. On the Select A Location For The Contoso2 Network, click Public Location. Notice that you don't need administrative credentials to configure the network as Public because Windows Firewall will aggressively protect the computer from incoming connects on the Public network, reducing security risks.

7. On the Successfully Set Network Settings page, click Close.

Notice that WEP encryption required you to type a passphrase. Whether you connect one computer or 1000 computers to the WEP-protected network, you'll use the same passphrase. For that reason, it's difficult to manage. For example, if you decide you don't want a particular client to connect to the wireless network in the future, you would need to change the WEP encryption key on the wireless access point and on every single wireless client. In a business environment you would need to change the WEP key every time an employee left the organization—making it impossible to manage if you have more than about a dozen employees.

▶ **Practice 3: Configure a WPA-PSK Encrypted Wireless Access Point**

In this practice, you connect to a wireless network protected by WPA-PSK. To complete this practice, you must have a wireless access point and a Windows Vista computer with a wireless network adapter.

1. Access your wireless access point's configuration page. Typically, you can manage wireless access points using a Web browser. Specify an SSID of "Contoso3" with WPA2-PSK security if available, or WPA-PSK (also known as WPA-Personal) security. Provide a complex passphrase between 8 and 63 characters—the longer, the more secure. Make note of that key.

2. On your Windows Vista computer, click Start, and then click Connect To.

    The Connect To A Network Wizard appears.

3. On the Disconnect Or Connect To Another Network page, notice that Windows Vista doesn't distinguish between networks protected with WEP or WPA; all networks with any level of encryption are shown the same way. Select Contoso3, and then click Connect.

4. On the Type The Network Security Key Or Passphrase For Contoso3 page, type the same security key you provided at the wireless access point. Then, click Connect.

5. On the Successfully Connected To Contoso3 page, click Close.

6. On the Select A Location For The Contoso3 Network, click Public Location.

7. On the Successfully Set Network Settings page, click Close.

Notice that WPA-PSK encryption required exactly the same process as WEP (besides allowing a longer passphrase). WPA-PSK is more secure against attacks that attempt to break the encryption. However, you'd still have the same management challenge because every client computer uses the same key.

Lesson Summary

- Wireless networking is extremely easy to deploy because you don't have to run cables through a building. Additionally, it's easy to manage in public locations because the networking gear can be locked away. However, because wireless networks are not physically protected, they can be much more difficult to secure.

- Windows Vista includes several important wireless networking improvements, including:
  - Friendlier user interfaces.
  - Single sign-on.
  - WPA2 support.
  - Support for hidden wireless networks.
  - Integration with NAP.

- Windows Vista supports the following wireless security protocols, in order from least to most secure:
  - WEP
  - WPA-PSK
  - WPA2-PSK
  - WPA-EAP
  - WPA2-EAP

- To connect to a wireless network that is currently in range, click Start, and then click Connect To. You can also configure wireless networks using Group Policy settings or the Netsh command-line tool.

- To change settings on a wireless network you have previously connected to, open Network And Sharing Center, and then click Manage Wireless Networks. Then, right-click the wireless network and click Properties.

Lesson Review

You can use the following questions to test your knowledge of the information in Lesson 1, "Configuring Wireless Networking." The questions are also available on the companion CD if you prefer to review them in electronic form.

NOTE Answers

Answers to these questions and explanations of why each answer choice is right or wrong are located in the "Answers" section at the end of the book.

1. Which of the following wireless security technologies provides the strongest security?
    A. No security
    B. Wired Equivalent Protection (WEP)
    C. Wi-Fi Protected Access, preshared key (WPA-PSK)
    D. Wi-Fi Protected Access-Wired Equivalent Protection (WPA-EAP)

2. You want users to be able to authenticate to your wireless network using a smart card. Which of the following wireless security protocols can you use? (Choose all that apply.)
    A. Wired Equivalent Protection (WEP)
    B. Wi-Fi Protected Access, preshared key (WPA-PSK)
    C. Wi-Fi Protected Access-Wired Equivalent Protection (WPA-EAP)
    D. Wi-Fi Protected Access 2-Wired Equivalent Protection (WPA2-EAP)

3. Which of the following types of credentials are supported for connecting to a wireless network protected by Wi-Fi Protected Access-Wired Equivalent Protection (WPA-EAP)? (Choose all that apply.)
    A. Domain credentials
    B. Static key
    C. A certificate stored on the local computer
    D. A certificate stored on a smart card

Lesson 2: Advanced Wireless Configuration and Troubleshooting

Most users will have no problem connecting to the wireless network configurations described in Lesson 1, "Configuring Wireless Networking." However, many enterprises use more complex wireless security leveraging Active Directory credentials or certificates. As complexity increases, so does the likelihood of problems. For that reason, troubleshooting wireless network problems is extremely important.

This lesson describes how to configure advanced wireless networks (such as WPA-EAP) and how to troubleshoot common wireless networking problems.

After this lesson, you will be able to:
- Set the priority of wireless networks.
- Create an ad hoc wireless network.
- Configure a client computer to connect to a WPA-EAP protected wireless network.
- Change the wireless network profile type from all-user to per-user.
- Troubleshoot common wireless network problems.
- Use Event Viewer to analyze wireless connection problems.

Estimated lesson time: 20 minutes

Changing the Priorities of Wireless Networks

Many locations have multiple wireless networks available at the same time. For example, if your office is located over a coffee shop, you might be able to connect to either your office wireless network or the coffee shop's public wireless network. To complicate matters more, you might specifically want to use the coffee shop wireless network when you're not in the office and use your office wireless network at all other times.

To ensure that you connect to the correct network when multiple wireless networks are available, you can prioritize wireless networks. To set the priority of wireless networks, follow these steps:

1. Click Start, right-click Network, and then click Properties.
2. In the left pane, click the Manage Wireless Networks link.
3. In the Manage Wireless Networks window, select a wireless network profile, and then click Move Up or Move Down.

When multiple networks are available, Windows Vista will always connect to the network listed first. If Windows Vista connects to the wrong network, click Start, click Connect To, and then manually connect to the network you would prefer to be connected to.

Creating an Ad Hoc Wireless Network

Most wireless networks use a wireless access point. Just like a hub or a switch in a wired network, all wireless clients connect to the wireless access point, and all peer-to-peer communications pass through the wireless access point.

Occasionally, traveling users might want to share files or other network resources when they don't have access to a wireless access point. For example, if two users are in an airport, it would be nice if they could share resources across a network without installing any infrastructure. Ad hoc wireless networks enable this.

In an ad hoc wireless network, two or more wireless clients communicate directly with each other without connecting to a wireless access point. To create an ad hoc wireless network, follow these steps:

1. Click Start, and then click Connect To.
    The Connect To A Network Wizard appears.
2. On the Disconnect Or Connect To Another Network page, near the bottom-left corner, click the Set Up A Connection Or Network link.
3. On the Choose A Connection Option page, click Set Up A Wireless Ad Hoc (Computer-To-Computer) Network. Click Next.
4. On the Set Up A Wireless Ad Hoc Network page, click Next.
5. On the Give Your Network A Name And Choose Security Options page, type a unique Network Name. Other users who connect to your ad hoc network will choose this network to connect.
6. In the Security Type list, you can choose between No Authentication, WPA2-Personal, and WEP. You should always choose WPA2-Personal because No Authentication or WEP might allow uninvited users to connect to your ad hoc network or view your network traffic. Then, type a security key, as shown in Figure 11-6.

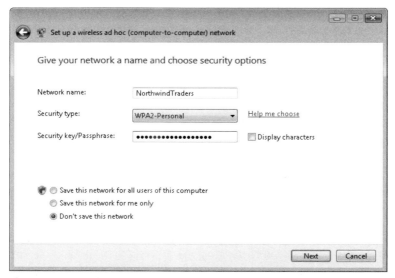

Figure 11-6   Using an ad hoc wireless network

7. Click Next.

8. On the final page, click Close.

Now that you have established the ad hoc wireless network, you can connect to it from other computers using the same process you would use to connect to a wireless access point.

Configuring WPA-EAP Security

The static keys used by WEP and WPA-PSK aren't manageable in enterprise environments. If an employee ever left, you'd need to change the key on the wireless access point to prevent the employee from connecting to the network in the future. Then, you would need to update every wireless client computer in your organization.

Remember, the EAP in WPA-EAP stands for Extensible Authentication Protocol. Because it is extensible, you can authenticate using several methods:

■ PEAP-MS-CHAPv2 to enable users to connect to a wireless network using their domain credentials

■ Certificates stored on the user's computers

■ Certificates stored on smart cards

Whichever authentication method you choose, Windows Vista uses the same authentication process. As shown in Figure 11-7, the wireless client computer passes the credentials to the wireless access point, which forwards them to a RADIUS server, which then authenticates the user against the Active Directory. Although Figure 11-7 shows the RADIUS server and the domain controller as separate servers, you can install both services on the same physical computer.

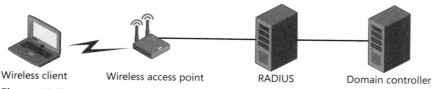

Wireless client   Wireless access point   RADIUS   Domain controller

Figure 11-7   How WPA uses a RADIUS server for authentication

Windows Server 2003 includes the Internet Authentication Service (IAS), which acts as a RADIUS server that is tightly integrated with Active Directory. When configuring IAS, you can specify a domain security group that will be granted access to the wireless network. For this reason, you should create a group specifically for users with the right to access the wireless network.

NOTE   Configuring a RADIUS server

Because this certification exam focuses on Windows Vista, this chapter will not discuss how to configure the RADIUS server in detail. However, Practice 2 at the end of this lesson walks you through the process of configuring an IAS server and a wireless access point to enable users to authenticate to a wireless network using their Active Directory credentials.

By default, when you connect to a new WPA-EAP or WPA2-EAP network, Windows Vista is configured to use the Secured Password (EAP-MSCHAP v2) authentication method to allow users to authenticate with their domain credentials. If users should authenticate using a certificate (whether stored on the local computer or on a smart card), create a wireless network profile for the network using the default settings and then follow these steps to configure the wireless network security:

1. Click Start, right-click Network, and then click Properties.
2. In the left pane of the Network And Sharing Center, click the Manage Wireless Networks link.
3. Select and right-click the network, and then click Properties. Then, click the Security tab.
4. Click the Choose A Network Authentication Method list, and then click Smart Card Or Other Certificate, as shown in Figure 11-8.

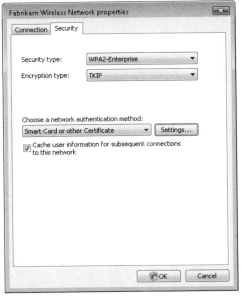

Figure 11-8   Manually editing a wireless network profile's properties to authenticate using a certificate

---

NOTE   Requiring users to insert smart cards

Notice that the Cache User Information For Subsequent Connections To This Network check box is selected by default. If you want users to insert their smart cards every time they connect to the network, clear this check box.

---

5. Click the Settings button. If the certificate is stored on the local computer, select Use A Certificate On This Computer in the When Connecting group, as shown in Figure 11-9. If you are using a smart card, select Use My Smart Card.

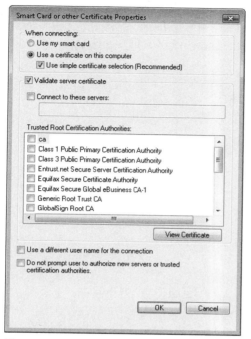

Figure 11-9   Choosing between storing a certificate on the local computer or on a smart card

---

NOTE   Validating the server certificate

Notice that the Validate Server Certificate check box is selected by default. This verifies that the RADIUS server has a certificate from a trusted CA before sending the credentials. That's important because you wouldn't want to send your credentials to a malicious server, which could then misuse them. However, it will cause the client to reject the RADIUS server if the RADIUS server has a certificate from an Enterprise CA (or any CA that isn't trusted by default), and the client computer hasn't connected to the domain since the Enterprise CA was added to the domain. To work around this the first time you connect to a domain (after which the client computer will trust the enterprise CA), clear the Validate Server Certificate check box, connect to the wireless network and to the domain, and then select the Validate Server Certificate check box again.

---

6.   Click OK twice. Respond to the UAC prompt when it appears.

The next time the user connects using the profile, Windows Vista attempts to automatically find a suitable certificate. If it cannot find one or if the user needs to insert a smart card, Windows Vista prompts the user to select a certificate, as shown in Figure 11-10.

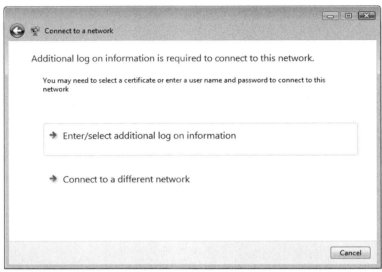

Figure 11-10   How Windows Vista prompts the user if a certificate cannot be automatically found

Configuring Wireless Network Profile Types

Most mobile computers are used by only a single user. However, if mobile computers in your organization are shared among multiple users, you might want to configure wireless networks to use per-user profiles. With per-user profiles, one user can connect to a wireless network without other users being able to use the same wireless network connection.

Per-user wireless profiles are important if, for example, a user configures a shared mobile computer to connect to his or her home wireless network. The default configuration of all user profiles would allow any other user of that computer to visit the original user's home and connect to the wireless network without being prompted for a security key—even if the wireless network uses security.

To change a wireless profile to per-user instead of all-user, follow these steps:

1. Click Start. Right-click Network, and then click Properties.
    The Network And Sharing Center appears.
2. In the left pane, click the Manage Wireless Networks link.
    The Manage Wireless Networks window appears.
3. Click Profile Types.

4. In the Wireless Network Profile Types dialog box, select Use All-User And Per-User Profiles, as shown in Figure 11-11.

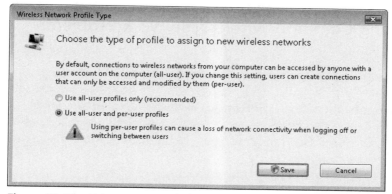

Figure 11-11   Using per-user wireless profiles to prevent users from sharing wireless connection configurations

5. Click Save. When prompted, provide UAC credentials.

After enabling per-user profiles, all existing wireless profiles will still be available to all users. However, the next time you connect to a new wireless network, Windows Vista will prompt you to choose how you want to store the wireless network profile, as shown in Figure 11-12. If you want to convert an existing wireless network profile from all-users to per-user, delete it and re-create it.

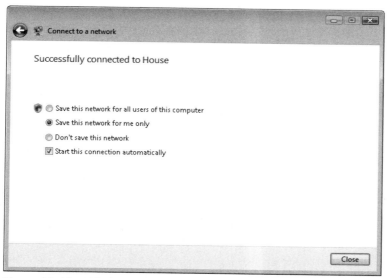

Figure 11-12   Windows Vista prompts you to create a new wireless network profile as per-user or all-user

One of the unwelcome side-effects of per-user wireless profiles is that the computer is disconnected from the wireless network when a user logs off.

Troubleshooting Common Wireless Network Problems

Some of the most common wireless networking problems include the following:

■ **Network adapter cannot see any wireless networks**   If your network adapter cannot see any wireless networks even though wireless networks are available, the network adapter might be turned off at the hardware level. Most mobile computers include either a dedicated hardware switch or a key combination that turns the wireless radio on or off. As shown in Figure 11-13, Windows Network Diagnostics will correctly detect this condition.

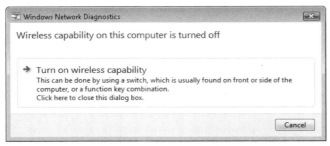

Figure 11-13   One of the most common wireless problems: a radio that has been turned off at the hardware level

You should also use Device Manager to verify that your wireless network adapter was detected and has a valid driver. To launch Device Manager, click Start, type **devmgmt.msc**, and press Enter. Then, expand Network Adapters. If the wireless radio is off, Windows Vista will still detect the network adapter—it just won't be able to use it.

■ **Weak wireless signal**   The farther you move from the wireless access point, the weaker the signal is going to be. The weaker the signal, the slower the network performance. You can, however, do several things to improve the range of a wireless signal:

❑ Move the wireless access point away from metal cabinets, computers, or other objects that might block the wireless signals.

❑ If attempting to connect from outdoors, remove screens from windows. Screens do not block a wireless signal, but they introduce a significant amount of noise.

❑ Adjust the antenna on the wireless access point. For greatest efficiency, have someone slowly move the wireless access point antenna while a second person monitors the signal strength from a computer at the target location.

❑ Use a high-gain antenna, also known as a directional antenna. Low-gain antennas (also known as a omnidirectional antennas) broadcast in all directions relatively equally. High-gain antennas are very directional. If you need to cover a specific area, point a high-gain antenna at the location. Some wireless network adapters also support high-gain antennas. For best efficiency, use a high-gain antenna on both the wireless access point and the computer.

NOTE Using a high-gain antenna

Many people incorrectly believe that high-gain antennas are more powerful. The antenna itself can't increase power—that's controlled by the transmitter within the wireless access point. The antenna does, however, control the direction of the signal. High-gain antennas just focus the transmitting power in a specific direction, offering a stronger signal in some areas while decreasing the signal in other locations.

❑ Increase the power at the transmitter. Many wireless access points allow you to configure the transmitter power. Although the default setting is typically the maximum, another administrator might have reduced the transmitter power.

❑ Increase the power at the client computer. All network connections are two-way. Therefore, in order for a connection to be established, the signals transmitted by the computer must be strong enough to reach the wireless access point. Many wireless network adapters allow you to configure the transmitter power from the wireless network adapter properties dialog box, as shown in Figure 11-14. This will be different for every wireless network adapter. Increasing the transmitter power can also increase battery usage.

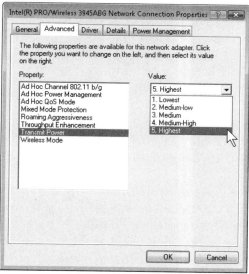

Figure 11-14 Some wireless network adapters allow you to configure the transmitter strength

---

NOTE How to view wireless signal strength

You can view the wireless signal strength by clicking the network icon in the status bar or by opening the Network And Sharing Center.

■ **Windows Vista cannot reconnect to a wireless network** Typically, if you cannot connect to a wireless network that you have previously connected to, it is because security settings on the network have changed. For example, if the wireless network uses WEP, an administrator might have changed the key. To change the security key, follow the steps in the section entitled "Reconfiguring a Wireless Network" in Lesson 1, "Configuring Wireless Networking." Alternatively, you could simply remove the wireless network profile and connect to the network as if it were a new network.

■ **Poor performance** Several factors can cause poor network performance:

  ❑ A weak wireless signal, as discussed earlier.

  ❑ Interference. 802.11b, 802.11g, and 802.11n use the 2.4GHz radio frequency, while 802.11a uses the 5.8GHz frequency. Cordless phone or other wireless devices on the same frequency can introduce performance problems.

  ❑ Overlapping wireless access points. Wireless access points can broadcast on one of 11 channels (from 1-11). If two wireless access points broadcast on the same channel or on a channel within five channels of another wireless access point, the performance of both can be reduced. For best results, use channels 1, 6, and 11 when wireless access points overlap.

  ❑ Multiple wireless frequencies. 802.11n and 802.11g are backward-compatible with 802.11b. However, supporting 802.11b clients on either 802.11n or 802.11g networks can significantly reduce performance. If possible, upgrade all wireless clients to the fastest wireless network standard supported by your wireless access points. Then, configure your wireless access point to use "802.11g Only" or "802.11n Only" modes.

  ❑ Significant network traffic. All wireless clients compete for a limited amount of bandwidth. If one client is downloading a large file, that can affect the performance of all clients.

■ **Intermittent or otherwise unexplained problems** Wireless network protocols have changed a great deal in a short time. Unfortunately, it's common that wireless network hardware from different vendors will have difficulty interoperating. For example, many vendors released wireless access points based on the 802.11n standard before the standard was finalized. If you're using a wireless network adapter that fully implements 802.11n and you're attempting to connect to a wireless access point based on pre-802.11n standards, you might not be able to connect, you might experience intermittent failures, or performance might be reduced. For best results, upgrade all wireless access point firmware and network adapter drivers to the latest versions. Then, work with the hardware vendor's technical support to continue troubleshooting the problem.

Using Event Viewer to Analyze Wireless Connection Problems

If a user calls you to discuss a problem connecting to a wireless network, that user might not have all the critical technical details that you need to know. Although the user might remember the SSID, the user probably doesn't know the security type required by the network or whether the network was 802.11b, 802.11g, or something different. Fortunately, Windows Vista records these technical details every time a user connects to a network.

To view the details of wireless networks a user has connected to, follow these steps:

1. Click Start. Right-click Computer, and then click Manage.
2. Under Computer Management, expand System Tools, Event Viewer, Applications And Services Logs, Microsoft, Windows, and WLAN-AutoConfig. Then, select Operational.
3. In the middle pane, select an event log entry.

This event log shows the details of attempted and successful connections to a wireless network. Figure 11-15 shows an example of Event ID 8001, which provides the details of a successful wireless network connection. As you can see, it shows the wireless network's SSID (Contoso4), the wireless network type (802.11g), and the authentication type (WPA2-Enterprise).

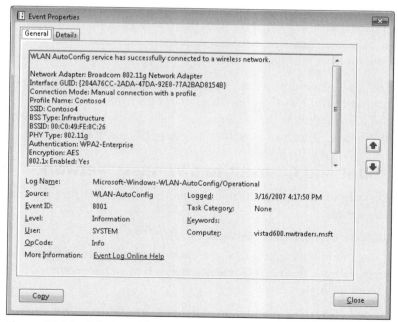

Figure 11-15 Windows Vista creates an event when it successfully connects to a wireless network

Figure 11-16 shows an example of Event ID 12103, which indicates a wireless authentication failure. As you can see, this event shows the wireless network's SSID (Cotoso4) and the reason for the failure (Explicit Eap Failure Received). Using the time of the event, you could correlate the authentication failure with an event on the RADIUS server or the domain controller.

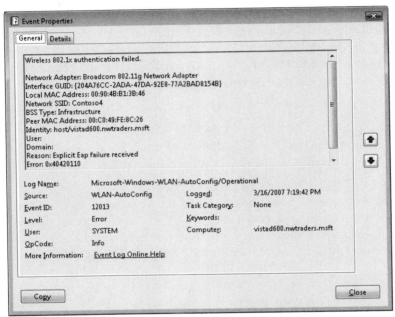

Figure 11-16   How Windows Vista records detailed information about wireless network problems

Windows Vista adds several events for any successful or unsuccessful connection. Additionally, if the user started Windows Network Diagnostics for troubleshooting assistance, you might find useful information in the System event log and the Applications And Services Logs\Microsoft\Windows\Diagnostics-Networking\Operational event log.

Practice: Troubleshoot and Connect to a Wireless Network

In these practices, you troubleshoot a wireless network connection, and then connect to a WPA-EAP wireless network.

▶ **Practice 1: Troubleshoot a Wireless Network Problem**

In this practice, you attempt to connect to a wireless network that has been previously configured with incorrect settings. To complete this practice, you must have completed Practice 1 in Lesson 1, "Configuring Wireless Networking."

1.   Access your wireless access point's configuration page. Typically, you can manage wireless access points using a Web browser. Specify an SSID of "Contoso" with WEP or WEP

Open security. Provide a complex key if your wireless access point does not automatically generate one for you, and make note of that key.

2. On your Windows Vista computer, click Start, and then click Connect To.

   The Connect To A Network Wizard appears.

3. On the Disconnect Or Connect To Another Network page, select Contoso.

   This time the Connect To A Network Wizard shows an error message. Because you had previously configured the Contoso wireless network with no security, it cannot automatically connect.

4. Right-click Contoso, and then click Diagnose.

   Wireless Network Diagnostics attempts to identify the problem.

5. In the Wireless Network Diagnostics dialog box, click View Wireless Security Settings To Verify That Correct Encryption Type Is Selected.

6. The Contoso Wireless Network Properties dialog box appears, allowing you to change the wireless security settings. Click the Security Type list, and then click No Authentication (Open). Then, click the Encryption Type list and click WEP. In the Network Security Key box, type the key you provided to the wireless access point. Then, click OK.

7. The Wireless Network Diagnostics dialog box reappears. Select Click Here When You Are Done to have Wireless Network Diagnostics retest the connection.

8. Click Close when Windows Network Diagnostics notifies you that the problem was resolved.

Now open Microsoft Internet Explorer to verify that you can connect to the Internet across your wireless link.

▶ **Practice 2: Configure a WPA-EAP Encrypted Wireless Access Point**

In this practice, you connect to a WPA-EAP protected wireless network. To complete this practice, you must have a wireless access point and a Windows Vista computer with a wireless network adapter. Additionally, you must have configured your Windows Server 2003 domain controller as an enterprise CA. For detailed instructions, complete Practice 3 of Lesson 1, "Configuring and Troubleshooting Internet Explorer Security," in Chapter 5, "Protecting Internet Explorer and Other Applications."

1. Log on to your Windows Server 2003 domain controller.

2. Click Start, Administrative Tools, and then Active Directory Users And Computers. Right-click Nwtraders.Msft (or your domain name), and then click Raise Domain Functional Level. In the Raise Domain Functional Level dialog box, select Windows Server 2003, and then click Raise. Then, click OK twice. The domain must be at the Windows Server 2003 functional level to support remote access policies.

3. In the Active Directory Users And Computers console, right-click Users, click New, and then click Group. Specify a Group Name of Wireless Users. Then, click OK. Double-click

the new group and click the Members tab. Use the Add button to specify the user account you will use to connect to the wireless network.

4. Click Start, Control Panel, and then Add Or Remove Programs.

5. In Add Or Remove Programs, click Add/Remove Windows Components.

   The Windows Components Wizard appears.

6. On the Windows Components page, select Networking Services. Then, click Details.

7. In the Networking Services dialog box, select the Internet Authentication Service check box. Then, click OK.

8. On the Windows Components page of the Windows Components Wizard, click Next.

   The Windows Components Wizard installs the IAS, which enables Windows Server 2003 to act as a RADIUS server. The wireless access point will send authentication requests for wireless clients to the RADIUS server, which in turn will check the Active Directory to determine if the wireless client should be allowed.

9. On the Completing The Windows Components Wizard page, click Finish.

   Now you need to configure the IAS to accept requests from the wireless access point.

10. On the Windows Server 2003 computer, click Start, click Administrative Tools, and then click Internet Authentication Service.

11. Right-click RADIUS Clients, and then click New RADIUS Client.

   The New RADIUS Client Wizard appears.

12. On the Name And Address Page, type a Friendly Name of Wireless Access Point. In the Client Address, type the IP address of your wireless access point, as shown in Figure 11-17. Click Next.

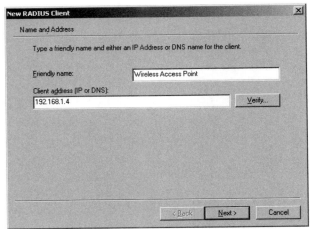

Figure 11-17   Configuring your wireless access point as a RADIUS client to use WPA or WPA2 in any mode other than PSK

13. On the Additional Information page, leave RADIUS Standard selected as the Client-Vendor type. Then, type a shared secret passphrase in the Shared Secret and Confirm Shared Secret boxes. Make note of this passphrase; you'll need to provide it on your wireless access point. Click Finish.

14. In the Internet Authentication Service console, right-click Internet Authentication Service, and then click Register Server In Active Directory. Click OK twice when prompted.

15. In the Internet Authentication Service console, right-click Remote Access Policies, and then click New Remote Access Policy.

    The New Remote Access Policy Wizard appears.

16. On the Welcome To The New Remote Access Policy Wizard page, click Next.

17. On the Policy Configuration Method page, verify that Use The Wizard To Set Up A Typical Policy For A Common Scenario is selected. Then, type a Policy Name of **Wireless Access**. Click Next.

18. On the Access Method page, select Wireless, as shown in Figure 11-18. Then, click Next.

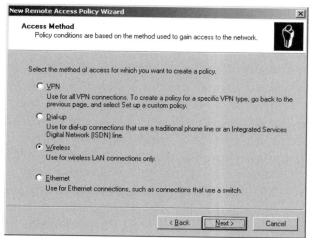

Figure 11-18   The Windows Server wizard for creating a wireless access policy

19. On the User Or Group Access page, verify that Group is selected. Then, click Add, select the Wireless Users group, and click OK. Click Next.

20. On the Authentication Methods page, select the default setting of Protected EAP (PEAP). Click Next.

21. On the Completing The New Remote Access Policy Wizard page, click Finish.

22. Access your wireless access point's configuration page. Typically, you can manage wireless access points using a Web browser. Specify an SSID of "Contoso4." For the security type, select WPA2 (which might be shown as WPA2-Enterprise, WPA2-EAP, WPA2 with 802.1X, WPA2 with RADIUS, or simply WPA2). If your wireless access point does not

support WPA2, select standard WPA—but choose the option that supports authenticating to a RADIUS server rather than using a static key. For the RADIUS server, specify your Windows Server 2003 computer's IP address, a port number of 1812, and the shared key you specified.

23. On your Windows Vista computer, click Start, and then click Connect To.

    The Connect To A Network Wizard appears.

24. Click Contoso4, and then click Connect.

25. If you are prompted to verify the certificate authority, click OK.

26. On the Successfully Connected To Contoso4 page, click Close.

Setting up WPA-EAP took significantly longer than any other wireless security method. However, connecting to the wireless network was simpler than any other method because it did not require the user to specify a security key. The user's Active Directory account was the only authentication required, providing single sign-on for wireless access. Additionally, when users leave the organization, you only need to disable their accounts to prevent them from accessing the wireless network—you don't need to reconfigure the wireless access point at all.

Lesson Summary

- You can change the priorities of wireless networks from the Manage Wireless Networks window. Windows Vista will connect to networks higher on the list when multiple networks are available.

- Ad hoc wireless networks enable two or more wireless computers to network without a wireless access point. To create an ad hoc wireless network, click Start, click Connect To, click Set Up A Connection Or Network, and then click Set Up A Wireless Ad Hoc (Computer-To-Computer) Network. Then, follow the prompts that appear.

- WPA-EAP and WPA2-EAP provide the strongest protection for wireless networks. Properly configured, users can connect to networks protected with one of these security standards without being prompted. However, using WPA-EAP or WPA2-EAP requires a RADIUS server.

- Wireless network profiles are available for all users by default, which means that any user can connect to a network created by any other user. You can change this behavior, however, so that users are prompted to create a wireless network for all users or just for their user account.

- The most common wireless network problem is turning off a mobile computer's wireless radio; this is solved by turning the wireless radio back on. Other common problems include weak signal strength, poor network performance, incompatibilities, and wireless network settings that have changed since the network was first configured.

■ You can use the Applications And Services Logs\Microsoft\Windows\WLAN-AutoConfig \Operational to determine which networks a user has connected to and view any problems that occurred.

Lesson Review

You can use the following questions to test your knowledge of the information in Lesson 2, "Advanced Wireless Configuration and Troubleshooting." The questions are also available on the companion CD if you prefer to review them in electronic form.

NOTE Answers

Answers to these questions and explanations of why each answer choice is right or wrong are located in the "Answers" section at the end of the book.

---

1. A user complains that she attempted to connect to a wireless network, but the connection failed. She didn't write down any details of the connection. In which log would you look to find the details of her connection attempt?

   A. Applications And Services Logs\Microsoft\Windows\Diagnostics-Networking \Operational

   B. System

   C. Applications And Services Logs\Microsoft\Windows\Wired-AutoConfig \Operational

   D. Applications And Services Logs\Microsoft\Windows\WLAN-AutoConfig \Operational

2. You attempt to connect to a wireless network by clicking Start and then clicking Connect To. However, Windows Vista does not detect any wireless networks in the area. You look at the person next to you, and he is able to connect to a wireless network. You verify that Device Manager shows a wireless network adapter under the *Network Adapters* node. Which of the following might be the cause of your problem? (Choose all that apply.)

   A. You do not have a wireless network adapter installed.

   B. Your wireless radio has been turned off at the hardware level.

   C. The wireless network is configured to not broadcast a service set identifier (SSID).

   D. The wireless network is secured and you have not been granted access.

3. You and a coworker are traveling to a customer location and are waiting in a crowded airport for your flight to board. You've made some modifications to a presentation and need to send the updated presentation to your coworker's computer. You'd like to use a wireless network, but there is no wireless access point available. You decide to create an ad hoc network, but you don't want anyone else in the airport to be able to connect to your network or view your traffic. Which security types can you apply to your ad hoc network? (Choose all that apply.)

    A.   Wired Equivalent Protection (WEP)

    B.   Wi-Fi Protected Access, preshared key (WPA-PSK)

    C.   Wi-Fi Protected Access-Wired Equivalent Protection (WPA-EAP)

    D.   Wi-Fi Protected Access 2-Wired Equivalent Protection (WPA2-EAP)

4. Which of the following is required to configure a wireless network with Wi-Fi Protected Access-Wired Equivalent Protection (WPA-EAP) security?

    A.   An enterprise certification authority (CA)

    B.   An Active Directory domain

    C.   A Remote Authentication Dial-In User Service (RADIUS) server

    D.   Smart cards

Chapter Review

To further practice and reinforce the skills you learned in this chapter, you can

- Review the chapter summary.
- Review the list of key terms introduced in this chapter.
- Complete the case scenarios. These scenarios set up real-world situations involving the topics of this chapter and ask you to create a solution.
- Complete the suggested practices.
- Take a practice test.

Chapter Summary

- Connecting to wireless networks is simple enough for most users to do without assistance. Typically, you just need to click Start, click Connect To, and then follow the prompts that appear. For organizations that need to automate the configuration of wireless networks, you can also configure wireless network profiles using Group Policy settings or scripts.
- If more than one wireless network is available at a single location, you can configure the priority of the wireless networks to control the order Windows Vista uses when connecting to them. If no wireless access point is available, you can create an ad hoc wireless network to allow two or more wireless computers to connect directly to each other.

Key Terms

Do you know what these key terms mean? You can check your answers by looking up the terms in the glossary at the end of the book.

- hotspot
- SSID
- Wired Equivalent Protection (WEP)
- Wi-Fi Protected Access (WPA)

Case Scenarios

In the following case scenarios, you will apply what you've learned about how to connect to and troubleshoot wireless networks. You can find answers to these questions in the "Answers" section at the end of this book.

Case Scenario 1: Teaching a User to Connect to Wireless Networks

You are a desktop support technician for City Power & Light. You receive a phone call from Parry Bedi, who just received a new mobile computer and is planning to take a trip to a customer site. Parry needs to be able to connect to wireless networks at the airport and hotel to check e-mail.

Questions

Answer the following questions for Parry:

1. How can I connect to a wireless network at the airport?
2. Are there any security risks using public wireless networks?
3. If the network is unencrypted, how can I protect the privacy of my data?
4. Will Windows Vista automatically connect to wireless networks as I travel?

Case Scenario 2: Troubleshooting Problems Connecting to a Wireless Network

You are a desktop support technician for City Power & Light. You receive a phone call from Parry Bedi, who is attempting to connect to the wireless network at the airport but is experiencing problems. Parry can connect to the network, but the connection doesn't seem stable—e-mail is downloading extremely slowly, and occasionally the connection disappears completely.

Questions

Answer the following questions about Parry's problem:

1. What is the most likely cause of Parry's problem, and how can Parry fix it?
2. What are some other possible causes of Parry's problem?

Suggested Practices

To successfully master the configure and troubleshoot wireless networking exam objective, complete the following tasks.

Configure and Troubleshoot Wireless Networking

For this task, you should complete at least Practices 1 and 2. If you want a better understanding of how wireless networks are used in the real world, do Practice 3 as well. To understand the real-world strength or weakness of WEP encryption, complete Practice 4. To better understand the Network Location Awareness service, view the virtual lab described in Practice 5.

- **Practice 1: Testing Wireless Range**   Connect to a wireless network with a mobile computer. Open a command prompt and run the command **ping -t** gateway to continuously ping your default gateway. The ping loop enables you to monitor whether you are connected to the local area network. Now, begin walking away from the wireless access point. How far do you get before you start to lose your connection? How does Windows Vista behave?

- **Practice 2: Browsing from a Public Hotspot**   Visit a coffee shop, airport, or other location with a public wireless hotspot. Connect to the wireless network and use it to browse the Internet.

- **Practice 3: Wardriving**   Walk or be driven through an urban area with a Windows Vista mobile computer. Open the Connect To A Network Wizard and regularly refresh the list of available wireless network connections. Make note of the number of available wireless networks, as well as the percentage of them that are unsecured.

- **Practice 4: Cracking WEP**   Download free tools from the Internet to crack WEP-protected wireless networks. Then, attempt to crack into your own 64-bit WEP-protected wireless network. Do you have the necessary hardware? If so, how long does it take you to break in? Now, repeat the process with 128-bit WEP. Are you successful, and if so, how long did it take? How long in total did you spend researching, configuring, and running the software?

- **Practice 5: Viewing a Virtual Lab**   View the virtual lab titled "Network Location Awareness Virtual Lab" at *https://msevents.microsoft.com/CUI/EventDetail.aspx?EventID=1032339411*.

Take a Practice Test

The practice tests on this book's companion CD offer many options. For example, you can test yourself on just the content covered in this chapter, or you can test yourself on all the 70-622 certification exam content. You can set up the test so that it closely simulates the experience of taking a certification exam, or you can set it up in study mode so that you can look at the correct answers and explanations after you answer each question.

MORE INFO   **Practice tests**

For details about all the practice test options available, see "How to Use the Practice Tests" in this book's Introduction.

Chapter 12

Managing Shared Desktops

Windows Vista includes two separate remote access features, each of which allows you to connect to the desktop of a remote computer in a different way. Whereas Remote Desktop allows you to establish your own user session on a remote computer, Remote Assistance allows you to connect to a remote user's live session.

For the 70-622 exam, you are expected to know how to implement, configure, and troubleshoot both of these remote access technologies.

Exam objectives in this chapter:
- Configure and troubleshoot remote access.

Lessons in this chapter:

Before You Begin

To complete the lessons in this chapter, you must have

- A domain controller running Microsoft Windows Server 2003 named dcsrv1.nwtraders .msft.

- Two Windows Vista Enterprise, Business, or Ultimate computers named Vista1 and Vista2, respectively. Both Vista1 and Vista2 must be members of the Nwtraders domain.

- A Windows XP Professional computer named Xpclient that is a member of the Nwtraders domain. Xpclient must *not* have the Terminal Services Client 6.0 update for Windows XP (KB925876) installed.

Real World

JC Mackin

Though this won't be covered on any IT certification exam, there is a "trick" you should know for the real world that lets you enable Remote Desktop remotely. Of course, you're supposed to enable Remote Desktop locally on any box that you later want to reach through a Remote Desktop Connection, but there are bound to be cases when you will need to RDP in to a computer that doesn't yet have the feature enabled. When you're in this kind of a situation, use Regedit on the local computer and the Connect Network Registry command to connect to the Registry of the remote computer. (Of course, you will need to be an administrator on the remote machine.) Then browse to HKEY_LOCAL_MACHINE\SYSTEM\CurrentControlSet\Control\Terminal Server on the remote Registry, and set the fDenyTSConnections key to 0.

Do yourself a favor and memorize this trick. If you work as a technical support specialist, it's certain to be useful.

Lesson 1: Managing Remote Desktop Connections

Remote Desktop is a feature built into Windows that lets you interact with the desktop of a remote computer as if you were logged on to that computer locally. You can use a Remote Desktop Connection to connect from any Windows computer to any other Windows computer on which Remote Desktop is enabled.

> **After this lesson, you will be able to:**
> - Configure Remote Desktop security options.
> - Troubleshoot Remote Desktop connections.
>
> **Estimated lesson time: 60 minutes**

Understanding Remote Desktop

Remote Desktop is actually a combination of two features. The first feature is the client software that you use to connect *to* another computer's desktop. This client software is called Remote Desktop Connection, and you can access it from the Start menu in all versions of Windows Vista. The second feature of Remote Desktop is the portion responsible for accepting connections *from* the Remote Desktop Connection client. This is the Terminal Services component and, among versions of Windows Vista, appears only in Windows Vista Enterprise, Business, and Ultimate.

Between these client and server components, Remote Desktop Protocol (RDP) is used to establish a Remote Desktop connection.

Exam Tip   On the 70-622 exam, the term "sharing a desktop" is used to refer to connecting to another computer through a Remote Desktop Connection.

Understanding New Remote Desktop Security Features

Although Remote Desktop is not new to Windows Vista, the version of Remote Desktop native to Windows Vista includes important new security features. You need to understand these security features so that you can configure them properly and be aware of any compatibility problems they might cause.

NOTE   **Remote Desktop update for Windows XP and Server 2003**

You can download an update to Remote Desktop for Windows XP and Windows Server 2003 that allows these versions to be compatible with the new security features in Windows Vista. However, be sure not to install this update until you have completed the Practice section of this lesson. The address for the update is *http://support.microsoft.com/kb/925876*.

Understanding Network Level Authentication

In previous versions of Windows, Remote Desktop established a connection to a remote computer before the user was authenticated. In other words, anyone could connect to a computer with Remote Desktop enabled and be presented with the Log On To Windows screen of that computer. If you could provide the credentials of an account with sufficient privileges, you could then log on and receive a desktop.

However, this behavior was not secure. First, by providing a Log On To Windows screen, Remote Desktop gave attackers an easy method with which to try out user name and password combinations. Second, even if attackers could not guess credentials that worked, every connection attempt to the remote computer demanded relatively significant resources of that computer. This behavior made Remote Desktop–enabled computers particularly susceptible to denial-of-service attacks.

This security problem is addressed by a feature called Network Level Authentication (NLA), which is included in Windows Vista. NLA ensures that a user is authenticated before an RDP connection to the remote computer is established.

When a user running Windows Vista attempts to connect to a remote computer through Remote Desktop, the user receives an authentication prompt such as the one shown in Figure 12-1.

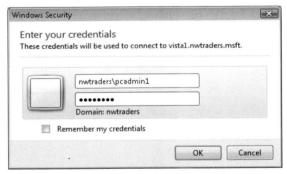

Figure 12-1   Remote Desktop credential prompt

If the remote computer performs NLA, user authentication is completed before the RDP connection is established. If the remote computer is not NLA-compatible, the RDP connection is established first, and the credentials just entered are supplied to the remote computer for authentication.

Server Authentication

Another Remote Desktop security feature new to Windows Vista is server authentication. Server authentication avoids network spoofing by verifying that you are connecting to the correct remote computer or server. By default, Remote Desktop Connection in Windows Vista requests server authentication. If from a Windows Vista computer you attempt to use Remote Desktop to connect to a computer running any earlier version of Windows, you will first receive the warning message shown in Figure 12-2.

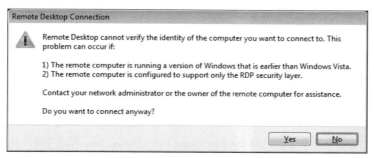

Figure 12-2   Warning of no remote server authentication

Configuring Remote Desktop Connection

You can open Remote Desktop Connection from the Start menu by pointing to All Programs, clicking Accessories, and then clicking Remote Desktop Connection. The Remote Desktop Connection dialog box is shown in Figure 12-3. To connect to another computer, simply type a computer name in the Computer text box, and then click Connect.

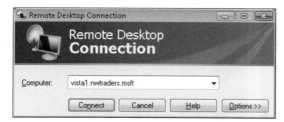

Figure 12-3   The Remote Desktop Connection dialog box

Clicking the Options button in the Remote Desktop Connection dialog box reveals the Remote Desktop Connection configuration tabs. The following section describes the options available on these tabs.

- **General tab**   This tab allows you to save all the configuration settings specified in the other tabs, along with a computer name to which to connect, in an RDP file. After you save the file, you can then connect to the remote computer with the desired settings simply by clicking that file.
- **Display tab**   This tab allows you to specify the dimensions and color depth of the remote desktop.

- **Local Resources tab** This tab allows you to choose the local resources (such as printers, clipboard information, and disk drives) that you want available on the remote desktop. It also lets you determine the conditions under which local keystrokes such as ALT+TAB are registered on the remote desktop and whether remote sounds should be played locally.

- **Programs tab** This tab lets you automatically configure a program to start on the remote desktop whenever an RDP connection is established.

- **Experience tab** This tab allows you to enable and disable graphics features that require additional network bandwidth.

- **Advanced tab** This tab allows you to set client options related to server authentication. Three options are available:

  □ **Always Connect, Even If Authentication Fails (Least Secure)** With this option, when Remote Desktop Connection attempts to connect to a computer unable to authenticate itself (a computer running a version of Windows earlier than Windows Vista), the connection continues without warning.

  □ **Warn Me If Authentication Fails (More Secure)** This is the default option. When you select this option, if Remote Desktop Connection attempts to connect to a computer unable to authenticate itself (a computer running a version of Windows earlier than Windows Vista), the warning message shown in Figure 12-2 is displayed before the connection is established.

  □ **Don't Connect If Authentication Fails (Most Secure)** When you select this option, if Remote Desktop Connection attempts to connect to a computer unable to authenticate itself (a computer running a version of Windows earlier than Windows Vista), the connection is blocked.

  The Advanced tab, along with these three authentication options, is shown in Figure 12-4.

Figure 12-4   The Advanced tab of Remote Desktop Connection

Allowing Remote Desktop Connections

To configure a Windows Vista computer to accept Remote Desktop connections from other computers, you need to enable the feature in the Remote tab of the System Properties dialog box. To access this tab, first open the System Control Panel. (You can open the System Control Panel by first clicking System And Maintenance and then System in Control Panel. Alternatively, you can open the properties of Computer in the Start menu or even just enter the keystroke Windows + Pause/Break.) Then, in System Control Panel, click Remote Settings on the Tasks menu, as shown in Figure 12-5.

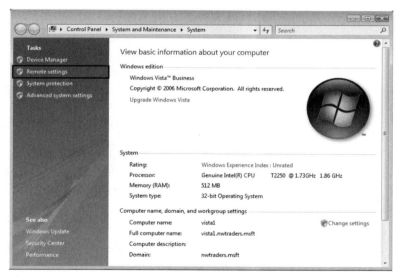

Figure 12-5   Accessing Remote Desktop settings in Control Panel

This procedure opens the Remote tab of the System Properties dialog box, shown in Figure 12-6.

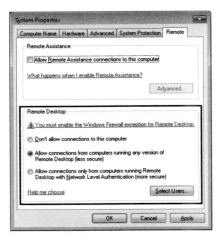

Figure 12-6   Enabling Remote Desktop

By default, in the Remote Desktop area of the tab, the Don't Allow Connections To This Computer option button is selected. This setting disables or blocks incoming Remote Desktop connections. To allow incoming Remote Desktop connections from any version of the Remote Desktop Client, choose the second option (selected in Figure 12-6). This option is considered less secure because it allows incoming connections from older clients to be established before the remote user is authenticated. If instead you want the local computer to perform user authentication before an RDP connection is established (and thereby reduce susceptibility to denial-of-service attacks), choose the bottom option, Allow Connections Only From Computers Running Remote Desktop With Network Level Authentication. Be aware, however, that this option will block most incoming connections from Windows XP and Windows Server 2003 computers.

Also note that when you enable Remote Desktop in this tab by selecting the second or third option, you are automatically creating a local firewall exception for incoming Remote Desktop connections. You would need to create this firewall exception manually only if it were deleted. But even in that case, you could also just disable and then reenable Remote Desktop in the Remote tab to re-create the firewall exception.

Exam Tip   On the 70-622 exam, expect to see questions related to these settings. For example, if a Windows XP computer cannot connect to a Windows Vista computer through Remote Desktop but other Windows Vista computers can, you know that the third option is selected. To allow the Windows XP computer to connect, choose the second option. Also be aware that you need to be familiar with the term "Network Level Authentication."

Adding Users to the Remote Desktop Users Group

When you enable Remote Desktop in the System Properties dialog box, the only users who are able to connect to that computer through Remote Desktop are by default administrators on the local computer. To allow other users to connect through Remote Desktop, add them to the Remote Desktop Users group on the local machine. The easiest way to do this is to click the Select Users button in the Remote tab. This procedure opens the Remote Desktop Users dialog box, as shown in Figure 12-7. To add users to the Remote Desktop Users group, simply click Add, and then type in the names of the desired user accounts. (To specify a domain user, be sure to enter the name in the form *domain\user name.*)

Figure 12-7   Adding users to the Remote Desktop Users local group

---

NOTE **Allow Log On Through Terminal Services**

Technically, a user doesn't really need to be a member of either the Administrators group or the Remote Desktop Users group to connect through Remote Desktop. The user account just needs to be assigned the Allow Log On Through Terminal Services user right. However, all members of both the Administrators and Remote Desktop Users groups are automatically assigned this right.

Troubleshooting Remote Desktop

Aside from networking issues, only five problems can typically block a Remote Desktop connection. If a remote computer is Remote Desktop compatible, yet a local user cannot connect to it through Remote Desktop, be sure to verify that all five of these conditions are met:

1. Remote Desktop cannot be disabled on the remote computer. You can enable and disable Remote Desktop in the Remote tab of the System Properties dialog box.

2. The authentication options defined in the Remote Desktop Connection client cannot prevent a connection to the Remote Desktop server type.

3. The NLA options defined at the remote computer (server) cannot prevent a connection from the Remote Desktop Connection client type.

4. The connecting user needs to be a member of Administrators or Remote Desktop Users on the Remote Desktop server (computer accepting Remote Desktop connections).

5. In Windows Firewall a firewall exception needs to be defined for Remote Desktop on the computer accepting incoming Remote Desktop connections. (This firewall exception is created by default when you enable Remote Desktop, but it can be deleted.)

Quick Check

1. Which local groups by default are granted the Allow Log On Through Terminal Services user right?
2. Where do you configure connection options related to server authentication?
3. Where do you configure connection options related to NLA?

Quick Check Answers

1. Administrators and Remote Desktop Users.
2. You configure connection options related to server authentication in the Remote Desktop Connection options in the Advanced tab of the Remote Desktop Connection dialog box.
3. You configure connection options related to NLA in the Remote tab of the System Properties dialog box.

Practice: Implementing and Troubleshooting Remote Desktop

On the 70-622 exam, you are expected to be familiar with various types of Remote Desktop errors, especially in connections between Windows Vista and Windows XP computers. In this series of practices, you will observe various error messages resulting from such connection attempts, and then you will provide fixes for these errors.

NOTE **Substituting Windows Server 2003 for Windows XP**

If you do not have access to a Windows XP Professional computer, you can use Dcsrv1 instead. If you do so, however, it's a good idea to use Local Security Policy to ensure that the Allow Log On Through Terminal Services user right is assigned to the Remote Desktop Users group on Dcsrv1. Also note that when you perform these practices, there will be slight differences between what you see in Windows Server 2003 and what you would see in Windows XP. The wording in the practices reflects the Windows XP user interface.

Even if you do have a Windows XP Professional computer to use for this series of practices, make sure that Dcsrv1 is started before you begin.

▶ **Practice 1: Troubleshooting a Remote Desktop Connection to Windows XP, Part 1 (Enabling Remote Desktop)**

In this practice, you will attempt to establish a Remote Desktop connection from Vista1 to Xpclient.

1. Log on to Nwtraders from Vista1 as a standard user (not an administrator).
2. From the Start menu, point to All Programs, point to Accessories, and then click Remote Desktop Connection.

    The Remote Desktop Connection dialog box opens.
3. In the Remote Desktop Connection dialog box, type **xpclient.nwtraders.msft** in the Computer text box, and then press Enter.

    The Windows Security dialog box opens.
4. In the Windows Security dialog box, type the name of the currently logged-on standard user in the form **nwtraders***user name*. Then type the associated password and press Enter.

    The Remote Desktop Disconnected message box appears and informs you that the local computer cannot connect to the remote computer.
5. Click OK to dismiss the error message.
6. If necessary, spend a few minutes investigating the settings on Vista1 and Xpclient, and then answer the following question:

    What is the reason that you have received this particular error message?

    Answer: Remote Desktop has not been enabled on Xpclient.
7. Log on to Nwtraders from Xpclient with a domain administrator account.
8. On Xpclient, open the System Properties dialog box. (You can find the System Control Panel icon in the Performance And Maintenance category. Alternatively, you can just open the properties of My Computer or enter the keystroke Windows + Pause/Break.)
9. In the Remote tab of the System Properties dialog box, select the Allow Users To Connect Remotely To This Computer check box.
10. If a Remote Sessions message box appears, read the message, and then click OK.
11. In the System Properties dialog box, click OK.
12. Return to Vista1.
13. In the Remote Desktop Connection dialog box, verify that "xpclient.nwtraders.msft" is still visible in the Computer text box, and then click Connect.
14. In the Windows Security dialog box, type once again the name of the currently logged-on standard user in the form **nwtraders***user name*. Then type the associated password and press Enter.

    The Remote Desktop Connection dialog box appears.

15. Take a few moments to read the message. Note that the message allows you to connect to the remote source, if desired.

16. Answer the following question:

    Would you have received this message if you were connecting to another Windows Vista computer?

    Answer: No. This particular message appears by default in Windows Vista whenever you use Remote Desktop to connect to a computer that does not support server authentication. (Server authentication for Remote Desktop is not available by default in Windows XP or Windows Server 2003.)

17. Click No to close the Remote Desktop Connection message box. Leave the Remote Desktop Connection dialog box open and proceed to Practice 2.

▶ **Practice 2: Troubleshooting a Remote Desktop Connection to Windows XP, Part 2 (Server Authentication)**

In this practice, you will alter the default Remote Desktop Connection settings on Vista1 and observe the resulting behavior.

1. On Vista1, in the Remote Desktop Connection dialog box, click Options.

2. In the Advanced tab, in the Authentication Options drop-down list box, select Do Not Connect if Authentication Fails, and then click Connect.

3. In the Windows Security dialog box, type the name of the currently logged-on standard user in the form **nwtraders\\user name**. Then type the associated password and press Enter.

4. A Remote Desktop Connection error message appears.

5. Read the error message. Note that you are no longer given the option to connect.

6. Click OK to dismiss the error message, and then, in the Advanced tab of the Remote Desktop Connection dialog box, select Always Connect, Even If Authentication Fails from the Authentication Options drop-down list box.

7. Click Connect.

8. In the Windows Security dialog box, type the name of the currently logged-on standard user in the form **nwtraders\\user name**. Then type the associated password and press Enter.

    The Log On To Windows dialog box appears from the remote Windows XP computer. Then, a Logon Message message box appears and informs you that the local policy of this system does not allow you to log on interactively.

9. If the Logon Message box has not disappeared on its own, click OK to close it.

10. If the Log On To Windows dialog box for the Windows XP remote desktop has not disappeared on its own, click the Cancel button to close it.

11. In the Remote Desktop Connection dialog box, click the Options button to remove the configuration tabs from view.

12. Leave the Remote Desktop Connection dialog box open and proceed to Practice 3.

▶ **Practice 3: Troubleshooting a Remote Desktop Connection to Windows XP, Part 3 (User Rights Issues)**

In order for a user to connect to a computer through Remote Desktop, that user needs to be a member either of the Remote Desktop Users group or the Administrators group on the machine in question. In this practice, you add your standard user account to the Remote Desktop Users group and then fix another user-related issue blocking the Remote Desktop connection.

1. While you are logged on to Nwtraders from Xpclient as a domain administrator, open the System Properties dialog box.

2. In the System Properties dialog box, in the Remote tab, click Select Remote Users.

   The Remote Desktop Users dialog box appears.

3. In the Remote Desktop Users dialog box, click Add.

   The Select Users Or Groups dialog box appears.

4. In the Select Users Or Groups dialog box, in the Enter Object Names To Select text box, type the name of the standard user account with which you just attempted to connect to Xpclient from Vista1. Remember to type the account in the form **nwtraders*user name*.**

5. In the Select Users Or Groups dialog box, click OK.

   In the Remote Desktop Users dialog box, the user account you just added should now be listed in the form NWTRADERS*user name*.

6. In the Remote Desktop Users dialog box, click OK.

7. In the System Properties dialog box, click OK.

   The procedure you have just performed adds the standard user account to the Remote Desktop Users group on the Windows XP computer.

8. Return to Vista1.

9. In the Remote Desktop Connection dialog box, verify that "xpclient.nwtraders.msft" is still visible in the Computer text box, and then click Connect.

10. In the Windows Security dialog box, type the name of the currently logged-on standard user in the form **nwtraders*user name*.** Then type the associated password and press Enter.

11. A Logon Message message box appears and informs you that another user is already logged on.

12. Answer the following questions:

   a. Including local users and remote users, how many users in total can be logged on to a domain-joined Windows XP client computer at once?

      Answer: 1

     b. Under which circumstances can one user remotely kick off a locally logged-on user in order to log on to Windows XP?

        Answer: Only an administrator can kick off another user. In addition, a standard user can kick off another logon session belonging to the same standard user.

13. If the Logon Message message box has not disappeared on its own, click OK to close it.

14. Return to Xpclient and log off the current user.

15. Return to Vista1. In the Remote Desktop Connection dialog box, verify that "xpclient.nwtraders.msft" is still visible in the Computer text box, and then click Connect.

16. In the Windows Security dialog box, type the name of the currently logged-on standard user in the form **nwtraders*user name***. Then type the associated password and press Enter.

17. The Remote Desktop connection from Vista1 to Xpclient is successfully established.

18. Answer the following question:

     Which four conditions need to be met in order to remotely log on as a standard user to a Windows XP Professional computer from a Windows Vista computer?

     Answer:

        a. Remote Desktop needs to be enabled in the System properties of the Windows XP Professional computer.

        b. The server authentication options in the Remote Desktop Connection on Windows Vista need to be configured to allow the connection even when authentication fails.

        c. The standard user account with which you are trying to connect must be a member of the Remote Desktop Users group on the Windows XP Professional computer.

        d. No other user can currently be logged on to the Windows XP computer in question.

19. On Vista1, use the Start menu in the Remote Desktop connection to log off the connection to Xpclient, and then log off Vista1.

▶ **Practice 4: Troubleshooting a Remote Desktop Connection to Windows Vista (Network Layer Authentication issues)**

In this practice, you will configure Remote Desktop settings on Windows Vista. You will then attempt to use Remote Desktop to log on to a Windows Vista computer from Windows XP Professional computer and observe the resulting behavior.

1. Log on to Nwtraders from Vista1 with a domain administrator account.

2. Open the System Control Panel.

3. In the System window, beneath Tasks, click Remote Settings.

4. In the User Account Control consent prompt, click Continue.

5. In the Remote tab of the System Properties dialog box, select Allow Connections Only From Computers Running Remote Desktop With Network Level Authentication (More Secure).

6. Click the Select Users button.

7. In the Remote Desktop Users dialog box, click Add.

8. In the Select Users Or Groups dialog box, type the name of a standard user account (not an administrator) in the form **nwtraders*user name*, and then press Enter.

9. In the Remote Desktop Users dialog box, click OK.

10. In the System Properties dialog box, click Apply. Leave the System Properties dialog box open.

11. Switch to Xpclient.

12. Log on to Nwtraders from Xpclient with the same standard user account you specified in step 8.

13. Open a Remote Desktop Connection by clicking Start, pointing to All Programs, pointing to Accessories, pointing to Communications, and clicking Remote Desktop Connection.

14. In the Remote Desktop Connection dialog box, type **vista1.nwtraders.msft** in the Computer text box, and then press Enter.

15. In the Remote Desktop Connection credential prompt, enter the credentials of the locally logged-on user. Be sure to specify the user name in the form **nwtraders*user name*.

    The Remote Desktop Disconnected error message appears and informs you that the remote computer requires NLA.

16. Answer the following question: Why doesn't the local computer support NLA?

    Answer: NLA by default does not appear in the Windows XP version of Remote Desktop Connection. By default, it appears only in the versions of Remote Desktop Connection native to Windows Vista and later.

17. Click OK to close the Remote Desktop Disconnected error message and proceed to Practice 5.

▶ **Practice 5: Connecting to Windows Vista Through Remote Desktop**

In this practice, you will fix the problem introduced in Practice 4. You will then create a Remote Desktop connection from Windows XP to Windows Vista.

1. While you are still logged on to Vista1 as an administrator, in the Remote tab of the System Properties dialog box, select Allow Connections From Computers Running Any Version Of Remote Desktop (Less Secure).

2. In the System Properties dialog box, click OK.

3. Return to Xpclient. In the Remote Desktop Connection dialog box, verify that "vista1.nwtraders.msft" is still visible in the Computer text box, and then click Connect.

4. In the Remote Desktop Connection credential prompt, enter the credentials of the locally logged-on standard user. Be sure to specify the user name in the form **nwtraders \user name**.

   The Remote Desktop Connection security prompt appears.

5. In the Remote Desktop Connection security prompt, click Yes to connect to the remote computer despite the certificate errors.

   A Logon Message appears. The message informs you that another user is already logged on to Vista1 and that if you continue, the user will have to disconnect from the computer.

6. Click Yes to continue, and then quickly switch to Vista1.

   On Vista1, a Remote Desktop Connection dialog box appears on the desktop and informs you that another user is attempting to connect.

7. On Vista1, read the message, and then click OK.

   Note that if you don't respond within 30 seconds, the local session will automatically be disconnected (but not logged off), and the Remote Desktop connection will be allowed.

   Also note that in Windows Vista, the locally logged on user can always choose to cancel the remote user session, even when the remote user is an administrator.

8. On Vista1, the local user session is disconnected. On Xpclient, a Remote Desktop connection to Vista1 is established.

9. On Xpclient, use the Start menu to log off the Remote Desktop connection to Vista1, and then log off the local computer.

10. Answer the following questions:

   a. Can a remote desktop user force a local user to log off Windows Vista?

      Answer: No, but if the local user does not respond, the user session is disconnected (not logged off). No data is lost in the local user session.

   b. Can more than one user stay logged on to a domain-joined Windows Vista computer?

      Answer: Yes, but only one user at a time can be connected to a Windows Vista desktop.

Lesson Summary

- Remote Desktop allows you to connect to the desktop of a remote computer as if you were logged on to that computer locally.
- To connect to another computer through Remote Desktop, the feature needs to be enabled on the remote computer, and you need to be a member of either the Administrators group or the Remote Desktop Users group on that remote machine.
- Remote Desktop in Windows Vista comes with two optional new security features: Network Level Authentication (NLA) and Server Authentication. These features are not compatible with Remote Desktop versions in Windows XP or Windows Server 2003 by default.
- NLA ensures that a user is authenticated before a Remote Desktop connection is established.
- Server authentication avoids network spoofing by verifying that you are connecting to the correct remote computer or server.

Lesson Review

The following questions are intended to reinforce key information presented in this lesson. The questions are also available on the companion CD if you prefer to review them in electronic form.

NOTE Answers

Answers to these questions and explanations of why each answer choice is right or wrong are located in the "Answers" section at the end of the book.

1. You work as a desktop support technician for a company with 200 employees. Approximately half of the company's client computers are running Windows Vista Enterprise. The remaining clients are running Windows XP Professional.

   Whenever a user named SallyB attempts to use Remote Desktop to connect to a Windows Vista computer named Vista1 from her Windows XP Professional computer, she receives an error informing her that the remote computer requires Network Level Authentication.

You want to allow SallyB to use Remote Desktop to connect to Vista1 from her Windows XP computer. What should you do?

A. Add SallyB to the Remote Desktop Users group on Vista1.

B. Add SallyB to the Administrators group on Vista1.

C. In the Remote Desktop Connection options on Vista1, configure the Server Authentication settings to always connect, even when authentication fails.

D. In the System Properties dialog box on Vista1, configure the Remote settings to allow connections from computers running any version of Remote Desktop.

2. You work as a desktop support technician for a company with 200 employees. Approximately half of the company's client computers are running Windows Vista Enterprise. The remaining clients are running Windows XP Professional.

A user named FredL wants to use Remote Desktop to connect to a Windows XP Professional computer, XPClient2, from his Windows Vista computer, Vista2. However, whenever he attempts to do so, he receives an error stating that the connection cannot proceed because Remote Desktop cannot verify the identity of the remote computer.

You want to allow Fred to use Remote Desktop to connect to XPClient2 from Vista2. What should you do?

A. Add FredL to the Remote Desktop Users group on XPClient2.

B. Add FredL to the Administrators group on XPClient2.

C. In the Remote Desktop Connection options on Vista2, configure the Server Authentication settings to always connect, even when authentication fails.

D. In the System properties on Vista2, configure the Remote settings to allow connections from computers running any version of Remote Desktop.

Lesson 2: Offering Remote Assistance

Windows Remote Assistance is a Windows Vista feature that allows one user, called a helper, to connect to another user's desktop session on a remote computer. Once connected, the helper can view and optionally interact with the assisted person's desktop. This lesson describes step by step how to offer technical assistance to another user through this tool.

After this lesson, you will be able to:
- Request Remote Assistance from another user.
- Answer a Remote Assistance request.
- Offer unsolicited Remote Assistance to another user.

Estimated lesson time: 40 minutes

Enabling Remote Assistance

To allow a helper to connect to a computer by using Remote Assistance, you first need to enable Remote Assistance on that computer. To do so, select the Allow Remote Assistance Connections To This Computer check box in the Remote tab of the System Properties dialog box, as shown in Figure 12-8.

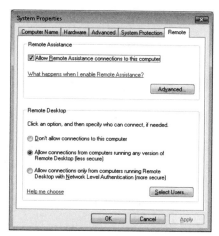

Figure 12-8   Enabling Remote Assistance

As mentioned in the previous lesson, to locate the Remote tab, first open the System window, and then click Remote Settings on the Tasks menu, as shown in Figure 12-9.

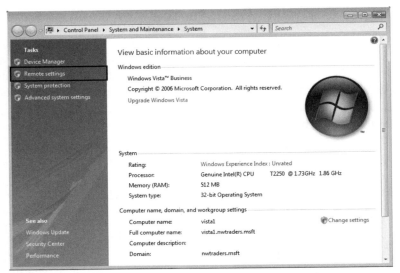

Figure 12-9   Accessing the Remote tab of System Properties

After Remote Assistance is enabled on a computer, a Remote Assistance connection to that computer can be initiated in one of two ways: by the user's requesting assistance from the helper or by the helper's offering unsolicited assistance to the user. Of these two methods, the first is simpler to implement.

NOTE   **Remote Assistance firewall exception**

When you enable Remote Assistance, Windows Vista automatically adds a local firewall exception for Remote Assistance.

Requesting Remote Assistance

A user can request remote assistance from a helper by creating a Remote Assistance invitation. To create a Remote Assistance invitation, first open the Windows Remote Assistance wizard by clicking Start, pointing to All Programs, clicking Maintenance, and then clicking Windows Remote Assistance.

The first page of the Windows Remote Assistance wizard is shown in Figure 12-10.

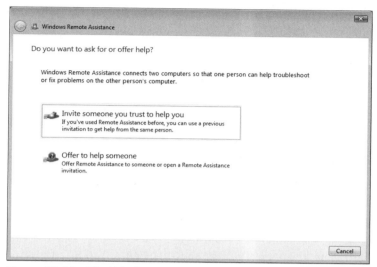

Figure 12-10   The Windows Remote Assistance wizard

To request remote assistance, on the first page of the wizard, click the option to invite someone you trust to help you. This step opens the page shown in Figure 12-11.

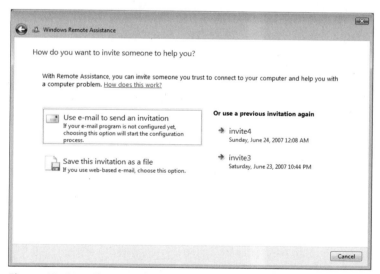

Figure 12-11   Choosing a Remote Assistance invitation method

On this page you can choose whether to send the invitation file to the helper through e-mail or simply to save the invitation in the file system so that the helper can later access it through a network share or another means. In either case, the invitation file must be password protected.

After you choose the password and complete the wizard, the Remote Assistance toolbar, shown in Figure 12-12, appears on the user's desktop. Note the toolbar's status message of "Waiting for incoming connection...".

Figure 12-12   The Remote Assistance toolbar

At this point the helper must use the Remote Assistance wizard to open the invitation he or she has received. To do so, the helper first chooses the Offer To Help Someone option on the first page of the wizard. This step opens the page shown in Figure 12-13. To open the invitation file, the helper uses the Browse button or enters the path to the file in the appropriate text box and then clicks Finish.

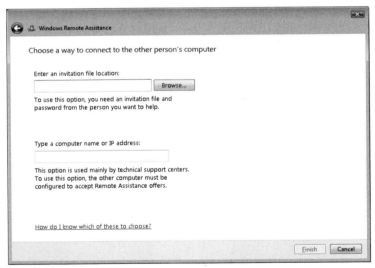

Figure 12-13   Opening a Remote Assistance invitation

The helper is then prompted for the password of the file. If the helper can successfully enter the password, the assisted party receives a Windows Remote Assistance offer message, such as the one shown in Figure 12-14.

Figure 12-14 Accepting a Remote Assistance connection

Offering Unsolicited Remote Assistance

Before you can successfully offer unsolicited Remote Assistance to a user running Windows Vista, you need to perform a number of preparatory steps:

1. Add the following local firewall exceptions on the assisted party's computer:

    a. Msra.exe (program). When Remote Assistance is enabled on the user's computer, this exception is created automatically.

    b. Raserver.exe (program). You must add this firewall exception manually.

    c. TCP 135 (port). You must add this firewall exception manually.

2. In Local Computer Policy or Group Policy, enable the Offer Remote Assistance policy setting for the assisted party's computer. You can find this policy setting in a Group Policy object (GPO) by navigating to Computer Configuration→Administrative Templates →System→Remote Assistance.

    a. To enable this setting, you must add at least one user account to the Helpers list in the policy setting. Once added in the policy setting, these user accounts also appear in the Offer Remote Assistance Helpers security group on the local machine.

    b. By default, when you enable this policy setting, the designated helpers are allowed to view and control other users' computers. However, in this policy setting you can also choose the option to allow helpers only to view remote computers.

The Offer Remote Assistance policy setting is shown in Figure 12-15.

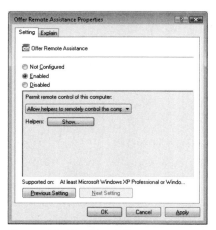

Figure 12-15   The Offer Remote Assistance policy setting

IMPORTANT   Remote Assistance helpers list
Only users added to the helpers list can offer unsolicited Remote Assistance.

After you have performed these preparatory steps, you can easily offer Remote Assistance to another user by using the Remote Assistance wizard. On the first page of the wizard, select the Offer To Help Someone option. Then, after you provide the name or address of a computer to help, the wizard immediately initiates a Remote Assistance connection to that computer. At this point the assisted party receives a Remote Assistance offer message identical to the one shown in Figure 12-14.

Establishing the Remote Assistance Session

When the assisted party approves the Remote Assistance offer, the status message of the Remote Assistance toolbar on his or her local machine changes to "Connected to your helper. Your helper can now see your desktop." At the same time, the assisted party's desktop appears within a Windows Remote Assistance window on the helper's desktop, as shown in Figure 12-16.

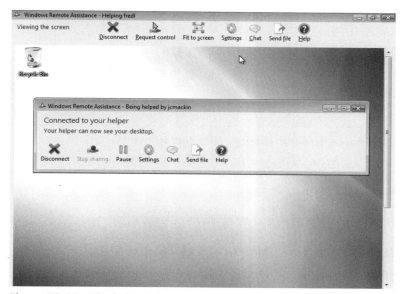

Figure 12-16   The helper's Remote Assistance window

At first, the helper can only view and not interact with the assisted user's desktop. If the helper wants to interact with the remote user's desktop, the helper must click the Request Control button on the Windows Remote Assistance window menu bar. This step opens the message, shown in Figure 12-17, on the remote user's desktop.

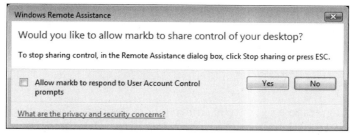

Figure 12-17   In Remote Assistance, the assisted user always voluntarily grants control to the remote helper

Of particular importance in this message prompt is the option to allow the helper to respond to User Account Control (UAC) prompts. If this option is *not* selected, the helper's Windows Remote Assistance window will go blank whenever a step requiring elevation is performed on the assisted user's computer. The helper will be able to regain control of the remote desktop only when the assisted user handles the UAC prompt by providing administrator credentials or clicking Continue, as appropriate. If, on the other hand, this option is selected, UAC prompts will be passed to the helper during the Remote Assistance session. Note also that selecting this option itself requires elevation.

After control is granted to the helper, the helper can interact with the assisted user's desktop. The assisted user can pause the session at any point by clicking the Pause button and resume the session by clicking Continue. To end the session, either party can click the Disconnect button on the toolbar.

NOTE Remote Assistance through Windows Live Messenger

In addition to requesting and offering Remote Assistance through methods built into Windows Vista, you can also request and offer Remote Assistance through Windows Live Messenger. This functionality, though interesting, is not covered on the 70-622 exam and is therefore beyond the scope of this training kit.

Windows Remote Assistance Compatibility Issues

Windows Remote Assistance is not new to Windows Vista, but there are enough feature differences with earlier versions to create certain limited compatibility problems.

- You cannot offer unsolicited Windows Remote Assistance from Windows Vista to either Windows XP or Windows Server 2003.

- In Windows XP and Windows Server 2003, Remote Assistance supported voice capability. Voice capability is no longer supported in Windows Vista.

- In Windows XP and Windows Server 2003, you can't pause a Windows Remote Assistance session. If the assisted party is running Windows Vista and pauses a session while connected to a helper running Windows XP, the helper will not be notified that the session is paused.

Quick Check

1. A remote user agrees to let you share control of her desktop. After you attempt to open Computer Management on her computer, your Windows Remote Assistance window goes blank. What is the likeliest cause?

2. Can you offer unsolicited Remote Assistance from a Windows Vista computer to a Windows XP computer?

Quick Check Answers

1. When agreeing to let you share control of her desktop, the remote user did not select the option to allow you to respond to UAC prompts.

2. No.

Practice: Offering Remote Assistance

In this practice, you will create a Remote Assistance invitation and allow a remote helper to take control of your computer.

▶ **Practice 1: Creating a Network Share for Remote Assistance**

In this practice, you will create a network share in which to place Remote Assistance invitations.

1. Log on to Dcsrv1 as an administrator.
2. Create a new folder in the root of the C drive. Name the folder Remote Assistance Invitations.
3. Open the properties of the Remote Assistance Invitations folder.
4. In the Sharing tab, click Share This Folder, and then click the Permissions button.
5. In the Permissions for Remote Assistance Invitations dialog box, assign Everyone the Allow – Full Control permission, and then click OK.
6. In the Remote Assistance Invitations dialog box, click the Security tab.
7. In the Security tab, assign the Users group the Allow-Modify permission.
8. Click OK to close the Remote Assistance Properties dialog box.

▶ **Practice 2: Creating a Remote Assistance Invitation**

In this practice, you will create a Remote Assistance invitation on Vista2 and save the invitation to the network share you created in Practice 1.

1. Log on to Nwtraders from Vista2 as a standard user (not an administrator).
2. Open the System Control Panel by right-clicking Computer from the Start menu and then selecting Properties.
3. Beneath Tasks, click Remote Settings.
4. In the UAC credential prompt, enter the credentials of an administrator.
5. In the Remote tab of the System Properties dialog box, select the Allow Remote Assistance Connections To This Computer check box, and then click OK.
6. Close the System window.
7. Open Windows Remote Assistance by clicking Start, pointing to All Programs, clicking Maintenance, and then clicking Windows Remote Assistance.
   The Windows Remote Assistance wizard opens.
8. On the Do You Want To Ask For Or Offer Help page, click Invite Someone You Trust To Help You.
9. On the How Do You Want To Invite Someone To Help You page, click Save This Invitation As A File.
10. On the Save The Invitation As A File page, type **\\dcsrv1\Remote Assistance Invitations\RAinvite1** in the Enter A Path And File Name text box.

11. Enter a password in the Password and Confirm The Password text boxes, and then click Finish.

12. The Windows Remote Assistance toolbar appears with the status message "Waiting for incoming connection..."

13. Proceed to Practice 3.

▶ **Practice 3: Answering a Remote Assistance Invitation**

In this practice, you will use the Remote Assistance invitation created in Practice 2 to provide Remote Assistance to Vista2 from Vista1.

1. Log on to Nwtraders from Vista1 as an administrator.

2. Open Windows Remote Assistance.

3. In the Windows Remote Assistance wizard, on the Do You Want To Ask For Or Offer Help page, click Offer To Help Someone.

4. On the Choose A Way To Connect To The Other Person's Computer page, type **\\dcsrv1\Remote Assistance Invitations\RAinvite1** in the Enter An Invitation File Location text box, and then click Finish.

5. In the Windows Remote Assistance dialog box, enter the password you assigned to the invitation in the Enter Password text box, and then click OK.

6. The Windows Remote Assistance window opens with the status message "Waiting For Acceptance."

7. Switch to Vista2.

   On the Vista2 desktop, a Windows Remote Assistance dialog box has appeared and asks you whether you would like to allow the remote helper to connect to your computer.

8. Click Yes to accept the Remote Assistance connection.

   On the Windows Remote Assistance toolbar, the status message has changed to "Connected to your helper – Your helper can now see your desktop."

9. Return to Vista1.

   On Vista1, the Windows Remote Assistance window has changed to "Viewing the screen." Within the window, you can see the Vista2 desktop.

10. Spend a few moments browsing the desktops on both Vista1 and Vista2. Do not change any settings.

11. Answer the following question:

    Who currently has control of the session, the user on Vista1, the user on Vista2, or both?

    Answer: The user on Vista2.

12. On Vista1, in the Windows Remote Assistance window, click Request Control.

    On Vista2, a new Windows Remote Assistance dialog box has appeared on the desktop and asks you whether you would like to allow the remote helper to share control of your desktop.

13. On Vista2, in the Windows Remote Assistance dialog box, click Yes.

14. On Vista2, the status message in the Windows Remote Assistance toolbar has changed to "Connected to your helper – Your helper is sharing control of your computer."

15. Switch to Vista1. Spend a few minutes experimenting with the control of the Vista2 desktop and exploring the various options on the Windows Remote Assistance toolbars.

16. On Vista1, click Disconnect, and then click Yes to confirm.

17. Close all open windows on both computers.

Lesson Summary

■ Windows Remote Assistance allows one user, called a helper, to connect to the live session of another user on a remote computer. Once connected, the helper can see the remote user's desktop and (if allowed) interact with it.

■ For a computer to receive Remote Assistance, the feature must be enabled in the Remote tab in the System Properties dialog box.

■ Remote Assistance can be solicited or unsolicited. When Remote Assistance is solicited, a user creates a Remote Assistance request and sends it to the helper. With unsolicited Remote Assistance, the helper does not need a request, but this method requires significant preparation.

■ There are a few compatibility issues between Remote Assistance in Windows Vista and earlier versions of Remote Assistance. Most important, a helper in Windows Vista cannot provide unsolicited assistance to a user running Windows XP.

Lesson Review

The following questions are intended to reinforce key information presented in this lesson. The questions are also available on the companion CD if you prefer to review them in electronic form.

NOTE Answers

Answers to these questions and explanations of why each answer choice is right or wrong are located in the "Answers" section at the end of the book.

---

1. You work as a desktop support technician in a large company whose network consists of a single Active Directory directory service domain. All client computers are running Windows Vista Business.

    While working at the help desk, you receive a call from an employee in another building who is receiving an unexpected error whenever he performs an elaborate procedure within an application. He is having difficulty describing the procedure and would prefer to show it to you on the computer.

    Which of the following is the best way to watch the user perform the procedure that generates the error?

    A. Use Remote Desktop to connect to the user's computer.

    B. Ask the user to connect to your computer through Remote Desktop.

    C. Ask the user to create and send you a Windows Remote Assistance invitation file through e-mail.

    D. Create and send the user a Windows Remote Assistance invitation file through e-mail.

2. You work as a desktop support technician in a company whose network consists of a single Active Directory domain. You want to be able to offer unsolicited Remote Assistance to a user by specifying her computer name in the Windows Remote Assistance wizard.

    If both of your computers are running Windows Vista Business, which of the following is NOT a requirement to achieve this?

    A. Your user account must be added to the Offer Remote Assistance Helpers group on the remote computer.

    B. In Group Policy, enable the Offer Remote Assistance policy option.

    C. Add firewall exceptions for msra.exe, raserver.exe, and port 135.

    D. Your user account must be a member of the Administrators group on the remote computer.

Chapter Review

To further practice and reinforce the skills you learned in this chapter, you can

- Review the chapter summary.
- Review the list of key terms introduced in this chapter.
- Complete the case scenarios. These scenarios set up real-world situations involving the topics of this chapter and ask you to create solutions.
- Complete the suggested practices.
- Take a practice test.

Chapter Summary

- Remote Desktop is a Windows feature that allows you to connect to the desktop of a remote computer as if you were logged on to that computer locally.
- To connect to another computer through Remote Desktop, the feature needs to be enabled on the remote computer, and you need to be a member of either the Administrators group or the Remote Desktop Users group on that remote machine.
- Remote Desktop in Windows Vista comes with two optional new security features: Network Level Authentication (NLA) and Server Authentication. These features are not compatible with Remote Desktop versions in Windows XP or Windows Server 2003 by default.
- Remote Assistance is a Windows feature that allows one user, called a helper, to connect to the live session of another user on a remote computer. Once connected, the helper can see the remote user's desktop and (if allowed) interact with it.
- Remote Assistance can be solicited or unsolicited. When Remote Assistance is solicited, a user creates a Remote Assistance request and sends it to the helper. With unsolicited Remote Assistance, the helper does not need a request, but this method requires significant preparation. In either case, for a computer to receive Remote Assistance, the feature must first be enabled locally.

Key Terms

Do you know what these key terms mean? You can check your answers by looking up the terms in the glossary at the end of the book.

- helper
- Network Level Authentication (NLA)
- Remote Desktop Protocol (RDP)

Case Scenarios

In the following case scenarios, you will apply what you've learned in this chapter. You can find answers to these questions in the "Answers" section at the end of this book.

Case Scenario 1: Configuring Remote Desktop

You work as a desktop support technician in a large company whose network consists of a single Active Directory domain, Nwtraders.msft. The company network includes 10 servers running Windows Server 2003 and 100 client computers running Windows Vista Enterprise.

A certain computer named Client1.nwtraders.msft is running a network monitoring application. You are using Remote Desktop to connect to Client1 periodically so that you can view statistics generated by this application. You are a member of the Administrators group on Client1.

1. A user named MonicaV has received authorization to connect to Client1 through Remote Desktop. You have been tasked with the responsibility of allowing MonicaV to connect to the computer without providing her with administrative privileges on the machine. What should you do?

2. You want to ensure that user authentication to Client1 is performed before any full Remote Desktop connection is established. What should you do?

Case Scenario 2: Offering Remote Assistance

You work at a call center for a software company. Your job is to provide technical support to customers all over the world by answering their questions on the telephone and occasionally by connecting to their computers through Windows Remote Assistance.

A customer named Fred calls in to the tech support center and describes to you problems configuring the software. You have decided that the best way to help Fred is to connect to his computer by using Remote Assistance.

You have verified that both your computer and Fred's computer are connected to the Internet.

1. Given the network environment, what is the best way to establish a Windows Remote Assistance connection to Fred's computer?

2. You want to be able to perform adjustments to Fred's computer without requring him to continually approve UAC messages. What should you do?

Suggested Practices

To help you successfully master the exam objectives presented in this chapter, complete the following tasks.

Enable Remote Desktop Remotely

■ **Practice: Connect to Another Computer that Has Remote Desktop Disabled**   Connect remotely to the registry of a remote Windows Vista computer and configure the appropriate key value to enable Remote Desktop on that computer. (This key is described in the Real World section at the beginning of this chapter.) Then, connect to that computer by using Remote Desktop.

Offer Unsolicited Remote Assistance

■ **Practice: Offer Unsolicited Remote Assistance**   Make the necessary firewall exceptions and Group Policy configurations to offer unsolicited Remote Assistance to another computer in the same Active Directory domain.

Accept a Remote Assistance Request from a Friend

■ **Practice: Offer Remote Assistance to a Friend over the Internet**   Guide a friend through the steps of creating a Remote Assistance request and have the friend send you the request over the Internet. Use the request to share your friend's desktop with his or her permission.

Take a Practice Test

The practice tests on this book's companion CD offer many options. For example, you can test yourself on just one exam objective, or you can test yourself on all the 70-622 certification exam content. You can set up the test so that it closely simulates the experience of taking a certification exam, or you can set it up in study mode so that you can look at the correct answers and explanations after you answer each question.

MORE INFO   Practice tests

For details about all the practice test options available, see the "How to Use the Practice Tests" section in this book's Introduction.

Answers

Chapter 1: Lesson Review Answers

Lesson 1

1. **Correct Answer: D**
   - A. **Incorrect:** Application compatibility testing is of minimal importance in this scenario because only Microsoft Office 2007 has been specified as required software. In addition, you do not need to evaluate application compatibility as soon as hardware assessment.
   - B. **Incorrect:** User interviews are valuable but not essential. In a scenario in which deployment should occur as quickly as possible, user interviews should not occur first, if at all.
   - C. **Incorrect:** User data migration is an essential phase of deployment, but it is not the first step to take.
   - D. **Correct:** You should conduct hardware assessment as early as possible because you need to know which computers need to be upgraded or replaced to support Windows Vista. After this, you can begin the process of obtaining budgetary approval to purchase additional hardware.

2. **Correct Answer: A**
   - A. **Correct:** Although it is beneficial to preserve user desktop settings when you are moving from one operating system to another, doing so is not essential.
   - B. **Incorrect:** Users need and expect their documents to be preserved during deployment.
   - C. **Incorrect:** Application settings are very important to preserve because they are needed to allow the users to perform their work functions. In addition, reconfiguring application settings in the new operating system is time-consuming.
   - D. **Incorrect:** Users need and expect their e-mail messages to be preserved during deployment.

Lesson 2

1. **Correct Answer: B**
   - A. **Incorrect:** The ACT is used to help an organization resolve application compatibility issues that arise as a result of deploying Windows Vista. It does not help you determine whether a given machine can run Windows Vista.
   - B. **Correct:** The WVUA is the best way to determine whether a small number of computers meet the hardware requirements of Windows Vista.
   - C. **Incorrect:** WVHA is most useful as a means to determine whether many computers on the network meet the hardware requirements of Windows Vista. It is more complex than is necessary for the task described in this scenario.

      D.   **Incorrect:** Manually comparing the local system information to a published list of Windows Vista hardware requirements is not an efficient way to determine the readiness of a single computer to run Windows Vista. Running the Windows Vista Hardware Assessment (WVUA) is far simpler.

2. **Correct Answer: C**

      A.   **Incorrect:** Creating a script is not the most efficient way to determine the readiness of the computers because a tool already exists (the Windows Vista Hardware Assessment [WVHA] tool) that can perform this function.

      B.   **Incorrect:** Using the WVUA in this scenario is not the most efficient solution because it must be run separately on each computer. In addition, this tool does not provide any way to compile the results into a single document.

      C.   **Correct:** The WVHA tool is the best method to achieve the task described in this scenario because you need to analyze the upgrade readiness of many computers and publish the consolidated results of this analysis.

      D.   **Incorrect:** You can't use the USMT 3.0 to analyze the readiness of computers to run Windows Vista.

Lesson 3

1. **Correct Answer: B**

      A.   **Incorrect:** USMT 3.0 is used to migrate user data, not to evaluate software compatibility with Windows Vista.

      B.   **Correct:** The ACT 5.0 helps you to find and resolve software incompatibilities with Windows Vista on your network.

      C.   **Incorrect:** Windows Easy Transfer is used to migrate user data, not to evaluate software compatibility with Windows Vista.

      D.   **Incorrect:** The WVHA tool is used to evaluate the hardware readiness of computers for Windows Vista, not to evaluate software compatibility with Windows Vista.

2. **Correct Answer: A**

      A.   **Correct:** Windows Easy Transfer is the best tool to use when you want to migrate a small number of users to a new Windows Vista computer. For a small number of users, the process is fast and requires little preparation or expertise. In addition, the tool is built into Windows Vista, so it is readily available.

      B.   **Incorrect:** You can use USMT 3.0 to migrate a single user, but because it requires knowledge of precise command-line syntax, it is an unnecessarily complex solution in this scenario. In addition, you need to download and install the tool before you can use it.

      C.   **Incorrect:** Complete PC Backup refers to the built-in backup utility in Windows Vista that allows you to create a virtual hard disk (.vhd) of a computer. Complete PC Backup does not allow you to migrate user settings to a new installation of Windows Vista.

D. Incorrect: The WVUA is a tool that verifies the hardware readiness of a given computer for Windows Vista. It does not allow you to transfer user data to a new installation of Windows Vista.

3. **Correct Answer: D**

A. **Incorrect:** The /v switch allows you to specify the level of verbosity in the Loadstate log.

B. **Incorrect:** The /all switch allows you to migrate all users.

C. **Incorrect:** The /q switch allows you to migrate the user data of the locally logged-on user without administrative credentials.

D. **Correct:** The /c switch allows Scanstate and Loadstate to continue to run despite nonfatal errors.

Chapter 1: Case Scenario Answers

Case Scenario 1: Performing Upgrades

1. Three. You already know that the four computers with 256 MB of RAM have insufficient memory to support Windows Vista.
2. Windows Easy Transfer with a Windows Easy Transfer cable.

Case Scenario 2: Migrating Data

1. To the network storage
2. USMT 3.0
3. USMT 3.0

Chapter 2: Lesson Review Answers

Lesson 1

1. **Correct Answer: A**

A. **Correct:** BCDEdit allows you to modify the BCD store. The BCD store configures operating system loading preferences in a multiboot system.

B. **Incorrect:** Boot.ini is the text file used in previous versions of Windows to configure operating system loading preferences in a multiboot system.

C. **Incorrect:** PEimg is used to view and modify the contents of a Windows PE image.

D. **Incorrect:** Diskpart is a command-line utility that allows you to perform maintenance on hard disks.

2. **Correct Answer: B**

    A. **Incorrect:** An unattended installation can be performed with or without the Windows Vista product DVD.

    B. **Correct:** Windows SIM allows you to create the answer files required for an unattended installation of Windows Vista.

    C. **Incorrect:** Sysprep allows you to prepare an image for capture, but it does not help you perform an unattended installation.

    D. **Incorrect:** Windows Deployment Services helps you deploy Windows images, but it does not allow you to perform unattended installations of Windows Vista.

Lesson 2

1. **Correct Answer: D**

    A. **Incorrect:** Sysprep is used to prepare a disk for imaging.

    B. **Incorrect:** Copype.cmd is a script that installs the Windows PE files into a folder.

    C. **Incorrect:** PEimg is used to modify WIM files of Windows PE installations.

    D. **Correct:** Oscdimg is the command-line tool used to create an ISO.

2. **Correct Answer: A**

    A. **Correct:** The /mountrw switch is used with ImageX to mount a WIM file into the Windows file system for read-write operations.

    B. **Incorrect:** The /mount switch is used with ImageX to mount a WIM file into the Windows file system for read-only operations.

    C. **Incorrect:** The /export switch is used with ImageX to transfer an image from one WIM file to another WIM file.

    D. **Incorrect:** The /capture switch is used with ImageX to capture a disk image into a WIM file.

Lesson 3

1. **Correct Answer: A**

    A. **Correct:** When you install Windows Vista by means of the product DVD, all removable drives are scanned for an answer file named Autounattend.xml.

    B. **Incorrect:** You can place the answer file on a floppy disk, but it has to be named Autounattend.xml, not Autounattend.txt.

    C. **Incorrect:** The local hard disk is not a location that the Setup program scans to locate an answer file.

    D. **Incorrect:** The file needs to be named Autounattend.xml, not Autounattend.txt.

2. **Correct Answer: D**

    A. **Incorrect:** To specify an answer file, you must use the /unattend switch.

    B. **Incorrect:** To launch Windows Vista Setup, you must use the Setup command, not the ImageX command.

    C. **Incorrect:** To launch Windows Vista Setup, you must use the Setup command, not the ImageX command.

    D. **Correct:** To use an answer file with Windows Vista Setup, type the Setup command with the /unattend switch.

Chapter 2: Case Scenario Answers

Case Scenario 1: Choosing a Deployment Technology

1. SMS. WDS would require two infrastructures, one for each domain.
2. WDS. This is possible because of the Active Directory domain. SMS would require an additional investment.

Case Scenario 2: Preparing a Master Image

1. You should first install Windows Vista on a single master client computer and then customize it with all the applications and settings that you want to include on the standard WIM file image.
2. You should run the Sysprep utility with the /generalize switch.
3. You should use the ImageX utility with the /capture switch.

Chapter 3: Lesson Review Answers

Lesson 1

1. **Correct Answer: B**

    A. **Incorrect:** You need to configure only one policy. In that policy you need to select the option to apply the redirection policy to earlier Windows operating systems.

    B. **Correct:** You need to configure the policy from a Windows Vista computer. Only in Windows Vista can you choose the option to apply the redirection policy to Windows 2000, Windows XP, and Windows Server 2003 operating systems.

    C. **Incorrect:** You need to configure the policy from a Windows Vista computer. Only in Windows Vista can you choose the option to apply the redirection policy to Windows 2000, Windows XP, and Windows Server 2003 operating systems.

    D. **Incorrect:** You need to configure the policy from a Windows Vista computer. Only in Windows Vista can you choose the option to apply the redirection policy to Windows 2000, Windows XP, and Windows Server 2003 operating systems.

2. **Correct Answer: A**

    A. **Correct:** To ensure that users can access their data after the policy is removed, you want to have their data moved automatically to the local user profile. Otherwise, after the policy is removed, users will have to connect to the network share manually to find their old data. In addition, this option needs to be selected before the policy is removed; selecting the option after the policy is removed will be too late to have any effect.

   B.   **Incorrect:** See the explanation for A.

   C.   **Incorrect:** See the explanation for A.

   D.   **Incorrect:** See the explanation for A.

3.   **Correct Answers: C and D**

   A.   **Incorrect:** The Documents folder can be redirected by means of the Folder Redirection feature.

   B.   **Incorrect:** The Desktop folder can be redirected by means of the Folder Redirection feature.

   C.   **Correct:** Desktop background settings, as opposed to files stored on the desktop, cannot be configured to roam with users by means of the Folder Redirection feature. Such settings are stored in Ntuser.dat, which cannot be redirected.

   D.   **Correct:** Folder redirection allows you to redirect the user profile folders only. If you store data in another location (such as a new folder on the root of the C drive), you cannot redirect this folder by means of the Folder Redirection feature.

Lesson 2

1.   **Correct Answer: A**

   A.   **Correct:** This is the only policy that actually helps detect why a running application has failed.

   B.   **Incorrect:** Enabling this policy lets a user be notified when drivers are blocked because of compatibility issues. The policy does not help diagnose why an application has failed.

   C.   **Incorrect:** This policy helps diagnose application installation failures. In this question the application has already been installed successfully.

   D.   **Incorrect:** This policy helps diagnose application installation failures. In this question the application has already been installed successfully.

2.   **Correct Answer: B**

   A.   **Incorrect:** 16-bit applications can run in the 32-bit version of Windows Vista. They cannot, however, run in the 64-bit version of Windows Vista.

   B.   **Correct:** Because of the new User Account Control (UAC) feature of Windows Vista, programs that require administrator privileges must be rewritten to handle the approval messages that appear when administrative tasks are performed.

   C.   **Incorrect:** Because of the file and registry virtualization feature of Windows Vista, the operating system intercepts application requests to write to protected areas of the registry and performs the write instead to a safe area. Because Windows Vista has been designed to perform this sort of redirection, this type of application is not the most likely to require updates to run properly in Windows Vista.

    D. **Incorrect:** Because of the file and registry virtualization feature of Windows Vista, the operating system intercepts application requests to write to system files and performs the write instead to a safe area. Because Windows Vista has been designed to perform this sort of redirection, this type of application is not the most likely to require updates to run properly in Windows Vista.

Chapter 3: Case Scenario Answers

Case Scenario 1: Supporting Roaming Users in Windows Vista

1. Configure Folder Redirection to redirect the Documents folder to the My Documents folder on the central share. In the Folder Redirection policy, choose the option to make the folder redirection compatible with Windows 2000, Windows XP, and Windows Server 2003.

2. She can find her Windows Vista user profile in a folder named SallyB.V2 on the network share \\server3\profiles.

Case Scenario 2: Configuring Application Compatibility Settings

1. You should investigate whether the application can be installed on a Windows Server 2003 computer to which members of the Advertising team can connect. If so, users can run the application by using Remote Desktop to connect to the Windows Server 2003 computer.

2. Enable the Detect Application Install Failures policy setting in Group Policy.

Chapter 4: Lesson Review Answers

Lesson 1

1. **Correct Answers: A, C, and D**

    A. **Correct:** The Local Computer Group Policy object applies to all users on a computer.

    B. **Incorrect:** Marsha is not a member of the Administrators group. Therefore, the Non-Administrators Group Policy object applies to her account, rather than the Administrators Group Policy object.

    C. **Correct:** The Non-Administrators Group Policy object applies to all users on the computer who are not members of the Administrators group.

    D. **Correct:** Every user on the computer has a Local Group Policy object that applies only to that specific user account.

2. **Correct Answer: D**

    A. **Incorrect:** Windows Vista will apply the Local Computer Group Policy object to Sam's account. However, any settings defined in the Administrators Group Policy object and Sam's user Group Policy object will overwrite settings in the Local Computer Group Policy object.

B.   **Incorrect:** Windows Vista will apply the Administrators Group Policy object to Sam's account. However, any settings defined in Sam's user Group Policy object will overwrite settings in the Administrators Group Policy object.

C.   **Incorrect:** Sam is a member of the Administrators group. Therefore, the Non-Administrators Group Policy object has no effect on his account.

D.   **Correct:** Windows Vista processes Multiple Local Group Policy objects (MLGPOs) from most general (the Local Computer Group Policy object) to most specific (the user Group Policy object). Settings in more specific policies always overwrite settings in less specific policies. Therefore, the settings in Sam's user Group Policy object will have precedence over all the other settings.

3.   **Correct Answer: B**

A.   **Incorrect:** Domain Policy always overrides Local Group Policy objects. However, in this case there are two Domain GPOs. By default, the Mobile Computer domain GPO will override even the Default Domain Policy.

B.   **Correct:** Domain Policy overrides Local Group Policy objects. If there are multiple Domain Group Policy objects, a GPO linked to an OU will override the Default Domain GPO.

C.   **Incorrect:** Domain Group Policy objects always override Local Computer Group Policy objects. In this example the Local Computer Group Policy object would be overridden by all other GPOs, including the Non-Administrators Local Group Policy object.

D.   **Incorrect:** Domain Group Policy objects always override Local Computer Group Policy objects.

4.   **Correct Answers: B and D**

A.   **Incorrect:** User Local Group Policy objects only contain definitions for User Configuration settings.

B.   **Correct:** The Local Computer Group Policy object contains definitions for both Computer Configuration and User Configuration settings.

C.   **Incorrect:** The Non-Administrators Local Group Policy objects only contain definitions for User Configuration settings.

D.   **Correct:** The Default Domain Group Policy object contains definitions for both Computer Configuration and User Configuration settings.

Lesson 2

1.   **Correct Answers: A, B, and D**

A.   **Correct:** Like Windows XP, Windows Vista processes user Group Policy settings when the user logs on.

B.   **Correct:** Windows Vista, unlike Windows XP, processes Group Policy settings when the user connects to an internal network using a VPN.

C. **Incorrect:** Group Policy settings are never pushed from domain controllers; they are always pulled by the client computers. Client computers do query for Group Policy updates on a regular basis, but they cannot determine when a Group Policy change has been made.

D. **Correct:** Windows Vista processes Group Policy when the power state changes, such as when a computer resumes from Sleep.

2. **Correct Answers: A and D**

A. **Correct:** With Windows Vista, administrators can grant users the right to install certain classes of devices or specific device IDs without requiring the users to have administrative privileges. This was not possible in earlier versions of Windows.

B. **Incorrect:** You can use Group Policy settings to prevent users from offering Remote Assistance. However, you can also configure this setting for Windows XP.

C. **Incorrect:** You can use Group Policy settings to configure programs to run at user logon with Windows 2000 or later operating systems, using the User or Computer Configuration\Administrative Templates\System\Logon\Run These Programs At User Logon setting. It is not new to Windows Vista.

D. **Correct:** Requiring the Secure Desktop is an option of User Access Control (UAC), which is a Windows Vista–only feature.

3. **Correct Answer: B**

A. **Incorrect:** This Group Policy setting configures User Account Control (UAC), which was not a component of Windows XP. Modifying this setting would have no impact on compatibility but could improve security.

B. **Correct:** By default, Windows Vista handles AutoRun differently from Windows XP. You can modify this Group Policy setting to return Windows Vista to the Windows XP behavior, which automatically executed the AutoRun mandates on removable media.

C. **Incorrect:** You might modify this setting if you want to aggregate and analyze error reports in your organization, rather than sending them directly to Microsoft. However, changing this setting would not directly impact application compatibility.

D. **Incorrect:** The Program Compatibility Assistant (PCA) is enabled by default, which improves application compatibility with Windows XP. Therefore, changing this setting from its default would reduce compatibility rather than improve it.

Lesson 3

1. **Correct Answers: A and C**

A. **Correct:** If the policy was successfully processed, you will find an Event ID 8006 shortly after the Event ID 4006. Successful processing generates an Event ID exactly 4000 higher than the Event ID created when processing began.

B. **Incorrect:** Events in the 4000–4299 range indicate that Group Policy processing is beginning, not ending.

C. **Correct:** Events in the 6000–6299 range indicate that Group Policy processing ended with a warning. Because the last digit is the same as the Event ID that started it (the Event ID is exactly 2000 higher), the Event IDs correlate to each other.

D. **Incorrect:** Correlating Event IDs will be exactly 1000, 2000, 3000, or 4000 higher than the Event ID added when processing began.

2. **Correct Answers: B, C, and D**

A. **Incorrect:** You can choose Basic User as the security level for any software restriction type except certificates.

B. **Correct:** You can choose Basic User as the security level for hash rules. When you choose the Basic User security level, a program cannot run with elevated privileges.

C. **Correct:** You can choose Basic User as the security level for path rules.

D. **Correct:** You can choose Basic User as the security level for network zone rules.

3. **Correct Answer: B**

A. **Incorrect:** You cannot use security templates to define software restriction policies.

B. **Correct:** The Change The Time Zone setting is located within Computer Configuration\Windows Settings\Security Settings\Local Policies\User Rights Assignment in a Group Policy object (GPO), which is duplicated within a security template. Only GPO settings within the Computer Configuration\Windows Settings\Security Settings node can be defined by a security template.

C. **Incorrect:** You cannot use security templates to define logon scripts.

D. **Incorrect:** Security templates do not contain settings for Internet Explorer.

4. **Correct Answers: B and D**

A. **Incorrect:** The Security Templates snap-in enabled you to view and edit security templates. Security templates do not include settings for software restrictions, however.

B. **Correct:** Event Viewer logs all blocked applications to the Application Event Log and includes the globally unique identifier (GUID) for the Group Policy object (GPO) that contained the software restriction policy. You can then run GPResult /Z to find the GPO name that corresponds to that GUID.

C. **Incorrect:** The Security Configuration And Analysis tool enables you to compare a computer's current configuration to a security template. Security templates do not include settings for software restrictions, however.

D. **Correct:** Running GPResult /Z outputs a list of all Group Policy objects (GPOs) that affect the current computer, including the globally unique identifier (GUID) for each GPO. You can use this output to identify the name of the GPO based on the GUID included with the software restriction event in the Application Event Log.

Chapter 4: Case Scenario Answers

Case Scenario 1: Configuring a Windows Vista Computer for a Kiosk

1. You should use Windows Vista. Windows Vista is the securest Windows client operating system, and it provides flexible configuration options for kiosk computers.

2. Your manager didn't want the computer to provide any way for an attacker to get to your internal network. So you shouldn't make it a member of your domain. If you did, an attacker might be able to gain domain privileges by installing a Trojan horse or keylogging tools onto the computer. Using the Control Panel would be very time-consuming, and it wouldn't provide the full set of configuration options provided by Group Policy settings. So your best choice is to use the MLGPO capability of Windows Vista and to keep the computer a member of a workgroup, rather than your Active Directory domain.

3. Windows Vista provides Group Policy settings that enable you to block removable storage devices. You should enable these settings. Additionally, you should provide as much physical protection for the computer as possible by locking the computer inside a case.

Case Scenario 2: Troubleshooting Group Policy Objects

1. You should look in the Application Event Log to identify the GUID of the GPO that contains the software restriction. Then you can use the GPResult command-line tool to find the name of the GPO. Alternatively, you could use the RSoP graphical tool to view all software restrictions applied to Carol's computer and user account. However, RSoP will not indicate exactly which caused her specific problem; it will only allow you to browse active software restrictions.

2. No, the domain software restrictions will override the local software restrictions.

3. Most likely Simon moved Carol's user account into the Temps OU, causing Carol's user account to inherit those software restrictions. The computer account is probably not causing the problems because Arlene said she applied them to the User Configuration node of the GPO.

Chapter 5: Lesson Review Answers

Lesson 1

1. **Correct Answers: B and D**

   A. **Incorrect:** An expired certificate would cause Internet Explorer to display a different message.

   B. **Correct:** If an attacker redirected traffic to a malicious server with an SSL certificate, the malicious server's SSL certificate probably wouldn't be issued for the same name by a trusted CA. Therefore, Internet Explorer would alert the user that the common name listed in the certificate doesn't match the name in the shortcut.

   C. **Incorrect:** An untrusted CA would cause Internet Explorer to display a different message.

   D. **Correct:** The most likely cause of this error is that the user typed a valid hostname for a legitimate server, but the server's certificate was issued for another name. SSL certificates can contain only a single hostname (such as CONTOSO-SERVER), but the server might be available by different names (such as 192.168.10.10, contoso-server.contoso.com, or www.contoso.com). Any name except the single name listed in the certificate will cause Internet Explorer to display this error.

2. **Correct Answers: B, C, and D**

   A. **Incorrect:** Internet Explorer can render animated GIFs, or any images, without requiring a Protected Mode prompt.

   B. **Correct:** Embedded audio requires a plug-in even if it uses Windows Media Player. Before the plug-in is activated, the user must click the Information Bar to enable the plug-in.

   C. **Correct:** Embedded video requires a plug-in, even if it uses Windows Media Player. Before the plug-in is activated, the user must click the Information Bar to enable the plug-in.

   D. **Correct:** Viewing the source code of a webpage requires Internet Explorer to open Notepad. This requires elevated privileges, which causes Internet Explorer to display a Protected Mode confirmation prompt.

3. **Correct Answer: B**

   A. **Incorrect:** The compatibility layer doesn't need to virtualize storing a cookie.

   B. **Correct:** If an add-on attempts to store a file in the Documents folder, the compatibility layer will redirect the file to \%userprofile%\AppData\Local\Microsoft \Windows\Temporary Internet Files\Virtualized to protect the user's security.

   C. **Incorrect:** Web applications can prompt the user to upload a file without the request being redirected.

   D. **Incorrect:** Add-ons can store files in the Temporary Internet Files folder without the compatibility layer virtualizing the request.

4. **Correct Answers: B and C**

   A. **Incorrect:** To run an ActiveX control, the user must click the Information Bar. Right-clicking the webpage will not provide that as an option.

   B. **Correct:** The easiest way to enable an ActiveX control is to click the Information Bar.

   C. **Correct:** It's typically safe to add intranet sites to the Trusted Sites list. Sites on the Trusted Sites list automatically run most ActiveX controls.

   D. **Incorrect:** Disabling Protected Mode will not cause ActiveX controls to run automatically.

Lesson 2

1. **Correct Answer: B**

   A. **Incorrect:** If you rely on employees to manually launch Windows Update, they will inevitably forget. As a result, computer security will suffer in the long term because important updates will not be installed.

B. **Correct:** For small organizations it is typically not worth the effort to configure a WSUS server. Therefore, the default configuration of downloading updates directly from Microsoft is sufficient.

C. **Incorrect:** For small organizations that do not have a requirement to approve updates, WSUS is unnecessary.

D. **Incorrect:** SMS is designed for enterprises with complex software management needs. It would be unnecessarily time-consuming to deploy SMS for a small organization.

2. **Correct Answer: C**

A. **Incorrect:** If you rely on employees to manually launch Windows Update, they will inevitably forget. As a result, computer security will suffer in the long term because important updates will not be installed.

B. **Incorrect:** Configuring Windows Update to retrieve updates directly from Microsoft would not give IT the opportunity to review and approve updates prior to deployment.

C. **Correct:** WSUS will give the IT department the ability to approve updates before deployment.

D. **Incorrect:** SMS is designed for enterprises with complex software management needs. It would be unnecessarily time-consuming to deploy SMS for most organizations with only 100 computers.

3. **Correct Answer: D**

A. **Incorrect:** Earlier versions of Windows used the Update.exe tool to install updates. Windows Vista uses the built-in Wusa.exe tool instead.

B. **Incorrect:** Use Msiexec.exe to install Windows Installer files with an .MSI extension. You cannot use Msiexec.exe to install Windows Vista updates from Microsoft, however.

C. **Incorrect:** Although updates for earlier versions of Windows were published using .exe files, updates for Windows Vista are not executable files.

D. **Correct:** Windows Vista updates are distributed in .MSU files. Windows Vista includes the Wusa.exe command-line tool for installing updates from a batch file or at the command line.

Lesson 3

1. **Correct Answers: A and D**

A. **Correct:** Windows Defender adds events to the System event log when changes are blocked or when the user chooses to respond to a Windows Defender notification.

B. **Incorrect:** Windows Defender does not use the Application event log. Instead, it writes events to the System event log.

C. **Incorrect:** Windows Defender does not use the Security event log. Instead, it writes events to the System event log.

D. **Correct:** You can always view Windows Defender actions in the Windows Defender History.

2. **Correct Answer: A**
    A. **Correct:** Windows Defender adds an event to the System event log when it updates definitions, whether the update is successful or not.
    B. **Incorrect:** Windows Defender does not use the Application event log. Instead, it writes events to the System event log.
    C. **Incorrect:** Windows Defender does not use the Security event log. Instead, it writes events to the System event log.
    D. **Incorrect:** The Windows Defender History records actions about changes that Windows Defender monitors and whether they were permitted or blocked. It does not contain information about definition updates, however.

3. **Correct Answers: A, B, and D**
    A. **Correct:** Windows Defender real-time protection can alert the user if a new service is installed.
    B. **Correct:** Windows Defender real-time protection can alert the user if a program configures itself to start automatically.
    C. **Incorrect:** Windows Defender cannot analyze the contents of Word documents.
    D. **Correct:** Windows Defender real-time protection can alert the user if an add-on is installed.

Lesson 4

1. **Correct Answer: B**
    A. **Incorrect:** You cannot publish programs under Computer Configuration; you can only assign them.
    B. **Correct:** Publishing a Windows Installer package under the User Configuration node of Group Policy causes the package to be available to users from within Control Panel. Additionally, if they attempt to open a document that is associated with the program, Windows Vista will automatically install the package, so the user can open the document.
    C. **Incorrect:** Assigning programs automatically installs them, which would inconvenience users connected using a low-bandwidth connection.
    D. **Incorrect:** Assigning programs automatically installs them, which would inconvenience users connected using a low-bandwidth connection.

2. **Correct Answer: D**
    A. **Incorrect:** The FC tool compares two files. It does not install Windows Installer packages.
    B. **Incorrect:** RACAgent is a scheduled task that collects data for Reliability Monitor. You cannot use it to install Windows Installer packages.
    C. **Incorrect:** WUAgent is the Windows Update Agent, which retrieves updates from Microsoft or from a WSUS server. You cannot use it to install a Windows Installer package from a script.
    D. **Correct:** You can use MSIExec to install Windows Installer packages without prompting the user.

3. **Correct Answer: C**

   A. **Incorrect:** Disabling the Turn Off User Installed Windows Sidebar Gadgets policy does not prevent users from running any Windows Sidebar Gadgets. Disabling this setting enables users to install Windows Sidebar Gadgets and to use the Sidebar itself.

   B. **Incorrect:** Enabling the Turn Off User Installed Windows Sidebar Gadgets policy does not prevent users from running Windows Sidebar Gadgets.

   C. **Correct:** Enabling the Turn Off Windows Sidebar policy prevents users from running Windows Sidebar Gadgets.

   D. **Incorrect:** Using a software restriction policy does not prevent users from running Windows Sidebar Gadgets.

Chapter 5: Case Scenario Answers

Case Scenario 1: Unwanted Internet Explorer Add-On

1. You can remove it using the Manage Add-Ons dialog box. To open that dialog box, launch Internet Explorer, click the Tools button on the toolbar, click Manage Add-Ons, and then click Enable Or Disable Add-Ons.

2. Yes. Internet Explorer will not automatically install add-ons from most websites. Instead, it will display an information bar, and users will need to click the information bar to install the add-on. Additionally, Protected Mode will require administrative privileges before some types of add-ons can be installed (but Protected Mode will prompt the user only if the add-on requires elevated privileges). Finally, Windows Defender will alert the user to any changes made by an add-on that might be unwanted, such as changing the user's home page.

3. You can use the Group Policy settings in User Configuration\Administrative Templates\Windows Components\Internet Explorer\Security Features\Add-on Management to enable or disable specific add-ons throughout your organization. For example, you could use this to list all add-ons created by your internal development team in the Add-On List setting and then enable the Deny All Add-Ons Unless Specifically Allowed In The Add-On List setting to block other add-ons.

Case Scenario 2: Distribute Updates

1. Although it's not always required for offices this small, WSUS would provide the ability to test and approve updates before deployment. SMS could also provide this capability, but the infrastructure and cost aren't justifiable for a network this small.

2. Yes, WSUS must be installed on a server. In this case, you could install it on the Windows Server 2003 computer.

3. Yes, WSUS works with both Windows XP and Windows Vista clients.

4. You could use Active Directory Group Policy settings to configure the client computers.

Chapter 6: Lesson Review Answers

Lesson 1

1. **Correct Answers: A, B, and D**

   A. **Correct:** The forwarding computer must have the Windows Rights Management service started to forward events.

   B. **Correct:** The collecting computer must have the Windows Rights Management service started to receive events.

   C. **Incorrect:** Internet Information Services is not required for Windows Rights Management Services even though Windows Rights Management uses HTTP for communications by default.

   D. **Correct:** The forwarding computer must receive incoming Windows Rights Management connections. Therefore, a Windows Firewall exception must be enabled. The winrm quick-config command does this automatically.

   E. **Incorrect:** Event forwarding is not enabled by default.

2. **Correct Answer: C**

   A. **Incorrect:** You can use the Event Viewer snap-in to create and manage subscriptions. However, Event Viewer does not enable you to set a custom interval. Instead, you must use the Wecutil command-line tool.

   B. **Incorrect:** The Windows Remote Management Command Line Tool (Winrm) is used to configure the Windows Remote Management service. You cannot use it to manage subscriptions.

   C. **Correct:** The Windows Event Collector Utility (Wecutil) is the correct tool for changing subscription settings that cannot be changed from the Event Viewer snap-in.

   D. **Incorrect:** Use the Windows Events Command Line Utility (Wevutil) to manage events and event logs. You cannot use it to manage subscriptions.

3. **Correct Answer: A**

   A. **Correct:** Choosing Minimize Latency sets the interval to 30 seconds. However, it might take longer for events to synchronize depending on factors such as waiting for the Windows Remote Management service to start.

   B. **Incorrect:** The default setting for subscriptions, Normal, has a timeout of 15 minutes.

   C. **Incorrect:** Minimize Latency sets the interval to 30 seconds, not 30 minutes.

   D. **Incorrect:** If you choose the Minimize Bandwidth subscription optimization, six hours is the default setting.

4. **Correct Answer: D**

   A. **Incorrect:** This command is required only in workgroup environments; you do not need to run this command in Active Directory environments.

   B. **Incorrect:** This command is required only in workgroup environments. Additionally, you need to run this command on the collecting computer, not the forwarding computer.

   C. **Incorrect:** In an Active Directory environment, you do not need to change group memberships on the collecting computer.

   D. **Correct:** To allow a subscription to work with the default authentication setting of Machine Account, you must add the collecting computer's machine account to the forwarding computer's Event Log Readers local group.

Lesson 2

1. **Correct Answer: B**

   A. **Incorrect:** By default, the Performance Monitor snap-in does not support comparing two windows.

   B. **Correct:** To compare two windows, you must run Perfmon.exe with the /sys parameter.

   C. **Incorrect:** By default, the Performance Monitor snap-in within the Computer Management console does not support comparing two windows.

   D. **Incorrect:** You should use the /sys parameter, not the /compare parameter.

2. **Correct Answers: B and C**

   A. **Incorrect:** The LAN Diagnostics performance counter logs networking data but does not log processor utilization.

   B. **Correct:** The System Diagnostics data collector set includes performance counters for processor utilization.

   C. **Correct:** The System Diagnostics data collector set includes performance counters for processor utilization.

   D. **Incorrect:** The Wireless Diagnostics performance counter logs networking data but does not log processor utilization.

3. **Correct Answer: B**

   A. **Incorrect:** The LAN Diagnostics performance counter logs networking data but does not gather information about hardware devices.

   B. **Correct:** The System Diagnostics data collector set generates a report that includes a list of any devices that are currently experiencing errors.

   C. **Incorrect:** The System Performance data collector set is focused on gathering performance data and does not collect hardware information.

   D. **Incorrect:** The Wireless Diagnostics performance counter is focused on diagnosing networking problems and will not report on malfunctioning hardware.

Lesson 3

1. **Correct Answers: A and D**

   A. **Correct:** You can configure scheduled tasks to launch at a specific time and at regular intervals, such as daily, weekly, or monthly.

    B.   **Incorrect:** You cannot tie scheduled tasks to users launching a process. As an alternative, you might create a script that launches both the user's e-mail and the task you need to run and replace the user's e-mail shortcut with the script.

    C.   **Incorrect:** You cannot tie scheduled tasks to launch when the screen saver starts. However, you could configure a scheduled task to launch at the same idle interval as that used by the screen saver, which would have the same effect.

    D.   **Correct:** You can configure scheduled tasks to run when the computer is idle. The Windows process that indexes files for easy searching uses this technique.

2. **Correct Answer: C**

    A.   **Incorrect:** Task Scheduler is the graphical console for managing scheduled tasks. It cannot be used from a command file.

    B.   **Incorrect:** At.exe was a command-line tool for scheduling tasks in earlier versions of Windows.

    C.   **Correct:** SchTasks.exe is the correct tool for managing scheduled tasks from the command prompt or a command file.

    D.   **Incorrect:** TaskMgr.exe is the Windows Task Manager. It cannot be used from a command file, nor can it be used to manage scheduled tasks.

3. **Correct Answers: A, C, and D**

    A.   **Correct:** You can use a scheduled task to start a program.

    B.   **Incorrect:** You cannot use a scheduled task to directly restart the computer. However, you could create a batch file that called the Shutdown.exe tool and schedule that batch file to run from a scheduled task.

    C.   **Correct:** You can use Task Scheduler to create a task that sends e-mail messages.

    D.   **Correct:** You can use Task Scheduler to display a message to the user.

Chapter 6: Case Scenario Answers

Case Scenario 1: Monitoring Kiosk Computers

1. You could configure event forwarding from the kiosk computers to your computer and forward just the important event.

2. You should use the Minimize Latency bandwidth optimization technique because it's important to receive the new events as soon as possible, and the number of computers is small enough that bandwidth should not be a problem.

3. You could configure a scheduled task with a trigger for Event ID 4226. Then you could configure an action for the scheduled task that sends an e-mail to your computer or mobile phone.

Case Scenario 2: Troubleshooting Client Computer Problems

1. Yes, Windows Vista collects a great deal of information about changes users make to computers and problems that arise. The quickest way to identify these changes and problems is to use the Reliability Monitor.

2. Yes. You can use data collector sets and reports to quickly build a report based on the system configuration. The built-in System Diagnostics data collector set will provide most of the information you need, and you can extend it to capture files or registry settings that your applications use to store configuration data.

Chapter 7: Lesson Review Answers

Lesson 1

1. **Correct Answers: A, B, and D**
   A. **Correct:** You can authenticate to a shared folder using credentials from Credential Manager.
   B. **Correct:** You can authenticate to a shared printer using credentials from Credential Manager.
   C. **Incorrect:** Credential Manager cannot complete the user name and password fields in an HTML form.
   D. **Correct:** If the website uses Hypertext Transfer Protocol (HTTP) authentication, which causes the Web browse to prompt the user for credentials rather than using an HTML form, Credential Manager can automatically supply the user name and password.

2. **Correct Answer: B**
   A. **Incorrect:** Windows XP required developers to replace the Graphical Identification and Authentication (GINA) interface in order to provide custom authentication mechanisms. Windows Vista has completely replaced the GINA interface with the credential provider. As a result, replacement GINAs are not supported.
   B. **Correct:** Windows Vista does have smart card authentication built in.
   C. **Incorrect:** Smart cards store certificates, such as those generated by a public key infrastructure (PKI).
   D. **Incorrect:** In Windows Vista users can reset their own PINs.

3. **Correct Answer: B**
   A. **Incorrect:** The Audit Logon Events audit policy logs local authentication attempts, as well as authentication attempts to the local computer from domain user accounts. However, enabling success auditing would log successful authentication attempts in which the user's credentials were correctly validated. It would not log unsuccessful attempts.
   B. **Correct:** The Audit Logon Events audit policy logs local authentication attempts, as well as authentication attempts to the local computer from domain user accounts. Selecting failure

auditing adds an event when the user fails to authenticate for any reason, including providing invalid credentials.

C. **Incorrect:** The Audit Account Logon Events audit policy only audits authentication requests received by domain controllers. Therefore, it would have no impact on a Windows Vista member computer.

D. **Incorrect:** The Audit Account Logon Events audit policy only audits authentication requests received by domain controllers. Therefore, it would have no impact on a Windows Vista member computer.

4. **Correct Answers: A and D**

A. **Correct:** Enabling auditing for logon attempts audits all authentication attempts to the local computer, including logging on locally.

B. **Incorrect:** Enabling auditing for logon attempts audits all authentication attempts to the local computer but not remote computers. However, the remote web server might add an audit event to its own event log if auditing is enabled.

C. **Incorrect:** Enabling auditing for logon attempts audits all authentication attempts to the local computer but not remote computers. However, the remote file server might add an audit event to its own event log if auditing is enabled.

D. **Correct:** Enabling auditing for logon attempts audits all authentication attempts to the local computer, including authentication at a UAC prompt. This includes UAC prompts that simply require the administrator to click the Continue button.

Lesson 2

1. **Correct Answer: C**

A. **Incorrect:** BitLocker Drive Encryption is not related to EFS.

B. **Incorrect:** The Computer Management console includes many snap-ins, but it does not include the Certificates snap-in.

C. **Correct:** Use the Certificates console to back up and restore EFS certificates. This allows you to access EFS-encrypted files after moving them to a different computer.

D. **Incorrect:** You can use the Services snap-in to manage services. However, you cannot use it to manage certificates.

2. **Correct Answer: A**

A. **Correct:** Encrypting File System (EFS) certificates are located in the *Certificates – Current User\Personal\Certificates* node.

B. **Incorrect:** Encrypting File System (EFS) certificates are not stored in this node.

C. **Incorrect:** Encrypting File System (EFS) certificates are per-user and not per-computer.

D. **Incorrect:** Encrypting File System (EFS) certificates are per-user and not per-computer.

3. **Correct Answers: B and C**

   A. **Incorrect:** After the BitLocker Drive Preparation Tool runs, the C:\ volume will consume all available disk space.

   B. **Correct:** The BitLocker Drive Preparation Tool creates a 1.5-GB S:\ volume and then allocates the rest of the disk to the C:\ volume.

   C. **Correct:** The BitLocker Drive Preparation Tool creates a 1.5-GB boot volume and assigns it the drive letter S.

   D. **Incorrect:** The S:\ boot volume is 1.5 GB, not 2.1 GB.

4. **Correct Answers: A, B, and D**

   A. **Correct:** If a computer has a TPM, you can enable BitLocker without requiring the user to enter a key or connect a USB flash drive.

   B. **Correct:** If a computer has a TPM, you can configure Windows Vista to prompt the user for a PIN before loading the operating system.

   C. **Incorrect:** If a computer does not have a TPM, your only option is to have the user insert a USB flash drive at startup. You must have a TPM to use PIN security at startup.

   D. **Correct:** With or without a TPM, you can configure BitLocker to require the user to insert a USB key at every startup.

Lesson 3

1. **Correct Answer: D**

   A. **Incorrect:** The Audit System Events policy audits events such as restarting or shutting down a computer. It does not track access to files.

   B. **Incorrect:** The Audit Privilege Use policy audits the usage of user rights. It does not track access to files.

   C. **Incorrect:** The Audit Process Tracking policy audits events such as program activation and process exiting. It does not track access to files.

   D. **Correct:** The Audit Object Access policy enables auditing of access to files and registry entries.

2. **Correct Answer: B**

   A. **Incorrect:** SecPol.msc is the Local Security Policy console. You can use this to configure auditing settings interactively, but it is not useful from the command line or from a script.

   B. **Correct:** You can use the AuditPol.exe command-line tool with the /set parameter to change auditing settings from the command line or from a script. You could also configure auditing settings to use a security template and the SecEdit.exe command-line tool.

   C. **Incorrect:** Mmc.exe is the Microsoft Management Console. You can use it to load the Group Policy Object Editor or the Local Security Policy snap-ins to edit auditing settings. However, you cannot use it from the command line or from a script.

D. **Incorrect:** ReLog.exe creates new performance logs based on data in existing performance logs. It cannot be used to configure auditing settings.

3. **Correct Answers: A, B, C, and D**

A. **Correct:** All events include the time the event was created.

B. **Correct:** Object audit events include the process that accessed the object.

C. **Correct:** Object audit events include the user name the process was running in.

D. **Correct:** Object audit events include the Access Request Information section, which details the rights the process requested to the file.

Chapter 7: Case Scenario Answers

Case Scenario 1: Recommend Data Protection Technologies

1. No. File permissions protect data only while the operating system is running. If an attacker has physical access to a computer, the attacker can easily load a different operating system that ignores NTFS file permissions.

2. Yes, encryption protects data even if an attacker has physical access to a computer. Windows Vista includes two types of encryption: EFS and BitLocker. EFS encrypts individual files, while BitLocker encrypts the entire system partition.

3. Both EFS and BitLocker allow you to share files across a network. In fact, neither type of encryption provides any protection across the network.

Case Scenario 2: Troubleshoot Permission Problems

1. This is an authorization problem. If it were an authentication problem, Ken would be prompted for credentials.

2. UAC won't always prompt the user to elevate privileges if a program wasn't created for Windows Vista. However, you could right-click the program and then click Run As Administrator to force UAC to grant elevated privileges to the program. Although that might temporarily solve the problem, it wouldn't be a good solution for Ken because he doesn't have an administrative user account.

3. The easiest way to solve Ken's problem would be to make Ken a member of the Administrators group and configure the program to always run as an administrator. However, this would reduce overall computer security by granting Ken excessive privileges. Instead, you should solve Ken's problem by identifying the exact resources the ExcelAnalyzer.exe tool requires and granting Ken's user account those additional privileges. To identify the exact resources, enable failure object access auditing, and then examine the Security event log. Alternatively, you could use the Process Monitor tool, available for download from Microsoft.com.

Chapter 8: Lesson Review Answers

Lesson 1

1. **Correct Answer: A**

   A. **Correct:** By default, the built-in Administrator account is disabled after an upgrade from Windows XP if another local administrator exists. If you need to access the built-in Administrator account, simply enable the account.

   B. **Incorrect:** If you cannot log on with the built-in Administrator account normally, you typically will not be able to log on in Safe Mode. In addition, Safe Mode is a restricted environment and would not allow a user full access to his or her settings.

   C. **Incorrect:** Migrating the built-in Administrator's profile to another account is unnecessary. You only need to enable the account.

   D. **Incorrect:** Migrating the built-in Administrator's profile to another account is unnecessary. You only need to enable the account.

2. **Correct Answer: D**

   A. **Incorrect:** This solution would make sense if the manager frequently needed administrative privileges. However, he needs to perform an administrative task only every few days. For this reason, it is safer not to promote his account to an administrator account.

   B. **Incorrect:** It is unnecessary for the manager to log off and log back on with an administrator account. He needs to provide administrator credentials at a credential prompt only when he needs to perform an administrative task.

   C. **Incorrect:** It is unnecessary for the user to switch accounts to a new administrator account. He needs to provide administrator credentials at a credential prompt only when he needs to perform an administrative task.

   D. **Correct:** Because the manager needs to perform administrative tasks only occasionally, it is safer to keep his account a standard user account and to provide him with the credentials needed to perform administrative tasks when necessary.

Lesson 2

1. **Correct Answer: B**

   A. **Incorrect:** This policy setting does not enforce any particular user interface behavior for standard users. It only affects administrators.

   B. **Correct:** This policy setting provides a credential prompt for standard users so that they can elevate to perform administrative tasks when required.

   C. **Incorrect:** This policy setting effectively disables User Account Control (UAC) behavior for all users. It does not provide standard users with an elevation prompt.

    D. **Incorrect:** This policy setting does the opposite of what is required: it blocks access to administrative tools without providing any elevation prompt for standard users.

2. **Correct Answer: C**

    A. **Incorrect:** This setting would ensure that administrators see a consent prompt every time they perform a task that requires elevation.

    B. **Incorrect:** This setting would force a credential prompt to appear every time administrators attempt to perform a task that requires elevation.

    C. **Correct:** This setting allows administrators to perform administrative tasks without being prompted to provide consent or credentials for elevation.

    D. **Incorrect:** Although this setting would achieve the desired outcome, it would also cause undesired effects. For example, standard users would no longer be prompted for elevation when they attempted to perform an administrative task.

3. **Correct Answer: D**

    A. **Incorrect:** This setting ensures that administrators are prompted for consent whenever they attempt to perform an administrative task, but the setting does not affect standard users.

    B. **Incorrect:** This setting ensures that administrators are prompted for credentials whenever they attempt to perform an administrative task, but the setting does not affect standard users.

    C. **Incorrect:** This setting ensures that standard users are prompted for credentials whenever they attempt to perform an administrative task, but the setting does not affect administrators.

    D. **Correct:** If neither standard users nor administrators are receiving elevation prompts, User Account Control (UAC) is disabled. By setting this policy to Enabled, you will turn on UAC at the domain level and ensure that both standard users and administrators receive the default UAC prompts.

Chapter 8: Case Scenario Answers

Case Scenario 1: Configuring User Account Control

1. Set the Run All Administrators In Admin Approval Mode security policy setting to Enabled.
2. Set the Behavior Of The Elevation Prompt For Standard Users security policy setting to Automatically Deny Elevation Requests.

Case Scenario 2: Troubleshooting User Account Control

1. Open a new command prompt by using the Run As Administrator option.
2. Configure the application to run as administrator.

Chapter 9: Lesson Review Answers

Lesson 1

1. **Correct Answer: D**
   - A. **Incorrect:** Every computer must be assigned a unique IP address.
   - B. **Incorrect:** If DHCP is enabled, it means the computer attempts to retrieve an automatic IP address configuration. If DHCP were disabled, that would indicate that an administrator had manually configured the IP address.
   - C. **Incorrect:** Windows Vista computers might generate a random IP address if a DHCP server is not available. However, having DHCP enabled does not indicate whether the computer has a random IP address.
   - D. **Correct:** When DHCP is enabled, it means the computer is configured to retrieve IP configuration settings from a DHCP server.

2. **Correct Answers: A and B**
   - A. **Correct:** To view a computer's IP address from Network And Sharing Center, click the View Status link.
   - B. **Correct:** You can run IPConfig from a command line to view the current IP address.
   - C. **Incorrect:** The Network Map allows you to view your computer in relation to other network resources and hosts. However, you cannot use it to view your current IP address.
   - D. **Incorrect:** Use Network Explorer to browse available network resources. You cannot use Network Explorer to view your current IP address.

3. **Correct Answer: C**
   - A. **Incorrect:** Network Explorer is not affected by using DHCP or a manually assigned IP address.
   - B. **Incorrect:** Network Explorer is not affected by using DHCP or a manually assigned IP address.
   - C. **Correct:** For Network Explorer to display network resources, Network Discovery must be enabled. Network Discovery is disabled by default on Public and Domain networks—it is enabled by default only on Private networks.
   - D. **Incorrect:** Clicking Start and then clicking Network opens the Network Explorer, which does not depend on Network Mapping. Only the Network Map requires Network Mapping to be enabled.

4. **Correct Answer: B**
   - A. **Incorrect:** Network Discovery is disabled by default on Public networks to reduce security risks.
   - B. **Correct:** Network Discovery is enabled by default on Private networks.

C.   **Incorrect:** Network Discovery is disabled by default on domain networks.

D.   **Incorrect:** By default, wireless networks are assigned the Public network profile, which has Network Discovery disabled.

Lesson 2

1.   **Correct Answers: B and C**

A.   **Incorrect:** You could use Ping to determine if the mail server is connected to the network. However, Ping will not indicate whether the mail server is responding to incoming e-mail requests—it's possible that the mail server is online, but the mail service itself has stopped.

B.   **Correct:** You can use Telnet to connect to the TCP port you use to download incoming e-mail. If the mail server responds to the Telnet request, you know that the mail server is responding correctly and that no firewall is blocking the connection attempt.

C.   **Correct:** Like Telnet, you can use PortQry to determine whether the mail service is responding on the mail server. PortQry is not included with Windows Vista, however.

D.   **Incorrect:** PathPing determines whether a host and every router between your computer and the remote host are responding. It has the same weakness as Ping; however, it does not determine whether the mail service itself is responding.

2.   **Correct Answer: D**

A.   **Incorrect:** This is a private IP address. However, Automatic Private IP Address (APIPA; the technique Windows Vista uses to assign an IP address when no DHCP server is available) does not use this range.

B.   **Incorrect:** The special IP address 127.0.0.1 always refers to the local host, whether or not DHCP configuration was successful.

C.   **Incorrect:** This is a private IP address. However, Automatic Private IP Address (APIPA; the technique Windows Vista uses to assign an IP address when no DHCP server is available) does not use this range.

D.   **Correct:** Any IP address starting with 169.254 is an Automatic Private IP Address (APIPA) address. Windows Vista assigns an APIPA address when a DHCP server is not available.

3.   **Correct Answer: A**

A.   **Correct:** Nslookup sends a query to a Domain Name System (DNS) server and reports whether the DNS server was available and whether the name could be resolved.

B.   **Incorrect:** Ipconfig reports the current IP configuration. Additionally, with the /release and /renew parameters, you can use it to retrieve a new IP address from the DHCP server. Although you could use it to determine your Domain Name System (DNS) server's IP address, you would not be able to use it to test the DNS server.

C.   **Incorrect:** Ping tests connectivity to a remote host. Although you could try pinging your Domain Name System (DNS) server, that wouldn't tell you whether you were able to successfully resolve hostnames.

D. **Incorrect:** Netstat shows current connections and cannot be used to identify name resolution problems.

Chapter 9: Case Scenario Answers

Case Scenario 1: Choosing a Network Configuration Method

1. You should use DHCP to configure the client network settings. Manually configuring the IP addresses would be okay to begin with, but you'd need to update the settings when network management added a second router.
2. No, DHCP does not require Active Directory.

Case Scenario 2: Troubleshooting a Network Problem

1. First, have Gordon run Windows Network Diagnostics. That will diagnose the most common network problems and can automatically fix some problems.
2. To determine whether the problem is with the local network, have Gordon attempt to contact a network resource on his local network. For example, have Gordon attempt to ping his default gateway or use PathPing to test the connection to a resource on the WAN. If he can reach the default gateway but not resources on the WAN, the problem is related to the WAN.
3. Have Gordon attempt to contact a network resource using the IP address, rather than the hostname. For example, if Gordon can browse *www.microsoft.com* using one of the website's IP addresses but cannot browse the website using the hostname, the problem is definitely related to name resolution.

Chapter 10: Lesson Review Answers

Lesson 1

1. **Correct Answer: A**

    A. **Correct:** If the filter were not configured as mirrored, the security requirement defined in the filter action would be applied in only one direction.

    B. **Incorrect:** Because both computers are members of the Nwtraders domain, Kerberos is the best authentication method to use.

    C. **Incorrect:** Because both computers are members of the Nwtraders domain, Kerberos is the best authentication method to use.

    D. **Incorrect:** If encryption is occurring in only one direction, the specific nature of the filter action is not the cause of the problem because the filter action is configured the same way on both computers.

2. **Correct Answer: D**

   A. **Incorrect:** This rule would block traffic to and from computers outside the domain.

   B. **Incorrect:** This rule would block connections from computers outside the domain.

   C. **Incorrect:** Kerberos is the best choice of authentication method because you want to authenticate data within the domain only. There is no need to create a certificate infrastructure since Active Directory (Kerberos) authentication is already available.

   D. **Correct:** This choice would enable ClientA to authenticate all data from within the domain but would not require authentication from sources outside of the domain.

Lesson 2

1. **Correct Answer: B**

   A. **Incorrect:** The problem reported is related to a newly installed application and not to an unsigned driver.

   B. **Correct:** This step is likely to fix the problem because unless an exception is made for the program, Windows Firewall will block incoming connections from other computers running the same application.

   C. **Incorrect:** This solution is insufficient because we don't know whether the remote computers running the application are members of the same domain. In addition, the stated allowed rule is restricted only to secure connections, and we don't know whether the remote clients can be authenticated or whether they are even IPSec-aware.

   D. **Incorrect:** This procedure is unnecessary because outbound connections by default are already allowed.

2. **Correct Answer: C**

   A. **Incorrect:** This setting would prevent firewall exceptions from being configured in Control Panel but would not affect firewall notification messages from being displayed.

   B. **Incorrect:** This setting would prevent firewall exceptions from being prohibited but would not affect firewall notification messages from being displayed.

   C. **Correct:** This setting would prevent firewall notification messages from being displayed on user desktops.

   D. **Incorrect:** This setting would have the opposite effect of what is desired: it would prevent administrators from being able to disable firewall notification messages.

Chapter 10: Case Scenario Answers

Case Scenario: Troubleshooting Network Security

1. Determine whether a firewall exception or inbound allow rule has been configured for the application. If one does not exist, create one.
2. Assign the Client (Respond Only) IPSec policy.
3. On Res1, create a Connection Security Rule requiring authentication.

Chapter 11: Lesson Review Answers

Lesson 1

1. **Correct Answer: D**
   A. **Incorrect:** Any user can connect to an unprotected wireless network.
   B. **Incorrect:** WEP provides authentication and encryption for wireless networks. However, the encryption is very weak and easily cracked by a knowledgeable attacker.
   C. **Incorrect:** WPA-PSK is very difficult to crack. However, all users use a single key. Therefore, if one of the users shares the key or his or her computer is compromised, an attacker could access your wireless network. Changing the WPA-PSK key is very difficult and time-consuming.
   D. **Correct:** WPA-EAP provides the highest level of security. It is inherently more difficult to crack than WEP, and because all users do not share a single key, you don't have the risk of losing the key that WPA-PSK provides.

2. **Correct Answers: C and D**
   A. **Incorrect:** WEP requires clients to authenticate using a static key. Smart cards cannot be used.
   B. **Incorrect:** WPA-PSK, also known as WPA-Personal, requires clients to authenticate using a static key. Smart cards cannot be used.
   C. **Correct:** Both versions of WPA-EAP support authentication using certificates stored on smart cards.
   D. **Correct:** Both versions of WPA-EAP support authentication using certificates stored on smart cards.

3. **Correct Answers: A, C, and D**
   A. **Correct:** Using a Remote Authentication Dial-In User Service (RADIUS) server, a wireless access point using WPA-EAP can authenticate a user with their domain credentials.
   B. **Incorrect:** WPA-EAP does not support using a static key. Wi-Fi Protected Access, preshared key (WPA-PSK) does, however.

    C. **Correct:** WPA-EAP supports authentication using a certificate, including certificates stored on the local computer.

    D. **Correct:** WPA-EAP supports authentication using a certificate, including certificates stored on a smart card.

Lesson 2

1. **Correct Answer: D**

    A. **Incorrect:** The Diagnostics-Networking log does contain useful information logged by Windows Network Diagnostics. However, the information is not as detailed as that contained in the WLAN-AutoConfig log.

    B. **Incorrect:** The System log does contain information from Windows Network Diagnostics, however, the information is not as detailed as that contained in the WLAN-AutoConfig log.

    C. **Incorrect:** The Wired-AutoConfig log contains information about connecting to wired networks, not wireless networks.

    D. **Correct:** The WLAN-AutoConfig log contains the details of all wireless connection attempts, whether successful or unsuccessful. That log will allow you to determine which wireless network the user attempted to connect to and the reason for the failure.

2. **Correct Answers: B and C**

    A. **Incorrect:** If you didn't have a wireless adapter installed, Device Manager would not show it under Network Adapters.

    B. **Correct:** If the wireless radio is turned off, it will still be visible in Device Manager. However, you will not be able to view any wireless networks—which exactly match your symptoms.

    C. **Correct:** If the wireless network does not broadcast a service set identifier (SSID), you need to manually create a wireless profile before you can connect to the network. Most wireless networks do broadcast an SSID, however, so although this is a valid option, the most likely cause is that the wireless radio has been turned off.

    D. **Incorrect:** Authentication failures occur only after you attempt to connect to the wireless network.

3. **Correct Answers: A and B**

    A. **Correct:** Ad hoc networks support WEP, but the security is not as strong as WPA-PSK.

    B. **Correct:** Ad hoc networks support WPA-PSK. All users must type a passphrase to connect to the network.

    C. **Incorrect:** WPA-EAP requires the use of a Remote Authentication Dial-In User Service (RADIUS) server and therefore cannot be used with an ad hoc network.

    D. **Incorrect:** WPA2-EAP requires the use of a RADIUS server and therefore cannot be used with an ad hoc network.

4. **Correct Answer: C**

   A. **Incorrect:** You can use an enterprise CA to generate a certificate for your RADIUS server, and clients can authenticate to the wireless access point using certificates generated by an enterprise CA. However, you can generate a certificate for the RADIUS server using any CA, and users can authenticate using their domain credentials rather than certificates.

   B. **Incorrect:** Using an Active Directory domain makes it easier to implement WPA-EAP and allows users to authenticate using their domain credentials. However, an Active Directory domain is not required for using WPA-EAP—you can also authenticate with certificates.

   C. **Correct:** Wireless access points always pass credentials to a RADIUS server for authentication. Therefore, a RADIUS server is required regardless of how you configure WPA-EAP.

   D. **Incorrect:** WPA-EAP supports smart card authentication when used with Windows Vista. However, smart cards are not a requirement.

Chapter 11: Case Scenario Answers

Case Scenario 1: Teaching a User to Connect to Wireless Networks

1. Click Start, and then click Connect To. Select your wireless network, click Connect, and then follow the prompts that appear.

2. Absolutely. Most public wireless networks are unencrypted, which means anyone can see all your network traffic.

3. You can enable security in your applications. For example, most mail servers accept encrypted connections. For better protection, connect to an internal virtual private network (VPN) that will encrypt all your data.

4. Not the first time you connect. If you connect and choose to save the connection, Windows Vista will automatically connect if it sees the same SSID in the future.

Case Scenario 2: Troubleshooting Problems Connecting to a Wireless Network

1. Parry probably has a weak wireless connection. To fix it, Parry should move closer to the wireless access point. If you managed the wireless network, you might be able to improve it by moving the wireless access point, adjusting the power of the transmitter, or replacing the antenna. However, at a public wireless access point, you do not have control over these factors.

2. Compatibility problems can also cause unreliable wireless connections. For example, if the wireless access point uses a poor or outdated implementation of the wireless standards, the wireless connection might experience those symptoms.

Chapter 12: Lesson Review Answers

Lesson 1

1. **Correct Answer: D**
    A. **Incorrect:** The error that SallyB receives is not related to her user rights on Vista1.
    B. **Incorrect:** The error that SallyB receives is not related to her user rights on Vista1.
    C. **Incorrect:** This option would allow SallyB to use Remote Desktop to connect to a Windows XP Professional Computer from a Windows Vista computer. SallyB wants to connect to a Windows Vista computer from a Windows XP computer.
    D. **Correct:** If a user receives an error stating that the remote computer requires NLA, the remote computer's System properties are restricting Remote Desktop connections to those versions native to Windows Vista and later. To allow earlier versions to connect, select the option in the Remote tab to allow connections from computers running any version of Remote Desktop.

2. **Correct Answer: C**
    A. **Incorrect:** The error that FredL receives is not related to his user rights on Vista2.
    B. **Incorrect:** The error that FredL receives is not related to his user rights on Vista2.
    C. **Correct:** If a user receives this type of error, the Remote Desktop settings on the local computer are preventing connections to computers that do not support Network Level Authentication. You can change these settings in the Advanced tab of Remote Desktop Connection options.
    D. **Incorrect:** This option would allow FredL to use Remote Desktop to connect to Vista2 from a computer running Windows XP. It would not allow him to connect to a Windows XP computer from Vista1.

Lesson 2

1. **Correct Answer: C**
    A. **Incorrect:** If you connect to the remote computer through Remote Desktop, the user will no longer be able to see or control his desktop.
    B. **Incorrect:** Allowing the user to connect to your computer through Remote Desktop only allows him to establish a session on your computer. It does not allow him to show you the procedure on his computer.
    C. **Correct:** To see the user demonstrate the problem on his computer, he should use Windows Remote Assistance to create an invitation file. Then, after you receive a copy of the file, you can use Windows Remote Assistance to connect to his computer and watch him perform the procedure.

D. **Incorrect:** Sending the user an invitation file will not help you share the remote user's desktop. Such a file would be useful only if you wanted the remote user to share your desktop.

2. **Correct Answer: D**

A. **Incorrect:** This is a requirement if you want to offer unsolicited Remote Assistance. This step is performed automatically by adding your account to Helpers group in the Offer Remote Assistance policy option in Group Policy.

B. **Incorrect:** You need to enable this policy option in Local or Group Policy if you want to offer unsolicited Remote Assistance.

C. **Incorrect:** In order for a Windows Vista computer to accept unsolicited Remote Assistance, you need to add these firewall exceptions.

D. **Correct:** You do not need to be a member of the Administrators group to offer Remote Assistance.

Chapter 12: Case Scenario Answers

Case Scenario 1: Configuring Remote Desktop

1. Add MonicaV to the Remote Desktop Users group on Client1.
2. In the Remote tab of the System Properties dialog box on Client1, select the option to allow connections only from computers running Remote Desktop with Network Level Authentication.

Case Scenario 2: Offering Remote Assistance

1. You should ask Fred to create a Remote Assistance invitation and to send the invitation to you through e-mail.
2. When Fred is prompted to allow you to share control of his desktop, he should select the option to allow you to respond to UAC prompts.

Glossary

access token A digital "admission ticket" that a user receives when logging on to Windows Vista and that allows the user to access certain parts of the operating system.

ActiveX A technology that enables powerful applications with rich user interfaces to run within a Web browser.

Admin Approval Mode A default mode of User Account Control in which administrators are prompted to give consent before any task requiring administrative privileges is performed.

administrative template A file (or a set of multiple files, if supporting multiple languages) that defines custom Group Policy settings that change registry values on target computers.

Automatic Private IP Address (APIPA) An IP addressing technique that assigns an address in the range 169.254.0.0 through 169.254.255.255. APIPA allows computers that don't have IP address settings to communicate across a local area network (LAN).

BitLocker Drive Encryption A Windows Vista feature capable of encrypting the entire system volume, thus protecting the computer in the event of attacks that bypass the operating system security.

Catalog (.clg) file A binary file that lists the state of all the settings and packages in a Windows image.

consent admin An administrator operating in Admin Approval Mode.

consent prompt The elevation prompt that administrators see in Admin Approval Mode.

credential prompt The elevation prompt that standard users see by default when User Account Control is turned on. Credential prompts allow standard users to perform administrative tasks if they can supply an administrator's credentials.

cryptographic service provider (CSP) A Windows Vista component that provides tools for encrypting, signing, and hashing data that any application can leverage.

elevation The process of using administrative privileges to perform a task.

Encrypting File System (EFS) A Windows Vista feature capable of encrypting specific files and folders, thus protecting the data in the event of attacks that bypass the operating system security.

event forwarding The process of sending specific events from a forwarding computer to a collecting computer where an administrator can more easily monitor them.

Firewall exception An allowance for a specified type of network connection to pass through a firewall.

Group Policy A mechanism for storing many types of policy data—for example, file deployment, application deployment, logon/logoff scripts and startup/shutdown scripts, domain security, and Internet Protocol security. The collections of policies are referred to as Group Policy objects (GPOs).

Group Policy object (GPO) The Group Policy settings that administrators create are contained in GPOs, which are in turn associated with selected Active Directory containers: sites, domains, and organizational units (OUs).

helper A user who connects to the live desktop session of another user on a remote computer.

hotspot A wireless network intended for public use. Most hotspots do not have any security. Some hotspots require users to pay before they can access the Internet.

ImageX   A command-line utility used to capture, apply, and edit Windows images.

Internet Control Message Protocol (ICMP) The messaging protocol built into IP on which the Ping and Tracert utilities are based.

Internet Protocol Security (IPSec)   An Internet Engineering Task Force (IETF) standards-based suite of protocols whose purpose is to provide data authentication and encryption for IP networks.

Kerberos   The data authentication protocol native to Active Directory.

latency   In network communications, the time it takes for a packet to travel between hosts. High latency connections don't necessarily cause bandwidth or throughput to drop. However, latency will cause problems with real-time communications such as Voice over IP (VoIP).

Mandatory Integrity Control (MIC)   A Windows Vista feature that labels processes, folders, files, and registry keys using one of four integrity access levels: system, high, medium, and low.

Media Access Control (MAC) address   The address that is used for communication between network adapters on the same subnet. Each network adapter has an associated MAC address.

multifactor authentication   Requiring two or more authentication techniques to validate a user's credentials. For example, users might be required to both insert a smart card and type a password.

Multiple Local Group Policy objects (MLGPOs) A feature of Windows Vista that provides different Local Group Policy objects (GPOs) for the local computer, Administrators and Non-Administrators, and each user. Earlier versions of Windows only had a single Local Computer GPO, which meant that computers that were not a member of a domain could not easily be managed by using GPOs.

name resolution   The process of converting a hostname to an IP address. Domain Name System (DNS) is by far the most common name-resolution technique.

Network Level Authentication (NLA)   A protocol that ensures that user authentication occurs before a Remote Desktop connection is established.

Ntuser.dat   A file in the user profile that preserves user-specific settings such as desktop background settings, audio settings, and printer settings.

Protected Mode   A feature of Internet Explorer 7.0 (available only with Windows Vista) that causes Internet Explorer to run with very limited privileges. This provides protection even if malicious code on a website successfully exploits Internet Explorer.

Protected Mode Compatibility Layer   A feature of Internet Explorer 7.0 when running on Windows Vista that redirects requests for protected resources to safer locations. For example, any requests for the My Documents folder (known as the Documents folder in Windows XP) are automatically redirected to \%userprofile%\AppData \Local\Microsoft\Windows\Temporary Internet Files\Virtualized.

pull delivery mode   In the context of event forwarding, the collecting computer initiates a connection to the forwarding computer to retrieve events.

push delivery mode   In the context of event forwarding, the forwarding computer initiates a connection to the collecting computer to send events.

Remote Desktop Protocol (RDP)   The protocol in Microsoft Windows that allows a desktop session to be sent over a network.

Restart Manager   A feature of Windows Vista that enables programs to coordinate with Windows Vista to free up resources that need to be upgraded, with the goal of reducing the number of reboots required by updates.

roaming user profile A user profile that stays with a user as he or she logs on to different computers in an Active Directory domain.

rootkit A form of malware that runs at a lower level than the operating system. Rootkits can be very difficult, or completely impossible, to detect.

security template A physical file representation of a security configuration that can be applied to a local computer or imported to a Group Policy object (GPO) in Active Directory. When you import a security template to a GPO, Group Policy processes the template and makes the corresponding changes to the members of that GPO, which can be users or computers.

single sign-on A general term for technologies that enable users to access different network resources with a single set of credentials.

SSID The name of the wireless network.

standard users In Windows Vista, users who do not have full administrative privileges.

Sysprep A tool used to prepare a master installation for imaging by removing data specific to the master computer.

User Account Control (UAC) A feature new to Windows Vista that separates standard user privileges from administrator privileges. If you are logged on to Windows Vista as an administrator, UAC by default prompts you to confirm any task you want to perform that requires administrator privileges.

user profile The personal collection of data and settings that makes up a user's environment. In Windows Vista the user profile is kept by default in C:\Users in a subfolder named after the user.

Windows Aero A set of enhancements to the graphical user interface of Windows Vista available only on Windows Vista Premium Ready computers.

Windows Defender A tool that informs users about changes programs make to their computers and that gives users greater control over which programs are installed.

Windows Deployment Services (WDS) A set of services that allows a new computer to locate and download a Windows operating system from the network. WDS is an upgrade to Remote Installation Services (RIS).

Windows Driver Display Model (WDDM) A driver display model new to Windows Vista that allows for advanced visual effects in the user interface of Windows Vista.

Windows Imaging (.wim) file A file containing one or more compressed Windows images.

Windows PE A bootable 32-bit environment that can run off of a CD-ROM and that replaces MS-DOS disks.

Windows Server Update Services (WSUS) A version of the Microsoft Update service that you can host on your private network. WSUS connects to the Windows Update site, downloads information about available updates, and adds them to a list of updates that require administrative approval.

Windows SIM A graphical tool used to create answer files.

Wired Equivalent Protection (WEP) An early wireless security standard that is now easily cracked by a knowledgable attacker.

Wi-Fi Protected Access (WPA) A wireless security standard that improves upon WPA by offering much better data protection. WPA is available as either Wi-Fi Protected Access, preshared key (WPA-PSK; also known as WPA-Personal), which uses a passphrase for authentication, or Protected Access-Wired Equivalent Protection (WPA-EAP; also known as WPA-Enterprise), which uses domain credentials or a certificate for authentication. WPA2 offers improved security over WPA with similar functionality.

Index

Windows Vista™ Resources for Administrators

System Requirements

We recommend that you use an isolated network that is not part of your production network to do the practice exercises in this training kit. The computer that you use to perform practices requires Internet connectivity. If you decide to use a virtual machine instead of standard computer hardware, you can still perform all of the practices.

Hardware Requirements

To complete all practices in this book, you will need four computers or virtual machines:

- One Microsoft Windows Server 2003 (Standard, Enterprise, or Datacenter) computer
- One Windows Vista (Enterprise, Business, or Ultimate) computer
- One Windows XP Professional computer (optional but strongly recommended)
- One computer with no software yet installed

Your computers or virtual machines should meet (at a minimum) the following hardware specifications:

- Personal computer with a 1-GHz or faster processor
- 512 MB of RAM (2 GB if you plan to use virtual machine software)
- 40 GB of available hard disk space (80 GB if you plan to use virtual machine software)
- DVD-ROM drive
- Direct X capable graphics card with 32 MB of graphics memory
- Keyboard and Microsoft mouse or compatible pointing device

Software Requirements

The following software is required to complete the practice exercises:.

- Windows Vista Enterprise or Ultimate edition.
- A computer running Windows Server 2003 Standard, Enterprise, or Datacenter that can be configured as a domain controller. You can download evaluation software for Windows Server 2003 Standard or Enterprise from Microsoft at *http://technet.microsoft.com/en-us/windowsserver/bb430831.aspx*.
- To run computers as virtual machines within Windows, you can use Virtual PC, Virtual Server 2005 R2, or third-party virtual machine software. To download Virtual PC 2007, visit *http://www.microsoft.com/windows/downloads/virtualpc/default.mspx*. To download an evaluation of Virtual Server 2005 R2, visit *http://www.microsoft.com/technet/virtual-server/evaluation/default.mspx*.

What do you think of this book?

We want to hear from you!

Do you have a few minutes to participate in a brief online survey?

Microsoft is interested in hearing your feedback so we can continually improve our books and learning resources for you.

To participate in our survey, please visit:

www.microsoft.com/learning/booksurvey/

...and enter this book's ISBN-10 number (appears above barcode on back cover*). As a thank-you to survey participants in the United States and Canada, each month we'll randomly select five respondents to win one of five $100 gift certificates from a leading online merchant. At the conclusion of the survey, you can enter the drawing by providing your e-mail address, which will be used for prize notification only.

Thanks in advance for your input. Your opinion counts!

* Where to find the ISBN-10 on back cover

Example only. Each book has unique ISBN.

Microsoft
Press